W9-DJN-752

The Subject
in the Dictionary Catalog
from Cutter to the Present

The Subject in the Dictionary Catalog from Cutter to the Present

FRANCIS MIKSA

AMERICAN LIBRARY ASSOCIATION
Chicago 1983

Designed by Ellen Pettengell

Composed by FM Typesetting Company in Linotype Baskerville

Printed on 50-pound Natural Glatfelter, a pH-neutral stock, and bound in C-grade Holliston cloth by Braun-Brumfield, Inc.

Library of Congress Cataloging in Publication Data

Miksa, Francis L., 1938–
      The subject in the dictionary catalog from
Cutter to the present.

      Bibliography: p.
      Includes index.
      1. Subject cataloging.   2. Catalogs, Subject.
3. Catalogs, Dictionary.   4. Cutter, Charles Ammi,
1837–1903.   I. Title.
Z695.M62   1983   025.4'9   83-2556
ISBN 0-8389-0367-3

*Dedicated
to
Shawne, Joel, Frank, Beth
and
especially
Mary*

Contents

Figures

Preface

The original impetus of the present work began with my dissertation on Charles Ammi Cutter when I found it necessary to make some sense out of Cutter's subject heading system. Seymour Lubetzky had provided a key for understanding Cutter's approach to entry in descriptive cataloging, but no writer had gotten to the heart of Cutter's subject cataloging, especially the meaning of his idea of "specific entry." The best that was concluded in the most extensive treatments of his ideas was that his work was shrouded in mystery, inconsistently applied, inappropriate for present-day subject cataloging needs, and the main source for permanently disabling modern subject heading work. None of these conclusions seemed to correlate with what I had learned of Cutter's systematic approach to various other library matters, but that was beside the point. The best I could do at the time was to admit to the perplexing nature of the matter and promise myself to investigate it more thoroughly later.

Another source for this work has been my desire to find out if subject heading work has any overarching rationality to it. I have experienced subject cataloging both by doing it and by teaching it. In my teaching, I have not found many sources to consult in order to gain understanding about it. Cataloging textbooks have always seemed to me to paint subject heading work with exceptionally light and vague strokes. And critical writers not only have had little good to say of it at all, but occasionally have worked themselves into frenzied diatribes about it. Few of their comments were particularly helpful in the classroom unless I too wanted to teach the art of casting aspersions. Given the general lack of explanation of the work, however, it has been difficult to feel comfortable about it all. More than once I have found myself apologizing to students for the topic as if it were akin to using a ouija board. All of this was only reinforced by my own experiences in using subject headings in the public catalog and by those of my colleagues, both librarians and teaching faculty, whose comments ranged from incredulity that anyone took subject headings seriously to humorous and, at times, not-so-humorous epithets. Mostly, however, I and others as well, have felt stuck with subject headings, without anything approaching a decent explanation of how they work (or are supposed to work), where they came from, and how they have changed (if at all). Instead, there was only the unsteady assertion that they came from Cutter (sort of), were modified by the Library of Congress (sort of), and have not changed much over their entire existence except to increase in inconsistencies. Furthermore, there was not much anyone could do about them. In the face of that rather negative experience, I have simply wanted to know why.

Something of a breakthrough came in the fall of 1974 when I stumbled across the Scottish philosophical thought that Cutter had been exposed to during his college years. The most startling aspect of that discovery was to be reading in Thomas Reid's *Essays on the Intellectual Powers of Man*, especially Essay V, "Of Abstraction," and find myself thinking that I was reading Cutter's subject rules—so close, in fact, was the resemblance.[1] The result of that discovery was to find a glimmer of hope that Cutter's subject heading work might indeed have had some rationality to it. And, of course, with that glimmer came the possibility of finding some kind of rationality in present-day dictionary subject cataloging as well.

A first attempt at drawing out some conclusions on the nature of Cutter's subject thinking came with the publication in 1977 of a volume of Cutter's writings. At the beginning of 1978 I began a second attempt, a brief paper for the Library Research Round Table of the A.L.A. the following summer. The result was a paper four times the intended length, with a shorter summary paper, and a presentation of the entire matter in twenty minutes—none of which I would be anxious to defend today. In that particular version of the topic I attempted two things: first, to give some explanation of how Cutter's system worked; and second, to show that present subject heading practice is not essentially related to Cutter's work. The motive was clearly to rescue Cutter's work from the charge that it was plainly incompetent and the cause of the ills of present-day practice.

Subsequent submission of the manuscript to A.L.A. Publishing Services, its return with the reviewer's well-put comments, and the need to make clarifications before publication set me to further study. The result was to recast the work entirely. For one thing, my original statement of Cutter's system needed redoing. I owe no small debt in that regard to Patrick Wilson's *Two Kinds of Power* where I was introduced to a stimulating range of thoughts and sources related to the question, To what does a subject heading refer?[2] As a result, the section on Cutter hopefully responds to that query more adequately. Second, my original effort to relate Cutter directly to present-day subject cataloging proved to be highly unsatisfactory. By withdrawing Cutter from direct relationship to the modern situation, I had improved the thesis about the genesis of modern work only slightly. It still appeared as if subject cataloging had not changed much. The only difference was that now the period of time had been shortened to a beginning at the turn of the century. The trouble with that view is that it does not square with what a literature search on subject cataloging will show, that is, that there have been changes. As a result of further investigations, the second theme of the original paper has also been redone.

The finished work now has the proportions of a full-scale history of dictionary subject cataloging beginning with Cutter. But that conclusion is partly deceptive. The work remains notably uneven in emphasis. Chapters 1 through 7 are concerned primarily with Cutter and reflect the earlier interest solely in Cutter's work. Chapters 8 through 12 deal with developments since Cutter. While divided into useful, mostly chronological eras, there is enough overlap between them to suggest that ultimately there may be a better way of framing the topics discussed. Furthermore, because writing the latter part was more like a process of fission than direct exposition—sections within sections growing into chapters seemingly of their own accord through the process of rewriting—and because they were developed somewhat independently of the first part of the work in both time and interest, a certain amount of redundancy in statement has crept in. Where not expunged, I hope the reader will be indulgent. Despite these difficulties, it is hoped that the finished work will help both students of subject cataloging and practicing subject catalogers to gain a new understanding of how the dictionary subject catalog functions and how it has arrived at its present state.

A word must also be said about terminology. What to call the subject portion of the dictionary catalog was a problem. The term "subject headings" by itself is not unique to the dictionary catalog and does not suggest the idea of a catalog system. The term "alphabetical subject catalog" likewise has a wider meaning than the dictionary catalog. In the end, I chose to use "dictionary subject catalog," knowing that there is no such thing as a dictionary subject catalog in and of itself, but hoping at the same time to pin down in a single phrase the catalog type (dictionary) as well as the idea of a subject system. The term "specific entry" also presents difficulties, at least to the extent that its idea of specification has changed since Cutter first used it in the 1870s. It has been particularly difficult in that respect to capture the modern meaning of the specification element of the term, where the emphasis is on encapsulating the entire topical contents of a book in the form of a subject heading. (This differs from indexing, of course, where what is specified may be only a portion or a theme of a document or where conscious specification of this sort is avoided altogether in favor of simply accessing a document in terms of the incidence of its vocabulary). I had originally intended to use "coextensivity" following British usage concerning specification until it was pointed out that that particular term has a wide variety of overtones that might hinder its use as a way to refer to specification. Therefore, I have coined a term, "scope-matching," that, while obviously clumsy, sets my more casual meaning of specification in a distinct light. I have also tried to avoid the use of the term "complex subject" mainly because it is my opinion that no such thing exists. Complex descriptions of subjects exist, but that is a far cry from the metaphysical overtones of the former phrase. More will be said of this in the notes to chapters 2 and 3 where terminology related to subjects is discussed.

It should also be noted that Cutter's *Rules for a Dictionary Catalog* are regularly referred to in the text as his *Rules*. Unless otherwise indicated, references are to the fourth edition, published posthumously in 1904. Citations are simply abbreviated *RDC*.[3]

Finally, I wish to take the opportunity to convey my sincerest gratitude to Elaine Svenonius, who listened patiently while I tested ideas on her as the Cutter section of the text progressed; to Kathryn Weintraub, who pointed out critical distinctions regarding classification that have helped immeasurably; to Edith Scott, who has been very encouraging and who also located special hard-to-find materials for me at the Library of Congress; and to Joel Lee, the A.L.A.'s own librarian's librarian, for likewise coming to my aid for sources when I most needed them. Most of all, however, I owe inestimable thanks to Lee Shiflett, my colleague on the faculty of the Louisiana State University School of Library and Information Science, who has patiently parsed my beginner's sentences throughout the entire manuscript, and to Mary Spohrer Miksa, who not only read every page and offered invaluable suggestions as an esteemed colleague, but who has offered untold encouragement as an endearing wife. Needless to say, the final product, complete with its intellectual fuzz and grammatical warts, is my own responsibility.

F.M.

CHAPTER 1

Statement of the Problem

The Historical Framework

> *On seeing the great success of the Library of Congress cataloging, I doubted whether it was worth while to prepare and issue this fourth edition of my Rules; but I reflected that it would be a considerable time before all libraries would use the cards of that library, and a long time before the Library of Congress could furnish cards for all books, long enough for libraries to absorb another edition and use it up in that part of their cataloging which they must do themselves. Still I cannot help thinking that the golden age of cataloging is over, and that the difficulties and discussions which have furnished an innocent pleasure to so many will interest them no more. Another lost art.*
>
> C. A. CUTTER (1904)1

> *The principles of subject cataloging have nowhere been fully stated as yet, but they have nevertheless been fairly faithfully and consistently followed by all libraries. In the present cooperative cataloging undertaking it was therefore very easy to get the libraries concerned to agree that the Library of Congress practice be the sole guide and criterion. The check on adherence to this guide and criterion is secured by a staff of revisers in the Library of Congress itself. Proof is not lacking that the work of these revisers has brought a large measure of consistency and uniformity to the varied product of the approximately thirty-five cooperating libraries.*
>
> D. J. HAYKIN (1937)2

> *It is no wonder that the subject catalog provides for librarians, catalogers, and the public a first-class guessing game.*
>
> G. SCHEERER (1957)3

These quotations provide a convenient historical framework for the common understanding of the history of dictionary subject cataloging

1

in America. They portray an essential continuity between the near past and the present—from Charles Ammi Cutter through the Library of Congress to contemporary practice. With the continuity there is the tacit hint of periods of development. The creative period of thought took place before the turn of the century—the "golden age of cataloging," a time of idyllic "innocent pleasure" when the fundamentals were set down. Since then, the hard work of applying the fundamentals to the subject headings found on the tops of catalog cards (or, in the 600s fields of a MARC display) has been the principal activity. Paul S. Dunkin characterized the continuity and the periods by the phrase "the Prophet and the Law." Cutter was the former, of course; and all efforts to reduce his words to procedures, especially by Library of Congress subject catalogers, the latter.[4]

The quotations also give recognition to two subject cataloging traditions intertwined as one: local subject cataloging on the one hand, Library of Congress subject cataloging on the other. The first is bound necessarily to the leadership of the second—a marriage of mutual respect or the institution of slavery, depending on one's point of view. Lastly, the quotations above strongly indicate that more recently a change in attitude has taken place. Haykin's comment in 1937 speaks of an age that was fundamentally positive in tone about dictionary subject cataloging. Were other quotations to be added to his from the period before World War II, one would not find indifference or blindness to problems in subject cataloging work, but rather an optimistic attitude that such problems would be solved as more study was pursued and more effort expended.

During the 1940s and 1950s many studies were conducted, especially on the needs of users and on the terminology of special fields of study. But by the end of the 1950s the mood of optimism had already begun to sour. Frarey's summary report on the state of the dictionary subject cataloging art in 1960 hints at one reason for the change in attitude: the studies of the previous twenty or so years had not led to the solution of many of the problems.[5] If anything, the studies had led only to exasperating dead ends, their findings indicating more often than not that few if any solutions were to be found.

Another reason for the change in mood was the explosion of new forms of subject access during the 1950s. The capacities inherent in developments such as analytico-synthetic classification and machine-based coordinate indexing systems not only provided a basis for criticizing dictionary subject cataloging, but also fostered the impression that the older means of subject access was no less than a dinosaur that had survived into the modern period through some historical accident.

It was from this perspective, in fact, that Scheerer made his own comment, likening the work to a "first-class guessing game."

By the 1960s the general mood had changed even more, so that articles and books written about dictionary subject cataloging took on an even more negative tone. Deficiencies in subject heading work, especially as represented by *Library of Congress Subject Headings,* were documented almost to a point of dreariness. The most common canon of criticism (whether plainly stated or not) was what its managers concluded was unavoidable variation and irregularity in subject heading choice and form, but which its critics considered unconscionable inconsistencies.

By the 1970s and lasting into the present, still another mood appears to have become prevalent—resignation. One reason for this may be the slowness of change. Some calls for alterations in Library of Congress practices have been successful—for example, the expunging of a modicum of objectionable subject headings. But many others, especially those that would fundamentally change the system, have gone unheeded. Upon reflection, one might conclude that the calls for alterations were like trying to make a brontosaurus change direction by throwing sticks at it. Or worse, requiring that it become something else altogether—clearly a futile exercise.

Still another reason for the mood of resignation may be that there are too many other changes in librarianship to worry about in its place. Or again, the advent of massive copy-cataloging made available through bibliographic utilities makes it less and less necessary for subject catalogers to open their Sears or Library of Congress lists of headings to devise subject headings from scratch. And as any subject cataloger knows, it is when the list of headings is opened that trouble begins. In short, out of sight, out of mind.

Despite the mood of resignation, however, the essentially negative attitude toward subject heading work has continued. To those librarians who of necessity continue to make a dictionary subject catalog available for their patrons, its operational principles and its practices remain only slightly less than inscrutable. There are so many individual quirks about it that to learn it thoroughly would appear to require a lifetime of attention to detailed exceptions by which one acquires "the mind of LC."[6] (As a side thought, one might seriously question whether it is worth the investment in time to learn it thoroughly. There are few rewards for doing so. And once having learned it, with whom does one then share his or her knowledge? So rarefied is the work, in fact, that it remains one of the last bastions in librarianship where professionalism is measured by the extent of one's esoteric knowledge.)

On the other hand, if the dictionary subject catalog were replaced, what might stand as a reasonable substitute? There are few who contend that some other system is to be preferred on all points, especially for the supposed general reader to whom the dictionary catalog has often been delegated. Is there, in fact, anything that is really better? This question, when asked by a subject cataloger who has invested much of his or her time in subject heading work, often has serious overtones. Is there really any better system that a typical subject cataloger is equipped to learn and that the library of such a cataloger, with its limited budget, is able to afford? Is "better" synonymous, for example, with machine technology and specialist information retrieval systems that appear to be as problematic in their own ways as dictionary subject cataloging is in its? In short, eighty years of subject heading work appear to have resulted in the common attitude that not only the dictionary subject catalog but in fact all subject access systems are, when considered together, enigmas.

The Etiology of the Dictionary Subject Catalog

One important aspect of the period since the 1940s has been an ongoing attempt to explain how and why dictionary subject catalogs operate as they do. This effort has in turn led to the conclusion that contemporary practice goes back directly to Charles Ammi Cutter's *Rules for a Dictionary Catalog.* The idea that contemporary practice is directly descended from Cutter's work is a compelling notion. Indeed, the main characteristics of contemporary practice—(1) an appeal to a concept of specific entry; (2) consideration of the user as the principal basis for subject heading decisions; (3) the practice of standardizing terminology and choosing between synonyms; (4) the use of cross-references to show preferred terms and to show hierarchical and coordinate relationships between terms; and (5) some of the rationalizations used for term order—all of which appeared by and large for the first time in Cutter's *Rules,* would seem to leave little doubt that Cutter's work is seminally related to contemporary practice, although how that connection has been accomplished has never been spelled out.

Furthermore, if one allows the legitimacy of the direct connection between Cutter and contemporary practice, only a short step in logic is required to reach still another conclusion that has gained equal currency, that shortcomings in contemporary practice may also be traced to Cutter. In this respect commentators on dictionary subject cataloging work may be divided roughly into two groups: those who are highly critical of dictionary subject catalogs and those essentially favorable to them. Neither group has been wanting in describing the inconsistencies and shortcomings of dictionary subject catalogs, and both groups generally have concluded that whatever basic problems exist in contemporary practice may be found at its beginning in Cutter's work. The only difference between the two groups is that those who are opposed to dictionary subject catalogs have tended to find Cutter's work the source of unredeemable error, while those essentially favorable to it have generally found Cutter's system fundamentally sound, needful only of modifications to make it more amenable to the modern situation.[7]

The forcefulness of the argument that Cutter's system is seriously problem-ridden may be seen by enumerating the most essential problems described by commentators. These problems arise from attempting to answer the following basic questions: To what does a subject heading refer? How should a subject heading be written? To what extent shall subjects be collocated?

TO WHAT DOES A SUBJECT HEADING REFER?

It might seem superfluous to ask what a subject heading is supposed to refer to. Indeed, a cursory glance at the literature of subject heading work will reveal a surprising consistency in answering this question. A subject heading should express or match in some essential way the topical contents of a work. Margaret Mann stated this equation well:

> As a general rule books must be entered under their most specific subject heading. This means the heading which will most accurately fit the book. The term must express the content of the book sharply and accurately, not vaguely and loosely.[8]

This description of a subject heading's referent implies something of a quasi-quantitative measure—"quantitative" in the sense that a subject heading is to correspond to a thing called a "subject" that itself has a vaguely sensed substantiality or quantitativeness to it, but "quasi-" in the sense that the measure is one of casual rather than formal correspondence. In other words, the topical contents of a document are not precisely measured in the same manner that one measures an object with a ruler or with some other agreed upon objective scale (Figure 1).

Given a document S, its subject may be represented by the arbitrary figure a,b,c,d; the description of the subject by a'b'c'd'; and the name of the subject that is useful as a subject heading and that portrays the essential nature of the subject by S'. The usefulness of the arbitrary

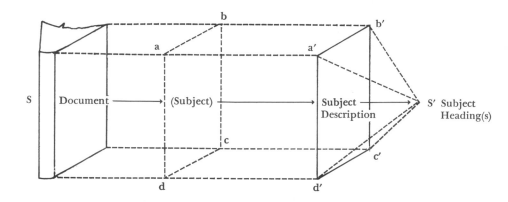

Document	Subject Descriptions	LC Subject Headings
1.	Title: The Birds of New England Elaboration: Descriptive guide to native birds of N. E.	BIRDS–NEW ENGLAND–IDENTIFICATION
2.	Title: Franklin D. Roosevelt, a Profile Elaboration: Mainly biography on Roosevelt, especially his career	ROOSEVELT, FRANKLIN DELANO
3.	Title: History of Libraries in the U.S. Elaboration: (same)	LIBRARIES–UNITED STATES–HISTORY
4.	Title: Libraries of Baton Rouge Elaboration: Historical sketches	BATON ROUGE–LIBRARIES–HISTORY
5.	Title: The Biological Origin of Human Values Elaboration: Psychobiology applied to values	1. PSYCHOBIOLOGY 2. VALUES
6.	Title: Before Civilization: the Radiocarbon Revolution and Prehistoric Europe Elaboration: Radiocarbon dating is explained & applied to European prehistory and its monument	1. MAN, PREHISTORIC–EUROPE 2. MEGALITHIC MONUMENTS 3. RADIOCARBON DATING
7.	Title: All in Good Time: Love Poetry of Shakespeare, Donne, Johnson, and Marvell Elaboration: A critical literary study	1. LOVE POETRY, ENGLISH–HISTORY AND CRITICISM 2. ENGLISH POETRY–EARLY MODERN, 1500-1700–HISTORY AND CRITICISM

FIG. 1.   Specificity as Scope-Matching

figure lies not in a supposed geometrical analogy, as if subject content could ever be represented analogically by a precise geometrical figure, but rather only in the sense that the figure suggests the subject to have a certain undefinable substantiality or scope to it. It is not usual, of course, to represent the topical content of a document by a geometrical figure. Rather, it is much more common to think of subjects as words and to speak of a subject content by means of its more or less precise name, or by an extended description of it (often in the form of a title), or both.[9]

The task of the subject cataloger is to move from S to S', that is, to devise a subject name for the subject content of the document. The task is considered to be successfully achieved if the name or names employed suggest, represent, fit, match, etc., the supposed substantiality of the topical contents. The most appropriate way to represent that process is by an analogy in which the extensivity or scope of the topical contents is matched by a term, a subject heading. The process may, therefore, be conveniently labeled *scope-matching*—the process by which the extent of the topical content of a document is matched by means of a subject heading, whether or not the actual heading accurately scope-matches the work by some other more formal and exact measure.[10]

To illustrate something of the matching process, a list of titles and elaborated subject descriptions together with Library of Congress subject headings that purport to match them has been added to the diagram in Figure 1. Regardless of whether or not one considers multiple headings to be a legitimate substitute for single-entry item specification, the implication remains that the headings provided are an attempt to scope-match the perceived subjects of each document listed.

HOW SHOULD A SUBJECT HEADING BE WRITTEN?

The second basic question in subject heading work follows closely on the first. Once having determined what a document is about, the description must be converted into a formal subject heading.[11] It is here, especially, that the classical features of the dictionary subject catalog are most felt. To begin with, the subject heading decided upon must be in common use among the patrons of the library. It will not do, for example, to use CONSUMPTION for documents on tuberculosis when patrons will most likely look under TUBERCULOSIS for them. Of course, not all the topics of books have names that are in common use. Therefore, if no commonly used subject name can be found, one alternative procedure is to enter the document under a broader heading that is itself commonly used and of which the immediate topic of the document is a part.

The subject cataloger must also be careful to choose only one term where more than one is equally valid in order to gather all the documents on the same subject together in the catalog. This activity applies equally to choices between terms altogether different (e.g., between BIRDS and ORNITHOLOGY) and between terms different because of the order of their elements (e.g., between ANCIENT HISTORY and HISTORY, ANCIENT). Finally, one essential mark of dictionary subject catalogs is that the terms chosen as the subject headings for documents must be directly rather than indirectly written. It will not serve the purposes of the patron, for example, to enter a document on frogs under a heading that is itself the last element of an "echelon of subjects" as in ZOOLOGY–VERTEBRATES–AMPHIBIANS–FROGS.[12] This form of entry is the mark of classified catalogs—in this case, the mark of an alphabetico-classed catalog. The dictionary subject catalog, on the contrary, requires that the term FROGS be directly accessible. This is accomplished by placing the term FROGS directly in the main alphabetical sequence of headings in the catalog.

HOW SHALL SUBJECT RELATIONSHIPS BE SHOWN?

A third, although derivative, area of concern in dictionary subject cataloging follows from the first two. If one has devised headings that scope-match the subjects of documents and then arranges them directly in an alphabetical sequence, the sequence that results will not admit of any order except that of the alphabet. Topics represented by the headings will often be found in strange juxtapositions (e.g., ABSCESS next to ABSENTEEISM, COMMUNION followed by COMMUNISM) and others that are logically related (e.g., LITERARY HISTORY and BIBLIOGRAPHY, CHRISTIANITY and THEOLOGY) will be separated by great distances in the catalog.[13] But subjects never exist in vacuums. All have some logical relationships to other subjects. And patrons often search for subjects with those semantic connections in mind. Therefore, a derivative activity for the dictionary subject cataloger is to employ some device to show the relationships between subjects deemed most useful to patrons—in other words, to collocate subjects.

Collocation is ordinarily done in one of two ways: (1) by a system of cross-references (the "see also" cards in a card catalog) which, when combined with references that show choices between terms ("see" references), provide a syndetic or connective infrastructure in the catalog; and (2) by carefully manipulating word order in multiword terms (e.g., using SILK, RAW instead of RAW SILK, bringing the term in close proximity to others beginning with the word SILK) to gather related subjects together in collocated groups.

DIFFICULTIES

The foregoing classical features of the dictionary subject catalog are notable for their simplicity and straightforwardness. But over the years they have been the source of great difficulties and, consequently, much heated debate. The main reason for criticism of the cataloging system is that it appears to be a greatly oversimplified process. It cannot easily accommodate subjects that have complex descriptions, a category that the subjects of many documents fall into. For example, how shall one provide subject access to documents concerning "the manufacture of multi-wall kraft paper sacks for the packaging of cement" or "the efficacy of the aqua mephitica alkaline in calculous disorders."[14]

The lack of accommodation arises from the fact that the injunction to enter documents under scope-matched headings runs afoul of the equally important injunction to use only those subject names that can be verified by common usage. Furthermore, if some alternative method is used to achieve the scope-match, the results are questionable. Some examples of alternative methods are subdivision, as in CEMENT–PACKAGING–SACKS–PAPER–KRAFT–MULTI-WALL–MANUFACTURE;[15] a phrase heading, as in MULTI-WALL KRAFT PAPER SACKS FOR CEMENT PACKAGING, MANUFACTURE OF; multiple entry, as in MULTI-WALL KRAFT PAPER SACKS, MANUFACTURE OF and CEMENT PACKAGING, both of which are broader than the scope of the work; and a broader term per se, as in CALCULUS (*in Medicine*) for the second example above.

Subdivision of headings appears to be the same as the indirect entry ordinarily associated with alphabetico-classed catalogs. Multiple and single entry under broader terms offer no single subject heading that scope-matches the work. And in all cases where more than one word is involved, the choice of a lead word and the subsequent order of the other words are uncertain. When problems such as these are then expanded by other issues related, for example, to how one determines common usage or how one determines the most appropriate collocative cross-references, the so-called simplicity of the dictionary subject catalog vanishes. More important, from the standpoint of the etiology of the system, it appears that these difficulties were present in Cutter's work at the very beginning of dictionary subject catalog development.

CUTTER AND SPECIFIC ENTRY

The core of Cutter's approach to the dictionary subject cataloging process turned on his use of the idea of specific entry. This idea appeared in the very first of his subject cataloging rules.

161. Enter a work under its subject heading, not under the heading of a class which includes that subject.

Ex. Put Lady Cust's book on "The cat" under CAT, not under ZOOLOGY or MAMMALS, or DOMESTIC ANIMALS: and put Garnier's "Le fer" under IRON, not under METALS or METALLURGY.

This rule of "specific entry" is the main distinction between the dictionary catalog and the alphabetico-classed.16

Upon close examination the idea of specific entry as it is used here appears to indicate two things. First, a heading should scope-match the topical contents of the book to which it is assigned. As a corollary, it should not be broader than the topic of the work. Second, although less obvious, the heading should be placed directly in the alphabetical sequence of headings. It should not, for example, be a subheading under a broader term.

What could be simpler than entering a work on cats under the subject heading CATS, or a work on iron under IRON? The headings achieve perfect scope-matches and are direct in form. The precision of the scope-matches assumes, of course, that both items are general works about their respective subjects, that neither of them speaks of some particular part or aspect of their topics. In other words, both are of the variety "All, or almost all, you ever wanted to know about cats, or iron," and are not restricted, say, to cats as pets alone, or to the specific gravity of iron. If each were restricted in scope, one would then hesitate to say the headings chosen were indeed scope-matched. But this is precisely the point at which trouble arises with Cutter's system. He seems to have been unable to accommodate easily works whose subjects are qualified in this way—works, in other words, that contain subjects that may be named only in some complex way.

Cutter suggested a lack of accommodation of this sort in his often-quoted discussion appended to this rule. He stated that some subjects have either no names or no usable commonly accepted names. He went on to say that in such cases, a work must be entered under the class heading to which its so-called unnamed topic belongs. For example, if one determined that the phrase "cats as pets" was not a commonly accepted name, a work on that topic must be entered under CATS, even if this heading did not result in a precise scope-match between heading and topic. In the same way, a work on the specific gravity of iron would be entered under IRON if no other commonly accepted name for this particular topic was found. Furthermore, Cutter made the restriction even more severe by prohibiting the use of contrived headings that, although precise in their scope-match formulation, were not in common use. Thus, one could not use the name CATPETS or even the phrase CATS AS PETS unless it was in common use.[17] The difficulty with these restrictions is obvious. They preclude precise scope-matching of many works, and particularly of works that are about topics with complex descriptions, for no other reason than the fact that such subjects often have no commonly accepted names.

The problem of an inadequate scope-match is further complicated by another restriction in Cutter's subject rules. If a work is about a particular topic but the discussion of the topic is limited to a particular place, Cutter indicates that the work should be entered under the place with only a "see also" reference from the topic.[18] This action is taken rather than entering the work under a heading that combines both place and topic name, a heading that would appear to be a much more effective scope-match. For example, Cutter noted that a work on the birds of New England should be entered under the heading NEW ENGLAND with only a cross-reference under ORNITHOLOGY telling the inquirer to "see also" NEW ENGLAND.[19]

This pattern of entry is provided in contrast to a heading such as ORNITHOLOGY OF NEW ENGLAND, or, by implication, one such as ORNI-THOLOGY—NEW ENGLAND. Cutter's reason for rejecting ORNITHOLOGY OF NEW ENGLAND was that, even though the heading met the requirement of scope-matching when considered by itself, it began with a term which indicated a class as opposed to starting with the place name which is an "individual." And faced with a choice between these two types of terms, Cutter concluded:

> Of course the dictionary catalog in choosing between a class and an individual prefers the latter. Its object is to show at one view all the sides of each object; the classed catalog shows together the same side of many objects.[20]

In other words, entering the work under ORNITHOLOGY would provide a classed sequence in the catalog with other entries that begin with the same term—a sequencing practice that "the dictionary catalog is expected to avoid."[21]

In the light of such instructions as these, one might reasonably ask, what happened to the basic scope-match principle? Cutter seems to have added conditions to this principle that allow one to achieve a scope-match more often only in the breach than in regular practice. Coates, for one, strongly indicted Cutter for these basic subversions of scope-match practice. He concluded that Cutter must have had little understanding of "complex subjects" and that his lack of understanding was a result of his living in a time in which

> knowledge still consisted of a number of accepted spheres of thought, each comfortably separate from the others. "Subjects" were islands of knowledge separated from one another by oceanic voids. This was a great convenience and aid to tidy minds, no longer, alas, available. In our day the various islands have become so thoroughly interconnected that it is often very difficult to see any ocean at all. In fact, the geographical metaphor has to give way to a biological one. Any subject may impinge upon almost any other and the chances are that such a union will produce a brand new offspring.[22]

He went on to say that Cutter was even more simple-minded in regard to subject names usable for subject headings. He supposed that Cutter had in mind a set of stock subject terms

> under one of which each book had to be accommodated. If the subject matter of a book is more restricted in scope than any of the stock terms, then the book must be placed under the most restricted stock term which contains its subject, just as the purchaser of ready-made clothing buys the nearest larger stock size to his actual size. The whole difficulty is that no definite criterion can be addressed to determine what shall be in the stock list of subjects. While it is true that some subjects are more "established" than others, there are infinite gradations and no fixed demarcation of the "unestablished" is possible.[23]

Coates had stated the same issue in a different form seven years earlier when he wrote in his review of Haykin's *Subject Headings*:

> The day is surely past when clearly defined subject fields lacking a name capable of use as a catchword in an alphabetical sequence should be hidden amongst material of general scope at the nearest generic head. A subject without a name can, and for a maximum usefulness should, be indicated by a descriptive subheading.[24]

Opposing Coates's criticism is an argument offered by John Metcalfe, who suggested that no matter what might be desired with regard to naming complex subjects, Cutter was not being naive in his insistence that only commonly used names could legitimately be used as the indexing vocabulary. The very idea of a verbal index suggests that the terms be known, not contrived. An alphabetical index is, in other worlds, a list of "known terms in known order."[25] Metcalfe's argument is sensible. But its application, at least in Cutter's *Rules,* leaves much to be desired because Cutter does not clearly spell out how he determined whether any particular subject name was commonly used and thus constituted a legitimate index term. In the long note to the initial subject catalog rule being discussed here, Cutter described several cases of subject name choices in the following words:

And it is not always easy to decide what is a distinct subject. Many catalogs have a heading PREACHING. Is Extempore preaching a sufficiently distinct matter to have a heading of its own? There are a number of books on this branch of the subject. In this particular case the difficulty can be avoided by making the heading "PREACHING WITHOUT NOTES." Many such questions may be similarly solved, with perhaps more satisfaction to the maker of the catalog than to its users; but many questions will remain.

Then, mixed with this, and sometimes hardly distinguishable from it, is the case of subjects whose names begin with an unimportant adjective or noun,—Arc of the meridian, Capture of property at sea, Segment of a circle, Quadrature of the circle. All that can be said in such cases is that, if the subject be commonly recognized and the name accepted or likely to be accepted by usage, the entry must be made under it.[26]

Although Cutter seems to have made choices that were satisfactory to himself, the basis of his choices is not apparent. For example, his choice of PREACHING WITHOUT NOTES for Extempore preaching apparently provided a name for a topic that he considered a distinct subject. Its use thus avoided the difficulty of giving class entry under PREACHING to works on that topic. But he leaves unsaid both why he used PREACHING WITHOUT NOTES instead of, say, EXTEMPORE PREACHING, and how he identified PREACHING WITHOUT NOTES as a usable heading in the first place. Thus, his sanguine, though ironically, qualified opinion that other such problems "may be similarly solved" offers little help.

Many writers generally conclude that the basis for Cutter's choices was actually his belief in the notion of common usage. That is to say, Cutter chose between alternative terms on the basis of what terms he surmised people who search in the catalog were likely to use. He seems to have indicated as much by describing usable names as those "accepted or likely to be accepted by usage" and by his reference to the discussion he appended to rules 174–175 (on compound headings) where the idea of common usage is referred to in greater detail. But this solution to the problem is not particularly helpful either, as an examination of that idea below will show.

In summary, given these various criticisms, one might well agree that Cutter's specific entry rule fails on three basic counts: (1) that it is born of an oversimplified view of complexity in subjects; (2) that it promotes an oversimplified view of subject names; and (3) that its dependence on determining commonly used names is vague and of little help.

To these, a fourth criticism of Cutter's idea of specific entry may also be added. In this case, however, the criticism has to do with what appears to be a fundamental inconsistency in Cutter's method. It seems obvious that Cutter did not envision subdivision of subject headings as a way to achieve precise scope-matches. For example, in a discussion of the topic Movement of fluids in plants, he seems never to have conceived of a heading of the form PLANTS—CIRCULATION, a form common to present-day subject heading lists. There would appear to be an inconsistency in the way Cutter proceeds, however. For example, he stated that the foregoing subject did not have a distinct and usable common subject name. Thus, a work on the topic would be entered under the name of its including class. In this example, however, the term he settled upon was BOTANY *(Physiological)*. BOTANY is, of course, a synonym for Plants. But he seems also to have subdivided that term with the word physiological. Having already faced his stricture on building classed sequences, how did he then rationalize a subject heading that is clearly subdivided by another term? Is that not a classed sequence? Dunkin clearly thought so in his evaluation.[27]

To make matters worse, one finds still other instances in Cutter's *Rules* of what appear to be subdivision practice for the purpose of scope-matching. For example, Anatomy would appear to be subdivided by inversion in the phrase ANATOMY, *Morbid,* and Spain by the addition of the subject word Architecture in the construction SPAIN; *Architecture.*[28] Furthermore, Cutter regularly subdivided the files of entries under countries in his Boston Athenaeum catalog.[29] In fact, in a section in his *Rules* on "Arrangement of Entries" some fifty pages later than his subject rules section, Cutter not only condoned and encouraged the practice of subdivision, but called it "classification."[30] His rationalization of the practice, implied in several places in his *Rules,* was that while the practice appeared similar to classed subdivision, in reality it amounted only to the division of subjects by their aspects. And subdivision by aspect was not prohibited by the specific entry principle. The difficulty with this explanation is, however, that the difference between subject subdivisions and subject aspects is not clear. Thus, the probability that either the subject cataloger or the catalog user could distinguish between them seems equally questionable.[31]

CUTTER AND SUBJECT HEADING FORM

The question of subdivision practice, because it is a matter of term order, brings to mind still another confusing aspect of Cutter's *Rules* —that is, how subject headings should be written. It is confusing primarily because of what appears to be Cutter's general appeal to the notion of common usage as a way to make decisions.

Cutter's more general statements on common usage have the appearance of a fundamental manifesto of subject heading work. In a short introductory preface to the second section of his subject rules entitled "Choice between different names," he wrote:

> General rules, always applicable for the choices of names of subjects, can no more be given than rules without exception in grammar. Usage in both cases is the supreme arbiter—the usage in the present case, not of the cataloger but of the public in speaking of subjects.[32]

This echoes the even more often quoted statement in the preface of the fourth edition of his *Rules*:

> The convenience of the public is always to be set before the ease of the cataloger. In most cases they coincide. A plain rule without exception is not only easy for us to carry out, but easy for the public to understand and work by. But strict consistency in a rule and uniformity in its application sometimes leads to practices which clash with the public's habitual way of looking at things. When these habits are general and deeply rooted, it is unwise for the cataloger to ignore them, even if they demand a sacrifice of system and simplicity.[33]

That Cutter's appeal to the idea of common usage is fundamental to his subject system generally has already been suggested by its apparent role in his basic subject rule and the determination of commonly used subject names. But his appeal to common usage for determining appropriate subject heading form appears to be even more pervasive. Choosing between alternative forms of headings might occur as a choice between different words that are synonymous (e.g., BUTTERFLIES or LEPIDOPTERA) or as a choice between different forms of approximately the same words (e.g., FLORAL FERTILIZATION, FLOWER FERTILIZATION, or FERTILIZATION OF FLOWERS). In the first of the examples here, Cutter wrote, "prefer the one that is most familiar to the class of people who consult the catalog."[34] And in the second case he stated, "When there is any decided usage (i.e., custom of the public to designate the subjects by one of the names rather than the others), let it be followed; . . ."[35]

Common usage also appears to play an important role in questions of term order, specifically in choosing between a heading that is written directly and its inverted form. For example, in devising a heading for the topic History of the ancient world, one might choose between the alternatives ANCIENT HISTORY and HISTORY, ANCIENT. In this case, Cutter suggested that inversion could be allowed when some word other than the first word of the compound heading "is decidedly more significant."[36] That one word rather than another should be more significant appears to have meaning only in the light of the idea of common usage.

The most pervasive difficulty that arises in the appeal to common usage is that Cutter provided no apparent criteria for assessing usage, except, perhaps, his reference to relating the use of a particular subject name to an identifiable "class of people who consult the catalog." But even he seems to have recognized the lack of criteria. In the choice between FLORAL FERTILIZATION, FLOWER FERTILIZATION, and FERTILIZATION OF FLOWERS, Cutter suggested at first that if one of the three alternatives—in his example, the third of the three—were the "more customary" phrase, it should be chosen. But then he concluded pessimistically, "As is often the case in language, usage will not be found to follow any uniform course."[37] If, however, even Cutter found the idea of common usage to be helpful only some of the time, what other criteria did he use as a basis for writing subject headings? In answer to this question, several alternatives are available, but Cutter's statement of them also raises serious questions.

With regard to choices between different, but synonymous terms, Cutter listed several criteria other than common usage. Among these was choosing a term that "brings the subject into the neighborhood of other related subjects."[38] Here, Cutter seems to be suggesting that the capacity of a term to collocate related subjects with terms already in use in the catalog is a viable basis for choice between alternative terms. Although the examples he appended to the rule are limited to terms denoting works of collective biography that may be collocated with the biographee's major activity (e.g., of the terms CONJURING, JUGGLING, LEGERDEMAIN, PRESTIDIGITATION, and SLEIGHT OF HAND, choose CONJURING or PRESTIDIGITATION because one could then collocate CONJURERS or PRESTIDIGITATORS with them), other catalogers since Cutter have appealed to this rule as a strong justification for choosing collocative forms of headings of all types, especially inverted forms. The difficulty, of course, is that the idea of collocating related subjects through term choice appears to be no less than a muted form of classification, especially when inverted headings are included. And Cutter had already spoken out strongly against the inclusion of classed headings and sequences.

Even allowing that Cutter did not intend such an extended interpretation, the reader of his *Rules* has little reason for assurance that Cutter was aware of the cross-purposes that seem to be in operation. In other words, Cutter appears here to allow the use of classed headings, or at least classed sequences, in an otherwise specific entry system. Furthermore, even if one concluded that classed infractions due to the application of this alternative would occur infrequently, there is no assurance that this would be the case in actual operation. Cutter followed his criteria for choosing between synonyms with the note, "Sometimes one and sometimes another of these reasons must prevail. Each case is to be decided on its own merits."[39] Deciding each case on its own merits not only appears to indicate a lack of principle, but also suggests that choosing between synonyms because of their capacity for collocation might well be applied and justified without reserve.

Questions raised by common usage and an alternative to it are also apparent in Cutter's discussion of compound subject names. Cutter discussed compound names at length in the notes appended to rules 174–175. The critical problem that he addressed initially was what is appropriate word order for multiple-word headings, particularly for headings that include adjective-noun and noun-noun combinations. For example, given works on the topics Comparative anatomy, Morbid anatomy, Death penalty, and Ancient history, one must decide how to write suitable headings to indicate these topics. If no alternatives are available that reduce the concepts to single words, multiple-word headings must be used. However, these headings could be written as they appear, or they could be inverted, using, for example, the form HISTORY, ANCIENT rather than ANCIENT HISTORY. The latter alternative had been formulated in Cutter's day by Jacob Schwartz as the "noun rule" for inversion.

Cutter seems to have concluded that any singular solution to the problem of inversion was unwarranted. If all compound headings were to be used as they read, some, particularly those in phrase or sentence form, would doubtless be lost to the user who might not expect to find them in their natural word order. On the other hand, Cutter surmised that consistent inversion would place some headings under words not considered the searching word. For example, entering the topic Alimentary canal under CANAL, ALIMENTARY would place it among works about canals as waterways. He, therefore, proposed the following rule as a solution:

> 175. Enter a compound subject-name by its first word, inverting the phrase only when some other word is decidedly more significant or is often used along with the same meaning as the whole name.[40]

Commentators on Cutter have generally considered this rule to be a model of inexactness bearing little help to one who is actually engaged in subject cataloging work. For example, how shall one determine those occasions when "some other word is decidedly more significant?" Cutter offers no direct answer to the query. Is this rule, in fact, a veiled reference to common usage? In a long discussion of this rule, Cutter did refer to the idea of common usage. But, having already pointed out the indeterminateness of common usage as a useful approach and Cutter's own seeming pessimism toward the idea, here as well one must look elsewhere for Cutter's alternative basis for making a choice. Cutter's alternative in this case is an extended rationalization of the direct entry of such headings.

Cutter analyzed the constituent elements of headings such as CAPITAL PUNISHMENT (in which an adjective is placed before a noun) and DEATH PENALTY (in which a noun used like an adjective is placed before a noun), noting that the second word in each instance was "the name of a general subject, one of whose subdivisions is indicated by the adjective." To invert the phrases or to use an alternative form such as PENALTY OF DEATH would, in effect, produce a classed heading and, with other headings beginning with the same general subject word, would introduce a classed sequence into an otherwise specific entry catalog. He explained further that

> we can have various headings for Death considered in different lights, among others as a penalty; and we can have headings of various sorts of penalties, among others death. It is evident that this collection of penalties taken together makes up a class, and therefore this belongs to a style of entry which the dictionary catalog is expected to avoid; but the series of headings beginning with the word Death would not make a class, being merely different aspects of the same thing, not different subordinate parts of the same subject.41

On the basis of this reasoning, therefore, Cutter concluded that headings should be used for the most part as they read, and, that given a choice between an adjective-noun heading and a heading in which the ruling noun is placed first as in PENALTY OF DEATH, the adjective-noun heading should be used.

Cutter's entire rationalization raises two serious questions, however. First, how is one to determine in each case which of the two words being considered is the broader and which is the narrower? Coates, for one, considers this approach to be "a highly questionable theoretical justification."42 Second, why, after already allowing incursions of classed headings into his specific entry catalog in at least two other instances— that is, classed headings for nameless subjects and classification-like sequences in choices between synonyms based on the use of collocative headings—should Cutter argue here so strongly against them, especially since this rule, allowing inversion as it does on the basis of consideration of a word being "decidedly more significant," might produce classed headings despite such a rationalization? On the basis of questions such as these, one might reasonably conclude that Cutter's approach to word order and inversion, like his approach to choices between synonyms, is both indeterminate and confusing and lacks the clarity necessary to produce consistency in choices.

CUTTER AND SUBJECT COLLOCATION

A third aspect of Cutter's work that also creates confusion is the role of subject collocation in his dictionary subject catalog, particularly in the form of cross-references. Difficulties arise not so much from what he proposed, but rather from the method by which it might be accomplished and, given its accomplishment, the value of what is achieved. Cutter knew that his specific entry system would obliterate any display of the normal classificatory relationships of subjects. Particular subjects that are logically related to each other would be scattered randomly throughout the alphabetically arranged catalog. While specific entry contributed to "facility of reference," it hindered those readers whose subject searching was aided by displays of the classificatory relationships between subjects. To overcome that loss, Cutter added a structure of cross-references ("see also" references) to his specific entry system. These consisted of a thoroughly devised set of references from broader to narrower subjects, occasional references between related subjects (subjects related nonhierarchically), and very occasional references from narrower to broader subjects. When instituted, his system of cross-references had the effect of tying the randomly arranged subjects together in a logical manner. They contributed, in other words, to the syndetic, or interrelated, nature of the catalog and held the promise of securing for the reader "some of the advantages of classification and system."[43]

Three difficulties arise with Cutter's cross-reference structure. First, the idea of displaying the relationships between subjects, while perhaps adequate for what has already been described as Cutter's generally simple world of subjects, does not seem particularly realistic for the complex world of subjects faced by subject catalogers today. It is one thing, in other words, to show the relationship between MAMMALS and CATS by the reference MAMMALS, see also CATS, but quite another to show appropriate references from MULTI-WALL KRAFT PAPER SACKS FOR CEMENT PACKAGING, MANUFACTURE OF to other subjects related to it either hierarchically or coordinately. Furthermore, even should appropriate references be devised for subjects like the latter, as the number of complex subject names increase, the cross-references required by them will necessarily increase in even greater numbers. A catalog of that sort will eventually become clogged by its cross-reference system.

Second, the value of the kinds of cross-references, while apparently settled in Cutter's mind, is not particularly clear. Why, for example, is there a greater value placed on downward directed references than on upward directed ones? Cutter's only answer was that the upward kind, while admittedly useful, were simply too numerous to make. Thus, he required the catalog user simply to understand their value and search for subjects based on them on his or her own. Chiefly downward references would be supplied. The difficulty with his reasoning is that it seems predicated on the amount of labor and space required rather than on the value of the references to the reader. Considering his supposed emphasis on the "convenience of the public," his argument appears to be out of place. Furthermore, his requirement that the reader understand the nature of upward references seems unjustified. One could argue that the user should understand downward subject relationships so that they could be omitted as well.

The third difficulty raised by Cutter's cross-reference structure concerns how it might be accomplished. Cutter appears to have had in mind the conditions of making a printed book catalog in which one could, upon having compiled all the various subject entries, view the various subjects as elements of a limited and closed system of subject relationships. Indeed, a limited number of subjects would greatly facilitate identifying the logical relationships involved. Today's catalogs and, perhaps, many of those in Cutter's time as well, are not limited in that way. Rather, they are constantly acquiring new subjects, many of which are very complex and which do not admit with any great clarity the references that should be made. This difficulty, when combined with the other two already mentioned, makes it reasonable to question both the value and the viability of making a cross-reference system of the kind that Cutter proposed.

Conclusions and Conflict

The nature of the criticisms leveled at Cutter regarding the various basic issues discussed here makes it difficult to avoid two general conclusions. First, Cutter's approach to dictionary subject cataloging appears to incorporate basic difficulties of such magnitude as to suggest that it was fundamentally unsound. Specifically, he appears to have written his rules on the basis of principles (e.g., specific entry and common usage) that were at one time or another not carried out consistently, at cross-purposes with each other, insufficiently explained, or indeterminative and unhelpful. Second, given the supposition that more recent practice is based on Cutter's work, one may also conclude that regardless of what corrective measures, if any, may have been taken by those who followed him, the same difficulties that are evident in Cutter's work are present today.

As forceful as these conclusions may seem, however, there are two significant reasons to question them. First, to accept the conclusion about Cutter's work, one must assume that Cutter was out of character in a most unusual way. This writer's previous general study of Cutter shows that his library work arose from a highly rationalized general view of life and society, an intellectual framework of reference that, while not expressed directly by him, nevertheless permeated the entire range of his accomplishments. The effect of this intellectual framework of reference and its attendant demands on Cutter's methodology was to cause him to approach any particular task as a conscious effort at systematization. In fact, one may most aptly describe him as a library systematizer or system-maker.[44] This is not to say, of course, that Cutter blindly failed to recognize the impossibility of rationalizing all elements of any particular task or that he naively thought that he could foresee all effects of any particular decision or course of action. It does suggest, however, that he was highly cognizant of illogic and irrationality—that in fact he chafed at it to an extraordinary degree—and that he attempted to eradicate it whenever he could. When he could not do so, he ordinarily took pains to explain why.

That Cutter applied the same goal of systematization to subject cataloging work as he did to other aspects of his library endeavors is nowhere more impressively recorded than in his words of introduction to the entire subject section of his *Rules*:

> The importance of deciding aright where any given subject shall be entered is in inverse proportion to the difficulty of decision. If there is no obvious principle to guide the cataloger, it is plain there will be no reason why the public should expect to find the entry under one heading rather than another, and therefore in regard to the public it matters not which is chosen. But it is better that such decisions should be made to conform when possible to some general system, as there is then more likelihood that they will be decided alike by different catalogers, and that a usage will grow up which the public will finally learn and profit by, as a usage has grown up in regard to the author-entry of French names containing De, Du, La, etc.[45]

His words are forceful. If there is little importance in making right decisions—that is, decisions derived from basic principles—then, obviously, individual decisions will be much more difficult, each having to be made in an ad hoc manner with little guidance. On the other hand, if great importance is attached to achieving right decisions based on principles, then individual decisions will be easier because consistent guidance will be available. As a corollary, if decisions are made without recourse to basic principles, then the public will not be able to approach the subject catalog with any expectation of consistent results in searching and, consequently, will not care how the catalog works. On the other hand, a subject catalog based on a system will lend itself to the growth of use patterns by patrons and to consistent cataloging among librarians.

In short, Cutter meant that a subject catalog should first of all be a system of elements that will produce reasonably consistent results. This view does not, of course, accord with the general conclusion about Cutter's system noted above. If, in fact, his subject heading work was fundamentally problem-ridden, then in this particular area of his work he must have suffered a decided lapse of mind and motivation—this, when he was approaching the height of his powers.[46]

A second reason for questioning the above conclusions is that the nature of the connection between Cutter and present-day practices has never been seriously examined. No thorough study of the historical development of dictionary subject cataloging has yet been made. Conclusions have been drawn now and again as to the character of the more general developments in subject access, but these have tended to treat dictionary subject cataloging more or less as a static phenomenon that has experienced few changes of significance.[47]

One result of this approach to dictionary subject cataloging history has been that the role of Cutter's work in twentieth century practice has remained, at best, a shadowy presence. In the absence of any serious study of Cutter's work as a system, commentators on dictionary subject cataloging have found it convenient simply to refer selectively to sections of his writings (for the most part to his *Rules*) without undue concern for understanding what Cutter meant in terms of his overall point of view. In other words, it has been assumed that what Cutter meant by one or another idea or practice corresponds to what is meant by those ideas and practices today. This has tended to transform Cutter's work and his name into something of a totem. Earlier advocates of dictionary subject cataloging tended to invoke the name of Cutter as a way, seemingly, to add the weight of authority to their own conclusions. Since the 1938 publication of S. R. Ranganathan's *Theory of Library Catalogue,* one may add to that tendency the steadily increasing practice of citing Cutter as a negative influence on contemporary work.[48] The latter tendency has led to the opposite extreme, the uncritical rejection of Cutter's work in the same manner that earlier advocates uncritically accepted it. At its worst, this attitude uses Cutter as little more than a scapegoat.[49]

Still another result of this approach to dictionary subject cataloging has been to neglect the ideas and practices of twentieth-century persons as if their contributions had little originality and were of little importance to contemporary practices. Likewise, the influence on dictionary subject cataloging of such striking twentieth-century developments as the differentiation of the library movement into types of libraries or the rise of the information revolution, has not been closely scrutinized.

The picture that has resulted from this approach to dictionary subject cataloging is singularly deficient. Present-day problems have been identified and criticized and something of an etiology has been given for them. But when the results are closely examined, it appears to this writer that, with the exception of Metcalfe, little of a convincing nature has been said as to how dictionary subject cataloging has arrived at its present state.

The present work constitutes an attempt to provide a meaningful alternative to the view of dictionary subject cataloging just described. Both the ideas and the practices of notable dictionary subject catalog advocates will be closely examined, beginning with Cutter and continuing with others who have been influential during the present century. In addition, the influence on dictionary subject cataloging of other more general trends in subject access in the twentieth century will be assessed.

CHAPTER 2

Subjects as Subjects Alone

It may seem strange to ask at the start what Cutter meant by the idea of a subject or subjects. Most writers appear to have assumed this term to be more or less self-explanatory, there being relatively few extended discussions of the matter.[1] Indeed, Cutter himself offered little formal help in the matter. His two most nearly formal definitions of subject are:

> *Subject*, the theme or themes of the book, whether stated in the title or not.[2]
>
> Subject is the matter on which the author is seeking to give or the reader to obtain information; . . .[3]

Elsewhere he spoke of books as being written about "object(s) of investigation," "objects of inquiry," and "matters of investigation."[4] But, none of these references are particularly helpful for explaining what Cutter considered a subject to be per se. The first two offer only synonyms for the term (i.e., theme and matter) and the last three cloud the issue by referring to indistinct or nameless subjects. Nowhere, in fact, does Cutter define the idea of a subject distinctly and conclusively. Nevertheless, some clarification in the matter is offered by a distinction (only implicit here but elsewhere spoken of more directly by Cutter) between questions of the locations of subjects and questions of what subjects are. Cutter suggested this distinction when, in describing theological subjects, he spoke of their distinctiveness as a characteristic that pertained to them regardless of their location—that is, "whether in books or only in thought."[5]

In other words, subjects have characteristics that exist before one's speaking of them in terms of their location. Indeed, Cutter's various writings about subject access are filled with an almost bewildering variety of terms that, while used to describe now and again the subjects of particular books, are not dependent on books as vehicles in which they are found. Rather, the terms refer to an orderly way to think of

24

subjects—that is, to a structure in which subjects are naturally found.

The most common terms that he employed are: general subjects, comprehensive subjects, more (or less) extensive subjects, subordinate subjects, general subordinate subjects, subdivisions (or parts, chapters) of subjects, classes of subjects, individual subjects, specific subjects, special subjects, and particular subjects, to name the most important. He also referred constantly to particularly named subjects, identifying them now and again with one or another of the foregoing categories. Given this specialized vocabulary that Cutter employed when speaking of subjects, it is important first to sort out the terminology involved and second to venture some conclusion as to its origin. Then questions of how he thought of subjects in relationship to books and in relationship to the public may be broached. Together, these three discussions (the contents of this and the following two chapters) will provide a more specific referent to Cutter's use of the idea of subject.

Kinds of Subjects

Cutter constantly spoke of subjects in terms of a very particular nomenclature, in which he differentiated between subjects on the basis of what they referred to. In his thinking, all subjects were of two distinct groups: general subjects and individual subjects.

> It is worth noting that subjects are of two sorts: (1) the individual, as GOETHE, SHAKESPEARE, ENGLAND, the MIDDLE AGES, the ship ALEXANDRA, the dog TRAY, the FRENCH REVOLUTION, all of which are concrete; and (2) general, as MAN, HISTORY, HORSE, PHILOSOPHY, which may be either concrete or abstract.[6]

The chief difference between the two groups is that individual subjects were reflections of whole, particular (i.e., unique, singular), concrete things, often denoted by proper names, whereas general subjects consisted of conceptual categories, themselves ultimately reflections of the qualities of particular things rather than particular things in and of themselves.

Furthermore, Cutter also divided general subjects into two subgroups: abstract and concrete. That is to say, one kind of general subject consisted of conceptual categories that directly reflected concrete things, whereas the other kind of general subject consisted of conceptual categories that reflected only abstractions. For example, Cutter called MAN and HORSE concrete general subjects because they directly reflected actual men and horses. On the other hand, HISTORY and PHILOSOPHY did not reflect for him any concrete thing, but rather only the abstractions of history and philosophy.

In summary, for Cutter there were actually three kinds of subjects: individual subjects, concrete general subjects, and abstract general subjects. These three kinds of subjects included in their purview all possible subjects. And any particular subject of necessity had to be one of these three kinds.

Subjects and Classificatory Relationships

Besides categorizing subjects, Cutter also spoke of subjects in terms of the classificatory distinctions of class and subclass relationships. Cutter defined a class at its most fundamental level as "a collection of objects having characteristics in common."[7] In this general sense, the collection might be of any kind of objects, tangible or intangible, such as books, plants, or angels. Thus, a collection of a dozen books, all of which have some characteristic in common—for example, their size, color, or subject matter—constitute a class of tangible items, in this case, of course, a book class. If the book class is gathered on the basis of a subject characteristic, such as the fact that all the books are in some way about cats, it might then be given the label CATS or some other arbitrarily assigned symbol. The books themselves are the "objects" that make up the class and their common characteristic—that is, the basis for their being grouped together—is the fact that each of them treats the topic Cats.

When the idea of a class is applied to subjects per se, the sense of what are the objects so collected changes because the objects are now "subjects"—that is, nontangible intellections spoken or written down. A class of subjects is, thus, "a grouping of subjects which have characteristics in common."[8] Said in a different way, a class is a superordinate subject that includes in its purview other subordinate subjects, all having something in common that allows them to be a part of the class. Likewise, the constituent subjects included in a class may themselves include still other subordinate subjects that have some common characteristic that allows them to be considered parts of their superordinate subject. For example, Mammals may be considered a subject, but also a class of subordinate subjects that includes all the particular animals or all of the particular kinds of animals that are mammals. And when enumerated, each of the kinds of mammals may not only be considered a subject, but also may be considered a class in that it includes all the different species of that particular mammal. Thus, Cats, a constituent subject of the class Mammals, is itself a class when all the various kinds of cats are considered. Similarly, one particular kind of cat, say Siamese cats, may also be considered a class when all particular varieties of Siamese cats or when all particular Siamese cats are listed under it.

For Cutter, to consider subjects in this way was to speak of the inclusion relationship that pertained to them when in conjunction with one another. Cutter referred to the idea of class inclusion frequently in his writings, particularly when he spoke of subjects as more (or less) extensive. For example, he described the subject Theology in terms consonant with this picture:

> THEOLOGY, which is itself a subject, is also a class, that is, it is extensive enough to have its parts, its chapters, so to speak (as FUTURE LIFE, HOLY SPIRIT, REGENERATION, SIN, TRINITY), treated separately, each when so treated (whether in books or only in thought) being itself a subject; all these together, inasmuch as they possess this in common, that they have to do with some part of the relations of God to man, form the class of subjects THEOLOGY.9

Cutter elsewhere spoke of the same relationships as a matter of subject extent or breadth. He referred to comprehensive or less comprehensive subjects, extensive or less extensive subjects, and, with each of these, he sometimes spoke of their subordinate subjects, parts, or branches, or of their divisions and subdivisions. For example, in speaking of the syndetic or cross-reference structure of the dictionary catalog, Cutter provided a discrete picture of the hierarchical class structure upon which this view of subjects was based:

> *Syndetic,* connective, applied to that kind of a dictionary catalog which binds its entries together by means of cross-references so as to form a whole, the references being made from the most comprehensive subjects to those of the next lower degree of comprehensiveness, and from each of these to their subordinate subjects, and vice versa.10

In addition Cutter sometimes used the alternative terminology "general" subjects and "special" or "specific" subjects to express the same sense of differences in breadth. For example, he sometimes described the extent of any particular subject in terms of how specific it was, that is, whether it was more or less extensive. He wrote in one place, "The dictionary catalogue gives information . . . *all* about a subject, if it is very specific, so that there are no subordinate subjects."11

In other places he occasionally spoke of specific subjects in relationship to general subjects as elements of the same continuum of subject extent. For example, in speaking of the cross-reference system in the dictionary catalog, he wrote, "References are needed not merely to the specific from the general but to the general from the more general and to that from the most general,"12 and also, "Make references occasionally from specific to general subjects."[13] Likewise, Cutter occasionally used the phrase "special subject" synonymously with "specific subject" in the same sense of subject breadth difference, although he limited this usage to his article "Library Catalogues." For example, Cutter described the dictionary catalog as one

> in which the attempt to subordinate individuals to classes, and classes to one another, is abandoned, and the subjects, special or general, are arranged like the words in a lexicon.[14]

And in comparing the merits of Ezra Abbot's Harvard College library alphabetico-classed catalog with a dictionary catalog, he wrote,

> The Abbot system is best adapted for the thorough investigation of comprehensive subjects; the dictionary system for finding quickly what relates to a person, a place, or a special topic.
>
> [Footnote to the above]:
> This may be illustrated by a comparison with the use of scientific works. One can study chemistry, for instance, best in a systematically arranged treatise; one could also study it well in an encyclopedia, in which the great divisions of chemistry should be arranged in alphabetical order, and the minor topics treated together under those heads; but it would be very hard to study in Watt's Dictionary of Chemistry. Yet to the practical chemist, desirous of instant information about carophyllin or arsenides of methyll or sulphotriphosphamide, Watts is indispensable, and his arrangement decidedly the best.[15]

Cutter's comparison leaves little doubt that the idea of a "special topic" is synonymous with "specific subject." That is to say, it indicated a subject of considerably narrower rather than broader extent.

Two words of caution should be noted in this picture of classificatory relationships. First, the use of the adjectives "special" and "specific" with the term "subject" is not without confusion, since Cutter also used them in still other ways, namely, in relationship to a significance order among subjects and in relationship to books. Both of these uses will be explained later. Second, Cutter's sense of classificatory relationships is not technical in the sense in which a logician might have explained the terms involved or in the sense that modern mathematical logic might approach the same ideas. Cutter's sense of classificatory relationships appears much more akin to the common-sense logic of the man in the street. Thus, for example, a class is literally any group of objects, regardless of whether the constituency of the group consists of individual objects or still other subgroups of objects.[16]

Classes and Kinds of Subjects

Cutter's idea of a class, as fundamental as it was to his idea of inclusion relationships between subjects, was qualified by a special distinction. Although he had delineated three kinds of subjects—abstract general, concrete general, and individual—he considered only the two kinds of general subjects to be classes. He wrote concerning the relationship between the terms "subject" and "class,"

> A little reflection will show that the words so used partially overlap, the general subjects being classes and the classes being subjects, but the individual subjects never being classes.[17]

In other words, general subjects, because they were notions capable of being divided into constituent notions of lesser extent were automatically classes "more or less extensive."[18] This did not mean that every general subject represented a very extensive class. Obviously, some general subjects were of such limited extent that their divisions might not be apparent. For example, Cutter apparently considered the general subjects Carophyllin, Arsenides of methyl, and Sulphotriphosphamide to be relatively indivisible as classes.[19]

Individual subjects, on the other hand, most often occurring as particular things or animals (e.g., particular ships, buildings, dogs, horses, etc.), as particular persons, and as particular places, did not consist of a group of subjects having like characteristics, but rather only of single unique objects. It was unthinkable for him, for example, to consider that some individual person might also connote some group of persons of like characteristics. Thus, individual subjects could not be considered classes.

Cutter's approach to the above distinction between general subjects and individual subjects with respect to whether they were classes has a strong ring of common sense about it. But his conclusion that individual subjects were never classes was not without difficulties in some instances. For example, Cutter recognized that to always consider particular places as individual subjects could cause some confusion. A particular place could, for example, be considered a class depending upon its use.

> It is plain enough that MT. JEFFERSON, JOHN MILTON, the WARRIOR IRON-CLAD are not classes. Countries, however, which for most purposes it is convenient to consider as individual, are in certain aspects classes; when by the word "England" we mean "the English" it is the name of a class.[20]

A particular place could also be considered a class of yet more localized places, or at least as consisting of parts that are themselves more localized places. For example, Middlesex County, Massachusetts, could be considered a class, the elements of which consist of all its various towns, their common characteristic being their location within the area called Middlesex County.[21] In the same way, an individual person might be considered a class made up of a group of anatomical parts. Of course, one might argue as well that these latter examples are not strictly equal to the idea of a general subject and its subdivisions as Cutter understood them. The "parts" of general subjects, regardless of whether they reflect even concrete objects, are, at their base, categories based on abstract differentia. The parts of individual subjects are not so differentiated but rather represent still other individual subjects. The relationship that each has with the individual subject of which it is a part is extrinsic and not based on abstract qualities. Regardless of these difficulties, however, Cutter proceeded on the assumption that individual subjects were for all practical purposes essentially different than general subjects in that they could not be considered classes.

Inclusion Relationships and Significance Order

Although Cutter viewed the relationships between subjects in general as a matter of classificatory inclusion, it is difficult to identify what method or approach he employed to determine the inclusion relationships between any particular combination of subjects—that is, to determine which one of a coordinated set of two subjects was superordinate and which was subordinate. To use such examples as Mammals-Cats-Siamese cats or Theology-Future life-etc. is somewhat misleading in this respect because the class-subclass order in these cases can be seen as a function of more or less explicitly defined and commonly agreed upon differentia. Other combinations, such as Circulation of the blood, Fertilization of flowers, Death penalty, Geology and revelation, New England ornithology, or Ancient history, to name a few such combinations that he referred to in his *Rules,* would not seem to yield the same distinctions with equal clarity.

Of course, Cutter may have appealed to some master classification scheme as an authority for such decisions. But that conclusion, while possible, seems unlikely because Cutter also held the opinion that subjects had innumerable relationships (with new ones occurring all the time) and that new subjects were themselves constantly appearing. Thus, the existence of any such authority device was a practical impossibility. Furthermore, he spent a lifetime working on a classification scheme, although he believed that formal classification schemes were ultimately founded on public consensus and, thus, likely to change over time.

Nevertheless, it remains that Cutter did approach all subject relationships as matters of classificatory inclusion. In fact, it is of the utmost importance to determine his approach to this matter, since it provided a basis for how he ultimately listed subjects in a subject catalog—his citation order, in modern terms—and thus how he went about what he called specific entry. The key to his approach can best be characterized as the order of significance that he attached to kinds of subjects.

In searching for clues as to how Cutter approached the relationships between particular sets of subjects, the section of his *Rules* on compound subjects (rules 174–175) is particularly helpful because there more than anywhere else Cutter referred to subjects coordinated with one another. One of the most instructive comments occurs where Cutter concluded that the combinations Comparative anatomy and Capital punishment could be considered in the following way: "the noun is the name of a general subject, one of whose subdivisions is indicated by the adjective."[22] In other words, Anatomy and Punishment were to be considered classes and, therefore, superordinate subjects, while Comparative (an adjective) and Capital (when used as an adjective) were to be considered subdivisions of the classes. Written in modern heading-subheading form as classed sequences, these would appear as ANATOMY–COMPARATIVE and PUNISHMENT–CAPITAL. From this one might conclude that Cutter's method for determining the class inclusion relationships that exist between subjects was to reduce subject combinations to adjectival relationships in which the qualified term would always be considered the including class, the qualifying term the included class. And viewed this way, it appears that he based significance order ultimately on grammatical relationships.

This conclusion is only incidental to what was a more important factor to Cutter. Cutter was not satisfied that this example fully illustrated what he was attempting to show. He suggested that while Comparative and Capital functioned as subdivisions and, therefore, limited the scope of the nouns as classes, they did not at the same time "imply any general subject."[23] That is to say, the examples did not yield a subject-to-subject relationship in the strictest sense of the idea.

Cutter went on to examine another pair of examples—ANCIENT HISTORY and MEDIEVAL HISTORY—that more fully represented what he meant. First, he repeated the same general analysis that he had used in the first pair of examples—"History the class, Ancient history and

Medieval history the subdivisions."[24] But then he shifted the focus of his discussion by reformulating the subject combinations as ANTIQUITY: *History* and MIDDLE AGES: *History*, constructions analogous to the genitive formulations, History of Antiquities and History of the Middle Ages. His purpose for doing so was to draw one's attention to the likeness of these formulations to still another subject combination, EUROPE: *History*. The importance of this likeness to his analysis is that it allowed him to refer the reader to a previous section (rules 164–165) where he had already discussed the same kinds of combinations in a rule pertaining to general subjects and places. His discussion both in the earlier rule and reiterated in the present case sheds considerable light on his thinking.

Cutter described subject combinations involving general subjects and places in two ways.[25] If in a single subject combination or in a series of such combinations, the general subject preceded the place—as in Ornithology of America, Ornithology of New England, Ornithology of Scotland, or, likewise, History of Europe, History of Antiquities,—the resulting combinations were to be considered class-inclusion relationships. If, however, the combinations were reversed, the place preceding the general subjects, the resulting combinations were not to be considered class-inclusion relationships.

Cutter's reasoning for this was fundamentally related to his nomenclature of subjects. A place was for him an individual subject. As such, it could not include any other subjects because it stood at the absolutely narrowest point of subject specificity or scope. By the same reasoning, an individual subject, when combined with any general subject, would be considered included in the general subject because any general subject was ultimately made up of individual subjects. From these examples, one may see immediately that Cutter was not interested in the adjective-noun grammatical construction for its own sake. He was interested in it because underneath it resided a more compelling rationale for determining inclusion relationships—that is, the significance order of the kinds of subjects involved in such constructions.

Of course, one may likewise conclude on the basis of these singular examples that the range of combinations thus explained is actually limited only to combinations of general subjects and individual subjects. The significance order of other combinations, especially those in which no individual subjects were involved, are not themselves explained. The table of examples in Figure 2, based on Cutter's full nomenclature of kinds of subjects, serves to illustrate such combinations.

By the reasoning already described, in numbers one to three in Figure

1. INDIVIDUAL SUBJECT / ABSTRACT GENERAL SUBJECT
   Example: The History of New England

2. INDIVIDUAL SUBJECT / CONCRETE GENERAL SUBJECT
   Example: New England Railroads

3. INDIVIDUAL SUBJECT / CONCRETE GENERAL SUBJECT / ABSTRACT
   GENERAL SUBJECT
   Example: The Behavior of New England Collies

4. INDIVIDUAL SUBJECT / INDIVIDUAL SUBJECT
   Example: Lassie and Rin Tin Tin compared

5. CONCRETE GENERAL SUBJECT / ABSTRACT GENERAL SUBJECT
   Example: The History of Railroads

6. CONCRETE GENERAL SUBJECT / CONCRETE GENERAL SUBJECT
   Example: Railroad Machinery

7. ABSTRACT GENERAL SUBJECT / ABSTRACT GENERAL SUBJECT
   Example: The History of Theology

Underlining key: ————— = Individual subject
                   - - - - - = Concrete general subject
                   . . . . = Abstract general subject

FIG. 2.   Examples of Cutter's Significance Order

2, where individual subjects are combined with general subjects of either kind (abstract or concrete), the individual subject, because of its nonclass and specific characteristics, will always be considered the included subject as far as significance order is concerned. But, the question remains, how shall one determine significance order when the two kinds of general subjects are combined?

Some suggestion of how Cutter thought regarding this wider range of combinations is contained in his extended comments about examples previously referred to. Cutter described the combination of New England with Ornithology not only as a relationship of individual subject with a general subject, but also as a relationship between objects and aspects (or sides). In comparing the two citation orders possible—one common to classed catalogs, the other to dictionary catalogs, and the reason why he preferred the latter—he wrote:

> Because entry under ORNITHOLOGY OF NEW ENGLAND . . . is, when taken in connection with the entries that would be grouped around it (ORNITHOLOGY, ORNITHOLOGY OF AMERICA, ORNITHOLOGY OF SCOTLAND, etc.), in effect class-entry; whereas the similar grouping under New England does not make that a class, inasmuch as NEW ENGLAND BOTANY, NEW ENGLAND HISTORY, NEW ENGLAND ORNITHOLOGY are not parts of New

> England, but simply the individual New England considered in various aspects. Of course the dictionary catalog in choosing between a class and an individual prefers the latter. Its object is to show at one view all the sides of each object; the classed catalog shows together the same side of many objects.[26]

In other words, the combination individual subject–general subject is tantamount to a sequence of object and aspect (or side), the reverse combination a sequence of side and object. In his examples of ANTIQUITY: *History* and MIDDLE AGES: *History* (in rule 175), he referred to the same formulation with only a slight variation in terminology: "The adjectives (Ancient, Mediaeval) imply a subject and the noun (History) indicates the aspect in which the subject is viewed."[27] He had converted the adjectives to their individual subject forms to show more clearly that the important comparison here was between individual subjects and general subjects, not simply adjectives and nouns.

Now, again, one might suppose that the significance of "object" in comparison to "aspect" is no more than that of individual subject to general subject. If this is indeed the case, then the reader is no further ahead than before in identifying a significance order between subject combinations not involving individual subjects. But, a final example suggests that the significance of "object" did not reside simply in its being an individual subject, but rather in the concreteness that an individual subject implied. His example was the subject combination Death penalty, notable because it included two general subjects, rather than a general subject and an individual subject. He wrote:

> e.g., we can have various headings for Death considered in different lights, among others as a penalty; and we can have headings of various sorts of penalties, among others death. It is evident that the collection of penalties taken together make up a class, . . . but the series of headings beginning with the word Death would not make a class, being merely different aspects of the same thing, not different subordinate parts of the same subject.[28]

In his explanation the terminology for the nonclassed sequence—thing/aspect—is clearly parallel to that of his previous examples—object/aspect and subject/aspect. In this case, however, "thing" is a concrete general subject (Death) and "aspect" an abstract general subject (Penalty). The significance of "object" and "thing" is not, therefore, that they are particular kinds of subjects, but rather that they have a greater degree of concreteness and, therefore, a greater degree of subject-scope narrowness than the "aspects" or sides with which they have been combined.

Seen in this light, Cutter's significance order is therefore greatly extended. Among the three kinds of subjects, the basic order of significance for determining inclusion relationships is abstract general/concrete general/individual. An abstract general subject, when combined with either concrete general subjects or individual subjects, includes them both as elements or divisions; a concrete general subject, when combined with individual subjects, includes them as elements or divisions; but individual subjects stand alone with no divisions. Conversely, an individual subject never includes either concrete general or abstract general subjects. And a concrete general subject never includes an abstract general subject. As a corollary, the relationship of individual subject to general subject of either kind and of concrete general subject to abstract general subject—that is, when subjects of the more concrete kind are qualified by those of a more abstract kind—is one of object or thing to aspect.

Applied to the examples in Figure 2, this significance order would mean that the subject Railroads is a subdivision of History in number five, but that conversely, History is only an aspect of Railroads. Likewise, the significance order for class inclusion in number three would be Behavior-Collies-New England, but conversely, New England is qualified by the aspects Collies and Behavior, and Collies is qualified by the aspect Behavior.

The Problem of Indeterminancy

Cutter's significance order was apparently satisfactory to him as a practical method for determining inclusion relationships between combinations of the three different kinds of subjects in his subject nomenclature. But it presented problems when extended beyond those combinations to combinations of the same kinds of subjects—specifically, to those shown in numbers four, six and seven in Figure 2. The chief difficulty is that the subjects in such combinations cannot be differentiated on the basis of sweeping differences pertaining to kinds of subjects.

It seems likely, therefore, that it was at this point that Cutter's knowledge of generally held opinions about particular subject relationships may have influenced some of his classificatory decisions. At least, that would seem to be the case in examples such as Mammals/Cats, etc. and Theology/Future life, etc. But that approach would seem to have been helpful only in those situations in which the subjects were closely related within a subject discipline and thus contained obvious bases on which to differentiate them. In other cases where the subjects were of different orders altogether, Cutter may well have appealed to common opinion and tradition or the convention of taking the noun in an adjective-noun combination to be the "more general idea, and the other i.e., the adjective as limiting it."[29] No other explanation seems capable of explaining his respective conclusions that History was an aspect and not a subdivision of Theology (number 7 in Figure 2) or that Machinery was an aspect rather than a subdivision of Railroads (number 6 in Figure 2). Both examples are found in his Boston Athenaeum catalog.

In many other cases, Cutter simply allowed indeterminate combinations to stand as they were, treating the subjects so combined as if each were without an inclusion relationship to the other. With respect to combination of individual subjects, this procedure is an understandable resolution. Since individual subjects could not be considered classes, no one individual subject could include another (except, of course, for a case such as Middlesex County, Massachusetts, noted above). Thus, in the concocted example in number four of Figure 2, Lassie and Rin Tin Tin could never be in an inclusion relationship to each other. Elsewhere in Cutter's writings and in the Boston Athenaeum catalog, this resolution is a common occurrence.

In many other cases where subjects of the same kind were simply too disparate to allow a judgment, Cutter simply bypassed the issue altogether by treating them as separate subjects that could not be related to one another in an inclusion relationship. Cutter took the latter approach in one especially instructive comment on the relationship of Geology to Theology as twin topics of a particular work. He wrote:

> It might be said, for example, that "Geology as a proof of revelation" would have for its *subject-matter* GEOLOGY but for its *class* THEOLOGY— which is true, not because class and subject are incompatible but because this book has two subjects, the first GEOLOGY, the second one of the evidence of revealed religion, wherefore, as the EVIDENCES are a subdivision of THEOLOGY, the book belongs under that as a subject-class.[30]

That is to say, of the two general subjects, Theology and Geology, Cutter was concerned that one not end up with the class-subdivision combination THEOLOGY–GEOLOGY, based on the idea that Geology was the direct subject matter of the work and was in some way narrower in scope and therefore subordinate to Theology. Thus, after pointing out that the particular subject matter of the work was the more limited subject Evidences (i.e., Evidences of revealed religion, a subdivision of Theology), he stated that that subject alone was subordinate to

Theology. In his analysis of the relationship between Geology and Evidences, he concluded only that two subjects were present and did not attempt to determine their significance order.

Result of Cutter's Approach to Inclusion Relationships

The most significant result of Cutter's approach to inclusion relationships was that it enabled him to identify with reasonable confidence what he considered to be the "most specific" subject in a large number of sets of coordinated subjects. Given the application of his significance order to combinations of different kinds of subjects or given cases in which like subjects presented relatively clear instances of understandable differentia, the subject within each combination that was at the most extended end of the chain of subjects—that was, in effect, "included" by all the other subjects—could be said to be more specific or narrower in subject scope than any of the others. Thus, in Figure 2 the individual subjects in numbers one to three and the concrete general subject in number five would obviously be the most specific subjects in their respective sets because of the inclusion relationship pertaining to kinds of subjects in general. According to the reasoning already explained regarding six and seven, Railroad and Theology would be the most specific subjects in their respective sets. Of course where the inclusion relationship was indeterminate—for example, between the two individual subjects, Lassie and Rin Tin Tin in number four—or between other particular combinations of like kinds of subjects that could not easily be compared, a most specific subject could not be determined in this way. Instead, the subjects would be considered equally most specific.

Cutter and Scottish Common Sense Realism

The foregoing description of subject nomenclature and significance order in Cutter's subject thinking provides a useful first step toward understanding how he approached the overall issue of subject access in libraries. And that description has been obtained only by culling hints from various portions of his writings. Cutter provided no formal explanation of these matters as prolegomena to his subject thinking. Because the ideas referred to arose from what, among at least the educated readers of Cutter's own generation, was a common intellectual framework of reference regarding the human thinking process and the ability to acquire knowledge, Cutter would have found it superfluous and redundant to include such an extended explanation for what his readers would have known already and what they would have considered a starting point in making a subject access system possible.

The specific source of Cutter's thinking about subjects was the psychologized epistemology of British empiricist thought that had begun with John Locke in the eighteenth century. Within that tradition the particular source of many of Cutter's ideas was the school of thought called Scottish common sense realism.[31] Scottish realism arose out of that spectacular flowering of intellect, the eighteenth century Scottish enlightenment, in which Scottish education, in pursuit of the idea of scientific and moral progress, replaced the then relatively sterile English academic community as the dominant intellectual force in the Anglo-American scene. This school of thought represented on the one hand a cohesive statement of epistemology, and on the other a general philosophy of individual and societal life and ethics. As an epistemology it occupied the labors of several notable philosophers. Those most commonly listed as its adherents were Thomas Reid (1710–96), his disciple Dugald Stewart (1753–1828), Thomas Browne (1778–1820), and somewhat later, Sir William Hamilton (1791–1856). It also included many other writers (e.g., Francis Hutcheson, Adam Ferguson, and Adam Smith) noted for their views on moral and social issues and widely influential in England, France, and America.

The intellectual breadth of the movement was impressive. In science, its adherents, appealing to Isaac Newton as their exemplar, contributed heavily to the fields of chemistry, astronomy, and physics, and to what afterward became the social sciences of economics and political science. They also exercised an overwhelming interest in mathematics because it represented for them the purest exercise of human reasoning. Their most spectacular achievements were in the realm of psychology, however, for in their concern to discover with Newtonian precision how one "knows," they extended the psychologizing tradition begun by John Locke into more detailed analyses of human mental processes.[32]

The original concern of the Scottish realists was to counter the epistemological skepticism of David Hume regarding how and what one knows about the world. Their goal was to state the knowing process in such a way as to preserve a rational basis for both scientific inquiry and moral activity. This goal arose in turn from a conviction that all phenomena were elements of a harmonious and rational universe created by a benevolent deity and capable of being discovered by analytical procedures. Their chief method for discovering the knowing process was to observe and record how their own thinking processes functioned. In sum, Scottish realists sought to do what Immanuel Kant, their contemporary, also dealt with in his own critical inquiries when he attempted to explain how one obtains knowledge of the world. But, instead of resorting to a fundamental division between the noumenal and the phenomenal worlds and a set of fundamental categories of mind through which we know the latter as Kant had done, they outlined a broad-ranging realism that accounted for all phenomena (material as well as nonmaterial) and closely analyzed the mental processes involved in both perceiving that world and acquiring the knowledge about it that was important for personal and societal conduct.

Their fundamental tenet, stated first by Reid, was that one perceives real objects, not simply ideas, as Hume and Berkeley had asserted, and that the reality of those objects, accepted by one's common sense, assures us that what is perceived really does exist. Furthermore, the objects so perceived are not limited simply to physical phenomena, but include fundamental nonmaterial phenomena as well—for example, fundamental relationships relating to value, such as the perception of right and wrong and of merit and demerit. Finally, given a basic font of perceptual knowledge to work with, one could mentally process that information to acquire knowledge of the true and harmonious relations of both nature and society and to conduct oneself in a manner that would reflect that harmony. The ultimate goal of the acquisition of knowledge was, therefore, to discover the first principles of nature and society. In fact, this goal was the fundamental meaning of science. Discovering the first principles was more than an individual activity, however, because it involved a cumulative societal process. Furthermore, the quest was viewed optimistically as already well under way in the physical sciences in the eighteenth century. It was also believed that the first principles of the social realm would soon be discovered as well.

Learning about nature and society was not automatic, however. The processes by which one might arrive at true knowledge of first principles and, ultimately, of action were dependent upon how the mind itself functioned. Thus, in a manner patterned after the investigations of Newton and others who studied the physical world and with a methodology that was deeply indebted to Locke, Berkeley, and Hume, Scottish realists systematically analyzed their own mental activities in order to see how the mind functioned. As a result of their investigations, the British tradition of empiricism was further psychologized in that form sometimes called faculty psychology. So strong was this tradition, in fact, that it was ultimately superseded only after the mid-nineteenth century through the criticism of the utilitarian John Stuart Mill, the labors of British idealist philosophers, and the advances brought about by experimental psychology.

One important facet of Scottish common sense realism was that the views of its proponents were transplanted to America as early as 1768 in the work of John Witherspoon at Princeton. Afterwards and especially throughout the ante-bellum period, Scottish realism enjoyed an influence on American thought and life that was overwhelming. It tenets were present among Revolutionary leaders such as Franklin, Paine, and Jefferson. It had a permanent effect on American religion after the prerevolutionary Calvinist era. And it became important as an underlying motif in American literature.

Most important, however, Scottish realism became the fundamental philosophy underlying the development of American higher education. As a formal system of mental and moral philosophy, it was presented to students in an unbroken tradition of courses and textbooks. Some of the latter were condensed versions of Reid and Stewart; others were unabashed adaptations of those earlier writers. The American version of the philosophy was not presented primarily as philosophical investigations, however. Having adopted the Scottish view of the intellectual faculties with little critical thought, American proponents dwelled more heavily on that realm of the school of thought that analyzed one's active powers. And from that body of knowledge American writers developed extended treatments and courses of moral philosophy. Usually taught by college presidents to graduating seniors, these courses and textbooks produced for them typically ranged far and wide over normative ethical issues related to contemporary social issues. This education factor is important because, with few exceptions, all early leaders of the American library movement who were educated before the Civil War were exposed to the tenets of Scottish thought.

Charles Ammi Cutter was himself thoroughly exposed to Scottish realism in the Unitarian movement in which he was reared and educated. Scottish thinking had been adopted in the American Unitarian movement almost from its beginning early in the nineteenth century. By 1851 when Cutter enrolled in Harvard College, then a bastion of Unitarian thought, the philosophy had become a basic element of Harvard's intellectual tradition. Cutter expressed the Scottish tradition in one way by taking much of his coursework in science. This included four years of mathematics from the notable American mathematician Benjamin Peirce. Furthermore, immediately after earning his A.B. degree, he enrolled in Harvard's Lawrence Scientific Institute in order to continue the study of mathematics under Peirce. But this came to naught and he resigned after one semester, subsequently enrolling in the Harvard Divinity School. Of greater importance is the fact that during his college years he received a thorough grounding in Scottish mental as well as moral philosophical principles under the teaching of Francis Bowen. The textbooks for his courses and from which he prepared his themes and recitations included American editions of Reid and Stewart produced by Bowen and Harvard president James Walker. He also seems to have retained some continuing interest in the ideas represented in this tradition because he found occasion after his graduation to borrow various volumes of their works, especially those of Stewart, from the Harvard library.[33]

Mental Faculties and Subject Structure

Cutter's view of subject structure closely reflected the general theory, fundamental to Scottish thought, of how the mind was structured and how it functioned in acquiring knowledge. Although the details of the theory varied from writer to writer, there were certain facets that remained essentially the same among them all and which formed the basis for Cutter's use of the theory in his subject system. A schematic representation of how that general theory was enumerated in Stewart's *Elements of the Philosophy of the Human Mind* and *Outlines of Moral Philosophy* might appear as sketched out in Figure 3.

The words on the diagram represent mental faculties. A mental faculty should not be viewed as a structural partition of the mind, but rather as a function, an ability, a process, or a power of the mind. Neither should the faculties be understood to operate in some sort of a rigid and sequential time frame. All of the realists readily agreed that the various faculties functioned simultaneously, or at least, in a constant interaction. The mental faculties were thus convenient abstractions, useful only to conceptualize a total process—the movement from initial perception to knowledge and action.

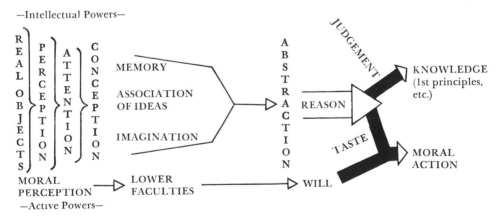

FIG. 3.   Mental Faculties: Scottish Common Sense Realism

It should also be noted that the diagram does not represent the full range of the mental faculties. The various mental faculties were generally divided into two basic groups: the intellectual powers (shown here) and the active powers of the will (referred to only briefly along the bottom of the diagram). The latter tended to be further divided into two subgroups: those that functioned rationally (moral perception, obligation, duty, and self-love) and those lowest powers that represented the basic propensities of the human personality (affections, desires, appetites). All three groups (intellectual powers/moral powers/ basic propensities) interacted with one another. But the lofty goal of moral philosophy was ultimately the balanced control of the three together, the lowest powers being held in check by the highest. Only the intellectual faculties are shown here because they are most directly related to Cutter's subject thinking.

The following important points should especially be noted. To begin with, the knowledge acquisition process has two primary foci: the perception of individuals and the conceptualization of general notions. Perception is the knowledge one obtains from sensing real or concrete objects. It thus represents the conversion of sense data into mental activity. The objects perceived are unities or wholes and when perceived present themselves to the mind as unique individual things. When thought of they then become individual notions. Individuals include such things as particular persons, places, cities—in fact, any particular thing that is distinguished from all other particular things. Perception is thus only of individuals and it takes place constantly.[34]

Upon perceiving individuals, however, the mind has powers that enable it to process its basic perceptual knowledge in a variety of ways. For example, the power of conception aided by the powers of memory and imagination enable one to form notions of absent objects of perception or of sensations which were formerly felt. The power of the association of ideas (described by Stewart as a series of laws) controls the patterns and sequences of the way such conceptions come about. Principles of association include "resemblance, analogy, contrariety, vicinity in place, vicinity in time, relation of cause and effect, relation of means and end, relation of premises and conclusions."[35]

The power of abstraction when disciplined by the power of reason enables one to describe and define (i.e., to make predications of) both perceived individuals and other general notions. As such, the predications are based on the attributes of individuals and represent notions of increasing generality. The continuous activity of the faculty of abstraction results in the formation of notions of still greater generality that are themselves combinations of notions of lesser generality. Their ultimate form is, in fact, the statement of the first principles of the true nature and relationships of all individually existing things, notions of the greatest generality of all. The functioning of this faculty is itself controlled by the powers of reasoning including both inductive and deductive logic, and the powers of judgment and taste.

The most striking feature of all the faculties beyond that of perception is that the knowledge with which they deal consists solely of general ideas. That is to say, the ideas produced by their operation, ultimately derived as they are from the attributes of individuals, are by definition categorical rather than individual. Furthermore, because they are categorical, they become the basis of classificatory relationships in which ideas are related to each other in a hierarchical or inclusive manner. The nature of the classificatory relationships had an important aspect, however. Some general notions were obviously related to each other on the basis of their specific logical connections. For example, cats were related to mammals because of the particular connotations and denotations that adhered to each general term. This aspect of classificatory inclusion relationships amounted to nothing less than the use of traditional logical distinctions between terms.

But the Scottish model of the mental processes went further by also providing a classificatory order between kinds of ideas. Ideas of greater abstraction were, from a classificatory point of view, superordinate to any ideas of lesser abstraction and greater concreteness. And conversely, concrete ideas were subordinate in a classificatory sense to any ideas of greater abstraction. This was the case regardless of whether or not the particular ideas were intrinsically related in terms of their specific connotations and denotations. Given this way of relating kinds of ideas, all ideas could be viewed as elements of a single classificatory hierarchy regardless of the combinations in which they might be found.

The structural features of Cutter's view of subject structure provided by the Scottish realists' theory of mental structure and knowledge acquisition are twofold. First, Cutter's division of all subjects into those that are individual and those that are general reflects the Scottish division between perception on the one hand and the remainder of the faculties on the other. It also reflects the two different kinds of knowledge gained from each of these loci of mental activity. Second, Cutter's sense of classificatory inclusion relationships and significance order reflects the Scottish idea of increasing levels of abstraction or generality as the mind proceeds from individual to general ideas, and among general notions from those that are more concrete to those less concrete (or, from those that are of lesser generality to those of greater generality).

Although described only briefly, the relationship between Cutter's view of subject structure and Scottish realist thought is important to this discussion in two respects. First, it demonstrates something of the connection that Cutter had with the intellectual life of his day. Cutter's subject thinking was neither conceived nor developed in an intellectual vacuum. It was, in fact, much more indebted to a broadly based philosophical background than might otherwise seem apparent. On the other hand, the datedness of Cutter's intellectual framework of reference is all too obvious. He expressed a view of subject relationships and intellectual processes that was already a century old by the time he wrote his *Rules*. In fact, even as he was writing, the intellectual currents of the times were changing. Scottish common sense realism, especially the moral philosophy that was its chief American expression, having held sway in ante-bellum American academia, was already at the point of losing credence as a viable basis for either instruction or educational philosophy. The process of its rejection was subsequently completed by the beginning of the twentieth century, its place taken by a philosophy of pragmatism.

Second, and more important, the relationship of Cutter's thinking to Scottish realism was not confined to the brief picture described here. The entire range of Cutter's concerns in librarianship was affected by the intellectual framework of reference that Scottish thought represented. The same pervasiveness also occurred in his subject system thinking, a matter that will become more obvious as the next two contextual elements of his subject access ideas are described—subjects in relation to books and subjects in relation to the public.

CHAPTER 3

Subjects in Relation to Works

Cutter's classificatory approach to subject structure and, especially, his significance order were related to his specific entry process solely because both matters employed the notion of a specific subject. To discover the nature of the relationship, however, the second contextual element of Cutter's subject system must be explored—that is, the way Cutter understood subjects in relation to books.

Specific Subjects and Document Classes

For Cutter, providing subject access for books was, at its most fundamental level, the process of classification. As already noted, Cutter defined classification as grouping objects by means of their shared common characteristics. Book classification consisted of "bringing together books which have the same characteristics."[1] In modern terminology, when a group of books or their surrogates is thus assembled, one has created a document class. The basis for any particular document class—that is, the characteristic held in common by the books within a group—might be any of a variety of things, including in Cutter's words, "size, binding, or publisher." However, he observed that books were usually gathered together "because they have the same authors, or the same subjects, or the same literary form, or are written in the same language, or were given by the same donor, or are designed for the same class of readers." Of these, Cutter noted that "classification by subject and classification by form are the most common."[2]

The critical question for the discussion at hand is how one might define the subject characteristic on the basis of which any particular subject document class is formed. Cutter's answer to this query was plainly stated. Books were brought together in a subject document class because they "treat of the same subject specifically."[3] Elsewhere, he referred to the same thing in the form of a definition of specific entry:

45

Specific entry, registering a book under a heading which expresses its special subject as distinguished from entering it in a class which includes that subject.[4]

This statement differs very little from his first rule of subject entry:

161. Enter a work under its subject heading, not under the heading of a class which includes that subject.[5]

Although Cutter did not say in this rule that the subject heading of a work was to indicate its special subject as he had stated in his definition of specific entry, the examples included at each place indicate that this is what he meant.[6]

In each of these formulations Cutter consistently indicated that the basis for inclusion of a book in a document class was its "special" or its "specific" subject. Cutter used these two phrases synonymously in speaking of the subject entry process.[7] The difficulty with these phrases lies in what Cutter meant by a work's specific or special subject.[8] It is obvious, for example, that Cutter did not mean that the subject under which a book was to be placed should be narrow (i.e., specific) as opposed to broad or comprehensive in some absolute or unqualified sense. The dictionary catalog, being "an alphabetical list of specific subjects,"[9] included books of relatively broad as well as relatively narrow subject extents. Thus, the specific subject of a work of broad subject extent would be the name of a broad subject rather than the name of some other subject that was "specific" or narrow per se. Cutter referred to this sense of the term when he wrote, "A dictionary catalog contains class-headings, inasmuch as it contains the headings of extensive subjects, but under them there is no class-entry, only specific entry."[10]

One possibility of what Cutter meant by "specific subject" is that the subject of a book occupies a particular hierarchical position in a subject structure. In other words, given any particular book and its subject, that subject might also be conceived as a subject in a classification of subjects. Cutter's injunction then would mean to enter a work under that subject and not under an implied subject of greater extent that includes the subject of the work at hand. This interpretation is supported by the use of the examples that follow his initial rule on subject cataloging.

Ex. Put Lady Cust's book on "The cat" under CAT, not under ZOOLOGY, or MAMMALS, or DOMESTIC ANIMALS: and put Garnier's "Le fer" under IRON, not under METALS or METALLURGY.[11]

The subject CATS implies the broader subjects, ZOOLOGY, MAMMALS, and DOMESTIC ANIMALS, and IRON implies METALS or METALLURGY as classes inclusive of them, although the subject of each work is respectively CATS and IRON. Conversely, CATS and IRON are the most specific subjects in their respective classificatory hierarchies that fit the books in question. Hence, the specific subjects of the two works are also the most specific subjects in a classificatory structure of subjects.

Now, although this appears to be a satisfying explanation of the meaning of specific subject in these two examples, it appears to fail as an explanation in other instances. For example, Cutter instructed the subject cataloger to place a work on New England ornithology in the subject document class NEW ENGLAND rather than under either OR-NITHOLOGY or ORNITHOLOGY OF NEW ENGLAND, and a work on Gothic architecture of Spain under SPAIN rather than under ARCHITECTURE or GOTHIC ARCHITECTURE (or GOTHIC ARCHITECTURE OF SPAIN, a combination that he did not even consider).[12] And in his Boston Athenaeum catalog, other examples of the same thing may be found in abundance—including, for example, books on the Circulation of the blood entered under BLOOD, those about a variety of topics related to the Alphabet (Medieval alphabets, Application of the Roman alphabet to Oriental languages, Phonetic alphabets, etc.) entered simply under ALPHABET, those about Solar eclipses and Sun spots entered under SUN. And even his example of Lady Cust's book on Cats is suspect when its full title, "The History and Diseases of Cats," is displayed.[13]

Obviously, Cutter's procedure for identifying the specific subjects of works on these various topics was not entirely equal to the equation set out above—that is, given a book with a particular subject, enter it under that subject, not under an implied broader subject that includes the specific subject in a classificatory hierarchy of subjects. While he did not enter the above works under implied subjects of even greater extent (for example, works on Ornithology of New England under ZOOLOGY or those on Gothic architecture of Spain under FINE ARTS, etc.), neither did he enter them under what seems to be their most specific subjects. Ornithology of New England appears to be, after all, a more restricted and therefore narrower topic than NEW ENGLAND alone, and Gothic architecture of Spain likewise would appear to be narrower in scope than either GOTHIC ARCHITECTURE or SPAIN alone. When these cases are considered, it appears that Cutter failed to identify the specific subject that was not supposed to be entered inclusively under some implied subject of broader extent.

A possible answer for this discrepancy might be that Cutter actually applied a different procedure to these works because their specific subjects were composed of multiple terms. In these instances, he seems to have gone one step further. From among the words that composed the specific subject of the work, he chose the term that was most specific according to the significance order among subjects. An analysis of some of the topics just discussed according to his significance order would yield the results found in Figure 4. Three of the examples (1, 3, and 4) are self-explanatory inasmuch as there is a clear choice in each case of a single term that is more concrete than the others. Those terms (New England, Cats, and Blood, respectively) serve as specific entries in their respective subject descriptions.

The other two examples raise additional considerations. In number two, there is no question as to which term is the specific entry according to Cutter's significance order inasmuch as Spain is an individual subject whereas Gothic, the only other possible choice, being an adjective, functions as a concrete general subject. It should be noted, however, that Gothic and Architecture, if considered a single subject together, would be an abstract general subject. In number five, something of the same situation applies. If Movement and Fluids are considered separately, there might be some question as to which of two

Subject Description	Specific Entry Term
1. Ornithology of New England (GS) + (IS)	New England
2. Gothic architecture of Spain (GS) + (IS) or (CGS) + (AGS) + (IS)	Spain
3. The history and diseases of cats (AGS) + (AGS) + (CGS)	Cats
4. Circulation of the blood (AGS) + (CGS)	Blood

5. Movement of fluids in plants
   (AGS) + (CGS) + (CGS)
   or   (AGS, i.e., + (CGS) Hydrology)
	Plants

GS = General subject
   AGS = Abstract general
   CGS = Concrete general
IS = Individual subject

FIG. 4.   Application of Significance Order to Compound Subject Descriptions

concrete general subjects, Fluids or Plants, is the specific entry. If, however, Movement and Fluids are seen together as a single abstract general subject (i.e., Hydrology), then the question of a specific entry is better defined. Plants, in that situation, would be the more concrete term.

The important thing in the above considerations is that the entry words are the most specific subjects according to Cutter's significance order. Seen in this light, his choice of the subject words in such instances appears to be rationalized by what amounts to a second procedure. Cutter wrote only one extra rule that specifically delineated a procedure of this sort—Rule 165 for the first and third examples in Figure 4—but perhaps it is what he intended, nonetheless. Furthermore, this process does not conflict with the initial procedure of entering a work under its specific subject and not under an implied inclusive subject if that process is seen to apply to subjects of only a single word.

The difficulty with this interpretation is, however, that while it appears to explain these examples, there are still others that it does not explain. There are some instances in which Cutter simply chose for the subject document class those multiple word headings that appear to match the particular topic of a book in the initial manner indicated. Works on the Arc of the meridian, Capture of property at sea, Capital punishment, Ancient history, and even Signers of the Declaration of Independence, to name just a few, were to be entered under those multiple-word phrases as headings rather than under a single word within the phrases.[14] And, should the reader wonder if these examples represent only a few exceptions, one need only peruse the pages of the Boston Athenaeum catalog to find dozens of similar cases. Furthermore, Cutter did not include a specific rule to delineate those occasions when a subject cataloger should use a multiple-word heading rather than analyzing it according to his significance order.

Both of these explanations of Cutter's subject entry procedure—noninclusive entry and entry according to significance order—fail to explain fully what Cutter understood the specific subject of a work to be. The reason for this, however, is not that Cutter simply failed to observe simple rules of consistency or logic (as modern commentators have suggested), or that he had a naive view of subject complexity. Nor is it because he used the idea of specific subject in more than one sense: one for this classificatory subject nomenclature, the other for his subject entry procedure. Rather, it is simply because Cutter had a fundamentally different view of subjects in relation to books than is held today; a difference in perspective that involves two basic elements: the notion of what "the subject" of a work is, and, concomitantly, how one names that subject.

The Modern Notion of the Subject of a Book

Modern commentators have come to regard the notion of the specific subject of a book as a quantitative measure of the scope of a work's subject matter, as characterized by the geometrical analogy in the first chapter. By delineating the specific or special subject of a work, one highlights either the whole subject of a work or at least that chief portion of the whole subject of the work that adequately describes the work's "aboutness." "The subject" of a work means, therefore, the entire subject as opposed to only a portion of the subject. Concomitantly, the chief goal of the subject analysis of a book is to identify its subject entirety (i.e., its complete aboutness), and the chief task of providing subject access is to make the book available to searchers by means of a label (or labels) that will indicate that subject entirety. Subject access is accomplished in a verbal subject access system by entering the book under one or more words in one or more combinations that will indicate that subject entirety as precisely as possible. The role of the subject heading (or headings) is thus to be expressive of "the subject" of the book. It is intended, in other words, to characterize the subject completely.[15]

There are several instances in which Cutter's expressions about subjects in relation to books suggest this sort of measure. For example, he defined a subject in one place as "*the matter* on which the author is seeking to give and the reader to obtain information."[16] He spoke of subject catalogs as those in which "the entries are arranged according to *the subjects* of the books."[17] He also wrote the following brief statements:

> *Subject entry,* registry of a book under its subject.[18]
> Enter books under the word that best expresses *their subject,* whether it occurs in the title or not.[19]
> We cannot always take the "author's own definition of his book." He knows what the subject is, but he may not know how to *express it* for cataloging purposes.[20]

Cutter's use of the italicized phrases in the above quotations seems to suggest something approximating the topical entirety of books, their subject matter understood as a complete rather than as a partial thing.

Elsewhere, he appears to indicate the same thing in more extensive contexts. When describing the dictionary subject catalog he wrote:

> Each book is put under as specific a subject as possible. Thus, if it treats of natural history, it is put under that heading; if it treats of

zoology alone, that word is the rubric; if it is confined to mammals, it will be found under Mammals: and, finally, if one is looking for a treatise on the elephant, he need not know whether that animal is a mammal, he need not even be sure that it is an animal, he has merely to know his alphabet well enough to find the word Elephant, under which will appear all the separate works that the library contains on that subject.21

Obviously, a work that "treats of zoology alone," a work that is "confined to mammals," and "separate works" on elephants, all imply works wholly on those subjects. Thus, his injunction to enter them under "as specific a subject as possible" seems certainly to be a reference to characterizing the whole of each of the implied topics. Likewise, when referring to a search for biographical information on Thomas Home, Cutter differentiated between the treatment of Home in a biographical dictionary and that in an individual book about Home, calling the latter a "special life of him." What else could he have meant, one surmises, than that the individual work was wholly about Home, unlike the biographical dictionary which divided its attention among many biographees. Concomitantly, entry of the work on Home specifically would mean to enter it under that word which would expressly characterize the entirety of the topic—that is, Home.22

Despite the similarity between Cutter's use of the above terminology and the modern notion of "the subject" of a work as a quantitative measure, the correspondence appears to be a fleeting one at best, and the foregoing examples are best accounted for as an accident arising from the fact that the subject descriptions of the works in question were in fact single well-recognized terms. Elsewhere, Cutter shows little awareness of the concept. In fact, there are numerous instances where a quantitative measure is obviously not what he had in mind. If one were to have asked him what was the subject of Lady Cust's book entitled *Cats: Their History and Diseases,* his answer would doubtless have been, CATS!

That Cutter was not thinking of the full characterization of the "aboutness" of books is also suggested by another term that he typically used. In many places Cutter referred to the relationship between the subject characteristic by which a work was most appropriately placed in a subject document class and the work itself as only a matter of the book "treating of" the subject. For example, he wrote, "If a book purports to *treat of* several distinct subjects . . ." and "A work *treating of* a general subject with reference to a place . . ."23 Now, by itself, the phrase "treat of" is noticeably vague, admitting only that the work in some way contains the subject referred to. It does not require that the named subject is the only subject in the work or that it amounts to the full characterization of the work's "aboutness."

All of the foregoing may leave the reader puzzled about "When is the subject of a book not its subject?" The likely reason for this is that it has become so common to think of a book's subject in a quantitative way that it is not apparent that there are other ways of considering it. The subject of a book may actually mean any of a variety of things. This may be seen more clearly by asking the commonplace question, What is the role of a librarian? The term "role" is not self-defining. One might answer the question with a definition that fully characterizes the librarian's work and existence in all aspects, or by defining the librarian's role within certain contexts—that is, the librarian's role with respect to the public; the librarian's role with respect to the library staff; the librarian's role as a scientist; or the librarian's role as a professional. In the same way, the notion of a book's subject is not self-defining and has meaning only in terms of a contextual referent. The question here is, if the specific subject of a book does not categorically refer to the entirety of the book's aboutness, to what then does it refer?

Cutter's Referent for the Specific Subjects of Books

Some indication of what Cutter meant by a book's specific subject is contained in his basic definition of book classification. After stating that book classification was "bringing books together which treat of the same subject specifically," he added:

> That is, books which each treat of the whole of the subject and not of a part only.[24]

This comment does not require that each of the works in a subject document class be equal in their topical entirety to the aboutness that the subject document class connotes. Rather, the comment conveys a concern only that the works be of equal subject scope in relation to what can only be called a classificatory sense of subjects; namely, that each book be in the most specific document class available in a classification structure of subjects. The referent of specific subject is a classificatory measure that exists independent of the work itself and to which the work might be compared to find the most appropriate subject characteristic listed.

The process of identifying the most appropriate subject characteristic of a work by which it may be placed in a subject document class may be illustrated in the following way. Imagine a furniture factory that receives periodic shipments of lumber to be used in furniture construction. Because the shipments are mixed, they must be sorted according to categories such as kind of wood (e.g., cherry, maple, oak, yellow pine, white pine) and stated ranges of length (e.g., 4–6 feet, 6–8 feet, 8–10 feet, etc.). The person charged with sorting does not characterize each board according to all possible categories (e.g., common name, specific name, exact length, thickness, number of knotholes, position of knotholes, number of discolorations, position of discolorations, etc.) but only in terms of those categories that have been established—no matter what the source of their establishment. And if some of the boards do not immediately fit into the stated categories—for example, if the sorter comes across some oak boards only 3 feet long or if there are some 7-foot loblolly pine boards, the sorter might then place them in a category that they seem closest to, the first in the bin that holds oak boards, 4–6 feet; the second in yellow pine, 6–8 feet. (Loblolly pine is a variety of southern yellow pine.) Special categories might ultimately be made for these two particular classes of boards, but until they are, the sorter may only fit them into the system in an approximate fashion.

The most important thing the sorter does in the entire classificatory operation, however, is to make good use of the categories that are available by fitting the boards into the most specific categories available. It will not do, for example, to mix all pine boards when there are categories for white and yellow pine, nor to place 5-foot oak boards in a single bin for all oak boards when it is possible to identify them by the more specific category 4–6 foot boards. The categories of pine boards (in general) and oak boards (in general) if used, would include the more specific categories, but the scheme of categorization makes it possible to be more specific. On the other hand it would be fruitless to be more specific than the scheme allows since the more specific categories have not gained any currency or usefulness. To paraphrase Cutter in all of this, board classification is bringing boards together each of which give evidence of the narrowest category available into which they can be placed (given a scheme of categories)—that is, placing boards into specific categories and not into broader categories which only include the specific categories.

For Cutter, identifying the specific subject of a work was not an exercise in making the most complete description possible of a work's aboutness, using language as the ultimate measuring device. Rather, it meant to locate a work at the narrowest point possible in an already established order of subjects independent of the work. Determining a work's specific subject did not refer to assigning a label to a book that uniquely characterized its subject totality by some measure of entirety, but rather referred to assigning the work to a label that was the most appropriate one available in a system of labels already extant.

The Problem of Cutter's Referent

Now, to an extraordinary degree, this interpretation of Cutter's referent to specific subjects—a system of subject labels related to one another in a classificatory manner—will appear to have almost insurmountable difficulties with regard to conception and application. To begin with, if identifying specific subjects in this way meant identifying them as categories in a classification scheme of subjects, the process would make subject heading work only another form of traditional book classification work. It would be a process analogous to classifying with, say, the Dewey Decimal Classification, where one placed the book in the narrowest category enumerated. If indeed this is what Cutter meant, however, where then is the classification scheme to which he appealed for identifying the specific categories? Cutter nowhere mentioned the existence of such a scheme. Furthermore, even if such a scheme existed, it would appear to have been very enumerative and very simplistic. How else could one account for the subject of Lady Cust's book being called CATS instead of, for example, some combination of CATS with, say, HISTORY, the latter a normal standard subdivision in most present-day schemes.

Suppose, however, that Cutter was not referring to the use of a fully worked-out classification scheme, but rather only to a way of looking at subject names in a classificatory sense. It will be noted that this has already been proposed earlier as the first of two possible ways to understand his initial rule of specific entry. But, if this is what he meant, then one must contend with the chief problem also noted earlier in applying it, that one must know in advance, in cases involving subjects with multiple-word names, which multiple-word names might be used as they are and which must be analyzed according to Cutter's significance order to ascertain an appropriate most specific subject document class name. Cutter was aware of this difficulty. In fact, the commentary attached to his initial cataloging rule refers to the difficulty under the rubric of "subjects that have no name." He said, in effect, until the topical matter of a book had been "raised to the status of a subject," or had obtained "a certain individuality" as an "object of inquiry," or had, in fact, become "a distinct subject" *and* had thus been "given some sort of *name*," the specific entry rule could not be applied to it.[25] In such cases, the most specific subject name under which the work could be placed of necessity had to be the class of which the more particular topical matter of the book was only a part. In other words, the multiple-word descriptions of the topical contents of some works could not be used as they appeared not simply because the names themselves had not become "established," but more importantly because the lack of having become established indicated that the topical contents that such names represented had not as yet become legitimate subjects.

Considering the amount of space that Cutter devoted to this issue—two relatively brief paragraphs in the entire corpus of his writings—it would appear that he considered this issue either a minor problem or, what is more likely, self-explanatory to his reading public. It does not appear to be such a slight problem or a self-explanatory problem to modern subject heading workers, however. How, indeed, does a subject become a legitimate subject in its own right and thus receive a name that is then usable as the name of a subject document class? And what are the criteria by which one can judge whether or not this has occurred?

It was precisely at this point that E. J. Coates concluded that Cutter actually based his assessment of subject specificity on

> a set of stock subjects under one of which each book had to be accommodated. If the subject matter of a book is more restricted in scope than any of the stock terms, then the book must be placed under the most restricted stock term which contains its subject, just as the purchaser of ready-made clothing buys the nearest larger stock size to his actual size.[26]

Indeed, Cutter's reference to established subjects suggests something of this sort with perhaps only this difference, that the set of stock subjects were arranged in a more sophisticated classificatory structure than Coates indicated.

Convinced that his description of Cutter's idea of established headings was accurate, Coates cited two reasons why it is inadequate for subject work today. For one thing, he concluded that "no definite criterion can be adduced to determine what shall be in the stock list of subjects." For another, he was convinced that the subjects considered legitimate by Cutter and by his contemporaries were relatively unsophisticated. That is to say, they consisted of broad subjects or subject areas, simply named and relatively distinct from each other, rather than the kinds of specific or narrow topics now typically associated with books and that involve complex combinations of many subjects.[27]

Coates's explanation of Cutter's method, while it provides an answer to what can only be seen as an awkward cul-de-sac in Cutter's work, only does so at the expense of one's estimation of the intelligence of Cutter and, in fact, of all nineteenth-century subject catalogers who proceeded in the same way. This is especially apparent when it is realized that if Cutter proceeded in this way, his method would have had a serious and obvious contradiction built into it. In a given set of documents, it would appear that the very assumption that the documents have subjects and the subsequent describing of the subjects, whether by one word or several, is tantamount to establishing the existence of the subjects. If this is so, why then would Cutter pause to make a secondary judgment as to whether the already established subject was established according to a control list of legitimate subjects? Furthermore, since the control list of legitimate subjects appears not to have been of nearly detailed enough specificity, Cutter would have been in the position of consciously working at cross-purposes with regard to his goal of subject access. Knowing that the subjects of the books were of one level of specificity, he would, nonetheless, be identifying their specific subject level within the control list of subjects at a consistently inadequate level of specificity.

The difficulty that modern subject workers have in understanding Cutter's use of a classificatory referent does not lie in his methodology but rather in a far more fundamental issue—the very idea of a subject itself. For example, Cutter did not accord the particular topical matter of every book denoted by a complex description the "status of a subject." Furthermore, he assumed this as if it were understood by his readers. What kind of thinking process would allow a discrimination of this kind? To answer this, the more fundamental issue of what is a subject must be explored. To what did Cutter refer when he employed the term "subject" and how does that differ from the present day use of the concept?

The Modern Idea of a Subject

A common assumption today is that, with few exceptions, every book has a subject and that this subject exists as a unique property of the book. This is because subject and book content have, for all practical purposes, become synonymous. To speak of a book's content is, in fact, to say something automatically of its subject. To describe its content is tantamount to naming its subject. Subjects are thought of as belonging to books in the same way that personality is thought of as belonging to human beings. One cannot speak of the one without implying the other.

This equation between subject and the content of any particular book may be highlighted in still another manner. If one were to ask the modern subject cataloger whether or not there is a difference between speaking of subjects in relation to books and speaking of subjects in relation to classification schemes, the answer would likely be that the only difference is the context of their respective locations. To speak of subjects in relation to books is simply to identify particular subjects that have been written about. To speak of subjects in relation to a classification scheme is simply to place those particular subjects in the context of their relationships with other subjects. The essential likeness remains. Subjects in either case are singular mental loci of thought. They are, for all practical purposes, named intellections that have their own separate identities. They are the mental particles that make up the intellectual universe, much in the same manner that atomic particles make up the physical universe. They may be broad or narrow, simple or complex in denotation and connotation, abstract or concrete in their reference as the case may be, easily named with a single word or named only with great difficulty by the precoordination of several words, and so on through a variety of characterizations. The factor common to all subjects is not their location—that is, whether found in a book, in a portion of a book, in the form of a spoken address or other communication, or as a location signified by a symbol in a classification scheme—but rather that they are the thoughts of people expressed in some way. Moreover, given all thinking beings at all times, their named thoughts constitute a total set of such subjects. With this in mind, the arrangement of subjects in some classificatory order would appear to be posterior or extraneous to their existence. If unarranged, each would retain its own validity and identity. In fact, resorting to yet another analogy, if unarranged, they might be envisioned as a vast egalitarian democracy of named intellections, each necessarily related to others in terms of language and context, but each nonetheless a separately identifiable thing.

With this understanding of subjects in mind, the role of classification is to impose some arbitrary order on the democracy of intellections, regardless of where they appear or how they are named. If they have been expressed at some time or another, especially in the form of a unit of recorded knowledge, they may be given their appropriate location in a document classification system. This is because knowledge records are most often the vehicle for the expression of new subjects. Concomitantly, the role of an alphabetical subject heading system is simply to list the subjects found in any given set of knowledge records in an alphabetical order. In either case, a subject system represents the effort to provide access to these named intellections regardless of how that system might ultimately arrange them.

Cutter's Idea of a Subject

Cutter's understanding of subjects differed significantly from this picture. Some insight into that difference may be gained from another look at the epistemological model that Scottish common sense realism provided for him. It has already been noted that the Scottish realists' theory of mental faculties, particularly their differentiation between the perception of individuals and the formation of general notions and, with respect to the latter, their theory of the progressive generality of general notions, provided a basis for Cutter's division between individual subjects and general subjects and for his significance order. A second important aspect of the realists' understanding of how the mind generated knowledge had to do with how ideas become communicated. The realists' surmised that all knowledge, whether of individuals or of general notions, was communicated by means of some kind of representational vehicle or set of signs. Signs of this kind might be nonverbal, but their most developed and typical form had come to be language. Language was in effect a naming process for the knowledge that the mental faculties generated. As such it was considered an integral element of the intellectual powers of humanity—so integral, in fact, that Thomas Reid's discussion of the power of abstraction, the faculty in which the names of general notions are most pertinent, consisted totally of an explanation of the relationship of the role of language to the exercise of that faculty.[28]

All ideas, whether they consist of individuals or of general notions, are named in accordance with the needs of humanity. There is a noticeable tendency, however, to adopt special names that achieve stable use in communication. Individuals, for example, might be named by using general words qualified in such a way as to indicate their individuality. For example, one might refer to "the black cat down the street," and by so doing indicate an individual black cat rather than black cats in general. Or one might be more specific and refer to "the black cat owned by the Brown's at 4154 Tupelo Street." As often as not, however, in order to facilitate communication (for instance, within the Brown's household), the black cat that resides there will be given a proper name that will represent its concrete individuality. Thus, the cat might be referred to by a proper name, "Blackie," or "Oilspot," or whatever. A proper name assigned in this way, in Reid's words, is "intended to represent one individual only."[29]

General notions also go through a similar naming process, but in their case the process has significant differences. First, the names of general notions consist of general words. General words are different from individual names in that they do not signify any particular, concrete thing, but rather only some class of ideas that ultimately are derived from the attributes of individuals. Thus, what they signify does not exist other than as ideas. "House," for example, does not signify any particular house, nor any real thing, but only the idea of a house. Second, because general notions conceived through the power of abstraction have meaning only through the classificatory process of the power of reasoning, the names of general notions likewise have meaning only in a classificatory sense. In other words, any general word represents a more or less extensive class and has meaning only in a classificatory context. Third, all general words, like individuals, likewise achieve stability of use in communication according to the needs of humanity. Where the particular needs of groups of persons are great, there is likewise a noticeable tendency to invent special words to convey distinct general notions, no matter what their respective degree of intension or extension may be in a classificatory sense.

With that tendency, however, the process of naming is critical. If special words were not invented, people would be able to communicate only in the form of verbal circumlocutions. Circumlocutions would be used because the powers of abstractions and reasoning identify general notions of greater intension by using combinations of other already known notions of lesser intension. For example, having never seen a DC-10, one might describe what it is, that is, what kind of airplane it is, by referring to the more general word "airplane" qualified by still other general words regarding body shape, placement of engines, etc. Likewise, never having encountered the named general notion of hazardous waste disposal, one might name it by resorting to a lengthy description of the processes involved—the use of an impermeable clay-lined pit, the placement in it of drums of dry off-products of industry, and the description of the contents of the drums as heavy metals, etc., that are harmful to humans in their industrial state and not degradable by natural processes. Normally, however, the processes of communication will result in shorthand ways of indicating such distinct general notions—that is, by the consensus use of specialized general terms made up of single or multiple words. Hence, in the foregoing examples, the general term "DC-10" represents a class of airplanes and the general term "hazardous waste disposal" represents a class of disposal activities, each with their own particular differentia.[30]

A final characteristic of the naming process of general notions is that because the Scottish realists ultimately viewed it as a process related to the development of society, they considered it a cumulative process. In this respect Scottish realists obviously betrayed their Enlightenment spirit of rational social progress. Knowledge among mankind had accumulated slowly over many centuries. The slowness could be attributed to many reasons, not the least of which was the dominance of the lower faculties that led to the prevalence of superstition. In their own era, however, humanity had witnessed a great expansion in the use of the higher faculties, especially the exercise of reason, which had increasingly led to the discovery of new truths. The result of that progress could be seen especially in the societal accumulation of knowledge. A great explosion occurred in the naming of ever more sophisticated and abstract truths by an ever greater accumulation of specialized general words or terms that had come to be generally accepted as to their meanings.

Cutter's application of this general approach to the way language is related to the accumulation of knowledge, both by individual persons and by society at large, is directly reflected in his use of the word "subject" in two different ways. First, a subject did not refer simply to anything that had been thought of and expressed by any person at some time or another either orally or in the form of a printed book. Rather, it referred more particularly to those intellections (either individuals or general notions) that had received a name that itself represented a distinct consensus in usage. The importance of this distinction cannot be overstressed. When referring to subjects that "have no names" or those that by implication were indistinct, Cutter was not simply saying that they were subjects described in an indistinct way. *He implied that they were not subjects at all,* although they had the potential of becoming subjects. In other words, he did not have two categories of subjects in mind, some that were established and others that were not. The term "subject" referred *only* to that kind of intellection that was distinct and that, because of its distinctiveness, had received a name that was stable in usage.

The others were something else altogether. He apparently struggled for a way to describe them—for example, "objects of inquiry," "objects of investigation," "matters of investigation." His statement that they were "from time to time discussed" likewise implies the breadth of their location—they could be found in the multitudes of books that libraries bought or, perhaps, in the multitude of speeches, newspapers, or magazines that one might chance upon. Nevertheless, they were not subjects per se because they had not attained "a certain individuality" nor had they been "raised to the status of a subject." In other words, they had not yet come through the societal process in which their meanings had become stabilized in a name. Names in the latter sense should be understood as those terms, especially those that were brief, that keep reappearing in the discussions as labels for the object of inquiry. They did not refer to simply any description, and they especially did not refer to those descriptions that were in effect circumlocutions that changed as each person interested in the object of study described what they were speaking about. On the other hand, Cutter recognized the fact that some circumlocutions represented the best that society could do in the way of naming a general notion. And when that seemed apparent, Cutter recommended the use of such an otherwise lengthy description.

Cutter's second fundamental application of the Scottish theory of mental faculties and the role of language to his use of the idea of subject had to do with the Scottish idea that general notions had meaning only in terms of the classificatory nature of their mental origins. The very act of conceiving general notions was considered by the realists to be a classificatory activity. Thus, the connotation and denotation of any general notion were directly related to its classificatory relationships to other general notions with which it was connected. By implication, therefore, Cutter's distinction between all general notions and those general notions that had become subjects suggests that the process by which any particular general notion became a subject was actually a public classificatory process. When a general object of inquiry was expressed often enough to have been given a name, gaining a name was tantamount to the subject becoming publicly identified as a classificatory location among all other general subjects likewise publicly identified as classificatory locations. As a corollary, all subjects (as distinguished simply from all general notions) were by their very nature elements in a publicly derived and tacitly understood classification structure. This corollary is important because it suggests that the very statement that any particular general notion is a subject is likewise a statement of classification. In this sense, the modern idea suggested above that subjects exist first of all as individual identities which may afterwards be conveniently arranged in some classification order would have appeared absurd to Cutter. Subjects are by their very nature locations in a classificatory structure of publicly accumulated knowledge. One might discover the classificatory position of any particular general subject, but one does not in some way create its classificatory position as a posterior and arbitrary process. The very definition of a subject implies that it already has a classificatory position.

Of course, to say that the definition of the word "subject" fundamentally implies classification in the first place still leaves unsaid the whereabouts of the actual classificatory structure of which all subjects partake. Some illumination of the implications of this may be gained from a brief, although somewhat speculative, examination of the definitions of the word "subject" that have accumulated in Western thinking over the centuries.

The Use of the Term "Subject" in Historical Perspective

Among the various dictionary definitions and uses of the word "subject" (omitting the derivative term "subject catalog") that one will find—for example in the *Oxford English Dictionary*—three focuses appear to be relevant. A subject is spoken of as:

(1) that which forms a basic matter of thought, discussion, investigation, etc.: e.g., a subject of conversation or discourse.
(2) a branch of knowledge as a course of study: e.g., He studied four subjects his first year at college.
(3) the theme of a sermon, book, story, etc.

A MATTER OF THOUGHT AND A BRANCH OF KNOWLEDGE

The first of these has in a sense enjoyed the longest history, occupying, in fact, a significant portion of the corpus of Greek philosophical thought. Plato, in the form of his "dialectic" and, particularly, Aristotle, in that group of works afterward called the Organon, were concerned with delineating how man arrived at true knowledge through the thinking process. A person might indeed think about or discourse on anything. But, as Aristotle concluded, only by rigorous and logical thinking could what one talked about be considered verified or "scientific" knowledge. To Aristotle that meant first of all the appropriate construction of propositional statements. For advancing to still newer scientific knowledge, it meant manipulating existing knowledge and ordering it into a logically coherent system by means of a syllogistic method. Subjects, the things written, spoken, or thought of in this more rigorous sense, were, therefore, a special category of all the things that could be written, spoken, or thought of. And the process that produced them was bequeathed as formal logical method to the generations that succeeded the Greeks.

The second of the uses of the word "subject" springs naturally from the first and has had a comparable history. Having actively engaged in logical discourse, people from the time of the Greeks onward accumulated products of that labor—that is, the subjects spoken about, defined and verified in that rigorous and systematic way. It was natural, perhaps, considering their accumulation, to arrange the curricula of schools, designed to instruct students in both how to think and in the things already rigorously thought of, according to a nomenclature of those products. Thus, the typical school curriculum that arose out of the Greco-Roman period and that was afterwards bequeathed to the Middle Ages in the form of the seven liberal arts, had two parts: the trivium, composed of grammar, rhetoric, and the dialectic (afterwards, logic) and oriented around the methods of discourse and thinking; and the quadrivium, composed of established products of thought (or at least those deemed appropriate for study)—arithmetic, geometry, astronomy, and music.

The interplay between these two related senses of "subjects" during the long Medieval period was significant.[31] Through the first half of the period, method tended to be circumscribed by an Augustinian approach to Plato's dialectic in which subjects were arranged in a hierarchy of importance and their study submitted to a singular logic. Because of this, and also because much of the content of the subject studies had never been transmitted from the earlier Greco-Roman period, schooling stressed method (i.e., the trivium) to the practical exclusion of the study of "subjects," except, perhaps theology. Still, efforts directed towards making accessible what knowledge of subjects was available were characterized by arrangements that more or less reflected a systematic order of subjects, as they had been handed down. This was obvious in earlier classifications of subjects found, for example, in the works of Cassiodorus and Boethius. It was reflected in book arrangements in libraries and in the compendia and encyclopedias that were common to the Medieval period.

The arrival of Greek writings and, especially, the Aristotelian corpus of literature through the channels of Arabic scholarship brought about significant changes, however. Method, freed from its earlier Augustinian bias, gained a new and exacting rigor in the hands of the Schoolmen. Furthermore, through the labors of scholars such as Albertus Magnus, his principal student Thomas Aquinas, and others, method itself gradually became viewed as specific to subjects themselves. When combined with a new profusion of writings that represented nontheologically oriented "subjects"—at first, medicine and law, but increasingly other topics in natural philosophy—a renaissance of new and ever-expanding learning took place. Subjects—that is, things spoken, written, or thought of, but verified by rigorous logical method (regardless of how one views the validity of the method itself)—multiplied in a way not previously experienced by mankind.

By the sixteenth century even more significant changes had occurred. The notion of logical method, itself developed to such a formidable degree by medieval logicians that it required even greater amounts of schooling to master, came under increasing scrutiny and, eventually, revision. Revision occurred first of all as a simplification of the university curriculum in logical method and of the textbooks employed to learn the method. Afterward, it led to the rise of new methods altogether, including Bacon's emphasis on inductive reasoning, which eventually led to modern emphases on empirical methodology.[32] Still another change was the attempt to bring some order to the ever-increasing numbers of subjects that were being delineated.

The latter represented, of course, the birth of the modern idea of classification, and the person most commonly associated with it is Francis Bacon. It is important to realize, however, that Bacon and, later, the French encyclopedists were not engaging in some essentially new activity. Rather, they were simply giving expression to a Western intellectual tradition that the products of thinking—subjects verified and publicly established by logical method—had meaning only insofar as they had a location in a classificatory map of the universe of such established knowledge. Throughout the Medieval period thinkers had attempted to enumerate subjects in some systematic manner related to the establishment of their meanings. As late as the early sixteenth century such enumerations still retained their essentially medieval orientation to the classical curriculum of subjects. Bacon and those that followed him broke the hold of that earlier nomenclature by arranging subjects more nearly correspondent with a new approach to logical method. Still, the activity was basically the same. Referring to a subject essentially implied locating it as an established point in a classificatory map of all publicly verified topics.

However, this does not mean that a full-blown scheme of subjects was actually or always at hand with which one might "identify" subjects. Indeed, only since the sixteenth and seventeenth centuries has such an undertaking been attempted, principally because the number of subjects considered in this way was expanding so rapidly that revised schemata of knowledge seemed the only way to keep everything in order. On the contrary, throughout most of Western history the identification of subjects as locations in a classificatory map of the universe of knowledge had operated much more casually, more as a belief or as a general consensus of opinion than as an explicit mapping of things.

One may speculate that subjects were viewed in this informal manner because interest in subjects per se was the province of that relatively small proportion of the total population that was schooled. Still another reason was that the range and total number of subjects were relatively circumscribed. Their limited numbers and range were in turn a function of the methodology involved in verifying them. Subjects were identified by a generally deductive process of logical definition. This implied that they were relatively distinct in content and in name. Concomitantly, new subjects were admitted to the general classificatory map only after a relatively extended process of social argumentation. In this way subjects, considered as classificatory locations, remained limited, manageable, and not unduly changeable, thereby providing a stable basis for the very fiber of Western intellectual traditions. The very act of thinking seriously about anything meant disciplining one's thoughts by submitting them to the accepted categories of thought (thus, the disciplines)—that is, to subjects conceived of as part of an established universe of subjects.

While one could obviously think about any topic or matter within one's power of mind, serious and recognized intellectual endeavor, especially that which was recorded for posterity, was commonly identified or recognized primarily in terms of the categories of the established universe of subjects. Furthermore, to say that any particular matter of thought, whether recorded for posterity or expressed orally, treated of a particular "subject" was to proclaim its validity by speaking of it in the context of the total universe of all serious thought. On the other hand, to not identify a person's matter of thought in this particular manner was not necessarily to adjudge it unintelligible, but rather only to conclude that in the social process of the growth of the universe of publicly accumulated knowledge, the topic had not become sufficiently verified and distinct to have achieved the status of an established subject.

Subject formulation and naming may be seen as a personal experience of groping for what, by consensus, the subject of a book or even of a thought-about experience really is. Using a modern example, imagine that the ignition key of a car is turned, the accelerator is pressed, and the motor starts—only to come to a sputtering halt after a few moments. This happens several more times with the same result until finally only a whirring sound is heard when the key is turned. For a person not versed in automobile mechanics, describing the situation over the telephone to a friend may prove awkward because there are no names readily available to describe or name adequately the "subject" of the experience. A series of descriptive phrases may have to be given to enable the friend to assess the situation and to offer advice. In the end the friend will likely name the problem somewhat more explicitly with a phrase such as, "Sounds like you've flooded it," or "Sounds like the carburetor is acting up." If, however, it were necessary to search for an answer in a maintenance manual, the need for an even more precise name for the "subject" will be crucial in order to consult the manual.

Of course, the nature of the manual will make a difference in the kind of name that is required. A manual of the type supplied to a purchaser of a car may describe subjects in words that are little more than combinations of far simpler descriptions or names. It may, for example, have a section entitled "Common Causes of the Car Not Starting" and in a discursive way describe the subject of which the car owner is thinking. On the other hand, a manual exhaustive in scope and intended to be used by auto mechanics may use a series of precise names associated with the general subject of Carburetor malfunction, such as Frozen thermostatic coil, Stuck flap, Broken accelerator pump plunger, Floats, etc. Such words are specially contrived names that more accurately name the subject or subjects related to the carburetion process; they have gained some sort of stability in use in the accepted subject area of automobile carburetors. The point of this example is that in learning to name the experience that one has had, one proceeds from no subject names to descriptive names and, ultimately, to more precise names that represent an accepted, defined and, in some measure, classificatory structure of the entire topic.

The foregoing example is limited to a person's acquisition of subject names that have already been derived by society at large and which are simply unknown to that person. In a larger sense, however, the initial naming of subjects is a societal process that follows the same pattern. Subjects begin to be formulated but often go through a period in which they are not clear enough or widely enough discussed to have gained a distinct name representing stability of use and meaning. They are described only by using groups of terms which are themselves subject names of already established meaning and which, when combined, may vary in connotation from one instance to another. For example, studies have been made from time to time in the area of wildlife management on the general topic of the growth and development of fish productivity, but related to the use, variously, of flood plain areas, backwaters, oxbows, sumps, gravel and borrow pits, swamps, and the mouths of tributory streams. As yet, however, the various writings and discussions on this topic of investigation have not yielded a single, or at least concise, term that conveys a stability of use and meaning. Likewise, cancer as a name is very general and may be better divided more precisely into particular kinds of disease phenomena according to etiology. Thinking and expression on the topic, however, has not as yet congealed sufficiently to yield stable names with stable meanings for the new ideas. In both of the cases here, the only way to refer to the respective topics at the present time is to describe them with a series of words or groups of words that are no more than other named subjects placed in descriptive combinations. According to the idea of the public development of subjects described here, they will not become "subjects" per se until the classificatory implications of their meanings have become stabilized and, with that, they have been given names that will convey that stability.

The foregoing examples are useful for illustrating the idea of a subject becoming identified through a social process of differentiation and naming. They fail to show one important difference between the process in the present day and the process in the earlier period, however. Establishment of a subject in the present day may arise out of any of several methods, that is, by experimentation, by historical analysis, etc. In the medieval and early modern period subject differentiation and identification was tied principally to logical definition through the analysis of propositions. This had a positive effect on the classification of subjects in that the subjects that did obtain recognition had distinct names that could be neatly arranged according to a simple hierarchical (i.e., genus-species) order according to their intrinsic logical connotations. It had a negative effect, however, insofar as subjects whose names constituted combinations of terms not intrinsically related by meaning could not be accommodated by a simple logical hierarchy. For example, how could one logically classify the topic History of mathematics when History and Mathematics were not intrinsically related the way Cats and Mammals were related? To the degree that topics representing such disparate combinations of terms began to be recognized as subjects, the role of traditional classification in subject differentiation came under increasing strain. It was at that point, in fact, that subjects as the topics of books, the third meaning of the term, came to have its greatest effect because the topics of books increasingly came to represent a new and more complex notion of subject order altogether.

THE THEME OF A BOOK

With the enormous increase in the discovery of new knowledge that occurred with the Renaissance and with the enormous expansion of formal education to an ever-widening range of people that occurred especially with the Reformation, the categorization of subjects and the introduction of new subjects increased dramatically. Of particular importance was the development of printing technology, not only in the fifteenth century, but even more so in the nineteenth century because it became the principal vehicle for expressing the new discoveries. So dramatic was the change afforded by the rise of printed books and their readership that Ortega y Gasset felt compelled to characterize the four centuries between Gutenberg and the coming of the modern library movement as the period in which "the book" became essential to the very fiber of Western civilization and social structure. Simply stated, by the 1850s, books, their writers, and their readers were commonplace rather than unique as characterizations of Western society.[33]

It was with the rise of "the book" (understood in its most general sense) that the third definition of subject listed above—the theme of a sermon, book, story, etc.—came into its own. This is not to suggest that books had never before been considered as vehicles of subjects. The history of this use of the word appears to go back well into the ancient and medieval periods. In its fundamental meaning, however, this use began simply as a normal extension of the first two uses. To speak of the subject of a book was to refer to a basic matter of thought identified by its location in the classificatory map of the publicly established universe of knowledge. If not identifiable in this way the book still had a topic, but that topic had not achieved the status of a subject taken in the more restricted and technical sense of the word.

As the volume of books increased over the centuries, this restrictive and technical referent to the idea of a subject became increasingly inadequate. Printed books, like all published writings of the past, had enjoyed the reputation of representing for the most part serious thinking about "subjects," not simply about any topics of thought. As they and their authors increased in numbers, especially by the nineteenth century, the incidence of new topics of thought, often treating of very specialized matters restricted in topical scope and named by very complex correlations of already recognized subjects, also increased in numbers. In fact, the very role of the book underwent a change in the process. Where previously the book might have been looked upon as a report of discussions about subjects already recognized as elements of a universe of established public knowledge, the book increasingly became the forum for the introduction of new topics. Thus, it was only with increasing difficulty that one could identify one or another book in terms of the recognized subject that it treated. Yet, traditions as firmly entrenched as the idea of subjects as established locations within a classificatory map of the publicly accumulated universe of knowledge die or change only with great difficulty.

THE NINETEENTH CENTURY RESPONSE TO SUBJECTS

When Cutter and his nineteenth century contemporaries began their endeavors, they became the first generation of librarians to attempt seriously to provide comprehensive subject access to books. But their schooling was, almost without exception, in the older patterns of thought that considered subjects in the more restricted manner previously described. Cutter's exposure to Scottish thinking furnishes a primary example of this. In fact, the Scottish understanding of the acquisition of knowledge, which in great measure reflected the above approach to subjects, was the dominant model in American higher education until after the Civil War, thereby affecting all subject thinking until the very end of the nineteenth century.

When Cutter and his contemporaries endeavored to create subject access systems, it was with an intellectual framework of reference in which a subject of any sort was automatically, without question, an expression of a systematic structure of established subjects resident in the public realm. All forms of subject access were essentially the same, therefore, because they all dealt with the same thing—subjects that were by their very nature elements of a systematic structure of subjects. The importance of this factor must be thoroughly appreciated to understand Cutter's work.

Some have attempted to show that Cutter's alphabetical subject system was indebted to a greater or lesser degree to classification.[34] This conclusion, based as it often is on the notion that classification is more or less posterior or incidental to subject heading work, is far from an accurate assessment. For Cutter, alphabetical subject systems were not simply indebted to classification in some way. They were classification, pure and simple, because what were considered to be subjects in the first place were fundamentally defined only as elements of the systematic structure of the universe of knowledge. There simply was no alternative in Cutter's thinking. There were no subjects or subject systems that were not wholly classification elements or that were defined in some way other than being classification elements. In short, topics of thought were subjects because they were categories in a systematic structure of knowledge. To envision subjects, regardless of their temporal location—whether expressed orally or expressed in books —was to see them as categories in such a scheme.

The implications of this view of subjects for understanding Cutter's subject access thinking is significant. First, a subject was a technical referent to a category located in a classificatory map of the established public universe of knowledge. The universe of knowledge thus conceived preceded the existence of objects of thought in any particular book and provided a means for distinguishing whether the topic of any particular book was a subject. Second, a subject understood in this sense was indeed a matter of thought or investigation, but not all matters of thought were subjects per se since only those that had become categories in the established universe of knowledge by a social process of establishment and definition could technically be considered subjects. Other matters or objects of thought or investigation were possible, but those were not to be considered subjects until established by the same process. Third, the establishment of a topic of thought as a subject was evidenced by the fact that the topic had gained a name; that is, that it became referred to by a particular word or set of words by the various persons who wrote on the topic. The existence of a special name in this sense was tantamount to the subject having come through the social process in which its connotation and denotation were established and verified in the public realm. Fourth, to say that books had subjects referred to the evidence they gave of treating only of some topic that had become established in this manner. It did not refer to something considered necessarily to be their entire topical aboutness. This obviously implies a differentiation between *all* that a work treats (i.e., its entire topical aboutness) and that which it treats that *is established.* (It should be carefully noted at this point that the differentiation just described is relevant only to modern subject theorists rather than to Cutter and his contemporaries. For Cutter there was no explicit differentiation because the idea of subject meant only what today would be considered an established subject.) Fifth, to provide subject access to books meant to make books available in terms of the established topics treated in them. More specifically, to provide subject access to the subjects of books meant for Cutter to make books available in terms of their most specific established subjects. Again, as in point four above, confusion will enter if the idea of a subject is extended to include anything and everything a book is about. Cutter meant by the specific or special subject of a book only that which would now be called an established subject.

The subject heading system that Cutter built will obviously seem limited and, as previously described, contradictory to the degree that Cutter's restrictive idea of a subject is not understood or considered invalid. The very use of the qualification "established subject" betrays the seriousness of the difference in point of view. To say that a subject is established suggests that there is such a thing as an unestablished subject. Concomitantly, to omit unestablished subjects from a subject access system would seem to be admitting that only some subjects are being used in the system and that the resulting subject system is incomplete or partial. From that conclusion it is only a short step to the rationalization that Cutter and his contemporaries had only a simplistic idea of subjects and that the chief problem in using his system, at least from a modern point of view, is how to incorporate into it measures that would allow complete access to all topics of thought without qualifications as to whether they are established or unestablished.

Because Cutter did not view subjects in the way modern subject access workers do, he did not perceive a conflict between something considered the whole topical aboutness of a book and the allowable topic under which that book might be entered in a subject system. Nor would he find it understandable that the chief difficulty with his system for present-day subject catalogers is how to overcome that conflict. This is not to say, however, that his system had no difficulties or that it did not address significant problems. In fact, Cutter's subject system can best be described as an innovative attempt to solve significant problems related to his own view of subjects.

One such problem has already been broached in the context of the discussion of Cutter's view of kinds of subjects and the order of significance that the kinds of subjects had with respect to inclusion relationships. Previous notions of inclusion relationships were, as noted in the historical survey of the idea of a subject, tied closely to the notion of logical definition and the genus-species hierarchical order that resulted from that method. But inclusion relationships based solely on logical definition did not easily accommodate subjects not intrinsically related. Cutter found it possible to follow the traditional approach to inclusion relationships where subjects were intrinsically related. The classificatory relationship of Cats to Mammals, for example, and Salvation to Theology could be determined because the topics were related by definition. To this Cutter added, however, an extension of the idea of inclusion relationships that arose out of his Scottish training. Given three essentially distinct kinds of subjects ranging from the most abstract to the most concrete and an inclusion or significance order between the kinds of subjects that arose out of the analysis of the mental faculties and that accorded specificity to the subject that was most concrete, Cutter was able to determine inclusion relationships between subjects not otherwise intrinsically related. That subject considered to be most abstract included the others; and conversely, that subject considered most concrete, was included by—was most specific in relationship to—the others. This solution to classificatory inclusion relationships was "logical" insofar as the relationships between kinds of subjects were seen to be logical extensions of mental processes. But it went beyond the notion of logical definition that was fundamental to the earlier approach to classificatory relationships because it avoided the necessity of basing the relationships between terms on their explicit meanings, at least in a great many cases. This had a profound effect in turn on how Cutter viewed the respective capacities of the two main types of catalogs, classed and dictionary, to provide for specific entry— a matter to be discussed in chapter 5.

Another problem that Cutter addressed was how to make a subject system responsive to those who can generally be described as users. Users did not mean simply those who came into a library and opened a subject catalog, however; it referred to the entire range of thinking and habit that people brought to the consideration and interaction with subjects as already discussed here. This broad meaning of users must be kept in mind as the third contextual element of Cutter's subject thinking is described: subjects in relation to the public.

CHAPTER 4

Subjects and the Public

The investigation of Cutter's view of subjects as subjects alone and subjects in relation to books has been necessary because those topics are important to the construction of any subject access system. A third contextual element that is equally important is the nature of Cutter's view of the public. Specifically, it is necessary to understand how Cutter's view of the public was integral to the notions about subjects already discussed and how it was important in subject access decisions and requirements.

The Public and Usage

Cutter referred to the notion of the public in one form or another in many specific instances in his subject rules. Sometimes he simply advanced the idea of the public in general, as in his discussion of the propriety of double entry (i.e., entry under both class and specific subject) for the same book.[1] At other times he referred to specific categories of users, as in his rule on choice between country and general or scientific subject. There he mentioned two particular kinds of users among the public, "the geographical student" and "the scientist."[2] More often than not, however, his references to the public had to do with usage. Usage refers to the habits of the public in searching for subjects, that is, to the particular subject names people might use when conducting a search.[3]

Since at least the 1940s, Cutter's statements on usage have generally been considered so prominent that commentators have concluded that it was his chief concern and guiding principle in subject cataloging. This conclusion would appear to be confirmed in a general statement that precedes the section of his rules on choices between subject names, where he wrote:

> General rules, always applicable, for the choice of names of subjects can no more be given than rules without exception in grammar. Usage

in both cases is the supreme arbiter,—the usage, in the present case, not of the cataloger but of the public in speaking of subjects.[4]

The same conclusions about the importance of usage would also seem to be confirmed by Cutter's general statement in the preface to the fourth edition of his *Rules* where he stated that "the convenience of the public is always to be set before the ease of the cataloger." There, however, Cutter went one step further by suggesting that when there was a conflict between the cataloger's desire to make a consistent system and "the public's habitual way of looking at things," it would be better for the cataloger to follow the public's habits "even if they demand a sacrifice of system and simplicity." In other words, if usage in such matters appears to contradict the notion of making a subject "system," the cataloger should follow usage without regard for any loss of the latter.[5]

Although Cutter was greatly concerned about the public's subject searching habits and considered it necessary that catalog rules should be responsive to the way people might reasonably be expected to search for subject entries, there are three significant reasons for questioning whether he intended his view of the public and the corresponding notion of usage to be interpreted in the way they have subsequently been explained. First, two of his general statements about usage were actually written in the context of special cases, raising a legitimate question as to how he intended them to be applied to subject cataloging. His statement about the "convenience of the public" appears to have been prompted because of particular concerns that he had concerning descriptive cataloging.[6] And his often quoted general maxim about usage—"Usage . . . is the supreme arbiter"—was intentionally placed by him at the beginning of the section on choice between subject names rather than as a prefatory note to the entire section on subject cataloging. In fact, Cutter's general prefatory statement to the entire subject cataloging section strongly supports the idea of making systematic rules that discipline and shape usage rather than follow it.[7] The limitations inherent in the contexts of his most general statement on usage raise at least the possibility, therefore, that Cutter did not intend usage to overwhelmingly guide practice in the way that it has been interpreted.

A second reason for questioning the generally accepted interpretation of Cutter's view of the public and usage is that it generally implies that the public is essentially unsystematic and irrational in its habits or, at best, given only to limited patterns of consistent searching behavior. The public is also sometimes portrayed as a single undifferentiated group and sometimes as a combination of numerous particular groups often defined socio-economically or by their subject interests.

Regardless of whether there is one group or many, the chief characteristic of the public tends to be the mysteriousness, the unpredictability, or the almost infinite variability of its subject searching habits. The result is that subject cataloging decisions designed to accommodate usage must necessarily be made on an ad hoc basis. And decisions made in that manner imply inconsistency and a lack of system.

For Cutter, however, the public was notably regular in its habits. In fact, he spoke of the habits of the public as being prominent enough to be observed and in a certain sense charted. In his scenario of conflict between catalogers' rules and the convenience of the public, he stressed that "habits" (i.e., "the public's habitual way of looking at things") should not be disregarded because they are "general and deeply rooted." His words imply that the habits are widespread and consistent enough to be accommodated by careful exceptions if not by rules themselves. The result, certainly, is a loss of system and simplicity in the cataloger's ideal conception of a code and its use where rules followed without exception are easiest to conceive and apply. It does not imply the loss of system altogether, however, or even the loss of system in large measure, at least if Cutter's overall stress on systematic cataloging means anything.

A third and final reason for questioning the above interpretation of Cutter's view of the public and usage is that it does not do justice to the breadth that Cutter brought to the notions. For Cutter, usage was only a derivative aspect of the much larger issue of how people in general exercised their thinking capacities and expressed the desire to learn. Given that more general view, usage ceases to be a fundamentally perplexing phenomenon related to highly variable individual or group behavior. Indeed, this was precisely the starting point for Cutter, a general view of the intellectual habits of humanity—a psychology of the public—so encompassing that it provided a viable basis for subject cataloging decisions and requirements.

Scottish Origin of Cutter's View

The basis for Cutter's general view of the public was the Scottish epistemological model already described and particularly the Scottish view of the intellectual development of both individual persons and society at large. Scottish philosophers not only analyzed how individual people think and act, but also pictured the ideal intellectual and moral development of any particular person from childhood to maturity. According to their thinking, mental faculties, including both intellectual and active powers, may function well or they may function poorly. In order for them to function well they must be improved by specific exercises in a manner analogous to an athlete who trains his or her body and mind in order to achieve peak performance. When one has achieved a high degree of training of the mental faculties, it may be said that one has become "cultivated."[8] Furthermore, when many people of a particular society have achieved a high degree of training of their mental faculties, it may be said that that society as a whole has become mentally cultivated. In fact, the mental cultivation of any particular society was viewed by the Scotsmen as essential to that society's well-being and ideal advancement.

A commitment to the process of cultivation was also a commitment to education, particularly systematic education that incorporated mental and moral training of the kind the realists themselves emphasized. According to Dugald Stewart, education of this kind had two very specific objectives:

> First, to cultivate all the various principles of our nature, both speculative and active, in such a manner as to bring them to the greatest perfection of which they are susceptible; and, secondly, by watching over the impressions and associations which the mind receives early in life, to secure it against the influence of prevailing errors, and, as far as possible, to engage its prepossessions on the side of truth.[9]

Systematic education of the intellectual and active powers would develop and discipline a person's mental faculties and provide one with the mental and moral fortitude to search for truth rather than be victimized by error. Furthermore, the emphasis that this kind of education made on using sound methods and achieving intellectual and moral advancement and discovery would promote the overall growth of science as a societal phenomenon.

Not all people were at the same point in their intellectual and moral development, however. For various reasons, some of which had to do with such societal conditions as poverty, geographical isolation, etc., the intellectual and moral development of many had been arrested at relatively low levels of advancement. Thus, the knowledge which different people had acquired varied in character and extent according to what state of development their various mental faculties were in. Because of variations of this kind, Stewart measured the general progress of mankind against a scale of intellectual development. At one end were the vulgar, the great mass of common people, whose level of cultivation was generally low. These people tended to function mentally at either more elementary levels, or, when functioning at higher levels, without disciplined powers of reasoning and judgment. In short, they tended to be occupied mentally with perceptions of individuals and with general notions of lesser extent. They also tended to be particularly affected by the relatively unbridled operation of their lowest faculties, the chief result of which was a greater degree of error or imprecision in their knowledge and judgment.

At the opposite extreme were the philosophers, that relatively small segment of society whose mental faculties were highly trained. Their powers of abstraction were especially affected by highly disciplined powers of reasoning and judgment. The disciplined use of these powers made them capable of forming propositions about ultimate first principles concerning the true relations of all things. They were also particularly aware of moral perceptions and strove to conduct their lives in such a way that their higher powers, both intellectual and moral, gave direction and control to their lower.

Stewart described the difference between these two kinds of persons not as a greater or lesser amount of mental activity, but rather as a difference in the kind of knowledge they held. This difference was ultimately a reflection of their respective use of language.

> It is not that the former [i.e., the philosopher] is accustomed to carry on his process of reasoning to a greater extent than the latter; but that the conclusions he is accustomed to form are far more comprehensive, in consequence of the habitual employment of more comprehensive terms. Among the most unenlightened of mankind we often meet with individuals who possess the reasoning faculty in a very eminent degree; but as this faculty is employed merely about particulars, whether their pursuits in life lead them to speculation or action, it can only fit them for distinguishing themselves in some very limited and subordinate sphere. The philosopher, whose mind has been familiarized by education and by his own reflections, to the correct use of more comprehensive terms, is enabled, without perhaps a greater degree of intellectual exertion than is necessary for managing the details of ordinary business, to arrive at general theorums, which, when illustrated to the lower classes of men, in their particular applications, seem to indicate a fertility of invention, little short of supernatural.[10]

Between these two extremes were to be found those people who, having separated themselves to a greater or lesser extent from the general ignorance of the masses, were at middling stages of the cultivation process. In many instances, however, the ordinary business of life had led them to learn those specialized terms of both lesser and greater comprehension that principally were related to their occupations or to some circumscribed area of personal study. Stewart recognized the uniqueness of their intellectual expertise, but was not sanguine about the depth of their mental culture because they had in effect neglected their broader cultivation for their specializations and thus lived in mental and moral imbalance.

A Psychology of the Public

Cutter's subject access writing reflected the Scottish view of personal and societal development in that he adopted it in large part as a general psychological model for his notion of the public. The public here does not simply mean those who came to the library to search for books or information. Rather it referred to everyone, regardless of their particular occupations, socioeconomic status, ethnic backgrounds, or even their specific relationships to the library—that is, inquirers, authors of books, or librarians.

The general nature of the psychological model is insisted upon because it pointedly emphasizes Cutter's starting position in the matter. Cutter did not first view people in terms of some particular group to which they belonged and then characterize their relationship to subject access matters (e.g., preference for one or another subject name, preference between variations in word order) in terms of those groups. Instead, he began with a basic psychological model common to all people which he then used as a measure when considering one or another of the other kinds of groups listed above. Even then, however, his references to special kinds of groups were relatively limited. More often than not, he spoke of persons directly in terms of his basic model.

Cutter's use of this basic model appears repeatedly in his writings, for example, when he discussed librarians as an occupational group, when he discussed the relationship of librarians to educators, and especially when he discussed the reading habits of the general populace. With respect to subject access concerns, his fullest expression of it occurs in his characterization of inquirers, those persons who came to libraries seeking information or books.

Cutter divided inquirers into three categories:

> (1) those who want something quickly; (2) those who want to make a thorough study of some specific subject; and (3) those who want to study fully some general class of subjects.[11]

The general characteristics of these categories of inquirers closely parallel Stewart's scale of intellectual and moral development of people in general with the exception that Cutter's terminology specifically focuses on searching habits and the second and third groups tend to be considered together.

DESULTORY READERS

Cutter considered the first category of inquirers to be the "largest and loudest" of the three groups.[12] They constituted, in effect, the mass of common people who were for the most part unlearned. And they were most likely to be found in this dominant proportion in public or town libraries rather than in libraries with a more scholarly clientele, such as libraries attached to natural history societies. Cutter attributed two kinds of searches to this category of inquirers. They sought books on particular specific subjects or they looked for groups of books that constituted their favorite reading topics. Cutter characterized both of these kinds of searches, however, as essentially non-discriminatory. The search for particular specific subjects was conducted not from the standpoint of a critical investigation of the topic nor in light of the relationship of the particular specific subject to other related subjects, but was conducted simply to get "an answer" in the form of a book. The answer might be neither complete nor true. But that did not matter so much as the fact that some answer was found.[13]

The search for groups of books on a favorite topic was likewise conducted without a critical intellectual framework of reference but rather arose from "desultory" reading habits. Choices were commonly made from kinds and forms of literature (e.g., English poetry and fiction, and biography in general) or from broad topical subjects (e.g., religious works or scientific works, or, especially, works about particular places). That which characterized the choice of books within such a group was not so much a critical awareness of the topic as a subject but simply whether the books were "well-written and interesting." Both kinds of searches suggested that the intellectual use of books was essentially flaccid and imprecise. In this respect, Cutter concluded that the desultory reader was "averse to mental effort."[14] In both kinds of searches as well, inquirers simply wanted something to read. Furthermore, they wanted to find what they were looking for "quickly" or "at once." They had little patience for delay.

For these various reasons, it made little difference that the subjects which desultory readers sought were arranged in some meaningful order. A straightforward alphabetical list of subjects suggested little to them. Furthermore, they were not likely even to discriminate between synonyms because they were not ordinarily used to thinking of such alternatives. And if an alphabetical arrangement of subjects was at times a trial, then a catalog that listed books under systematically arranged subjects or even a synoptic table of subjects was sure to puzzle and confuse them, in the end delaying or perhaps even barring their use of the catalog. A simple, straightforward, alphabetical arrangement of the specific subjects of books would do as well as anything, facilitating to some degree the kinds of simple searches that this category of inquirers conducted.

ADVANCED READERS

The second and third categories of inquirers differed from each other only in the extent of their searches, not in the essential manner in which searching was conducted. The second category looked for books on a particular specific subject whereas the third type of inquirer looked for books on a group of subjects that were related by being in the same general class. The searches of each of these groups of inquirers could together be characterized in two important ways.[15] First, they were conducted as an expression of study rather than as simply a desire to find something to read. In this regard they planned their searches, often with considerable care. Moreover, they exercised patience and tenacity in conducting their searches. They were willing to spend time on a search, to come back for more than one try, and they accepted difficulty and the need to learn a system of subjects as part of the searching process. Furthermore, searching was done with an eye to thoroughness. On an elementary level this meant that readers critically chose among books on the same subject, comparing their merits. On another level, this meant that alternatives needed to be followed, either in the form of synonymous subject names or in the form of related subjects. And, at its most extended level, thoroughness involved searching not only for whole books on a subject or on a group of subjects, but also for parts of books, periodical articles, and notable articles in encyclopedias. Thoroughness also implied that one might well have to go beyond what a catalog offered to supplement the search.

The second common characteristic of these searches was that they were always conducted with the knowledge that all subjects were interrelated in a classificatory manner. In other words, the very nature of subjects implied the necessity of a classificatory approach to subject searching. A word of caution should be added at this point, however. Cutter's view of classificatory structure, deeply indebted as it was to Scottish epistemology, invoked a more expansive notion of classificatory relationships than what might be otherwise understood by the term. As noted in the previous chapter, traditional subject classification arose out of Greek and medieval methods of logical definition. As a result, the notion of subject order inherent in a classification of subjects was at first tied closely to the hierarchical (i.e., genus-species) relationships that adhered to that methodology. Scottish epistemology enhanced the traditional notion of logically determined inclusion relationships by positing a logical significance order between kinds of subjects as well as between subjects that were intrinsically related to one another. The source of this broader approach to inclusion relationships was, of course, the model of the mental processes inherent in the Scottish view of man. And it was this enhanced notion of classification that Cutter implied when he noted that there was a correspondence between searching for books by their subjects understood in a classificatory sense and the fundamental nature of the learning process.

The two basic characteristics of these searches—a study orientation and a classificatory orientation—obviously set these inquirers apart from the first category of inquirers. The second group, like the first, searched for particular specific subjects, but they went about the task in a studious rather than a desultory manner. Of course, the third group differed from both of the other groups in the intensity, commitment, and breadth of their searching.

These various searching habits set the three categories of inquirers apart for Cutter. It should be noted, however, that Cutter did not consider the picture thus derived to be static. In his opinion, most persons in the first category, although basically desultory in reading habit, "would prefer, if they knew how, to improve their minds and increase their stock of knowledge."[16] Thus, they could be helped to a better appreciation of knowledge and a more accomplished technique of knowledge gathering. In fact, one of the principal goals of librarianship as then articulated was to offer that sort of help and influence, especially among children. Likewise, there was movement between the other two groups, sometimes in the form of a person in the second category changing a search to that of the third. On the other hand, persons in both of the two advanced groups occasionally searched with the impatience of the first category.

Cutter also considered certain characteristics to be common to all three groups. Despite the fact that some of the first kind had trouble even with the alphabet, Cutter held the opinion that in general "everyone knows the alphabet."[17] Likewise, in general everyone knew the single well-known names of most subjects, especially of individual subjects. And among commonly known subjects, he concluded that "persons and places are the most common objects of inquiry."[18] Cutter also held the opinion that the public had, to a certain extent, "an unsystematic association of ideas," with the exception that there was a basic font of commonly understood subject relationships known especially by the second and third groups.[19] Finally, Cutter was also aware that certain characteristics of subject systems were bothersome to all inquirers. For example, no one liked double reference—being referred from one place to another in the catalog for the subject of one's search, especially for individual subjects. And no one liked what appeared to be strange subject collocations. On the other hand, even with respect to these various shared dislikes, some qualifications had to be added. The first category of inquirers disliked double reference from the standpoint of their general impatience, where the second and third, generally more patient, at least understood its necessity and would put up with it. Likewise, the first category of inquirers were likely to find all subject collocation strange, whereas the second and third categories, having a good deal of patience with subject collocation in areas they were not familiar with, tended to focus their dislike on what they considered to be untenable subject collocation in their own areas.[20]

One of the most immediate implications of this picture of the psychology of the public is that it should caution the modern reader about the way Cutter meant usage. When Cutter appealed to usage as a way to resolve subject cataloging dilemmas of choice, the basic user categories to which he appealed were, in fact, those described here. Thus, the reader of his subject rules must necessarily attempt to identify which categories of the public in his general scale he was referring to in particular instances. For example, one of the initial issues of choice based on usage that Cutter delineated concerned the matter of identifying legitimate specific subjects in terms of whether or not their names were distinct. His criterion for decision in that instance was not to determine the names for which inquirers who came into the library were habitually accustomed to looking. If it were, Cutter would have been appealing primarily to the judgment of desultory readers, "the largest and loudest" class of inquirers. But because of his description of this class of inquirers, using them as the basis for determining such a consensus is questionable. Rather, the criterion he intended was plain enough. Legitimate specific subject names were to be based on whether the books themselves used them. And a moment's reflection will strongly suggest that books, or rather the authors of books, did not represent Cutter's typical desultory reader. On the contrary, they represented, if anything, the other two groups of the public.

The other major area of choice for subject catalogers was between equally valid names for the same specific subject—the substance of the second section of his subject rules. Here, Cutter specifically directed attention to the habits of inquirers as the basis for choosing between synonyms and in certain cases for justifying alternative word orders in compound subject names. But here one also encounters a much more ambivalent attitude on Cutter's part about usage. There was, in fact, a strong inclination on his part to deny its practical value in favor of other solutions. (A more detailed discussion of these applications of usage will be reserved for later in this study. It is sufficient here simply to note that the appropriate basis for interpreting the notion in the first place is Cutter's general psychology of the public.)

The General Requirements of Subject Systems

While Cutter's psychology of the public is important to his concept of usage, the effect of the same view of the public is even more significant with respect to what he considered the general requirements of subject access systems. Cutter's incorporation of a general psychological model of the public strongly reinforced the equation, previously mentioned, that all subject access systems were necessarily expressions of classification. When that equation was discussed earlier, however, it had been in the context of a theoretical model of the human knowing process. Here, where the overall psychological model is invoked, there is a much closer connection of its results to what Cutter could observe in everyday life about him. A large portion of the public was untrained in the disciplines of the intellect and did indeed present a noticeable picture of aimless reading and unstructured interaction with ideas. Furthermore, it seemed obvious to Cutter that the public tended to search for the simplest kinds of subjects, those that were concrete, especially individual subjects. In contrast to this preponderant group were those who were educated to varying degrees and whose thinking processes were cultivated so that to greater or lesser degrees they dwelled on ideas of much greater abstraction and comprehension. Their interest in abstract and comprehensive ideas in turn affected the searching patterns they used, which tended to be based on a classificatory approach to subjects. In other words, Cutter's experience appeared to demonstrate the reality of the overall psychological model of how the minds of the public worked and of how the mental activity of groups of the public was translated into library habits.

From the perspective of an additional century, modern readers clearly have reason to question this entire explanation of subjects, their interrelationships, and their basis in a theoretical model of the mind. One might also question Cutter's description of the thinking and inquiring habits of people and particularly his relatively undifferentiated category entitled the desultory reader. Regardless of the viability of his explanation, however, the important thing here is that this is the way *he* explained things. And because it seemed connected with the real world about him, it provided him with a reasonable basis for subject system requirements.[21] Subject systems were necessarily expressions of classification because the very nature of thinking and the very nature of language were classificatory. This maxim was demonstrated to Cutter's satisfaction in the way people conducted themselves in relation to the library and, specifically, in the subject-inquiring process.

This view is significant because it shaped what Cutter considered to be the fundamental requirements of any subject system. To begin with, every subject system must necessarily contend with the classificatory nature of the subject access task. To disregard this would be to disregard the fundamental nature of the knowing process and, thus, the fundamental nature of the public. This emphasis, more than anything else, appears to be the source of Cutter's criticism of the "common" dictionary catalogs of his day—that is, dictionary catalogs of the kind made notable by William F. Poole—in which subject entries were based almost entirely on subject words taken from the titles of books and little, if any, attention given to a cross-reference structure. Such catalogs neglected what Cutter's sense of priorities demanded, that subject access to be true to its nature must express its classificatory foundations.

This requirement was further qualified by the "missionary" motivation of the early years of library development, a motivation of some importance. Cutter worked in an era when librarianship as a profession was just becoming organized. Among the various goals of the new profession, one of those most strongly stated was to bring cultural enlightenment to a general populace which was viewed as having little. For Cutter, this amounted to something of an intellectual program largely educational in overall proportions. Librarians were described by him as belonging to a helping profession dedicated to intellectual and cultural uplift. His writings are literally peppered with statements, often phrased in religious or general humanitarian language, that highlight this concern. His views on cataloging also gave evidence of the same orientation although it amounted to only one theme among many others that were much more technical in their import. For example, his advocacy of descriptive and evaluative notes in catalogs had strong overtones of intellectual guidance to catalog users who might not otherwise be capable of such discrimination by themselves.[22]

Cutter's notion of the public gave evidence of the same kind of thinking. Despite his view that desultory reading habits were generally aimless and uncultivated, and that well-intentioned librarians were not likely "to convert" readers of novels to something better, he also gave evidence of the optimism of his uplift motivations when he described desultory readers with the words, "most of whom would prefer, if they knew how, to improve their minds and increase their stock of knowledge."[23]

The combination of Cutter's general view of the public, the classificatory nature of subject access, and a missionary motivation provided a rationale for two other specific subject system objectives. First, regardless of the kind of subject system being constructed—whether alphabetical or classed in arrangement—the specific subjects of books must be identified in every instance. To not do so would require users to search for books on those specific subjects among undifferentiated groups of books entered under more inclusive subjects. The practical reason for demanding this was, of course, that it made subject retrieval of documents on specific subjects easier. One would not have to sift through dozens, perhaps even hundreds of entries, to locate such books. The more important reason for the demand, however, was that by Cutter's reckoning the largest number of inquirers—desultory by habit—were precisely those who, tending to search for the most concrete subjects, were least likely to know in which including class such specific subjects were likely to lie hidden. If these people were to be helped, even in the simple manner of getting them to nonfiction books about the least comprehensive, most concrete subjects, then subjects of that sort must of necessity be given access. And given the probability that the specific entry subjects of a large number of all the books that a library collected were individual subjects (concrete by definition) or concrete general subjects, the entry of those books under their most concrete subject names in every instance would fulfill the need.

Second, after the specific subjects of books have been identified, these should be given what today is called direct access. That is to say, they should be placed in the primary sequence of the catalog, rather than in some subsidiary position of access. The reason for this was twofold. On the one hand, as in the case above, this arrangement facilitated searching by that dominant class of inquirers who were least capable of finding the subjects when subentered under more inclusive classes. The latter is how they would appear, of course, in classed arrangements. In other words, assuming their general lack of intellectual acumen, users of this class would simply not know where to look for such subjects. Cutter also concluded that even better-educated inquirers would have similar difficulties if they were not familiar with the structure of the classification system used. Furthermore, because indexes to classed catalogs were rare in Cutter's day, this lack of direct access amounted to a critical problem. Of course, with a good index this problem would have been solved, at least for the better-educated user and for the desultory reader as well if the general impatience of that class of inquirer could be overcome. But Cutter was not sanguine about the latter. To place such books in an arrangement that could only have appeared complex would in his view have tended to court the frustration rather than the satisfaction of desultory readers. They desired books easily located and "at once" or not at all in his opinion.

Perhaps even more important, providing direct access to the specific subjects of books would overcome the normal dispersion of specific subjects that a classed arrangement engendered. A sense of the critical nature of this dispersion of specific subjects should be a matter of considerable awareness to those who look for books arranged, for example, according to the Dewey Decimal Classification. Books on cats will be found in 636.8 and also in 599.74428 as well as in a variety of other places; those on bridges in perhaps a total of more than ten different locations.[24] To point this out is not to criticize such dispersion. The very nature of a classification scheme requires it. But for Cutter such dispersion was critical, given the public he was serving, because the subjects that were most likely to be dispersed would be those of greatest concreteness and individuality. And it was precisely those subjects that the "largest and loudest" category of inquirers were not only likely to look for but, by Cutter's reasoning, would want gathered together as easily accessed groups of books on their favorite topics. If subject catalogers were to be responsive to the larger portion of inquirers, especially since these were the primary objects of the library's cultural endeavor, subject systems must be constructed that avoided the dispersion.

When the general requirements of subject access systems are stated in this way, as necessarily classificatory in nature but primarily designed to serve that portion of the public that is relatively incapable of approaching subject knowledge in its natural classified structure, the scene is set for making a subject system that is essentially upside down from a classifier's point of view. The system must carefully arrange and exhibit for the most immediate access those most concrete and individual specific subjects of books that would best serve that large proportion of the public to whom the mission, especially as it was conceived for public libraries in Cutter's day, was dedicated—the desultory reader. Then if some help could be provided for the fewer in number but more cultivated and advanced portion of the public, it might be added.

The specific form of subject system that Cutter devised to meet these requirements was the dictionary catalog, not in the form typical in the mid-nineteenth century, but rather in the form that he rationalized in his *Rules* as the "syndetic dictionary catalog." That the syndetic dictionary catalog should have been the best possible answer for Cutter may not be plainly evident, however, especially in the light of claims made on behalf of classified subject access by twentieth-century classifiers that strongly contest his conclusion. The ultimate reason why the dictionary catalog as he designed it was for him the best solution will become evident as the last of the contextual elements of his subject system work is examined—Cutter's view of the practice of subject cataloging in his day.

CHAPTER 5

Subject Catalogs and Cataloging

An examination of the notions of subjects as subjects alone and subjects in relation to books has provided a view of Cutter's fundamental intellectual framework of reference with regard to subjects. An examination of subjects and the public has provided a picture of the constraints imposed by his understanding of whom subject systems were designed to serve. Here, a discussion of a fourth and last contextual element of his subject system will show how Cutter viewed subject catalogs and cataloging in his day. This discussion will include the fundamental kinds of catalogs available, the basic structural features of subject catalogs in general, and, most important, the features common to each kind of catalog seen from the standpoint of both their ideal form and typical practice.

Kinds of Subject Catalogs

Cutter divided catalogs into types according to their basic arrangements. He defined a catalog as "a list of books which is arranged on some definite plan,"[1] and a subject catalog more particularly as "a catalog of subjects, whether arranged in classes or alphabeted by names of subjects."[2] Cutter's reference to both classed and alphabetical arrangement is important because these two terms indicated fundamental principles of arrangement, the differentia of which formed the basis of the four kinds of subject catalogs available. The two kinds of arrangement differed in the following way. Cutter viewed alphabetical arrangement, based as it was on the arbitrary order of the alphabet, as "external, mechanical." But class arrangement, encompassing as it did "the relations of subjects to one another," was "internal, chemical, so to speak."[3] In other words, the natural or intrinsic order of subjects was classed. Alphabetical arrangement, quite to the contrary, represented the application of an extrinsic order to subject arrangement that was useful only to the degree that it repre-

87

sented a convenience for those who were not otherwise aware of the natural order.

Over the course of subject catalog development, these two principles of order had produced four basic kinds of catalogs in Cutter's view: (1) the specific dictionary; (2) the alphabetico-classed; (3) the classed without subdivisions; and (4) the classed with subdivisions. Of these, only the specific dictionary catalog adhered fully to alphabetical order. It arranged all of its subjects "like the words in a dictionary, in alphabetical order."[4] The other three types of catalogs arranged their subjects in terms of classificatory relationships. The classed catalog with subdivisions placed the narrowest subjects under their next inclusive superordinate subjects (i.e., classes) and those in turn under superordinate subjects of even greater extent, and so on, the whole eventually being subsumed under a series of main classes themselves arranged in some logical order. Because of the foregoing pattern of organization, this kind of catalog was often called the systematically classed catalog. The alphabetico-classed catalog also arranged subjects in terms of their classificatory relationships with the exception that at each level of subdivision, subjects in the same array were arranged alphabetically instead of systematically. Thus, the main classes were arranged alphabetically, the divisions of each main class were subarranged alphabetically under their respective main classes, the subdivisions of each division were subarranged alphabetically under their respective divisions, and so on down to arrays of subjects at the narrowest level of subject scope. In addition, the alphabetico-classed catalog normally had many more subjects in its primary subject sequence than did the systematically classed catalog, narrow subjects often being placed there when their positions as subdivisions were in doubt. The classed catalog without subdivisions also arranged its subjects in a systematic order like the classed catalog with subdivisions. But because it contained no subdivisions, its only subjects were the principal array of main classes.

Cutter was also quite aware of other kinds of catalog arrangement. For example, several of the earliest catalogs in a comprehensive list of catalogs that he had compiled were arranged by size categories. And other catalogs were alphabetical arrangements only of the authors or of the authors and titles of works. But such arrangements had little bearing on his typology of subject catalogs. He also differentiated between particular varieties of the four kinds of catalogs discussed here. For example, he distinguished between his own specific dictionary catalog and other kinds of specific dictionary catalogs in terms of how rigorously they pursued specific entry. Differences of this kind were not matters of arrangement, however, but rather of how catalogs represented subjects in relation to works.

Cutter also discussed subject catalogs according to how they accommodated the kinds of considerations presented in the previous chapters. Before delving into his conclusions regarding those matters, Cutter's understanding of basic features of subject catalog structure, including the terminology that he used, must be described.

Structural Features of Subject Catalogs

Cutter employed several terms related to catalog structure in specialized ways. An "entry" referred to "the registry of a book in the catalog with the title and imprint," that is, the full record of its bibliographical details.[5] This was in contrast to a "reference" which Cutter defined as the "partial registry of a book (omitting the imprint) under author, title, subject, or kind, referring to a more full entry under some other heading."[6]

The position of the entry as a bibliographical description within the catalog was in turn determined by the heading of the entry. In catalogs of the types that Cutter described, all headings consisted of a word or words that denoted an access point to the work, either the name of the author of the work (or some substitute for the author), the title of the work, the name of the literary form in which a work was written, or, in the case of subject catalogs, the name of a subject treated in the work. In two instances Cutter referred to the heading as "the word" under which its bibliographical description was placed, rather than, for example, "the word or words," as noted here.[7] This reference should not be taken to mean that Cutter considered headings to be a single word in every instance or that only the first word of any multiple grouping of words was the heading. Cutter's equation of a word with an author's name, for example, would simply indicate that his use of "word" was synonymous with the more accurate distinction made today by the use of entry "term." A heading for Cutter was any term, whether it consisted of one word or more than one word. In sum, the heading determined "the place of the entry in the catalog."[8] And in a dictionary catalog, the heading was the word or words "by which the alphabetical place of an entry in the catalog is determined."[9]

When viewed in the foregoing manner, the entry (as a bibliographical description) and its heading produced a distinct visual effect in the printed catalogs of Cutter's day. The heading was positioned above—that is, *at the head* of—the bibliographical descriptions related to it. (The only exception was that the first of the descriptions in any such list was commonly placed immediately to the right of the heading. This was a printing convention designed to conserve space.) Conversely, the bibliographical descriptions were said to be "under" the heading, the descriptions and the heading together making a separately identifiable "file" within the entire catalog sequence.

Another way to view these structural elements is to consider those instances in which Cutter spoke of entry as an action, such as when he spoke of a work being "entered" in the catalog. In this sense the two elements, bibliographical description and heading, were considered as a single unit. One cannot register a book in a catalog without a heading because the very act of registering a book implies a heading which determines the place of the bibliographical description in the catalog. Thus, an entry could also be spoken of as both a heading and a bibliographical description—an author entry meaning the bibliographical description of a book together with the author heading under which it was placed; a subject entry meaning the bibliographical description of a book together with the subject heading under which it was placed, etc. This sense of entry was in turn affected by the relationship of the subject heading to the subject treated in the work and by the relationship of the heading to the main sequence of the catalog.

The relationship of a subject heading to the subject treated in a work was based on the notions already discussed—every book could be said to treat some specific subject and that every subject, including any specific subject, was by definition an element of a subject hierarchy consisting of a classificatory map of the universe of knowledge. From this Cutter concluded that two basic alternatives were available to indicate the relationship of a subject heading to the subject of a book, and therefore the act of entering a book under a subject as well. One could place the bibliographical description of a book under a subject heading that denoted the book's specific subject, or one could place the bibliographical description under a subject heading that, in terms of subject nomenclature, was broader than the book's specific subject. To follow the first course was to combine the work with what Cutter called a specific heading, meaning that the specific subject of the book and the subject named in the subject heading were matched in scope. To follow the second course was to combine the bibliographical description of the work with a classed heading, where the subject named in the subject heading represented a broader subject than the specific subject of the book.

For example, if one placed the bibliographical description of a book about the specific subject Cats under the subject heading MAMMALS, the heading MAMMALS would be a classed heading because the subject Mammals is a broader subject that, from Cutter's classificatory perspective, included the subject Cats. Likewise, if one placed the bibliographical description of a book about the specific subject New England (the book being "Ornithology of New England") under the subject heading ORNITHOLOGY, the heading ORNITHOLOGY would be a classed heading because the subject Ornithology is a broader subject that, from Cutter's classificatory perspective, included the individual subject New England. Of course, if the specific subjects of these two books had been Mammals and Ornithology respectively, the headings MAMMALS and ORNITHOLOGY would then have been specific headings. Of these two alternatives, Cutter obviously favored specific headings over classed headings in every instance.

Combining a subject heading with a bibliographical description in either of these two ways did not automatically make the result an entry, however. For Cutter, entry occurred only when the resulting combination was itself placed in the primary sequence of the catalog. This interpretation of the meaning of entry is suggested by Cutter's terminology for the dictionary catalog. Cutter defined a heading as the term by which "the alphabetical place of an entry is determined."[10] In a dictionary catalog the only place where a term used as a heading could function in this way was the primary alphabetical sequence of headings. Taking this conclusion one step further, if the relationship between bibliographical description and heading might be either specific or classed, the resulting placements in the primary sequence of the catalog might then be termed "specific entry" or "classed entry." In each case the resulting combinations of bibliographical descriptions with specific headings and classed headings respectively would be found in the primary sequence of the catalog. Here also Cutter preferred specific entry rather than classed entry as the standard procedure.

Still another way to view Cutter's appreciation of this standard procedure was that in each case of specific entry the work could be said to be entered "specifically"—placed directly under its specific heading, which itself was placed directly in the primary sequence of the catalog.[11] It is from this structural characteristic that the modern appreciation of specific entry as both specific *and* direct arises. However, one should be careful to note that in Cutter there are two important qualifications to the "specific and direct" rubric. First, the notion of specific itself does not mean the scope-match equation of modern subject access, but rather means Cutter's notion of specific subjects as publicly established and named subjects in the light of his classificatory significance order. Second, the modern appreciation of the idea of direct entry tends to focus on the heading itself, that is, on its position in the primary sequence of headings. For Cutter, direct entry had a double connotation. Not only was the heading directly in the primary sequence of headings, but the bibliographical description was likewise directly (i.e., specifically) under the heading.

Describing specific entry in this way and, particularly, suggesting that directness of entry includes the notion that the bibliographical description was also directly under the heading might seem troubling because Cutter regularly subarranged the bibliographical descriptions that accumulated under such headings by the use of terms interposed between the heading and the descriptions. In fact, since he considered the ideal file of entries under any one heading to total no more than "half-dozen to a score," when a file increased beyond that size he gave explicit directions that they be subarranged, if possible.[12] The location for those directions are not in his subject cataloging rules, however, but are in another section of his *Rules* entitled "Arrangement"—his filing rules. For example, if large enough, Cutter might have subarranged a file of works on the specific subject CATS (the file itself in the primary sequence of the dictionary catalog) by such terms as Bibliography, Physiology, and History. The result is that such subarrangements appear to be alphabetico-classed headings of the order CATS–BIBLIOGRAPHY, CATS–PHYSIOLOGY, and CATS–HISTORY, where the subarrangement terms appear to be subdivisions of the heading CATS.

The source of confusion here is actually not in Cutter's practice, but rather in present-day card catalog procedure. In modern card catalogs, terms such as Bibliography, Physiology, and History commonly reappear on individual cards that represent single works and are indiscriminantly called subdivisions.[13] In fact, they are purposefully assigned to works on an individual basis to satisfy the modern quest to specify the entire subject (and form) contents of each work in the catalog. As a result, the entire string-of-terms is commonly referred to as the subject heading rather than, for instance, only the initial term.

For Cutter, such subarrangement terms as those cited here were not subdivisions. A subdivision referred only to a term of greater concreteness subarranged under a term of greater abstractness according to his nomenclature of subjects and his notion of significance order. When the reverse was true, that is, when a term of greater abstractness was subarranged under a term of greater concreteness, the resulting relationship was not one of division to subdivision as in a classed system, but rather one of thing (or object) to aspect. Thus, in the example here, Physiology and History, being of greater abstractness, are not subdivisions but only aspects of CATS. And a term such as Bibliography is not a subdivision for the simple reason that it deals with form characteristics rather than subject matter. But if subarrangement terms were not subdivisions by Cutter's reckoning, what relationship did they have to the subject heading?

To begin with, such terms were not a part of the subject heading per se, nor, in his specific entry practice, part of the specific heading, but rather were only file dividers. Visually, they were separate from the heading and, in fact, regularly set in a different typeface than that of the heading. This difference was further reinforced by the fact that the bibliographical descriptions themselves were not positioned in some unique manner under such terms, as in indented paragraph style, but were all aligned evenly along a single margin under the heading itself. Furthermore, such terms were not assigned to individual books that were entered in the file. They were assigned to the subject heading file itself to break it up for more convenient searching. That they further specified a book in the modern sense of the idea is not at issue. Cutter was only concerned that the relationship of any particular bibliographical description under the heading at the top of the file remained specific rather than classed. If that held true and if the terms used for file arrangement were only of greater extent in relationship to the heading itself, or only indicated the form that the books themselves were in, then the file was by definition not subdivided but rather only subarranged.

If a term for subarrangement was actually of greater concreteness than the term in the primary sequence of the catalog, a classed relationship did result, regardless of the indention pattern used and the intention of the cataloger simply to subarrange the file of descriptions. For example, if a work on Mammals was placed under the terms ZOOLOGY (*Mammals*), the combination would be one of class to subclass or division to subdivision. However, given this situation, what constituted the subject heading in Cutter's view also changed. In Cutter's thinking, a subject heading considered visually was the particular term "under" which a bibliographical description was directly positioned. More importantly, it was that term alone that matched the book's specific subject, that functioned, in effect, as the book's specific heading. Thus, if a work on Mammals were positioned under the combination ZOOLOGY (*Mammals*), its actual subject heading would be Mammals because that would have amounted to its specific heading. Technically speaking, however, placing the bibliographical description under Mammals in that combination would not have constituted entry. Cutter would have considered it to be subentry. This is suggested by the terminology that he used to describe classed catalog entry procedure.

Cutter's understanding of the entry process in classed catalogs is not very apparent because his *Rules,* oriented as they were to dictionary subject catalog procedure, provide only fleeting glimpses of classed catalog structure. However, his annotated chart of the four types of catalogs (Figure 5) suggests how he conceived of the structure. Cutter observed in the list of characteristics to the right of the chart that three of the catalog types "contain specific subjects." The dictionary,

Alphabetical arrangement.
- Specific entry. (Common dict. catal.)
- Specific entry and class reference. (Bost. Pub. Lib., Boston Athenaeum.)
- Specific and class entry. (No example.)
  } Dictionary catalog.
- Class entry with specific or class subentry. (Noyes)
- Class entry with chiefly class subentry. (Abbot)
  } Alphabetico-classed catalog.

Logical arrangement.
- Class entry. (Undivided classed catal.)
- Class entry and subentry and finally specific subentry. (Subdivided classed catal.)
  } Systematic catalog.

Alphabetical arrangement.

	Specific headings in alphabetical order. A	Classes in alphabetical order. B	
Single subjects.	D Specific headings arranged logically in classes.	C Classes in logical order.	Classes of subjects.

Logical arrangement.

A,   Specific dictionary.
B,   Specific dict. by its cross-references and its form-entries. Alphabetico-classed catalog.
C,   Classed catalog without subdivisions.
D,   Classed catalog with subdivisions.
A,B   are alphabetical.
C,D   are classed.
A,B,D   contain specific subjects.
B,C,D   contain classes.

The specific entries of A and the classes of B, though brought together in the same catalogs (the class-dictionary and the alphabetico-classed), simply stand side by side and do not unite, each preserving its own nature, because the principle which brings them together—the alphabet—is external, mechanical. But in D the specific entries and the classes become intimately united to form a homogeneous whole, because the principle which brings them together—the relations of the subjects to one another—is internal, chemical, so to speak.

---

*Taken from *Rules*, Definitions: "Classed catalogs," p. 18. When Cutter indicates in the diagram that B and C have classes, he means headings under which books of either the class itself or one of its subclasses are gathered. Type A also has class terms, but they are used only for specific entry, not for class entry.

FIG. 5.   Kinds of Subject Catalogs

alphabetico-classed, and classed catalogs with subdivisions each had the potential for placing the bibliographical description of a book under a term that denoted its specific subject. A term that denotes a specific subject was, of course, a specific heading. Thus, the chart itself notes this potential in two of the three cases (A and D) with that slightly variant terminology.[14]

As noted above, all the headings in the dictionary catalog were arranged in a single primary sequence of headings and indicated the specific subjects of books. For this reason Cutter considered a specific heading in that situation to also be a specific entry heading. And the act of placing a book under it was specific entry.

The entry terminology for classed catalogs varied because of a different heading arrangement. In an ideally constructed classed catalog, only a relatively few main class terms would be directly accessible. Most of the terms under which actual bibliographical descriptions of books would be placed would appear as the subordinated elements of chains of terms that included the particular heading's superordinate classes. Cutter did not view as entry the process of placing a book under a subordinate heading; he called it subentry. It was subentry because only headings in the main sequence of terms were capable of entry in the strict sense of the word. Entry was synonymous with the notion of being directly accessible.

Given this understanding of entry and subentry, several other observations follow. If the subordinate heading under which a book was listed was also a specific heading—if by itself it matched the specific subject of the book—the result was specific subentry. If, however, the subordinate heading under which a book was listed simply "included" rather than matched the book's specific subject, the result was classed subentry. Concomitantly, if the main heading under which a book were placed only "included" rather than matched the book's specific subject, the result was classed entry. But if the main heading under which a book were placed matched the book's specific subject, the result was specific entry, regardless of the fact that it occurred in a classed catalog. It was in this sense that Cutter wrote:

> Even the classed catalogs often have specific entry. Whenever a book treats of the whole subject of a class, it is specifically entered under the class. A theological encyclopedia is specifically entered under THEOLOGY, and theology is an unsubordinated class in many systems.[15]

It might be suggested at this point that the preceding discussion turns unnecessarily on minor matters of terminology; that, in fact, it makes little difference whether one considers placing the bibliographical description of a book under its specific heading as specific entry or specific subentry. The result is essentially the same. A work is combined with the heading that best indicates its particular subject in either case regardless of the level at which it appears. The only real difference is that in one process the combination is direct; in the other it is indirect. This conclusion is understandable in the present era when the typical structure of classed catalogs has reached a highly developed state and when, in fact, the rigorous construction of indexes by formal means makes the indirect access to the subjects of books in a classed catalog at best only a slight inconvenience.

In Cutter's day, however, a far different situation prevailed. His was a world in which no firm principles of subject catalog construction had been discovered, much less accepted. The catalog alternatives that Cutter faced were frankly primitive by today's standards. In this respect, Cutter's emphasis on such details as those discussed here functioned as something of a statement of principles and practices to a cataloging community which had not yet learned to identify those issues that in later decades and in our day would make viable alternatives possible. That this was the case may be seen by observing Cutter's view of the typical subject cataloging practices of his day.

Cutter's View of Cataloging Practices

When Cutter began writing his *Rules* early in 1875, he had already gained considerable experience in making subject access systems of one type or another. Of particular importance in this respect were his seven and one-half years working with Ezra Abbot on the latter's innovative alphabetico-classed card catalog of the Harvard College Library (mid-1861–68) and some five years of labor on the printed dictionary catalog of the Boston Athenaeum (1870–74).[16]

Furthermore, while writing his *Rules* and his article "Library Catalogues" for the 1876 *Special Report,* he compiled a list of more than 1,000 American catalogs and their supplements printed between 1723 and 1876. He gathered entries initially by examining the collections of catalogs held by the Boston Athenaeum, the Boston Public Library, and the Harvard College Library. To these entries he added descriptions of catalogs provided by the United States Bureau of Education, gained through Commissioner of Education General John Eaton's efforts to acquire library statistics and materials. Finally, Cutter supplemented his list by information taken from Jewett's *Notices of Public Libraries in the United States of America* (1851) and Hermann Ludewig's article "Bibliotheken in den Vereinigten Staaten" published in the *Serapeum* in 1846. In addition to his writings and his compilation, Cutter also sent a questionnaire to seventy-five libraries to gain information on the costs and general assessments of catalogs then recently printed. The results of his study of catalogs provided the basis for his article "Library Catalogues."[17]

The immensity and industry of Cutter's work during 1875 and through mid-1876 are impressive, especially in the case of his survey of catalogs. During that period he personally examined scores of catalogs and catalog supplements, determining not only their general structure and scope, but in many cases such details as whether subject word entry occurred in addition to or in place of title entry and, occasionally, even the total number of subjects listed in alphabetical subject indexes. Furthermore, he did these various tasks while supervising the compilation and the printing of the Boston Athenaeum dictionary catalog, administering the Boston Athenaeum library, writing regularly for the *Nation,* and during the spring and summer of 1876, participating in preparations for the initial meeting of the American Library Association.

The most notable result of Cutter's extensive experience and, especially, of his strenuous efforts at data collection was that they provided him with a broad overview of the development of subject access systems then current. His list of 1,010 catalogs and supplements is especially revealing in this respect. While the list has some omissions, it appears to be complete enough to draw conclusions with some confidence.[18] First, the rate of production of printed catalogs had increased enormously over the period covered. When, for example, the entries in the list are divided into three approximately equal groupings (Figure 6), the time spans covered by each grouping grows significantly shorter, the first (1723–1850) covering 128 years, the second (1851–70) covering 20 years, and the last (1871–1875/76) covering only little more than five years. Even when the total of 1,010 entries is reduced by the number of entries that specifically denote supplements and newer editions so that the total represents only 886 unique catalogs (Figure 6 line 3d), the results still show that a dramatic increase in printed catalog production had taken place.

A second, but more tentative conclusion that one may draw from Cutter's data and one that corroborates the more recent general findings of Jim Ranz is that the period after 1850 witnessed the gradual triumph of the dictionary subject catalog over other subject catalog formats.[19] This conclusion is tentative because Cutter actually provided information on the arrangement of only 375 of the 886 unique catalog entries that he listed, his sample of specifically described items constituting only 42 percent of that total. Furthermore, some of the information

	a. 1723-1850	b. 1851-1870	c. 1871-1875/76	d. Totals
1. Total entries	338	339	333	1,010
2. Supplements, additions, etc.	48	38	38	124
3. Total catalog entries	290	301	295	886
4. Catalogs described[1]	131	168	76	375 (42%)

Of the catalogs described:

Classed Arrangements				
5. Classed by size	11			11
6. Classed systematically	49 (37%)	41 (24%)	16 (21%)	106 (28%)
7. Alphabetico-classed	2	4	2	8
8. Total all classed	62 (47%)	45 (27%)	18 (24%)	125 (33%)
Alphabetical Arrangements				
9. Author only[2]	54 (41%)	52 (31%)	13 (17%)	119 (32%)
10. Title only[3,4]	2	7	3	12
11. Subject word only[4]		1	3	4
12. Dictionary (various arrangements)[5]	13 (10%)	63 (38%)	39 (51%)	115 (31%)
13. Total, all alphabetical, not incl. alphabetico-classed	69 (53%)	123 (73%)	58 (76%)	250 (67%)
14. Total, all alphabetical, incl. alphabetico-classed	71 (54%)	127 (76%)	60 (79%)	258 (69%)
15. Total catalogs with subject access (lines 6,7,11, &12)	64 (49%)	109 (65%)	60 (79%)	233 (62%)

FIG. 6. Statistics on Cutter's List of 1,010 Catalogs

that he did supply was scanty. For example, of 125 classed catalogs listed, 22 (18 percent) were described simply as classed without enough information to pinpoint the nature of the classification system used.[20] And his listings of dictionary catalogs involved a large enough variety of combinations of entries to cause the reader to debate his use of the term "dictionary." (Figure 6, note 5). But despite its weaknesses, Cutter's detailed information does support Ranz's overall findings. For example, alphabetical arrangement of any sort (including alphabetico-classed arrangements) increased from 54 percent to 79 percent of the total number of catalogs specifically described in each period (Figure 6, line 14). And even if the alphabetico-classed arrangements are grouped with the systematically classed, the increase still remained

Of catalogs with subject access:

16. Classed access incl. alphabetico-classed	51 (80%)	45 (41%)	18 (30%)	114 (49%)
17. Alphabetical access, incl. subject word and dictionary	13 (20%)	64 (59%)	42 (70%)	119 (51%)

Source: Based on data in Charles A. Cutter, "Library Catalogues," pp. 577-622.

1. Does not include class lists of, for ex., the Boston Public Library, but does include lists of books to be purchased. Some catalogs were in multiple sections. For ex., the 1855 catalog of the N.Y. State Lib. (Item 386) had two sections, one for the law library and one for the general library. Most often, these had similar arrangements. Occasionally, the two parts were listed separately—for ex., Calif. State Lib., items 628(Cl.) and 678(A), which were counted separately. Generally, all such instances were dealt with individually. Also does not include one catalog arranged by donor and five that seem to have been arranged by price.

2. Includes 5 catalogs listed as A or T, or A,T, or SW; 3 catalogs listed as A&T, but not dictionary arrangement; and 1 catalog listed as A&SW, the predominant device being understood to be author arrangement.

3. Includes 2 catalogs listed as T&SW and TorSW, title arrangement being understood here as predominant.

4. With the exception of three items over 100p. each, all T and SW catalogs were relatively small, the median size in the 16 examples listed being 47p., the range extending from 16 to 188p.

5. Cutter apparently considered a dictionary catalog to be one where at least two entry types (e.g., A and T) were interfiled alphabetically. He seems not always to have been consistent in his typology, however, listing, for ex., some title and author or subject word catalogs separately and as dictionary catalogs, there being little appreciable difference in his descriptions. Because there are so many combinations included in the 115 dictionary catalog descriptions, it would be fruitless to attempt an exact accounting of them all. Some significant trends are evident, nonetheless. The earliest dictionary catalogs usually involved two entry types (usually author and title) and first appeared in 1817. By 1845 a new variety (author plus title or subject word) appeared. The most popular form overall (author, title and subject word) first appeared in 1852, accounting for 55 items or 39% of the total. Finally, Cutter's choice for an even better kind of dictionary catalog (author, title and subject) began appearing in 1858 with the Lower Hall catalog of the Boston Public Library. Cutter increased even its coverage in his own version of the dictionary catalog by including at least some form entries as well as mandatory cross-references, the result described by him as a "quadruple syndetic dictionary catalog."

about the same, from 53 percent to 76 percent (Figure 6, line 13). Furthermore, if only those arrangements that included obvious subject access features are considered (Figure 6, line 15)—that is, if one excludes catalogs classed by size and catalogs that only included alphabetical arrangements of authors or titles alone—the trend is even more pronounced. Classed arrangements (including alphabetico-classed) dropped from 80 percent to 30 percent of the total while alphabetical direct arrangements increased in a corresponding way from 20 percent to 70 percent (Figure 6, lines 16, 17).

It is unlikely that Cutter analyzed his data as closely as this, although he did occasionally resort to the use of statistical data in other matters. But he would not have needed to analyze the data closely to draw the general conclusions already noted about trends and developments in cataloging because those conclusions would have been too obvious to miss in even the most casual examination of his sample of catalogs. Thus, the historical trends as well as the typology of catalogs they imply are firmly reflected in Cutter's writings.

More importantly, Cutter also observed what can only be termed the general failure of typical catalogs to accommodate what he had come to consider the fundamental requirements of any subject system, matters already discussed in previous sections above: (1) the recognition of the specific subjects of books; (2) the recognition of the relationship of those specific subjects to classificatory structure; and (3) the need for catalog arrangements to incorporate these two factors in a way that would best serve the library's public. To see how he viewed this more general failure, each of the types of catalogs above will be examined to determine Cutter's understanding of its ideal structure and of the actual practices related to making it.

CLASSED CATALOG PRACTICE

If one takes for granted that books treat particular subjects and if those subjects are also assumed to be, by definition, elements of a classificatory map of subjects—that is, if the particular subject treated in any particular work is at the same time the most specific subject in any hierarchy of subjects—then ideally it stands to reason that the specific subject of a work could be positioned in a classed catalog as the last element of a hierarchical chain of subjects. Indeed, as already mentioned, Cutter saw that possibility although he called it specific subentry rather than specific entry. And the most common kind of catalog that organized books for subject access in this way was the systematically classed catalog.

Cutter found much to his liking in the ideal systematically classed catalog conceived in this way. He wrote:

> Generally an attempt is made to bring all books under a strictly philosophical system of classes, with divisions and subdivisions, arranged according to their scientific relations. It is a very attractive plan. The maker enjoys forming his system, and the student fancies he shall learn the philosophy of the universe while engaged in the simple occupation of looking for a book.[21]

The last sentence in the quotation above contained a good deal of irony. It had the sardonic tone of a gibe. But it was not entirely tongue-in-cheek. Cutter was raised in a tradition in which that goal was strongly believed. And, although being raised in such an atmosphere did not ensure that any particular student ever came to grips with the goal, there is strong reason to believe that Cutter personally responded very positively to it during his early years.

Furthermore, statements related to the teaching function of classification were not uncommon in the prefaces of classed catalogs of that time. In fact, one of the classic statements to that effect had been written by Cutter's mentor, Ezra Abbot, in the latter's classed catalog of the Cambridge High School library. A classed arrangement would, in Abbot's opinion, not only supply young students with something of a map of the universe of knowledge, especially as it pertained to their own subjects of interest, but would "animate them to press cheerfully through the somewhat tangled and thorny paths by which it is to be entered." Moreover, by following the guide the student would be building the good habit of ascertaining the interrelatedness of all knowledge. This was not only essential to the pursuit of truth and the making of a scholarly and cultivated approach to life, but would also prepare one to use much larger collections of books later in life.[22]

Cutter appears to have adopted this attitude as his own. In his 1869 article describing Abbot's Harvard catalog, he wrote in support of its classified structure:

> In fact, it is to be hoped that the catalogue will be a not insignificant addition to the educational apparatus of the university, leading the students, in spite of the perverse willingness of men to let any good escape them which cannot be obtained without some exertion, unconsciously to make classifications themselves, and assisting them in forming the very useful habit of laying up questions and facts in the mind, suitably labelled, and in their proper places.[23]

This goal had lost much meaning even by the time Cutter had written this statement. Nevertheless, he retained an essential interest in the classification of knowledge throughout the remainder of his life, concentrating almost all of his energies in his later years toward completing his *Expansive Classification.*

Cutter also found the systematically classed catalog particularly useful to those whose search for subject material was conducted in the light of the interrelatedness of subjects. Of this kind of investigator and his use of the classed catalog conceived in this way, Cutter wrote:

> He sees not merely the books on the particular topic in which he is interested, but in immediate neighborhood works on related topics, suggesting to him courses of investigation which he might otherwise overlook. He finds it an assistance to have all these works spread out before him, so that he can take a general survey of the ground before he chooses his route; and as he comes back day after day to his particular part of the catalogue he becomes familiar with it, turns to it at once, and uses it with ease.[24]

This is obviously a description of the searching habits of the second and third categories of inquirers, mixed with perhaps not a little of

Cutter's personal experience. It certainly is not a picture of the desultory reader. On the other hand, Cutter found at least some value in the systematically classed catalog even for the desultory reader, at least to the degree that this kind of inquirer found it "a convenience that their favorite kind of reading should all be contained in one or two parts of the catalogue and freed from the confusing admixture of titles of a different sort."[25] In other words, although not planned for use this way, the systematically classed catalog also functioned as a series of reading lists, provided that the desultory reader could find the appropriate sections among its printed pages. This would have been especially possible if the catalog were small and had few, if any, subdivisions of classes. The broad main subjects would then have appeared as a mixture of books about general topical areas, such as, for example, books on philosophy, or books on science. On the whole, however, one may conclude that Cutter perceived the value of the systematically classed catalog to be mainly oriented to the needs and capacities of the smaller numbers of persons that comprised the second and third categories of inquirers, rather than oriented to the desultory reader.

Balancing this view of the benefits of the systematically classed catalog were the criticisms that Cutter leveled against it even when it was well made. Desultory inquirers would have difficulty finding anything in it quickly. Moreover, a classificatory summary of the scheme would likely not help such readers either, but rather only further confuse them with its complexity. In fact, even scholarly readers would have difficulty with such a scheme when searching in subject areas outside their specialties. Cutter concluded that the complexity inherent in such schemes was what

> has made these catalogues so unpopular, and the unpopularity is increased by the want of agreement among classifiers, which prevents any system becoming common enough to be known to everybody and to seem the only natural one. And the occasional vagaries of otherwise excellent catalogues have had their influence in bringing classification into disrepute.[26]

Finally, Cutter noted that one remedy which would have made systematically classed catalogs much more useful—an alphabetical index of subjects—had been adopted by only a few such catalogs. Indexes were needed because subjects unfamiliar to the searcher could not always be located in a classified scheme and sometimes classifiers placed works in classes that would not be evident even to the most learned.

One might think that if the advantages and disadvantages of the systematically classed catalog listed here and encompassed in a brief three-page section of Cutter's basic article on library catalogs constituted all that he could say about this catalog form, then he obviously gave it short shrift. Certainly, one might surmise, there was more to say of it than this. The reason for his relatively brief treatment of it, however, was that his criticisms of the systematically classed catalog were of its ideal form, as ideal, at least, as one might have found it at that time. The fact is that systematic classed catalog practice was on the whole so far from even this limited ideal that it constituted not simply a lesser alternative, but in effect no alternative of any merit at all. Some indication of this is provided by the statistics (Figure 7) that may be derived from Cutter's list of catalogs.

Cutter listed 125 classed catalogs (including alphabetico-classed) among the 375 catalogs he described in detail in his list. Of these, 11 were actually classed by size, and another 22 were insufficiently described to be able to determine their classification structure. Of the 92 remaining, it is significant that fully 61 of them (66 percent) appear to have been classified at one level only. That is to say, they comprised his category (C) of the four kinds of catalogs, those "classed without subdivision." Furthermore, another 21 were classified at only two levels (i.e., with one level of subdivision). Thus, a total of 82 (89 percent) of

	a. 1723-1850	b. 1851-1870	c. 1871-1875/76	d. Totals
1. Total all classed catalogs listed	62	45	18	125
2. Total all classed by subject (omitting cl. by size)	51	45	18	114
3. Subjects = 1 level (i.e., without subdivisions)[1]	27	27	7	61[3]
4. Subjects = 2 levels	14	3	4	21
5. Subjects = 3 levels	1	6	1	8
6. Subjects = 4 levels		2		2
7. No indication of number of levels[2]	9	7	6	22

(rows 3 and 4 braced together with note [4])

Source: Based on data in Charles A. Cutter, "Library Catalogues," pp. 577-622.
1. Includes 5 of the 8 alphabetico-classed catalogs. The others were not described.
2. Includes 3 catalogs otherwise described as Baconian, Jeffersonian, and Bacon-Jefferson. No liberty was taken in assuming these to be at any particular level of classification structure because the levels involved could be single or multiple. If any notable scheme was used at multiple levels, it appears to have been Brunet's.
3. Of 114 catalogs classed by subject, 61 (54%) were 1 level (66% of the 92 described).
4. Of 114 catalogs classed by subject, 82 (70%) were 2 levels or less (89% of the 92 described).

FIG. 7. Statistics on Classed Catalogs from Cutter's List

the 92 systematically classified catalogs specifically described were classified at up to only two levels of hierarchical structure.

Classed subject indexes to other primary arrangements (mainly alphabetical) fared only somewhat better. Cutter listed a total of 66 indexes in his list. Of these, 16 were alphabetically arranged including six secondary indexes where a primary index was classified. The 50 remaining indexes were all classed, but only 34 were described in detail sufficient to categorize them by structure. In contradistinction, a much larger percentage of the total (47 percent or 16 total) were provided by two levels of hierarchical structure. But when added to those at one level (35 percent or 12 total), the combined total was still overwhelming (28 of 34, or 82 percent).

One cannot say, of course, in which particular instances the classed arrangements so described actually reached down to the level of the specific subjects of the books entered in them. But the likelihood is that they did not often do so, given the relatively large increases in books collected by libraries in Cutter's day and the probability that many of the books had subjects narrower in scope than a single or even double level of hierarchical structure would accommodate. In sum, classed catalogs and indexes most probably provided class entry or class subentry for books rather than specific entry.

These conclusions appear to be further corroborated by a brief analysis of 18 of the listed single-level catalogs correlated with the number of volumes they accommodated. The volume counts ranged from 1,130 to 20,000 with mean and median averages of 6,930 and 5,908 volumes respectively. The number of classes listed for the same catalogs ranged from nine to 79 with mean and median averages of 26.5 and 21.5 classes per system respectively. And if the number of volumes for each of the catalogs is divided by its respective number of classes to derive an artificial average of volumes per class, the results range from 112 to 769. Among the latter the mean average is 254, the median is 202. These figures could be considered of debatable value because of the small sample involved and because the average number of volumes per class is itself a debatable figure. Nevertheless, even if it were supposed that the specific subjects of some of the books would be matched by specific headings under which they were entered, there is a high probability that a large number of others would fail to be so entered.

Again, it is highly unlikely that Cutter resorted to a statistical analysis of this kind to determine whether or not typical classed catalogs provided access to the specific subjects of books. It would not have been necessary, however, because here too the conclusion was plainly evident to even the most casual observation. There is no way to avoid the fact that typical systematically classed catalogs regularly avoided giving access to the specific subjects of books in favor of classed entry or subentry. And this practice amounted to a massive failure to provide adequate subject access to both learned and unlearned inquirers alike. Cutter seemed to hint at this state of affairs when, in describing classed catalogs in general, he wrote:

> Among the logically arranged (classed or classified) catalogues there is a difference, according as they are more or less minutely subdivided. The larger the collection of titles, the greater need of division. For it is plain that if a hundred thousand titles are divided into only sixty or seventy classes, some of the larger divisions will contain several thousand, all of which the impatient reader must look through to find what he wants.[27]

What remained unsaid was that the latter situation pertained much more often than not.

Cutter provided no explanation for why this state of affairs had arisen. It is probable, however, that the situation came about in the following way. When provided, subject access to knowledge had always been approached in an ostensibly classificatory manner, at least through the first years of the nineteenth century. Moreover, the ideal catalog was normally considered to be in book format and, if done well, in printed book format. As long as the total number of books to be arranged in this manner remained relatively small and, by implication, as long as the total number of books having specific subjects not accommodated by the most obvious classes and subdivisions also remained relatively small, this approach to subject access remained reasonable. An arrangement of this kind remained easy enough to devise. And it was relatively easy to use when all that was required was to scan limited numbers of books under each heading.

But, as Ranz pointed out, library collections began to increase in size in a notable way by the middle of the nineteenth century. Furthermore, the inclusion of subject access in catalogs became accepted as a necessity rather than a luxury to be added if one felt inclined toward providing it.[28] The corresponding effect of these factors on classed cataloging is not difficult to envision. More books, commonly with more specialized subjects, raised the probability that classed catalogs subdivided at only one or two levels would not accommodate the new subjects.

Classed catalogers had two immediate alternatives for coping with the situation. One could either greatly extend the subdivisions to accommodate the increased number of special subjects at their appropriate hierarchical levels, or one could simply include the books that treated those special subjects under subject classes of greater extent. The first alternative was time-consuming, and it delayed the publishing and raised the cost of the catalog. The reason it was time-consuming appears related in turn to the lack of development of classificatory ideas. Cutter noted at one point that the "scientific relations" of subjects were not always clear. Even by the third quarter of the nineteenth century, the general idea of classificatory order appears not to have progressed much beyond the idea of the logical relationships inherent in subjects that were intrinsically related in their meanings. In short, when topics considered to be specific subjects employed terms not intrinsically related to each other—when they, for example, contained both concrete and abstract terms related to each other extrinsically, such as Ornithology is related to New England in the topic Ornithology of New England—there was no general consensus as to what was the including class. Cutter had solved the problem of inclusion relationships to his satisfaction by the use of his significance order based on a scale of concreteness. But the classed catalog tradition appears not to have adopted a similar resolution of the problem. This fact is nowhere better illustrated than in the typical treatment in classed catalogs of what Cutter considered individual subjects. With the exception of the general classes of history and geography, which when extended at all usually incorporated subdivision by place, one will find almost no classificatory subdivisions that included places (or, for that matter, individual persons). Instead, individual subjects were regularly invisible as divisions of any sort. Subdivision, when made at all, was usually warranted only by criteria based on logical definition. Individual subjects were not the only examples of insufficient subdivision, however. Classificatory subdivision was simply not developed to any great extent for any kind of subject. Considering the increasing number of special subjects treated in books, the lack of development in classification that would accommodate the new subjects amounted to a serious deficiency.

This did not mean that the potential of the classed catalog for providing access to the specific subjects of works might never be reached. But at the time that Cutter was writing his *Rules* (the mid-1870s), solutions for such essential technical problems as citation order, the fact that specific subjects could often be placed in more than one hierarchical chain of subject classes, phase relationships between subjects, and the making of competent indexes of classed schemes, were barely thought of, much less investigated and solved in a systematic way. In fact, the most fundamental step towards making the systematically classed indication of knowledge possible in the first place, the enumeration of subjects so as to see something of their complex relations and to come to terms with their citation order, would eventually occupy classifiers for more than four decades. Cutter, following Melvil Dewey, would eventually occupy a principal role in that enumeration era. And only after that would the clarifying work of Ranganathan and Bliss bring the science of classification to a fuller expression.

Cutter's most significant contribution to classed subject access and, in fact, to all modern subject access work preceded his formal effort in classified subject enumeration, however, and occurred precisely at the point of the two alternatives that faced the makers of classed catalogs. Failing in their technical ability to include the specific subjects of books in their classified structures, classed catalogers more often than not followed the second alternative rather than the first. They chiefly provided class entry or class subentry for books rather than specific entry or specific subentry. The propensity to follow this alternative also suggests why so few alphabetical indexes of the subjects in classed arrangements had been made. There was simply little need for such indexes when the number of formal subjects enumerated in a systematically classed catalog was so few. Moreover, should the catalogers of systematically classed catalogs have made indexes for the specific subjects of books to relate them to the general classes in which they might be found, they would have engaged in the work they had sought at first to avoid, and would have in fact produced something of an alphabetico-classed index. Furthermore, the specific subject index would have been tantamount to a second, perhaps even a more useful, subject access device in its own right, a dictionary listing of the specific subjects of books.

It was Cutter more than any other person who pointed out the deficiency of the second and common alternative to classed catalog practice, for it was he who codified and insisted on the principle that, to be adequate, subject access must include the specific subjects of books in every instance. With that insistence, modern subject access work was born.

It may seem strange to consider this a principle to be emphasized in this way because it is taken very much for granted in our day, even though the notion of what is a specific subject has itself changed. It is difficult to imagine a time when it was not a primary principle of subject access procedure. To point out Cutter's insistence on it, therefore, only emphasizes the critical point at which his work was located in the history of subject access development. At the same time, it should also be strongly emphasized that Cutter did not single-handedly discover, much less invent, the notion. Instead, he simply observed it in action between the late 1840s and 1870 in the most innovative development in subject cataloging yet to occur—the dictionary catalog.

DICTIONARY CATALOG PRACTICE

The dictionary catalog that had developed since the 1840s with the work of Charles C. Jewett, William F. Poole, and others represented another important alternative to those engaged in providing subject access. Its value resided precisely in the recognition, regularly avoided by most classed cataloging of the time, of the specific subjects of works and, because of its method, of the ease of making and using a catalog of this kind.

In common with other methods of subject access, typical dictionary cataloging began with the assumption that every work specifically treated a subject of one scope or another. But contrary to classed cataloging, it did not insist upon identifying the specific subject of a work as an element of a grand classificatory map of the universe of knowledge and, therefore, as the final link in a hierarchically related chain of subjects. Instead, it began only by insisting on the identification of the specific subject of a work alone, whether or not its appropriate classificatory position were ever made explicit. This did not mean that subjects so identified no longer partook of a classificatory connection in the minds of catalogers, but rather only that their classificatory connection was not made a necessary condition of their indication in a subject access system. Neither did it mean that specific subjects identified in this manner no longer could be considered as individual or general subjects, although their identification apart from their classificatory connection made distinctions of this sort far less important.

As a corollary and necessary condition for identification, typical dictionary catalog practice assumed that the explicit identification of the specific subjects of books was possible in most instances because the authors of most books named the subjects that they were treating, usually in the form of subject words found in the titles of the books themselves. The normal course of this practice was, when seeking to enter a book under a subject, for the cataloger to restrict the choice of terms to only those found in the title. If the subject word thus obtained was synonymous with subject words in other titles, each would be entered in their respective places. Thus, books with the title subject word Birds would be entered under that term in the catalog; those with Ornithology under that term. It was uncommon, however, to link such entries with cross-references. Furthermore, if the title lacked any distinctive subject word, the usual practice was to omit altogether what would be considered a subject entry, the book in that case limited to an author entry (if any) and to a first-word title entry. Using the titles of books as the chief source of subject words in this way was not thought to be foolproof because some titles were deceptive and others were not indicative of subject content at all. But nevertheless, as Ranz has summarized, it assumed that "subject-word entries, despite their many shortcomings, furnished a fair indication of the contents of most of the books."[29]

Having identified the specific subjects of works in this manner, typical dictionary catalog practice went one step further by providing access to the works through their subject entry rather than their sub-entry in the catalog. The subject-words and the bibliographical descriptions of the books that they indicated were placed in a single alphabetical sequence of the catalog, along with the author and title entries when made. As a result, not only was the specific subject of a work given access, it was also given access directly. One did not have to know anything of the subject structure to which any particular specific subject belonged in order to find it in its proper place among all the entries of the catalog arranged in one seemingly easy-to-consult alphabetical sequence.

Dictionary cataloging of the kind described here was relatively simple to do and thus possible to complete in a relatively brief period of time for even large library collections. And when combined with a title-a-line printing format in which entry information for each access point was limited to a single line of type, it also made a multiple-access catalog economically viable. In fact, it seems likely that the ease and economy of its construction not only contributed to its growth in popularity, but also to the demise of the classed catalog as well. It solved the problem of creating a hierarchical subject structure by avoiding it altogether, thereby opening the door to providing access to the specific subjects of books in almost every instance. As a viable alternative to systematically classed catalogs, it induced a lack of interest in grappling with the problems of that catalog form.

Cutter found some things unusually attractive about the dictionary catalog as an alternative to the classed catalog it was fast supplanting. For one thing he considered its emphasis on identifying the specific subjects of books to be extremely important because it served the needs of that large number of inquirers, either desultory or scholarly in their approach to subject searching and the use of knowledge, who were simply looking for a book or books on a single specific subject, more often than not an individual subject such as a person or a place. The arrangement served in the same way that indexes might have served with classed schemes had they been commonly made. Furthermore, the emphasis on direct entry of specific subjects made the arrangement particularly useful to those inquirers who placed a premium on speed. Finally, given the general knowledge of the alphabet, the dictionary catalog's direct entry of specific subjects in a single alphabetical sequence made the entire arrangement apparently simple to use.[30]

But Cutter was also deeply disturbed by certain practices common to dictionary cataloging as he found it. He was highly critical of its dependence on the titles of books for subject words. He expressed something of a disdainful attitude toward this practice, speaking of it in one place as making subject entries "merely under words taken from the title."[31] In his *Rules* he stated somewhat contentiously:

> It is strange that the delusion ever should have arisen that "a catalog must of necessity confine itself to titles only of books." . . . The title rules the title catalog; let it confine itself to that province.[32]

One way Cutter explained his dissatisfaction with the practice of deriving subject terms only from titles was that it confused what today would be called a known-item search with a categorical subject search. He wrote:

> The inconsistency of depending on title subject words originated from not distinguishing between the wants of the man who seeks a certain book and remembers not merely in a vague way its subject, but the very word which the author used to designate that subject, (who of course is best served by an entry under that word,) and the wants of the man who is studying a certain topic, (who is best served by the entry of all relating to that in one place.)[33]

Cutter noted that dependency on title subject words in this way would not accomplish the latter objective, although it should also be noted that the search objective itself, centering as it does on "studying," was a feature of the second and third categories of inquirers rather than of the first. What was needed to accomplish the search objective was uniformity in subject words, something that the indiscriminate use of title subject words could not assure.

> We cannot always take the "author's own definition of his book." He knows what the subject is, but he may not know how to express it for cataloguing purposes; he may even choose a title that misleads or is unintelligible, especially if his publisher insists on a striking title, as is the manner of publishers; and different writers, or even the same writers at different times, may choose different words to express the same thing.[34]

And in addition to these obvious difficulties, Cutter also pointed out that the misleading nature of title words could cause one to enter some books not simply under the wrong subject altogether, but under classed rather than specific headings.

A second criticism that Cutter leveled against the dictionary catalog as he found it was that in most cases it did not exercise control over synonymous terms.[35] This caused inconvenience to users in two ways. On the one hand, it made successful searching dependent on entering books under the term the inquirer brought to the catalog. If, however, the books which the library had on the subject were actually entered under a synonym because the synonym is what appeared in the title, the search would be unsuccessful unless the inquirer thought of that synonymous term and any others that the topic was likely to be entered under. On the other hand, if the library had several books on the same subject but entered them under several synonymous terms, to find all the books that the library had on that particular topic, the inquirer would have to look in more than one place, if, that is, he thought of the other terms. Cutter questioned this procedure by comparing it to the common practice of gathering together all the books by one author.

> Every one sees that to separate an author's works and oblige the reader always to look in two or three places for them is to cause a greater inconvenience than to refer him, two times out of three, from the name he looks for to the name chosen by the cataloguer. Why is it not likewise a greater inconvenience to be compelled always to look in two places for the works on a given subject than half the time to be referred from one heading to the other?[36]

A final criticism that Cutter leveled against dictionary cataloging as he found it was its neglect of the classificatory nature of subjects. Cutter described the fundamental alphabetical arrangement of a dictionary catalog as one "in which the attempt to subordinate individuals to classes, and classes to one another is abandoned, and the subjects, special or general, are arranged like the words in a lexicon."[37] Cutter's estimate of the dictionary catalog when it remained in this primitive state was that it was "a mere collection of fragments, unconnected and all alike. There is no light and shade, nothing to fix the attention."[38] In his *Rules* he was even more explicit:

> Its subject-entries, individual, general, limited, extensive, thrown together without any logical arrangement, in the most absurd proximity —ABSCESS followed by ABSENTEEISM and that by ABSOLUTION, CLUB–FOOT next to CLUBS, and COMMUNION to COMMUNISM, while BIBLIOGRAPHY and

LITERARY HISTORY, CHRISTIANITY and THEOLOGY, are separated by half the length of the catalog—are a mass of utterly disconnected particles without any relation to one another, each useful in itself but only by itself.[39]

The result, in Cutter's words, was to have little more than a "mob" of subjects.

This kind of arrangement had as its principal goal "facility of reference."[40] It assumed that persons were simply looking for a book or books on a single identifiable subject. Cutter pointed out that this approach to searching presupposed in turn that the library had a book or books "on just that subject."[41] If, however, "the library had no book or article sufficiently important to be catalogued on that topic," the search strategy must necessarily be changed. The nature of the change was to pursue the topic in terms of its classificatory relationships with other related topics. Thus, the searcher

must look (a) in some more comprehensive work in which he will find it treated, (as the history of Assyrian art is related in histories of Art,) in which case he will get no help whatever from any dictionary catalogue yet made, in finding the general work, but must trust to his own knowledge of the subject and of ordinary classification to guide him to the including class; or (b) there may be something to his purpose in less general works, (as books on Iron bridges or Suspension bridges might be better than nothing to a man who was studying the larger subject Bridges,) but in this case also he will seldom get any assistance from dictionary catalogues, and must rely entirely upon his previous knowledge of the possible branches of his subject.[42]

Given Cutter's estimate of the three kinds of inquirers, the continuation of a search in this manner was a concern of the second and third categories of searchers, not the first. If a simple search could not be expanded in this way, the third category of inquirers' search for subjects in a comprehensive area would not be able to be facilitated at all. Furthermore, the desultory readers' use of class lists that grouped favorite kinds of reading was also lost.

Cutter's criticisms of the common dictionary catalog of his day were extensive and somewhat harsh. They did not imply that he found no potential in it, however, because he ultimately used it as a beginning point for his own version of a dictionary catalog. Before he arrived at that solution, however, he found it necessary to deal with yet another possible method of providing subject access, the alphabetico-classed catalog.

ALPHABETICO-CLASSED CATALOG PRACTICE

The alphabetico-classed catalog represented something of a compromise among classed catalogs in that its classes, as well as their divisions, subdivisions, etc., were arranged alphabetically rather than logically at each level of the classificatory hierarchy. With such notable incursions of alphabetical order, it is tempting to think that the alphabetico-classed catalog had become very much like the dictionary catalog. But this was at best a superficial likeness. The two catalogs remained fundamentally different in that the alphabetico-classed provided class entry and class or specific subentry for most subjects while the dictionary catalog provided specific entry alone and admitted neither class entry nor subentry of any kind. In other words, the alphabetico-classed catalog remained a classed catalog fundamentally, a fact that no incursion of alphabetical order could erase.

When one considers the above factor in the light of Cutter's criticisms of systematically classed catalogs, Cutter's general attitude toward the alphabetico-classed catalog might seem strange. Fundamentally, he held this kind of catalog in singular esteem, a matter that is evident in various ways in his writings. For example, his 1869 description of Ezra Abbot's Harvard College library alphabetico-classed card catalog leaves no doubt about his opinion of its excellence. And in his 1876 article on library catalogs, rather than critically examining alphabetico-classed catalogs, Cutter simply surveyed three catalogs of that type. The result was little more than a mixture of praise and quibbling over details.[43]

Besides esteem, the most notable feature of Cutter's attitude toward this kind of catalog was that it was generally comparable to his form of the dictionary catalog. They were comparable because they were so closely matched in usefulness. In speaking of Abbot's catalog in relation to his own, Cutter wrote that,

> after fifteen years constant use of the two catalogues, I am convinced that there is very little difference in their convenience to a person who understands both. The Abbot system is best adapted for the thorough investigation of comprehensive subjects; the dictionary system for finding quickly what relates to a person, place, or other special topic.[44]

Several significant conclusions may be drawn from this comment. To begin with, Cutter's opinion represents a slight but significant change from a similar statement he made in 1869. Although Cutter had said at that time that "each plan has some merits which the other does not possess," he still concluded that the alphabetico-classed "deserved the palm of superiority." His conclusion was based on its usefulness to a relatively narrow range of users, however. The alphabetico-classed catalog was superior "for those who understand it and have learnt where to look for what they want. It is therefore well adapted to the library of a college or of a learned society."[45] In other words, the alphabetico-classed catalog best served either mentally cultivated users or those who were in the process of becoming mentally cultivated—the second and third categories of inquirers.

Cutter repeated this opinion in his 1876 evaluation of library catalogs. But the significant change that occurred by the latter date is that Cutter had identified and accepted the legitimate needs and searching patterns of desultory readers as well as study-oriented readers. And meeting those needs first constituted the principal goal of the dictionary catalog. Of course, the dictionary catalog with which he compared the alphabetico-classed in 1876 was no longer the common dictionary catalog that he himself had earlier criticized so harshly, but rather his own form of the dictionary catalog. His 1876 explanation did not tell why the two catalogs were comparable in use, however, but only how the two catalogs met the goals of respective primary groups of users. If the comparison were left at this point, it would be tantamount to comparing two essentially different things. One might conclude that both were needed to provide adequate access, each being inadequate by itself for the full range of inquirers. Thus, what Cutter implied is that each catalog, while doing well in its primary objective, also met the needs of the other catalog inquirers to some useful extent as well. The alphabetico-classed catalog, while mainly serving cultivated inquirers who were study-oriented, also served desultory readers to some extent. And the dictionary catalog, as Cutter had redesigned it, while mainly serving desultory and single-subject searches, also served study-oriented searching to some extent. In sum, the general effectiveness of the two catalogs was very close.

Because of the comparability of the two catalogs, Cutter felt especially obliged to distinguish between them. He wrote his often-noted dictum on specific entry with this in mind: "This rule of 'specific entry' is the main distinction between the dictionary catalog and the alphabetico-classed."[46] Elsewhere, when considering subarrangement practice under individual places in his dictionary catalog, he wrote, "It is not of the slightest importance that this introduces the *appearance* of the alphabetico-classed catalog, so long as the main object of a dictionary catalog, ready reference, is attained."[47] Finally, when considering the treatment of individual subjects in the two catalogs, he noted that the specific entry of individual subjects without exception was "the invariable and chief distinction between the two."[48]

Considering Cutter's esteem for the alphabetico-classed catalog and his sense of its comparability with his version of the dictionary catalog, one may wonder if the traditional picture of Cutter as advocate of the dictionary catalog is accurate. It might have been expected that Cutter, who is generally regarded as the champion of the dictionary catalog, would have been more enthusiastic about his own work as a well-defined alternative to each of the other catalog alternatives of his day and especially to the alphabetico-classed catalog. This not being the case, however, how then did Cutter perceive the importance of the alphabetico-classed catalog and what set his own dictionary catalog off from it, even if the difference was only slight?

The alphabetico-classed catalog was important to Cutter not because it represented a catalog alternative of growing popularity. Actually, there were relatively few alphabetico-classed catalogs in existence in the 1870s. Cutter listed only eight such catalogs among the 375 catalogs that he described in his list (Figure 6, line 7). And he listed only eight indexes out of a total of sixty-six that were constructed in alphabetico-classed format. Furthermore, of the catalogs he listed, only those that he commented on in his article seemed well enough developed to have merited his special attention. The real source of his thinking about the alphabetico-classed catalog was not a printed catalog at all. It was Abbot's Harvard College library catalog on cards.

Cutter's relationship to Abbot and to Abbot's catalog was much more formative and important than a bare accounting of his years at Harvard reveal. Abbot had taken an interest in Cutter's work as a student librarian at the Harvard Divinity School library (1858–59) and followed this with his support for Cutter's appointment to the college library staff in May 1860. Between 1860 and 1861 Cutter helped him plan the new catalog and in the summer of 1861, when Cutter had the opportunity of taking a better-paying job elsewhere, Abbot successfully argued for a substantial increase in his salary to keep him at Harvard. The fact is that Cutter was already so conversant with Abbot's catalog and so deeply committed to its success that, had he left three months after its beginning in May 1861, it might never have been made.

Furthermore, this essential relationship of Cutter to the catalog continued during most of his tenure at Harvard. Cutter did not simply work on the project; he was actually the chief supervisor of the project as it expanded by thousands of card entries per year, especially since Abbot was often absent from close contact with the work. The latter occurred because of Abbot's precarious health and partly because he followed his primary interest of theological scholarship. The only point at which Cutter relinquished some of that close control was a period of some twenty months in which he cataloged part-time at the

Boston Public Library for Charles C. Jewett. And in that case his experience appears to have helped him to compare the merits of dictionary and alphabetico-classed cataloging, perhaps even to come to a conclusion regarding the needs of desultory readers. In sum, Cutter's relationship to Abbot and his catalog was such that in many respects one might consider it as much his work as Abbot's.[49]

Within that context, Cutter developed a firm commitment to the alphabetico-classed catalog as the best form of subject access attainable, at least for inquirers with any sort of mental cultivation. Several years later, he stated that when he left Harvard for the Boston Athenaeum he had come to "swear by" Abbot's system. Thus, it is understandable that when the Athenaeum's trustees placed him directly in charge of the Athenaeum's catalog project in the spring of 1870, his first move was to convince them that the catalog should be redesigned along the lines of Abbot's work. His arguments toward that end did not prevail, however, and he was subsequently obliged to carry to completion the Athenaeum's catalog in a dictionary format. Nevertheless, Cutter's sense of what constituted the most appropriate features of a subject access system was not to be denied. In the end he changed what had been the common dictionary catalog into the complex instrument that his *Rules* represent. The nature of his revision is important because it consisted of incorporating into the common dictionary catalog format the fundamental features of a subject access system that he had learned while working at Harvard.[50]

Cutter's work at Harvard had four fundamental principles: (1) the consistent recognition of the specific subjects of books; (2) the need for uniform terminology; (3) an entry system that recognized the role of subject structure and its relationship to use patterns; and (4) the importance to the entry system of a cross-reference structure. Cutter carried the first two principles over into his dictionary catalog work virtually without change. The cataloger's recognition of the specific subjects of books as a starting point had not been a feature of typical systematically classed catalog practice, but it had been a fundamental feature of dictionary cataloging from the latter's beginning, at least to the degree that subject words taken from titles indicated such subjects. In keeping with his Harvard work, Cutter not only began by recognizing such subjects, but insisted that they be identified regardless of the nature of the titles of the books—that the identification of the specific subjects of books be based on the cataloger's estimation of the contents of books and be severed from an absolute dependency on title wording. Further, because subject identification was severed from title wording, the cataloger was free to choose between alternative terminology so that uniform terms might be used for all works on the same subject.

It is with the third and fourth basic principles that one begins to see where Cutter's later work diverged from the alphabetico-classed because their implementation in typical practice led to what Cutter considered the weakness of this catalog type. Alphabetico-classed cataloging began with the classed cataloger's ideal that each such specific subject was also the narrowest point in a hierarchical chain of subject relationships. The entry process placed the bibliographical descriptions of books under their specific headings. But the specific headings were subsequently subentered as the last elements of hierarchical chains of headings. For example, a work on cats in the field of zoology might be subentered under the chain ZOOLOGY–MAMMALS–CATS and one on cats from the point of view of veterinary science might be subentered under ANIMAL HUSBANDRY–VETERINARY SCIENCE–DOMESTIC ANIMALS–CATS. The position of the book in the catalog was thus dependent on the lead term in the chain. But on this point the alphabetico-classed procedure exercised a freedom not typically available to systematically classed catalogs. In the latter such strings-of-terms ordinarily were dictated by a preconceived notion of a limited number of basic main classes into which the universe of knowledge was logically divided and logically arranged. Thus, the lead term had to be one of those main classes. Because the initial terms of such strings-of-terms in the alphabetico-classed catalog were not dictated by a limited set of logically arranged canonical classes, but rather could include any subject and were arranged alphabetically, one had the option of including any subject in the main catalog sequence if indeed that was desirable. One could, in effect, place a string-of-terms in the main sequence at any of its hierarchical points. If it were deemed useful to segregate the classes MAMMALS and VETERINARY SCIENCE from their positions in their superordinate classes ZOOLOGY and ANIMAL HUSBANDRY, one might just as well place those terms, with the sequences that were arranged under them, in the main catalog sequence. There was no systematic way of choosing such instances. Rather, the choices were ordinarily related to considerations of use characteristics of a particular library's public. Because of their ad hoc bases, however, Abbot for one took pains to warn against making such decisions without serious consideration.[51]

The ability to place a subject string in the main catalog sequence at some lower hierarchical level proved invaluable not only when the string itself was not clear, but when the relationships of a particular subject admitted so many variations that the specific subject was unduly scattered about the catalog. Abbot used the topic of tobacco to illustrate the latter situation. Given several books specifically on that subject but which fell in several superordinate classes—for example, its culture (AGRICULTURE), its manufacture (COMMERCE), its uses in medicine (MEDICINE), its poisonous qualities (TOXICOLOGY), etc.—one might decide in the end to place all such works under TOBACCO, thus collocating all works on that topic under their specific entries.[52] This practice, like the truncation practice noted above, admitted to little systematization in application, but solved the problem of entry for the kinds of topics that had caused so much difficulty for classed cataloging in general.

Regardless of which way the previous cases were decided, indicating to the catalog user where a particular subject might be found was accomplished by an elaborate system of cross-references. In most cases this amounted to placing a reference in the main catalog sequence from the names of specific subjects to their respective classed locations throughout the catalog. Thus, an inquirer seeking works on cats would find in the main sequence references such as CATS, see ZOOLOGY—MAMMALS—CATS and ANIMAL HUSBANDRY—VETERINARY SCIENCE—DOMESTIC ANIMALS—CATS. In those instances where narrow topics had been given specific entry rather than subentry—for example, where books on TOBACCO had been entered under that term directly and it had been placed in the main catalog sequence—cross-references would be placed in the catalog at their otherwise appropriate positions in hierarchical chains of terms such as MEDICINE, see also TOBACCO; TOXICOLOGY, see also TOBACCO, etc., to indicate the reverse relationships.

This entire procedure had distinct benefits. For the most part, subject document classes were collocated in terms of classificatory relationships. Inquirers of the second and third categories were thus directly helped. This remained true whether they searched for entire comprehensive classes with their subdivisions or only for specific subjects of narrow scope. Furthermore, if narrower subjects had been given specific entry or if their including classes at a less comprehensive level had been given specific entry, the cross-reference structure would relate the less comprehensive but specifically entered lead terms to their own inclusive classes. It should also be noted that desultory readers were also helped by this arrangement to the degree that they could locate familiar and useful groups of their favorite kinds of reading.

Although helpful in the way just described, alphabetico-classed arrangements also had distinct difficulties. To begin with, as in any classed system, books treating narrower topics tended to be scattered throughout the scheme because those subjects were normally subentered under the final elements of classificatory chains. This did not mean that books on such subjects were necessarily inaccessible because, ideally speaking, cross-references placed in the main catalog sequence collocated their respective subdivision locations and informed the reader of their whereabouts. Nevertheless, to find all the various works on any particular specific subject of narrow scope, one might have to search in several places in the catalog.

This scattering of relatively narrow subjects, while not an insurmountable difficulty for searchers, was exacerbated by two far more serious problems—the failure to collocate individual subjects and the loss of accessibility to some individual subjects altogether. The failure to collocate individual subjects occurred when, in the process of subject classification, individual subjects were appropriately subentered, but no cross-references to their subentry locations were placed in the main catalog sequence. For example, typical alphabetico-classed procedure subentered a biography under the general class BIOGRAPHY. Thus a biography of Oliver Wendell Holmes would be found in the sequence BIOGRAPHY–HOLMES, OLIVER WENDELL. At the same time, it was not typical to place a cross-reference in the main catalog sequence of the type HOLMES, OLIVER WENDELL, see BIOGRAPHY–HOLMES, OLIVER WENDELL. Most likely no cross-reference was made because the typically large number of individual subjects of this kind in any library would require an unusually large number of such cross-references. Instead, it was expected that readers would learn that particular classed sequence and go directly to it to find biographical works.

Where materials about an individual were subentered only in the class BIOGRAPHY, searching indirectly for them could be considered a not unusually difficult thing to ask of patrons. But where materials about an individual were subentered in other classes as well, as when several works of criticism about the legal views of Holmes were subentered somewhere in the class LAW, there would likely be no cross-references to him at that alternative location either. In other words, no collocation of Holmes as an individual subject would have been provided even in the form of cross-references. Furthermore, given the nature of the subentry procedure itself, there was no collocation of works about an author with works by the author because the latter would have been entered under the author's name. One could surmise that the number of such instances might be either relatively limited or, as in the case of literary authors, relatively identifiable, so that in the most notable cases cross-references could be made to obviate this difficulty. And indeed, this was occasionally done by catalogers who realized the seriousness of the problem. But it was not typical.

This entire problem was even worse with countries or places considered as individual subjects. In a manner similar to biographies, works on countries were subentered in appropriate superordinate classes. Here, in contradistinction to individual persons, however, the number of the subentry locations was often even greater. For example, works on England might fall under HISTORY, GEOGRAPHY, ORNITHOLOGY, SOCIOLOGY, VETERINARY SCIENCE, as well as a host of other general subjects, many of which were themselves subordinate classes of varying subject scopes. And here as well, it was even more uncommon to identify such subentry locations by means of cross-references. Thus, even more so than with persons, places as individual subjects remained uncollocated at any position in the catalog. They were for all practical purposes lost to all except those who understood classed relationships.

Besides this general failure in collocation, alphabetico-classed procedure occasionally omitted specific subentry for individual subjects altogether. The occasion for not providing specific subentry at all was likewise a practical one. Given a relatively small subject document class, such as a total of only four works on alligators in the sequence ZOOLOGY–REPTILES–ALLIGATORS, only one of which was further limited to a place, say Louisiana, or again a total of three works on shipbuilding in the sequence NAVAL SCIENCE–SHIPS AND SHIPBUILDING, only one of which was about a particular ship, say The Shenandoah, typical procedure omitted the specific subentry altogether to avoid subject document classes that had few books and were not likely to grow in size. But as a result, the specific subjects involved would not have been given access at all, despite the first principle that all specific subjects of books should be identified. To the degree that this practice was extended to general subjects that were narrow in scope, they also would be lost to the searcher as well.

The scattering of specific subjects of narrow scope, especially individual subjects, the lack of their adequate collocation, and the occasional loss of their accessibility altogether in typical alphabetico-classed catalogs made searching for individual subjects not only more difficult but at times impossible. The inquirers most affected by these practices were chiefly desultory readers and those of the other two categories of inquirers who wished to study and compare critically books on some particular individual person or place.

It was precisely at this point that Cutter identified the critical difference between alphabetico-classed cataloging and his version of the dictionary catalog. It was a difference not of theoretical or ideal proportions, but rather of the exigencies of practice and use. Alphabetico-classed cataloging procedure potentially could have subentered all individual subjects and could have collocated their locations through an elaborate cross-reference structure. But it did not typically do so, most likely because of the great amount of labor involved and what was perceived as a relatively small increase in benefit to relatively cultivated inquirers who could be expected to make up the loss of access through their tenacity in searching. In other words, alphabetico-classed catalogs demanded of the reader that one supplement one's search for subjects of greater concreteness with one's personal labor in other sources.

Cutter's Dictionary Catalog

Cutter began with a different set of priorities. He estimated that the clientele of a library searched more commonly for the specific subjects of books and among those especially for individual subjects. He also surmised that the clientele searched less commonly for comprehensive subjects and their divisions or for individual subjects as natural subdivisions of their including classes. Given this understanding, he concluded that a more appropriate subject entry system would be one that always began with the specific subjects of books, especially individual subjects, and one that subsequently entered rather than subentered those specific subjects. He summarized how this dual emphasis set his idea of a dictionary catalog apart from the alphabetico-classed when he wrote:

> These are differentiated not, as is often said, by the dictionary having specific entry, but (1) by its giving specific entries in all cases and (2) by its individual entry.[53]

However, if only this were done, aid to the scholarly inquirer would be lost altogether. To recoup at least some of that help, he reformulated the cross-reference system so that it would "correspond to and [provide] a good substitute for the arrangement in a systematic catalog."[54]

The dictionary catalog that resulted from these procedures was different from the alphabetico-classed catalog in its formal structure because of the use of specific entry rather than specific subentry. The use of specific entry was tantamount to standing the alphabetico-classed catalog on its head. That is to say, the chains of terms of an alphabetico-classed catalog were permuted or rotated by one position. The specific subjects that were ideally placed at the ends of the chains in the alphabetico-classed catalog were brought to the beginning and filed alphabetically in Cutter's dictionary catalog. Subarrangement included only so much of the now displaced beginnings of the classed chains as were necessary for easy consultation of the specific subject files. Of course, subarrangement achieved this way tended to be classed. But Cutter was not disturbed about that prospect so long as "ready-reference," that is, immediate access, to the specific subjects of books and especially to individual subjects was obtained.

The formal structural difference was also ensured by the new use of the cross-reference system. Instead of being used primarily to refer patrons from specific subject names in the main catalog sequence to their subentry locations, cross-references became primarily a device to refer patrons from comprehensive subjects listed in the main sequence to other subject names also listed in the main sequence that were their immediate subdivisions. They became, in other words, an index to systematic relationships lost because of specific entry.

It is important to note, however, that despite its obviousness, the formal structural differences described here were not what Cutter considered to be the most essential difference between the two catalogs. On the contrary, the most essential difference in his mind was the extension of effective access that his arrangement achieved for a certain kind of subject. The dictionary catalog's rule of beginning subject access considerations with the specific subjects of books was an insistent and unyielding prescription that forced to completion what alphabetico-classed procedure sometimes neglected—the recognition of individual subjects among the specific subjects that were treated in books. Individual subjects became in effect the central focus of the dictionary catalog both in their identification and in their collocation. That this was the case is not only suggested by the definition cited above, but even more forcefully in Cutter's parenthetical statement that he added to that definition in the fourth edition of his *Rules*. Having stressed in the earlier editions the fact that alphabetico-classed cataloging did not "permit" individual entry, he observed:

> Since this was written the only alphabetico-classed catalog in existence has arranged its individual biography in the same alphabet with its authors, so far destroying the distinction between itself and the dictionary catalog.[55]

By itself this statement, most likely prompted by the refiling of the Harvard catalog in the 1890s in dictionary format, is vague mainly because it fails to specify that places, also individual subjects, would also need to be given specific entry rather than subentry for the distinction to be resolved. But despite the vagueness, it does serve to focus attention on what seemed to be Cutter's chief point of comparison—the respective capacities of the two catalogs to collocate and give access to individual subjects—rather than on other more formal differences such as directness versus indirectness of entries. If this is an accurate interpretation of his concerns, one wonders if he would have revised his opinion of the differences between the catalogs had the alphabetico-classed catalog collocated and provided even indirect access to individual subjects in the first place.

The dictionary catalog, rationalized in the manner described here, was set apart from the alphabetico-classed catalog for Cutter in an important way. This did not solve every problem, however, and in fact it raised some that were unique to its own methodology. But given the contextual elements of the subject cataloging process that have been discussed here—subjects as subjects alone, subjects in relation to books, subjects and the public, and subject cataloging practices—the methodology of the dictionary catalog as a subject access system as Cutter conceived it may now be more adequately examined.

CHAPTER 6

Cutter's Subject Rules

When approaching Cutter's subject rules, it is necessary to keep in mind two matters of importance related to their overall organization.* First, the subject rules do not include form entry. Cutter theoretically conceived of the dictionary catalog as the interfiling of four separate catalogs—author, title, subject, and form. Each of these catalogs had its own procedures. Thus, his subject rules are not only separate from author and title entry rules, but also from form entry rules. The latter differentiation sets his rules apart from modern subject cataloging where subject and form entry are normally intermixed. Of course, when a work was about a literary or practical form, the resulting name under which the work was entered was in fact a subject heading. But when a work (limited by Cutter for the most part to collections) was simply in a literary or practical form, the resulting heading was a form heading.

Form entry meant placing the name of the form in the primary sequence of headings. However, when a work was about or in a literary or practical form of literature but was limited to a country or a people, its normal indication in the catalog for Cutter was a combination of subject entry and form subarrangement. For example, collections of drama or fiction by German authors were entered under Germany and subarranged by the terms Drama and Fiction under the subheading Literature (e.g., GERMANY. *Literature. Drama.* or GERMANY. *Literature. Fiction.*). He allowed only few exceptions to this practice, some because of tradition—for example, ENGLISH DRAMA, ENGLISH FICTION, etc.—and others because the adjective in the corresponding phrase heading did not refer to a country—for example, HEBREW LITERATURE, LATIN POETRY, etc.[1]

---

*Because this chapter is written in the form of a commentary, although not always with accompanying text, it will be assumed that the reader has a copy of Cutter's *Rules* (4th ed.) on hand. This will reduce the need to reproduce the text and allow footnotes to be confined primarily to other sources or to other places in the *Rules* besides those being discussed.

The second thing to keep in mind regarding the overall organization of Cutter's subject rules is that their arrangement in sections is important to their use. The rules are divided into two main sections: "A. Entries Considered Separately" (rules 161–186); and "B. Entries Considered as Parts of a Whole" (rules 187–188). The first corresponds to rules for the entry system; the second to rules for the cross-reference structure. The first section is further divided into four subsections: "1. Choice Between Different Subjects" (rules 161–166); "2. Choice Between Different Names" (rules 167–175); "3. The Number of Subject Entries" (rules 176–180); and "4. Miscellaneous Rules and Examples" (rules 181–186).

The order of the first three of these subsections corresponds to something of an order of procedure for making entry decisions. Of these three, the first two constitute the basic sequence of subject cataloging rules. First, one must choose the subject under which a document should be entered. Second, one must determine the appropriate name form for that subject. In modern subject heading work, a choice procedure also takes place, but it is essentially choice *of* rather than choice *between* subjects. That is to say, it constitutes the act of subject analysis or summarization of a document. Because subject summarization is essentially a verbalizing process, it may be chiefly characterized as a word choosing and word ordering activity. Thus, choice of subject and choice between names have become close to being the same thing, at least for those such as the subject catalogers at the Library of Congress who have been responsible for the library's basic vocabulary list.

The procedure in Cutter's *Rules* is profoundly different. The first two subsections function much more like the relationship between choice of entry and choice of name form in author-entry rules. After determining the subject content of a book, one arrives at a subject description that is also an expression of what Cutter considered to be classificatory inclusion relationships and significance order. Considering the subject description in this way automatically gives the cataloger a series of options among which a choice must be made for the entry rather than the subentry of the item. The options meant here are not those of equivalency relationships, such as synonyms, variations in term order, etc., but of differing hierarchical levels of meaning. *Only after a choice among them has been made may the cataloger proceed to the second section.* The use of the second section is involved only if, in the process of choice between different subjects, more than one subject name for the same chosen subject has been obtained. In sum, Cutter's rules for choice between names are not intended to stand for determining what a book is about, but only as a subsidiary decision-making process to determine which of two or more equally legitimate names for the subject chosen in the first section should be used. To intermix the two sections in one's thinking will engender problems of which Cutter never dreamed.

The third subsection is also ancillary to the first section because it is applied only when the process of choosing among the options in section one produces two or more equally legitimate subjects under which a book may be specifically entered. Because a result of this kind seems to be so closely related to the first subsection and because choice between name forms applies equally to it as well as to the first subsection, one might persuasively argue that it logically follows immediately after the first section. But Cutter placed it in the third position, perhaps to emphasize the two primary activities involved most often in the basic entry process: choice between subjects and settling on an appropriate uniform term to use after that choice has been made.

The last section is unrelated to the decision process per se. It contains rules and discussions only for the entry of special kinds of items that illustrate special problems. For that reason no formal discussion of it will be presented.

The Entry System

Cutter's headnote to this section indicates the value he placed on arriving at a rational system of entry procedure and the amount of labor that he surmised such a system would require of the cataloger. The substance of the headnote has been discussed in chapter 1.[2] This was not the first time Cutter had broached the question of how much effort this kind of a system would require. In 1869 he had defended Abbott's system in a similar way:

> It has been objected to Mr. Abbot's plan, that not only will readers find such a catalogue hard to consult, but other librarians will find it hard to make. But any good index of subjects is difficult of construction. Rhetoricians say that easy writing is hard reading. In the same way a catalogue which is compiled without much trouble will be likely to cause considerable delay and disappointment to those who use it. No satisfactory result can be obtained without the expenditure of time and thought. Shall it be the time of the librarian, or the time of the reader? Certainly not of the latter; for their labor, spent in solving the question of the moment, will in each case benefit only themselves, —while the labor of the librarian, being put into a form permanently accessible, may help numberless persons inquiring into the same matter.

But let no cataloguer who undertakes the task, wishing to give as much assistance as possible, delude himself with the idea that the work will be easy or rapid.[3]

In the remainder of the article, Cutter illustrated how systematic decisions might be made in a variety of situations. Here, he approached the dictionary catalog in the same way. It is easy to object to his emphasis on making a rational system if one considers the usage of the public to be equivalent to a mass of individual habits that, if individually followed, would greatly reduce the probability of attaining such a system. As explained in chapter 4, however, Cutter did not view the public in this way. Rather, he supposed that the usage of the public could be reduced to general patterns that were identifiable enough to be followed. Furthermore, he was hopeful that usage could be taught.

CHOICE BETWEEN DIFFERENT SUBJECTS (RULES 161–166)

Cutter's first subsection contains six rules that deal with five basic considerations, each of which he conveniently captioned to indicate its intent:

a. Between general and specific (rule 161)
b. Choice between person and country (rule 162)
c. Choice between event and country (rule 163)
d. Choice between subject (or form) and country (rules 164–165)
e. Between subjects that overlap (rule 166)

Each of these are meaningful only in the context of what was discussed earlier, that considering what a book treats specifically is an expression of classificatory inclusion relationships and significance order. The first rule is fundamental, however; the other five are related to the first as special cases.

Rule 161, the principal statement of specific entry, reads, "Enter a work under its subject heading, not under the heading of a class which includes that subject."[4] When faced with a book, or with any part of a book that is being given subject access as a documentary unit, the subject cataloger's first task is to determine what it treats specifically, its specific or special subject. This refers to what the book treats of that a consensus of intelligent persons would denote as its distinct and meaningful content, a subject understood to be the narrowest location available on a classificatory map of the universe of "established" subjects. Evidence of the book's specific subject will be found in the form of a name consisting of one or more words that are commonly used by persons who know the subject well enough to communicate about it with reasonable consistency in meaning, that is, by authors who have also written on the matter. Determination of the specific subject of any particular book must, therefore, be correlated with other works on the same topic. Furthermore, the name of the specific subject should not be determined on the basis of titles alone, but on a consideration of all aspects of books—their titles, tables of contents, texts, etc.[5]

Cutter was aware that some books would fall into the gray area of treating just-emerging subjects, the names of which would still be susceptible to variations beyond that of being synonymous. The best one could say is that they were topics of investigation described only by coordinating the names of other established subjects in the form of verbal circumlocutions. For example, Cutter indicated that Iron was an established subject that met the criteria of stabilized meaning and name. But Movement of fluids in plants was hazy as a distinct subject in his day and consisted of a series of names of other already established subjects.

In cases such as the latter, the method Cutter appears to have followed for determining if the specific subject of a book was legitimately established was to examine several books that appeared to treat the topical matter to see if they offered some consensus concerning what was being talked about and how it was named. In his discussion of rule 161, Cutter implied this method in such phrases as "if several works were written on it," "late writings have raised it to the status of a subject," and "a number of books on this brand of the subject." He may not have elaborated on it as a method because he supposed that catalogers followed it as a course of habit. Cutter also did not say what one might do if only one book were written on a topic. It seems clear, however, should that case have arisen, he probably would have disqualified it as a candidate for having a distinct subject.[6] And indeed, that would be the case if by a nonestablished topic he meant especially one that had few if any points of contact with other topics that were established in a literature of reasonable size.

The process of determining what a document treats of will produce one of three results: (1) a distinct and established subject with a commonly used name (or with more than one commonly used name, each of which is equivalent to the other); (2) a topic of thought, unestablished as a subject in its own right, but consisting of other established subjects; (3) a content so indistinct as to be impervious to subject analysis. Rule 161 deals with the first two results. The third is mentioned in the subsection on number of entries (rule 180) and leads to no subject entry or subentry of any kind.

Given the first result, the subject name may be seen as the final term in an implied hierarchical chain of subjects. The name is at the same time the specific subject of the book and the specific heading under which the description of the book will be placed in the catalog. Cutter's injunction at this point is to enter the book under the specific heading rather than to enter it under the name of the implied class of which the specific heading is only a division. For example, a book that treats the specific subject Iron should be entered under IRON, not under METALS. And one treating the Segment of a circle should be entered under that name, not under GEOMETRY. The book could, of course, be subentered under their specific headings in a classed chain of terms —for example, METALS–IRON or GEOMETRY–SEGMENT OF A CIRCLE—but that alternative is not at issue here. If the cataloger has determined the specific heading, there is no need in a direct access system to make it accessible only indirectly.

Given the second result, a different procedure must be applied. The cataloger is not to invent a name for the topic but rather to enter the work in the class of which the topic is a part. For example, Cutter entered the topic Movement of fluids in plants under BOTANY (i.e., Plants). The entire description of the topic was itself a subdivision of Botany as a class. But because the entire description was not a commonly used name, Cutter entered the book that treated of it in Botany as its including class.

The method for determining which including class is to be the class entry term is not difficult to ascertain, given Cutter's notions of subject structure and significance order and how he understood the mind to work in devising new subjects. Any description of a topic of this kind is actually a combination of other established subjects. The choice is to be that subject among the combination of subjects which is the most concrete among those listed. In this example, the subjects listed in order of their concreteness would be Plants and Movement of fluids (or Hydrology), plants being synonymous in Cutter's work with descriptive botany rather than with systematic botany. Because it is the more concrete subject of the two (at least in Cutter's opinion), Plants would be the final term in the classification chain incorporating both terms and would be the appropriate choice for entry.

One may ask why, if this rule implies two separate procedures, Cutter did not explicitly distinguish between them? The answer is that just as the notion of subject structure and therefore the definition of a specific subject were for Cutter matters of common understanding that needed little or no explanation, an explicit exposition of the procedures needed to identify a specific subject was also a matter of common understanding that needed little explanation. The rule simply calls for a single result—the entry of a work under its specific subject. How one identifies a specific subject was not at issue. In fact, Cutter's discussion of the gray areas that made the notion difficult did not serve as a definitive exposition but only as a reminder of those difficulties. To have entered into such an explanation would have been the same as telling a coal miner how to determine what coal was. To modern catalogers, however, the notion of a specific subject has a different connotation, and thus it has been necessary to include an explicit description of the process of identification that Cutter used.

The remaining rules for choice between different subjects deal with special cases. Two of the rules deal with cases in which a book has two specific subjects, each of which is of the same categorical level in terms of subject nomenclature—that is, two individual subjects or two concrete (or abstract) general subjects—but one of which is more dominant than the other in terms of the focus of the work. For example, rule 162 deals with books which may variously be considered either biographies of a ruler of a country or histories of the country during that ruler's reign. Both are individual subjects, the first a person, the second a country. Rule 166, on the other hand, deals with books which may variously be considered to treat two different and not otherwise hierarchically related general subjects that in effect overlap in the work, such as a work on the origin of the earth that deals with both Astronomy and Geology. The resolution in each of these cases is to enter the document under the subject that is predominant. If, however, neither predominate, the decision is thrown into the third subsection of his rules—"Number of entries"—which will be dealt with later.

The other two special rules in this section deal with those situations in which an item treats two specific subjects, one of which is subordinate to the other in terms of significance order. Rule 163 deals with books which are about particular events or periods in the history of a country. The choice to be made is either the name of the event (or the period) or the name of the country. Both are individual subjects, but they are related to each other hierarchically as a whole is related to its parts. The War of the Roses is an individual subject but also a particular period in the history of England, the latter being the whole individual of which the War of the Roses is only a part. The key to deciding whether to enter such a book under England (perhaps subarranged by History and even by period if there are enough works) or under its own name is whether the event or period has a distinct proper name of its own. If it does, that name is to be used for the book's specific entry heading. If not, the document should be entered under the country.

Because this rule involves individual subjects only, it constitutes something of a critical problem. Cutter's intention in the dictionary subject catalog was to give precedence to any individual subject that had its own distinctive name over any other kind of subject with which it was coordinated. When individual subjects are combined with general subjects, the matter of choice is clear because individual subjects are automatically considered the most concrete subject in the combination. But in these cases the subject with which an individual subject is combined is another individual subject. And their relationship falls into that gray area of a whole individual and its individual parts. Thus, Cutter found it necessary to give some specific guidance where this conflict occurred. An individual part of still another individual subject is to be treated as a specific subject in its own right if it has a name that is distinct (or, in modern terms, if its name is nongeneric).

The last situation to be dealt with (rules 164–165) also involves an item with an individual subject—in this case a country. But unlike the previous case, the individual subject is combined with a general subject. To begin with, if the resulting combination forms an acceptable name in its own right, it is to be used as it appears. In this respect, Cutter noted that ORNITHOLOGY OF NEW ENGLAND and NEW ENGLAND ORNITHOLOGY were "merely different names for the specific subject," suggesting that if either entire phrase were customarily used, its use was tantamount to naming the special subject of the work. But Cutter also seems not to have been convinced that this kind of name was typical because he went on to treat the topic simply as a coordinated description. By treating it that way, entry became a choice between the terms within the description on the basis of significance order. As a result, he entered a book on that topic under the individual subject in the combination.[7]

To show the processes involved in this subsection, it is convenient to set them out in the form of a chart (Figure 8). The cases are systematically divided into three groups: (1) those in which the specific subject of a work is named but may be seen as related to an implied subject of greater extent; (2) those in which two specific subjects are identified but one is predominant; and (3) those in which the specific subject of a work does not have a commonly used name and another subject must be chosen.

CHOICE BETWEEN DIFFERENT NAMES
(RULES 167–175)

As already noted, the choices described in this subsection follow choices made in the first subsection. They occur when two or more

IS = Individual subject
GS = General subject
CGS = Concrete general subject
AGS = Abstract general subject

IS^b = Individual subject of implied
    broader extent
GS^b = General subject of implied
    broader extent

I. ONE SPECIFIC SUBJECT (i.e., has commonly used name)

Rule	Title	Named subject	Implied subject	Specific entry
161	Le fer	IRON (GS)	METALS (GS^b) METALLURGY (GS^b)	IRON
	The children's book of cats	CATS (GS)	ZOOLOGY (GS^b) DOMESTIC ANIMALS (GS^b) PETS (GS^b)	CATS
163	On the bicentennial of Dorchester	DORCHESTER (IS)	MASSACHUSETTS (IS^b)	DORCHESTER
	The massacre of St. Bartholomew	ST BARTHOLOMEW'S DAY (IS)	FRANCE (i.e., its history) (IS^b)	ST. BARTHOLOMEW'S DAY

II. TWO SPECIFIC SUBJECTS (but only one dominant)

Rule	Title	1st subject	2nd subject	Specific entry
162	Henry the Eighth of England	HENRY VIII, KING OF ENGLAND (IS)	ENGLAND (i.e., its history during Henry's reign) (IS)	The one that predominates[1]
166	The geology and geography of the earth	GEOLOGY (GS)	GEOGRAPHY (GS)	The one that predominates[1]

---

equally usable names are available for the same specific subject. In such situations, one name must be chosen so that all the books that treat that specific subject will be gathered together in one place in the catalog, a "see" reference being made from the term not chosen to the one chosen.

The headnote to this subsection has long been considered by commentators to confirm Cutter's dependence on usage (in the modern sense of the term) as a principal basis for subject cataloging decisions. Cutter wrote:

> General rules, always applicable, for the choice of names of subjects can no more be given than rules without exception in grammar. Usage

III. TOPIC WITHOUT COMMONLY USED NAME (i.e., not a "subject")[2]

Rule	Title	Subjects placed in significance order			Specific entry
161	Cattle diseases	DISEASES (AGS)	CATTLE (CGS)		CATTLE
	Movement of fluids in plants	HYDROLOGY (AGS) *or* MOVEMENT (AGS)	PLANTS (CGS) FLUIDS (CGS)	PLANTS (CGS)	PLANTS PLANTS (assuming it to be the most concrete)
163	The Civil War (i.e., of the United States)	CIVIL WAR (IS, but not distinct)	UNITED STATES (ISb)		UNITED STATES
164-165	New England ornithology	ORNITHOLOGY (GS)	NEW ENGLAND (IS)		NEW ENGLAND
	Memories of fishing under the High Street Bridge (i.e., in Aurora, Illinois)	FISHING (GS)	HIGH STREET BRIDGE (IS)[3]		HIGH STREET BRIDGE

1. Rule 176 makes it clear that if neither predominate, multiple entry should be made.

2. This assumes, of course, that the entire topic suggested by the title has no commonly used name, a matter that must be determined by some investigation.

3. This choice is based on the assumption that the individual subject and its name are established. If they are not, choice would have to be made on the basis of R163 in the same section. Even if they are, however, a choice between the particular name and the name of the larger individual subject of which the bridge is a part would have to be determined (cf. R163 in Section 1 above).

FIG. 8. Entry Choices for Cutter's Rules 161-166

> in both cases is the supreme arbiter,—the usage, in the present case, not of the cataloger but of the public in speaking of subjects.

Cutter obviously defended usage as a basis for making exceptions to general rules for choices between subject names. But two important factors must be kept in mind when one considers how he applied this notion. First, as described in chapter 4, Cutter's concept of the public was limited to three general categories of inquirers and had to do only with how those three types responded to or thought about subjects. He did not have in mind an infinite variety of use based on types of libraries and the supposed implications of the socio-economic characteristics of the users found in those libraries. Exceptions based on usage arose, therefore, from a very narrow range of alternatives.

Second, Cutter was not convinced that usage based on even that narrow range of alternatives would yield many clear decisions. Responding to the objection to catalogers' choosing names of subjects rather than taking the authors' own names for them as found in titles and the corresponding difficulty of inquirers determining what those names might be, he wrote:

> A seemingly strong objection, but of little practical account. In the first place, almost all individual subjects, and the majority of general subjects, have single well-known names; and in the case of pseudonyms or synonyms, he who is looking up any subject, not having a particular book in mind, is at least as likely to look under the name which the cataloguer has chosen as under any other. The heading is selected for the very reason that it is the most usual name of that topic or class of topics, the one under which most people would be likely to look; a vague and unscientific rule perhaps, but a thoroughly useful one; for the result is that in ninety-eight cases in a hundred there is not room for doubt where to look, and for the ninety-ninth the inquirer will hit the right heading at first, and therefore will be referred only once in a hundred inquiries.[8]

In other words, Cutter held the opinion that there were relatively few instances in which alternative names offered unclear choices.

Furthermore, he appears to have believed that even when a choice had to be made, users' preferences were not particularly determinative. In the discussion attached to rule 172 on choosing between title subject words and controlled vocabulary subject words, Cutter wrote:

> A man who is looking up the history of the Christian church does not care in the least whether the books on it were called by their authors church histories or ecclesiastical histories; and the cataloger also should not care if he can avoid it.[9]

Likewise, in a discussion of synonymous compound subject names, after suggesting that choice should be based on "decided usage"—that is, "custom of the public to designate the subjects by one of the names rather than the other"—Cutter wrote, "As is often the case in language, usage will be found not to follow any uniform course."[10] With that he enjoined the cataloger to choose between the terms on a systematic basis, perhaps with the thought, expressed in the headnote to the entire entry system section, that by doing so usage would eventually follow rather than determine practice.

As in the first subsection, captions reveal that Cutter was essentially dealing with five explicit problems:

f. Language (rule 167)
g. Synonyms (rules 168–171)
h. Subject-word and subject (rule 172)
i. Homonyms (rule 173)
j. Compound subject-names (rules 174–175)

Of these, three present no problems of any great difficulty. With respect to language variations (rule 167), English equivalents are preferred. When there is a choice to be made between subject title words and controlled vocabulary subject words (rule 172), the latter are to be used. And homonymous subjects (rule 173)—those spelled the same way but having different meanings—are to be strictly separated. For example, GRACE might refer to a prayer before meals, a quality of poise, a musical term, or a theological doctrine.[11] These must therefore be differentiated. Cutter nowhere stated in his *Rules* how their separation might be achieved. But in his Boston Athenaeum catalog he simply added an italicized statement in parentheses after a homonym to indicate its meaning, such as GRACE (*in theology*) and GRACE (*before meals*).

In the section captioned "synonyms," rule 171 actually deals with antonyms and suggests that where two exactly opposite meanings are always implied in the use of either of two terms—for example, TEMPERANCE and INTEMPERANCE—only one should be used, the other being referred from. With regard to synonyms per se, rule 168 states the obvious: a choice should be made between them in order to gather together books on the same subject. Rule 169 then provides five criteria for choice. The heading should be preferred that

(a) is most familiar to the class of people who consult the library
(b) is most used in other catalogs
(c) has fewest meanings other than the sense in which it is to be employed
(d) comes first in the alphabet, so that reference from the others can be made to the exact page of the catalog
(e) brings the subject into the neighborhood of other related subjects.

Three general observations may be made of these criteria. First, they do not constitute an order of preference. Cutter wrote in his discussion following the rule, "sometimes one and sometimes another of these reasons must prevail. Each case is to be decided on its own merits." Second, the equivalent terms being considered here are limited to synonyms, that is, names involving distinctly different words. They do not include, for example, equivalent terms that arise simply from alternative word orders. Those kinds of terms are dealt with in rules 174–175. Thus, the fifth criterion is not to be invoked as a rationale for inverting phrase headings. Third, choice between synonyms presupposes Cutter's fundamental emphasis on specific entry, especially of individual subjects, which is stated clearly in the preceding subsection.

Thus, while some choices based on clear knowledge of the preferences of inquirers might involve the use of class-entry terms (e.g., the choice of PENALTY OF DEATH over CAPITAL PUNISHMENT), the regular practice of choosing class-entry over specific-entry terms would suggest that the cataloger was not really committed to the fundamental emphasis that specific entry implies. On the contrary, in situations where there was any doubt whatsoever as to the public's preferences, Cutter assumed that entry terms were to be preferred which promoted the specific-entry ideal.

Of the five criteria, two are individually noteworthy. The first must be interpreted in the light of Cutter's general concept of the public. Cutter attached to the criterion the following comment:

> A natural history society will of course use the scientific name, a town library would equally of course use the popular name—BUTTER-FLIES rather than LEPIDOPTERA, HORSE rather than EQUUS CABALLUS. But the scientific may be preferred when the common name is ambiguous or of ill-defined extent.

That is to say, inquirers in a natural history society will, according to Cutter's analysis, prefer scientific names over common names. They will do so, however, not because of some special vocabulary patterns attached to natural history library users as a sociological group distinct from all other groups of library users, but rather because the users of natural history libraries will likely be of the second and third categories of inquirers. They will approach subject searching from a study-oriented point of view that includes an appreciation for precise terminology and classificatory structure. By Cutter's general reckoning, a dictionary catalog might not even be the best kind of catalog for them to use, although the value of its emphasis on directly accessible specific subjects was not to be deprecated. On the other hand, a town library, serving the entire range of inquirers including a preponderance of less cultivated, desultory readers, would necessarily provide common subject names even though the latter were often less precise in meaning.

The last criterion is also notable in that the examples that Cutter included are limited to the collocation of subject names indicative of collective biography (e.g., musicians) with subject names indicative of the fields in which the biographees functioned (e.g., music) when the subject names for each began with the same word roots. The limitation inherent in his examples suggests in turn that Cutter did not view this criterion in the same way that more recent subject heading workers have interpreted it—as a means to introduce collocative sequences into the dictionary subject catalog at every possible opportunity, regardless of whether or not such headings are contrary to the more fundamental rule of specific entry.[12]

The last issue to which Cutter directed his attention in this subsection is compound subject names (rules 174–175), and specifically, how one might choose between them and what alternative word orders are available for them. Cutter began by listing six kinds of subject names which one might encounter. All but the first involve more than one word and are therefore "compound" in their structures.

(a) single word
(b) adjective-noun
(c) noun (used like an adjective)-noun
(d) noun-preposition-noun
(e) noun-conjunction-noun
(f) extended phrase or sentence

He then listed three options for dealing with the word order of all but the first of these, critically evaluating each option in turn.

The first option is always to use compound subject names as they read in their normally spoken order. Cutter surmised that the chief weakness of this method was that it might be applied in an absurd manner in certain cases, such as entering Ancient Egypt under that name if it were asserted that "Ancient Egypt is a distinct subject from Modern Egypt, having a recognized name of its own, as much so as Ancient history."[13] Despite that weakness, Cutter concluded that this option was the "best," but only "if due discrimination be used in choosing subject-names." In other words, the success of the approach depends on how well the cataloger perceives what constitutes a legitimately established subject with a commonly used name, a prospect about which Cutter was obviously sanguine.

The second option for dealing with compound subject names is to use longer phrases (i.e., types e and f) as they read, but to enter two-word combinations (types b and c) and prepositional phrases (type d) "under what one might consider the significant word of the phrase, inverting the order of the words if necessary." The special character of this option should be carefully noted. Some subject names of these three types may be reduced to one of their constituent words without changing their meanings. For example, Theory of probabilities, Special providences, and Proper names might be entered respectively under the single terms PROBABILITIES, PROVIDENCES, and NAMES without indicating a significantly different subject than the original term implies. But others may not be reduced to a single word in the same way because deleting the remaining words would change their meanings. The latter may sometimes be inverted, however, because the inverted form does not change their meanings. For example, Figure of the earth and Origin of the species may be inverted to EARTH, *Figure of the* and SPECIES, *Origin of the,* respectively, without indicating significantly different subject names than the original phrases.

Cutter noted that the chief weakness of the second option was "that there would often be disagreement as to what is the most important word of the phrase, so that the rule would be no guide to the reader." Nevertheless, he concluded that this option, if followed judiciously, could moderate the first option in a useful manner. Thus, he devised a rule on the matter that combined both options:

> 175. Enter a compound subject-name by its first word, inverting the phrase only when some other word is decidedly more significant or is often used alone with the same meaning as the whole name.

Commentators have found Cutter's rule, his subsequent admission of its vagueness, and the discussion that followed it generally disconcerting and contradictory. He clearly advocated at least occasional inversion. But the basis for inversion appears to be vague because it requires the cataloger to judge the "significance" of some word in the name other than the first word. Of course, significance has been taken to mean significance in usage, that is, which word in such a heading would likely be looked for by patrons. More important, however, Cutter subsequently argued strongly against inversion because it violated the principle of specific entry. He focused his arguments first on the noun rule for inversion advocated by his contemporary, Jacob Schwartz, and secondly, on an analysis of word order in compound subject names. His rule appears, therefore, to advocate the selective use of inversion *against* the specific-entry principle on the basis of word significance that is all but indeterminate. Lois M. Chan, supposing this to be the case, attributed Cutter's conclusions in the matter to his notion of usage. "Cutter's misgivings about violating the principle of specific entry were evidently overruled by his policy of 'convenience of the public'."[14]

Conclusions of the preceding kind are attempts to explain what appears to be an obvious contradiction. They are misapplied, however, because Cutter was not contradicting himself. To see why this is so, one must carefully observe the order of his arguments in the entire discussion and the distinctions implicit in that order.[15]

To begin with, it is notable that Cutter formulated a rule for the treatment of compound subject names before he had discussed the third and final option for dealing with them. One would have thought that he would have discussed the pros and cons of all three of the options before coming to some conclusion about the most appropriate procedure. The reason why he formulated his rule at this point, however, lies in the way the characteristics of the third option allowed him to clarify the provisions of his rule.

The third option is to use all compound subject names except adjective-noun combinations as they read. The adjective-noun ones are to be reduced to their "equivalent nouns," or, if that is not possible, inverted, using the noun in the combination as the entry word. It should be noted that the special provisions of this option are restricted to only one of the types of headings (type b) that he listed. The value of discussing the third option at this point did not reside, therefore, in its special scope. It was almost as narrow in its approach as the first option. And it certainly was not as broad in what it covered as the second option which dealt with three kinds of combinations. Rather, the value of discussing the third option at this point resided in the fact that its provisions—reduction of adjective-noun combinations to equivalent synonyms and inversion—*represented for Cutter what he did not mean by similar provisions in his own rule.*

The reduction called for in the third option is different than the reduction specified in the second option and in his rule in the following way. Instead of reducing a compound subject name to one of its words as Cutter had required, reduction here means choosing a different word altogether, changing MORAL PHILOSOPHY to the single term ETHICS, for example, or SANITARY SCIENCE to HYGIENE. This in turn presupposes that the equivalent single-word synonyms are not the most commonly used subject names available. If they were, choosing them rather than the single words would be automatic. Cutter criticized this form of reduction on the basis that the reader might not know what the equivalent (but, by implication, less commonly known) term would be. Even with this difficulty, however, Cutter concluded that this procedure was "often a good one" when used with discretion.[16] Cutter's regard for procedure did not erase the fact, however, that the reduction it represents is markedly different than the reduction that he had advocated in his rule.

The other provision of the third option, inversion, is also significantly different than the inversion that Cutter had called for in his rule. Cutter stated after his rule that the inversion to which he referred was "somewhat vague and that it would be often of doubtful application." His reference was not to the vagueness of trying to guess which word of those in a phrase a patron might be inclined to look under. Cutter simply did not approach usage with that modern interpretation of its meaning. Even his call for choice among synonymous compound subject names (to be discussed later) did not refer to usage in that way but only to determining which entire name of several entire names patrons used. And in his criticism of the second option quoted above, he suggested that guessing at "significance" in an unqualified manner was erratic enough in its results to be of "no guide to the reader." Rather, the vagueness that Cutter referred to here was the difficulty of determining which phrases were so constructed as to be capable of being reduced or inverted *with no significant change in their meanings or with no subsequent confusion because of their placement in the catalog.* The problem is that such phrases have little in the way of distinctive characteristics in their own right by which Cutter could describe them. They consist of the residue of phrases that remain after one discounts the far greater number of compound subject names that may not be inverted under any circumstances. To clarify what he meant, therefore, Cutter found it more convenient to describe the compound subject names that should not be inverted. His discussion took the form of a critical evaluation of the inversion that the third option called for and, especially, its embodiment in Jacob Schwartz's noun rule—the practice of consistently placing the noun in adjective-noun combinations in the lead position.

Cutter found Schwartz's approach to inversion objectionable for two fundamental reasons. First, the adjective in the combinations sometimes so affects the meaning of the phrase that to invert the phrase has the effect of placing the term in a location that would be unexpected to the user and thus lost to the user during a search. For example, entering Alimentary canal under CANAL, ALIMENTARY would place books on that subject in a sequence with works on waterways where few users might think of looking for them. Cutter's provision for inversion, especially as illustrated in the examples that he appended to it, suggests that inversion should be done only for terms whose adjectives do not greatly alter the meaning of the whole term and that when inverted do not produce confusions of the above kind.

The second and far more important objection that Cutter had toward the inversion provision of this option was based on theoretical grounds. Cutter observed that the words in "most" of the adjective-noun combinations have a classificatory relationship to one another where "the noun expresses a class, the adjective limits the noun and makes the name that of a subclass . . . and to adopt the noun (the class) as the heading is to violate the fundamental principle of the dictionary catalog." Cutter noted that Schwartz knew of the propensity of his rule toward classed entries of this kind, but claimed it had practical advantages. Cutter argued against Schwartz's claims by advancing counterclaims of his own. But the real forcefulness of Cutter's objection to consistent inversion did not turn on pragmatic considerations but rather on his aversion to classed structure in subject headings.[17] Because Schwartz's noun rule makes the introduction of class structured headings a regularized exception to the specific entry system, it would consciously compromise the goals of the dictionary catalog and make it into a mixed system that would be difficult for the user to learn. Cutter was adamant at this point. He wrote:

> The specific-entry rule is one which the reader of a dictionary catalog must learn if he is to use it with any facility; it is much better that he should not be burdened with learning an exception to this, which the noun rule certainly is.

Cutter's provision for inversion does not cross this boundary. Inversion is not to be used if a classificatory relationship exists between the words in a compound subject name. Rather, inversion is to be applied only when the words in such a name are neutral in a classificatory sense; when, in fact, their deletion through reduction or their manipulation through inversion does not lead to classed headings or misleading placement in the catalog.

In summary, Cutter discussed the third option for dealing with compound subject names after devising his rule because its contrasting provisions served to define what he meant in his rule. In his rule, reduction of a compound subject name (i.e., actually only of types b, c, and d) is restricted to the use of one of the words of the heading itself rather than to a different single-word synonym. Inversion is restricted to phrases that when inverted will not be lost in confusing sequences and that do not have classificatory relationships between the words, such that inversion would result in class-subclass headings. Given these restrictions, Cutter's provisions for both reduction and inversion would not be used extensively. It is their limited use, in fact, that points to the actual forcefulness of Cutter's rule *that almost all compound subject names are to be used as they read.* His rule might therefore be paraphrased in the following way: Enter almost all compound subject names directly as they read, except for those relatively few that might be inverted or reduced to one of their component words in terms of the restrictions already discussed. Rendering his rule this way is in marked contrast to interpretations in which the reduction and inversion provisions of the second and third options have not been differentiated and where, consequently, the thrust of Cutter's rule has been an unqualified but contradictory call for a decision about inversion in every case, usually based on some assessment of users' random searching habits.

After finishing his discussion of the third option, Cutter was then free to return to the most important aspect of his rule, the entry of almost all compound subject names as they read and the most common problem that attends it, the necessity of choosing between synonymous compound subject names where more than one are available for the name of a subject. He began his discussion by listing two examples, each consisting of the three kinds of phrases (b, c, and d) pertinent to the second option and thus included for consideration in his rule:

EXAMPLE 1	EXAMPLE 2
(b) Capital punishment	Floral fertilization
(c) Death penalty	Flower fertilization
(d) Penalty of death	Fertilization of flowers

Of the examples, he asked, "Is there any principle upon which the choice between these three can be made, so that the cataloger shall always enter books on the same subject under the same heading?" His answer, "I see none," was his admission that there is no plainly obvious and absolutely consistent basis for making such a decision. Lacking that kind of a basis, he described two alternative procedures that might stand in its place. The first is usage. He wrote, "When there is any decided usage . . . let it be followed; . . . "

Cutter realized that following usage might produce contradictory results. For example, usage might dictate that of the above examples, a heading beginning with an adjective might be used for the one and a heading beginning with a noun for the other. Perhaps because of this, Cutter expected no great help from considerations of usage per se. He wrote, "As is often the case in language, usage will be found not to follow any uniform course." Reflecting on the two hypothetical cases he had delineated, he continued, "If usage manifests no preference for either name, we cannot employ the two indifferently; we must choose one, and some slight guide to choice in certain cases may perhaps be found." By a slight guide he meant a useful, although not absolutely foolproof, rationale that consisted of the analysis of the phrases in terms of the classificatory relationships of their components. The analysis is similar to that applied in the first subsection of his entry rules in which subject descriptions not considered to be commonly accepted subject names are scrutinized to pick the most concrete subject name among them. Here, in contrast, the purpose of the analysis is to determine which subject name begins with the most concrete term. The analysis is the same, of course. The most appropriate compound subject name to use is the one in which the first term is the most concrete and is "included" (in a classificatory sense) by the other terms in the phrase. When that occurs it is in effect the most specific subject name available.

Cutter's discussion of compound subject names came to a close with the foregoing discussion. His overall approach to compound subject names may be summarized in the following manner. First, the preferred form for almost all compound subject headings is their direct, unmanipulated form. Second, two-word phrases (types b and c) and prepositional phrases (type d) may be reduced to one of their constituent words or inverted, but only if the result does not place the heading in a confusing sequence or produce a nonspecific class-subclass entry. Third, if two or more synonymous compound subject names are available for the same specific subject, the one that begins with the most concrete word is to be preferred to preserve the specific entry principle.

THE NUMBER OF SUBJECT ENTRIES

The third subsection in the entry portion of the *Rules* deals with how many subject entries one might make for any particular document. The tone of the subsection is set by Cutter's headnote where he reminds the subject cataloger that "almost every book will appear several times in the catalog." After enumerating the various types of entries (author, title, subject, etc.) that might typically be made for any particular item and noting their necessity if the goals of the catalog are to be attained, he further cautioned the cataloger with the following:

> But inasmuch as the extent and therefore the cost of the catalog increases with the multiplication of entries, it becomes worthwhile to inquire whether some of these can not be dispensed with by devices which will suit the inquirer as well or nearly as well.

In other words, Cutter concluded that the growth of the catalog could be controlled by curtailing its entry system in some manner. Here, control meant curtailing the subject entry system. To do so created tension, however, because any curtailment must not be done by damaging the subject entry system. Thus, Cutter began this section first by reiterating the entry goal of his system and then by showing how that entry goal might be moderated. As a result, curtailment turned out to be not so much the omission of entries as their modification in form.

The initial rule, "Enter a polytopical book under each distinct subject" (rule 176), states the basic entry goal and represents a natural outcome of the entry process of the first subsection in the entry system. While the normal process of identifying the specific subject of a work might often result in a single subject, there are also occasions in which more than one specific subject will be the result. This will occur when two or more subjects of the same kind (e.g., multiple general subjects or multiple individual subjects) are identified among which no inclusion relationship can be determined. A book about Travels in Patagonia and Peru, for example, or one that is a Handbook of drawing and engraving would each yield two most specific subjects—in the first, the two individual subjects PATAGONIA and PERU, and in the second, the two general subjects DRAWING and ENGRAVING.

Ordinarily, each item would be entered under each subject because significance order does not make one inclusive of the other. Cutter noted, however, that if one of the subjects were treated only diminutively in the work, it might be omitted altogether, supposing that the relevance of the treatment would also be diminutive to anyone searching for literature on it. This is little more than a reflection of rules 162 and 166 in the subsection on choice between different subjects where Cutter enjoined the cataloger to enter some works under the subject that predominated. Cutter also suggested here, however, that sometimes "an analytical can take the place of full entry for the less important topic," that is, an analytical reference which briefly refers the reader to the full entry. The latter option does not do away with the subject entry as the first option above does, but it does reduce the amount of space required in a printed catalog.

Because an injunction to omit entries altogether might possibly be carried out without careful discrimination, Cutter also found it necessary to point out that still other books have more than one specific subject, one of which might not be readily apparent—for example, a collection of German portraits which is not only about the subject of the portraits (i.e., GERMANS) but illustrative of the portrait technique involved as well (i.e., PORTRAIT ENGRAVING or PORTRAIT PAINTING).

The remaining rules in this third subsection suggest other ways to control the number of subject entries. The most important is rule 177 where it is noted that although a polytopical book such as "a treatise on anatomy, physiology, pathology, and therapeutics" might be entered under each of its distinct specific subjects, it would alternatively be entered under the general subject (i.e., MEDICINE) that includes each of the specific subjects, if together they comprise "the whole or a great part" of the whole of the more extensive subject. Furthermore, "analyticals" might also be placed under the component subjects, but only "if the separate parts are by different authors."[18] Cutter supplied an even more complex example involving this same kind of procedure in the fourth subsection (rule 186) among the miscellaneous rules. He noted that theological books on the "Last things" actually cover seven distinct topics that together have six distinct names. Because so many works treat combinations of the specific subjects rather than the subjects individually, yet do not always include all the subjects, he suggested two ways to enter such books in the catalog. On the one hand, one might enter all the books under a single inclusive heading regardless of the particular subjects they cover. Or, more appropriately in Cutter's opinion, one might use four specific headings that represent the most common groupings of the specific subjects typically found in such books.

SUMMARY AND COMMENT

The main outline of Cutter's entry system has been briefly described by examining the first three subsections of Part A of his subject rules. His entry system has been shown to consist of the necessary identification of the specific subject of a book according to his notions of subject structure and significance order, the choice of a single subject name where the first process resulted in more than one subject name for the same subject, and a series of suggestions on how multiple subject entry might be controlled without damaging the essential nature of the specific entry ideal.

There are several places in Cutter's entry procedure where one might interpret Cutter's methods in such a way as to justify entries that do not accord with his specific entry ideal. For example, although Cutter prohibited class entry for a clearly delineated specific subject (rule 161), he did not specifically prohibit specific subentry although he implied its prohibition. Thus, one could provide specific subentry and rightfully claim that the specific subject of the work had been given access even though not directly. One might also rationalize the choice of synonymous headings or compound name forms that were in effect classed entries by claiming their convenience to the public.

But those who apply Cutter's entry system in this way have failed to appreciate fully the forcefulness of his specific entry ideal. Outside of explicit cases of "decided usage" (of which Cutter concluded there were few), when there was any doubt whatsoever in choices to be made, Cutter consistently chose those entries that best fulfilled the specific entry objective, that is, those that would provide direct access to the most concrete subject treated in a book. The final result of this methodology was to enter books under a host of essentially concrete subjects which were dispersed randomly throughout the catalog according to the way their names were spelled. Efforts to circumvent this goal by means of subtle (or not so subtle) manipulation of entry choices and names have arisen for the most part because catalogers have not been altogether comfortable with the massive dispersion of specific, especially concrete, subjects that this methodology entails. Classed entries (whether or not they include specific subentry) moderate the dispersion by providing at least some collocation of related subjects.

Cutter was committed to his specific entry ideal regardless of its dispersive effects. This did not mean that he considered it to have some absolute value against which the collocative ideal of a classed system palled in comparison. His comments suggest that he was very aware not only of the structural properties of each system, but also of their strengths and weaknesses. He was also aware of a tendency among advocates of each system to overestimate the value of their respective system. This was especially the case with those who promoted classed subject access. Having been such an advocate, his opinions of such claims have the ring of experience. The strength of well-made classed systems obviously resided in their potential to collocate related subjects. But Cutter questioned what he considered to be inflated opinions as to how completely that might be accomplished.

> Inasmuch, however, as it is absolutely impossible to devise a system of classification which shall exhibit each subject in all its relations to other subjects, and always bring together all the books which a course of investigation may oblige one to use, any classed-system, and still more the alphabetico-classed, will sometimes seem as inconvenient and as disjunctive as the dictionary. No catalogue can exhibit all possible combinations of thought. Enough if it exhibit the most common, and give some clew for tracing the rarer ones. Those that claim perfection for any system show that they have no idea of the difficulties to be overcome.19

The value attached to the collocative potential of the classed catalog was in turn justified by its perceived usefulness in searching. Here also Cutter questioned conventional wisdom by suggesting that persons searching for comprehensive general subjects and their divisions were really not as anxious for the enormous recall that this kind of search implied.

> It is objected to the dictionary catalogue, and with much truth, that it gives no help to the man who wishes to glance quickly over all the

literature on a comprehensive subject, including the books on its various branches, . . . It seems to me, however, that the objection is sometimes a little overstated, or too much is made of it. The inquirer above mentioned will find the general works under the general head, and with them a number of cross-references, perhaps five, perhaps fifty. If his needs oblige him to look them up, his case is indeed pitiable. But how often would that happen? Generally, he will run his eyes over the references, find two or three in which he is interested, look them up, and get reading enough for one day at least.[20]

While he did not moderate his view that direct access to the specific subjects of books was extremely useful and greatly to be desired, Cutter did bemoan the loss of the collocation of subjects that would enable inquirers to search for books from a classificatory orientation. In fact, he considered the dispersive effect of specific entry to be the "weak point" of the system. It resulted in entries being "thrown together without any logical arrangement" and being placed "in the most absurd proximity" to one another. In fact, so thorough and so random was the dispersion that he likened the result to a "mob" of entries. The dispersive effect of this system was, consequently, an "evil which it tries, not unsuccessfully, to reduce to a minimum, but can never away with altogether."[21] His attempt to ameliorate that evil took the form of a cross-reference system.

The Cross-Reference System

The second part of Cutter's subject rules—"B. Entries Considered as Parts of a Whole"—consisted of provisions for a cross-reference system. The cross-reference system referred to here is comparable for the most part to the "see also" references in current dictionary subject catalogs. It does not include cross-references between equivalent terms (i.e., "see" references) which were a function of the entry system.

Considered theoretically, the sequence of subjects in a specific entry display of the kind found in Cutter's specific entry catalog represented both the narrowest subjects under which the works listed under them could be entered and the final terms of classificatory strings-of-terms. If the specific subjects were subentered as the final elements of those strings, the catalog display would accomplish two things. First, the immediate classificatory context of an individual book would be identified from among various alternatives that might seem to apply to it. For example, a book entered under CATS would be placed in its correct classificatory chain, say, in either ZOOLOGY–VERTEBRATES–MAMMALS–CATS or DOMESTIC ANIMALS–CATS. Second, the arrangement of the word strings would provide a measure of collocation dependent on the kind of arrangement employed, that is, whether logical or only alphabetical.

The classificatory strings were not displayed in Cutter's specific entry system, of course. As a result there was a corresponding loss of the advantage to searching which their display would have promoted. The purpose of Cutter's cross-reference system was to restore at least some of those lost relationships. The extent of the restoration depended on the range of devices that Cutter employed and the thoroughness of their application. Cutter's two rules (187–188) here provide something approaching a minimal restoration, and even this restoration varied in terms of the categories of catalogs that he invoked—that is, whether "Full," "Medium," or "Short," these corresponding to printed catalogs of various degrees of completeness with respect to the bibliographical details included.[22]

DESCENDING AND COORDINATE REFERENCES

The first device Cutter employed was to make "descending" and "coordinate" references between the subject of a book being cataloged and related subjects already entered in the catalog (rule 187). Thus, if a zoological book on CATS is being entered in the catalog for the first time and the subject MAMMALS is already displayed in the catalog (or vice versa), a descending reference from the including class MAMMALS to the included class CATS (i.e., MAMMALS, see also CATS) should be made. In the same manner, should a work later be added that treats a specific variety of cats (say, SIAMESE CATS), a reference will also be necessary from CATS to that even narrower subject.

One important aspect of this downward chain of cross-references is that Cutter intended it to reach down regularly to the individual subject level. This extension appears especially in two cases. First, books that treat a general subject and a place and that are entered under the individual subject through application of Cutter's significance order in rule 165 are automatically to have cross-references made from the general subject to the individual subject used for entry. Thus, books on the Ornithology of New England, Spanish architecture, or English coins entered respectively under NEW ENGLAND, SPAIN, and ENGLAND are to have cross-references to those individual subjects from ORNITHOLOGY, ARCHITECTURE, and NUMISMATICS. (The references are to be in the form ORNITHOLOGY, see also NEW ENGLAND; ARCHITECTURE, see also SPAIN; NUMISMATICS, see also ENGLAND.) Second, persons as individual subjects are to have cross-references made to them from the classes that normally include them. Thus, works about Rembrandt van Rijn and Pierre Renoir should be referred to from PAINTERS (e.g.,

PAINTERS, see also REMBRANDT VAN RIJN, P. A. RENOIR). And those about Sir William Ramsay or Louis Pasteur as chemists would be referred to from CHEMISTS (e.g., CHEMISTS, see also LOUIS PASTEUR, SIR WILLIAM RAMSAY), the class headings in each case being used primarily for the entry of collective biography.[23]

Cross-references designed to connect related (i.e., coordinate) subjects occur most often within a single general class. Cutter's example of the combined network of cross-references among books on coins illustrates this in his discussion appended to rule 165:

> To show the procedure under this rule, suppose we have a collection of books on coins. Let the general works go under NUMISMATICS; let works on any particular kind of coin, as a PINE–TREE SHILLING or a QUEEN ANNE'S FARTHING, go under the name of the coin; let works on the coins of a country be put under its name; refer from the country to all particular coins on which you have monographs, and from NUMISMATICS both to all the separate coins and to all the countries on whose coinage you have treatises.[24]

The cross-references from NUMISMATICS to particular coins and countries are of the descending type. But the references from countries in which particular coins had their basis or perhaps their origin to the coins themselves are coordinate, representing something of an intersection of subject content.

Cross-references designed to connect illustrative subjects were described by Cutter primarily as those relating individual persons to other subjects to which their activities might offer some insight, between cities and "persons connected with them by birth or residence, or at least to those who have taken part in the municipal affairs or rendered the city illustrious," or between very general subjects such as HISTORY, LITERATURE, and ART to "rulers and statesmen," "authors," and "artists"—that is, from subjects "to the names of persons distinguished for discoveries in them or knowledge of them."

Two matters of significance are noteworthy with respect to the cross-reference procedure just described. First, Cutter suggested that the procedure would vary in thoroughness from catalog to catalog. While all catalogs would have a basic descending cross-reference structure, only "Full" catalogs would be most completely developed, incorporating a wide range of coordinate and illustrative references. "Short" and "Medium" catalogs were, on the other hand, encouraged by Cutter to "make such of these references as seem most likely to be used."

The second significant point about this procedure is that Cutter suggested it would result in an incomplete cross-reference structure if limited to those occasions when individual books were being cataloged.

He had in mind the idea, presumably, that during the actual cataloging process, cross-references would primarily be made from what would often be the relatively narrow specific subjects of the books in hand to their immediate subordinate subjects and also to them from their immediate superordinate subjects—in other words, to and from subjects that were immediately suggested by the subjects at hand. Given the emphasis in the specific entry system on making directly accessible what more often than not amounted to the relatively narrow-in-scope concrete subjects found in most books, the resulting cross-reference system would be more or less restricted to the more concrete end of the entire subject range.

To provide a successful restoration of the systematic subject structure lost by the specific entry process, however, the cross-reference structure that needed to be incorporated into the catalog must necessarily begin from the broadest general subjects and descend to all the various individual subjects to which a catalog provided direct access. Cutter wrote, "References are needed not merely to the specific from the general, but to the general from the more general and to that from the most general. There must be a pyramid of references . . ." To ensure this structural thoroughness and consistency, Cutter suggested that "a final revision" of the cross-reference system should be made just before printing, in which something of a synoptic chart of the subjects in the system would show those places where necessary cross-references had been inadvertently omitted. In rule 187 he elaborated:

> The best method is to draw off in a single column a list of all the subject-headings that have been made, to write opposite them their including classes in a second column and the including classes of these in a third column; then to write these classes as headings to cards and under them the subjects that stood respectively opposite to them in the list, to arrange the cards alphabetically, verify the references and supplement them by thinking of all likely subordinate headings and ascertaining whether they are in the catalog, and also by considering what an inquirer would like to be told or reminded of if he were looking up the subject under consideration. In this way a reasonably complete list may be made.

Some of these relationships would have been indicated, of course, while the actual entry process had ensued. And the procedure suggested a process in which a catalog had a stopping point—either the preparation of the catalog for printing or the completion of the cataloging of an initial collection of books for a new library. Furthermore, the revision process also engendered the possibility that references might be made from superordinate subjects which themselves had no actual works entered under them in the catalog. For example, given a series of books entered under CATS and corresponding references to that subject from MAMMALS, there might be no actual books entered under the latter heading nor under ZOOLOGY, the next superordinate subject. In Cutter's opinion, references of this sort, consistently incorporated into the catalog, would greatly increase its bulk. He therefore suggested, as a modification which would ameliorate that tendency, omitting the intervening including classes and making a reference to the more concrete subject only from the broadest class in the hierarchical chain. Thus, in the example above, a cross-reference would be made from ZOOLOGY directly to CATS, until, one supposes, books on the intervening subject MAMMALS might be purchased by the library. In that way something of the bare skeleton of the entire subject structure might be retained.

ASCENDING REFERENCES

The second major device Cutter employed to restore the subject relationships lost by the specific entry process was to make "ascending" cross-references from specific to general subjects (rule 188). Given the fact that "much information about limited topics is to be found in more general works," references from the limited topics might be made to those including classes where further information might be found, such as from CATHEDRALS to the including classes CHRISTIAN ART and ECCLESIASTICAL ARCHITECTURE.

Earlier in his career, Cutter seems to have held the opinion that such ascending references would be as thoroughly done as those of the descending kind. In 1870, when reporting to the Boston Athenaeum trustees, he included them in his description of work to be done before printing the Athenaeum's catalog began:

> The last work before sending copy to the printer must be, if we wish to have all safe, to go over the whole of the catalogue, make out a list of the subjects and see . . . whether the proper cross-references have been made from general to specific subjects . . . and also from specific to general, which is more important, because often the best things on special subjects are found in more general works, and from allied subjects to one another. . . . These references are often of very great value. They suggest courses of investigation which an inquirer in his hurry or in a momentary inability to collect his ideas, might not remember or think of.[25]

When writing his subject rules, however, Cutter purposefully limited making ascending cross-references to only occasional instances. There appear to be three reasons (two obvious and one implied) for this limitation. First, Cutter considered it impossible to make all required references of the ascending sort in some consistent manner because there would have been so many of them as to make the task impossible. Upon some reflection the reason for this will be obvious. The narrower the subject in scope, the more possibilities there are, theoretically at least, that it will be subordinate to many subjects of broader scope and, concomitantly, that it will be referred to in many works of broader scope. This is particularly true of very concrete general subjects and especially true of individual subjects.[26] Furthermore, not all such references would have had equal value, some of them referring to comprehensive subjects where the books listed there treated the subordinate subject in a substantial manner, but others referring to comprehensive subjects where the books listed under them treated the subordinate topic only insubstantially. In the light of this unequal usefulness, Cutter wrote:

> The cataloger may very excusably not think of referring to those subjects [i.e., broader topics] or, if he thinks of it may deem the connection too remote to justify reference, and that he should be overloading the catalog with what would be generally useless.

A second reason why this part of the cross-reference system was to be limited arose out of Cutter's appreciation of the searching patterns of the public. The cross-reference system was Cutter's attempt to reinstate in his specific entry system some aid for cultivated inquirers who searched for subjects in terms of their classificatory relationships. Cutter judged the searching patterns of these inquirers to have certain restrictions, however. He recognized, for example, that some might conduct what today is called a generic search, a search in which an inquirer "desired to take an absolutely complete survey of [a] subject, or who was willing to spend unlimited time in getting information on some detail." Thus, in a search for any particular subject, books directly on the subject, books on subdivisions of the subject, and treatments of the subject in works of broader or related scope would constitute, theoretically at least, the basic set of items considered relevant to the search. If a dictionary catalog were to aid in this kind of search, cross-references would be needed that branched out in all directions from any particular subject entered in the catalog.

It was precisely this kind of expanded search that Cutter mentioned sparingly, questioning whether it was ever carried on as seriously and thoroughly as implied. And because of his skepticism about this search procedure, he concluded that the one conducting it must use means other than simply the public catalog to complete it, in general relying on one's "knowledge and intelligence" to find what was needed.[27]

Searches for "comprehensive subjects" were of even greater importance than generic searches as a way to characterize catalog use by cultivated inquirers. In contrast to generic searches which branched out in all directions, comprehensive subject searches were primarily conducted as a descent through a hierarchically ordered structure of subjects. Cutter described this in 1869 as the basic search technique of the professors who constituted the chief clientele of the Harvard alphabetico-classed catalog and who, "engaged in some limited field of investigation," would learn the structural characteristics of that field.[28]

Cutter's use of the term "field of investigation," synonymous in this sense with "comprehensive subject," is important for the picture of the scholar it conveys. A scholar was one who, having learned by previous schooling that verified knowledge was also classified knowledge, approached the task of gaining new knowledge as an exercise in classificatory distinctions. One did not simply look for subjects as if they were unique entities isolated from all other subjects in a vast unorganized conglomerate, but rather as hierarchically located classificatory positions. Given any particular general subject, one expected that it would be subdivided (unless it was very concrete), and that its subdivisions considered together gave fullness to the concept represented by the subject itself. If one were not sure of the exact nature of the subject itself, it was then more appropriate to begin with the supposed including class of the topic that would add the prerequisite definition of the particular subject of interest in order to work down to it in a correct classificatory descent.

This approach demanded a lot from the inquirer. It especially required the reader to bring to the catalog a basic knowledge of classificatory relationships. Moreover, one would have to learn to adjust even that basic knowledge to the classificatory structure of the catalog at hand. Finally, if the including class of a subject were not immediately apparent, the scholarly inquirer was obliged to learn that relationship. Cutter knew that the lack of such knowledge made searching for unfamiliar subjects difficult at times for even the scholarly inquirer.

However, Cutter was also sanguine that the very nature of the scholarly mind and its training made up for the foregoing difficulties. In describing a hypothetical search for works on the badger by learned persons unfamiliar with the topic, he suggested that difficulty would be expected at the outset of the search. But he added:

A man generally does know some of the including classes of his subject. In the present case he would know that the badger is an animal, and would look for it in some zoological encyclopaedia. By the description there he would find to what subclass it belongs, and how he could pursue his inquiry farther, if he chose.29

Cutter's estimate of scholarly inquiry is obviously a classical picture of subject thinking and confirms more than ever the classificatory orientation he brought to what constituted appropriate subject access. In the present case it also provided the basis for the main outlines of his cross-reference system, that it must necessarily contain downward directed cross-references, but that it need include no more than a selection of coordinate or illustrative references and even fewer ascending references. The reason was obvious. Scholarly inquiry was by definition a descending classificatory activity.

A third and final reason why Cutter may have limited the use of ascending cross-references, but one that is only implied in his writing, has to do with subarrangement techniques in his specific entry system. Here, however, one must move away from his subject rules section per se to the section of his *Rules* entitled "Arrangement: Subjects" (rules 339–343), which deals with filing.

It has already been noted that one way to view Cutter's specific entry system is as a rotated version of the alphabetico-classed catalog based on the idea of significance order. In other words, given the identification of the specific subject of any particular book as the last element in a classificatory chain of subject terms, specific entry procedure rotated the chain of terms by one position to enter the work under the specific term. Thus, books on the concrete general subject Cats and books on the individual subject Italy would have classed and specific entry rotated chains as listed in the table in Figure 9A.

It is important to note that what follows each instance of the specifically entered subjects CATS and ITALY are in fact classified strings-of-terms which function as subarrangement words. Cutter did not allow such strings to remain in the catalog, however, except where the number of works under a specific subject merited their subarrangement in some further fashion. For example, if there were only a total of four works under CATS, one each in the first two categories and two in the last, he would have entered them as four single books under the specific entry term CATS alone (Figure 9B1). However, if there were, say, ten books on cats, of which six were on the first topic alone, he would have considered identifying at least that group by using some subarrangement device. He might have placed all the books except that group under a subarrangement term such as General works or even the term CATS directly and those six books under a subarrangement

A. *Table of Classed Entries Rotated as Specific Entries*

Classed Entry Strings	*Specific Entry Rotations*
DOMESTIC ANIMALS–CATS	CATS–DOMESTIC ANIMALS
VETERINARY SCIENCE–DISEASES–CATS	CATS–VETERINARY SCIENCE–DISEASES
ZOOLOGY–VERTEBRATES–MAMMALS–CATS	CATS–ZOOLOGY–VERTEBRATES–MAMMALS
ART–PAINTING–ITALY	ITALY–ART–PAINTING
ART–SCULPTURE–ITALY	ITALY–ART–SCULPTURE
LANGUAGE–ETYMOLOGY–ITALY	ITALY–LANGUAGE–ETYMOLOGY
LANGUAGE–GRAMMAR–ITALY	ITALY–LANGUAGE–GRAMMAR
LAW–ITALY	ITALY–LAW
ZOOLOGY–VERTEBRATES–ORNITHOLOGY–ITALY	ITALY–ZOOLOGY–VERTEBRATES–ORNITHOLOGY

B. *Table of Possible Subarrangement Patterns*

1. For books on Cats,
   1) If only 4 books total: Enter all directly under CATS
   2) If 10 books, of which 6 are on the first topic above:

CATS	or,	CATS
General works		(4 books here)
(4 books here)		
Domestic animals		*As pets*
(6 books here)		(6 books here)

2. For books on Cats or on Italy if classification substructure not retained:

CATS	ITALY
Diseases	*Art* (in general)
Domestic animals	*Language*
Veterinary science	*Painting*
Zoology	*Sculpture*
	Zoology

FIG. 9.   Subarrangement in Cutter

term such as Domestic animals, or, if merited, under some more explicit term such as *As pets* (Figure 9B1, second example). In a similar fashion, he sometimes combined groups to provide at least some useful subarrangement. For example, if there were three works each on painting and sculpture in a large file of entries under ITALY, he probably could have combined them as a single group of six works under –ART, awaiting some further time when the more specific subarrangement categories became necessary. Files extensively subarranged in this manner most often occurred under countries and, if carried out in the fullest manner possible, would amount to specific entry with classed subarrangement.

When subarrangement included even a single more inclusive term, however, it became important to Cutter's cross-reference system because in every such instance Cutter inadvertently included what amounted to an ascending relationship. That is to say, subarrangement terms that were more inclusive functioned as clues showing broader topics under which an inquirer might find other works that would be relevant to a search—for example, under ART for general works that might include the topic of Italian art, and under ZOOLOGY for general works that might include something on Cats among other topics treated. Thus, although strictly classified subarrangement was not consistently done in a specific entry catalog, to the degree that it was included it lessened the necessity to include formally stated ascending cross-references.

It should be noted at this point that Cutter was aware of and somewhat sensitive to the fact that his subarrangement procedure allowed the incursion of classification sequences (albeit only at subarrangement level) within a dictionary catalog that otherwise demanded specific entry. He knew that the entire sequence (including the specific entry itself) might appear as classification to the uninitiated inquirer. And when greatly carried out, classified subarrangement made his dictionary catalog appear like an alphabetico-classed catalog. One way he was able to reduce qualms about it was to insist that no more than a single subarrangement level be used under specific entry headings, these in turn to be arranged for the most part alphabetically or pragmatically. Thus, if there were sufficient works on Italian art in general, Italian paintings, and Italian sculpture or on both the veterinary science and diseases of cats separately, these should be subarranged in one-level sequences as shown in Figure 9B2.

Despite the conflict that it engendered, Cutter justified his subarrangement practice, describing its appearance under countries as a trend in dictionary catalog development.

> But the tendency of the dictionary catalog is toward national classification; that is, in separating what relates to the parts of a subject, as is required by its *specific* principle, it necessarily brings together all that relates to a country in every respect, as it would what relates to any other individual.[30]

And although he realized that it gave the appearance of an alphabetical classed catalog, it was not important because "the main object of the dictionary, ready reference"—the immediate access to the specific (especially those that are concrete and individual) subjects of books—had been attained.[31]

SYNOPTIC TABLE

A final device Cutter considered for restoring the subject relationships lost by the specific entry process was to include a "synoptic table" of the subject relationships in the system as an appendix to the catalog. By this he meant an index chart that placed the subjects in classificatory order, much like the method he suggested for revising the system of downward references. He suggested the possibility of providing a synoptic table in the first three editions of his *Rules.* And he had himself begun one at the time that he began printing the Boston Athenaeum catalog. By the last edition of his *Rules,* however, he not only concluded that, like complete ascending cross-references, the worth of such a table was questionable, but suggested that one could find such information already extant in the tables and indexes of the then current Expansive and Decimal classification schemes.[32]

It is perhaps fitting to close a commentary of Cutter's subject rules with the preceding point because in a very important way it symbolizes Cutter's true orientation in giving subject access to information. Cutter began and ended his more than forty years of library work by working on explicit classification systems—Harvard's alphabetico-classed catalog at the start, his own Expansive Classification at the close. The specific entry dictionary catalog did not represent a different kind of subject access, but rather only a permuted form of what was at its root a classificatory approach to knowledge. The outline of that classificatory base was decidedly nineteenth or even eighteenth century in much of its structure. Regardless of its structural origins, however, to view his system as something less than a particular form of classificatory thinking is not only to do it in an injustice, but also to invite its misinterpretation. And misinterpretation is, in fact, the best way to describe how his system has fared in the years since he made it.

CHAPTER 7

The Transition from Cutter to the Twentieth Century

Subject Heading Lists

Alphabetical subject catalogs appear to have gained widespread use only after the first general subject heading list, the American Library Association's *List of Subject Headings for Use in Dictionary Catalogs,* was published in 1895.[1] Before that, alphabetical subject catalogs when made at all were based on headings borrowed from notable printed library catalogs or simply on catchwords taken from the titles of books. The insistence that such catalogs incorporate uniform terminology and a system of cross-references, both difficult and time-consuming tasks, easily discouraged their construction.

The difficulty of their construction in concert with typical library organizational patterns may explain the early popularity of the shelf classification of books as the principal means of subject access. The shelves of library collections were typically closed to all but a few persons. Thus, requests for subject information, often phrased as general requests for reading guidance, were necessarily directed to the librarian. The shelves, arranged in classified order, served librarians well because librarians, having been educated by college curricula that typically stressed the classificatory nature of all knowledge, could respond to requests in terms of the classified categories of the shelf arrangement.

The rise of open-shelf policies during the 1890s altered this subject access picture drastically. Patrons now able to go directly to the shelves could browse easily enough for their favorite types of reading. But when they wanted books on particular subjects, an alphabetical subject index became necessary. Dictionary subject catalogs appeared to serve the latter need better than the subject indexes of classification schemes. They emphasized common subject names. And they listed entries directly under those common subject names rather than requiring the users to go from the index to the classified arrangement. The use of common subject names and a simple direct arrangement were im-

158

portant because they appeared to be best for the common people who came into the library. Common people were, of course, the chief object of the library movement's cultural uplift objective. In contrast, classified catalogs appeared to cater to those users who were more highly educated, those, in other words, who often represented the upper classes.[2]

The 1895 American Library Association *List* also represented a significantly new direction and opportunity in subject access work because it signaled the beginning of dependence on a published authority list of headings. The *List* incorporated the standard features of dictionary subject catalogs found in both Cutter and twentieth-century catalogs—such things as controlled vocabulary and cross-references. But one should be wary at this point of concluding that because such features were included the resulting work was a wholesale rendition of Cutter's subject system. Julia Pettee's reminiscence some years later suggests on the contrary that little of Cutter's connection between subject headings and classificatory notions about subjects was carried over.

> In these early first years, although Cutter had brilliantly outlined in his Rules a section on subject headings, his "syndetic" had not permeated our thinking [*sic*]. Our headings were mainly index captions, care being taken to weed out synonyms and put in obvious cross references. To the rank and file of catalogers the idea that the dictionary catalog had any relation to a systematic classification of knowledge had not dawned. We revelled in the new A.L.A. *List of subject headings* then just published, chose what seemed to fit the book and let the relationships go by the board. No wonder the results were sometimes appalling.[3]

Pettee's comment is instructive, but it reveals only a glimmer of what actually took place. The fact is Cutter's intellectual framework of reference and, especially, the most important features of his subject access thinking that that framework prompted—the classificatory nature of subjects in and of themselves, the relationship of subjects to books, and the relationship of subjects to the public—did not survive the transition to the twentieth century unscathed. Instead, they became transformed, taking on new meanings in the process. Recognition of the character of the transformation they underwent is fundamental to an understanding of how Cutter has been interpreted in the twentieth century. Moreover, it is especially pertinent to an understanding of the practices and the explanations offered by twentieth-century catalogers of what is involved in both subject access work in general and in dictionary subject cataloging in particular.

The Loss of Cutter's Contextual Elements

The most obvious characteristic of writings dealing with subject access during the post-Cutter era is their lack of reference to or apparent comprehension of the most fundamental contextual elements on which his system was based. For example, except for the prefatory footnote in the American Library Association's *List* that Cutter followed "the principle of concrete cataloging," there are no references at all to Cutter's sense of discrimination among kinds of subjects.[4] This does not mean that examples of particular subjects that belonged to one or another of his three categories of subjects (individual, concrete general, abstract general) were not referred to nor that there was no sense of differentiation in the breadth of subjects. Persons and places as subjects were, in fact, a constant matter of discussion. But persons and places were not set apart categorically as individual subjects. And references to general and specific subjects came to indicate only a general notion of relative subject breadth rather than Cutter's more rigorous attempt at denoting subject nomenclature.

The lack of differentiation between kinds of subjects was paralleled by a corresponding lack of reference to a significance order based on kinds of subjects, especially Cutter's notion that individual subjects were necessarily included in general subjects of any kind and thus were more specific in relation to them. This too did not mean that ideas of classificatory inclusion relationships were altogether lacking. Writers regularly referred to the subordination of specific subjects to those broader subjects that included them, superordinate and subordinate subjects together comprising the matter of broad classes of literature. But such notions functioned in only the most general way rather than with the greater precision that Cutter had given to them. The lack of precision is perhaps nowhere more apparent than in the tendency to denote uncritically any subheading as a subdivision of a topic rather than to differentiate, as Cutter had done between those that were technically subdivisions in an inclusion sense and those that represented broader concepts and that functioned therefore in a manner different than classificatory subdivision.

In a certain sense the failure of subject catalogers to retain Cutter's framework of reference should not be found strange. Even during the period in which Cutter was most active in American Library Association deliberations, there appears to have been considerable difficulty in accepting his system or even understanding it. For example, the association formed a Committee on an Index to Subject Headings in 1879 to devise a code of subject heading rules and a list of subject headings. Besides Cutter, the committee included Richard R. Bowker, Frederic B.

Perkins, Stephen B. Noyes, and William I. Fletcher, each of whom had the background and credentials to understand Cutter's work, particularly its classificatory background. The failure of the committee to achieve its objectives might be formally attributed to logistical matters, 1880 having been particularly difficult for association leaders. But it is also significant that in the final report of the committee in 1881, Fletcher attributed some of the committee's difficulties to the inability of its members to agree on a final authority in devising subject headings, either in the form of a code of rules or in the form of a cooperative method for deciding individual cases of subject heading choice and form. Even more important, while the final choice of a subject catalog—the dictionary catalog—was not in question, the only extant set of rules for such a catalog was Cutter's *Rules*. Fletcher referred to them as providing a useful discussion of particular points, but it is plain that he did not treat them as conclusive.[5]

The American Library Association did not again resume subject cataloging cooperation until 1892 when another committee was formed, this time charged more specifically with compiling an authoritative list of subject headings rather than a code of rules. Here again the dictionary catalog format was the accepted type of catalog. But in its 1893 report the committee recommended two important procedures—subarrangement *by place* under arts and sciences and the use of adjectival country names with literature headings (e.g., FRENCH LITERATURE instead of FRANCE. *Literature*). Both procedures were directly contrary to Cutter's *Rules*. In fact, the first of the two was specifically designed to break up what was considered to be "a confusing accumulation of sub-heads under the principal countries" produced by following Cutter's *Rules*.[6] This committee's decision is important not simply because it contradicted particular procedures in Cutter's *Rules*, but because it contradicted Cutter's fundamental notion of significance order in which places as individual subjects were considered the more specific terms in combinations including general subjects and thus required entry rather than subentry in the catalog.

The 1894 report of the committee showed even more disagreement with Cutter's procedures when it changed Cutter's condition for the exceptional inversion of compound headings from "decidedly more significant" to merely "more significant." Subsequently, the list published in 1895 incorporated such headings as HISTORY, ANCIENT and HISTORY, MODERN (contrary to Cutter's use of ANCIENT HISTORY and MODERN HISTORY), and prompted the inclusion of a "minority report" that expressed Cutter's contrary position.[7] Here again, the importance of the change is not simply the use of particular headings different than those that Cutter prescribed nor even what appears to be a minor change in terminology, but rather the failure to understand that be-hind Cutter's prescription for term order was a sense of classificatory relationships and significance that gave him a rationale for term order.

Cutter's Diminished Role

Besides the fact that public discussion of subject heading work was at odds with Cutter's approach, Cutter's personal role and influence in such matters was decidedly less extensive and enthusiastic than one might have expected. In fact, it may be concluded that, although Cutter held the opinion that the dictionary catalog was the most useful kind of catalog for libraries in general, he was singularly inattentive to dictionary subject catalog issues after 1876. He made no changes of any significance in the subject catalog section of his *Rules* in the second to fourth editions. This was in marked contrast to his work on its author catalog section where the issue of how to name corporate bodies influenced by his growing appreciation of common usage considerations prompted him to reformulate rules in a substantive manner. Although he orally reported Fletcher's opinion regarding the work of the Committee on an Index to Subject Headings in 1881 and chaired the meeting in which the second committee reported in 1893, he offered no recorded comment in either instance on the conclusions reached in the reports, despite the differing points of view they represented. Cutter was also a member of the committee that signed the 1895 A.L.A. *List,* but it is unlikely that he participated to any great extent in the compilation of the list, having been in Europe for almost the entire year of the committee's principal efforts (1893–94) and thereafter occupying himself with setting up the Forbes Library in Northampton, Massachusetts. Even his minority report in the initial A.L.A. *List* was provided only in the third person, suggesting thereby that it was not a direct offering from his own pen. His brief explanation of subject heading work, "Some Hints on Subject Cataloging in Dictionary Style," was included in the second edition of the *List* in 1898, but was no more than a summary of a few of the main points found in his *Rules.*[8]

None of this is meant to suggest that Cutter lost interest in subject access problems in general. In the face of those who argued that subject access was unimportant and too expensive for libraries to provide, he raised an early voice on behalf of its absolute necessity. But after 1876 the principal way Cutter expressed his concern for subject access was not in the particulars of the dictionary subject catalog. Rather it was in developing a viable shelf classification scheme, a task to which he assiduously devoted himself to the end of his days. He was convinced that a properly made shelf classification held greater promise than the dictionary subject catalog for direct and intelligent usefulness to the librarian's work.[9]

Another reason why Cutter's role and influence in subject heading thought was muted had to do with the increasingly circumscribed intellectual tradition which he represented as the century wore on. The intellectual framework of reference that formed the basis of Cutter's subject heading system was an American adaptation of Scottish thought that dated from the eighteenth century. Cutter had been schooled in it during his years at Harvard College before the Civil War. By the time he wrote his subject rules, however, the American expression of Scottish realism and especially the notion of mental faculties essential to it were already on the wane. As the professional library movement grew and accepted new librarians into its ranks who had been educated after the Civil War in a different philosophical tradition, the Scottish tradition increasingly became a less than familiar basis for discussing any philosophical question, let alone subject heading theory. It is no wonder, therefore, that what might have been plain for Cutter was not a matter of general concurrence among many of his younger colleagues.[10]

It is also likely that Cutter's subject access thinking underwent at least some significant changes during the same period. By 1879 Cutter was already claiming the principle of evolution as a basis for the logic of subject sequencing in at least the sciences portion of his classification scheme. Two decades later his claims regarding that principle were even more broadly applied.[11] Cutter's brief instructions to dictionary subject catalogers included in the A.L.A. *List* also give evidence of some change in terminology if not in meaning. He described the basic rule for subject cataloging in the following words:

> Every book should be entered under the word that most clearly expresses its main subject. This designation should be as exact as possible, neither too restricted, for then part of the book's contents will be wasted, nor too general, because it is not the purpose to make a classed catalog.[12]

That his reference to a main subject was synonymous with his more formal notion of a specific subject is confirmed by his use of the latter term in the succeeding paragraph. But "main" does not have nearly the classificatory bearing that "specific" suggests. And his suggestion that "part of the book's contents will be wasted" if a heading were "too restricted" could be interpreted as a loss of access to some element of the entire topical contents of a book rather than simply to some part of the book's known or validated subject. Interpreting both of his comments in the preceding ways seems unwarranted, given that the remainder of his instructions align so well with the procedures outlined in his *Rules*. Nevertheless, his statements here cause one to wonder whether the meanings behind his procedures were slowly shifting.

A final reason for Cutter's reticence to pursue dictionary subject cataloging further was the growing pragmatism of the times. Beginning in the 1870s and culminating in what has since been called the Progressive Era, American society underwent a major socio-economic shift which brought about a significant reorientation of its societal values. One of the chief marks of that shift was a growing interest in solving societal problems by practical means. Efforts to provide efficient bureaucratic organizations and expedient decision making overshadowed and eventually diminished interest in idealistic discussions and theoretical distinctions.[13]

One need look no further than the changing leadership of the library profession, especially in the person of Melvil Dewey and the scores of librarians trained at his School of Library Economy, to see how quickly that same spirit overtook the American Library Association. By the mid-1890s Cutter and other library leaders who had been educated in the philosophical currents of an earlier day had been effectively replaced in national library leadership roles by others who were deeply committed to achieving immediate and pragmatic solutions to library problems. The new leaders showed relatively little interest in pursuing the kinds of theoretical questions in cataloging that had been raised during earlier decades in writings such as Cutter's *Rules*.[14]

Even Cutter seems to have been pressed to pursue that course of pragmatic action. The stringent economies of his Forbes Library situation made it possible for him to catalog and classify only a small part of the 90,000 volumes accumulated there under his direction between 1894 and 1903. Thus, when schemes for distributing printed catalog cards became popular during the 1890's and when the Library of Congress began distributing its cards in 1901, Cutter welcomed such services despite whatever differences they represented in fundamentals. They offered him an expedient solution to a critical problem, and he seemed not inclined to argue about it on the basis of theoretical distinctions. Besides, he held the opinion that if one were not satisfied with the cards, it was easy enough once having received them to change them to what one felt was more appropriate. The task of completing his classification scheme, including its writing, printing, and promotion, also assumed exhausting proportions after 1893. Thus unlike the two previous decades, he discontinued all writing that involved substantial theoretical issues simply to get this work done.[15]

In the end, therefore, neither the pragmatic climate of opinion nor his personal situation made it favorable nor even useful for Cutter to investigate further, much less struggle with, the fundamental intellectual bases of a subject heading system. His earlier subject work amounted to a tentative foray into that realm. But by 1900 or so its conceptual foundations lay buried under a mountain of other more pressing changes and concerns.

Cutter's Contribution

The foregoing picture of Cutter's muted activity on behalf of subject cataloging work and the loss of the ideas most basic to his subject system makes a reevaluation of his role in the development of dictionary subject cataloging tradition necessary. The common view of Cutter's role has been that Cutter's subject system was adopted more or less *in toto* by those who followed him. Variations that did occur were only matters of degree and emphasis rather than differences of a more substantial nature. It seems obvious, however, that the transmission of Cutter's system suffered without the accompanying transmission of ideas as fundamental as those noted above, because regardless of what particular procedures of Cutter's might have been incorporated in the ongoing tradition, the result could not have been the same as Cutter had originally intended. And if that was the case, then there is good reason to ask what Cutter's role in the tradition actually was.

The first point in understanding the nature of Cutter's contribution is that Cutter's approach to subject heading work did not rise from a cooperative tradition. His subject rules were a personal creation. They represented his rationalization of procedures necessary to make a subject catalog that was logically consistent. His subject rules, like his author rules and later his *Expansive Classification,* were widely consulted by librarians and usually noted with appreciation even during his lifetime. But they appear never to have been adopted completely by any large number of libraries, and they never became the sole basis for fundamental discussions of meaning and theory within the library movement. In short, like many other innovations of that especially creative period of professional library development before 1900, Cutter's subject cataloging rules represented only one alternative among others. It was perhaps an unusually creative alternative, but it did not occupy the kind of dominant position that would have automatically made it the core of the tradition that subsequently developed.

A second point is that while his work represented a personal creative endeavor, it was nevertheless closely related to the dictionary cataloging movement that had preceded him. Dictionary subject cataloging came on the American scene in the late 1840s with the express purpose of making books accessible in terms of their specific subjects rather than in terms of the classes that included those subjects. The idea of a specific subject had arisen in the context of classed catalog development and the general philosophical ideas that were basic to that development. Because Cutter adopted that same idea of a specific subject for his system, his work was similar to that of his predecessors with respect to the meaning of subjects in the subject access process.

On the other hand, Cutter was displeased with the chief method that earlier dictionary subject catalogers followed for providing specific subject access—the use of undisciplined subject words taken from the titles of books. He was also displeased with the earlier practice of severing specific subjects from their classificatory origins. Thus, Cutter instituted procedures, such as the use of a controlled vocabulary and the use of cross-references, that made his version of the dictionary subject catalog very different from those of his predecessors. In sum, Cutter adopted without much change the idea of specific subject which was fundamental to the earlier tradition, but also instituted procedures which displayed specific subjects in an altogether different manner. Of course, the earlier idea of specific subjects does not appear to have been transmitted by Cutter to those who came after him. And this, when combined with the fact that Cutter's successors used his subject cataloging procedures with essentially different meanings, draws one to conclude that Cutter's most important contribution to the ongoing subject cataloging tradition resided neither in the realm of the idea of subjects nor in the realm of subject cataloging practices.

There was one aspect of earlier subject cataloging work adopted by Cutter that did survive into the twentieth century, however. In fact, it has become essential to current subject heading work. It resided neither in the realm of the idea of a subject nor in the realm of procedures, but rather had to do with the objectives of subject cataloging. The earlier dictionary subject catalog tradition differed from classed cataloging in that having chosen to give access to books in terms of specific subjects, it made it imperative for subject catalogers to focus on the specific subject of each book—to identify, in other words, that specific subject in every instance possible. Classed catalog procedure was not committed to identifying specific subjects in this way. In fact, the specific subject of any particular book might easily be bypassed in the rush to find an appropriate including class.

Cutter zeroed in on the concern of early dictionary subject catalogers to identify the specific subjects of books. In his hands, however, this objective did not remain a matter of convenience to be achieved only when book titles allowed it. Rather, Cutter made the goal of identifying the specific subject of each book a mandate. His most essential contribution to the entire dictionary subject cataloging tradition was, in effect, to clarify, discipline, and codify that goal so that it would be applied in every instance.

To conclude that Cutter's essential contribution to dictionary subject cataloging was this mandate might not seem important in the present day. Beginning with what is considered to be the specific subjects of books in every instance is now a commonplace assumption when providing subject access. It must be remembered, however, that Cutter wrote in a day when making the specific subjects of individual books the starting point for subject access work was a nebulous objective in a dictionary subject cataloging tradition that lacked any serious discipline. Cutter was the first cataloger to state the objective as an axiomatic goal. Dictionary catalogs, Cutter wrote, "are differentiated not, as is often said, by the dictionary having specific entry, but (1) by its giving specific entries in all cases and (2) by its individual entry."[16] "In all cases" is remarkable for the thoroughness that it demands. As previously indicated, no subject cataloging system then extant could make that claim.

The latter part of Cutter's definition indicated the context in which the idea of specific subjects was to be understood. "Individual entry" was Cutter's way of referring to the general ideas of subject structure and significance order which underlay his procedures for implementing the subject access goal. Those ideas did not survive him. But his emphasis on beginning with the specific subject of each book did. One finds Cutter to have been in the unique position of having passed on to the dictionary subject cataloging tradition the fullest expression of its mandate—book-by-book subject analysis—but without the meaning of subject under which his system operated. The meanings implicit in the pursuit of book-by-book subject analysis are what changed between Cutter and his successors. In fact, one will not fully appreciate how twentieth-century dictionary subject cataloging has developed without pinpointing the essential nature of those changed meanings, for they have given an entirely different use to the procedures which Cutter's successors borrowed from him.

Changed Meanings

BOOKS AND SUBJECTS ARE COMPLEMENTARY

The first difference in fundamental meanings between Cutter's work and what followed him is that while both began with the subjects of individual books in every instance, the latter brought to a focus what the dictionary tradition had only begun to express, that books and subjects are the natural complements of one another. In the newer tradition, books and subjects became identical for all practical purposes. Subjects gained their validity—became subjects by definition—simply by being the topical contents of books. This equation broke the grip of the older classificatory tradition that Cutter had attempted to incorporate in his work in which subjects were equated first and foremost with established elements of a socially determined classificatory map of the universe of knowledge. In the older tradition, a book might "treat of" a subject, but the subject itself was a subject not because it was the content of a book, but because it had gained prior validity in the social process of classificatory differentiation. To provide subject access to the book was no more or less than to identify whether the book treated a validated topic and to place the book in a document class with other books that also gave evidence of treating the same subject.

This change necessitated a reformulation of the idea of new subjects. In the new equation, any book written on any topic not previously denoted in any way represented a new subject. Therefore, new subjects constituted a problem of much greater intensity. New subjects were equated by and large with new books. And new books were appearing in ever-increasing numbers.

A SPECIFIC SUBJECT IS *THE SUBJECT* OF A BOOK

The second fundamental difference in meaning, following from the identification of subjects automatically with the topical contents of books, was a corresponding shift in the meaning of the idea of the specific or special subject of a book. In the older tradition, at least as Cutter represented it, a book's specific subject referred to the single most concrete subject treated in the book. Identifying a book's single specific subject in this way was dependent on the discrimination noted above between two kinds of topical contents—those that were recognized subjects in their own right no matter how named, and those that were indistinct topics described only by combinations of other established subject names. Indistinct topics were not, in other words, single subjects in their own right, but only several single subjects joined together to name a topic. The existence of two kinds of topical contents led to Cutter's two-fold procedure for the entry of books in the subject catalog. The first kind were entered directly under the entire term established as the legitimate name of the subject, rather than under a class of which that single subject was a part. The second kind was more of a problem, however, because the indistinct or unestablished description could not be used as is—that is, as a subject defined by classificatory relationships. "Specific" in that context meant that single subject element of the description that was most concrete and thus included in a classificatory sense by all the other subjects which made up the description.

With the loss of the distinction between established and unestablished topics, the topical contents of any book became its single specific subject no matter how named. "Specific subject" became, in other words, a denotation for the subject of any book, that is, for its essential and entire contents. In practical terms this meant that all books were approached as if they were in the first category of the two that Cutter had delineated.

SUBJECT CATALOGING MEANS SUBJECT NAMING

The third fundamental difference in meanings, following naturally from the shift in meaning of the notion of a specific subject, was that the primary activity of subject cataloging came to be redefined as the sheer problem of naming "the subjects" of books. Cutter's approach to the subject cataloging of any particular book had always begun by identifying the book's specific subject. The process of identification was in effect a choice between subjects. Only after choosing the subject did he technically deal with the form of name, that is, choosing between one synonym or another or, for subject names that included more than one word, choosing between different sequences of the words in the name. With the loss of a classificatory basis for discriminating between established and unestablished topical contents of books and the concomitant use of the term "specific subject" to denote the totality of what any book was about, the overall choice procedure was also significantly affected.

One choice remained the same, of course, choosing to enter a work under its own name (whatever that might be) rather than under the name of a class that included that name. It amounted to following Cutter's first procedure without the complications of the second. When the subject of a book was only a single word, that choice was simple indeed. For example, a book whose specific subject is Iron should be entered under that name. It should not be entered under an including class such as METALS. Nor by implication should it be subentered under its including class in a string-of-terms such as METALS–IRON. This choice was so apparent that it was really not much of a choice. But when subject names included a series of combined terms considered together to be the legitimate subject name in every instance, the problem of determining the including class was overshadowed by the implications of the name form itself. For example, subjects whose names were of the compound variety, such as combinations of Ornithology and New England or Movement of fluids and Plants, had to include all their elements in the name entered in the catalog in every instance. And where such instances increased in numbers as new subjects in new books appeared, the result was to struggle with what constituted a specific rather than a classed entry *form* of subject name.

Name form did affect whether the resulting entry was specific or classed even for Cutter. That is plain to see in his rules 164–165 where he dealt with combinations of individual and general or scientific subjects, and especially in his rule 175 on compound subject names. But there were important differences in the overall process between Cutter and those who dealt with the same problem afterwards. First, when entering a work with an unestablished topical content, Cutter distinguished between terms in order to choose an entry term from among those in the description, not to choose which one came first in a heading that included all the words. Second, because the very process of distinguishing between established and unestablished names tended to place many, if not most, of the combination name forms in the unestablished group, there were fewer legitimate subject names involving more than one word in Cutter's system than in the newer procedure where all name combinations were considered to be legitimate candidates for subject headings. Third, for Cutter the basis for choice of the entry word among all the words in a compound subject name, like his basis for choice of entry in unestablished topics, was itself predicated on a significance order that was lost to the ensuing generation. Fourth, even when entertaining the notion of writing a compound subject name in some unnatural order such as inversion, Cutter exercised that option only sparingly because in his opinion only a relatively few compound subject names passed his restrictions on the exercise of the option.

At the same time, there were also certain likenesses between the way Cutter and the way those who followed him handled subject naming problems. First, Cutter's use of subarrangement, especially when done regularly with, for example, places combined with general subjects, looked like an attempt on his part to use the combined elements of a subject description to indicate the topical contents of books in the catalog, regardless of the fact that entry itself had been formally limited by him to only the most specific term in the description.

Second, and far more important, the process by which Cutter determined whether the topical contents of a book was a legitimate subject in its own right and the process of naming a subject in subject heading work after him were almost indistinguishable. The process of determining whether the topical contents of a book was a subject in its own right required some measure by which Cutter could judge the validity of the topic. Lacking an explicit authority list of topics established as subjects, Cutter appealed to what a consensus among writers on the topic might show. He concluded that the legitimacy of the topic as a subject was demonstrated "if several works were written on it" and it was given a particular name in those works.[17] If this were the case, the topic could be considered a subject rather than simply an indistinct notion.

There is a certain practical truth to this procedure. Topics of thought do tend to become defined and thus "established" by a procedure of this kind. But this procedure is also close to another in which one attempts not to determine whether a topical content is established per se, but rather only to determine what an appropriate name for it should be. In other words, if the beginning question had been, "What should this topical content be called?" one may also look at several works not to see if the topic was something called a subject, but rather only to see how the topic already assumed to be a legitimate subject was named. The first procedure determined the validity or invalidity of the topic's status by noting the consistency of naming and, one supposes, the general alikeness of the various discussions about it. Failure to find consistency in naming made it necessary to enter the book under something other than the group of words that comprised its description. The notion of determining a name in the second procedure was not a judgment of validity or invalidity, but rather only a method of devising or writing a name. There was no failure in that process because failure to devise a name would have been simply failure to complete the process. In sum, the first process was one of conceptual discrimination, the second one only of description. The difference between the two processes was only a matter of one's point of view or intention. Cutter seems to have recognized this closeness implicitly when he noted in his discussion of specific subject choices that cases involving the determination of correct name form (a matter posterior to that process and placed by him in the second section of his subject rules) were "mixed with this, and sometimes hardly distinguishable from it."[18]

When, in subject heading work after Cutter, the idea of a subject became synonymous with the contents of books and the distinction between established and unestablished topics was lost, the principal problem that remained for subject catalogers was how subjects should be named. In fact, the whole of subject cataloging since Cutter's day may be seen as a development of that theme. One will find few if any substantial discussions of the need to choose between subjects because there are no such choices to be made. Most discussions of subject heading work now boil down to how to write subject names and, with the great increase in compound names, whether one or another formulation of a name is the most appropriate format. The various attempts to resolve that dilemma over the years, sometimes by analyzing the elements of names and other times by sheer appeals to usage, constitute one of the most fundamental characteristics of the development of subject heading work in the twentieth century.

SUBJECT CLASSIFICATION AND SUBJECT CATALOGING

The fourth and final fundamental difference in meanings follows from the first three differences already discussed. It centers on the relationship between subject classification and subject cataloging. In the older tradition, subject classification, a heritage of medieval and Greek philosophical thought, was concerned with the orderly arrangement of verified knowledge. It arose separately from the issue of what subjects were treated of in written records and was thus prior to and foundational to matters of subject catalog access. In short, the older classed catalog tradition arranged books according to categories of subjects which were anterior to and independent of the need to provide subject access to books.

This older view of classification was not without its limitations. Because the idea of a subject inherent in it was principally a function of logical definition, the number of topics generally enumerated as subjects was limited and their names were for the most part common, succinct, and uncomplicated in form. Further, the notion of subject order inherent in the older view was restricted in great measure to the hierarchical relationships that arose from the process of logical definition. But, as the number of new special subjects (especially as they were treated in books) began to increase and the new subjects increasingly had names that represented comparatively complex combinations of only extrinsically related terms, the capacity of traditional classification to represent adequately the new subjects in terms of their hierarchical structures failed. As a result, classed catalogs regularly resorted to class entry or class subentry rather than to any kind of entry that indicated the new subjects specifically.[19]

Cutter's use of classification in relation to subject cataloging represented an attempt to unite the older view of classification with the growing need to provide expanded subject access. As such, his view of classification combined some aspects of the older view with innovations of his own gained from his Scottish epistemology. He enhanced the classification methodology of the older tradition by an essentially unique solution to the problem of inclusion relationships. Because inclusion relationships based solely on logical definition could not accommodate subjects that were not intrinsically related, he added to that approach his notion of subject structure and inclusion relationships. Given three essentially distinct kinds of subjects ranging from the most abstract to the most concrete and a significance order inherent among them in which concreteness was tantamount to greater specificity, any set of co-ordinated subject terms might hypothetically have its most specific (i.e., its most concrete) subject component identified. This solution to classificatory inclusion relationships was significantly different than the earlier approach in that it did not depend solely on the implicit connotations and denotations of the terms involved, but rather on their categorical relationships. As a result, his approach to inclusion relationships significantly enhanced the older view.

Cutter also continued to observe the anterior position of classification in his formulation of the dictionary subject cataloging process. In spite of his insistence on beginning with books in every instance, he did not look for subjects in the modern sense in which the topical entirety of each book was automatically considered a subject. Rather, he looked for those topics treated in books that were validated by an anterior sense of classification. In fact, his notion of a specific subject has little meaning outside of that context. But by following this positional sense of classification, Cutter tied his system to the notion of distinct and stable subject names inherent in that older approach and, therefore to the need to distinguish subjects from other topics not considered to be subjects.

By the end of the nineteenth century, the growing insistence that subject cataloging should begin with the topics of books in every instance and the subsequent equation of the topical contents of books automatically with the notion of specific subjects—notions central to the dictionary subject cataloging movement and due in no small measure to Cutter's efforts—had the effect of severing the older anterior and preemptive relationship of classification to the subject cataloging process. One simply did not need a notion of prior classificatory origins in order to conclude that the topical contents of any particular book was a discrete subject, access to which must be provided in a subject catalog.

The severing of classification from its anterior relationship to subject cataloging had a profound effect on the role of Cutter's work. When combined with the loss to those who followed him of his notions of subject structure, it had the effect of making Cutter's entire approach to the relationship of classification and subject cataloging seem obscure. Lost were the older aspects of classification which he followed as well as his newer innovations with respect to inclusion relationships.

At the same time, the severing of classification from its preemptive position with respect to subject cataloging did not mean that classification was no longer related to subject cataloging. But the relationship assumed an accidental and unnecessary character. Classification became an operation accomplished after the subjects of books were identified, one that involved arranging or at least conceptualizing those subjects in some useful and often arbitrary order.

One major effect of severing classification from subject cataloging in this fundamental way was to give a dual focus to the idea of a subject itself. C. L. Drake observed this when he wrote in 1958 that the term "subject" appeared to have two essential meanings. The first had arisen out of the pedagogic delineations of departments of knowledge. This meaning corresponded to the meaning of subject basic to the older view of classification that depended heavily on relationships which arose out of logical definition. Drake suggested that, as such, a subject

> has, or is assumed to have, a more or less permanent, agreed, and definite content. It is part of the general body of knowledge which has been conventionally fenced off and given a more or less permanent and accepted form.20

The second meaning of the term "subject" focused in Drake's opinion on the topical contents of books themselves. In terms of the discussion here, this meaning of subjects represented the new tradition ushered in with dictionary subject cataloging. Drake described this sense of subject as indicative of

> something which is impermanent, changing, personal, unique. For, as the dictionary says, a subject may also be "that which forms or is chosen as the matter of thought, consideration or inquiry—a topic or theme" and, in particular, it may mean the theme of a literary composition, "what a book is about."21

The twofold identification of subjects that arose from the severing of classification and subject cataloging has been an important aspect of the development of subject access in the twentieth century. In one respect, one may view subsequent subject access theory as an attempt to re-relate the two views of subjects in some meaningful way, the most notable attempt being that of S. R. Ranganathan. Yet, the separation persists, especially in the specialized terminology which is seemingly applied to subjects in the two different contexts. For example, one finds reflections of this twofold view of subjects in the latest edition of the *Dewey Decimal Classification* where the editor speaks of subjects in two essentially different ways. He describes subjects rather uniformly as the main classes, divisions, subdivisions, etc., of the schedules. But then, using a somewhat different choice of terms, he also describes subjects as the property of books, that is, as their subject matter or what the books are about. When he speaks of them in the latter sense, the editor describes subjects as simple or as complex, and when complex, replete with "points of view," "aspects," "characteristics," etc. None of these terms were used to describe subjects when simply spoken of as the elements of a classification scheme.22

A second major effect of severing classification from subject cataloging was to open classification up to alternative conceptions of subject relationships and order. The older version of classification was closely tied to the process of deductive logical definition and as a result displayed subjects principally in hierarchical, genus-species relationships. But once the anterior relationship of classification to the notion of subjects in books was severed, the notion of subject order also gained a new freedom from the older notion of hierarchical subject order. Subjects, especially when seen as the contents of books, became in effect independent notions, the interrlationships of which were capable of being displayed in a variety of ways, not simply in terms of the older logical hierarchies.

It is interesting to note, however, that the potential implicit in the new freedom concerning subject relationships was not realized immediately. Classifiers experimented with different modes of subject order for decades. Cutter's use of a significance order based on degrees of concreteness seems never to have been adopted, for example, except perhaps in the context of alphabetico-classed systems.23 Those who first attempted to make book classification schemes seem to have returned instinctively to the older notions of genus-species order. Melvil Dewey's decimal classification, for example, consisted of a traditional hierarchical display of topics improved by the fact that it took more assiduous account of places as subdivisions.

Cutter also appears to have approached the classification of subjects in his book classification work with the same implicit recognition of traditional hierarchical order, his notions of significance order notwithstanding. At the same time, Cutter's constant experimentation with subject relationships in his classification work also brought him face to face with the fact that subject order was not necessarily bound to strict genus-species differentiation. The most prominent alternative order he advocated over the years was to arrange subjects according to their order in evolution. An even more important factor lay behind that subject order, however. Cutter justified evolutionary order because it represented a scholarly consensus. The importance of this rationalization is that ultimately it represented subject order justified on the basis of usage—that is, on the basis of how subject classifiers surmised the public thought about subjects—rather than on some implicit logical basis.

It was the discovery of subject order based on usage that eventually provided a basis for dividing classification into two fundamentally different approaches after the turn of the century. Classification schemes based on usage deemphasized theoretical distinctions in arranging subjects in favor of other pragmatic arrangements of implied greater practicality. Called book classifications, such approaches to subject order were contrasted with others based principally on theoretical conceptions of subject order, regardless of whether the conceptual structures were based on older hierarchical nomenclature or on some newer basis such as Cutter's principle of evolution. They were labeled theoretical classifications of knowledge and, because they emphasized theoretical distinctions in arranging subjects, implied for their detractors a greater impracticality.

Cutter eventually experimented with other subject arrangements even more directly based on usage. But he did not carry the principle of subject arrangement based on usage to its ultimate expression by making it the chief basis of subject order. His classification work remained fundamentally tied to what he perceived as some natural or implicit order of subjects with only some incursions of order based on usage. Others after him took up where he left off, however, especially those who devised the Library of Congress Classification at the turn of the century. Subject order based on perceived patterns of usage or at least on perceived practicality was central to that scheme, while subject order based on theoretical distinctions was for the most part restricted in it to the most obvious and general situations. An appreciation of the practical book classification emphasis of the Library of Congress scheme is important because, as it will be shown later, subject order based on usage ultimately affected the Library's subject heading work as well. And that effect was transmitted to the general dictionary subject cataloging tradition in America.

Summary

Ultimately, Cutter's major contribution to the dictionary subject cataloging which succeeded him was his decided emphasis on the notion that books were in every instance to be the starting point for subject access. A secondary contribution consisted of his provision of a good example of the structural features of a dictionary catalog subject heading system. At the same time, the intellectual framework of reference which had been the basis used by Cutter for subject differentiation was lost. Instead, the idea of a subject came to mean whatever any book was about. And subject cataloging became the straightforward process of naming those subjects and entering books in the catalog under them. Classificatory distinctions were retained. But they assumed a different relationship to subject heading work proper, relevant only to the issue of what constituted classed as opposed to not-classed headings and deeply affected by alternative conceptions of subject order, the most significant of which was order based on usage or practicality.

The conceptual changes discussed here did not occur immediately. Some of the earlier classificatory tradition extended well into the twentieth century, a matter which will become evident as this work proceeds. Even more important, the shift to the new tradition and meanings did not provide an upsetting, conscious change. The reason for this resided in the work of the single most influential agency that represented the new tradition, the Library of Congress, and especially in the ideas imposed on that work by its cataloging chief, J. C. M. Hanson. So overwhelming was his influence, in fact, the first two decades or so of dictionary subject cataloging work in the twentieth century may be appropriately labeled the Hanson era.

CHAPTER 8

Hanson and the Library of Congress

The Role of the Library

The initial publication of the A.L.A. *List of Subject Headings* at the end of the nineteenth century represented a revolution in subject cataloging. The list alleviated the practical problems of naming new subjects, of exercising control over vocabulary, and of providing cross-references. That more was needed—for example, clarity as to what a subject was, especially in relation to classificatory ideas—or that a significant conceptual change was already well under way in the very nature of the subject heading process, was not a major issue.

The *List* was relatively limited in what it included, especially for the subject naming needs of large libraries. Its initial sources were the subject catalogs of four notable libraries and the *American Catalog*, the heading forms made uniform by the work of the committee which compiled it. But the work of the committee was a volunteer effort and was not continuous. Not even a quickly issued second edition in 1898 could keep up with the demand for new headings, and a third edition was not issued until 1911.[1] What was needed was the ongoing work of an organization to keep a subject heading list current. Between 1901 and 1911 that need was fulfilled by the ascendancy of the Library of Congress as the chief source of subject heading work. The ascendancy of the Library of Congress was important because it imposed a control on subject cataloging that ensured a good measure of at least operational consistency to an extent unequaled by the A.L.A. *List* and never seen before in the cataloging world.

The public role of the Library of Congress began with the publication of its printed cards in 1901. At first, only a relatively few cards included subject headings because it was decided to include them only when new classification numbers were available. As more of the classification scheme was completed during the first decade of the century, the number of subject headings also increased. By 1909, 50 percent of all the cards issued contained them.[2] The subject headings

178

which appeared on the printed cards represented something of an unknown quantity during this period. They appeared as fragmentary pieces of a system of headings as yet unpublished in a single place. Furthermore, while the Library's subject cataloging staff used the A.L.A. *List* as one of its chief sources of headings, they could not be confined to it. The sheer volume of subject cataloging being done required that many subject names not represented in the A.L.A. *List* be devised anew. Thus, the headings which appeared on the cards went well beyond the *List* in many cases. On the other hand, there was good reason to trust the subject headings thus devised. The Library of Congress, committed to making a dictionary catalog system, found it necessary to discipline the forms of headings it was using in order to arrive at some consistency, at least in its own work. As the decade progressed it acquired a relatively large and well trained staff to accomplish its work. Of course, it functioned as its own authority in subject heading practice. But it was an authority which could be trusted to produce subject headings highly useful to local libraries.[3]

The influence of the Library's subject heading practice was significantly advanced with the publication in 1911 of the third edition of the A.L.A. *List* which deferred for the most part to the Library of Congress in such particulars as new heading choices and the form of headings and subdivisions under countries and cities. Conversely, the *List* differed from Library of Congress practice primarily in terms of completeness rather than in heading form and recommended use. With subject heading work becoming primarily a question of how to write subject names, however, this difference was relatively insignificant. Finally, the influence of the Library of Congress was made firm with the publication of its own list between 1910 and 1914. This list was followed by numerous supplements and then by a second edition in 1919. So encompassing was that achievement that the A.L.A. *List* was not published again.[4]

J. C. M. Hanson

The most important factor contributing to the trend-setting influence of the Library of Congress in subject cataloging was the work of James Christian Meinich Hanson, the chief of the Library's Catalog Department from 1897 to 1910 and the creator of the Library's subject heading system. Hanson was born in Norway in 1864 but was sent by his parents to the United States for his schooling. He received an A.B. degree from Luther College in Decorah, Iowa, in 1882 and for the next six years taught in an elementary school. From 1888 to 1890 he pursued graduate studies in history and political science under the tutelage of Charles Kendall Adams at Cornell University. The direction of his life changed dramatically in 1890 when he accepted a position as a cataloger at the Newberry Library in Chicago. Three years later he became the head cataloger for the University of Wisconsin library. And in 1897 he was appointed chief of the Catalog Department at the newly reorganized Library of Congress.[5]

Between 1897 and 1910, when he left the Library of Congress for the University of Chicago library, Hanson accomplished work that exercised an extraordinary influence over the course of cataloging and classification in the twentieth century. He was responsible for the creation of those systems related to the organization of knowledge that have been the basis of both the Library's work and the work of other libraries which have come to use the Library's bibliographical products. These products included the Library's descriptive cataloging practices, its subject catalog system, and through the work of Charles Martel, its shelf classification scheme.

The practices basic to these systems were widely disseminated through the distribution of Library of Congress cataloging copy and through the printing and distribution of its subject heading lists and classification schedules. In this way the Library's practices have become central to the national effort to achieve a cooperative cataloging program. Furthermore, Hanson was the major figure in the compilation of the 1908 *Catalog Rules,* and through his personal efforts that code achieved international success. Finally, Hanson's work at the Library was continued after he left by Charles Martel, who became chief of the Catalog Department in 1912 and carried out Hanson's original designs until his retirement in 1930.

Hanson became aware of the work of Cutter while at the Newberry Library where he used Cutter's *Rules* as the basis of his cataloging work. While at the University of Wisconsin, he added to this base a firm knowledge of Cutter's *Expansive Classification* when he applied the sixth expansion of that scheme to the library's collection. He also privately experimented with modifications of the main subject sequence of Cutter's scheme as well as with alternatives to its notation. Hanson later employed Cutter's *Rules* and *Expansive Classification* at the Library of Congress as important sources for its descriptive cataloging, subject cataloging, and shelf classification systems.

As influential as Cutter's work was in Hanson's career, it should be strongly emphasized that Hanson used no given system, including Cutter's, in its original state. Instead, he decidedly modified the systems he borrowed. Furthermore, Hanson did not develop systems that were rationalized every step of the way on the basis of philosophical premises as Cutter had done; he approached the organization of knowledge as a pragmatic matter in which one organized the means of achieving practical results into a coherent operating mechanism. This does not mean that he avoided philosophical issues or was disinterested in the philosophical bases of rationalized procedure. It does emphasize the fact that Hanson subjugated matters of philosophical import to the end in view, the resulting system better characterized by its eclecticism than by its philosophical consistency. Although a cataloger whose aim was to make a working system, he was also a consummate administrator of the machinery necessary to produce the system, especially to achieve a useful balance between means and ends. He was, in other words, a cataloging pragmatist at a time when persons able to make widely influential decisions which would solve relatively large problems constituted a new but highly valued kind of technician in growing bureaucracies. In this respect, Hanson appears to have had an extraordinary ability to calculate what was needed to achieve the necessary balance.

His accomplishments were all the more impressive given the conditions under which the work had to be done. He joined the Library's staff just as its new building was complete. With only minimal staff at first, he faced the recataloging and reclassification of the nearly one million volumes of the older collection as well as the need to care for a substantial increase in new acquisitions. And in each case he was ultimately responsible for devising or approving the systems by which the materials would be organized. Given these conditions and the energy and abilities he brought to meet them, J. C. M. Hanson rightly deserves to be called the first modern cataloger.

Hanson's Subject Catalog

The subject catalog Hanson developed for the Library of Congress exemplified his general pragmatism in library matters. Hanson began with Cutter's *Rules* as a basis for the main features of his system—that is, subject analyses that began with books themselves, the notion of entering books under uniform subject headings, the elimination of synonyms, and the use of cross-references that tied the subject heading system together. These features constituted only formal similarities between his work and Cutter's, however. With respect to the more significant issues of goals and the meaning of the idea of a subject, his work pursued a fundamentally different path than Cutter had taken.

The most fundamental difference and the one from which all other differences arose is that nowhere in Hanson's comments on dictionary subject cataloging does one find the same kind of classificatory considerations that Cutter brought to his work. There is no sense in which subjects were validated by means of an anterior sense of classification, no subject structure by which kinds of subjects could be differentiated, and no significance order by which to judge inclusion relationships or to determine the most specific (i.e., concrete) subject among those that were combined in complex descriptions. For Hanson the chief task of the subject cataloger was simply to give access to the topical contents of books considered as entireties, with no further qualifications about their status as subjects. His approach to the task of subject cataloging represented the triumph of the straightforward activity of subject description over any kind of subject heading work that began with classificatory distinctions of the kind that Cutter had used.[6] This is not to say that Hanson's system was devoid of a classificatory emphasis. In keeping with the changes in meanings discussed previously, however, Hanson's appeal to classification was also significantly different than Cutter's, a matter which will become evident as this examination proceeds.

By beginning with the straightforward identification of subjects with the topical contents of books, Hanson avoided the major problem with which Cutter and his nineteenth-century contemporaries had struggled, that of always finding it necessary first to identify established subjects treated in the books at hand. More importantly, Hanson brought to the process of subject cataloging a new dimension. The topical contents of all books now vied equally as subjects. This meant not only more subjects would be used in a subject access system, but also more subjects would have relatively complex names. Hanson did not invent this new dimension in subject access, of course. It had been implied in dictionary subject cataloging from its beginning. Cutter himself had contributed to establishing this new dimension by insisting on beginning with books themselves in every instance in subject heading procedure, although he attempted to control the explosion of "new" subjects by imposing a classificatory matrix of thought on it. It was left to Hanson, however, to provide the fullest expression yet given to the changed idea of subjects and to do so within the context of regularized formal features of alphabetical subject catalog structure. At the same time, Hanson's approach to subject cataloging generated serious new problems. Some idea of these problems may be seen in the following discussion of subject heading practices in Hanson's system.

Conventional Subject Names

The initial and perhaps most perplexing problem Hanson faced was how to formulate subject headings for the greatly increased numbers of subjects promoted by the new dimension in subject access goals. Giving access to the thousands of new subjects represented by thousands of new books was a problem because the activity of naming subjects remained wedded to the notion of conventional subject names central to previous subject heading work. Cutter had defined a subject heading as "the name of a subject used as a heading under which books relating to that subject are entered."[7] He meant that a subject heading functioned as a socially derived label that was reasonably stable in what it denoted. It took the form of one or more words written as a cohesive grammatical unit. It did not include names concocted by the cataloger and it certainly did not imply the use of an artificial vocabulary replete with special punctuation marks (such as dashes) that represented subject relationships in some technical way.

A preference for conventional subject names as headings is understandable given the generally circumscribed notion of subjects up to that point. At the same time, conventional subject names did not adequately accommodate the new dimension in subject access noted above, especially where the only adequate method for denoting the topical contents of a book as a subject involved the use of phrase subject names of more than one word. Cutter had also used phrase headings, but only after he had determined to his satisfaction that the phrases represented "established" subjects. When Hanson resorted to phrase headings, his determination of their validity was not a judgment about whether the topics denoted by such phrases were subjects as opposed to nonsubjects. Instead, his determination was only a judgment about the acceptability of the phrases in terms of common usage. If such phrases were judged acceptable as commonly used subject names, they could be used as subject headings that scope-matched the topical contents of the books to which they were applied. If not, some alternative method of entry had to be found.[8]

Given the enlarged goal of representing the entire topical contents of all books by means of subject headings, Hanson tended to use phrase headings much more freely than Cutter had. Despite their awkwardness, phrase headings remained true to the notion of conventional subject names. Some indication of his wide use of such phrases may be seen in Figure 10 where many of the subject descriptions listed in the first column are followed in the second column by

FIG. 10. Subject Terminology Used in Library of Congress Subject Catalogs under J. C. M. Hanson

A ASTRONOMY

a. Descriptions	b. Phrases deemed usable	c. Class entry terms	d. Subheadings used	e. Entry term inversions	f. Final list
Cipher and telegraph codes used in A.		CIPHER AND TELEGRAPH CODES	—ASTRONOMY		CIPHER AND TELEGRAPH CODES —ASTRONOMY
Clocks used in A.	ASTRONOMICAL CLOCKS				ASTRONOMICAL CLOCKS
A. in geography	ASTRONOMICAL GEOGRAPHY				ASTRONOMICAL GEOGRAPHY
Models used in A.	ASTRONOMICAL MODELS				ASTRONOMICAL MODELS
Astronomical observatories	ASTRONOMICAL OBSERVATORIES				ASTRONOMICAL OBSERVATORIES
Photography in A.	ASTRONOMICAL PHOTOGRAPHY				ASTRONOMICAL PHOTOGRAPHY
Photometry in A.	ASTRONOMICAL PHOTOMETRY			PHOTOMETRY, ASTRONOMICAL	PHOTOMETRY, ASTRONOMICAL
Refraction in A.	ASTRONOMICAL REFRACTION			REFRACTION, ASTRONOMICAL	REFRACTION, ASTRONOMICAL
Spectroscopy in A.		ASTROPHYSICS SPECTRUM ANALYSIS			ASTROPHYSICS SPECTRUM ANALYSIS
A. in the Ancient world	ANCIENT ASTRONOMY			ASTRONOMY, ANCIENT	ASTRONOMY, ANCIENT

A. in the Arabic world	ARABIC ASTRONOMY	ASTRONOMY, ARABIC
A. in the Chinese world	CHINESE ASTRONOMY	ASTRONOMY, CHINESE
A. in the Egyptian world	EGYPTIAN ASTRONOMY	ASTRONOMY, EGYPTIAN
A. in the Greek world	GREEK ASTRONOMY	ASTRONOMY, GREEK
A. in the Hebrew world	HEBREW ASTRONOMY	ASTRONOMY, HEBREW
A. in the Hindu world	HINDU ASTRONOMY	ASTRONOMY, HINDU
A. in navigation	NAUTICAL ASTRONOMY	NAUTICAL ASTRONOMY
A. in the Roman world	ROMAN ASTRONOMY	ASTRONOMY, ROMAN
Spherical and practical A.	SPHERICAL AND PRACTICAL ASTRONOMY	ASTRONOMY, SPHERICAL AND PRACTICAL

Source: Headings taken from *Subject Headings Used in the Dictionary Catalogues of the Library of Congress* (1910–1914) and [Supplement] *List of Subject Headings. Additions and Revisions* (1908–1917).

FIG. 10—*Continued*

B BOOKS

a. Descriptions	b. Phrases deemed usable	c. Class entry terms	d. Subheadings used	e. Entry term inversions	f. Final list
Appraisal of books		BOOKS AND READING			BOOKS AND READING
Binding of books	BOOKBINDING				BOOKBINDING
Chained books	CHAINED BOOKS				CHAINED BOOKS
Classification of b.		CLASSIFICATION	–BOOKS		CLASSIFICATION– BOOKS
Condemned books	CONDEMNED BOOKS				CONDEMNED BOOKS
Conservation and restoration of b.		BOOKS	–CONSERVATION AND RESTO- RATION		BOOKS–CONSER- VATION AND RESTORATION
Covers of books	BOOK COVERS				BOOK COVERS
Expurgated books	EXPURGATED BOOKS				EXPURGATED BOOKS
Format of books		BOOKS	–FORMAT		BOOKS–FORMAT
History of books		BOOKS	–HISTORY		BOOKS–HISTORY
Illustration of b.	ILLUSTRATION OF BOOKS				ILLUSTRATION OF BOOKS
Lending of books	INTER-LIBRARY LOANS				INTER-LIBRARY LOANS
		LIBRARIES	–CIRCULATION, LOANS		LIBRARIES– CIRCULATION, LOANS
Ornamentation of b.	BOOK ORNA- MENTATION				BOOK ORNA- MENTATION
Owners' marks in b.		BOOKS	–OWNERS' MARKS		BOOKS–OWNERS' MARKS

Plates in books	BOOK-PLATES		BOOK-PLATES
Poetry about books	BOOK VERSE		BOOK VERSE
Prices of books		BOOKS —PRICES	BOOKS–PRICES
Privately printed b.	PRIVATELY PRINTED BOOKS		PRIVATELY PRINTED BOOKS
Prohibited books	PROHIBITED BOOKS		PROHIBITED BOOKS
Repairing of books		BOOKBINDING —REPAIRING	BOOKBINDING–REPAIRING
Unauthorized reprints of books		COPYRIGHT —UNAUTHORIZED RE-PRINTS	COPYRIGHT–UNAUTHORIZED REPRINTS
Reviews of books		BOOKS —REVIEWS	BOOKS–REVIEWS
Selection of books		BOOKS AND READING	BOOKS AND READING
		BIBLIOGRAPHY —BEST BOOKS	BIBLIOGRAPHY–BEST BOOKS
Selling of books	BOOKSELLERS AND BOOK-SELLING		BOOKSELLERS AND BOOK-SELLING
Sizes of books		BOOKS —SIZES	BOOKS–SIZES
Book stamps		BOOKBINDING —STAMPED BINDINGS	BOOKBINDING–STAMPED BINDINGS
Subscription books		BOOKSELLERS AND BOOK-SELLING —COLPORTAGE, SUBSCRIPTION TRADE	BOOKSELLERS AND BOOK-SELLING–COLPORTAGE, SUBSCRIPTION TRADE

FIG. 10—*Continued*

BOOKS (*Continued*)

a. Descriptions	b. Phrases deemed usable	c. Class entry terms	d. Subheadings used	e. Entry term inversions	f. Final list
Tariffs on books		BOOKS	–TARIFF		BOOKS–TARIFF
Thefts of books	BOOK THEFTS				BOOK THEFTS
Titles of fictitious books	IMAGINARY BOOKS AND LIBRARIES				IMAGINARY BOOKS AND LIBRARIES
Books printed on vellum	VELLUM PRINTED BOOKS				VELLUM PRINTED BOOKS

C   HEART

a. Descriptions	b. Phrases deemed usable	c. Class entry terms	d. Subheadings used	e. Entry term inversions	f. Final list
Abnormalities and deformities of the h.		HEART	–ABNORMALITIES AND DEFORMITIES		HEART–ABNORMALITIES AND DEFORMITIES
Diseases of the h.		HEART	–DISEASES		HEART–DISEASES
Diagnoses of the diseases of the h.		HEART	–DISEASES–ANALYSIS		HEART–DISEASES–ANALYSIS
Fattiness of the h.	FATTY HEART			HEART, FATTY	HEART, FATTY
Homeopathic treatment of the diseases of the h.		HEART	–DISEASES–HOMEOPATHIC TREATMENT		HEART–DISEASES–HOMEOPATHIC TREATMENT

a. Descriptions	b. Phrases deemed usable	c. Class entry terms	d. Subheadings used	e. Entry term inversions	f. Final list
Displacement of the h.		HEART	–DISPLACEMENT		HEART–DISPLACEMENT
Hypertrophy and dilatation of the h.		HEART	–HYPERTROPHY AND DILATATION		HEART–HYPERTROPHY AND DILATATION
Palpitation of the h.		HEART	–PALPITATION		HEART–PALPITATION
Rupture of the h.		HEART	–RUPTURE		HEART–RUPTURE
Diseases of the valves of the h.		HEART	–VALVES–DISEASES		HEART–VALVES–DISEASES

D JEWS

a. Descriptions	b. Phrases deemed usable	c. Class entry terms	d. Subheadings used	e. Entry term inversions	f. Final list
Jews in Africa	JEWS IN AFRICA				JEWS IN AFRICA
Jewish antiquities		JEWS	–ANTIQUITIES		JEWS–ANTIQUITIES
Jewish charities		JEWS	–CHARITIES		JEWS–CHARITIES
Jews in Chicago	JEWS IN CHICAGO				JEWS IN CHICAGO
Jewish civilization		JEWS	–CIVILIZATON		JEWS–CIVILIZATION
Jewish cultus	JEWISH CULTUS			CULTUS, JEWISH	CULTUS, JEWISH
Jewish commerce		JEWS	–COMMERCE		JEWS–COMMERCE
Jewish education		JEWS	–EDUCATION		JEWS–EDUCATION
Jewish ethics	JEWISH ETHICS			ETHICS, JEWISH	ETHICS, JEWISH
History of the Jews		JEWS	–HISTORY		JEWS–HISTORY

FIG. 10—*Continued*

JEWS (*Continued*)

a. Descriptions	b. Phrases deemed usable	c. Class entry terms	d. Subheadings used	e. Entry term inversions	f. Final list
Jewish hygiene	JEWISH HYGIENE			HYGIENE, JEWISH	HYGIENE, JEWISH
Jews among labor and laboring classes		LABOR AND LABORING CLASSES	–JEWS		LABOR AND LABORING CLASSES–JEWS
Jewish law		JEWS	–LAW		JEWS–LAW
Jewish literature	JEWISH LITERATURE				JEWISH LITERATURE
Jews in literature	JEWS IN LITERATURE				JEWS IN LITERATURE
Marriage among Jews		MARRIAGE	–JEWS		MARRIAGE–JEWS
Jewish missions		MISSIONS	–JEWS		MISSIONS–JEWS
Jewish music		MUSIC	–JEWS		MUSIC–JEWS
Jewish numismatics		NUMISMATICS	–JEWS		NUMISMATICS–JEWS
Origin of the Jews		JEWS	–ORIGIN		JEWS–ORIGIN
Persecutions of Jews		JEWS	–PERSECUTIONS		JEWS–PERSECUTIONS
Jewish philosophy	JEWISH PHILOSOPHY			PHILOSOPHY, JEWISH	PHILOSOPHY, JEWISH
Political and social conditions of Jews		JEWS	–POLITICAL AND SOCIAL CONDITIONS		JEWS–POLITICAL AND SOCIAL CONDITIONS
Jewish religion		JEWS	–RELIGION		JEWS–RELIGION
Liturgy and ritual of Jewish religion		JEWS	–LITURGY AND RITUAL		JEWS–LITURGY AND RITUAL

a. Descriptions	b. Phrases deemed usable	c. Class entry terms	d. Subheadings used	e. Entry term inversions	f. Final list
Social life and customs of Jews		JEWS	–SOCIAL LIFE AND CUSTOMS		JEWS–SOCIAL LIFE AND CUSTOMS
Jews in the United States	JEWS IN THE UNITED STATES				JEWS IN THE UNITED STATES
Zionism among Jews		JEWS	–RESTORATION		JEWS–RESTORATION

E. PHOTOGRAPHY

Things used in Photography:

a. Descriptions	b. Phrases deemed usable	c. Class entry terms	d. Subheadings used	e. Entry term inversions	f. Final list
Photographic apparatus and supplies		PHOTOGRAPHY	–APPARATUS AND SUPPLIES		PHOTOGRAPHY–APPARATUS AND SUPPLIES
Testing of photog. apparatus & supplies		PHOTOGRAPHY	–APPARATUS AND SUPPLIES–TESTING		PHOTOGRAPHY–APPARATUS AND SUPPLIES–TESTING
Photographic films		PHOTOGRAPHY	–FILMS		PHOTOGRAPHY–FILMS
Photographic lenses	PHOTOGRAPHIC LENSES			LENSES, PHOTOGRAPHIC	LENSES, PHOTOGRAPHIC
Photographic negatives		PHOTOGRAPHY	–NEGATIVES		PHOTOGRAPHY–NEGATIVES
Photographic printing papers		PHOTOGRAPHY	–PRINTING PAPERS		PHOTOGRAPHY–PRINTING PAPERS

FIG. 10—*Continued*

PHOTOGRAPHY (*Continued*)

a. Descriptions	b. Phrases deemed usable	c. Class entry terms	d. Subheadings used	e. Entry term inversions	f. Final list
Photographic plates		PHOTOGRAPHY	—PLATES		PHOTOGRAPHY-PLATES
Photographic ray-filters		PHOTOGRAPHY	—RAY-FILTERS		PHOTOGRAPHY-RAY-FILTERS
Photographic studios and darkrooms		PHOTOGRAPHY	—STUDIOS AND DARKROOMS		PHOTOGRAPHY-STUDIOS AND DARKROOMS
Processes & aspects of photography:					
Artificial light in p.		PHOTOGRAPHY	—ARTIFICIAL LIGHT		PHOTOGRAPHY-ARTIFICIAL LIGHT
Business methods in p.		PHOTOGRAPHY	—BUSINESS METHODS		PHOTOGRAPHY-BUSINESS METHODS
Chemistry in p.	PHOTOGRAPHIC CHEMISTRY				PHOTOGRAPHIC CHEMISTRY
Photographic developing and developers		PHOTOGRAPHY	—DEVELOPING AND DEVELOPERS		PHOTOGRAPHY-DEVELOPING AND DEVELOPERS
Enlarging in p.		PHOTOGRAPHY	—ENLARGING		PHOTOGRAPHY-ENLARGING
Exposure in p.		PHOTOGRAPHY	—EXPOSURE		PHOTOGRAPHY-EXPOSURE
Failures in p.		PHOTOGRAPHY	—FAILURES		PHOTOGRAPHY-FAILURES

Fine arts aspects of p.	ARTISTIC PHOTOGRAPHY	PHOTOGRAPHY	PHOTOGRAPHY, ARTISTIC
Legal aspects of p.		PHOTOGRAPHY —LAW	PHOTOGRAPHY-LAW
Optics in p.	PHOTOGRAPHIC OPTICS		PHOTOGRAPHIC OPTICS
Printing processes in p.		PHOTOGRAPHY —PRINTING PROCESSES	PHOTOGRAPHY-PRINTING PROCESSES
Toning in printing processes in p.		PHOTOGRAPHY —PRINTING PROCESSES-TONING	PHOTOGRAPHY-PRINTING PROCESSES-TONING
Blue-printing processes in p.	BLUE-PRINTING	PHOTOGRAPHY	BLUE-PRINTING
Carbon printing processes in p.		PHOTOGRAPHY —PRINTING PROCESSES-CARBON	PHOTOGRAPHY-PRINTING PROCESSES-CARBON
Gum-biochromate printing processes in p.		PHOTOGRAPHY —PRINTING PROCESSES-BIOCHROMATE	PHOTOGRAPHY-PRINTING PROCESSES-BIOCHROMATE
Ozotype printing processes in p.		PHOTOGRAPHY —PRINTING PROCESSES-OZOTYPE	PHOTOGRAPHY-PRINTING PROCESSES-OZOTYPE
Platinotype printing processes in p.		PHOTOGRAPHY —PRINTING PROCESSES-PLATINOTYPE	PHOTOGRAPHY-PRINTING PROCESSES-PLATINOTYPE
Silver printing processes in p.		PHOTOGRAPHY —PRINTING PROCESSES-SILVER	PHOTOGRAPHY-PRINTING PROCESSES-SILVER

PHOTOGRAPHY, ARTISTIC

FIG. 10—*Continued*

PHOTOGRAPHY (*Continued*)

a. Descriptions	b. Phrases deemed usable	c. Class entry terms	d. Subheadings used	e. Entry term inversions	f. Final list
Recovery of wastes in p.		PHOTOGRAPHY	—WASTES, RE-COVERY OF		PHOTOGRAPHY–WASTES, RE-COVERY OF
Retouching in p.		PHOTOGRAPHY	—RETOUCHING		PHOTOGRAPHY–RETOUCHING

Kinds of Photography in terms of objects photographed:

a. Descriptions	b. Phrases deemed usable	c. Class entry terms	d. Subheadings used	e. Entry term inversions	f. Final list
P. of animals	PHOTOGRAPHY OF ANIMALS				PHOTOGRAPHY OF ANIMALS
Ballistic p.	BALLISTIC PHO-TOGRAPHY			PHOTOGRAPHY, BALLISTIC	PHOTOGRAPHY, BALLISTIC
P. of biological objects	BIOLOGICAL PHOTOG-RAPHY			PHOTOGRAPHY, BIOLOGICAL	PHOTOGRAPHY, BIOLOGICAL
P. of birds	PHOTOGRAPHY OF BIRDS				PHOTOGRAPHY OF BIRDS
P. of buildings	ARCHITEC-TURAL PHO-TOGRAPHY			PHOTOGRAPHY, ARCHITEC-TURAL	PHOTOGRAPHY, ARCHITEC-TURAL
P. of clouds	PHOTOGRAPHY OF CLOUDS				PHOTOGRAPHY OF CLOUDS
P. of insects	PHOTOGRAPHY OF INSECTS				PHOTOGRAPHY OF INSECTS
P. of interiors		PHOTOGRAPHY	—INTERIORS		PHOTOGRAPHY–INTERIORS
P. of landscapes		PHOTOGRAPHY	—LANDSCAPES		PHOTOGRAPHY–LANDSCAPES

P. of leaves	PHOTOGRAPHY OF LEAVES			PHOTOGRAPHY OF LEAVES
P. of marine objects		PHOTOGRAPHY	—MARINES	PHOTOGRAPHY—MARINES
P. of nature	NATURE PHOTOGRAPHY			NATURE PHOTOGRAPHY
Panoramic p.	PANORAMIC PHOTOGRAPHY		PHOTOGRAPHY, PANORAMIC	PHOTOGRAPHY, PANORAMIC
P. of plants	PHOTOGRAPHY OF PLANTS			PHOTOGRAPHY OF PLANTS
P. of the invisible	PHOTOGRAPHY OF THE INVISIBLE			PHOTOGRAPHY OF THE INVISIBLE

Kinds of Photography in terms of techniques or ends in view:

Aerial p.	AERIAL PHOTOGRAPHY	PHOTOGRAPHY, AERIAL	PHOTOGRAPHY, AERIAL
Amusement p.	TRICK PHOTOGRAPHY	PHOTOGRAPHY, TRICK	PHOTOGRAPHY, TRICK
Color p.	COLOR PHOTOGRAPHY		COLOR PHOTOGRAPHY
Composite p.	COMPOSITE PHOTOGRAPHY	PHOTOGRAPHY, COMPOSITE	PHOTOGRAPHY, COMPOSITE
Flash-light p.	FLASH-LIGHT PHOTOGRAPHY	PHOTOGRAPHY, FLASH-LIGHT	PHOTOGRAPHY, FLASH-LIGHT
Moving picture p.	MOVING-PICTURES		MOVING-PICTURES
Night p.	NIGHT PHOTOGRAPHY	PHOTOGRAPHY, NIGHT	PHOTOGRAPHY, NIGHT
Orthocromatic p.	ORTHOCHROMATIC PHOTOGRAPHY	PHOTOGRAPHY, ORTHOCHROMATIC	PHOTOGRAPHY, ORTHOCHROMATIC

FIG. 10—*Continued*

PHOTOGRAPHY (*Continued*)

a. Descriptions	b. Phrases deemed usable	c. Class entry terms	d. Subheadings used	e. Entry term inversions	f. Final list
Pinhole p.	PINHOLE PHOTOGRAPHY			PHOTOGRAPHY, PINHOLE	PHOTOGRAPHY, PINHOLE
Portrait p.		PHOTOGRAPHY	–PORTRAITS		PHOTOGRAPHY–PORTRAITS
Lighting & posing in portrait p.		PHOTOGRAPHY	–PORTRAITS–LIGHTING AND POSING		PHOTOGRAPHY–PORTRAITS–LIGHTING AND POSING
Submarine p.	SUBMARINE PHOTOGRAPHY			PHOTOGRAPHY, SUBMARINE	PHOTOGRAPHY, SUBMARINE
Time-lapse p.	CHRONOPHOTOGRAPHY				CHRONOPHOTOGRAPHY
P. on wood	PHOTOXYLOGRAPHY				PHOTOXYLOGRAPHY
The use of Photography:					
P. in astronomy	ASTRONOMICAL PHOTOGRAPHY				ASTRONOMICAL PHOTOGRAPHY
P. in the measurement of stars		STARS	–PHOTOGRAPHIC MEASUREMENTS		STARS–PHOTOGRAPHIC MEASUREMENTS
P. in commerce	COMMERCIAL PHOTOGRAPHY			PHOTOGRAPHY, COMMERCIAL	PHOTOGRAPHY, COMMERCIAL

	a. Descriptions	b. Phrases deemed usable	c. Class entry terms	d. Subheadings used	e. Entry term inversions	f. Final list
	P. in copying		PHOTOGRAPHY	—COPYING		PHOTOGRAPHY-COPYING
	P. in the reproduction of plans, drawings, etc.		PHOTOGRAPHY	—REPRODUCTION OF PLANS, DRAWINGS, ETC.		PHOTOGRAPHY-REPRODUCTION OF PLANS, DRAWINGS, ETC.
	P. in legal proceedings	LEGAL PHOTOGRAPHY			PHOTOGRAPHY, LEGAL	PHOTOGRAPHY, LEGAL
	P. in medicine	MEDICAL PHOTOGRAPHY			PHOTOGRAPHY, MEDICAL	PHOTOGRAPHY, MEDICAL
	P. in the military	MILITARY PHOTOGRAPHY			PHOTOGRAPHY, MILITARY	PHOTOGRAPHY, MILITARY
	P. in surveying	PHOTOGRAPHIC SURVEYING				PHOTOGRAPHIC SURVEYING
	Scientific applications of p.		PHOTOGRAPHY	—SCIENTIFIC APPLICATIONS		PHOTOGRAPHY-SCIENTIFIC APPLICATIONS
F	TAXATION					
	T. in a place, e.g., Louisiana		TAXATION	—LOUISIANA		TAXATION-LOUISIANA
	Law relating to t.		TAXATION	—LAW		TAXATION-LAW
	Exemption from t.	EXEMPTION FROM TAXATION			TAXATION, EXEMPTION FROM	TAXATION, EXEMPTION FROM
	Progressive t.	PROGRESSIVE TAXATION			TAXATION, PROGRESSIVE	TAXATION, PROGRESSIVE

FIG. 10—*Continued*

TAXATION (*Continued*)

a. Descriptions	b. Phrases deemed usable	c. Class entry terms	d. Subheadings used	e. Entry term inversions	f. Final list
State t.	STATE TAXATION			TAXATION, STATE	TAXATION, STATE
T. of articles of consumption	TAXATION OF ARTICLES OF CONSUMPTION				TAXATION OF ARTICLES OF CONSUMPTION
T. of articles of consumption in a place, e.g., La.		TAXATION OF ARTICLES OF CONSUMPTION	–LOUISIANA		TAXATION OF ARTICLES OF CONSUMPTION–LOUISIANA
T. of beet sugar		BEET SUGAR	–TAXATION		BEET SUGAR–TAXATION
T. of bonds, securities, etc.	TAXATION OF BONDS, SECURITIES, ETC.				TAXATION OF BONDS, SECURITIES, ETC.
T. of corporations		CORPORATIONS	–TAXATION		CORPORATIONS–TAXATION
T. of hearths	HEARTH-MONEY				HEARTH-MONEY
T. of income	INCOME TAX				INCOME TAX
T. of legacies	INHERITANCE AND TRANSFER TAX				INHERITANCE AND TRANSFER TAX
T. of liquors		LIQUOR TRAFFIC	–TAXATION		LIQUOR TRAFFIC–TAXATION

T. of personal property

TAXATION OF PERSONAL PROPERTY

T. of U.S. bonds

TAXATION OF U.S. BONDS

G UNITED STATES

a. Descriptions	b. Phrases deemed usable	c. Class entry terms	d. Subheadings used	e. Entry term inversions	f. Final list
Aliens in the U.S.		ALIENS	–UNITED STATES		ALIENS–UNITED STATES
Altitudes in the U.S.		UNITED STATES	–ALTITUDES		UNITED STATES–ALTITUDES
Annexations of the U.S.		UNITED STATES	–ANNEXATIONS		UNITED STATES–ANNEXATIONS
Antiquities of the U.S.		UNITED STATES	–ANTIQUITIES		UNITED STATES–ANTIQUITIES
Appropriations and expenditures of the U.S.		UNITED STATES	–APPROPRIA-TIONS AND EXPENDI-TURES		UNITED STATES–APPROPRIA-TIONS AND EXPENDI-TURES
Archives in the U.S.		ARCHIVES	–UNITED STATES		ARCHIVES–UNITED STATES
Church history of the U.S.		UNITED STATES	–CHURCH HISTORY		UNITED STATES–CHURCH HISTORY
Civil service in the U.S.		CIVIL SERVICE	–UNITED STATES		CIVIL SERVICE–UNITED STATES

FIG. 10—*Continued*

UNITED STATES (*Continued*)

a. Descriptions	b. Phrases deemed usable	c. Class entry terms	d. Subheadings used	e. Entry term inversions	f. Final list
Civilization of the U.S.		UNITED STATES	–CIVILIZATION		UNITED STATES–CIVILIZATION
Claims of the U.S.		UNITED STATES	–CLAIMS		UNITED STATES–CLAIMS
Climate of the U.S.		UNITED STATES	–CLIMATE		UNITED STATES–CLIMATE
Coast defenses of the U.S.		UNITED STATES	–COAST DE-FENSES		UNITED STATES–COAST DE-FENSES
Coinage of the U.S.		COINAGE	–UNITED STATES		COINAGE–UNITED STATES
Colonial question of the U.S.		UNITED STATES	–COLONIAL QUESTION		UNITED STATES–COLONIAL QUESTION
Commerce of the U.S.		UNITED STATES	–COMMERCE		UNITED STATES–COMMERCE
Commercial law of the U.S.		COMMERCIAL LAW	–UNITED STATES		COMMERCIAL LAW–UNITED STATES
Commercial policy of the U.S.		UNITED STATES	–COMMERCIAL POLICY		UNITED STATES–COMMERCIAL POLICY
Exploring expedi-tions of the U.S.		UNITED STATES	–EXPLORING EXPEDI-TIONS		UNITED STATES–EXPLORING EXPEDITIONS

The U.S. exploring expedition of 1838-1842	UNITED STATES EXPLORING EXPEDITION, 1838-1842		UNITED STATES EXPLORING EXPEDITION, 1838-1842
Express service in the U.S.	EXPRESS SERVICE	—UNITED STATES	EXPRESS SERVICE–UNITED STATES
Finance of the U.S.	FINANCE	—UNITED STATES	FINANCE–UNITED STATES
Flags of the U.S.	FLAGS	—UNITED STATES	FLAGS–UNITED STATES
Foreign mail in the U.S.	POSTAL SERVICE	—UNITED STATES–FOREIGN MAIL	POSTAL SERVICE–U.S.–FOREIGN MAIL
Foreign populations in the U.S.	UNITED STATES	—FOREIGN POPULATIONS	UNITED STATES–FOREIGN POPULATIONS
Foreign relations of the U.S.	UNITED STATES	—FOREIGN RELATIONS	UNITED STATES–FOREIGN RELATIONS
Fortifications of the U.S.	FORTIFICATIONS	—UNITED STATES	FORTIFICATIONS–UNITED STATES
History of the U.S.	UNITED STATES	—HISTORY	UNITED STATES–HISTORY
History of the U.S. from 1675-1676 during King Philip's War	KING PHILIP'S WAR, 1675-1676		KING PHILIP'S WAR, 1675-1676
History of the U.S. from 1689-1697 during King William's War	UNITED STATES	—HISTORY-KING WILLIAM'S WAR, 1689-1697	UNITED STATES–HISTORY–KING WILLIAM'S WAR, 1689-1697

conventional phrase subject headings that were considered acceptable as common usage names.

At the same time, however, using conventional headings resulted in serious problems. The basis for deciding which phrase headings were acceptable and which were not was necessarily vague, depending as it did upon the judgment of a subject cataloger in each individual case. Ordinarily this required the subject cataloger to observe how books named their own topical contents and then compare that name with names found in a variety of other catalogs, subject name lists, and other reference sources. If a particular name reoccurred as the most commonly used name, then it could be used as a subject heading. At other times, the only information that could be found about many new subjects was limited to a single work in which a particular topic was found. When that occurred, adopting a phrase heading was at best tenuous because of the sparse evidence for it being in common use. Hanson concluded, for example, that even though the topic Institutional church seemed appropriate as a heading, it should not be used "until more literature and consequently more information is available." As a result, books on that topic were placed under CHURCH WORK with a "see" reference from Institutional church.9

The most important result of adopting large numbers of phrase subject names was, however, that they necessarily scattered books on related topics over the entire catalog according to the diverse ways their names were written. Hanson noted with disapproval that to use the name Fasciation in plants (a particular kind of plant abnormality) would necessarily separate books on that topic from books on other kinds of plant abnormalities. To use the various common names of topics related to the Eastern question, such as Balkan question, Near Eastern question, Middle Eastern question, would scatter those topics excessively. And to use Beacon street as it appeared would separate that topic from others related to Boston. In each of these cases, Hanson turned to alternatives that either referred from the common name to another name, as in Fasciation in plants, see ABNORMALITIES (PLANTS), or used the name but only as a subheading, as in BOSTON–STREETS–BEACON STREET and EASTERN QUESTION–BALKAN.10 In other cases he had to contend with the common phrase names because he could not avoid their use. This is particularly noticeable for topics related to Astronomy, Photography, and Taxation when their straightforward phrase subject names are considered (Figure 10A, E, and F, column b).

Cutter had recognized the problem of phrase names but had controlled it in his system by limitations related to his notion of established (as opposed to unestablished) topics of thought and by his use of cross-references based on the orderly structure of subjects he had invoked. Scattering was a much greater problem in Hanson's catalog because the need to accept phrase headings was much more intense. Furthermore, Hanson's use of cross-references to control the scattering was more problematic not simply because phrase headings required so many more references that they tended to choke the catalog with additional cards, but because without Cutter's subject structure, such references could not be determined systematically. In short, scattering was a problem of such proportions that Hanson considered it to be an essential but negative result of following "the dictionary principle."

> As for economy of compilation, it is my firm conviction that strict adherence to the principle of specific entry under minute subjects to be arranged in regular order of their names, would in the long run prove well-nigh impossible in the catalog of a large and rapidly growing library. A subject catalog compiled according to this plan must, it seems to me, resolve itself in course of time into a mere subject index in which it becomes practically impossible to guard against the ultimate dispersion of the literature on one and the same topic under various headings.[11]

Referring to topics related to EASTERN QUESTION as an example, Hanson declared that it was the Library's intention "to keep the different phases of this subject together as far as possible."[12] The method resorted to in that case was to use class-entry terms with subdivisions, the result being specific subentry. Subdivision was not the only method available, however. Hanson noted that inversion vied equally with it when he wrote, "Hundreds of similar illustrations could be enumerated where by inversion or subordination, a specific subject has been made to stand with the general topic to which it bears relation."[13] And to both of these methods he added the practice already referred to above of using what is best described as undivided class entry, that is, the use of a broader term to stand for a narrower topic, but without subdivision.

> There are, however, numerous instances in which the specific entry is omitted altogether, and where it has seemed best to enter under a more comprehensive subject without subdivision, a reference from the specific subject directing the student simply to the general heading.[14]

Hanson's statement about the scattering tendencies of the dictionary subject catalog is significant because of its accurate evaluation of specific entry as he understood it and as he applied it to the subject access process. The fact is the use of conventional subject names, especially those in phrase form, could not help but scatter literature on related topics.[15] But Hanson's resolution of the problem of scattering is even more significant because of the importance it gave to the collocation of related subjects. Bringing related subjects together was only another way of saying that the cure for the scattering tendency of the dictionary subject catalog was to incorporate classification in it. Classification formed, therefore, the broader context of Hanson's subject heading work. From it he obtained specific measures that shaped his subject cataloging procedure. Because of the importance of classification for Hanson, his general understanding of it must consequently be reviewed before the remainder of his subject cataloging procedures can be explored.

Classification and Subject Cataloging

Hanson's appeal to classification—the collocation of related subjects —as an overriding principle in dictionary subject cataloging should not be considered unusual. Subject access thinking had originally arisen from notions about the classification of knowledge, a matter more than adequately illustrated in Cutter's work where the dictionary subject catalog represented little more than a systematic rearrangement of previously established classificatory relationships. What is important in Hanson's work was not, therefore, his bare appeal to classification. Rather, it was how he conceived of classification in the first place. The nature of that conception would necessarily have a profound effect on how he applied classificatory measures to his subject cataloging work. In this respect, two aspects of his classificatory thinking are particularly significant: his general approach to subject order, and his understanding of users in subject order.

SUBJECT ORDER

Hanson's general approach to subject order is notable because it reflected changes in subject access thinking that had occurred by the end of the nineteenth century. The older classification tradition, represented so well by Cutter, began with the assumption that subjects constituted a more or less single cohesive structure or universe of knowledge. The structure of subjects was singular and cohesive because the process by which subjects came into being—humanity's mental activity in acquiring knowledge—was itself viewed as a uniform activity among all people. Uniformity did not mean that all reasonably educated persons agreed on the validity and positioning of every particular subject within the classificatory universe of subjects, but rather only that all subjects could be viewed as belonging to a common classificatory structure. Given this assumption, it is understandable that when Cutter attempted to provide subject access, he did so primarily in terms of a principal or single basis of subject order. This factor is particularly evident in the subject structure underlying his dictionary subject catalog.

By the last decade of the nineteenth century, the conceptualization of the universe of knowledge as a single cohesive structure of subjects had already begun to disintegrate into something akin to a confederation of more or less related fields or areas of knowledge. This realignment appears to have arisen as a product of the growth of specialized and scholarly studies both within the academic context and in technical fields. Cutter's classification work in the last two decades of the century gives some evidence of his attempt to cope with the shift in thinking that was taking place.[16] He continued his effort to enumerate subjects on the basis of a single ordering principle, although in this case it was the idea of evolution broadly conceived rather than the structural categories of subjects that characterized his dictionary subject cataloging. Behind his appeal to evolution, however, was a still more profound rationalization for subject order—the usefulness of subject collocation to the readers. As long as the idea of usefulness was expressed in terms of a unified source and structure of the universe of subjects, the result was the same as if the idea of usefulness had been omitted. For Cutter this meant that evolution and the idea of a useful subject ordering principle were the same.

But Cutter also had to contend with the emerging idea that usefulness and therefore subject order varied among different users and among different fields of knowledge. Thus, one will find measures in his *Expansive Classification* that did not follow his basic principle of evolution but rather were pragmatically based on the needs of users in particular fields.[17] Still, Cutter's efforts at subject enumeration may be said to have been based primarily on a single ordering principle. Subject order based on pragmatic estimates of the needs of particular fields of knowledge functioned only as a slight incursion into an otherwise unified whole.

Hanson educated himself in classification work primarily by applying Cutter's *Expansive Classification* to the library collections of the University of Wisconsin between 1893 and 1897.[18] One may assume the experience exposed him to the ideal of a single unified general classification that integrated all subjects into a single structural whole. But Hanson was also exposed to the changing educational patterns of the times as one of the newer generation of American scholars educated at the graduate level in specialized scholarly fields. And he was an eyewitness to the chief effect that specialized scholarly fields of graduate study had on academic libraries—the rise of departmental libraries, a matter with which he took serious issue in his work at the University of Chicago library.[19]

When Hanson found it necessary to develop a new shelf classification for the Library of Congress soon after his arrival there in 1897, he showed little hesitancy in adopting the ideal of a general classification, replete with a uniform notation in which all subjects were given a basic location. But Hanson's proclivity to view the universe of subjects as a series of special fields of knowledge, combined with the exigencies of the Library's situation, gave the Library's classification scheme an altogether different cast than that of any previous classification. Hanson found it necessary to develop the full classification quickly. This required working on various parts of the scheme simultaneously, a task facilitated by the use of several persons who could specialize in particular subject areas and develop them as more or less specialized units of the entire scheme. Logical subject collocation related to particular fields of study was adopted when it could be easily ascertained and when it appeared as a reasonably confirmed consensus within the literature of a particular field of study. But no overall logical principle of subject order was adopted. The result was to give the classification scheme its most fundamental characteristic, that of appearing to be a conglomeration of smaller and more specialized classifications, the subjects of each collocated on the basis of a variety of logics and patterns appropriate to themselves.

A classification scheme carried out fully on the preceding basis would ultimately disintegrate into as many separate sections as specializations in the actual universe of subjects might allow. At the time at which the scheme was made, however, that prospect seems not to have been foreseen. Thus, the number of particular fields of knowledge enumerated as separate units was relatively small by today's standards. Nevertheless, even that small number of separate areas of knowledge tended to produce wide variations in subject order patterns in the scheme.

In addition to collocation patterns unique to the separate fields of knowledge, Hanson and Martel also made general use of a series of simple collocation patterns. They adopted this practice perhaps because developing even a limited number of fields of knowledge solely according to principles of subject order unique to each field was beyond the powers of a staff of modest size. Collocation patterns of this simpler kind included chronological arrangements of materials based variously on the history of the subject at hand or on the publication dates of the materials being arranged, geographical arrangements enumerated to varying degrees of fullness depending on the subject at hand, form arrangements based most often on publication characteristics (dictionaries, serials, collections, etc.) but including categories representing what since have been called aspects of subjects (history, law and regulations, study and teaching, etc.), and, the most common device of all, undifferentiated alphabetical arrangement of topics, often with interruptions providing preferred positions for special topics and catchall secondary alphabetical arrays.[20]

Practical and simple collocation patterns of this kind were used in combination with other logical patterns of arrangement deemed appropriate for individual sections. Nevertheless, they were so ubiquitous that they, rather than any logical patterns that they may have been combined with, came to characterize the overall organization of the classification. The presence of the simpler collocation patterns tended to mute the disjointedness that arose from developing areas separately because their repetitious use gave the appearance that a unified approach to subject order had been used throughout the scheme. The appearance of unity was deceptive, however, because the collocation devices offered only a formal rather than an integral cohesiveness.[21]

Pursuing subject collocation in the manner indicated effectively reversed the priorities Cutter and older classifiers had brought to subject enumeration. Previous subject classifiers had attempted to discover a logical order inherent in the universe of subjects, one that they had not invented but rather only brought to light. It was this process of discovery Cutter had referred to when he spoke of arranging subjects according to their "scientific relations." In the work of Hanson and Martel the effort to discover scientific relations was kept to a minimum. Instead, subject collocation was for the most part turned into a pragmatic activity. It was pragmatic in that it stressed subject arrangement that was touted as simple and practical rather than complex and philosophically justified. And because it was simple and practical, it was viewed as more useful to the Library's clientele.

The consequences of a pragmatic approach to subject collocation were profound. It produced subject collocation sequences that were highly variable throughout the scheme. Variable sequences would have offered little difficulty to those who devised them. But to those not privy to the rationalizations underlying them, they often could only have appeared to be the results of decisions made in an ad hoc manner. The authoritativeness of subject collocation was also placed on a new footing. Collocation based on a principle of self-evident subject order was devalued, replaced by trust in the decisions of classifiers who assessed what was practical and useful in each classification situation.

Basing the authoritativeness of classificatory order on the evaluation of use appeared warranted because of an essentially new view of users which made its appearance in Library of Congress work at the same time.

USERS AND SUBJECT ORDER

Appeals by classifiers to the way users understood subject relationships were not new. Cutter's understanding of the public was, for instance, an integral element of his subject access work. But Hanson's understanding of users in relation to subject order was strikingly different from others before him, and it was especially different from Cutter's understanding of the matter.

Cutter's approach to use and users grew out of the same model of mental processes that had produced for him a singular, cohesive universe of subjects. Because all users had the same mental processes, all dealt with or had the potential to deal with the same singular universe of subjects. All users were, in other words, members of a single continuum of users and use. Differences between kinds of users were thus based on how their mental faculties operated in relation to the singular universe of subjects. For example, desultory readers tended to be concerned with subjects of greater concreteness (i.e., individual subjects and concrete general subjects) whereas scholars added to this an interest in subjects of greater abstractness. Desultory readers also tended not to recognize classificatory relationships between subjects whereas scholars did.

Differences of this kind were not important as an independent measure, however, and did not function as an end in themselves. Rather, they focused on what ultimately was of greatest concern in Scottish thought, the development of one's inner character. Differing degrees of mental ability were, in other words, little more than an indication of what kind of a person a user was. This emphasis on character assessment was particularly important when one attempted to characterize what the idea of a scholar meant. To say that someone was a scholar was not simply a way to judge a person's intellectul ability to deal with kinds of subjects or to recognize classificatory relationships. It was a way to state that the person was mentally cultivated and that a person's mental faculties, both intellectual and moral, were developed and balanced.

The most notable aspect of the foregoing picture is there is no indication of the particular subject areas in which scholars had become interested. Nor is there any indication of the mental acumen that any scholar had displayed in dealing with his or her particular subject area. But the absence of this aspect is understandable when one considers how subjects fit into the overall Scottish framework. In the Scottish view of things, subjects as a class of thoughts were important first of all because they were of a higher order of ideas than indistinct matters of thought. Furthermore, they were all derived more or less through the same process of definition and were elements of a singular and cohesive universe of subjects. Thus, they did not stand as relatively isolated sections or bits of the whole. Finally, the most important differences between subjects were not what particular fields of knowledge they denoted but rather their relative concreteness or abstractness.

This view of subjects complemented the picture of scholarship already described. The idea that a scholar was devoted to a particular subject or subject field was not unimportant. One did, after all, identify particular subjects or subject fields with individual scholars, such as evolution with Darwin and physics, optics, and calculus with Newton. But the scholarship of particular scholars was not a measure of what they discovered and studied, but rather of how they studied. It concerned the general level of abstraction at which their intellectual faculties functioned and the balance and integration that had been achieved among all their intellectual and moral powers. They were scholars, persons characterized by their wisdom, first and students of a particular subject only secondarily.[22]

In the same way, to say that readers were desultory in their approach to subjects was not primarily a judgment about their lack of identification with a particular subject field or their lack of mental acumen in dealing with that field, but only a statement of their lack of mental cultivation. Their lack of understanding of the relationships between categories of subjects suggested an unbalanced character growth and the relative absence of the virtue of wisdom.

By the time Hanson was writing at the end of the century, the preceding picture of users and use had already changed dramatically. With the waning of the faculty psychology of Scottish realism, the connection between mental abilities and personal character also waned. With the diminishing of that connection, the way was cleared for mental abilities to become significant in their own right. This significance, when combined with the already mentioned change in which the universe of subjects came to be viewed as a confederation of separate subject areas, served to bring a new meaning to the idea of a scholar. A scholar came to be synonymous with one who by superior mental skills had investigated a particular subject or subject area of significance. A scholar was, in other words, an intelligent subject specialist.

This shift in meanings formed the context of Hanson's approach to user categorization. Hanson distinguished two basic kinds of users:

scholars, who were students and investigators; and nonscholars.[23] His categories of users were not derived from a model of human mental processes as Cutter's had been. At least, Hanson nowhere referred to such a model with respect to users, just as he had not referred to a model of that kind as a basis for a singular, cohesive universe of subjects. Rather, his categories appear to have arisen as a simple observation of two kinds of users in relation to his notion of scholarship.

Students and investigators were those who had received or were in the process of receiving specialized training in a particular subject field, much as Hanson himself had received specialized graduate training. Proof of their scholarship resided in the way they understood the subject matter pertaining to their area of specialty and to the mental skill they brought to solving problems within their area. A nonscholar was one who was not identified with a field of study. And because this person had no such training or orientation, a nonscholar tended to view subjects as separate things, ideas unencumbered by their positions within the fields of knowledge to which they belonged.

There is some similarity between Hanson's and Cutter's categories of users, of course, particularly in the idea that scholars had an understanding of classificatory relationships whereas nonscholars did not. But Hanson's categories of users diverged markedly from Cutter's, not only in their basic orientation to subject fields, but even more significantly in how the two categories were related. Hanson's two kinds of users stood in stark contrast to one another. They functioned as simple opposites unrelated in any necessary way. Rather than being elements of a continuum of users as in Cutter's view, they represented a profound discontinuity.

In some respects Hanson's approach to users was much simpler than Cutter's. It simplified the categorization of all users by dividing them into two large basic groups with sharp distinctions between them. There was no blending together of the categories that one found in Cutter's sense of continuum. Furthermore, Hanson's characterizations of users no longer carried the added burden of character assessment. The differences between his two basic categories were restricted to the single factor of whether or not subject relationships were understood as elements of a field of knowledge.

At the same time, Hanson's view of users was much more complex than Cutter's because the idea of scholarly users was no longer the simple cohesive category to which Cutter had appealed. As particular fields of knowledge multiplied in number, so also did the number of distinct groups of scholarly users. And as particular fields of knowledge were more or less independent, so also were the groups of persons who studied in those fields. What might satisfy the needs of any one group of scholar specialists in the way of subject collocation might not satisfy the needs of other groups in their respective fields.

It was the complex side of Hanson's view of users that fit in so well with his understanding of the basic requirements of subject order. The need to consider separately each group of scholars and specialists was the fundamental rationalization that Hanson's variable and seemingly ad hoc approach to subject collocation required. Subject order necessarily varied because the needs of scholars and specialists in various fields varied. And it was the task of subject access workers to determine those variations.

SUMMARY

This survey of Hanson's general approach to classification, including his approach to subject order and his understanding of users in relation to subject order, is necessary because it was this general understanding that underlay Hanson's appeal to the need for subject collocation. This general understanding, in fact, profoundly affected his subject catalog work in two distinct ways.

First, Hanson's understanding of specific entry as the dictionary subject catalog's basic methodology—that is, that it produced a "mere subject index" of the particular subjects of books without collocating the subjects—meant that the unmodified dictionary subject catalog was suitable principally to nonscholars. That assessment was important because Hanson was convinced that the primary clientele of the Library of Congress, those who would be most likely to use its subject catalog, were not the nonscholars that the dictionary catalog best served. On the contrary, he wrote, "The use of the Library of Congress will tend more and more to restrict itself to the student and the investigator." Because those users were "best served by having related topics brought together," he introduced modifications into the catalog that would result in purposeful subject collocation. He did so apologetically and claimed they were restricted to those that would not result in "a too serious violation of the dictionary principle."[24] That such modifications actually went far beyond Hanson's claim will be seen as his other subject cataloging procedures are reviewed.

The second way Hanson's understanding of classification affected his dictionary subject catalog resided in the nature of the subject collocation which he used. Hanson did not employ the orderly classificatory logic that characterized older approaches to subject relationships, but rather reproduced in his subject heading system the pragmatic variability that characterized his field-of-knowledge approach to classification and arrangement devices.

Class Entry as an Alternative

The first subject heading procedure which Hanson employed, following the straightforward use of scope-matching conventional subject names, was alternative class entry. The use of a conventional name for a scope-match subject heading depended on the name being a commonly accepted one. If no conventional name could be determined, some alternative method of entry had to be followed. The chief alternative that Hanson followed in such instances was to enter the book under a class heading, a conventional subject heading that "included" the topical description of the book.

Hanson's common use of this alternative is strongly suggested by a perusal of column c in the various sections of Figure 10. One should note, however, that Hanson nowhere specifically described this procedure or even mentioned it, despite its fundamental importance to his work. The absence of a reference to it is likely due to the fact that the procedure was too common to need an explanation. That is to say, when speaking of any subject that has no distinctive name, one normally describes the subject by referring to and qualifying the class to which the topic belongs. Furthermore, in classed procedure it had been a longstanding practice to subenter books on particular topics under their class. And Cutter had already described the practice in the long note to his first subject heading rule where he discussed the problem of subjects that had no names. Hanson thus had little motive to explain the procedure. He appears simply to have followed a commonly known and understood procedure.

The class entry choices in column c of Figure 10 appear at first to be no different than those Cutter would have made. Cutter had concluded that until topics had become established as subjects and had gained names of their own, they had to be given class entry. By this reasoning Cutter entered the topic Movement of fluids in plants under BOTANY (subarranged under Physiology if the size of the file under BOTANY merited it) and combinations of general subjects and places (e.g., Ornithology of New England, of Scotland, etc.) under their places.[25] In each case the entry term theoretically included the entire topical matter of the invalid phrase. BOTANY, for example, stood for all matters pertaining to Botany, including its Physiology, and NEW ENGLAND, SCOTLAND, etc., stood for all matters pertaining to those respective places including their Ornithology. Examples from Hanson's system shown in column c of Figure 10 ostensibly suggest that the same inclusion principle had been followed. They constitute conventional subject names that by the same reasoning "include" the entire phrase descriptions they replace.

While Hanson's alternative class entry choices appear to be like Cutter's, two characteristics suggest they were significantly different. First, Hanson regularly incorporated variations in his choices of class entry terms that Cutter's significance order would not have allowed. This difference is particularly evident in cases involving individual subjects. For example, although most of the class entry choices involving the terms Jews and the United States (Figure 10D and G, column c) are those two individual subject names, Hanson also chose the general subject term in other cases—MARRIAGE instead of JEWS for Jews and marriage, ALIENS instead of UNITED STATES for Aliens in the United States, etc. These might be accounted for as occasional lapses in using Cutter's approach to the matter. But in other cases the variation was even more acute. For example, among topical descriptions involving Taxation (Figure 10F), the general subject TAXATION was regularly chosen as the class-entry term over individual places, but not when combined with concrete general subjects such as BEET SUGAR and CORPORATIONS. In still other instances, such as topical descriptions involving the concrete general subject Books, sometimes the more concrete term was chosen, as in BOOKS for Conservation and restoration of books, but at other times the less concrete term was chosen, as in CLASSIFICATION for Classification of books.

The second characteristic consisted of those instances, fewer in number than the variations just noted, where Hanson's choice of a class entry term was not one of the terms in the original description. This practice was unlike Cutter's procedure of restricting such choices to terms from the original descriptions. For example, Hanson used POSTAL SERVICE as the class entry term for the unacceptable description Foreign mail in the United States, BOOKBINDING for Repairing of books, COPYRIGHT for Unauthorized reprints of books, and BOOKSELLERS AND BOOKSELLING for Subscription books. Likewise, he used ASTROPHYSICS as one of two class entry terms for Spectroscopy in astronomy (the other being SPECTRUM ANALYSIS, a synonym of Spectroscopy) and LIBRARIES as one of two terms for Lending of books (the other being INTERLIBRARY LOANS).[26]

The underlying reason why Hanson's alternative class entry choices differed from Cutter's is that the general understanding of classification that Hanson brought to the procedure was different from Cutter's and affected the way he determined such terms. Some indication of how this occurred may be seen by examining the second characteristic more closely, the practice of using a term for class entry that was not a part of the original topical description. It is very likely that Hanson's choices of class entry terms in such cases arose from treating the entire topical description in each case as a formal element of a classified enumeration of subjects. For example, the topical description Foreign mail in the United States may be viewed as a single subject that is wholly subordinate to the more general subject Postal service. When displayed as a classed sequence of terms such as POSTAL SERVICE–FOREIGN MAIL–UNITED STATES or as POSTAL SERVICE–UNITED STATES–FOREIGN MAIL, POSTAL SERVICE is clearly the next broader conventional heading inclusive of the entire original description.[27] Likewise, the choice of ASTROPHYSICS for Spectroscopy in astronomy is understandable when the full sequence ASTRONOMY–ASTROPHYSICS–SPECTROSCOPY is displayed, ASTROPHYSICS being the next more inclusive conventional term in the sequence.

Other examples also lend themselves to this analysis. Noting that Fasciation in plants was not a usable phrase heading, Hanson concluded the appropriate class entry term that included the topic was ABNORMALITIES (PLANTS). His reason for choosing ABNORMALITIES is more readily seen when the entire classed string-of-terms is displayed: PLANTS–ANATOMY–ABNORMALITIES–FASCIATION. Likewise, his choice of EASTERN QUESTION as the including term for Balkan question is an appropriate choice when the string POLITICAL SCIENCE–FOREIGN RELATIONS–EASTERN QUESTION–BALKAN QUESTION is displayed.[28]

This explanation of Hanson's class entry term choices not only provides sources for the terms in the examples, but also proposes a model of how Hanson viewed class entry relationships in general. It suggests that Hanson viewed class relationships primarily on the basis of the particular meanings of the terms involved. The immediate including class of any given term was that term which included the idea represented by the given term. Thus, as shown in Figure 11B, ABNORMALITIES is the only appropriate class entry choice for Fasciation in plants because it is the next broader term that includes the idea represented by Fasciation in plants.

Hanson's approach to class entry choices differed greatly from Cutter's. Cutter viewed class relationships in two different ways. On the one hand, the class relationships that existed between any given set of terms were a function of the significance order of the categories of subjects the terms represented. Viewed this way, Fasciation in plants has two single subjects: Fasciation, an abstract general subject, and Plants, a concrete general subject. The term Plants is included in the term Fasciation because it is the more concrete of the two. On the other hand, the class relationships that existed between a phrase and one of its elements, between Fasciation in plants and either of the two single terms Fasciation and Plants, was a matter of an elementary form of class algebra. Figure 11A shows that each of the single terms "include" the content of their intersection. The question raised by the need to

A. *Cutter*

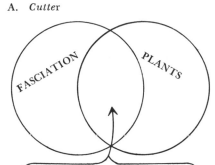

Each single term "includes" the subject "Fasciation in plants." However, in Cutter's subject heading system the most appropriate class entry term was that which was most "concrete." In this case, the most concrete term is "Plants."

B. *Hanson*

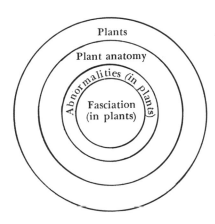

The appropriate class entry choice is *only* that term which, in the light of its particular meaning, is the next broader term that "includes" the term in question. In this case, the next broader term is "Abnormalities."

Since the relationships of the particular terms are based on their particular meanings within an enumeration of subjects, they may also be displayed as shown below in their hierarchial order.

or

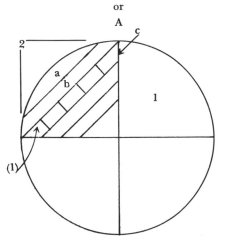

A. PLANTS
1. Plant physiology
2. Plant anatomy
   a. Vegetative organs (in plants)
   b. Reproductive organs (in plants)
   c. Abnormalities (in plants)
   (1) Fasciation (in plants)

FIG. 11.   Class Entry Choices in Cutter and Hanson

choose a class entry term for the phrase was which single term would be the most appropriate. Since Cutter's system gave preference to the most concrete term as entry choice, in this case the most appropriate was Plants. It is the most concrete of the two when the terms are examined in the light of his significance order.

Because Hanson did not have Cutter's significance order at his disposal, his subject catalogers had to determine class entry choices on the basis of the particular meanings of terms in every instance. But this requirement turned Hanson's alternative class entry choice procedure into a conceptual determination, requiring each subject treated in this way to be given an absolute classificatory location based on its meaning. This practice amounted to a reintroduction into the subject cataloging process of the kind of formal classificatory thinking that dictionary cataloging had originally attempted to avoid. Given the general restriction of earlier forms of classification to differentiation based on logical definition, determining the appropriate classed sequence for many subjects had become so difficult that the first dictionary subject catalogers bypassed the operation altogether. They simply entered books directly under the names of the particular subjects they treated.[29]

Cutter wanted to preserve the classificatory context of the specific subjects of books even in the dictionary catalog. But he did so by approaching classification in an essentially different way, that is, by appealing to the significance of kinds of terms in the descriptions of the topical contents of books rather than to their particular meanings. The effect of his categorical approach to classification was to raise the potential of classification to chart effectively the relationships of a much broader range of subjects. It also simplified the procedure for determining alternative class entry choices because it required of the subject cataloger no more than a knowledge of kinds of subjects rather than a knowledge of the meanings of terms in relation to each other.

The most serious problem raised by Hanson's use of classification based directly on the particular meanings of terms was that, with the greatly increased number of subjects validated by his equation of subjects and the topical contents of all books, something akin to a formal enumeration of subjects was required as a guide for making alternative class entry decisions. One would have difficulty in deciding what an appropriate class entry term was without a well-developed classification scheme. It was precisely the lack of this resource that had stymied earlier classed catalog work and had made the simple dictionary catalog an attractive alternative. Even by Hanson's day, the state of enumerative classification was still primitive. Existing schemes were for the most part clearly inadequate for the large number of subjects represented by the books in the collections of the Library of Congress.[30]

Hanson's partial remedy for this need was to draw classificatory relationships from the Library's own classification scheme then being made under Charles Martel's direction. At least this appears to be the case for a considerable number of class entry choices. For example, the sequences involving Fasciation in plants and the Balkan question as well as the greater part of the class entry decisions related to the topics in Figure 10 may be found directly in the schedules of the Library's classification scheme. The use of the Library's classification scheme also appears to be reflected in Hanson's policy that subject headings were not, for the most part, to be printed on catalog cards for books whose subjects fell in topical areas not completed in the classification scheme. The stated reason for not doing so was to avoid having to withdraw all such cards to add their appropriate classification numbers. But another pertinent reason was doubtless the desire to avoid having to change subject headings because the work of the classifiers afterward had determined a different subject order and thus possibly different class entry choices in particular cases.[31]

Correlating alternative class entry choices with the Library's classification scheme unavoidably brought to the subject heading system the kinds of variations in subject order that were basic to the scheme. For example, the topics History of books and Classification of books have the opposite alternative class entry terms, BOOKS and CLASSIFICATION (Figure 10B, column c), because they are treated in an opposite manner in the Z schedule of the classification. In the Z schedule the topic Books (in general) has History of books as a subdivision. But the topic Classification of books is itself a subdivision of or at least implied in Classification.[32]

Likewise the class entry terms for some of the topics related to Jews (Figure 10B, column c) such as LABOR AND LABORING CLASSES, MARRIAGE, MUSIC and NUMISMATICS, simply reflect the scattering of those topics in other general classes in the Library's classification scheme (schedules HD, HQ, ML, and CJ respectively). In each case the topic Jews is a subdivision of those topics rather than being inclusive of them. It was appropriate therefore for Library of Congress subject catalogers to use those topics as class entry terms rather than the term JEWS. Most of the other topics related to Jews (Figure 10D) justifiably have the term JEWS as their class entry term because they are found in schedule DS in the classification scheme where the general sequence History–Jews–[topic] made the term JEWS the next most inclusive class. This same reasoning also accounts for the class entry term variations in the area of Taxation (Figure 10F, column c) as well as some of the variations for topics related to the United States (Figure 10G, column c).[33]

At the same time, the fact that many, if not most, alternative class entry decisions followed the Library's classification scheme does not explain the presence of all the variations to be found. Some variations frankly contradicted the order of the scheme rather than followed it, and some represented no more than the failure to use the full hierarchical sequence of the Library's scheme. For example, PHOTOGRAPHY, the class entry term for topics such as Photography of interiors and Photography of landscapes (Figure 10E, column c), does not reflect the fact that those kinds of photographic topics were actually subdivisions of the topic Photography in the TR schedule. Their full sequences were Photography–Artistic photography–Photography of interiors, –Photography of landscapes, etc. In other words, the next broader class entry term ARTISTIC PHOTOGRAPHY was omitted in each case in favor of the still broader class entry term PHOTOGRAPHY.

Still other variations were even more directly a denial of the subject order found in the scheme. For example, the use of JEWS (Figure 10D) for Jewish education (LC) and Jewish charities (HV) and the use of UNITED STATES (Figure 10G) for Church history of the U.S. (BR), Coast defenses of the U.S. (UG), and for topics related to economics such as Appropriations and expenditures of the U.S. (HJ) and Commerce of the U.S. (HF), clearly reverse the subject order found in the schedule locations listed in parentheses after each topic.

Hanson's rationalization of variations that were made independently of the Library's classification scheme was rooted in his general approach to usefulness in subject order. In its broadest sense, useful subject order implied an area-of-knowledge approach to subject collocation. Since the Library's classification scheme was based on an area-of-knowledge approach to collocation, following the scheme (including its variations) was tantamount to incorporating useful subject order. But useful subject order was not restricted to the subject order represented by the classification scheme because not even the scheme represented every useful subject order that was available. Sometimes, its order could be viewed as only one of several possible alternatives. For that reason, there were occasions when even its collocation patterns could be justifiably disregarded. In this respect, Hanson wrote:

> Occasionally our decision has been influenced by a desire to supplement the classification, an arrangement under place having been determined upon because the opposite order is already provided in the classification schedules.[34]

Hanson's reasoning explains not only the source of the variations in subject order in topics related to the United States (i.e., considered as a place), but also by extrapolation the variations concerning Jewish education and Jewish charities. Variations made independently of the classification scheme simply provided supplementary or simplified subject order alternatives.

The desire to simplify or supplement the subject order found in the Library's classification scheme explains how such variations were justified. But it does not provide the source of the particular alternatives used. The ideas for particular alternatives may well have come from a variety of sources. One source that seems to have been very important for Hanson was current opinion among librarians as to which subject order patterns and thus which alternative class entry choices were most appropriate for library patrons. Hanson's regard for such opinion is reflected in his treatment of topics that combined places and general subjects. He supported the decisions made in 1893 by the A.L.A. Committee on Subject Headings to moderate Cutter's practice of always choosing a place as the alternative class entry term when a place and a general subject were combined. The committee preferred to enter such topics related to science and technology under the general subjects rather than under the places.[35]

Hanson found it ncessary to go well beyond the suggestions of the committee, however, because the larger number of topics included in the Library's subject catalog required more detailed guidelines. He eventually found the collocation patterns in the subject heading system made by Henry C. L. Anderson for the Public Library of New South Wales in Sydney, Australia, to offer the most help. When topics combining general subjects with places fell in the areas of science and technology and, for the most part, in the areas of economics and education, Hanson favored the general subject as the class entry term. But he chose the place as the class entry term when the general subjects were in the areas of history, description (i.e., travel), political science, and sociology.[36]

As a general statement of procedure, this division of topical areas was necessarily incomplete because it did not include the fact that in some instances Hanson simply followed the classification scheme rather than the breakdown here. It was also necessarily vague because the topical divisions were themselves vague. In this respect, Hanson stated apologetically:

> It is needless to say that there are a number of subjects so nearly on the border line that it has been difficult in all cases to preserve absolute consistency in decisions. Here and there will be found under place some heading that might seem to belong logically under the subject, and vice versa, a few headings in which place is not subordinated to subject might well be treated by the reverse method.[37]

Actually, variations were not restricted simply to borderline subject areas. Class entry term choices such as UNITED STATES for the topic Coast defenses of the U.S. but FORTIFICATIONS for Fortifications of the U.S. and UNITED STATES for Appropriations and expenditures of the U.S. but FINANCE for Finance of the U.S. (Figure 10G, column c) were variations that had arisen within the same subject areas. These and others like them could not easily be explained as anything but inconsistencies.[38]

Hanson was aware of the presence of inconsistencies but preferred to think that cross-references would ameliorate them. He wrote:

> In all such cases our chief consolation has been that the reference will presumably furnish the necessary clue to the location of entries and thus disarm to some extent the criticisms sure to be hurled at us for inconsistencies, real as well as apparent.[39]

The general validity of this reasoning is questionable, however, because Hanson's approach to subject collocation had effectively reduced the clarity of the reference structure in the catalog. "See" references used to overcome the effect of pragmatically (and sometimes mistakenly) determined alternative class entry terms simply compounded the problem of the use of "see" references for conventional subject names; that is, they tended to choke the catalog with extra cards. This was aggravated by the effect of that same approach to subject collocation on the "see also" cross-reference structure in the catalog. The role of the "see also" reference structure in Cutter's system had been to recover the classificatory relationships of subjects lost because of adherence to his concept of entry under the most concrete terms. But because the application of a significance order between kinds of subjects made it possible to determine the classificatory order of different kinds of terms, it also made possible the systematic determination of cross-references.

Hanson's system did not have a similar consistent basis upon which to make "see also" cross-reference choices. Worse still, his cross-references varied in their clarity in the same way that the class entry choices they were related to varied. They reflected subject relationships based on pragmatic assessments of users' subject order needs rather than any logical patterns of real subject relationships. As such, both devising them and using them could only result in a cumulative sense of confusion. That Hanson placed much faith in them as a means to rectify the ad hoc nature of subject order in his subject heading system would appear therefore to be unjustified.[40]

In summary, Hanson agreed with Cutter's practice that books whose topical descriptions did not yield conventional subject names had to be entered under class entry terms that included their topical descriptions. However, Hanson did not approach alternative class entry choices in the same manner as Cutter had done. Rather than basing such choices on a significance order among categories of subjects, Hanson chose terms on the basis of their particular meanings viewed in the context of an enumerative classification. But this practice caused his class entry choices to reflect the same kind of variability which characterized his approach to subject order and classification in general. The result introduced into an otherwise straightforward index of conventional subject names a means by which related subjects could be collocated according to the pragmatically assessed needs of specialist users. It did so at the expense of consistency within the system and, consequently, of the predictive nature of subject entry patterns.

Subarrangement

Subarrangement, the organization of a file of entries listed under a conventional subject heading into smaller subgroups, was the second major subject heading procedure Hanson used following the straightforward use of conventional subject headings. Like alternative class entry, it too was affected by Hanson's general approach to classification. In addition, it also suffered from lack of clarity in function.

The subarrangement of the books listed under conventional headings had originated as a feature of classed catalogs. Subarrangement terms, when not simply form categories, functioned as subdivisions of the main subjects under which they were placed and made possible the classed or specific subentry of the books displayed under them. It was this original function that gave subarrangement both its basic character and its common name—the "subdivision" of subject headings.

Early dictionary catalogs did not often resort to subarrangement because they were relatively small and the use of specific subject words usually made the individual files of books under each of the words small enough to make subarrangement unnecessary. But as dictionary catalogs grew in size and the number of entries under particular headings multiplied, searching through such files became more difficult. The use of subheadings could help readers consult such lengthened subject heading files by breaking them up into smaller groups of entries that were easier to consult.

The subarrangement of subject heading files in dictionary catalogs varied according to the way such files grew. Where the entries in a large subject heading file were entirely about the topic of the heading, subarrangement often took the form of grouping the entries by date of publication, by language of publication, or by some literary or practical form inherent in the books themselves. But when a large subject heading file included books that were narrower in scope than the subject heading—a phenomenon produced by the practice of alternative class entry—the nature of subarrangement took on a different character altogether. A large increase in the number of books under the class entry headings listed in Figure 10, column c, for example, would make the files of entries under such terms especially difficult to consult if searches were restricted to the limitations inherent in the topical descriptions. Thus, patrons searching for the subject JEWS or UNITED STATES limited by any one of the term coordinations found in the descriptions of those subjects (Figure 10D and G, column a) would find most of the books relevant to their searches entered under only JEWS or UNITED STATES if the files of entries under those headings were not further subarranged. This situation would arise regardless of the reason or methodology employed in the alternative class entry procedure; whether, for example, it was because a topical description was not considered a subject and the class entry term was chosen as the single most concrete established subject among the terms of the description (Cutter) or because a topical description was not considered established in common usage and a class entry term was chosen as the most appropriate broader term according to the particular meaning of the terms in question (Hanson). In either case, books on the various particular topical descriptions would not only be intermixed under the class entry terms chosen, but would also be intermixed with books whose topical scopes were matched by the entry terms.

The chief method by which the difficulty could be alleviated was to subarrange lengthy files by topical subheadings of the kind found in Figure 10, column d for the various class entry terms listed. To do so brought the charge, however, that the dictionary subject catalog was resorting to the methodology of subject subdivision common to classed catalogs and especially to alphabetico-classed catalogs. This was a relevant charge because topical subheadings looked like and appeared to function like the subject dividing process on which classed catalogs were based. One need only peruse the subheadings used with HEART, for example, or with PHOTOGRAPHY or JEWS (Figure 10C, D, and E) and attempt to demonstrate why any particular one should not be considered a subject subdivision to sense the nature of the problem.[41]

Cutter had been sensitive to this similarity. His goal of choosing the single most specific term in a topical description according to his notion of significance order gave him confidence in declaring that his use of subarrangement was essentially different from that of classed subdivision. Because his topical subheadings were categorically greater in abstractness and subject breadth than the entry terms under which they were placed, they could not be considered logical divisions of the entry term. He called them aspects of the entry term to distinguish them from logical divisions. Cutter knew that multiple-level subheadings below the level of the entry term would themselves be classified if he retained the structure of the strings-of-terms that when rotated produced the specific entries. But this operation was not necessary nor was it favored by Cutter. When used, however, classed substrings did not obviate his specific entry principle.

Hanson, unlike Cutter, could not claim that he had avoided classed subdivision in his subarrangement practices. In fact, he freely admitted not only that he had used classed subdivision, but also that he had used it extensively. He illustrated his use of classed subarrangement by referring to the topic Balkan question, showing how that topic as well as others had been subordinated to the more general topic Eastern question in the construction EASTERN QUESTION–BALKAN, EASTERN QUESTION–CENTRAL ASIA, etc. He then stated:

> Hundreds of similar illustrations could be enumerated where by inversion or subordination, a specific subject has been made to stand with the general topic to which it bears relation.[42]

The proportion of the "hundreds" of collocations that could be attributed solely to classed subarrangement is not known. But the evidence is strong that it was considerable because Hanson's topical subarrangement terms, like his choice of alternative class entry terms, appear for the most part to have been drawn from the Library's classification scheme. And if the combinations of entry terms and subheadings were in classed relationships in the classification scheme, there is little reason to believe that they were not classed when used as subject headings. For example, just as the class entry term PHOTOGRAPHY constituted the next larger conventional subject name that according to the scheme "included" many of the particular topics in Figure 10E (especially those topics in the first two sections, Things used in photography and Processes and aspects of photography), so also did the topical subarrangement terms listed in Figure 10E, column d constitute the subdivisions of the topic of photography as found in the TR schedule. The same may be said, in fact, of almost all of the various topical subheadings in Figure 10. Where the class entry terms were based on the structural enumeration of the classification scheme, the topical subheadings used to subarrange the files of entries under the class entry terms will also be found in the scheme as subdivisions of the class entry terms.

This fidelity to the classification scheme was retained even when the class entry terms represented opposite classificatory decisions. In such cases the subheadings followed the same reversed patterns. The topics Classification of books and History of books (Figure 10B), for example, were, following the Z schedule, not only given the opposite class entry terms CLASSIFICATION and BOOKS, but were provided with subheadings—CLASSIFICATION–BOOKS and BOOKS–HISTORY—that followed the scheme as well. In the same way, Jewish antiquities and Marriage among Jews (Figure 10D) were written as JEWS–ANTIQUITIES and MARRIAGE–JEWS, and Taxation in Louisiana and Taxation of beet sugar (Figure 10F) were written as TAXATION–LOUISIANA and BEET SUGAR–TAXATION. The same may be concluded of many of the other examples of opposite class entry term decisions found in Figure 10.

One might conceivably make a distinction between those cases of subordination specifically explained by Hanson in which the Library's subject catalogers had purposefully used class entry terms and subheadings even when conventional subject headings were available, and those in which class entry terms and subheadings had been used because no conventional subject names appeared to have been found. The distinction suggests that only the first kind could be considered true classed relationships. The second kind, one might argue, having been in a sense forced on subject catalogers, could not be considered classed subdivision because there was in a sense nothing to divide. The class entry terms in those cases already represented the narrowest available conventional subject names. And one cannot logically subdivide that which by definition is already "the narrowest." Subdivision, in this view, is really a function of the availability of conventional subject names that scope-match the topical contents of books. It takes place only when a conventional subject name that by itself scope-matches the topical contents of a book has been subordinated. It does not take place if the subheading used with a class entry term does not scope-match the book to which it is applied.

Hanson did not advance the foregoing distinction as a way to claim that the topical subheadings in his system were generally not classed.[43] Even had he advanced the argument, however, the distinction would not have helped anyone who wished to determine whether any particular heading-subheading combination was classed or not. The crux of the distinction was whether the class entry term was in fact the narrowest conventional subject heading available. But only those privy to the deliberations behind conventional subject name determination would know if that criterion had been met. Those not privy to those deliberations could only try to reconstruct the reasons for the choices or trust that the Library's subject catalogers had made accurate choices.

Trusting the Library's subject catalogers to have been guided by strict adherence to a clearly defined procedure for determining conventional subject names would have been questionable, however. Despite the fundamental role that conventional subject names played in the Library's subject cataloging system, Hanson's desire to collocate subjects was so overwhelming that not even conventional subject names remained unaffected. This will become more evident when the manipulation of conventional subject names is discussed in the next section. Here it is sufficient to say that the object of collocation was intrusive enough to have required rather than simply suggested giving precedence to class entry heading-subheading combinations over conventional subject names. Thus, conventional subject name choices were deeply compromised by the potential of classed sequences to collocate related subjects. Conventional subject names were often avoided, perhaps unconsciously, because class entry heading-subheading combinations fulfilled the collocation goal better. This seems to be, in fact, the most obvious reason why so many of the class entry heading-subheading combinations clearly reflected the Library's Classification scheme.[44]

In the same way, Hanson's desire to collocate related subjects appears to have been the most likely reason that class entry heading-subheading combinations were also given precedence over another possible but lesser used method of subject display—the use of qualified specific entry headings. Qualified specific entry headings entailed the use of a subheading as the entry heading, qualified in parentheses by its inclusive class term. For example, topical subheadings used with PHOTOGRAPHY such as –FILMS, –NEGATIVES, –PRINTING PAPERS could also have been given the forms FILMS (PHOTOGRAPHY), NEGATIVES (PHOTOGRAPHY), PRINTING PAPERS (PHOTOGRAPHY), etc., much in the manner that Hanson had chosen ABNORMALITIES (PLANTS) instead of PLANTS–ABNORMALITIES for the topic Fasciation in plants. The specific reasons why qualified headings were employed in the relatively few instances of their use is not known. But it seems apparent, in a fashion characteristic of the entire collocation goal, that qualified headings were generally avoided because they would have scattered related topics.[45]

Hanson's approach to subarrangement was thus deeply affected by his desire to modify the scattering effect of the dictionary principle. It would be wrong to conclude, however, that, because much of his use of subarrangement was motivated by that desire, all of it was. There were other cases in which his use of subarrangement was clearly not classificatory in nature. Subarrangement on the basis of form, a device he also used extensively, was an example of this. Where class entry heading-subheading combinations reflected subject relationships the reverse of those found in the classification scheme, one may also conclude that nonclassed topical subarrangement had been used, given the authoritative nature of the scheme as a classificatory enumeration. For example, because the classification scheme subdivided the topic Education with, among other things, the subtopic Jews, the use of the reverse order in the subject heading systems—JEWS–EDUCATION (Figure 10D)—may be considered a nonclassed combination. On the same basis, the combinations JEWS–RELIGION, HEART–DISEASES, and UNITED STATES–ALTITUDES, –CHURCH HISTORY, –CLIMATE, –COAST DEFENSES, –COMMERCE, etc. (Figure 10C, D, and G), all of which were opposite the order found in the classification schemes, may also be considered not-classed in their structure.

The occasions in which the foregoing use of nonclassed subarrangement occurred do not appear to be numerous. But their existence, along with the use of subarrangement by form categories, points out that Hanson's use of subarrangement was mixed in function. Subheadings used for subject subdivisions, for nonclassed topical subarrangement, and for form subarrangement were all intermixed. One could not easily tell in any one situation, especially cases involving topical rather than form subheadings, which function was in effect. As a result, differences between subheadings became less important.

The mixture of functions was further aggravated and confused by the presence of still another factor—the effect scope-matching had on the use of subheadings. The goal of Cutter's specific entry process had been to enter each book under its narrowest (i.e., special or specific) conventionally named distinct subject. The idea of "narrowest," "special," or "specific" was controlled by his significance order and based on degrees of concreteness. Cutter's chief concern was to ensure the fidelity of the entry term to his notion of specificity. What occurred in the way of subarrangement after the specific entry goal had been achieved was little more than a matter of practicality.

The ideal of Hanson's system, as distinguished from Cutter's, was to scope-match "the subjects" of books by the use of commonly accepted conventional subject names. Problems involved in reaching that goal, such as the difficulty of ascertaining conventional subject names and the scattering tendencies of those names, led to a heavy use of alternative class entry choices, which in turn required the extensive use of subarrangement terms as a way to organize individual subject heading files.

But the use of subarrangement, regardless of whether subheadings were considered classed or not classed, served still another purpose. Although alternative class entry choices purposefully did not scope-match the topical contents of books, the careful use of subheadings under such entry terms did. The topics Negatives used in photography and

Classification of books, for example, were inadequately indicated by their class entry terms PHOTOGRAPHY and CLASSIFICATION. But when the subheadings –NEGATIVES and –BOOKS were added, not only were the files subarranged for easier access, but also the topical contents of books about Negatives used in photography and Classification of books had been scope-matched. Scope-matching had been achieved, however, by the use of artificial term constructions rather than by conventional subject names. In other words, carefully devised class entry heading-subheading combinations could accomplish the scope-matching that adherence to conventional subject names could not—given, that is, a scope-match interpretation of specific entry.

The use of subheadings in this way does not seem to have been originally intended. In fact, Hanson seems to have been much more concerned with the twin capacities of subheadings to collocate related subjects and to organize large subject heading files rather than with their capacity to scope-match the topical contents of books. But the scope-matching effect could not be denied. In time, the use of subheads became an alternative to conventional subject headings as a method for achieving the scope-match objective. In turn, their capacity for reaching this objective appears to have become even more important than any issue related to whether they were classed or not classed.

One of the reasons why the use of subheadings for scope-matching assumed a role of such importance was due to the practice begun by the Library of Congress of placing subheadings on catalog cards that otherwise specified individual books. If, as Cutter had originally noted, the use of subheadings was only important for file organization and the principal concern of the subject cataloger was to determine the special subject of any particular book, then placing subheadings on cards for individual books was in many respects superfluous. Their presence on cards served, however, to emphasize the notion that a subject heading was not simply the initial term in any such string-of-terms, but rather was the entire string-of-terms because the entire string achieved the scope-match objective.

Of course, the Library's subject catalogers' use of subheadings was directly related to their own subject catalog. They devised subheadings for their own collocation and file dividing needs. Thus, they could rightly claim that there was a distinction between headings and sub-headings. But for those outside the Library and, in many respects, for subject catalogers who served at the Library in later years, subheadings clearly assumed the function of promoting the scope-match interpretation of specific entry. In short, subheadings were needed for that purpose and arguments about whether they were classed or not classed were both confusing and superfluous.

In summary, Hanson's use of subarrangement assumed an entirely different character than its function in Cutter's system. Ostensibly a device to subarrange extensive subject heading files in a nonclassed manner, in Hanson's system the practice also came to be used as a means to incorporate still greater subject collocation and as an alternative method of achieving specific entry interpreted as scope-matching. The subject collocation the procedure brought into the system followed, of course, Hanson's version of subject order—variable, pragmatic, and oriented to the assessment of the needs of scholars in particular fields of knowledge. His incorporation of subject collocation into his system in this way, as diverse as it was, did not end there, however. Rather, it reached its highest development in the last of his basic subject heading procedures, the manipulation of conventional subject headings.

Manipulation of Conventional Subject Headings

Hanson's initial subject heading procedure was to scope-match the subjects of books by means of conventional subject headings. But conventional subject headings by their nature scattered related topics throughout the alphabetically arranged subject catalog, an effect with which Hanson was extremely dissatisfied given his opinion that the principal users of the Library's catalog required the collocation of related subjects. But since he was committed to the dictionary subject catalog at least in its general structural appearance, any attempt to make the catalog more acceptable to the students and investigators who made up the Library's principal clientele had to be accomplished within the confines of that general structure. That meant, in effect, that he had to use conventional subject headings when they were available.

It is a truism that the scattering of topics in a conventional subject name system is unavoidable and that the only way to correct every instance of scattering is to use permuted multiple entries under every substantive word in every term. Hanson did not intend such a remedy for the problem. What concerned him was not that all related subjects were scattered, but that those that in his own opinion should have been collocated were scattered. Which subjects should have been collocated was dependent on Hanson's approach to classification, especially on his estimate of which specialist users in which fields of knowledge should be principally served.

Hanson's use of alternative class entry, a procedure necessary as a complement to his use of conventional subject names, when combined with his use of subarrangement, eliminated much of the scattering.

First, he was able to choose entry terms which would gather together books on topics that seemed important to gather. Sometimes class entry terms were chosen because no scope-match conventional headings were available. But, as explained in the preceding section, at other times class entry terms were chosen purely on the basis of their collocative potential even when conventional subject names were available. Regardless of the reasoning behind any particular case, however, the result ensured that the most important subject collocations were achieved. This is presumably the reason why some related topics were collocated differently. For example, books on many topics related to the UNITED STATES were gathered by entering them under that class entry term, presumably because searchers would look for them under that term. But books on other topics limited to the UNITED STATES were entered under such class entry terms as ALIENS, ARCHIVES, CIVIL SERVICE, etc. (Figure 10G, column c), presumably because searchers would look for them under those terms. Second, Hanson was able to subarrange any given set of coordinated topics in a useful fashion, a matter amply illustrated in Figure 10, column c.

In the long run, even the use of alternative class entry together with subarrangement was limited because Hanson's commitment to conventional headings meant that still other important groups of related topics would be unavoidably dispersed. Sometimes the effect was slight, as in the case of topics related to Heart where only a single straightforward conventional heading, FATTY HEART (Figure 10C, column b), upset an otherwise cohesive display of related topics. At other times it was moderate, as in the case of topics related to Astronomy (Figure 10A, column b) where about one-half of the conventional headings listed destroyed the major collocative sequence. But at times it was very severe, as in the case of kinds of Photography (Figure 10E, column b) and topics related to Books (Figure 10B, column b).

Hanson's solution to this difficulty was to use extensively another procedure, the manipulation of conventional headings. In its most general sense this meant choosing conventional headings carefully with an eye to their collocative capacities or, failing that, writing the order of their words in a way that would collocate the headings with other related topics.

Choosing conventional headings carefully means that given two or more synonymous ways of expressing a subject, each of which is equally acceptable in common usage, one should choose the one that places the term in proximity with other important topics to which it is related. Because this procedure was so close to the basic act of determining a conventional heading in the first place, one cannot say with any precision if and when it was practiced by Hanson outside of having available a record of the actual conventional headings choice procedure.

Lacking that evidence, two other points may be made that support the conclusion that it was used extensively in Hanson's system. First, the strength of Hanson's desire to collocate related subjects, when combined with the fact that evidence for the acceptability of particular conventional headings was often vague, strongly suggests that given the opportunity to practice this method of choice, Hanson's subject catalogers would have done so. There was, in effect, little reason for them not to do so. Second, and more important, the existence of series of conventional headings that are formulaic in nature, such as those that begin with the words JEWS IN . . . (Figure 10D, column b) and those that begin with the words PHOTOGRAPHY OF . . . (Figure 10E, column b), strongly suggests that such a choice mechanism was in operation.[46] Since the collocation patterns for topics related to those two areas demanded that headings begin with the terms JEWS and PHOTOGRAPHY, to have used other conventional headings such as AFRICAN JEWS, CHICAGO JEWS, etc., or ANIMAL PHOTOGRAPHY, BIRD PHOTOGRAPHY, etc., at least some of which would have been acceptable as well, would have been counterproductive to the collocative task. In fact, to have used even a few such variations would have required still further manipulation to arrive at the point where the entry term in the various headings would have brought the related topics together.

The chief difficulty with this procedure is there was only a fine line separating the purposeful use of formulaic headings as quasi-conventional headings, headings that simply looked conventional regardless of whether they were strictly in common use or not, and those that were truly conventional. Given even the occasional use of such extensive formulaic headings, it is difficult to see how their use could easily be held in check. The impetus to collocate related topics was simply too strong to quibble over the use of such sequences, even though following the practice over a period of time resulted in the introduction of a conventional method of making headings which were no more in common use than the contrived strings-of-terms that characterized the Library's use of subheadings.

The manipulation of conventional headings by changing the order of their words occurred in two ways. First, terms which if entered separately might well be separated in the filing order were occasionally combined in conjunctive phrase headings, such as SPHERICAL AND PRACTICAL ASTRONOMY and BOOKSELLERS AND BOOKSELLING. This could usually be justified if books were ordinarily written about both topics together. Second, and by far the most important means of manipulation, phrase headings were often inverted in such a way as to bring the term basic to a collocative sequence to the entry position. So extensive was this practice in Hanson's system that a separate column in Figure 10—column e—has been provided to show how its use affected the examples there. By the judicious use of this method, Hanson was able to complete the collocation of some related topics with only a minimum of effort, a matter suggested by his use of HEART, FATTY to bring that lone topic together with others using HEART as a class entry term (Figure 10C, column e). By its more extensive use, Hanson was able to collocate other related topics that would have been inordinately scattered, for example, topics related to Astronomy and kinds of Photography (Figure 10A and E, column e). Furthermore, Hanson could employ the device selectively, using it only occasionally, as in some topics related to Jews that he chose to collocate elsewhere (Figure 10D, column e), or not at all, as is evident with topics related to Books (Figure 10B).

In short, entry term inversion allowed Hanson to do what could only be partially achieved by his other methods—*the very extensive yet selective incorporation of subject collocation into his otherwise conventional name and specific entry subject catalog.* With that practice, in fact, the specific measures that Hanson drew up to overcome the scattering effect of the conventional heading dictionary subject catalog reached their highest point of development.

Hanson's extensive use of inversion was not without problems. The use of inverted phrases even occasionally, let alone in the large numbers that Hanson's system required, made the filing order of subject headings in the catalog difficult. How, in other words, should the punctuation in headings of this type be understood? One might, of course, disregard punctuation altogether and file all headings in a straightforward word-by-word order. Indeed, many subject catalogers have traditionally filed subject headings this way. But to do so belies the fact that inverted phrase headings theoretically are different subjects than their entry terms alone or their entry terms with subheadings. Filing all such headings together intermixes headings with different meanings. On the other hand, one may argue that the mixture of the functions of subheadings made such a generalization untrue except in those cases where subheadings were neither subdivisions nor extensions of an entry term explicitly intended to indicate a different topic than the class entry term.

Thus, interfiling different kinds of headings makes little difference. In the end, Hanson solved the filing problem by imposing a rigid group order among the various heading types. An entry term with its subheadings always preceded other conventional headings that began with the same entry term. He also separated inverted headings from unmanipulated phrase headings, filing the former as a group before the latter. This appears questionable from a theoretical viewpoint since all such headings, whether inverted or not, were alike in representing distinctly different topics from the entry term alone or with subheadings. The practice had some usefulness as a practical measure, however, in that when inversion was restricted to a particular kind of phrase heading in any one collocative sequence—for example, where it was used mainly with ethnic qualifiers, in the Astronomy section (Figure 10A, column d)—the separation of such headings into an identifiable group served as an elemental form of facet indication.

The second problem Hanson faced with the use of inversion was its appearance. It patently violated the idea of conventional headings by resorting to a format that was obviously patterned after the alphabetico-classed catalog's use of subdivision. Hanson appears to have justified its use in two ways. The first arose out of his understanding of what constituted a conventional heading. As noted earlier, a conventional heading was for Hanson the commonly used name of a subject. It functioned like any other name, therefore, in that if preserved as a cohesive grammatical unit, its integrity as a name was also kept intact. The implications of this view may be illustrated by the way personal names are ordinarily treated. John Lawrence Jones might be used as it reads or it might be inverted in the form Jones, John Lawrence. Because the integrity (perhaps understood simply as the order) of the name has been preserved even in the inversion—by convention everyone conversant with English usage knows that the surname has been put first and what follows are the given name and a middle name—the name is considered unchanged. Only if some element of the original order is disturbed, for example, by reversing the given and middle names to produce Jones, Lawrence John, would the result be considered something different.

Hanson appears to have applied this understanding of personal names to subject names. A conventional subject name might be inverted, fulfilling thereby his collocation objectives, without destroying its integrity as a name as long as the original order was preserved. Only when the name's integrity was tampered with—for example, by changing the comma to a dash and breaking the heading into two separate names that would then be swallowed up in a welter of subheadings—would the name cease to exist in its original sense. It was this action, in fact, that caused Hanson to write to Mary W. McNair, the editor of the second edition of the Library's subject heading list published in 1919, protesting her decision to convert many inverted headings to entry term-subheading combinations "whenever practicable."[47]

The second reason why Hanson could rationalize his use of inversion was that it, like so many of the other procedures that he used, could be found in Cutter's *Rules*.[48] Hanson did not articulate this reason, but it was undoubtedly on his mind insofar as he had followed his understanding of Cutter's *Rules* in his other practices. It makes little difference that he did not use Cutter's procedures with the same meanings that Cutter had given to them. The important thing is that he was able to use them in a cohesive manner. In fact, there is a unique sense in which all of Hanson's uses of Cutter's procedures are perfectly understandable given the change in fundamental meanings that occurred between Cutter and his successors.

Conclusion

Hanson's version of the dictionary subject catalog began with what by the end of the nineteenth century was an essentially changed view of subjects. He proceeded on the assumption that subjects were the topical contents of books, without any further qualifications related to classificatory thinking of the kind Cutter had invoked. This caused the basic goal of Hanson's catalog, although expressed in terms of specific entry, to differ fundamentally from Cutter's. Nevertheless, Hanson adopted the principal features and procedures of Cutter's subject catalog system for his system—conventional subject names, alternative class entry, subarrangement practices, and other practices related to the writing of headings and the use of cross-references—using them in a manner consonant with his goal. He subsequently modified those features even more radically by using them to achieve at every appropriate instance the additional goal of collocating related subjects. When one recalls, however, how this understanding of collocation was deeply affected by his general approach to subject order and to the users who needed access to subjects, the conclusion is inescapable that Hanson's system was not simply somewhat different from Cutter's, it was profoundly different.

In some respects Hanson's catalog may not even rightly be called a dictionary subject catalog. Rather, it was a hybrid catalog, alphabetical in its basic arrangement, but laced with incursions of pragmatically determined classification sequences that had little to do with specific entry even as Hanson understood that notion. Hanson appears to have recognized that his catalog was unique. He freely admitted that there was undeniably a strong tendency in the Library of Congress catalog to bring related subjects together by means of inversion of headings, by combinations of two or more subject-words, and even by subordination of one subject to another.[49]

In fact, he observed that the tendency toward subject collocation was so "noticeable" that it might seem to critics

as if an effort were being made to establish a compromise between the dictionary and the alphabetic-classed catalog, just as the latter was intended as a compromise between the systematic and the alphabetic plans of arrangement.[50]

Hanson raised the spectre of a compromise not to refute the charge, however, but so that he could explain why it had been done. Yet, in the process of providing an explanation, he severely understated the radical nature of the compromise. He suggested that collocation was appropriate for the Library's users "so far as that can be accomplished without a too serious violation of the dictionary principle."[51] By his own admission, however, the instances of collocation were very extensive, and by the analysis here, it is apparent as well that they went well beyond simple violation. In the face of what really occurred, one can only wonder what "a too serious violation of the dictionary principle" meant.

Hanson also suggested that while collocative procedures made the compilation of the catalog more economical to accomplish, those who favored strict subject-word entry could be served by the Library making additional catchword entries above and beyond its regular subject headings. This too was an understatement in that no number of catchword entries based on titles overlaid on the system that he had begun could even begin to make a syndetic dictionary catalog. A catchword index based on title-words was not, in fact, what a controlled dictionary catalog consisted of. Furthermore, it is doubtful that Hanson was or even could have been serious about the offer. He admitted that it would be an extra expense and that it could not be undertaken until the Library had "reached a normal condition." Considering the enormous workload the Library was experiencing and thus the unlikely possibility that the Library could take on still another project anytime within the then near future, the offer seemed less than realistic.[52] In sum, one may reasonably conclude that both of Hanson's reasons for the Library's compromised catalog were actually adroit comments designed to focus on what Hanson considered the strong points of his version of the dictionary catalog rather than on its comparative worth as a compromise. By rationalizing his work that way he succeeded in disarming to an appreciable degree any criticisms that might have been offered.

From the perspective of an additional three-quarters of a century, it is tempting to make value judgments as to the wisdom of Hanson's creation of this particular version of the dictionary subject catalog. The fact remains, however, that regardless of such judgments, Hanson's work was a concerted effort to deal with what was essentially a significant change from an older to a new understanding of subject access needs.

Hanson had relatively little in the way of help to accomplish building the bridge necessary between the older and newer situations. He also found it necessary to build the bridge under the constraints offered by a particularly intense library situation. Given those factors, his accomplishment was little short of brilliant. His Library of Congress subject catalog was not a rendition of Cutter's subject system, although it obviously borrowed much from it. It would be more accurate to say that Cutter's system was totally absorbed and surpassed by Hanson's work. Neither was Hanson's catalog a rendition of any other system, although he borrowed much from his other contemporaries. In the final analysis, it was a unique creation befitting the appellation given to Hanson earlier as the first modern cataloger.

Hanson's accomplishment was also significant in that it fulfilled a unique need in the wider world of subject cataloging. The larger cataloging community not only welcomed Hanson's work but, in the form of cataloging copy and the Library's subject heading lists, also used its results with relatively little critical comment for the first twenty years after the turn of the century. To the extent that Hanson's system was adopted either directly, or indirectly by following its general patterns, the notions of dictionary subject cataloging, of the nature of subjects, and of the role of users in making a subject system, as well as other matters fundamental to alphabetical subject heading work, were also adopted.

CHAPTER 9

Dictionary Subject Cataloging before 1940

Early Public Discussion

The advent of readily obtainable subject heading copy in the form of the first A.L.A. list of subject headings and of headings on Library of Congress printed cards made it possible for the first time for libraries of all sizes and clienteles to provide the subject element of the dictionary catalog. But that possibility almost immediately raised another important issue, that is, the extent to which a dictionary catalog should be simple or complex in its structure and in the format of its headings.

The relative simplicity or complexity of the dictionary subject catalog was important because of how readers and libraries had come to be viewed by the beginning of the twentieth century.[1] As already noted in relation to Hanson's work, readers were generally divided into two groups: those who used books in a serious and scholarly manner, and those who did not. The latter group was considered to be vastly greater in numbers than the first group, but notably inferior in bibliographical and intellectual motivation and skills. The members of the latter group were characterized as "average" or typical readers, whereas members of the first group were "above average." The fundamental assumption of the library movement that the ultimate goal of the library was to aid readers in achieving self-culture and self-improvement meant that subject access tools should likewise be self-help devices. They were to be made in such a way that readers could consult them by themselves with comparative ease. The respective characteristics of the two kinds of users required, however, that subject access tools necessarily be different for each group. Above average readers could use subject tools that arranged subjects with some regard to their classificatory relationships, whether this meant classificatory incursions in the dictionary subject catalog, classified catalogs, or more specialized subject bibliographies. The bibliographical and intellectual deficiencies of average readers required, on the other hand, that the bibliographical tools prepared for them be as simple as possible. This meant not only that

236

bibliographies and classified catalogs could not be used, but that the dictionary subject catalog itself had to be simple in such matters as vocabulary choices and subject heading format and file structure.

Libraries looked upon as mainly serving average readers were smaller and medium-sized public libraries and the branches of large urban libraries. They also included any library or library department which served children. With respect to children, some questioned whether even the simplification of dictionary subject catalogs for smaller and medium-sized public libraries was enough in this regard and, consequently, called for even greater simplicity for children's subject catalogs. Others held that a better solution would be to make all such catalogs at a level adequate for children, thus ensuring their usefulness for bibliographically unskilled adults as well.[2]

Despite the promise the initial A.L.A. *List* held for helping catalogers to include reasonably controlled subject access in their catalogs, the goal could only be achieved in the face of serious obstacles. For one thing, the initial A.L.A. *List* was relatively brief and was not kept up-to-date. Thus, subject catalogers were unable to provide subject access with any great ease for books about new subjects not included in the list. Library of Congress printed cards, available after 1901, were seen by some as a solution to that problem. But for others they amounted to more trouble than they were worth. They often contained far greater bibliographic description than the brief cataloging already present in the typical library catalog. And at first they did not always contain subject headings. Worse, the subject headings they did contain were often incompatible with those already in use.[3]

Another difficulty encountered by subject catalogers was the lack of directions on how to do subject cataloging. Cutter's *Rules* were considered too complex and out-of-date and his list of directions included in the A.L.A. *List* were far too brief. Furthermore, no available directions dealt with the practical problems of subject cataloging in the context of using a subject heading list.

By 1905 the issues provoked by the availability of subject headings brought about a relatively intense period of public discussion. The discussion began with the publication in 1905 of the first twentieth-century cataloging text, Theresa Hitchler's *Cataloging for Small Libraries*. And it continued the following year with William Warner Bishop's address at the annual meeting of the American Library Association entitled "Subject Headings in Dictionary Catalogs." (The address afterward became the chapter on subject heading work in his cataloging textbook.)[4] Ultimately, however, the chief focus of the discussion centered on the project to produce a new edition of the A.L.A. *List of Subject Headings.*

HITCHLER AND BISHOP

The most striking characteristic of Hitchler's and Bishop's treatments of dictionary subject cataloging was the way they expressed the concerns of the times. Both began with the assumption that the character of a library and of its readers dictated what was required of its subject catalog. Because Hitchler directed her work toward the needs of small public libraries that served average readers, she commented on such topics as vocabulary choices and analytical entries that were especially relevant to those situations. For example, she advised subject catalogers not to choose "the most abstruse or the more erudite form of heading, but the one most likely to be used by the borrowers of your library."[5] And with respect to analytics she wrote:

> Bring out *all* the subjects treated in a book, particularly if they seem of the least interest to your community. This is most important in a small library, as the subjects included in the book may not appear in your library in separate works. Make first the subject heading that covers the entire book, the general heading, in short; then bring out the various chapters not covered by this general heading under their specific subject headings.[6]

Bishop was concerned with the larger library (or those that expected to become large) and with its principal clientele—students.[7] Assuming that "ease of consultation" was the primary goal, Bishop warned subject catalogers in large libraries to guard against making the subject catalog into a "formidable and intricate machine which only an expert can use." He wanted to avoid a subject catalog that, having not been constructed on the basis of thoughtful policies, incorporated "medleys of opposing decisions of different catalogers." Thus, he advised subject catalogers to pursue uniformity in their decisions.[8] The remainder of his address consisted of the policies and procedures he thought appropriate for larger libraries. His requirements for dictionary subject catalogs were, therefore, different than those set out by Hitchler. For example, vocabulary choices were to be based on precise meanings. And owing to the potential size of the catalog, analytical and duplicate subject entries had to be kept to a minimum.

Another striking way Hitchler and Bishop expressed the concerns of their times was by portraying subject cataloging as an activity primarily concerned with subject heading format and file structure. Each devoted most of their comments to what constituted the most appropriate practices regarding such issues as topic-place combinations, the use of national adjectives, literary form headings, conjunctive headings, the use of subdivisions, and the practice of inversion. Because Bishop made special demands on preciseness of terminology, he also devoted much space to the nature of names and especially geographical names. The effect of their overwhelming emphasis on such concerns was to portray dictionary subject cataloging as "subject heading work" rather than as subject access work more broadly conceived.

There can be no denying the importance of matters having to do with subject heading format and file structure in dictionary subject cataloging. In 1906, however, that concern was especially significant. First, it seems to have arisen as a natural result of the appearance of subject heading lists and copy. Subject headings were the great new "given" for subject catalogers. They represented the means by which one could provide subject access in a dictionary catalog. The operation was seemingly a straightforward one. Books by definition contained or were about subjects. The chief difficulty had come to be the process of devising suitable and uniform names for the subjects. Easily available subject heading copy overcame that difficulty by providing a ready source of names. One need only match a book with a particular name to achieve subject entry. And even if the copy lacked the particular name needed, it often provided patterns by which one could devise an appropriate one.

Unfortunately, the subject names thus supplied came in a confusing variety of forms that ranged from single-word terms to multiple-word constructions and that had varying degrees of added complexity arising from the practice of inversion and the use of subheadings. The variety of term formats would not have been unduly troubling but for the fact that many subject names could be written in more than one way. A book whose subject content involved both a place and a topic could be listed under one term subdivided by the other or even under both. A phrase heading could also be written as a subject word-subheading combination. If one decided to enter topic-place combinations regularly under topic subdivided by place, a decision then had to be made regarding the use of phrases that began with national adjectives. An alternative available was to invert the latter, but that played havoc with the filing order of the headings.

Problems such as these as well as others like them were primary concerns of subject catalogers in 1906 because no public standards had as yet been reached as to what constituted the most appropriate subject name forms to use. And the notion of appropriateness was further complicated by the conviction that different sizes of libraries having different kinds of readers required different heading formats and file arrangements. Although the makers of the initial A.L.A. *List* had intended to provide some sort of answers to such issues, the *List* served more to sensitize subject catalogers to the issues than to settle them.

This was particularly the case as subject heading copy from the Library of Congress began to diverge noticeably from the headings in the initial A.L.A. *List*. Given these developments, Hitchler's and Bishop's focusing on such issues as the central concern of subject cataloging is understandable.

A second and even more important way the focus on subject heading work was significant was that it tended to mask the more fundamental issue of the purpose and method of subject access—what, in other words, assigning subject headings was supposed to accomplish. Instead, the purpose and method of subject heading work was simply taken for granted. This caused Bishop and Hitchler to incorporate what now appear to be fundamental confusions in their work.

The purpose and method of subject heading work for both Hitchler and Bishop was plainly to denote the topical contents of books by the use of subject headings. To the extent that they both required specific headings as the chief means of accomplishing the task, one might conclude that both writers were giving expression to the idea of scope-matching already discussed. Bishop not only described the process in this way, but also insisted that it was a generally accepted principle.

> Everybody is agreed on the fundamental principle that in dictionary cataloging the "specific" subject must be our norm. We want to get exactly the caption which fits our book and no other.[9]

Likewise, the previously quoted statement by Hitchler that the subject cataloger should first determine "the subject heading that covers the entire book, the general heading, in short," conveys the same impression.[10]

A closer examination of their statements suggests, however, that their idea of a match between the subject of a book and a subject heading was modified in a significant way. The key to the modification was the way they juxtaposed the idea of a specific subject and its specific subject heading with the idea of a general subject and its respective general subject heading. Hitchler wrote:

> Choose a specific subject heading whenever possible. That is, enter a book on Ants under the specific heading ANTS, not under the more general heading INSECTS: a book on Birds under BIRDS, not under ZOOLOGY, etc.[11]

Bishop followed his above quoted words with the similar statement:

> Especially do we wish to avoid general headings for treatises covering a limited field. A man looking for a book on trees does not want to be sent to look through all the cards on botany, nor does the inquirer for

> information about Nelson want to see all the cards on British naval history and biography. He wants what we have about Nelson. As I have said, everybody admits this. The smallest possible unit must be sought out and made the basis for the subject heading.[12]

One might conclude that the referent of the terms "specific subject" and "general subject" is no less than the topical contents of books considered as entireties. In other words, specific subjects are those that match the entire topical contents, and general subjects are those that are broader than the entire topical contents. But Bishop's further elaboration on the matter suggests that the referent was not some notion of a book's entire subject, at least not for its principal meaning. Rather, the referent was a classificatory structure.

> But the library has also books—many thousands of books, probably —which do not deal with one small, particular topic. It has treatises on Botany and British naval heroes. Hence there arises of necessity a set of subjects of a general nature, which are in effect identical with the large divisions of the classifications. We have general treatises on Philosophy, on Religion, on Sociology, on Philology, and so forth. And, further, we have general works on such topics as Physics, Electricity, Mathematics, Latin literature, Hydraulics, Political Science, Psychology, side by side with works of equal bulk and importance on divisions of those subjects, such as Heat, Alternating currents, Differential invariants, Latin pastoral poetry, Canal locks, Proportional representation, The Sense of touch.[13]

The juxtapositions of the terms are revealing. Small particular topics, specific subjects, and specific headings were together placed opposite subjects of a general nature, general subjects, and general subject headings. General subjects were the same, however, as the large divisions, the major classes, of "the classifications." By implication, specific subjects are the same as the subdivisions of the major classes in "the classifications." In other words, subjects, whether specific or general, referred to the elements of known classification enumerations. Some were larger, some smaller, but all were identified as subjects by virtue of their locations within such schemes. As a corollary, books "had," "treated of," or "were about" such subjects, whether general or specific, not in the sense that the subjects were qualities of the books per se, but rather only in the sense that they simply resided in the books. In that respect, a book might be considered general because a general subject resided in it, or specific because a specific subject was found there. But that was only a way of speaking. It did not indicate a concern with the topical entirety of the book except in a secondary sense.

Subject heading work, understood in the light of this classificatory referent, was something akin to an enormous game of matching. There were thousands of books, each the repository of a general or specific subject (and sometimes the repository of more than one). The task of the subject cataloger was first to identify the general or specific subject in a book and then to match that subject with an appropriate subject heading found in an authoritative list of subject headings. It did not mean, primarily at least, devising a heading for the topical scope of a book as if that topical scope had an existence independent of subjects that were known by virtue of already having been plotted in classification enumerations.

Cutter, too, had identified subjects as classificatory locations independent of the books that happened to contain them. Moreover, his goal in subject access had likewise been to enter books under their specific or special subjects (actually, under their *most* specific subjects) rather than under general subjects that included their specific or special subjects. The likenesses between Cutter's approach to the matter and the one found here stops at this point, however. In fact, that there is any likeness at all is probably due only to the fact that the two views had a common source in nineteenth century classificatory thinking rather than because the views discussed here were built on Cutter's view.

Cutter's classificatory referent was at the same time far less fixed and far more inclusive than Bishop's. It was far less fixed in that it was not based on subjects being explicitly enumerated in known classification schemes, as Bishop had suggested by his reference to "the classifications." Rather, it was based only on the much vaguer idea of scholars having come to some consensus on the meaning of a particular term. For Cutter, evidence that a topic was a subject and not simply an indistinct matter of investigation came from the way it was treated, defined, and named in writings. The idea that a subject could be identified by having already been named in an authoritative modern enumeration of subjects was a development that came after Cutter had devised his dictionary subject catalog system, an idea in fact to which he himself had contributed.

Cutter's classificatory referent was also far more inclusive than Bishop's because Cutter, not being tied to one or another authoritative enumeration of known subjects, found it theoretically necessary to provide for all subjects. He accomplished this by his threefold range of subject categories he had derived from Scottish thinking about how a person acquires knowledge of the world. His epistemology also provided a scale of concreteness by which he could determine which subject in any particular combination of subjects was the most specific.

The most specific subject was, of course, the one that was the most concrete.

Bishop's classificatory referent was severely circumscribed compared to Cutter's. His two categories of subjects, specific and general, accommodated only that relatively narrow range of topics that were related intrinsically. In other words, self-evident inclusion relationships —which subject in any combination of subjects was the specific and which was more general—were determined solely on the basis of the logical definitions of the particular terms involved. Physics was a general subject that included the specific subject Heat, for example, because Heat was by definition an element of Physics. Likewise, Electricity included Alternating currents, Mathematics included Differential invariants, Latin literature included Latin pastoral poetry, Hydraulics included Canal locks, Political science included Proportional representation, and Psychology included Sense of touch because in each case the term denoted as the specific subject was *by definition* an element of the term denoted as the general subject. In each case, the relationship of one term to the other was an intrinsic one.

This approach to subjects and their relationships had philosophical origins of great antiquity, of course. But it was inadequate for a subject catalog because it could not state automatically and on the basis of principle the inclusion relationship for subjects related only extrinsically. Bishop could not, in other words, determine which term was specific and which term was general and thus inclusive of the specific term in such combinations as topics and places (e.g., Geology and California; Ornithology and New England) and topics not otherwise related by definition (e.g., Physics and History; Railroad rails and Steel). And where the inclusion relationship could not be determined with any ease, neither the most specific entry term nor the order of terms in a term-subdivision combination could be identified. In fact, the injunction to avoid class entry made little sense in such situations. There was simply no way to determine in a combination such as Ornithology of New England, which term, Ornithology or New England, was more specific.

Bishop ultimately solved the problem of what to do in such situations, but he did so in the same manner that Hanson had solved it. He appealed to such practical measures as how subjects were listed in known classification schemes or how readers supposedly thought about subjects. The latter is particularly important because it essentially changed the basis of entry from class inclusion to what seemed practical and useful to readers, that is, to what a reader was likely to look under first. Bishop's appeal to practical measures is well illustrated in his conclusions regarding entry choices in place-topic combinations.

> I believe that the British Museum practice and that of the Library of Congress are more nearly in line with the habit of readers and the viewpoint of the makers of books. If we leave out the historical sciences, the main interest is the topic and not the region. . . .
>
> I advocate, then, a deliberate policy of restricting the entries under the country or region to those topics which have a strictly local interest, *i.e.*, the field of the historical sciences and such of the social sciences as depend for their value on local conditions. . . .
>
> I would limit the subheads under a country to those which seem absolutely necessary. For everything else which might be expected under country I would make a subject reference card. This may be begging the question. It may be abandoning the search for a guiding principle. But it seems to me that the habit of most readers and authors is a fair guide for us. After all it is for them that the catalog is made.[14]

Bishop's approach to determining subject relationships affected his overall subject cataloging instructions in a striking way because it caused him to interpret the relationship of classification to dictionary subject cataloging in a confusing manner. On the one hand, he was adamant about not giving books class entry. He portrayed that alternative as the wrong use of general subject headings.

> Because some headings must be the same in any sort of catalog, and because some which are definitely group headings have to be used as a practical matter of common sense in a dictionary catalog, you will find catalogers continually reverting to these class headings. It is vastly easier to label a book Sociology than to pin its contents down to one particular phase of social inquiry. We all tend to move unconsciously along the lines of least resistance. We shall never get our catalog of specific headings without constant self-vigilance, constant self-criticism, and drastic revision. We must have class headings so long as our libraries are not composed wholly of theses for the doctorate. And we must avoid them as much as possible.[15]

In other words, dictionary subject catalogs necessarily had to use what in "the classifications" were general or class headings. But one had to be careful that such headings were used only when the subjects contained in books entered under them matched those headings in their subject scope. This concern was not unfounded. Subject catalogers had traditionally found it easier to provide entry under inclusive general classes rather than under the specific subjects included in the general classes. And this led to extensive subject files of books entered under class headings that actually varied widely in their respective subject scopes.

On the other hand, Bishop also regularly spoke of any subheading used in subarrangement as a subdivision of a subject. Topics were to be subdivided by places, by other topics, and by chronological divisions. He justified such "subdivisions" by suggesting that they were useful in bringing related topics together systematically. To the objection that the reader was then obliged to examine complex subarrangements like those found in classed catalogs, Bishop claimed only that such sequences were unavoidable. Thus, it was better for them to be alphabetically rather than systematically subarranged.

In addition to the above, Bishop also spoke of form subheadings as classificatory subdivisions that should be used with class or general headings.

> Moreover, a first-rate dictionary catalog will use under these class headings—or headings common to both sorts of catalogs—a few of the simple and large subdivisions of classification, such as *History, Essays and addresses, Outlines, syllabi, etc.*[16]

One might disregard his statement because form subheadings are not now nor were they then generally considered evidence of classification. Still, Bishop appears to have considered them as classificatory sequences. And the effect of treating them as classificatory sequences was to instruct the dictionary subject cataloger to use classification in the specific entry catalog. Then, after having instructed the subject cataloger to use classification, he stated, "In doing this it will not violate the dictionary principle."[17] Unfortunately, he did not explain why no violation would occur.

In sum, Bishop was in the position of adamantly prohibiting the use of classed entry in the dictionary subject catalog while at the same time encouraging the use of classificatory sequences in the form of subarrangement practices. In retrospect, one can see that Bishop was struggling with the need to accommodate what amounted to essentially different kinds of term relationships. All such relationships fell into three categories: subjects related intrinsically, subjects related extrinsically, and subjects related to terms denoting form categories. He considered all such term combinations as manifestations of classification, perhaps because the classification schemes of his day did not distinguish between such relationships but displayed them all as class-subdivision sequences. Of the three kinds of term relationships, however, Bishop considered only one, subjects related intrinsically, as truly representative of classificatory inclusion. Thus, it was only that relationship that he warned subject catalogers against using because only it represented for him the denial of specific entry. The others, while representing classification, were legitimately usable and in fact necessary to the dictionary subject catalog.

All of this may have been clear to Bishop, but to one not conversant with the idea of subjects and subject access, his instructions, provided without any basic explanation, could only have appeared confusing. Moreover, Bishop's instructions likewise could only have substantially blurred the relationship of classification to subject cataloging. If the dictionary subject catalog found it necessary to resort to classification, what then was the essential difference between it and any formal classification scheme? This question, not apparently seen in Bishop's time, came to occupy a position of paramount concern in later decades when subject catalogers attempted to explain in a more theoretical way the essential characteristics of the dictionary subject catalog.

A.L.A. LIST OF SUBJECT HEADINGS, THIRD EDITION

Hitchler's and Bishop's forays into subject heading work may well have provided the impetus for further action by the American Library Association. In late 1906 the Association's Publishing Board announced plans to publish a third edition of the A.L.A. *List*.[18] The concerns of the public discussion of dictionary subject cataloging were thereafter almost totally taken up with that project, perhaps because it represented the opportunity to set standards for subject heading format that would permanently affect how dictionary subject catalogs would be constructed.

The character of the discussion followed the patterns set by Hitchler and Bishop in that it was almost completely concerned with subject heading format and file structure rather than with issues related to the fundamental purpose of the subject catalog. Thus, commentators again went over the same kinds of subject heading format problems that had been raised earlier, except the issue of entry under place or topic when a book was about both receded into the background as a principal issue.

The discussion also adhered to the ideal that a subject catalog should be constructed with a library's clientele in mind. In this case, however, the premise of user considerations was greatly expanded. Both Hitchler and Bishop, following current opinion, had based their approaches to subject heading work on the two different kinds of users libraries served. However, saying that subject heading format and file structure should be adapted to one or the other of the two kinds of users, while an understandable goal, did not in and of itself suggest how that might be done. The habits of readers were, in other words, easy to hypothesize but difficult to define and ascertain.

Hitchler had pointed the way to a resolution of what was meant by that notion when in 1905 she described something of the method that a subject cataloger had to follow. She suggested that subject catalogers in small libraries had to be aware of two chief factors in their work—their own intelligence and familiarity with bibliographical processes, and the lack of those same qualities on the part of the average reader. Because the average reader was "ignorant," especially "so far as the use of the catalog is concerned," catalogers had to be wary of being too technical or too precise in their work.[19] Technical perfection and precision based on subject catalogers' desire to make systematic subject access instruments would likely be wasted efforts for such users. Rather than beginning with that kind of a goal, subject catalogers should begin with an appreciation of the average reader. This implied that the average reader should be observed.

> Observe carefully the "ignorant" borrower; from him you may gain much *if you will but make careful note of what he asks for and how his mind works in regard to the entries he seeks.* Be open to suggestions from anybody and everybody, culling the best.[20]

Translated into subject heading procedures, this meant that decisions about subject heading format and file structure might be settled if the ways that readers used subject terminology in their thinking could be determined.

Discussion regarding the new edition of the A.L.A. *List* took up Hitchler's challenge directly. In January 1907 Esther Crawford, the first editor of the project, published an extensive list of questions designed to answer not only what things the new list might best include or exclude, but also what alternatives in particular subject heading format were the most appropriate for smaller and medium-sized public libraries.[21] In the October 1907 *Library Journal* she clarified the goal she had in mind. She stated that she wished to base the new edition on "the experiences of thoughtful loan and reference workers who had tried to satisfy the calls of readers with the catalogs constructed upon the usages of the past 20 years."[22] The observations of reference workers seemed to her to provide the most reliable source of information about how users thought.

Crawford subsequently noted that on the basis of preliminary talks with reference workers, several "tendencies" already seemed apparent about the way "the average adult intelligent American" looked for subjects. Among these was the conclusion that average readers tended to look under place first only for historical or local interest topics when places and topics were combined. Otherwise, the reader generally looked for topics first. More important, Crawford concluded that the reader normally did have specific and definite subject requests in mind, but these were often obscured by using a general term for a specific subject request. Furthermore, this latter tendency was ordinarily governed "by the extent to which the newspapers, the magazines and the readers' associates used the generic for the specific term."[23] She concluded that vocabulary choices must follow such variations.

> The principle is reducible to this: How closely does the reader actually classify the subject in his own thought (but not necessarily his language) to cover his own needs? This, rather than consistency, should govern the closeness of entry in the catalog. It must rest upon what the reader really does think and not upon what you believe he ought to think, nor upon what you vaguely hope he may be brought to think if you "educate" him long enough.[24]

Stated in terms of subject heading work, Crawford had concluded that nothing less than term-by-term decisions would do, the results being as variable as readers' habits of thinking.

One might argue that to follow this course of action would mean the end of all consistency in the subject catalog. A better alternative would be to construct the catalog on the basis of consistent subject heading format practices to begin with and to teach the reader to search according to those consistent patterns. Crawford sensed that that alternative was on the minds of at least some catalogers, and supported the necessity of her own position with an argument concerning the average reader's learning capacity. She noted that on the one hand the average reader

> positively refuses to be "educated" by any catalog. He doesn't want his vocabulary increased—at least not in that forced way—and when you try, you succeed in enlarging it only along the line of profanity.[25]

On the other hand, the average reader still desired

> vital information—the spirit which quickeneth, not the letter which killeth—and the more quickly you get him to it and to exactly the right information, the more he will be likely to extend his research to related and including subjects.[26]

The average reader was, in other words, "intelligent in desires and comprehensions but untrained in methods of bibliographic research or in the use of card catalogs."[27] Average readers knew what they wanted but did not go about searching for it with the precise vocabulary and logical sense of subject relationships that librarians and scholars did. Furthermore, this situation was likely to remain unchanged as long as the social and educational environment of average readers remained unchanged.

More hopeful, however, was the thought that if average readers were enabled efficiently to find the immediate information they were looking for—and this meant searching through headings that arose from their vocabulary and not from the more precise and systematic vocabulary of librarians and scholars—then they would have the reading materials that would educate them and help them of their own accord later to expand their searches through more systematic searching. The education of readers was a process, in other words, that came after subjects were found, not before readers began their searching. Crawford wrote disparagingly of requiring readers' education at the start of their searching.

> Any attempt *at this stage* to force the larger or more comparative view of the subject is an impertinence. It cannot and will not be taken in mind until the smaller want has been filled and the new energy generated thereby begins to crave something more comprehensive and explanatory of causes. This seems to be one of the reasons for discontent concerning subjects which are so bewildering in a card catalog by reason of their great bulk.[28]

In sum, Crawford was convinced that the best way to serve average readers was to aid them in finding the immediate subject matter for which they searched. This meant using whatever subject terminology the reader used, even if that led to choosing generic headings for specific subjects in some cases and specific headings for specific subjects in others. The key was to determine the right heading in each case and to avoid all other matters of subject heading format and file structure complexity. Toward this end, Crawford called on librarians in smaller and medium-sized public libraries and in the branches of larger urban public libraries to study readers and to report their experiences as to what headings were needed. In fact, she published articles in the next two succeeding months that asked a plethora of questions about dozens of particular headings and heading patterns, hoping in each instance to receive answers that would provide a basis for providing headings in the new edition of the list.[29]

Crawford's attempt to determine the vocabulary and habits of thinking of average readers was consistent with the ideal that subject catalogs should be adapted to the readers who will use it. But it was also a gargantuan task. It involved reaching a consensus on every notable heading and heading pattern likely to be used in such catalogs. Not only did it involve more effort and time than any single person or perhaps any group of persons could expend, its method, based mainly on the opinions of reference librarians rather than on direct questioning of readers, led more often than not to inconclusive results.

Crawford eventually turned the editorship of the project over to Mary Josephine Briggs, who brought the new list to completion in 1911. Briggs, like Crawford, believed that because subject headings had to be chosen with the reader constantly in mind, overall consistency within a catalog was impossible and even an undesirable goal.[30] But Briggs also had to deal with the results of Crawford's work, that not only did the ideal make overall consistency within any one catalog impossible, but also it made consistency among libraries impossible as well. Diametrically opposed opinions between librarians over many matters suggested, for example, that there was little basis for agreeing on even the same kinds of irregularities. This was especially the case with the three interchangeable kinds of heading forms available for any compound subject: straightforward adjectival phrases, inverted adjectival phrases, and noun-subdivision strings-of-terms. If librarians could agree on the use of one or another of these forms in particular cases, they could at least set standards among them, although on a case-by-case basis. Briggs found, however, that not even this was possible. She concluded:

> In the end, all efforts to frame the desired rule resolved themselves into something like this: It is necessary to use all three forms of headings; noun with subdivision, adjective phrase, and inversion. Each case must be decided upon its own merits, and that form used under which it is believed that the majority of readers will look—the majority of readers in each particular library, be it understood. A university library will use many subdivisions because it is convenient for professors and students to have much of the material brought together under large subjects. A medical library will use few, if any, headings beginning Medical because Medical is understood.[31]

Briggs's statement is significant because she in effect recast the ideal of making the subject catalog closely responsive to the mental habits of readers. First, she noted that rather than attempting to base the catalog on the habits of all readers of one kind, it should be based on the habits of a majority of readers *in a particular library*. Her revision was important because it accommodated Crawford's findings that little agreement could be found among libraries. Briggs said in effect that such consistency was not possible or necessary.

Second, Briggs provided some explanation of what a majority of readers meant. Her examples suggested that the idea of a majority meant typifying the readers a library served and choosing subject headings on the basis of the characteristics associated with that "type." University libraries served readers with characteristics which represented one kind of usage. Medical libraries served readers which represented still another.

Typifying the readers for whom a subject catalog was to be constructed was eventually to become an important part of subject cataloging discussions in later decades when types of libraries would become an essential factor for consideration. From its beginnings in comments such as the one found here, however, the argument suggested something of its own weaknesses. First, typifying a library's clientele is a notably intuitive matter, especially when no serious methodology for determining the characteristics of the group is included. Second, the public library for which the A.L.A. *List* was ostensibly being prepared was omitted from Briggs's examples. The fact is that public library readers, of all the types of library readers that might be delineated, are those most difficult to characterize. One might even conclude that the public library represented the lack of a distinctive set of characteristics. For these reasons, Briggs's resolution appears to have been little more than a convenient rationalization to explain the impasse to which the original ideal of making subject catalogs responsive to readers and Crawford's pursuit of them had led. This conclusion seems probable, in fact, because having suggested the resolution, Briggs discontinued her discussion of it to address the chief issue at hand, the characteristics of the new list she had edited. Her description of the procedures she had followed suggests that consideration of the reader played at best only a minor role.

Briggs noted that, contrary to the pursuit of the ideal of devising subject headings that reflected the mental habits of readers, the chief practical constraints in devising the new list were, first, providing consistency between it and the initial list, and second, making the new list compatible with headings supplied by the Library of Congress. With respect to the first constraint, some headings in the initial list were changed, but only when opinion based on Crawford's findings had been decisive. With respect to the second constraint, Briggs noted that in all cases where evidence of the most appropriate heading was inconclusive, "the usage of the Library of Congress, if known, was the determining factor in the decision." Briggs was clear about the implications of the latter procedure. "The Library of Congress headings are admittedly devised to meet conditions in the Library of Congress—certainly very different conditions from those of a public library."[32] She did not explain why she followed this alternative, but the reason is not difficult to see. Devising subject headings specifically for a public library clientele was next to impossible because there was simply too much variation to accommodate. In fact, the ideal if pursued would make a standard list of headings impossible. A standard list was what was desired, however, and there was no better basis available for it than the highly reputed subject heading list of the nation's most prestigious library. The Library of Congress had in fact begun to publish its own list of headings in 1910 and thereafter continued to be the chief source of up-to-date subject heading copy.[33]

Making a subject catalog responsive to the vocabulary and thinking patterns of a library's readers could still be accomplished, but it would come in a local library context and not in the form of a standard national list. Briggs stated this alternative directly when she wrote:

> The list is not intended as a guide to be followed blindly, but to be adapted to individual needs, by the exercise of common sense—perhaps the most necessary part of the cataloger's equipment.[34]

In other words, the subject cataloger should begin with the list as a standard, and where the situation demanded it, vary the headings in the list to serve the local needs.

RESULTS OF THE PUBLIC DISCUSSION

With Briggs's remarks, the initial public discussion of dictionary subject cataloging was in a very real sense brought to a close. Almost nothing new and significant was written in American publications about subject cataloging for more than a decade afterward.[35] The discussion was determinative in fixing the practice of dictionary subject cataloging work, however. Theoretical issues, such as the nature of subjects, the essential goal of subject cataloging, and the relationship of subject cataloging and classification, had been left dangling between nineteenth-century ideas and the changing patterns of twentieth century thought. The ideal of constructing subject catalogs in the light of readers' needs was more thoroughly investigated. But it proved to be so impervious to implementation that it was relegated to the role of a more or less intuitive procedure.

At the same time, the practical activity of subject cataloging, interpreted primarily as subject heading work, settled into the task of accommodating the most dominant reality that subject catalogers faced—the assignment of subject headings to the increasing acquisitions of the times. The activity was at best a mixture of tensions, however. On the one hand, the cataloger faced the cold fact of the authoritative nature of subject heading lists and copy. These constituted their principal "given"—A.L.A. subject headings for some, but for many others the increasingly useful Library of Congress headings. At the same time, using subject headings supplied by authorities only served to reinforce the identification of subject heading work with the mechanical and monotonous side of cataloging that was so much the center of concern at the 1915 Catalog Section discussion on "Training for Cataloging Work."[36] On the other hand, subject catalogers were called on to use their common sense in adapting the subject headings provided in a list to the specific needs of their users. But this proved to be at best a subjective procedure. And when combined with vague notions of what subject headings were supposed to denote and of the relationship of subject headings to classification, the entire process of subject heading work found itself laced with a strong dependency on intuitive procedures—an interpretation of the task that eventually came to be considered the "art" of subject heading work.

Problems Encountered by the 1920s

Although the public discussion of dictionary subject cataloging had diminished during the decade following Briggs's remarks, the problems that subject catalogers faced did not abate. The problems were not new but rather only extensions of issues that had been expressed earlier. But they arose with a greater urgency because of the slowly changing context in which they were expressed. That context included larger numbers of libraries attempting to provide subject access within the dictionary catalog and larger numbers of acquisitions to be accommodated by subject headings. The problems encountered were expressed in terms of the size and types of libraries.

LIBRARY SIZE

The relative size of a library had been a central issue during the initial period of discussion primarily because size was the principal way for librarians to differentiate the varying conditions of particular libraries. Small libraries were identified with average readers and the need for simple subject catalogs whereas larger libraries were identified with above average readers and the need for more complete and more sophisticated subject access tools and catalogs. There was a practical truism to that equation because small libraries often were those that served children or a general public in a town rather than a large urban setting. Thus, their readership often had less schooling and thus fewer bibliographical skills. But taken at face value, the association between the size of a library and its cataloging needs was only an accidental rather than an essential relationship.

By the 1920s the equation of a library's relative size with its basic cataloging conditions was fast being augmented by a different equation—that a library's basic cataloging needs could be better expressed as a function of its type. The size of a library remained an important factor, but it was qualified in two important ways. First, that a library was small was important only for children's libraries and smaller and medium-sized public libraries, whereas that a library was large was important principally for university libraries and large urban libraries. Size tended not to be a principal issue for other types of libraries, such as special or college libraries. Second, the issue of library size, when considered by itself, actually revolved about the logistics of subject heading work, that is, with the problems related to obtaining just those headings which would produce files of subject entries of adequate size, neither too large nor too small.

Despite the publication of a third edition of the A.L.A. *List,* smaller and medium-sized public libraries and libraries that served children continued to find it difficult to meet their subject cataloging needs for the same reasons they had had difficulties during the earlier period. The third edition, like the initial list, was a one-time publication that was neither updated nor improved as time passed. And those who depended on it found it increasingly inadequate for their needs. Using the Library of Congress subject heading list (completely available in a preliminary edition by 1914, supplemented occasionally afterward, and finally reissued in a formal second edition in 1919) likewise offered only a sparing solution to those problems. Supposing the librarian of a small library even knew of the existence of the Library of Congress list (let alone of its supplements) and could justify obtaining it, the process of using it was formidable. The needed headings had to be extracted from what, in comparison to small library needs, was an enormous list of terms; this made even the straightforward act of finding an appropriate heading an arduous task. And the headings in the list were often incompatible with those already in use either by being based on distinctions that were too precise and thus confusing to choose between or by differences in heading format. Incompatibility of headings was also the chief problem in using the headings supplied by the Library of Congress on its printed cards. In the latter case, however, the headings, if used without reference to the Library's list, were further confounded by their lack of explicit connection to an integrated subject heading system. They became disparate particles that helped to make one's entire subject catalog uneven and uncoordinated.

The most important result of the logistical problems small libraries had in obtaining and using subject headings was the publication of special lists of headings geared especially to their needs. Margaret Mann's *Subject Headings for Use in Dictionary Catalogs of Juvenile Books* (1916) was an attempt to provide headings for the subject cataloging needs of children's libraries. It represented the headings of a single library, the Carnegie Library of Pittsburgh, and followed earlier efforts to supply headings in a joint venture by that library and the Cleveland Public Library. It was limited, however, by being oriented to children's catalogs vaguely defined rather than to types of children's libraries, by being from a single library rather than representing the needs of several libraries, and most of all by being a one-time publication that was not updated periodically. Her work was surpassed in 1933 by Elva S. Smith's *Subject Headings for Children's Books in Public Libraries and in Libraries in Elementary and Junior High Schools.* This work attempted to rectify the weaknesses of Mann's list by being more up-to-date, by not being limited to the headings of a single library, and by taking into special account the needs of school libraries as a special type of library.[37]

Of even greater importance than Smith's work was the publication by Minnie Earl Sears in 1923 of a new shortened list of subject headings for smaller libraries. Proclaimed as an alternative to both the Library of Congress and the earlier A.L.A. lists, it nevertheless filled a role similar to that of the A.L.A. lists in claiming as its justification the special needs of smaller libraries. Like the A.L.A. *List*, it represented the headings of a group of libraries, except in this case the nine libraries used as a basis for it were all public libraries in smaller towns and cities. At the same time, the forms of headings and choices between synonyms were generally based on Library of Congress patterns just as they had been in the third edition of the A.L.A. *List*.[38]

So popular did Sears's list become that a second edition was published three years later (1926, reprinted in 1928). It was a distinct improvement over its predecessor because it included all "see" and "see also" cross-references, including "refer from" references, those that since the 1940s have regularly been listed as "xx" references. By including "refer from" references, Sears made the list a syndetic subject heading system, unlike the Library of Congress list which excluded them and thus displayed to catalogers only part of the syndetic structure of its system.[39]

Large libraries also had difficulties when using Library of Congress subject heading copy and lists. Problems of the extraction of headings from the Library's work, such as those noted above, were always present where the books in a particular subject area held even by a large library were significantly fewer in number than those cataloged by the Library of Congress. This situation tended to be complicated by the occurrence of the opposite situation as well, that is, when subject areas in large libraries had many more books than the Library of Congress.

In the latter situation, the large local library needed more headings or better specified headings than the Library of Congress supplied. This need forced libraries to devise their own headings and heading subdivisions with the concomitant risk of their choices later conflicting with Library of Congress expansions in the same areas. For some institutions both situations were strained because the lack of general explanation for and understanding of the nature of subject heading work promoted inconsistencies. On the other hand, because larger libraries tended to have more people who specialized in cataloging and who took considerable pains with their work, subject cataloging also gave evidence of being overdone, laced as it was with double-entry procedures and smothering incursions of cross-references.

Subject heading work in local situations as well as the sheer size of rapidly growing catalogs led to still another critical issue that had arisen by the 1920s, that of cost. As early as 1909, Hanson had already broached the problem of cost for the Library of Congress in terms of the expense of catalog administration, the sheer physical size of catalogs, and the enormous files of entries which tended to accumulate under certain subject names that had been thought to be of adequate specification when first created.[40] This last problem made continual revision of subject headings necessary, particularly through subarrangement techniques. These same kinds of problems in the catalogs of other large libraries came especially into focus in a 1924 A.L.A. roundtable discussion, the proceedings of which were edited by Henry B. Van Hoesen and published under the title *Selective Cataloging*.[41] The title itself indicates something of the answer that larger libraries proposed, that is, limiting certain cataloging practices. But the very nature of the discussion indicated a more important change taking place—that is, that the problems of cataloging in general and of subject cataloging in particular were being affected by a relatively new factor, the library administrator, whose responsibility included controlling costs. The subject cataloging situation of the first two decades had apparently proceeded without much concern about cost. Catalogers did what they thought necessary to achieve a viable, though relatively uncriticized, cataloging procedure. The effect of the new factor, felt in a continuous way over the decades that followed, was to force catalogers to examine their work and to justify it.[42]

TYPES OF LIBRARIES

The second major way catalogers tended to express the problems that had developed in dictionary subject cataloging was in terms of the libraries in which they found themselves. Thinking of libraries in terms of their types was in many respects the natural result of the growth of the library as a social institution. Although libraries had always borne distinguishing names such as "college" libraries, "town" libraries, or "historical society" libraries during the initial period of the library movement in the nineteenth century, the most significant differentiation that librarians then made between them was whether they regularly allowed some portion of the public into them or were essentially private. Most were of the first category and were thought of as elements of a more or less unified endeavor to bring cultural uplift to society at large. In that respect, all such libraries were considered "public" libraries. Beginning about the 1890s, however, librarians who found themselves in similar institutional contexts increasingly identified their libraries as specialized manifestations of the library in general. By the 1920s this conscious progress of institutional differentiation had resulted in a nomenclature of types of libraries that has persisted to the present day—academic, public, school, and special libraries.[43]

Thinking of libraries in terms of categorical types affected subject cataloging by providing an enhanced basis for pursuing the goal of constructing subject catalogs that were closely responsive to library users. The previous categorization of libraries as either large, with above average or scholarly readers, or small, with average or general readers, had been clearly too vague a basis upon which to pursue the goal. Type-of-library thinking provided not only more categories, but categories that suggested a more clearly delimited set of parameters within which to characterize readers. And if readers could be more accurately portrayed, then the goal of making the subject catalog more closely responsive to readers stood a better chance of being reached.

This approach to dealing with subject cataloging problems was not without its special problems and peculiarities. To begin with, library-size considerations not only continued to be expressed, but came to be intertwined with type-of-library considerations in such a way as to make their differentiation unclear. Furthermore, the characterization of public library readers as a type of library clientele was conspicuously absent in the subject cataloging literature of this period. One may speculate that that absence appears to have arisen from the very process of institutional differentiation that had taken place.

The public library was in many respects the general model or prototype from which other types of libraries and their clienteles were originally set apart. Thus, once the other types of libraries had been effectively differentiated from the prototype, it appears that librarians assumed that what remained was, so to speak, the real public library, the modern public library unmixed in one's thinking with specialized manifestations of the library in general. But librarians then appear to have been satisfied that the general characteristics previously attributed to the readership of the prototype applied as well to the now more clearly separated modern public library. In other words, the original characterization of the average readers attributed to small libraries now became the characterization of the general modern public library as well. Since those characteristics had already been described, there was really no need to characterize public library readers further except to the extent that any public library also included elements of some other kind of library, such as a children's room or a special business service. In those cases, however, the special element appears to have been considered independently of the whole and functioned as an additional rather than an ameliorating feature of the general characterization. A public library in that situation remained a public library that was simply augmented by another kind of library element. It did not become some distinctly separate kind of library.[44]

The last special feature of type-of-library thinking had to do with the particular characteristics which came to be attributed to each type. Sometimes these included difficulties and vagueness as in children's libraries, and sometimes striking advances as in special libraries. These will be examined here in terms of three types—children's, special, and academic libraries—each with their respective clienteles and, therefore, each having special features of subject heading work.

Children's Libraries. One of the first types of libraries to be set apart with respect to subject cataloging was children's libraries, considered either as separate institutions or as children's departments in public libraries. The characterization of this type of library was intermixed with the special problems of small libraries because most children's collections were relatively small. Thus, issues related to the size of children's libraries were normally spoken of together with the special needs of children as readers. But beyond these problems were two others of special note.

First, it was generally concluded that subject headings for children demanded the use of simple terms. The idea of a simple term was not without difficulties, however, and between Mann writing in 1916 and Smith writing in 1933 one can see some signs of those difficulties. Mann wrote:

> The style and content of books for children naturally lead one to select a simple word; for example, a book on candy making for children does not discuss the other forms of confectionary, so one is not tempted to use that heading merely because it is used in the adult catalog, but the book is put under the heading Candy without further

consideration. A book of flowers which does not discuss the classification of plants does not warrant the heading Botany, so one is not led to adopt the scientific term. Textile fabrics in the adult catalog should be replaced by Cloth in the juvenile catalog, because the first term is not the common one.[45]

Mann's first example suggests the idea of a simple term was related to the relative scope of a term. Candy making is obviously more circumscribed in what it denotes than Confectionary. Supposing that a child's book covered no more than what the term Candy denoted, the book should be placed under that term and not under the broader term. The two terms, Candy making and Confectionary, are related in a classificatory sense, the latter being a class which includes the former. This suggests that Mann was simply providing a formula similar to those found in Bishop and Hitchler that a heading should indicate the particular narrow subject a book is about and not the class of which the narrow subject was a part. This conclusion is reinforced by her second example, using a heading that denotes Flowers rather than Botany if the book placed under it is only about flowers and not also about the scientific classification of plants.

Given this approach to the idea of a simple term, one might be tempted to consider it only a modified version of the then current idea of specific entry. This is further suggested by the fact that Mann's examples in the section of her text that was entitled "Definite and specific terms" are for all practical purposes the same as the two cited here.[46] The principle of specific entry was modified only in the sense that particular, specific topics in books for children became synonymous with simple subjects and therefore with simple terms or headings. Thus, the admonition to enter books under simple terms was little more than the usual specific entry equation with one element missing or understood: specific subjects = [simple subjects] = simple terms.

Because the admonition to use simple terms, when understood in the preceding manner, did not require anything of the subject cataloger which would not have been expected of subject heading work for adults, its significance as a special provision for subject heading work for children was diminished. It seems obvious, however, that Mann thought more to be involved. Her third example, Cloth for Textile fabrics, indicates something of this because the difference between these terms for Mann did not turn on their relative breadth, but rather on vocabulary preference. Mann considered Cloth to be the "common" term, Textile fabrics by implication to be the uncommon term, uncommon, that is, to children. In other words, in the third example, the simple term was a matter of usage, not a matter of classificatory breadth. And Mann's admonition in choosing between equivalent terms was to use the term used by children, not the one used in adult catalogs by adults.

One may surmise that here, too, there was a hidden but understood element of the equation, similar to the one noted above, that terms commonly used by children were simple terms by reason of the fact that children used them. Mann did not extend this sense of the idea of simple terms further. In fact, she was explicit about the limitations in the use of common terms, noting that some represented little more than poor usage. Consequently, to choose them for the catalog might either suggest "talking down" to children (e.g., using Bunnies for Rabbits; Bugs for Insects) or give the impression of promoting poor usage (e.g., Stuffed animals or Mounted animals for Taxidermy). She advised subject catalogers not to use such terms despite the fact that children might use them. She did not explain her reasoning in the latter example except to say, "The child old enough to make use of this heading should learn the correct term."[47]

Seventeen years later, Elva S. Smith, using Mann's text as a point of departure, reiterated the call for simple terms. But in keeping with the ever-growing stress on making subject catalogs closely responsive to catalog users, she gave a much greater emphasis to usage, the second of Mann's two sources for the meaning of simple terms. Smith began her section on "Use of Simple Terms" as Mann had done, by noting that once having identified the subject of a work, a subject cataloger next had to "choose the term which will best express this subject." To do so was nothing less than to follow the specific entry process. Like Mann, however, she also noted that because of the "style and context" of children's books, the terms needed could not be just any terms. Rather, they had to be simple terms. Simple terms were those terms "naturally used by children" or "sufficiently explicit and already familiar to children!" They consisted of "simplified phraseology" that arose from "the children's own wording." Simple terms were, in other words, "the vocabulary of children."[48]

Smith's heavy emphasis on usage as a way to define simple terms is significant because she shifted the idea of a simple term from that of a measure of the term's content to a measure of how the term was perceived, in this case, by children. Said otherwise, "simple" was no longer a quality of a term per se, but rather a quality of the user or use of a term. Furthermore, using simple terms in a catalog became a process of catalog simplification.

The effect of this shift in essential definition on subject heading procedure was immediately to engage the subject cataloger in a serious conflict. The basic principle that terms should be chosen that "best express" the subjects of books implied that adult terms should be used. Adult terms were words commonly employed by adults and used in general catalogs for adults. Adult terms were not simplified. They expressed subjects with greater precision and suggested all the various connotations and denotations that the subject expressed by them required. In comparison to children's terms for the same subjects, they were "difficult." And in contrast to the use of catalogs by children, they demanded that a catalog user approach subject searching "intelligently."[49]

The problem with applying the basic goal of using expressive terms to the children's subject catalog was, in Smith's view, that "the vocabulary of children does not always adapt itself to the requirements of the catalog."[50] In other words, children's terms did not accomplish the task of best expressing the subjects of books. Thus, using children's terms, although required by the goal of making catalogs closely responsive to its users, would cause one to fail in best expressing the subjects of books. Conversely, to use adult terms that best expressed the subjects of books would cause one to fail in achieving the goal of making the catalog user responsive.

Smith's resolution of this conflict was to call for the use of children's terms, but only in a careful manner. She wrote:

> Practical usefulness need not be sacrificed in order to insure uniformity with the terms commonly employed, but there should be definite reasons for variations. Candy may be substituted for Confectionery, Birds for Ornithology, Cooking for Cookery, because these are the words that will most invariably be looked for and they are adaptable to the phraseology of a catalog. The term Plays is preferable to Amateur theatricals and Handicraft to Amateur work, for psychological reasons.[51]

Her first reason, that terms which will be used by children in searching are to be chosen, is clear enough. The second reason, "for psychological reasons," is a little less clear but can refer to nothing else but the fact that certain terms are "explicit" to children and thus should be used in preference to others that are not.

Smith emphasized the need for care in choosing such terms because of three factors encountered in the course of children's cataloging. First, the very process of childhood education suggested that children's terms were at best only transitory. The very nature of schooling was to teach children to use adult terms. Adult terms were, of course, those that teachers used and taught. Therefore, to incorporate too many children's terms in the children's catalog would conflict with the natural process of education. This factor caused Smith to recommend that when one had to choose between two equivalent terms such as Cloth and Textile fabrics, the first, being the simpler of the two and commonly used outside of an educational framework, might be chosen for the public library, whereas the second, being the teacher's term and thus an adult term that children were expected to learn, might be used in a school library catalog.

The second factor that led Smith to advise care in choosing children's terms was that some terms represented "unnecessary simplification" and were aimed primarily at very young children. To use those terms in a children's catalog would have the effect of "talking down" to older children.

The third factor which made care in choice necessary, at least in the opinion of some, was the assumption that if many children's terms were used, the children who used them would afterward have difficulty in using general catalogs with adult terms. Smith denied that this was a relevant matter. She noted that many subjects had no equivalent simplified terms. Thus, adult terms had to be used for them even in the children's catalog. She concluded that "the number of such terms simplified in the specialized catalog is only a small percentage of the total."[52] Furthermore, because children learned adult terms naturally and with relative ease, the small percentage of the total number of terms that were children's terms would require of them only "minor changes" as they grew up.

Smith's approach to choosing children's terms may be summarized in the following manner. Smith recognized that there was a conflict between using children's terms to fulfill the goal of making a user-responsive catalog and using adult terms to fulfill the goal of specific entry. She rationalized the use of children's terms, however, because she believed that the total would not be too large and because those that were chosen would not significantly disrupt the child's ability to learn adult terms. To ensure that result, therefore, she advocated that such terms only be chosen with great care.

Despite the straightforward nature of Smith's approach to the matter, it was not without serious difficulties both with respect to its assumptions and with respect to its procedure. Like Mann, Smith's call for the use of simple terms was clearly an expression of the idea that types of libraries had particular clienteles. Furthermore, such clienteles had unique vocabularies that, if identified and pressed into service, would make the dictionary subject catalog closely responsive to those who used it. In this case, the unique vocabulary consisted of terms used by children. It would be a mistake, however, to assume that Smith's call for the use of such a vocabulary was also an attempt to demonstrate the validity of the assumption that such a vocabulary indeed existed. Rather than being a demonstration, Smith simply took the existence of the vocabulary to be a fact.

It would also be a mistake to assume that by describing children's terms as simple terms that Smith was demonstrating anything of the nature of the simplicity involved. The equation that children's terms are simple terms is, like the existence of a children's vocabulary, not a demonstration but rather only an assumption. To press it into the role of a definition or an explication on the order of, say, the statement that children's terms are simple because they are used or understood by children, is unwarranted. In the end, the nature of the supposed "simplicity" that she claimed for children's vocabulary remained undefined.

The nature of Smith's assumptions and especially the vagueness of the idea of "simplicity" are important because they are likely the cause for a similar vagueness in the procedures she outlined. Having claimed the existence of a children's vocabulary that was simple in contrast to adult terms, Smith provided some interesting examples of what she meant, but no explicit criteria for determining what that vocabulary was. The fact is that having only assumed its existence and nature, the process of determining it was at best a highly subjective and intuitive matter. Furthermore, having made a case for using children's simple terms, she then suggested since their numbers were so comparatively few and hedged in by qualifications, they were not all that significant. On the basis of the lack of criteria and her admission of the lack of significance of the terms, it is reasonable to question the validity, the practicality, and the worth of concerning oneself with determining the supposed vocabulary in the first place. Of course, perhaps an analysis as close as this was not really the issue. Smith's discussion was, after all, more a rationale for her procedure than one to be used by subject catalogers. Subject catalogers, being essentially dependent on subject heading lists, needed only to be convinced that Smith's work was itself cognizant of the ideals spoken of and therefore trustworthy. Supposing the latter to be true, subject catalogers could then use the list she had supplied with only minor attention to procedure.

The second special problem that children's subject catalogers faced had to do with the idea of specific or "definite" subjects. Mann wrote in 1916 in a section entitled "Definite and specific terms":

> Definite subjects should not be covered up by larger and more inclusive subjects; while this is a repetition of an old rule, it deserves special emphasis when making a catalog of juvenile books. A book on

> Parties should be entered under Parties and not included under the heading Amusements or Entertainments. The child cannot classify material nor does he want all kinds of amusements when he is looking for Parties.[53]

Smith reiterated Mann's comments although with more explicit reference to children's thinking patterns and without using the adjective "definite."

> One of the fundamental principles of dictionary cataloging is the use of specific subject headings. Although the rule is not new it deserves repetition and emphasis when it concerns the cataloging of juvenile books, for it agrees so perfectly with the mental habits of children, who, as already indicated, ask for books or information on specific topics rather than general subjects—for Parties or Picnics instead of Amusements; for Bees or Beetles, instead of Insects; for the Telephone or the Telegraph rather than Inventions. Boys and girls do not classify material logically under the more comprehensive headings.[54]

Both writers were aware of the fact that they were simply reiterating the idea of specific subject entry as stated earlier in the century by Hitchler and Bishop. In that scheme of things, specific subjects were relatively small subjects included by definition in larger or general subjects, the general subjects being classes. But because general readers more often than not wanted access only to small specific subjects and because they did not think of such subjects in a classificatory manner, books about them had to be placed directly in the main alphabetical sequence of headings under the names of the smaller subjects rather than being given class entry under the broader general subjects. Books should in other words be given direct and specific subject entry rather than indirect classed entry.

Mann and Smith found that approach to specific subject entry especially pertinent to children's subject catalogs because they were convinced that of all the readers for whom subject catalogs were prepared, children most exemplified this approach to subject searching. In their views, children were indeed mainly interested in definite, particular, small specific subjects. And children did not approach such subjects in a classificatory manner, but rather approached them as if they were separate particular topics. Therefore, specific and direct entry was even more needed for children.

At the same time, the problems that attended accomplishing this goal were also intensified in children's subject cataloging. For one thing, the children's subject cataloger had to carefully identify just those small specific subjects that were likely to be of interest to children. In many cases that meant no more than placing a book under a direct heading which indicated its entire contents because the subject of its entire contents was already considered to be a small specific subject. In other cases, however, it meant entering a book about a general subject under the specific subjects included in the general subject because those subjects were of greater importance to children. And occasionally it meant avoiding specific subjects deemed excessively minute. Smith and Mann justified this last case by claiming that such topics rarely had substantial writings devoted to them. Mann wrote:

> There are a few subjects which include divisions so small that it is quite improbable that they will be discussed separately. For example, Spices would best be used as a heading for books treating of the various spices, as one would seldom or never have material on cinnamon, cloves, etc., alone. References may be made if necessary from the various spices treated in the books entered under the general heading.[55]

Smith expanded on Mann's statement even more explicitly:

> Specific subject headings do not imply unnecessarily minute headings. There are subjects which include divisions so small that it is quite improbable they will be discussed separately. There are others for which there is little material in children's books. Children may ask for information about allspice, cinnamon, or cloves, or about the plane or the saw; but the available material for each is slight and several spices or various tools may be treated in one short chapter, or even in a section of a chapter. Separate headings would necessitate so many cards and cross-references that it is better in such cases to use the general subject with reference from the specific headings.[56]

In the end, identifying just those subjects deemed pertinent to children's thinking was similar to and no less a subjective and intuitive operation than determining which headings were simple and which were adult. But approaching the identification of specific subjects in this manner was considered necessary because only by this means could one fulfill the goal of making a subject catalog closely responsive to the patrons, that is to the children, who would use the catalog.

If simply determining the specific subjects that children needed to find in the catalog was difficult, another equally difficult problem was that certain subjects could not be accommodated by the rule of direct and specific subject entry. Subjects that consisted of a topic coordinated with a place, for instance, or of a topic coordinated with a form category ostensibly demanded a classified form of entry string that was contrary to the direct and specific rule. These were dealt with in a manner not unlike that found in Hitchler and Bishop, that is, by surmising those patterns of usage most likely to be followed by readers and making subject headings which follow those patterns. For children this meant dispensing in some cases with the complex heading altogether. Both Mann and Smith concluded, for example, that children did not attach any importance to the place that circumscribed some topics. Therefore, they recommended entry in those situations to the topic alone and suggested that while subdivision by country could thereafter be made, the latter practice would usually prove unnecessary.[57] It should be noted that the question of which topics were considered not to have a place significance attached to them varied slightly. Mann, for example, concluded that generally all but History and Local geography fell into that category.[58] Smith agreed with this but excluded Folklore which she concluded "is not used by children as a subject, but which is correlated with their study of geography."[59]

On the other hand, Mann and Smith both not only followed the opposite practice with respect to History and Geography (as well as Folklore for Smith), but also assumed that for at least the chronological periods of a country's history, classed heading structure had to be used. Smith, for example, set the two patterns in opposition:

> An exception to the rule of specific and alphabetical entry is made in most general catalogs in the treatment of history, all the material being collected under the name of the country with subdivisions arranged chronologically.[60]

Classed structure was also deemed necessary for various form categories. Even in the case of History, however, the specific and direct rule was to be applied if at all possible. For example, wars and other events likely to be looked up by children under their own distinctive names were to be entered directly in the main alphabetical sequence of the catalog under their own names.

One may summarize the activity of using specific and direct headings for children's catalogs by seeing it in the position of an ideal. Specific subjects were equated with topics, relatively circumscribed in scope, that had uncomplicated one-word names and that could be entered directly in the catalog's main heading sequence for direct access. They were tantamount, in other words, to the particular topics that catalogers supposed children were most commonly interested in. The task of the subject cataloger was to identify those topics in books and to place those books under the names of the subjects directly in the main alphabetical sequence of the catalog's headings. Of course, when the naming procedure would not allow that direct approach, alternative procedures that involved what were considered classed heading structures had to be used. But these were looked upon as compromises made necessary by the limitations of language. They were to be kept to a minimum. And in keeping with the entire approach to subject heading work that sought to fulfill the goal of making a catalog closely responsive to the children who would use it, the occasions when such a procedure should be followed, along with the entire process of determining the appropriate specific subjects in the first place, could best be accomplished by applying one's experience and intuitive understanding of children's needs to the situation.

Special Libraries. Another early expression of the implications of types of libraries and their clienteles on subject cataloging occurred with the rise of special libraries and the parallel documentation movement.[61] The chief significance of these movements for the discussion here is that together they represented two unique twentieth-century phenomena: the further growth of specialized fields of knowledge and the rise of modern research ideals. The first of these phenomena has been discussed already in conjunction with the development of Library of Congress subject heading work under Hanson. It need not be repeated here except to say that while subject catalogers at the Library of Congress expressed the impact of specialized fields of knowledge on subject work by conceiving of subject collocation to be oriented to such fields, the constraints under which they worked still demanded that they ultimately integrate the subjects of special fields of knowledge into the total organization of knowledge, whether that be in the form of classification on the shelves or in the form of the subject portion of a dictionary catalog. For that matter, even the documentation movement, if thought of especially in terms of the work of the Institut Internationale de Bibliographie, labored under that same constraint.

Special libraries, however, commonly operated under no such universal knowledge conditions. Subject workers in libraries related to special fields of knowledge could, therefore, generally confine themselves to only those special fields that were central to their collections. This narrowing in focus provided opportunities for more exacting attention to the subject cataloging details of their fields, such as those having to do with terminology and the unique characteristics of subject collocation. It should also be noted that by itself the idea of special libraries is very broad, encompassing a great variety and number of institutional situations. Obviously some, perhaps even a great many such libraries were conducted in very traditional ways, including the way their subject cataloging work was treated. What is of particular importance here are those special libraries that, especially by the 1920s, already represented the vanguard of the scientific and technical revolution that was to become pronounced in the coming decades. These constituted a special class not simply because of their emphases on special fields of knowledge, but because their emphases became intimately correlated with their participation in a new research ideal.

The second of the two twentieth-century phenomena—research ideals—may appear to some to be wrongly placed, having its origins in great part in university graduate education. Indeed, research methodology, having been originally influenced by the German university seminar, saw its most striking early representation in university settings. As such it deeply affected university library collection growth rates and subject interests. The most immediate effect of research on subject access procedures appears not to have occurred within university library settings, however, bound as they were to universal knowledge schemes and to a national pattern ultimately set by the Library of Congress. Rather, it occurred with the growth of special libraries that were relatively free from such constraints.

Subject catalog access work under these freer conditions could be characterized by its response to several unique factors. First, special fields of knowledge had come to be viewed as the locus of special terminology which had arisen with those particular fields. The notion that specialized language exists among scholars was not new, of course. A long tradition had held that subject catalogs for public libraries should use popular terms and those for libraries serving scholars should use scientific terms. The difference here was the notion of specialty even within science. The source of specialized terms was not simply a common realm called science or scholarship, but rather more specifically the specialized fields of knowledge themselves. This did not mean that a special field of knowledge had a language so unique that it operated apart from all other special fields or essentially apart from all other languages. Obviously, specialists within any one field had to express themselves in terms of commonly known and used languages. Furthermore, because concepts within particular special fields were often expressed in terms also common to many other fields, they were constantly cross-fertilized. Still, each special field of knowledge came to be viewed as having, in addition to what it shared with others, its own unique terminology. This was sometimes expressed as specially invented jargon, sometimes as accretions or different emphases given to more widely shared terms, and sometimes as unique combinations of terms representing unique complexes of ideas. The effect of the foregoing development of special terminology on subject catalog access within such contexts is obvious. If a specialized field of knowledge had unique terminology, then persons active within the field would use the terminology in subject searches. Consequently, a library had to use that terminology in its subject catalog if it intended to serve its specialist clientele effectively.

Second, special fields of knowledge also came to be viewed as the locus of special patterns of subject collocation. Hanson's earlier work had emphasized the breakdown of a singular and unified conception of the universe of knowledge. His choice of devices by which subjects could be coordinated was of particular interest in that shift. While he continued to use coordination patterns based on older hierarchical notions, he also coordinated other subjects with little reference to that understanding of subjects. In fact, constrained by the need to provide a universal scheme, Hanson tended to use simple patterns of collocation rather than ones based on complex conceptual differentiation.

By the 1920s and 1930s, subject catalog workers in special libraries were already grappling with what were considered more fundamental approaches to the subject collocation in their particular fields. Such efforts continue to the present day and may be especially characterized in the following way: Subjects, rather than being seen as strictly defined members of an older hierarchical universe of knowledge or as discrete entities to be collocated by means of simple arrangement devices, have come to be thought of commonly as elements of any one of a number of complex idea structures, each having its own kind of conceptual framework. What distinguishes this view from previous views, especially from those up to and including Hanson's, is the variety of relationships involved, actually or potentially. So complex is this variety that efforts to express it have included biological metaphor, linguistic and atomistic models, mathematical models involving set or graph theory, and mathematical logic. More recently, attempts to understand such conceptual structures have involved the study of the sociological characteristics of their origins. The most important point to be made with respect to special library contexts, however, is that since such patterns arise from the special fields themselves, subject catalog access must be particularly attentive to the collocation patterns within the field in question. This point is a particularly crucial one because, like all subject access systems that have aimed to serve scholarly users, collocation has always been considered the *sine qua non* of the subject cataloger's efforts. The reason for this is based on the idea that scholars and specialists search for subjects with their own collocative patterns in mind. Subject catalog access must therefore attempt to incorporate those patterns. Freed from the demand to provide more universal collocation patterns which were less sensitive to individual fields, special libraries became a natural point for experimentation with specialized collocation. As a result, the subject cataloger in special libraries became specialized, if for no other reason than the sheer intellectual effort involved in the work.

A third factor affecting subject catalog work in special libraries and one more closely allied with the very essence of the documentation movement was the idea of what special library users needed to find in subject searches. The opinion had been long held that one mark of scholarly endeavors was thoroughness. Cutter had suggested this in his description of scholars as "those who want to study fully some general class of subjects" and in his opinion that there are some who wish "to glance over all the literature on a comprehensive subject, including the books on its various branches."[62] It should be noted, however, that Cutter's notion of thoroughness was strongly bound to the nineteenth-century context in which he worked. For him, thoroughness was a function of breadth of view rather than of what has come to be considered "recall" in modern terms. In fact, Cutter expressed some doubt as to whether scholars ever wanted to get access to literally everything on a topic. His view of thoroughness is best pictured as a mind seeking knowledge within a hierarchically classed framework where none of the component elements of the subject structure had been omitted.

Cutter's picture of scholarly searching may be usefully compared to one drawn by Samuel Bradford in the 1930s and representative of new developments in scientific research. Bradford pictured scientific research as a cumulative process, the work of one generation of scientists or, better yet, the work of even a single scientist essentially dependent on the work of predecessors and other contemporaries. The critical point was gaining access to the past and present record of accomplishments—the more complete the access, the better the chances that progress would ensue. In Bradford's view, the role of the librarian, or rather the "documentalist," followed from this need.

> Documentation is an art of practical necessity, practised by brotherhood of enthusiastic devotees, whose painstaking altruistic labours contribute, in modest obscurity, towards the progress of society. For progress depends on access to information. And the art of documentation is the art of collecting, classifying and making readily accessible all kinds of intellectual activity. It is the process by which the documentalist is enabled to put before the creative specialist the existing literature, bearing on the subject of his investigation, in order that he may be made fully aware of previous achievements in his subject, and thus be saved from the dissipation of his genius on work already done. Documentation proceeds from the need to put in order the processes of acquiring, preserving, abstracting and supplying, as re-

quired, books, articles and reports, data and documents of all kinds. It is the result of the realisation of the gap between the making of a record in any sphere of activity and the placing of that record in the hands of the individual who can use it as the basis of new achievement. The principal medium for recording progress is the periodical press, which speaks in so irregular and incoherent a manner, that it is impossible, without documentation, to obtain a clear and concise view of any particular branch of knowledge, large or small. This disorder reigns in the production of documents of all kinds. Documentation is the necessary remedy.[63]

From this statement and other writings by Bradford, several important conclusions may be drawn that set the work of the documentalist apart from traditional library service and from traditional subject cataloging. The differences are important not so much for their uniquenesses, as for the sharpness and necessity of their focuses. First, the range of materials required for accessibility is notable for its breadth, focusing on *all* pertinent literature and on *all kinds* of literature. This emphasis obviously went beyond the traditional library concern with monographs and extended to all types of materials, including technical reports and periodical literature. Access to periodical literature in traditional library service had already become separated from subject cataloging by the willingness of librarians to accept commercial indexing in place of their own subject analysis. Bradford was not only noting that access to periodical literature was more important to scientists than access to books, but also that access to all materials should be integrated.

A second conclusion from Bradford's statement, one at least implied, is that the depth of subject cataloging must be commensurate with the scientists' needs. This conclusion has two aspects. On the one hand, the unit of recall and thus of subject specification may not be confined to the traditional entire book or to the traditional entire periodical set. It has to focus on all levels—that is, on entire books, on periodical articles, and more importantly on parts of such items. This need also implies that the specification of those more discrete information levels should be adequate, even though the subjects in them are minute or involve multiple relationships and require complex methods for their indication in a catalog. On the other hand, the unit of recall is constrained especially by relevance. It must be what the scientists actually need for their work, not simply what the subject worker thinks is appropriate. A third conclusion is that the first and most essential focus of the documentalist's activities must be directed toward achieving order. The order implied here is not simply casual order or pragmatic order but rather systematic order. And this injunction implies two further requirements. The systematic order implied must accommodate complex subject relationships, and the documentalist, striving after the model displayed by the scientists for whom one labors, must apply scientific methods to achieve that order. In this sense, therefore, the "art" that Bradford referred to was actually a technical art, that is, one founded ultimately on a scientific basis.

A final conclusion to be drawn from Bradford's statement is that the scientists themselves are interested in and will be helped by the breadth of the information structure thus composed and by the order inherent in it. They will, in other words, be engaged in exhaustive but relevant searches for information. The name for that goal as time passed became generic searching—subject searching notable for its breadth, depth, and relevance and for the intricacy and complexity of the subject relationships it followed.

One result of these various factors on subject cataloging in special libraries was the compilation of lists of subject headings specially adapted to special fields of knowledge. The publication of such lists became rather notable during and after the 1920s. To the extent that such lists followed the alphabetical subject heading patterns already standardized according to Library of Congress practices, their chief contribution was to make accessible to the wider subject cataloging community the specialized terms and their meanings considered basic to such fields.[64] As a result of their general availability, their specialized terminology also began to appear in the subject catalogs of more general institutions. To the degree that such lists also represented more radical departures from traditional dictionary subject heading format and collocation practices, and to the degree that they represented subjects which were expressed with much greater verbal complexity than in traditional lists, they stood as evidence to those in more general institutions of greater precision in and knowledgeability of subject access requirements.[65]

The latter kinds of specialized lists were a manifestation of a growing separation of special library and documentation subject access work from traditional subject cataloging. As such they indicated a second general result of subject work in special fields—the prompting of a mood of questioning among those involved in general subject access situations. At first, the phenomenon of special subject access seems to have been seen by traditional subject catalogers as a model upon which to draw. Grace O. Kelley writing in 1930 could picture the process of becoming acquainted with a special subject field, especially with the uniqueness and complexity of its subject relationships, as a useful approach to both teaching and learning subject access procedures.[66] Throughout the 1930s and afterward, the theme that she noted was increasingly sounded in calls for subject catalogers to be better trained in subject specialties. As already suggested, the situation in which general libraries found themselves tended to frustrate such emphases. The tension created brought about a good deal of questioning by the mid-1930s, however, and led academic libraries, especially those in research-oriented institutions, to become the third of the four general types of libraries to address problems in subject cataloging.

Academic Libraries. It took academic librarians longer to more fully delineate the unique problems they had in dictionary subject cataloging because they tended to retain their identification with the public library movement the longest; this was in part because the general kind of knowledge base was similar, in part because earlier liberal education goals were similar to the cultural uplift goals of the public library movement, and in part because given the typical range of users in an academic library, even the clientele remained somewhat similar.[67]

By the 1930s, however, the identification of academic libraries with the new research ideals was fast gaining ground. This meant that at least portions of the clientele—faculty, graduate students, and to an increasing degree, students in professional curricula—could be more readily identified with the unique subject access requirements of special fields of knowledge. By the late 1930s and early 1940s, the firm establishment of the idea of research universities having research libraries further bifurcated the academic library field, impressing upon subject cataloging interests even further the uniqueness of subject access within the academic community.[68]

The effect of grappling with the particular problems of subject catalog access in academic libraries was not, however, to denote any special considerations other than those already noted within the special library and documentation movements. Instead, the chief effect of the identification of academic library subject cataloging needs was to provide a context in which the idea of dictionary subject cataloging could be examined with an expenditure of effort unlike that ever accomplished in the past. This examination had two focal points. First, the academic context provided the first widely accepted impetus to do research in dictionary subject cataloging. Second, the academic context provided the first laboratory for subject catalog investigation, at least insofar as initial studies of catalog use centered there. Before looking at the nature of that examination, however, prior attempts to explain subject cataloging procedure that took place by the late 1920s must first be explored.

New Explanations of Subject Cataloging

One important response to the growing intensification of subject cataloging problems was the publication of new explanations of subject cataloging procedure between 1927 and 1933. The need for new explanations had been occasionally expressed during the period after Briggs's article in 1912, but it did not immediately come to fruition. The Hitchler and Bishop texts on cataloging, supplemented by New York State Library School materials (reissued in a second edition by Dorcas Fellows in 1922) and by the introductory pages of Mann's 1916 list of children's subject headings, remained the principal sources of explanation throughout the period.[69] But these works had serious deficiencies related to the early twentieth-century context in which they had been written.

The situation began to change by the late 1920s with the A.L.A.'s publication of Susan G. Akers's *Simple Library Cataloging* (1927) and Margaret Mann's classic, *Introduction to Cataloging and the Classifications of Books* (1930). Each was notable for its concerted effort to explain subject cataloging work cogently and effectively and may be attributed in part to the effort that ensued in the wake of the Williamson report to improve library instruction. These two works were joined in 1933 by Elva S. Smith's *Subject Headings for Children's Books,* discussed earlier, and the third edition of Minnie Earl Sears's *List of Subject Headings for Small Libraries,* both of which contained explanations of subject cataloging procedures.[70]

These four works and their subsequent editions provided the chief sources of explanation of dictionary subject cataloging in America during the 1930s and 1940s, especially for library school students and for new librarians. They provided in effect the basis for the subject cataloging education of at least a generation of American librarians. Unfortunately, the picture one receives of subject heading work in them is not without severe difficulties. While these works attempted to present subject cataloging as a rational procedure, their explanations gave evidence of deep tensions that made the results ambiguous. Some indication of this ambiguity may be seen in an examination of two themes treated in them: the idea of specific entry and the role of the subject cataloger's consideration of the user in subject cataloging.

SPECIFIC ENTRY

The new writers of the late 1920s and early 1930s were the first (besides Cutter a half century earlier) to consistently call the basic operation of assigning subject headings "specific entry" instead of simply the assignment of "specific headings." The new caption suggested a shift in emphasis insofar as it seemed to indicate that a subject heading should express or match in some essential way the entire subject content of a book rather than simply a subject, either specific or general, that a book contained. Margaret Mann expressed the new emphasis in a representative way in the following words:

> As a general rule books must be entered under their most specific subject heading. This means the heading which will most accurately fit the book. The terms must express the content of the book sharply and accurately, not vaguely and loosely.[71]

Although this kind of definition might appear to more nearly represent the kind of scope-match approach to subject headings that Hanson's work had stressed, the explanations that surrounded it limited its application. For example, Sears, after providing a lengthy section on identifying "the real subject of a book," a process fundamental to the scope-matching goal, then explained that a second step in the subject cataloging process was to

> find the subject heading which will fit the subject as presented in the book, and at the same time will fit other books of a similar character. (The use of a printed list of subject headings is assumed.) Before taking this second step it is essential to understand an important general rule. That is, that the cataloger must in the end consider not just one book in hand but also other books which treat of the same subject, sometimes under different titles, in order to select a subject heading which will do for the entire group of books as well as for the one book.[72]

Her ensuing example involved placing a cookbook consisting of recipes not under COOK BOOKS, "the heading that would best fit the book" and the one that "the inexperienced cataloger would probably think of first," but rather under COOKERY. When placed under COOKERY it would be brought together with other books that contained at least some recipes and whose subjects were related to COOKERY. It would also be placed in proximity to books entered under COOKERY FOR THE SICK, a related topic. Mann, perhaps the source of Sears's explanation, had also referred to the same practice three years earlier and had also provided similar examples.[73]

Entering a book best denoted by the specific heading COOK BOOKS under the term COOKERY, which is a broader and including term, is class entry rather than specific entry and as such directly violates the specific entry idea. The purposeful way the explanation is written suggests, therefore, that while specific entry as a scope-matching process was the appropriate place to begin, it was limited or moderated by a second ideal related to the gathering objective of the subject catalog. That ideal might be stated in the following way: The objective of the subject catalog is to gather books together in small groups related by subject likeness. Thus, if following specific entry results in no such groups being gathered, one should abandon the specific entry ideal in order to produce such groups.

This twofold procedure contains serious ambiguities, however. First, the second goal is not really elaborated by these writers. In fact, it is referred to in a more or less casual way, as if the subject cataloger were simply being reminded of something already well known. Having mentioned it in this way, both writers immediately return directly to the topic of specific entry as the avoidance of class entry, seemingly failing to recognize that their twofold procedures appear to have called for class entry. Second, even the manner in which the second goal is described is ambiguous. Sears states in the initial part of her explanation (quoted earlier) that books of a "similar" character constitute the basis for such groups, but shortly thereafter describes the basis as books with the "same subject." There is, of course, considerable difference between "similar" and "same." Moreover, both seem to imply the class entry result in their respective discussions of subarrangement practices. Subarrangement is spoken of not only as a way to break up long subject heading files, but also as a way to differentiate works that had not been sufficiently differentiated in their subject matter in the first place. This suggests that books had purposefully been given class entry at the start.[74] Third, the twofold procedure is ambiguous because of the way the writers explain how or when it was to be carried out. The best they do is to imply that gathering books in little groups is more useful for recall, to speak of the procedure as particularly applicable for small libraries, or to relate the operation to the maxim that experience will tell.[75]

Given these ambiguities, it seems appropriate to ask what role the goal of specific entry as scope-matching was supposed to play. If that goal applied in an unadulterated manner was not the sole basis for the catalog, how was the catalog's organizing principle conceived? The beginning of an answer to these questions is suggested in the following considerations.

The ideal of a catalog as a device to gather books about subjects in small cohesive groups was not simply a long-standing conception, but was fundamental to subject catalog definition. The essential purpose of a subject catalog had always been to gather books on the same subject together. How else could one interpret the intentions of all those procedures that insisted on uniform terminology? Even Cutter's principal subject catalog objective—"To show what the library has on a given subject"—implied that the library had at least two and perhaps even more books on any given subject or that it would have that many as time passed.[76]

The assumption that books will automatically fall into groups according to their subjects was little more than an extension of traditional classificatory thinking. Subjects were considered to be defined as categorical elements of a classificatory universe of knowledge. The word "subject" was a technical referent to a special kind of matter of thought, that is, one that had become established. Subjects were, consequently, a more or less limited subset of all the matters of thought. Books on the other hand were simply repositories of "subjects" considered in this technical sense. Certainly, they were not thought of as equivalent to subjects or even as nearly equivalent. Books thus represented many attempts to treat what in comparison to their numbers was a relatively few established topics called subjects. The task of the subject cataloger was to identify which subjects among the comparatively circumscribed total were treated in books and to enter the books under the plainly accepted names of those subjects.

Early classed catalog procedure tended to reinforce this approach to subjects and books. Classed catalog procedure began with a unified but circumscribed universe of subjects. That is, all subjects were elements of a basic set of older, well-established broad classes and grew in numbers only in the sense that classificatory subdivision produced new and smaller elements of already existing subjects. Subject catalogers who worked within that tradition inadvertently prejudiced how they provided subject access because they began with what subjects were known in terms of the classificatory structure and applied that to books, rather than beginning with some idea of the subject of a book per se, attempting thereafter to accommodate it to the classificatory structure.

Given this approach to subjects and books, it was sensible to suppose that books would fall into substantial groups on the same subjects. This was not to deny that new subjects came into existence (i.e., become established) nor to deny that a new book would likely be the repository of a new subject about which no other books had yet been written. But, as Cutter had said, until a new topic of that kind had attained "a certain individuality" as an object of inquiry and had been "given some sort of *name*" in several writings, the prejudice was to treat the topic only as an indistinct matter of thought named only by a circumlocution that combined older established subjects.[77] The most specific subject of such a book was not the description of its unestablished topic, but rather an established subject that included its unestablished topic. And to enter the book under the including established subject would automatically place it in a group with other books that also treated the same established subject.

That this older approach to subjects and books had persisted into the twentieth century is evident in the writings of Hitchler and Bishop. And that at least a vestige of it was preserved among the present writers seems evident not only in the way it explains their emphasis on the subject catalog as a gathering device, but also more directly in a statement that Mann appended to her description of the gathering objecttive of the subject catalog. Mann wrote that a subject heading that would fulfill the gathering objective

> shall apply to a group of books covering one field. In other words, it should be a term which *shall stand for a subject and not for one book*.[78]

A subject heading that stood both for a subject apart from any book and for a group of books in one field was basic to the older classificatory approach to subjects and books and, in fact, had little meaning apart from that view. Mann described subjects and books in this way in her discussion of subject cataloging only in this single instance. Its significance for her does not appear to be of the same intensity as that which has been described here—a direct and conscious application of classificatory thinking. Rather, it appears only as an offhand remark, an additional factor in a subject heading procedure that otherwise stressed specific entry as scope-matching.

But the two approaches to subject access for books were contradictory, at least to the extent that classification theory had not yet arrived at a point in which the topical contents of books per se considered to be "the subjects" of books could also be expressed in terms of complex classificatory categories. Cutter had, in a sense, made the conflict possible. Despite holding a classificatory approach to subject identification, he had insisted on beginning the subject access process by identifying the specific subjects of books themselves rather than simply ending up at the specific subjects by means of a process of classificatory fission. This had the effect of opening the floodgates to a consideration of the subjects of books apart from any essential classificatory reasoning process. Thereafter, Hanson and the subject catalogers of the Library of Congress (as well as subject catalogers in other large libraries), pressed to name the subjects in thousands of new books, increasingly treated subject headings without reference to a self-evident classificatory order of the universe of knowledge. Consequently, subjects came to be considered the attributes of the books themselves rather than the established elements of a unified and singular order of established knowledge. Mann's bringing of the two approaches together, without an awareness of their differences and with apparently only a diminutive appreciation of the older view, represented not only a meeting of the old with the new but also, for all practical purposes, the triumph of the new.

The shift from the older to the newer approach to subject identification engendered a profound and serious difficulty for those who had grown up with the older method. Specific entry as scope-matching, if carried out fully, would eventually lead to many books, if not a preponderance of them, being entered under headings that were unique to each of them. In modern terminology it would produce a notable and disturbing number of single-item document classes. If that were to happen, the traditional *raison d'être* of the subject catalog—its capacity to assemble small groups of books on the same subject—would be sabotaged. The subject catalog, instead of appearing as a gathering instrument, would be fractured into a thousand little pieces.

Of course, given a large number of books to catalog (as was the case at the Library of Congress), that prospect might be unlikely or at least less noticeable. It would be noticeable, on the other hand, in catalogs made for relatively small general collections where the number of books that might even come close to making groups of the "same" subjects would be small or, conversely, the number of books likely to fall into single-book categories would be great. Indeed, this appears to have been the issue at stake with these writers. They were explaining subject heading practice especially for small libraries in which the fracturing would be more likely. The tendency to produce single-item categories would also have been made more probable with the use by small libraries of subject heading lists in which headings originating from larger libraries would be "unnecessarily minute." For smaller libraries, the tendency of such headings to obscure the traditional role of gathering attributed to the subject catalog would be great—so great, in fact, that it would appear as a failure on the part of the subject catalog.

Specific entry interpreted in a purely straightforward manner as a process of indicating the subjects of books was thus not the ultimate goal these writers had in mind. The ultimate goal was to produce subject document classes that fulfilled the common notion of subject catalog gathering. This did not mean that indicating the subjects of books was unimportant. But it was only a starting point rather than the chief objective. The potential that specific entry as scope-matching had for very detailed, even complete, subject content specification was to be invoked only to the point needed and no more.

Specific entry as scope-matching, viewed in this limited way, may be illustrated as the process of focusing on a subject as an "emerging" topic rather than as a completely identified topic. Given a book with a complex subject description such as Schools for the blind in the United States, one might interpret specific entry either in terms of complete specification or alternatively only in terms of an emerging topic. In the first case, all three elements of the description, Schools, Blind, and United States, would automatically be included in the subject heading. In the second case, only so much of the topical description as was necessary to cause the subject to "emerge" from other related subjects in the catalog which already consisted of document classes of viable size would be included in the subject heading. If one had many works on Education in general and three or four on Schools per se, that might mean placing the book under some term indicating Schools along with those other three or four works. But if many works were already entered under the topic Schools as well, some term indicating Schools for the blind could be used. Specific entry in this sense begins with entering a work under a "not classed" heading. But it also means not placing the work under such a minute heading that it gets lost in the catalog *because of its individuality.*

It should be noted, too, that not even the issue of subject heading structure intervened here. If specification with all three elements was required, subject heading structure practices might cause the result to be SCHOOLS FOR THE BLIND–UNITED STATES, the subdivision itself rationalized as "not classed" according to the idea of it being only a geographical aspect rather than an included subject. But how one rationalized the heading form made little difference in the end. The important thing was that a useful grouping device had been created.[79]

It is reasonable to ask how subject catalogers would know if a particular heading was "unnecessarily minute" for use in a particular library. They might, of course, have set a goal of gathering only a certain number of entries under each heading. What is more likely, however, was that in most cases the controlling factor was the use of a subject heading list. If, for example, the A.L.A. *List* or Sears's *List of Subject Headings* were being followed, a subject cataloger could use the narrowest heading delineated in the list. In the example above, if the list simply went to the specification level of Schools for the blind, the heading indicating that level of specificity could be used without question. While this procedure did not solve all such questions and in fact led to injunctions by Mann and Sears to occasionally modify the scope-matching goal, it did provide an operational method for many, if not most, situations.

That the foregoing was indeed the most common way of answering the question of how minute a heading should be is suggested by the heavy use made of such lists of subject headings by the 1930s, so much so that subject heading work had become virtually list-dependent by that time. Sears noted specifically that "the use of a printed list of subject headings is assumed."[80] And Mann at least implied that specification level was a function of such lists when she added the word "available" to her rendition of the specific entry rule in the second edition of her work: "As a general rule, books must be entered under the most specific subject heading available."[81] Her reference to availability can mean nothing else but the availability of a subject heading in a list.

Interpreting specific entry as scope-matching in the foregoing way—that is, as just enough "not classed" specification to create subject document classes of relatively reasonable numbers of items—also appears to be confirmed by the generally muted way the positive side of the idea was explained by those who wrote about it during the 1930s. The first and most notable feature of those explanations was their negative interpretation of the notion. Specific entry was defined by what it was not, rather than by positive statements stressing its full specification potential. This was the case even with Hanson's statements concerning Library of Congress practice. For him, specific entry was described in two ways: not subentered as an included subdivision in alphabetico-classed format and not entered under a superordinate conventional heading. Of course, Hanson violated both of those practices purposefully, the first occasionally and with apologies, the second regularly, especially through the practice of inversion. He justified the latter by claiming the retention of the heading as a cohesive grammatical unit did not lead to formal alphabetico-classed appearance. Moreover, he did not have to appeal to the notion of preserving the gathering principle because he had a higher purpose in mind—the collocation of subjects for a scholarly clientele. In fact, even though the Library of Congress did end up with one-item categories, the overall state of its system easily buried such instances among many other categories well-stocked with entries under them. Despite their cataloging volume, however, one wonders what percentage of even Library of Congress subject cataloging was actually based on the negative and "emergent" interpretation of specific entry.

The second feature of contemporary explanations that tends to confirm the foregoing "emergent" interpretation of specific entry was the general lack of concomitant space given to how subject headings were to be derived for the subjects of books. This is significant because if specific entry had been interpreted in a positive way, the first step after one determined the topical contents of a book would have been to convert that description into a comparable but conventional subject heading. It was precisely at this point that the positive approach to specific entry would have been encountered because the attempt to convert a topical description to a heading arose from the idea of scope-matching for its own sake. But such explanations were not provided and their absence, or at least the absence of this conversion procedure, would indicate as well the absence of a positive meaning for the scope-matching ideal.

It is noteworthy that the Library of Congress, while apparently following the procedure of attempting to specify books in terms of conventional headings, never published any description of that procedure for the general public. Perhaps the procedure was thought to be understood. Or perhaps it was thought to be plainly evident in Cutter's *Rules.* At any rate, one notable feature of the works being discussed here is that none of them treated this aspect of subject heading work. One finds them going immediately from the notion of using subject headings that expressed "the real subject" of a book to considerations of subject headings that were not classed on the one hand and not too minute on the other. The only context in which the acceptability of headings was discussed was not in relation to whether they expressed the entire subjects of books but only in choices between scientific or nonscientific terminology.

In sum, although specific entry was primarily described as the act of entering books under headings that denoted their entire subjects, in practice specific entry meant entering books under headings only specific enough to produce subject document classes of reasonable size. Subject catalogers were enjoined to achieve a balance between broad class entry in which direct access to books by means of their subjects would be lost, and overly precise entry, where the subject catalog would be fractured into a multitude of bits and pieces called specific subjects. The chief means for achieving the balance was to work from a basic list of subject headings, varying the choices offered by it according to the specificity levels needed.

This approach to specific entry is understandable because it directly countered the potential loss of the subject catalog's gathering function. Nevertheless, it led to dire results. On the one hand, it required the subject cataloger in some instances to retreat from the narrowest specificity level of even a given list of subject headings. When this entailed no more than the decision not to use a subarrangement term, the choice was not overly difficult. But when it required not using one conventional heading in favor of another broader conventional heading, solely for the purpose of preserving the gathering function, the basis for choosing was at best a vague appeal to experience. On the other hand, this procedure also at times confronted the subject cataloger with the need for subject headings even more specific than those provided in the list of headings. In some cases a heading could be constructed by means of patterns provided, particularly where a greater degree of specificity could be achieved by subarrangement practices. But where a greater degree of specificity required a new conventional heading, especially one of any major complexity, the subject cataloger was more or less at a loss. There were no directions for either creating complex conventional headings or for determining their acceptability according to common usage. The very use of lists of subject headings as control devices discouraged the creation of such headings in favor of working within the confines of the list—except, that is, at the ultimate source of such lists, the Library of Congress. Even among Library of Congress subject catalogers, however, the tendency was to work within the confines of the names and subarrangement patterns already established and to avoid the hasty creation of what could only be complex phrase headings.[82]

One result of the foregoing tendency was to resort to multiple entry, that is, to use two or more separate headings considered together to provide the needed specification. Thus, Mann noted that Jean Piaget's book *The Language and Thought of the Child* would have the two separate headings, CHILD STUDY and LANGUAGE AND LANGUAGES; and a book on gold mining in Colorado was to be entered under GOLD MINES AND MINING and MINES AND MINING—COLORADO. In neither case did she indicate that some other heading that combined the various elements of the respective subject descriptions would actually be possible. She also gave no explanation of the choices that she did make, although one could suppose that the answer was the same as in those cases in which one retreated from specificity altogether—that is, that experience would tell.[83]

Application of the idea of specific entry—the achieving of a balance between not-classed and overly specified entries—was a product ultimately of experience tied to dependency on lists of subject headings. But what could be more vague than an appeal to experience, especially when the kind of experience required was not defined? The result was to cause specific entry to appear as an intuitive exercise. It made the choice of a subject heading akin to divining some sort of self-evident core or main subject of a book, the subject heading for which could be decreased or increased in specificity as the occasion demanded. At the same time, the appeal to experience did not appear to be out of place because it fit well with the second feature of the explanations—user considerations.

USER CONSIDERATIONS

A second way that these writers expressed notable ambiguity revolves around the role that user considerations played in constructing the dictionary subject catalog. The idea that a subject catalog should and could be made closely responsive to the needs and mental habits of the readers who would use it had been raised to the status of a principal goal of subject cataloging during the first decade of the twentieth century. During the succeeding years, the most substantive change that took place in the way the ideal was conceived was to transfer the principal basis for characterizing readers from the size of a library to the type of a library.

By the 1930s the ideal had become very much taken for granted. The earlier discussion of Smith's treatment of children's subject heading work demonstrated her unquestioned acceptance of the ideal. Akers, Sears, and Mann also approached the ideal in the same unquestioning way. But their treatments of it were relatively limited in scope. Akers and Sears little more than alluded to the ideal, chiefly in the context of choices between synonyms. In a section entitled "Choice of subject headings," Akers wrote:

> Of two equally correct and specific headings, namely, Birds and Ornithology, the choice depends on the type of library, and a reference should be made from the one not chosen. In a public or high school library choose the heading Birds as being the term commonly used by the readers. In a special ornithology library, use the heading Ornithology, for the users of the library will be quite familiar with the scientific terms relating to that subject.[84]

In a section entitled "Scientific or Popular Headings," Sears wrote the similar words:

> Subject headings are chosen to fit the needs of the people who are likely to use the catalog. The average reader looking for a book on grasses will look under that word and not under AGROSTOLOGY, the scientific name for grasses which might be used in a special library. In like manner general books on birds will be looked for under BIRDS, not under ORNITHOLOGY. What general reader looking for a book on adenoids would think to look under NASOPHARYNX–ADENOID VEGETATIONS, altho this is the correct heading for a large and special

library? Common usage should always be considered and the entries in a good general encyclopedia are often a help in case of doubt. Here, as in other parts of the catalog, the needs of the individual library call for consideration. After deciding on the common name as entry word, the scientific name will be cared for by a reference to the form used.[85]

Neither writer elaborated on the implications of the ideal further than these words indicate. Akers, however, quoted Cutter's words on choice between synonyms—"In choosing between synonymous headings prefer the one that—(a) is most familiar to the class of people who consult the library . . . "—as her authority for this particular practice.[86] Her reference to Cutter was unusual since it was not typical to cite Cutter specifically during this period. Her reference to Cutter was significant as well because she obviously took Cutter's phrase "class of people" to be the same as a type of library's particular clientele rather than a reference to Cutter's by-then-forgotten psychology of users and its attendant categories of readers.

Mann's general approach to the ideal, including her typology of libraries, was more complex than what Akers and Sears had written, at least in her general discussion of librarianship. When speaking of book selection goals in the introductory chapter of her work, she stated:

> Books in a library are tools collected for public use. They are usually chosen to serve the specific needs of a definite group of people. This group may be the inhabitants of a limited community, a village, town, or city; or it may be a student body, as in university or college libraries. Again, the library may aim at serving a group of specialists by building a collection limited to one subject, as Art, Engineering, or Medicine.[87]

Categories such as these were important in her opinion because they set the stage for assessing special uses of materials made by the various groups of users noted. In other words, the use of similar materials would vary according to the type of library. She continued:

> Particular regard must be given to those libraries serving a very special class of readers so that proper emphasis can be given to books according to their use. The medical library will find one use for a book, while an engineering library may wish to use the same book for a different purpose.
>
> It is surprising to find how many interpretations can be given to the same treatise. Taking a rather homely example, the books on occupational diseases may illustrate the possible variations to which books may be put. To the medical library the value of these books lies in the information they give about the cause and treatment of a disease; in

the technical library they are used to study the effect a certain product may have on health; for the insurance library they contribute to the question of a certain risk; in the civic library they make a contribution to a phase of the labor question; to the financial library they give information about investing in a business where a certain risk exists; while to the public library will come readers seeking the subject from one or all the points mentioned here.[88]

Having delineated a relatively complex nomenclature of types of readers related to types of libraries, Mann had set the stage for relating subject cataloging decisions to those categories. She failed to do so, however, employing instead only two basic categories of libraries of initial importance in making subject heading decisions—libraries that have a particular subject focus (i.e., special libraries) and libraries that do not (i.e., general libraries).[89] The first group, one might assume, would offer some explicit help in choosing precise terminology. But Mann did not deal with them further. Instead, she limited her work to general readers and the libraries that served them. The second group consisted of general libraries that included by implication either all of the various approaches to subject materials of the first group considered as a whole or, what is more likely, none of those approaches precisely. It was for this group of libraries that she particularly attributed the value of the dictionary catalog. To these categories Mann subsequently added still another consideration, that is, whether a general library was small or large. All things being equal, most of her particular instructions regarding choices to be made on the basis of a library's particular clientele had to do with the needs of smaller libraries that served general readers—that is, how certain measures in small libraries serving general readers were different from those in larger libraries also serving general readers.

Considering the importance of the ideal of making subject catalogs closely responsive to the needs of the readers who would use them and especially the idea that readers' mental habits could be characterized by grouping them according to type of library, one may wonder why these three writers either treated the entire matter in a cursory fashion or failed to broach very adequately the differences that pertained to the users of various types of libraries. One might suppose that because the entire matter was so difficult, the writers simply were not able to deal with it and thus chose to avoid it. There is some truth to the idea that the topic was avoided purposefully, at least in Akers and Sears. But their avoidance of the matter did not arise from their inability to deal with it, but rather from their assumption that it was too complex a topic for their readers. Akers aimed her work at those who had no professional library training at all and Sears at the beginning cataloger. As a result, both were intent on presenting subject heading work in its simplest light, avoiding for the most part those aspects that were perplexing to beginners in the work. And user considerations were above all perplexing.[90]

The willingness of Akers and Sears to forego discussion of user considerations for beginners raises a curious problem, however. If the idea of user considerations was indeed central to subject heading work, its perplexity is not a sufficient reason for omitting it from discussion. To do so would not only leave their subject heading work instructions incomplete, but would suggest that the writers had attempted to portray an operation that by its very nature was complex and difficult as an unduly simplistic matter. On the other hand, it is also apparent that these writers strongly believed they could write about the simple aspects of subject heading work without dealing with the complex aspects, or at least without dealing with a substantive part of the complex aspects. But this immediately places the idea of user considerations in a strange position in subject heading work. After having been cast in the role of being both essential to the task and at its base an exceedingly perplexing and difficult notion, the idea of user considerations has seemingly been set aside as not necessary to an elementary understanding of subject cataloging.

The writers apparently concluded they were able to proceed in the manner they did without shortchanging the very idea of user considerations because of the way they applied the idea of a type of library to their work. A factor common to all four of these writers is they all dealt with what may be called general libraries. A general library may be defined on the one hand as a library with a policy of collecting items covering the entire range of knowledge. As such, general libraries may be contrasted to special libraries, defined as those whose policy is to collect items on only some limited portion of the entire range of knowledge. On the other hand, a general library may also be defined as one which chiefly serves general readers. When defined this way, general libraries may be contrasted with those libraries which chiefly serve specialist or scholarly readers. Both pairs of characteristics provide a way to describe any particular library. Put in the form of a chart, the various combinations of the four characteristics along with types of libraries exemplifying each combination can be found in Figure 12.

The four writers focused their work chiefly on those libraries which exemplified relatively small general collections used by general readers —those in the upper left section in Figure 12. That these libraries fell together as a common group may well account for these writers' limited comments about user considerations. There appeared to be simply too few differences and too many likenesses among the users of each type

	General Collections	Special Collections
General Readers	Children's libraries School libraries Smaller & medium size public libraries Branches of large urban libraries	Special sections of public libraries(?)
Scholarly Readers	College libraries University libraries Large urban libraries (main collections)	Special libraries

FIG. 12. Characteristics of Libraries

of library in that group to make much of variations among them. As a corollary, type-of-library thinking really only came into play when one moved from one of the quadrants in Figure 12 to another—for example, from relatively small general collections used by general readers (upper left section, Figure 12) to relatively large general collections used by scholarly readers (lower left) or to special collections used by scholarly or specialist users (lower right).[91]

An even more significant aspect of this categorization is that the readers who used the groups of libraries treated by these writers were thought to have an essentially simple approach to subject searching. Smith's call for simple terms for children's subject catalogs (regardless of the difficulties that adhere to the meaning of simple terms) and her conclusion that children searched for subjects as separate particular terms rather than as elements of a classified structure of knowledge is essentially the same as Mann's description of the general reader in public libraries. Mann stated that the dictionary catalog in such libraries was "for the person who wants a definite bit of information and who is neither pursuing general investigation nor trying to exhaust a subject."[92] Although she apparently attributed this characterization of the general reader to Cutter as the meaning of Cutter's phrase "facility of reference," it actually owed its origins to J. C. M. Hanson. It was Hanson who had singled the general reader out as one interested in separate, particular bits of information rather than information collocated in a classificatory structure, and Mann's "definite bit of information" can mean little else than that.[93]

In sum, the readers who used the various libraries in this common group had essentially the same simple needs. And because they had the same simple needs, the catalogs designed for them were not only to be simple, but to be simple in the same manner, regardless of the particular type of library within the common group. Finally, the simple catalog that was for all practical purposes the same in any of these libraries could be constructed on the basis of simple directions. There was no need, in other words, to broach the problem of user considerations within this particular group of libraries because their needs, being the same, implied few special variations or complex subject heading requirements. Sears implied this when she concluded that fewer subdivisions of subjects were needed in a small library.

> The advantage of having all books on a subject under one subject heading without subdivisions, in case the entries are few, is that this simpler, less complicated entry makes the catalog easier to comprehend and to use, as long as the entries remain few.94

The fewer the subdivisions, the simpler were the directions needed for the subject catalogers as to how to choose them or when not to use them.

A final reason why the role of user considerations appeared to play only a diminutive role for these writers is that each of them described subject heading work as essentially dependent on subject heading lists. Smith and Sears both supplied their own special lists, although Sears allowed that for new subjects the list might have to be supplemented from other sources. Akers and Mann, on the other hand, simply advised the subject cataloger that a list be chosen and used consistently. The significance of list-dependency for the idea of user considerations was striking. Regardless of what might be said even in a minimal way of making one's subject catalog closely responsive to the readers who would use it, the fact is an authoritative list of subject headings generally circumvented any decision making that needed to be done to fulfill the ideal. In other words, if one had chosen to follow a list and the list used the term INSECTS rather than BUGS or BIRDS rather than ORNITHOLOGY, to concern oneself with whether the terms not used were better for one's clientele would be a superfluous consideration. Indeed, if the list being used had been predesigned to serve the group of libraries of which one's library was a member—in this case, for general collections serving general readers—then most decisions, particularly those related to choices between equivalent terms, would already have been made for the subject cataloger.

One may summarize the foregoing discussion by saying that although the role of user considerations was generally taken for granted as an essential component of the ideal of making subject catalogs closely responsive to the readers who used them, to make an explicit connection between one's formally characterized readers and a particular subject heading choice was at best only a tenuous and ambiguous matter. The fact is readers in this group of libraries continued to be characterized as they had been at the beginning of the century. They were "general readers," chiefly notable for their "simplicity" in mental habits. If choices needed to be made at all, they were made primarily as a way to accommodate that supposed simplicity. This was, of course, no different than the way choices were made with respect to specific entry. It implied little more than the exercise of a subject cataloger's intuition.

All of this suggested ambiguity in subject heading work on a large scale. But one other factor made that ambiguity even more intense. These four writers assumed that the most appropriate vehicle for catalog subject access in the libraries they wrote about was the dictionary subject catalog. This opinion was not new, of course, having been stated long before by Cutter, although for essentially different reasons. What is significant is the form of the dictionary subject catalog these writers considered to be basic. Without exception, these writers referred to the normative dictionary subject catalog as that which had heading formats and subdivision practices patterned after those devised by J. C. M. Hanson for the Library of Congress. They showed little awareness in other words that the dictionary subject catalog of the Library of Congress was by no means a pure dictionary subject catalog, even by Hanson's own definition. The dictionary subject catalog used by the Library of Congress was a hybrid vehicle laced with subject collocations effectively hidden in the context of conventional subject heading manipulation and in the vague use of subheading procedure. Yet, it was this catalog that was the principal model on which the subject heading practices of these writers were based. And it was this catalog that was the principal model for the headings found in the lists these writers supposed would be used for general libraries. As a result, the dictionary subject catalog that these writers considered the most appropriate vehicle for general libraries because it was a simple, straightforward vehicle for readers with relatively simple, straightforward subject needs, was not nearly as simple as they implied. It was an ambiguous tool in its own right. And that put these writers in the curious position of needing the idea of user considerations not simply as a means to make subject headings that responded to the needs of readers, but also as a way to show how subject headings that had already been chosen were appropriate for the readers they served.

Ultimately, then, the entire idea of user considerations could not escape from bearing the most ambiguous implications for the actual details of subject cataloging work. Nevertheless, the idea of user considerations remained a normative and potent idea in subject cataloging work, perhaps because it so reinforced the general philosophy of librarianship which placed the reader at the center of its activities. The potency of the idea, especially in the form of the idea of types of libraries, helped to set the stage for the revolution of the 1940s and 1950s in which a burst of energy in the subject cataloging community led to investigations of and changes in subject cataloging, the effects of which are still being felt.

CHAPTER 10

Revolution in Subject Access

A significantly different stage in the search for explanation in subject cataloging began to take shape by the early 1940s. The preceding period had been notable for the ambiguity and general simplicity of its statements, the new for its attempted rigor and scholarship. The initial context of the new search consisted of academic programs in library science, at first at the University of Chicago, by the 1950s also at Columbia University, and thereafter at an ever-increasing number of library schools. By the late 1940s the academic context was augmented by the concerns and work of librarians involved in governmental special libraries. As the 1950s wore on, these two sources of new ideas were joined by persons in other special libraries and in an increasing number of academic information science programs.

The most significant results of the new search for explanation took the form of journal articles, conference proceedings, and specialized treatises instead of the classical textbooks which had characterized the previous period. New general cataloging textbooks continued to be written, but they tended not to incorporate the substance of what findings were made, perhaps because the findings themselves were most often couched as analytical observations rather than as precepts of cataloging practice.[1] The mode of investigation was at first a combination of both descriptive and analytical methods. Descriptive research was initially expressed in the form of catalog use studies. First carried out primarily in academic library settings, use studies reflected an attempt to identify subject searching patterns and needs that might be used as a basis for making revisions in subject cataloging goals and procedures.[2] Analytical investigations, often in the form of commentary on traditional practices, were important not only for their newfound rigor, but also for their attempts to identify the origins of dictionary subject cataloging as practiced in the contemporary world. It was in the latter context that Cutter's subject cataloging work came to be identified as the chief source of modern alphabetical subject heading procedure.

292

The Discovery of Cutter

Previous writers had mentioned Cutter in different contexts but never in the sense that his work was the chief source of current subject cataloging practice. Sometimes he was cited as one source among others listed for the benefit of those who wished to study the matter further or in connection with the observation that no uniform principles of subject cataloging had been widely adopted. Occasionally, too, he was mentioned as the source of one or another particular idea, the most common being specific entry.[3] The most usual manner of expressing the character of subject cataloging work for the entire earlier period, however, was to note that dictionary subject cataloging was without a stated code of rules and that it was primarily dependent on lists of subject headings that were themselves ultimately patterned after Library of Congress practice.[4] This kind of expression was accompanied by a tradition, beginning with Dorcas Fellows in 1922 and continuing to the end of the 1950s, that a comprehensive statement of subject cataloging work and principles was either in the planning stages or of the first order of business in the subject cataloging community.[5]

With the publication of Ranganathan's *Theory of Library Catalogue* in 1938, however, this situation changed. Ranganathan treated Cutter's *Rules* together with elements of Mann's work as the definitive statement of dictionary subject cataloging. He submitted them to a scathing analysis, particularly for what he considered to be their chief weakness, an intuitive technique that led to inconsistencies. The results of his critique, based as they were on comparing the Cutter "tradition" to an almost anthropomorphic representation of his own laws and canons of library science, were not nearly so important as the linear connection that he posited between Cutter and current practice:

> Why has nobody done more than reproduce Cutter's old rules in less terse and more ambiguous terms? Is it not due to the tyranny of blind tradition? Should we not get out of this slough of inertia?[6]

Thereafter, American commentators tacitly assumed the linear connection as well. Maurice F. Tauber, writing in 1942, exemplified that new assumption when he stated:

> On the basis of knowledge accumulated from the experiences of reference and circulation librarians, it becomes apparent that the procedures for assigning subject headings as set down by Cutter in 1904 are as valid today as they were two decades ago.[7]

Even more notable was the first extended American treatment of Cutter's *Rules* in 1944 included by Patricia B. Knapp in the first part of her study of the use of the subject catalog in college libraries. She described Library of Congress subject cataloging as the principal pattern which local subject cataloging followed, but stated of that pattern:

> The rules formulated by Cutter in the United States Report of 1876 and revised three times are the foundation upon which Library of Congress is based.[8]

This conclusion provided a basis for her subsequent analysis of selected rules from Cutter, the purpose of which was to show the manner in which then contemporary practice either followed or varied from them. But her analysis could only reveal the obvious, that Cutter's *Rules* were not entirely followed. That Cutter's rules were not followed was especially apparent in the formulation of headings for books with complex subject descriptions.

Having searched for the reason that such variation had arisen, Knapp also became aware of the fact that common dictionary subject catalog practice in the United States was actually not fully traditional but rather followed "the Library of Congress modification of it." Knapp referred directly to Hanson's 1909 article in which something of the nature of that modification had been stated. Nevertheless, following Hanson, she concluded that the modification was only a minor tendency. It amounted only to the incorporation of "certain characteristics of the classified catalog" through the "juggling of terms" identifiable principally as the flexible interpretation of two of Cutter's rules.[9]

Following Knapp's work, the connection understood to pertain between Cutter and everyday dictionary subject cataloging mediated by the labors of the Library of Congress was assured. Julia Pettee gave it a historical base in her 1946 work, *Subject Headings: the History and Theory of the Alphabetical Subject Approach to Books.* After observing that "Subject headings because of the complex relationships and the uncertain demand of readers for topical material do not as readily lend themselves to fixed rules," she stated:

> Catalogers have struggled along with no more authoritative rules for subject headings than the half dozen pages in Cutter's *Rules*, first set forth for the printed catalog nearly three quarters of a century ago.[10]

After Pettee, every important discussion of dictionary subject cataloging assumed the connection explicitly. The only significant exception to this was David J. Haykin's *Subject Headings, a Practical Guide,* an authoritative description of Library of Congress practice, which referred to Cutter only sparingly. This may well have been because Haykin, who finished his work in 1951 at the end of his tenure as Chief of the Library's Subject Cataloging Division, was in the best position to realize the uniqueness of the Library of Congress system.

User Considerations

Beyond the discovery of Cutter's work, the first, and in many respects, the most significant finding of the new search for explanation was the confirmation of the importance of user considerations in subject cataloging work. By the 1950s the focus on the user had assumed such importance that one could refer to its centrality to subject cataloging without having to explain the matter. The ascendancy of user considerations to that central position did not occur without difficulty, however. Some appreciation of its development may be seen by considering its most significant aspect—user categories.

At first, the major focal point of user considerations continued to be the categorization of users by type of library. In a notable 1940 call for technical services in libraries to be based on the study of users, William M. Randall assumed such categorization implicitly. Eventually, this emphasis led not only to user studies that assumed categorization of this kind as a valid starting point for research, but also to forums such as those held in 1952 and 1953 in which user needs were explicitly examined in types of library categories.[11]

In some respects Julia Pettee's 1946 work represented the acme of this tradition. She not only distinguished even more sharply the categories of libraries Mann had used, but also emphasized more than anyone before her how an understanding of the user was fundamental to all aspects of subject heading work. Pettee divided libraries and thus the users of libraries into the following categories:

1. Small libraries including book wagons
2. Children's libraries—an age group
3. Special libraries. These libraries are designed primarily to promote the interest of some special field. Their function differs greatly from that of the general library.
4. General libraries. These are of two groups:
   a. Public libraries and all medium-sized general collections designed for popular reading and ready reference. Their function is cultural and to serve as purveyors of general information.
   b. Research collections existing primarily to serve the needs of advanced scholarship.[12]

Pettee's categories are not without difficulties. Her list in some respects intermixed the two kinds of differentia noted in the discussion of Mann: special/general and small/large. As a result, her categories are somewhat confusing. It makes no sense to differentiate small libraries from either special or general libraries because small libraries may be either special or general. Again, it does not make sense to differentiate children's libraries from either small libraries or general libraries because children's libraries may also be small and most likely are general. Furthermore, her qualification of children's libraries as "an age group" offers little help because she did not explain its significance.

Pettee recognized that her categories overlapped but considered the overlapping to be insignificant. She concluded that small libraries and children's libraries were insignificant for her discussion because they were adequately cared for by Sears's and Smith's lists of subject headings and because their catalogs were of "minor importance" for subject access in comparison to the use of shelf arrangements by the patrons of these libraries.[13]

By considering the first two categories of libraries to be insignificant, what remained for Pettee was in some respects a repetition of Mann's two fundamental categories of libraries and their users: special and general. Of course, Mann had divided the latter category into those that were small and those that were large. Pettee appears to have used a different stated basis of subdivision for general libraries, research and non-research. But there are also overtones of a size differentiation in her criteria as well. Research collections have always been associated with either established academic libraries of notable size or established large public or private libraries whose size is considered to be an especially important factor in their usefulness for research. Other general libraries, including public libraries and "medium-sized general collections"—the latter can only mean all the various college libraries of moderate or small size—would be considered nonresearch libraries not because one could not do research in them, but because by virtue of their size they did not present themselves as thoroughgoing research collections.

At the same time, Pettee went well beyond Mann's library and user considerations. To begin with, her differentiation of special libraries was especially severe. She considered them so unique in their subject orientation that regular subject headings and, one supposes, the regular subject heading procedures of dictionary subject cataloging did not apply to them at all. She wrote:

> Special libraries form a type quite distinct from general collections. In each of these libraries the special interest of its clientele is devel-

> oped. The whole point of view of a special library is from one particular angle of the field of knowledge. General lists of subject headings have been compiled for them, and they have developed their own particular methods.[14]

This conclusion strongly reinforced the opinion, increasingly widespread during her time and fundamental to the documentation movement, that special libraries, especially those oriented to the role of disseminating scientific and technical information, were fundamentally different from other types of libraries, not only in vocabulary needs, but also in how subject access systems should be structured.

Pettee also went well beyond Mann in her characterization of the users of the two types of general libraries. First, she identified the two types of libraries and their users with the two traditional categories of users distinguished by Cutter, Hanson, and other earlier writers. She concluded that the first type of general library (public and college) had primarily nonscholarly users whereas the second type of general library (research) had primarily scholarly users, chiefly graduate students and faculty. She discounted the role of undergraduates in such settings, suggesting that they were often supplied with their own special college collections.[15]

Second, Pettee characterized in detail the subject searching habits of each kind of user. The first sought "popular and current literature," "casual informative literature," or "casual information." A search was approached as a "specific request for information" rather than as an involved bibliographic exercise. Thus, the user preferred "a few selected entries to a trayful." And searches were conducted with special emphasis on "quick access," because this kind of user was "in a hurry."[16] The second kind of user, the scholar, had some specific information requests. But more often than not, the scholar was involved in "an exhaustive study of his particular interest." This implied intense bibliographical work in the context of extensive collections where the scholar, working primarily from a knowledge of the authors associated with an area of study, examined scores of works and, like a detective, uncovered many disparate bits of information not otherwise accessible because they were scattered and often buried within such works.[17]

Last, although she assumed the dictionary catalog would be the standard form of subject catalog access found in each type of library, Pettee considered the structural requirements of the dictionary catalog to be different for each kind of user. The casual, informational, and popular nature of nonscholarly searching required the dictionary catalog to approach "encyclopedic completeness," at least so far as it supplemented current indexes and reference works.[18] By this she meant that the catalog should be a key aid in locating material on a wide variety of current topics likely to be looked for by this kind of user. It should be like an encyclopedia in its coverage—wide, but not necessarily deep. This implied the necessity of analytical subject entries as well as regular specific subject entries to give access to the widest range of distinct, current, and popular topics. It also implied entry under a variety of popular literary form categories. Finally, it implied a high degree of access point redundancy, such as the selective use of double entry of the same heading under its different elements and of entry of the same item under both specific and general headings. At the same time, the searching characteristics of the nonscholar militated against the full specification of works if that resulted in excessive scattering of the desired topics into tiny document classes, often of only single items. Instead, reasonably sized document classes also had to be preserved. In this respect, Pettee wrote:

> As the choice between the most specific term (which can be used as a heading) and a more inclusive one depends entirely upon the number of items which will be likely to collect under the more inclusive term, a safe rule would be to prefer the more inclusive for less than a dozen titles which would be likely to collect under it.[19]

Because scholarly users also had at least some informational needs as well as highly developed author access needs, Pettee also concluded that the dictionary catalog format was generally appropriate for this class of user as well. At the same time, Pettee concluded that the dictionary catalog was not very useful for the scholar's principal activity of extensive and in-depth searching. In fact, the kind of bibliographical listings it provided could not begin to match those of specialized bibliographies. A scholar might use it "for material outside his main theme or as a first step in assembling the multitude of books through which he expects to search patiently for all clues which contribute to his work," but at best it would provide only "a meager bibliography for him."[20] This occurred because no catalog could ever give access to books to the depth and degree of responsiveness required by scholarly detective work. For that reason, Pettee recommended that the subject aspect of the catalog in research libraries be severely curtailed, especially in light of the great expense that subject heading work in research libraries entailed. For example, form entries for popular literature should be discontinued. Redundancy in entries should be kept to a minimum with a stress on making no more than single specific entries for each item. On the other hand, where materials did collect under particular topics, especially those involving chronological and type of treatment differences, every effort should be made to subar-range those entries in useful subsequences.

It might seem on the face of things that Pettee's characterization of user considerations was hardly more than a logical extension of what had been stated before by others. Her view of the first type of user as impatient and generally desiring popular literature reflected the views of all previous writers. Her emphasis on general users as interested mainly in subjects as separate entities reflected Hanson's and Mann's views. Her insistence that general readers wanted only ready reference materials reiterated Mann's views. And finally, her characterization of scholarly searching habits as bibliographical detective work had a tra-ditional cast to it.

Despite such resemblances, however, Pettee's characterization of users was significantly different from previous conceptions. The most striking aspect of that difference resided in how sharply she distin-guished between the two basic kinds of users. For Cutter, all readers, although divisible into various categories, remained in a single con-tinuum of users. Hanson, assuming that there were only two basic cate-gories of readers, separated the two categories severely enough to create a hypothetical discontinuity between them. He did so by assuming that each kind of user approached subjects in different ways—nonscholars in terms of discrete entities, scholars in terms of collocative patterns. He also implied, of course, a difference between them in terms of their respective demonstrations of intellectual rigor. But Pettee went beyond even Hanson. She did not simply separate the two basic kinds of users. She separated them radically. Nonscholars searched for casual and popular information. She did not define "casual," but the word im-plies some combination of imprecision, lack of substance, temporari-ness, and a lack of intellectual focus so severe as to suggest ephemer-ality. The scholar did bibliographical detective work in a realm so rarified and specialized that it implied subject relationships that were disparate, highly abstract, and subtle to the point of extreme intel-lectual complexity. The result was the two kinds of users ended up in intellectual worlds so different as to have no common meeting ground whatsoever.

The corresponding implications of this radical separation for sub-ject access vehicles were likewise severe. Pettee suggested that subject headings made for a dictionary catalog designed for the first kind of user "do not assume theoretical completion but are practical aids to actual needs."[21] She did not define "practical" further, but one may assume she meant that the headings had to respond to this kind of user's characteristics. That could only mean that the catalog would need to capture the same ever-changing, popular, at times imprecise and frivolous character inherent in user searching. On the other side, a dictionary catalog for scholars was at best only a starting aid. The scholar's real subject searching needs were so complex and refined as to be beyond the capabilities of any dictionary subject catalog and perhaps beyond any formal subject catalog at all. As a result, the maintenance of the dictionary subject catalog was a default arrangement made necessary by its partial usefulness. Because of this, it had to be trimmed in format to its barest essentials.

Still another way in which Pettee's characterization of users was significantly different was in her idea of scholarly subject access. Previous pictures of scholarly access turned primarily on the idea of subject relationships—for example, on hierarchical inclusion relationships in Cutter and sheer subject collocation in Hanson. Taking her cue from the documentation movement, perhaps, Pettee added to those characteristics the notion of exhaustive searching. The very idea of scholarship meant for her a desire on the part of scholars to find all there was on the subject at hand. This included especially disparate pieces and bits of information buried within documents. The discovery of those bits of information could only be accomplished through highly complex verbal constructions because they were, in comparison to the subjects of books themselves, very "specific" or "tiny" bits of information. But Pettee did not consider the dictionary catalog to be a powerful enough subject retrieval instrument to provide such access. At best it could specify narrow topics by chronological and form subarrangement techniques. But her stress on exhaustive searching remained notable because, despite her opinion that specialists and special libraries constituted an altogether separate category of users, her description of the research library user equated that user directly with the specialist as the latter was coming to be defined in the documentation movement. Both, in other words, were users who, for the sake of scientific advance, exhausted the resources available for every hint of useful information.

Pettee's implied identification of scholars in research libraries with specialists in special libraries signaled, in a certain sense, the future direction of user categorization. Writers on subject heading work continued into the 1950s to appeal to types of libraries as a basis for user considerations. But the appeal to types of libraries eventually proved to be perplexing. Jean K. Taylor expressed that perplexity well at the 1952 conference on the subject analysis of library materials jointly sponsored by Columbia University and the American Library Association:

> It has always puzzled me to find our profession drawing hairlines between types of reference libraries and trying to set up elaborate dis-

tinctions between public libraries, college libraries, research libraries, special libraries, etc.[22]

What Taylor was apparently trying to express was that no fundamental distinction by which the entire population of any one type of library could be set off from the users of other types of libraries had ever been established. By the mid-1950s, in fact, Pettee's more detailed analysis of user characteristics appears to have taken hold because by that date an essentially new and far more simplified nomenclature of users came to be expressed—that is, that there are only two essentially different categories of users: specialists, including Pettee's scholarly users; and general users, or nonspecialists.[23] A type of library might still be distinguished from other types of libraries in its usage. But the distinctiveness of its use came to reside in whether one or the other of these two general categories of users predominated. If the first, it was a specialist library; if the second, simply a general library.

The idea of analyzing user habits as closely as Pettee did, when combined with the specialist-general user nomenclature, had both positive and negative effects on subject heading work. On the positive side it not only served to reemphasize the need of catalogers to think of users specifically when making subject heading decisions, but also provided a model—specialist use—for doing so. Specialist use served as a model because specialists, especially researchers in science and technology, tended to fall into identifiable groups which could be studied and measured with respect to terminology and subject searching habits. Studies of that sort raised the hope that subject access work in general and subject heading work in particular could be made to respond much more precisely to the needs of users than previously thought possible. The positive emphasis on measuring use more precisely was also reinforced by the rediscovery of Cutter. In an effort to pin down the source of user considerations in the American subject heading tradition, commentators concluded that it had arisen with Cutter himself; that, in fact, Cutter's own emphasis on common usage made his subject heading system almost totally dependent on such considerations. Paul S. Dunkin typified this reassessment of Cutter when he wrote in 1956 that

> Cutter fell back on his old standby, readers' habits, and in elaborate annotations on his rules he tried to explain and justify choice of words, compound phrases, inverted headings, and the like.[24]

Later, in the same article, he extended his assessment of the consideration of the user and usage in Cutter's *Rules* even further, claiming it to have enjoyed a position there beyond that even of a principle:

> Cutter sets the user above and outside the basic principles and the rules. Whenever he felt that the reader's habits would conflict with the logic of the principles, he followed what he thought was the reader.[25]

Consideration of the user in the way described by Pettee also had a profoundly negative side to it. To begin with, the radical separation of the two kinds of users and the concomitant focusing on the specialist-scholar as the model for usage led to a general disparagement of the nonspecialist user as a meaningful category. While Pettee did not appear to intend this effect, even her description of general users tended to characterize them as generally flaccid in thought and not given to more than minimal intellectual sophistication. And among commentators that followed her, nonspecialist users fared little better.[26] The result was the general user came to be characterized as not representative of simply a somewhat lower level than specialist searcher but, in a sense, representative of the lowest common denominator in use. This attempt to summarize the way general users were characterized must be moderated, however, because even more important than the generally low estimate attributed to them was the habit of avoiding a positive description of the category altogether. The general user was often not specifically defined at all. Instead, the category was by implication taken to be neither more nor less than the obverse of the specialist. General users were simply "not specialists," that is, readers who plainly lacked those qualities or abilities which characterized specialist subject searching.

A concomitant effect of characterizing the general user in the foregoing manner was to suggest that the dictionary subject catalog, which had long been considered to be a tool primarily for the general user, by its nature had to be just as vague as its users were. As noted earlier, Pettee had called for an essentially different approach to the dictionary subject catalog when made for general users than when made for scholar-specialists. Upon close examination, however, her prescriptions for its structure suggest that the job was forbidding, if not impossible. She required the catalog made for the general user to be pragmatic, shifting with every current subject interest change the public might follow, although she provided little direction for determining how such currency might be assessed or achieved. She also required it to stress a variety of specification procedures, sometimes scope-matching, sometimes class entry, and sometimes depth analysis, each of these, however, just as likely to change. Here again, she provided no reasonable indication of when and how these various measures should be applied beyond the general injunction of placing no more than twelve items under each heading. Finally, she required the catalog made for the general user to emphasize popular and more or less unsophisticated terminology. But here too she gave little indication of how such terminology might be determined. In short, Pettee suggested that a dictionary subject catalog appropriate for the general user could only be constructed by an intuitive technique. At least that is what the notion of user considerations and its practical application in the form of common usage suggested, considering the vagueness of the general user category.

Vagueness in the notion of user considerations was not limited to the general user category, however. The application of common usage decisions to anything but the most clearly defined specialist situations did not present clear alternatives either. This was particularly the case for those subject catalogers whose clientele consisted of a mixture of both general and special users. Common usage for college catalogers, for instance, implied the need for opposite decisions depending on who was being served and when they were being served. When so fundamental a contradiction was then added to the general opinion that the dictionary catalog was really a basically imprecise subject instrument more fit for general than for specialist use, it is no wonder that the literature of the 1950s saw not a few calls for some kind of new subject system altogether. It is interesting to note, however, that even calls for new systems were ordinarily justified by appeals to user considerations, the users commonly characterized as specialists, or at least of a higher order than the general user category.[27] As it turned out, however, even strictly specialist use was subject to imprecision, vagueness, and even contradiction. By the end of the 1950s the intensive study of specialist searching was beginning to show a variety that made the consideration of even that category of user difficult to convert into common usage decisions. For example, Voigt's summary of findings related to researchers' information needs and his division of them into the three categories—current, everyday, and exhaustive—suggested that there was much more complexity present than was previously realized and certainly much more than the comparatively simple picture drawn by Pettee some thirteen years before.[28]

In the final analysis, therefore, the notion that user considerations are important to the subject cataloging process, while evolving from type of library basis to specialist and general user categories and from a more or less assumed importance to an all encompassing centrality, engendered a notable amount of frustration. It constituted a high ideal that was fundamentally vague. And when pursued within dictionary subject cataloging, it fostered the breakdown of that system by incorporating justified inconsistencies based on intuitive procedures.

Dunkin summarized something of this aspect of the notion in 1967 when, in commenting on Sidney Jackson's landmark use study of a decade before, he asked rhetorically:

> Is there such a creature as "the user"; or are there (as with costs) many users each with his individual habits? Can such a study include many kinds of libraries and succeed? Even if we find "the user," can we safely build our practice to fit him—or shall we have to keep on making studies to find out if "the user" (just as you and I) changes habits and ways of thinking from time to time?[29]

He obviously felt that the quest for "the user" was not only vague, but close to impossible. Two years later, when reviewing dictionary catalog development in the United States, he expressed his opinion even more sardonically. Cutter's idea of the convenience of the public, he noted,

> has a noble ring; who can deny that libraries exist to serve? One would as soon attack mother love or home. On the other hand, it is convenient; it gives us an excuse to do almost anything in the catalog.[30]

Given a subject heading procedure that begins with the intention of building something of a rational system, the effort ultimately fails because

> whenever the going gets tough we turn aside to Cutter's notion that we must follow the convenience of the public regardless of what that presumed convenience may do to the convenience of a bibliographical system.[31]

Despite the difficulties that the notion of user considerations entailed, however, it retained its position of importance. Moreover, it exercised considerable influence on other discoveries as well. This was particularly the case in the development of a new understanding of specific entry.

Specific Entry

The second significant aspect of the quest for explanation in subject heading work during the 1940s and 1950s consisted of the analysis and enhancement of the idea of specific entry. The most obvious result of the discoveries that were made was to divide specific entry into two distinct parts: directness of entry form and extent of specification. The general significance of the division will become apparent as the most important writings concerning the idea are examined. Before that can be done, however, the general background of confusion that had enveloped specific entry by the beginning of the 1940s must first be reviewed.

The confusion that had come to characterize specific entry as an operational measure came from two sources. The first source, already referred to in the discussion of Mann and Sears, was the essentially negative way in which the idea was applied. Specific entry was circumscribed by the way the gathering function of the catalog was understood. It was also made dependent on an intuitive sense of the needs of the clientele served. And it was affected severely by the use of printed subject heading lists. The result was choices of headings highly varied in how they indicated or specified the topical contents of books. In situations where a printed list of subject headings provided terms considered too specific, subject catalogers retreated from scope-matching in favor of headings that were consciously more inclusive than scope-matching rightly demanded. Sometimes this amounted to no more than not using a subheading that the list provided. But at other times it meant using an entirely different term than the one best fitted for the book. In situations where the list was not specific enough, the need to scope-match a work sometimes led not to a process of devising a new heading but rather to the use of multiple headings. None of the individual headings specified the entire topical contents of the books by themselves, of course. Instead, each represented a more inclusive heading. Nevertheless, it was apparently thought that the headings together specified the work.

No original source for the use of multiple headings as one solution to the problem of specification has even been definitively traced. It seems likely, however, that their use was patterned after multiple entry for books that actually had separate topics within their covers, as in the case, for example, of a book on dogs and cats entered under two terms, one for each of the two subjects. That kind of example, when combined with the absence of any regular explanation of how new headings were to be devised and with a dependency on printed subject headings lists, perhaps made it seem normal to use multiple headings for new complex topics as well. When one considers the fact that lists of subject headings represented authoritative decisions made by subject catalogers who were highly reputed (especially subject catalogers at the Library of Congress), this resolution is understandable. At the same time, it is also clear that by the 1940s the use of multiple headings for new complex topics had also become an established practice among Library of Congress subject catalogers. The conclusion is unescapable, therefore, that by that date, and perhaps even much earlier, the subject naming procedure used by Library of Congress subject catalogers had itself become circumscribed to a significant extent by adherence to its own list of printed headings.

Regardless of the reasons for the practice, however, the use of multiple entry in this way, combined with choices of headings that were conscious efforts to keep specific entry from being either too broad or too narrow, could not help but cause specific entry to appear confusing as an operational procedure.

As confusing as the foregoing operation might have appeared, it was overshadowed by a second source of confusion related to specific entry—the variety of heading formats that by the 1940s had come to characterize dictionary subject cataloging, especially in relation to subjects which could only be indicated by means of complex descriptions. At its most fundamental level, the question of appropriate heading form was based on the notion of conventional headings. As already observed, Hanson, when beginning the Library of Congress subject heading system, attempted to achieve the initial goal of specific entry interpreted as scope-matching within the confines of conventional heading format. This limitation sometimes led to the creation of complex phrases for headings. In cases where extended or complex conventional headings were unacceptable in terms of common usage, however, he then resorted to entry under broader or inclusive conventional headings that were less complex in their structure but acceptable in their usage. But more inclusive or broader headings of this kind left the books they described intermixed and undifferentiated among other books in the same subject files, some of which were fully specified by the heading for the files and others of which were unspecified in the same manner as the books in question.

The chief method for overcoming the intermixing which took place in large files was to subarrange the entries by means of subheadings. One effect of subarrangement was in many cases to achieve the scope-matching specification originally sought by the use of a conventional heading. Specification achieved in that way fell outside the confines of conventional headings, however. It used what may be conveniently labeled strings-of-terms with specialized punctuation. As a result, Hanson's procedures created two basic methods for converting what was considered to be the subject of a book into a subject heading: conventional headings, and strings-of-terms that involved an inclusive heading subarranged by a qualifying term. The first method was preferred because it followed conventional naming practices. The second was an alternative justified by the reasoning attached to the initial decision about the lack of a common usage name.

Given the growing forcefulness of the scope-match interpretation of specific entry together with the inadequacy of conventional subject headings, the strings-of-terms format became not simply a convenient alternative but rather a necessary tool of the cataloger in pursuing the scope-matching ideal. The presence of that format had become so pervasive by the 1940s that it changed the very idea of what constituted a legitimate subject heading. Instead of the older view that differentiated between a conventional heading per se and other terms that were subheadings, a subject heading became, at least in common parlance, the entire set of words written across the top of a catalog card entry that denoted the document's subject. This understanding of what constituted a legitimate subject heading was further reinforced by the fact that once a decision had been made to subarrange any particular heading by the use of subheadings (rather than to use an extended conventional phrase of some kind), it was much more convenient and much less expensive over the long run to keep using the subarrangement device than to change back to a conventional heading even though it might at some later point have become justified by common usage considerations. That led in turn to a proliferation of strings-of-terms headings.

One may summarize the foregoing development by stating that given the growth of the idea of specific entry as scope-matching, strings-of-terms headings became an overwhelmingly important and in many respects a more conveniently applied competitor of conventional headings as a way to fully specify the subjects of books, especially those that could be described only by compound terms. And this applied regardless of any modification of scope-matching related to the preservation of the gathering capacity of the subject catalog. The question that remained for subject catalogers was which form might be justified for any particular book. But since there was no consensus about how to devise specific entry headings, the question of appropriateness was not answerable.

Confusion did not stop with the bare conflict between specification formats, however. It was exacerbated by variations within the formats themselves. For example, strings-of-terms justified by the initial subject naming procedure were intermixed with other strings-of-terms that were conscious choices of class-subclass arrangement. Also, complex conventional headings were consciously manipulated into class-subclass formats by means of inversion. Moreover, the tendency of subject catalogers to convert inverted conventional headings into strings-of-terms format only reinforced the use of strings-of-terms as a specification procedure. As a result of these variations, there were by the 1940s four fully developed means of providing specific entry headings for complex subject descriptions: conventional headings used in a straightforward manner; conventional headings that had been manipulated, usually by inversion; strings-of-terms justified by the subject naming procedure; and strings-of-terms that had obvious class-subclass meanings. When such variations were added to the confusion already inherent in the idea of specific entry itself and also to the common use of multiple entry, the result was a welter of subject heading choices and formats with little indication as to which was appropriate in any one situation.

Fundamental Issues

Given this confusing situation, the renewed and close questioning of the fundamental nature of the dictionary catalog that took place during the 1940s is understandable. The foci of that questioning revolved around two basic but related issues. First, how did specific entry serve to differentiate the dictionary catalog from any other catalog type and, more specifically, from the alphabetico-classed catalog? Second, how could one justify the long-held opinion that the dictionary catalog was by its nature simple and straightforward if one considered the complexity in heading format and choices that had arisen?

UNIQUENESS

The issue of what made the dictionary subject catalog fundamentally different from other catalogs, especially from the alphabetico-classed catalog, was important for no other reason than the strength of the long-held opinion that specific entry did indeed express the difference between the two. Cutter had been unequivocal in his statement of the equation more than a half-century earlier when he wrote, "This rule of 'specific entry' is the main distinction between the dictionary catalog and the alphabetico-classed."[32] Although they did not always refer directly to Cutter's statement, commentators after Cutter regularly reiterated the equation. The difficulty with the equation was, however, that common dictionary subject catalog practice did not appear to support the difference.

On the level of appearance alone the regular use of strings-of-terms subject descriptions had all the marks of alphabetico-classed sequences, at least to the generally uninformed subject cataloger. When these forms were regularly intermixed with incursions of subject descriptions that were purposefully class-subclass in structure, the general impression one received was that the dictionary catalog was becoming an alphabetico-classed rather than a specific entry subject access vehicle. This conclusion became even more a matter of concern if one also concluded that, however they were rationalized, subject headings that appeared to be alphabetico-classed in structure were absolutely necessary to achieve anything approaching the scope-matching ideal or anything approaching control over otherwise unwieldy subject document files. Alphabetico-classed headings appeared to be mandatory, in other words, if specific entry as scope-matching was to be achieved, an obviously contradictory conclusion.

The foregoing conclusion was superficial, of course, based as it was only on appearances. Specific entry and alphabetico-classed headings could not ultimately be differentiated by format. Even Cutter had noted this when, in discussing the use of subheadings under countries, he had stated, "It is not of the slightest importance that this introduces the *appearance* of an alphabetico-classed catalog, so long as the main object of a dictionary, ready reference, is attained."[33] Cutter could make this distinction because the difference between the two kinds of formats resided in the class relationships they connoted rather than in their appearance, and his categorical approach to subjects enabled him to speak about class relationships with considerable clarity. But neither Hanson nor those who followed him retained Cutter's underlying classificatory referent. As a result, they had no clear way to explicitly rationalize how any alternative to a conventional heading that involved the coordination of terms was not classed rather than classed in its meaning.

Obviously, many such coordinated strings-of-terms were plainly not classed. A topic subarranged by form as in CHEMISTRY–DICTIONARIES did not involve a hierarchical class-subclass relationship between subjects. In fact, not only were form categories not considered subjects per se, but dictionary catalogs had used such subheadings for decades without raising any objections as to whether they represented alphabetico-classed sequences. Even Cutter had treated subheadings of that kind in a separate section in his *Rules*. But the A.L.A. *List* as early as 1895 and Hanson's system as well had not only included other subheadings in the same category as form subheadings, but also had treated them as nonclassed as well. Chief among such additional categories were geographical and chronological subsequences and such special subtopics as Biography, Philosophy, Study and teaching, and Law and legislation.

By the 1940s subheading sequences of this kind had not only become standard, but also had been expanded greatly as well. For example, Sears's *List* also included HISTORY and STUDY AND TEACHING among its standard subdivisions as if those were also form treatments.[34] And the fourth edition of the Library of Congress list of subject headings (1943) need only be cursorily examined under a topic such as

CHEMISTRY and its inverted extensions (CHEMISTRY, INORGANIC, etc.) to see how Hanson's earlier practice of intermixing subheadings had expanded over the years to include many other types of subheadings as well—for example, subheadings that focused on an intended audience such as —JUVENILE LITERATURE and subheadings of a topical nature that had little relationship to form considerations such as —MANIPULATION; —NOMENCLATURE; —NOTATION; and —SYNTHESIS.[35]

The difficulty with all subheadings that went beyond purely formal relationships was that without a formal structure of kinds of subjects to refer to and without a more extensive understanding of class-subclass structure than genus-species or whole-part relationships, the relationships implied by topical subheadings could only be rationalized on an individual basis to distinguish those that were not classed from those that were. Most such rationalizations were never recorded, however, but rather lay buried in the past memories of Library of Congress subject catalogers. Therefore, no convincing systematic explanations could easily be offered for them. Furthermore, because there was no way to prove that the use of subheadings was not classed in such instances, there was also no way to prove that they were specific entries either, at least in any classificatory sense.

This confusion in identity led to a curious problem of semantics when one wished to state how specific entry made the dictionary catalog distinctive. Specific entry might mean that a string-of-terms heading was not classed. If, however, there was no evidence to support that conclusion, one might then appeal to the other meaning that specific entry had gained since Hanson's day—that is, that such a heading scope-matched the topical contents of the book to which it was applied. The use of this meaning of specific entry did not make the dictionary catalog unique, however. Furthermore, since scope-matching was often modified in practice for reasons already discussed, it could not be appealed to with any assurance that it had been carried out or even intended.

SIMPLICITY

The second focus of the questioning about the dictionary subject catalog of the 1940s had to do with the supposed simplicity and straightforwardness that the catalog embodied. This assumption, like that of specific entry as the chief differentia of the dictionary subject catalog, also had a long tradition.

The dictionary subject catalog had long been perceived as best suited to the needs of general rather than specialist or scholarly readers. The reason for this equation had changed over the decades, however. Cutter considered the maxim to be true because of the way specific entry required books to be entered (not subentered) under the most concrete subject they treated. His emphasis on "ready reference" meant that the kind of subject (i.e., concrete subjects) a general reader was most likely to look for was the kind of subject most readily available in the dictionary subject catalog. And the ready availability of concrete subjects was what made the dictionary subject catalog simple and straightforward and best-suited to the needs of the desultory reader.

Hanson modified the idea of simplicity by basing it not on easy access to a certain kind of subject but rather on access to any subject that was distinct. He had concluded that what set general readers apart from scholars was their tendency to search for subjects as discrete, separate ideas that had distinct conventional names rather than as elements of subject collocations related to special fields of knowledge. The dictionary subject catalog served general readers well by making conventionally named distinct subjects directly available in the main sequence of subject headings.

The writers of the 1930s reiterated Hanson's approach to the matter but modified it with conditions related to types of libraries. They concluded that the direct accessibility to distinct topics afforded by the dictionary subject catalog—what, in the end, made it simple and straightforward—was particularly relevant to those kinds of libraries that did not have specialist users. Pettee further modified even this conclusion by attributing to the dictionary subject catalog made for general readers a pragmatic adaptability and impermanence. For her, simplicity implied direct accessibility not just to any subject, but especially to the fleeting and imprecisely named topics searched out by general readers. In other words, the dictionary subject catalog was especially suited to any library dominated by an intellectually shallow and generally unsophisticated, impatient clientele that wanted immediate access to generally unsophisticated and noncomplex topics. The dictionary subject catalog served these readers especially well because its primary purpose was to make such topics directly available through a variety of methods that often stressed redundancy in entry.

It is especially important to note that regardless of the particular reasoning employed to show why the dictionary subject catalog was best adapted to the general reader, each interpretation had this in common, that the basis for simplicity was the direct accessibility of subjects. The subject headings understood to be those most desired by general readers were to be placed in the main alphabetical sequence of headings. As long as subject headings remained single-word conventional subject names, this conclusion offered little difficulty. But it became a problem when the subject cataloger had to resort to compound phrase headings to name subjects. Some method for choosing between alternative phrases or between alternative word orders in a single phrase had to be devised. Cutter simply applied his understanding of subject structure to the problem. His method was systematic, therefore, at least within the confines of his understanding of the nature of subject relationships. Hanson did not have the same overall understanding of subject structure to appeal to, however. His decisions were based instead on judgments about which choices would collocate subjects most usefully for scholars and still not violate too radically the direct entry method that the dictionary subject catalog ordinarily employed. But because usefulness for scholars was based on pragmatic assessments about subject structure in special areas of knowledge, his method was systematic only to the degree that his underlying assessments of special fields of knowledge were systematic. For libraries not dominated by scholars, however, the best that one could do was to appeal to vague notions of how a particular clientele was likely to look up individual subjects that had compound phrase names. Decisions made that way were highly intuitive rather than systematic.

The methods used by subject catalogers to make choices related to compound phrase names ranged from those that were very systematic to those that lacked any systematic approach at all. When choices related to term order in strings-of-terms headings and to headings involving inversions were added to those related to straightforward phrase names (choices that Cutter had not for the most part had to face), not only did the ability of subject catalogers to decide such questions become confusing and strained, but also the very simplicity that was previously attributed to the dictionary subject catalog became lost entirely. The alleged simplicity of the dictionary subject catalog simply could not be maintained when so many of the subjects that were looked for even by general readers necessarily consisted of complex term formulations or were buried among a welter of other complex term formulations. The only kind of library ultimately capable of claiming its dictionary subject catalog was simple and straightforward was one of small size where subarrangement was kept to a minimum, or one that contained documents on relatively broad subjects, the names of which were older and thus both well-established and uncomplicated.

The most obvious conclusion that may be drawn from both of the foregoing issues is that by the 1940s the uniqueness of the dictionary subject catalog could not be maintained in any meaningful way either by recourse to a basic definition or in terms of the simplicity of its structure. The two foci of concern were related because they both arose from the presence of headings that involved the complex coordination of terms. But the appropriateness of such terms and a systematic approach to their use were little understood. Furthermore, notions of user considerations served only to make the dictionary subject cataloging process more mysterious. It was in this context that the appearance of Knapp's study offered something of a new direction in the attempt to understand the nature of the dictionary catalog and its idea of specific entry.

Patricia B. Knapp

Besides being the first American writer to closely appeal to Cutter's *Rules* as the source of American subject heading work, Knapp also set something of a standard for the investigation of dictionary subject cataloging. Her article, representing the findings of her master's thesis at the University of Chicago Graduate Library School, incorporated a skillful blend of all the various elements of subject cataloging already discussed—user considerations, the problems of fundamental definitions, and considerations related to subject heading format.[36] The impetus of her study was a concern about the usefulness of the dictionary subject catalog to college library users, especially since making one entailed high costs. She was particularly interested in establishing whether the dictionary subject catalog fulfilled the claims made about its essential characteristics and the benefits to be derived from them. The findings of her study were thus aimed at more fully understanding the nature of the catalog and at offering suggestions as to how it might be made more useful if that were found necessary.

Knapp began with a description of the origins and structure of the dictionary subject catalog and followed this with the results of her interview survey of students who were searching in the catalog for books by means of their subjects. In her survey she measured the failure rates of students' searching in terms of the difference between their search terms and the most appropriate subject headings in the catalog that would have answered their requests. The eleven resulting categories of failure, numbered in their order of frequency, included such things as students looking under conventional headings that were either broader or narrower than was necessary (categories 1 and 5), wrongly looking under a heading directly rather than indirectly, or failing to look for a topical or form subheading at all when one was involved (categories 2, 7, and 8), wrongly looking under a place when the subject was entered under a topical term and looking under a topic when the subject was entered under a place (categories 3 and 6), and other failures related to the up-to-dateness and word order or spelling of headings (categories 4, 9, 10, and 11).

Perhaps the most notable of her findings was that nearly half of the categories of failure (2, 3, 6, 7, and 8) had to do with the failure on the part of students to appreciate subheading practices, a matter that directly reflected the problem of simplicity already discussed. And when the failure to proceed as far as a subdivision (7, 8) is added to the propensity of students to define a topic either too broadly or too narrowly to begin with (1, 5), it is clear that students had little understanding of either how to formulate search headings that matched their requests in topical scope or how the various headings formats were used to accomplish that goal. The latter could only have been exacerbated by the confused state of specific entry as an entry practice. As already noted, makers of dictionary subject catalogs incorporated considerable variations in both how they interpreted scope-matching and in the heading formats they used. In the end, therefore, Knapp's study strongly suggested that the dictionary subject catalog was as difficult to use as to make, at least for the type of user that she had studied.

Knapp's findings were even more significant with respect to characterizing the nature of the dictionary catalog. As already noted, she observed that the then current form of the dictionary catalog was not a pure example of subject heading practice, but incorporated Hanson's classed catalog thinking. She was thus able to discount conscious incursions of alphabetico-classed structure in her effort to determine the essential difference between the two catalog types.

Knapp's most significant discovery related to definitions arose out of her discussion of compound heading practice. Of subjects that required more than one word for their expression, Knapp observed not only that entry under the words separately failed to specify the subject precisely, but that when the multiple terms were precoordinated, four heading formulations were possible: strings-of-terms, adjectival phrases, prepositional phrases, and inverted adjectival headings. She subsequently noted that any of the compound topics she used as examples could be expressed by each of the four formats. For example, Organic chemistry could be expressed as CHEMISTRY—ORGANIC (or ORGANIC MATTER—CHEMISTRY); ORGANIC CHEMISTRY; CHEMISTRY OF ORGANIC MATTER; and CHEMISTRY, ORGANIC. Finally, she concluded that regardless of their respective formats, each heading form was legitimate because each met *"the primary rule of specific entry."*[37] That is to say, each scope-matched the subject precisely.

The importance of Knapp's conclusion about the relationship of heading form to scope-matching cannot be overestimated. She articulated for the first time what previously had only been implied, that one of the most important aspects of the meaning of specific entry had to do with how precisely a subject heading matched the scope of the subject it was intended to indicate rather than with whether it simply appeared as a not-classed heading. Her conclusion was significant for dictionary subject catalog practice. If the compound headings in the catalog scope-matched the topics they denoted, they could be considered specific entry headings, regardless of their format. Conversely, the scope-matching capacity of a dictionary catalog is what made the catalog unique, that is, what made it a specific entry system.

Knapp's conclusion was not without difficulties. If carried to the extreme, it would have required, for instance, that she deny that the form of headings had anything to do with the dictionary catalog's uniqueness.[38] But such a conclusion would have flown in the face of the long-held opinion that specific entry meant "not classed" and that "not classed" in turn meant not like an alphabetico-classed sequence in appearance. Perhaps sensing the conflict involved, she suggested felicitously that the reason why any particular heading format actually came to be used was "apparently" due to "a differing solution of meeting the needs of the user."[39] In other words, variations in heading form arose from the thoughtful application of conclusions about user needs. And perhaps to bolster that conclusion, she subsequently noted that many variations arose from the conscious decision on Hanson's part to collocate subjects—to incorporate some useful and necessary classification in the catalog. Even that extended reasoning was questionable, however, for it ultimately meant that variant forms had not only arisen in great part from alphabetico-classed needs, but also that what appeared to be alphabetico-classed sequences were the only alternative by which one could meet the needs of specific entry defined as scope-matching.

Marie Louise Prevost

Knapp ended her study without drawing further conclusions about the uniqueness of the dictionary subject catalog or the character of specific entry. Two years later, however, Marie Louise Prevost published a strongly worded article which took Knapp's analysis still further. Prevost was particularly incensed over the inconsistencies of subject heading practice that arose from making expedient decisions based on the vagaries of user considerations. Expediency of that sort had in her opinion made the dictionary subject catalog into a "maelstrom." She traced the regular incorporation of inconsistency back to Cutter's statement that "the public's habitual way of looking at things" must not be ignored, even if it led to "a sacrifice of system and simplicity." She concluded that inconsistency was allowed in the dictionary catalog by Cutter and others from its very beginning because, having actually pinned their hopes for a systematic approach to subject access on the classification schemes they were also developing, they could not only allow inconsistency based on user considerations to appear in the dictionary catalog without much concern, but also could treat it as a virtue. In her opinion, however, the clientele of a general library on which such an expediency was based was so diverse as to make the idea of a single unitary public into "a patent absurdity."[40] In other words, the habits of users, especially general users, in subject searching could not provide a basis for devising subject headings.

Prevost subsequently focused her discussion on the problem of subject heading terminology and proposed an alternative approach to the diversity found in contemporary subject heading format. Applicable especially to compound subjects that did not include places and personal names, it involved the strict control of heading syntax by the invariable use of the fundamental idea in a compound heading as its lead term. She interpreted the fundamental idea of a compound subject name generally as that "primary noun" or "direct subject noun" which other terms were simply intended to qualify. To use the fundamental idea as the lead term, her method required that it be recast in the form of a noun. It was that practice that caused her to name her method the "noun approach" to subject heading formulation.[41] Once the noun was determined, other terms in the subject descriptions were to be subarranged after it as qualifiers. For example, given subject descriptions such as Access to books in libraries, Library accession department, Library accounting, Library administration and Agricultural libraries, all of which were ways of speaking about Libraries, she suggested that these be given headings in the forms LIBRARIES–ACCESS TO BOOKS, LIBRARIES–ACCESSION DEPARTMENT, LIBRARIES–ADMINISTRATION, and LIBRARIES–AGRICULTURAL. By consistently following this method of subject heading formulation, she concluded that filing would be simplified and the expectations of at least intelligent users would be satisfied.

Prevost's emphasis on meeting the needs of intelligent users suggests how she resolved the problem of user considerations in subject catalog construction. Although she criticized Cutter's handling of the matter, she did not thereafter deny the usefulness or the need of the idea. She simply concluded that intelligent users were ultimately the only viable audience that the subject cataloger could aim at. Of the less intelligent she wrote:

> The less intelligent must lean on professional competence—as, in fact, they always have done. In other words, we must make plain the truth

> that no one can use a catalog who does not know how, and, for those who do know how, we must make its use quicker, easier, and more sure, disavowing openly and without shame the pretense that it can be, successfully, a free-for-all.[42]

In contradistinction to the less intelligent, Prevost considered specialists to be the proper target group for catalog design. Specialists, particularly those who used a public library for its business and commercial information, were of equal, if not of greater, importance in user considerations than that other portion of the public who were plainly too deficient in intelligence to use a library and its catalog with any facility.[43]

One cannot help but admire the boldness Prevost displayed as she attempted to outline a rational and systematic approach to subject heading terminology. In the course of twelve pages she managed to question and revise nearly every important convention that had dictated subject heading practice since the turn of the century. The same iconoclastic spirit may well have been the reason why so little of what she said seems to have altered opinion and practice within the dictionary subject cataloging community in any immediate or significant way.

At the same time, Prevost served as something of a bellwether of the times because she focused attention on several critical issus related to subject heading work. She reiterated Knapp's conclusion that the meaning of specific entry turned primarily on scope-matching. This was plainly evident in her opinion regarding the use of subheadings.

> Again, it should not for a moment be thought that this breakdown of a subject by use of subheads only works against the "specific" service we have from the start (and no doubt rightly) sought to give. "Schools-Commercial" is precisely as specific as "Commercial schools," and, with our direct-noun key in mind, just as immediately findable.[44]

Unlike Knapp, however, she did not concern herself with whether the resulting heading forms were classed or not classed according to some preconceived idea of proper heading format nor with whether the resulting catalog was uniquely a dictionary catalog rather than some other form. She was able to ignore these traditional concerns because she had already dispensed with them by rejecting the idea of catering to supposedly uninformed readers for whom not-classed headings and the uniqueness of the dictionary subject catalog were aimed.

Prevost also addressed the problem of the directness of headings and thus the simplicity of catalog structure. But she essentially recast the issue of directness and simplicity as a question of how a user anticipated looking up a heading rather than as a question of conventional versus nonconventional heading form. In other words, directness of headings was more properly conceived of as a function of consistency in search procedure rather than as a function of the vagaries of the language of naming things. Given subject headings with consistent citation orders based on a minimal knowledge of the parts of speech (i.e., knowledge of the difference between nouns and adjectives), a user could directly find whatever one was looking for with a higher probability of finding it on the first try than if conventional subject names were used. It was this that caused her to use the terms "direct-noun" and "specific subject-noun" as synonymous labels for this approach. And it was this as well that supported her claim that the catalog would subsequently become simpler in use.

Beyond the notion of specific entry itself, the sheer power of analysis that Prevost applied to subject terms brought out still other matters of importance. In the first place, she did not allow coordinated subject descriptions to remain in their conventional grammatical formats. Instead, she factored every such set of coordinated terms into its constituent parts to reconstruct the heading according to what was in effect a formal rather than an informal vocabulary and syntax. Prevost held the opinion that conventional composite headings of the phrase variety, when left in their natural state, were notable sources of vagueness in subject headings, not only in their semantic value, but also (as if reiterating Hanson's conclusion) for the seemingly random places they ended up in the catalog. In this respect, she condemned phrases that incorporated the conjunction "and" because that word in her mind "either kills the possibility of definite indication, hitches on a useless appendage or presents . . . no real subject area."[45] She considered prepositions to be somewhat more suitable for use, but relegated the prepositions themselves to parentheses in a manner somewhat akin to the relational "operators" that Farradane and others would come to propose during the succeeding decades.[46]

Prevost also paid special attention to those subject descriptions that had two "key headings" rather than only a single focus. She concluded that such headings should be entered under each "key" appropriately coordinated in each case by the second term in the combinations, rather than being entered only once under one of the "keys" with a "see" reference from the other. Agricultural education would by this method be entered under both AGRICULTURE–EDUCATION and EDUCATION–AGRICULTURE.[47] Such complex headings had been present since the beginning of dictionary subject cataloging work and had been dealt with either by the use of one phrase heading with a "see" reference from the other form or by multiple entry. In the context of Prevost's analytical approach to subject heading structure, however, their identification in the manner suggested served to highlight them in a far more sophisticated way than before—that is, as a precursor of analytically determined phase relations, needful of specially important considerations in their indication, or alternately as an early attempt to express what would later become important to the future of the documentation movement, the development of indexing vocabularies based on the logic of classes.

Despite what amounted to an orientation to the future, the immediate effect of Prevost's work on dictionary subject cataloging was slight. Furthermore, developments subsequent to her article, chiefly in the work related to the Technical Information Program of the Library of Congress, turned the interpretation of specific entry into a direction much more amenable to the preservation of practices already established.

C. Dake Gull

In 1949, C. Dake Gull, writing of his experience as editor-in-chief of the Library of Congress's Science and Technology project, provided what was eventually to become the final direction to be taken in this period concerning the meaning of specific entry.[48] The project, begun just after the end of World War II, was charged with creating a totally new armed forces technical report file. An alphabetical subject heading catalog was chosen for the task over a classified approach because it was less involved to plan and construct and therefore could be made more quickly. Having chosen that type of catalog, however, Gull found it necessary to rationalize the process involved in devising subject headings for the many complex subject descriptions encountered among the specialized documents.

Gull described the subject heading process as having two key elements: the extent of specification inherent in headings that were chosen; and the format of the headings. From these two elements, two pairs of considerations became necessary in every choice of a heading. First, a heading might be either specific or nonspecific. It might, in other words, either match or be more general than the topical scope of the document being given subject access. Second, the heading might be either direct or indirect. It might be written in a straightforward manner beginning with the first normal word of its conventional name. Or it might use as its entry word "the basic idea represented by a compound heading," taking the form of an inverted phrase or alternately the form of a string-of-terms.[49] A table (Figure 13) using Gull's example topic, Ballistic cameras, illustrates the difference.

	Specific	Non-specific
Direct	BALLISTIC CAMERAS	CAMERAS
Indirect	CAMERAS, BALLISTIC	PROJECTILES-BALLISTIC-CAMERAS

Source: Based on discussion in C. D. Gull, "Some Remarks on Subject Headings," *Special Libraries* 40 (March 1949): 84.

FIG. 13.   C. D. Gull's Two Pairs of Considerations in Subject Heading Choices

Gull used these examples to show that the two elements of heading choice were actually separate considerations. The extent to which a heading scope-matched a work was not a function of its form. The headings in each of the columns in Figure 13 were either specific or nonspecific, although in each case one was direct and one indirect. Conversely, the form of a heading—whether it was direct or indirect— did not bear on a heading's specificity. Each line of headings in Figure 13 was either direct or indirect, although in each case one was specific and the other nonspecific. The fact that the two considerations were essentially different made it necessary to make decisions concerning them separately. Because specificity was considered to be the more important of the two, the order in which decisions were to be made was specificity first, directness of heading form second. Furthermore, given the four choices possible, Gull noted that the project eventually decided to restrict its headings as much as possible to those in the upper left portion of the chart, that is, to those that were both specific and direct.

The decision to use specific and direct headings was apparently not made at the start, however. At first specific but indirect headings in the form of inverted phrases were also allowed. But Gull noted that "the opinions of those attending the Symposium on Medical Subject Headings led us to revise our inverted headings in preparation for the subject index which closed out the work of 1947." Indirect inverted headings were subsequently revised and put into direct form. Gull then related that, "Our experience in the past five months continues to confirm our reliance upon the direct form of very specific subject headings." To show the reasoning behind the choice made, Gull then devoted the remainder of his article to demonstrating the superiority of direct and specific headings over indirect and nonspecific headings.[50]

One important result of Gull's description of subject heading procedure was to confirm the findings of Knapp and Prevost that the idea of specific entry had two basic elements and that what was indicated by a heading was a separate issue from how a subject heading might be written. Gull also recovered for dictionary subject cataloging a process that had been clear in Cutter's work but that had been subsequently obscured—that what a heading is supposed to indicate is a decision that must be made before any decision about how to write it. Hanson and those who succeeded him had eroded that order of procedure by their tendency to convert all subject heading decisions into questions of how to name subjects. Of course, it must also be observed that Cutter and Gull held differing opinions about what a subject heading was supposed to indicate. Cutter's interpretation was dependent on identifying the most specific (i.e., concrete) subject treated in a book, whereas Gull's was dependent on identifying the entire subject of a work without recourse to categories of subjects. Thus, Gull's recovery of Cutter's methodology was limited.

Despite the clarity with which Gull characterized specific and direct headings, his rationalization of their use was not without severe difficulties. In the first place, Gull's arguments concerning their superiority over nonspecific and indirect headings were both slanted and specious. They were slanted because he used only one kind of indirect heading—noun entry form of the kind promoted by Prevost and written in the form of a string-of-terms—in his comparison. He did not, in other words, also demonstrate the superiority of direct and specific headings over indirect and specific headings of the inverted type. Perhaps he concluded that to argue successfully against the noun form of indirect headings was also to argue successfully against inverted headings. But this cannot be easily maintained. One is led to suspect, therefore, that what Gull was really attempting to demonstrate, although without formally stating it, was the superiority of alphabetically arranged conventional subject names over alphabetico-classed headings that took the form of strings-of-terms.

Gull's claims of the superiority of direct and specific headings were also specious in two respects. In one instance, the same arguments he leveled against indirect headings, that they were long and that they harbored unclear semantic relationships, could also be leveled against direct headings as well, at least when direct headings took the form of lengthy conventional phrases. In a second instance, he used a single argument—the potential that headings had for collocating related subjects—in two different ways, as a weakness of indirect headings but as a strength of direct headings. That is, collocation was a negative quality when achieved by indirect headings because it was made a more important goal than achieving direct access to conventionally named subjects. But collocation was a positive quality when achieved by direct headings (through carefully drawn filing procedures) because having been made only a secondary goal it did not greatly hinder direct access to conventionally named subjects. In summary, Gull did not really successfully argue the superiority of direct over indirect headings. At best he simply offered comments on the assertions that direct headings were better because they were direct and indirect were inferior because they were indirect. The problems raised by his arguments did not detract, however, from the forcefulness with which he characterized specific entry—that two aspects rather than only one must be taken into account when determining its meaning.

The second major difficulty that accompanied Gull's description of his use of direct and specific headings had to do with the idea of the extent of specification itself. It may be said at the onset that Gull's stress on devising headings that were "very specific" was an emphasis not typically found in dictionary subject cataloging as generally explained during that time. On the contrary, explanations of specific entry were, as already noted, clouded with confusion. Of course, Gull's emphasis on great specificity was demanded by the nature of his project. The process of giving subject access to upwards of 100,000 specialized government reports on military technology, most of which likely had topics that could only be indicated by complex descriptions and many of which were closely related in content, could not expect to avoid the necessity of being very specific.

At the same time it would also be erroneous to conclude that the specificity conceptualized by Gull was for the first time a purely defined notion uncontaminated by other modifications. On the contrary, Gull clearly noted that "very specific" had practical limitations. It did not mean "anything as specific as the indexing found in books" regardless of the implication that the requests made of the system might require a level of subject indication that complete. To give subject access at that level would, in effect, have required analytical subject indexing or depth indexing. But even the less intense idea of specificity that turned on entering each report "under its subject" was clouded by the already established belief that extent of specification was actually a function of the number of items likely to be gathered in a single document class. The latter was strongly suggested by Gull's statement that the staff "considered it axiomatic that the larger the catalog grew, the more specific the subject headings ought to be."[51] Thus, Gull reiterated what Mann and Pettee had already suggested, that the subjects of documents should be indicated more specifically only to the degree that files became too unwieldy to search. And as an implied corollary, they should be indicated more generally if the document classes they were placed in were too small.[52]

A final difficulty that attended Gull's description of his use of direct and specific headings had to do with the briefly stated procedure he advocated for documents which had subjects with multiple aspects. For example, pumps might be written about in terms of their construction (e.g., rotary) or in terms of their use (e.g., fuel). When a document treated both aspects, Gull advised the cataloger to use two separate headings—in this case, ROTARY PUMPS and FUEL PUMPS—instead of devising a single complex heading that included both aspects. He justified this by concluding that the document actually had two overlapping subjects rather than one complex subject.[53]

Gull's double entry procedure was not unusual for dictionary subject cataloging, having been clearly stated by Mann and having apparently been common to Library of Congress practice. But despite the traditional nature of it as a solution and the brevity of Gull's statement about it (it occupied only forty-six words of his text), the procedure was significant for its symbolic value. For one thing, it symbolized the natural limits of dictionary subject cataloging. In the attempt to apply rigorously to a specialized reports collection the idea that the topical contents of documents should be indicated in a catalog, dictionary subject cataloging found itself strained to the limit by its dependence upon conventional subject name headings. The subjects of such documents required descriptions far too complex to be accommodated by conventional subject names without, as even Hanson had recognized, requiring a tortured exercise of usage determination that far exceeded the subject cataloger's ability. Likewise, the alternatives in heading structure that had developed over the years, laced as they were with structural inconsistencies and justified by a wide variety of rationalizations, were also limited.

Gull's procedure also symbolized the confrontation of dictionary subject cataloging with a new era of subject access developments that was just getting underway. Three years after Gull wrote, his multiple entry procedure was highlighted in still greater detail by Eleanor J. Aronson, one of his successors on the science and technology project. Significantly, Aronson's explanation of the procedure became central to Mortimer Taube's subsequent comparison of coordinate indexing with dictionary subject cataloging.[54] And Taube along with others who were his contemporaries represented a break with the dictionary subject cataloging tradition. It is important to gain some perspective on the advances represented by this break since they provided the backdrop for the significant restatement of dictionary subject cataloging at the Library of Congress made by David J. Haykin.

New Types of Subject Access Systems

New types of subject access systems developed since the 1950s have proceeded in three general directions: analytico-synthetic classification systems, coordinate indexing systems, and natural language text indexing systems.[55] The first of these, analytico-synthetic classification, developed for use primarily in classified catalogs, had perhaps the most solid connection with the past. Introduced originally to the library community by S. R. Ranganathan in 1933 in the form of his Colon Classification, this approach attempted to bridge the gap between the complex descriptions of the topical contents of documents and a systematic classification of knowledge. Ranganathan connected these two factors by analyzing the subject fields of his classification scheme into such thoroughly drawn subject structures that the precise subject of any document could be formulated or synthesized from the elements of the scheme. It was this procedure that gave the name "analytico-synthetic" to the method.

The goal of Ranganathan's system was no different than the goals of older, more traditional "enumerative" classification schemes. But Ranganathan's system was immensely different in both its methodology and its results. Ranganathan resorted to five conceptual categories (facets) of subject field division—Personality, Matter, Energy, Space, and Time—these consisting in turn of still other analytical elements. The citation order of the facets and other analytical elements of each subject field was also carefully set. The citation order provided a syntax for subject descriptions, regardless of whether the descriptions were symbolized by a notation or written in verbal form for index entries. And last, since this approach provided first of all a single statement of the subject description of any document, indirect index access to other elements of any such subject description was also provided by the rigorous application of what Ranganathan called a chain-indexing procedure.[56]

During the 1950s, Ranganathan's approach to subject access was enthusiastically applied to special document collections by such British advocates of the method as B. C. Vickery, B. I. Palmer, A. J. Wells, E. J. Coates, and D. J. Foskett. The same people formed the Classification Research Group and their subsequent researches into Ranganathan's analytico-synthetic method expanded it in two principal directions. First, the idea of how subjects were related to one another was extended far beyond the analytical schema that Ranganathan had developed. Second, the weakest point of Ranganathan's scheme, its postulated main classes, was ultimately replaced. A schema of entities (i.e., individual or whole "things," including natural substances and organisms, manufactured products, and human ideas), based in many respects on a combination of the concepts inherent in Ranganathan's personality and matter facets, were grouped according to levels of complexity. The basic entities were then subdivided rigorously in an analytical manner by activities, processes, and other categories similar in part to Ranganathan's other facets. It was hoped that with an adequate citation order and notation, representations of the subjects of any individual document could be made in a manner similar to the original analytico-synthetic method. But by the mid-1970s the intense difficulties of enumerating and ordering the fundamental entities, especially at any level more complex than purely inanimate things, and the appearance of still newer indexing techniques that in many respects preempted the need for such a classification, left future developments of the effort in doubt.

Among the newer indexing systems, perhaps the most notable is the PRECIS system in operation with the British National Bibliography since 1974. PRECIS is in many respects the principal heir of the analytico-synthetic approach to subject access as expanded by the Classification Research Group, although it remains primarily an alphabetical indexing system rather than a classification system. It divides subject terms in a manner similar to the entities-activities structure the group had originally formulated. And it enforces a rigorous citation order for the strings-of-terms headings produced as subject descriptions for documents. PRECIS differs from the alphabetically arranged chain-indexes of analytico-synthetic classification schemes, however, not simply by providing alternative entries for most of the other terms in the strings, but by including the entire string-of-terms at each alternative entry point. The latter is accomplished by "shunting" the terms along in a two-line format, recognition of the elements of the string aided by the use of different typefaces. Moreover, the entries are generated automatically by computer.

PRECIS also differs from its immediate predecessors in that its chief architect, Derek Austin, claims that the rationale for its fundamental citation formula, object-activity-entity (entity meaning "subject," as in the subject of a sentence) is derived from the idea of "deep-structure" found in the transformational grammar of contemporary linguistics. Because that theoretical justification is related to the PRECIS indexing technique in a more or less *a posteriori* and nonessential manner, however, its value may be questioned. And finally, because a formal classification scheme is clearly a derivative product of the system, it remains to be seen whether such a scheme will in fact be produced and, if produced, whether it will contribute any arrangement of subjects that substantially advances the work of the past.

A second approach to subject access which also arose during the 1950s was coordinate indexing. The analytico-synthetic classification approach to subject access, although differing from traditional approaches in its analytical methods, shared with traditional methods the trait of precoordinating compound subject descriptions. In all such systems, the coordination of the parts of a subject description occurred at the input stage of subject cataloging, before the use of the system. For that reason, a user of the system had to look for compound subjects under the coordinated forms to achieve any reasonable success in searching.

Coordinate indexing reversed that traditional process. At input, the only "entries" made for any document were the separate terms that made up compound subject descriptions. By searching in the system for documents that had each been separately associated with particular terms, a user in effect coordinated the terms at the output stage of the system. The coordination of subjects at the search stage was conceived in terms of an algebra of classes or, as it is now more commonly called, in terms of Boolean operators. Because the coordination of terms was carried on only at the search stage, this kind of indexing has generally been called postcoordinate indexing to differentiate it from those systems that precoordinate compound subject descriptions.

The most notable of the early postcoordinate systems were those of W. E. Batton, Calvin Mooers, and Mortimer Taube. These systems varied according to the type of file materials used (Batten: Hollerith hole-punched cards; Mooers: edge-notched "Zatocards"; Taube: columnar index cards), according to the method of matching used (Batten: optical coincidence, afterward done with light beams; Mooers: a simple mechanical selector or sorting device; Taube: visual comparison of item registry numbers on index cards), and according to whether they were item-on-term systems (Batten, Taube) or term-on-item systems (Mooers). They also varied according to the extent to which they controlled or otherwise organized the vocabulary used. Batten, for instance, used a highly selected vocabulary and arranged it in a classified manner. Searching could therefore be restricted to portions of the entire file. Mooers also used a selected vocabulary but did not restrict it to single words. Instead, he used selected single or combined words which he called descriptors. Taube, alone among the three, used only natural or textual language, that is, terms derived from the publications themselves. Furthermore, the terms were restricted at least initially to single words (hence, the name Uniterm or, rather, unit-term), and no attempt was made to control them by avoiding synonyms.

Ultimately, it was Taube's Uniterm system which became highly popular among indexers in America, perhaps because it was a relatively easy and low-cost system to construct and also because it was the most adaptable to automatic processing equipment. Furthermore, Taube resorted to an algebra of classes to elegantly characterize the term relationships and, consequently, the search strategies necessary to retrieve citations from his system. The lack of even minimal vocabulary control in Taube's concept of coordinate indexing, while lowering the cost of input, eventually proved to be its chief weakness, especially when applied to large and growing collections of documents. The use of synonymous words made it difficult both to conduct searches and to retrieve a reasonable number of all the documents relevant to a search request. The restriction to single words combined with the vagueness of the semantic relationships between the words produced disturbing numbers of useless or false coordinations. Devices to correct these features, such as links between words, indicators of the roles of words in relation to one another, and a new emphasis on terms as concepts regardless of whether they involved more than single words, made their appearance later in the 1950s. These were joined by the appearance of the thesaurus, a listing of a system's terms indicating something of their semantic relationships. Originally designed for searchers to improve their search strategies, thesauri came to be used at least in part as aids in the input operation as well. By the mid-1960s, thesaurus construction began to benefit as well from research done in classification, at least to the extent that it adopted classificatory arrangements (e.g., the thesaurofacet) or otherwise included the kinds of term relationships which had become common in analytico-synthetic classificatory thinking.

The third major form of subject access to grow out of this period was natural language indexing. Indebted primarily to the growing capacities of computers not only for manipulating large quantities of data, but also for being employed in the indexing process itself (hence, the term "automatic indexing"), natural language indexing made its initial appearance in the late 1950s in the form of machine-produced keyword-in-context (KWIC) and keyword-out-of-context (KWOC) indexes. These were joined during the next decade by full or partial text systems that enabled the searcher to conduct postcoordinated searches on all substantive terms in the texts. Powerful techniques have also been developed to overcome the same kinds of semantic problems that plagued the original postcoordinate systems as well as to alleviate the unique problem caused by the massive amount of data for which machine-searching time is necessary. The techniques devised, combined with the growing capacities of computers to accept greater amounts of data and to manipulate the data, have led F. W. Lancaster to predict a reasonably useful future for such systems.[57] More important, the appearance and growth of natural language systems strongly suggest that the romance of subject access workers since the early 1950s with the ideal of devising highly controlled and structured vocabularies may well be coming to an end. It would appear that natural language systems, aided by the increasingly sophisticated capacities of computer technology, cannot do worse than the structured systems of the past and possibly have the potential to do much better.

New Developments for Dictionary Subject Cataloging

Several characteristics of the foregoing developments in subject access could profitably be examined for their implications concerning dictionary subject cataloging. Such characteristics include the rise of information systems theory, especially in the form of general notions about communication, and the growing capacities and uses of computers. The two most significant characteristics of those developments for the present discussion, however, are related more directly to the nature of subjects and users.

The first major characteristic is the way the new developments reflected an essentially changed view of the world of subjects. For the lack of a better description, this view may be described as an atomistic view of subject indication. The nature of the universe of subjects had gone through a virtual revolution in understanding by the 1950s. The revolution began when the nineteenth-century understanding of subjects—expressed so well by Cutter as a technical referent to only a portion of all the possible topics of thought that humanity might hold and afterward discuss in books—was replaced by a new view by the beginning of the twentieth century. The new view, particularly obvious in the work of Hanson at the Library of Congress, considered the topical contents of all documents to be subjects without further qualification.

Although there was little change in that assumption after Hanson's day (except perhaps for it becoming a widespread and thoroughly accepted view), the general appreciation of the documents that contain subjects changed greatly. Documents increased in numbers and in kinds, of course. More importantly, documents came to be viewed as different in the very nature of their contents.

The older, well-established, well-known (sometimes characterized as broader) subjects contained in books remained. But these were joined by far larger numbers of works on special subjects related to the growth of special fields of knowledge. Ranganathan characterized the increase in documents with special subjects as representative of a new world of "microthought."[58] And almost all subject access writers began to note both the complexity of their subject descriptions and the multidimensional nature of their relationships with other subjects within the realm of knowledge. In the end, the difficulty of naming or otherwise indicating such subjects in a consistent manner and of showing their relationships assumed gigantic proportions.

The greatest difficulty that dictionary subject cataloging increasingly encountered over the decades was how to indicate such topics in the catalog in some meaningful way. The subject heading techniques devised by Hanson, particularly his use of subdivision procedures, constituted an initial attempt to accommodate that changing world of subjects. From the onset, however, the techniques Hanson developed were hampered by adherence to conventional subject names as headings. They were also constrained by an essentially negative interpretation of specific entry despite the positive tone that the idea contained when interpreted as scope-matching. The discoveries related to dictionary subject cataloging made during the 1940s may, in a corresponding way, be seen as the first serious examinations of the extent to which dictionary subject cataloging, operating under such constraints, had met the changed subject situation.

Newer developments in subject access since the 1950s, particularly those involving the systematic coordination of subjects, in their pursuit of the goal of indicating subjects, especially those that had complex descriptions, avoided the traditional constraints associated with dictionary subject cataloging and approached all complex subject descriptions as sets of separate elements that for the purposes of subject access could be broken apart and recombined in the form of an orderly, although artificial, syntax. In other words, these developments considered subject descriptions to be analogous to molecular or atomic structures, the individual words or terms much like the elements or particles in such structures. The most appropriate way to indicate them in subject access systems was to list their elements in an orderly and systematic manner rather than using the normal but unsystematic grammer of everyday speech.

Ultimately, the rise of an enlarged and changed view of subjects and the documents that contain them functioned as a great continental divide in the topography of subject access work. Modern subject access developments crossed the divide by an atomistic approach to subject indication. Dictionary subject cataloging encountered the same divide and, while not totally unaffected by the newer developments, went about its crossing in a different manner.

The second major point to be noted of the new developments, one that in many respects provided the impetus to proceed with the atomistic approach to the indication of subjects, was that all such developments have been predicated on the separation of subject access into two relatively distinct realms—subject access for specialists and subject access for general users or nonspecialists. Dividing subject access in this way was not new, of course. But it is especially noteworthy at this point because all important developments in subject access since the 1950s have been rationalized at their most fundamental level as aid to specialists, regardless of the way "specialist" has been defined in any one instance. Nonspecialist or general users on the other hand have tended to be neglected, their needs often considered to be satisfied by subject access systems more "traditional" in nature. Said in another way, almost all subject access workers since the 1950s have accepted the assumption that traditional dictionary subject cataloging (and, for that matter, traditional shelf classification as well) is unalterably general in its intent and thus appropriate for the most part only to general users. In contrast, all new forms of subject access have been vivified by their specialist orientation. The reason for the latter is obvious. In the opinions of their makers, only the newer developments have been able to indicate in a consistent and positive manner the complex subject descriptions deemed necessary to specialist needs.

The supposition that specialists, scholars, and researchers need some more refined or at least alternative vehicle for subject access was a legacy from the nineteenth century, the principal alternatives being classified catalogs and subject bibliographies. Even Cutter recognized the distinction between the needs of each group, although he was confident that the dictionary subject catalog (as he understood and constructed it) would meet most of the needs of scholars as well as the needs of desultory readers.

Since the 1920s, the call for improved subject access vehicles for specialists and scholars took something of a different turn. Pollard and Bradford set the tone of that change in 1930 when, in attempting to show what sort of subject access instrument was most appropriate for specialists, they not only advanced the classified catalog as the most appropriate form, but also strongly castigated alphabetical subject heading arrangements as well. They found it necessary to criticize the dictionary subject catalog severely because, having become the normative approach to catalog subject access, it had in their opinion assumed a stranglehold on subject access thinking. Their arguments pro and con were not essentially related, however, because the contention that the dictionary subject catalog is inappropriate for specialists does not lead to the conclusion that the classified catalog is any better or that it is a viable alternative at all, although it might be considered so on some other basis.[59] Ranganathan's advocacy of the classified catalog took the same approach. But in his 1938 *Theory of Library Catalogue* he appeared to advance the argument by showing that because classificatory distinctions preceded and underlay alphabetical arrangement, it was the more fundamental format. Alphabetical subject access must arise from it, not stand in opposition to it.[60]

American subject catalogers seemed not to have been impressed by such arguments. One may speculate that this was the case because to admit them would have been tantamount to admitting a four-decade mistake. But what was most likely the cause of their intransigence concerning the matter was the fact that the classified catalog had simply not been refined to such a degree that it could be considered a definitive alternative. And one does not rationally pursue what amounts to an enormous and costly change unless the evidence for the worth of the change is overwhelming. Thus, when calls for a change became more frequent during the 1940s, the classified catalog assumed no greater importance as an alternative than, say, the revival of the subject bibliography ideal.[61] Most important, the classified catalog remained not nearly as important as the supposed improvement thought possible in the dictionary subject catalog itself, especially when it was assumed that the dictionary catalog could be tailored to the needs of types of libraries and their types of clienteles.

The latter assumption, particularly characteristic of the 1940s, set the scene for subsequent developments in dictionary subject cataloging. Those in the mainstream of subject catalog development, especially David J. Haykin at the Library of Congress, retained the belief that the dictionary subject catalog could be improved to adequately care for the needs of the entire range of users, both general and special. Measures were adopted to make the dictionary subject catalog more responsive to the changing perceptions of the world of subjects. When, however, increased numbers of user studies eventually suggested that types of libraries had little to do with subject access per se, that in fact there were really only two types of users after all, specialists and nonspecialists, and that the dictionary catalog seemed unalterably attached to serving the needs of nonspecialists, the opinion that the dictionary subject catalog could be improved in some significant way also began to be seriously questioned. This attitude only reinforced the belief that something new was needed. The previously described developments of the 1950s amounted to one response to that need. The other was to make changes in the dictionary subject catalog itself. The chapters that follow will attempt to chart the course of those changes.

CHAPTER 11

Haykin and the Library of Congress

One significant result of the Hanson era was to bring into existence a second major dictionary subject cataloging tradition. The first tradition was centered in the work and practices of local subject catalogers in libraries of all kinds and sizes. With the creation of the Library of Congress dictionary subject catalog, an additional tradition was created that from the very start brought an enormous influence to bear on the local tradition. Hanson and those who followed him made the subject cataloging work of the Library of Congress available to the wider library community through subject heading copy on its printed cards, through its published list of subject headings as well as other special publications that enhanced that list, and through the occasional participation of its leading catalogers in public discussions of subject cataloging problems.

Not every library chose to use the products of Library of Congress subject work. And others used it only with difficulty. But even where alternatives were available, such as the third edition of the A.L.A. *List* and the Sears and Smith lists, the influence of the Library of Congress was important, especially in matters of vocabulary choices and subject heading form. The relationship between the two traditions was very close. It was this closeness that doubtless caused the domination of the dictionary subject catalog over other forms of subject access in the United States. And it was the awareness of this closeness that made it seem appropriate for some to explain dictionary subject cataloging as a singular phenomenon. Mann, Akers, Sears, and others recognized differences between Library of Congress needs and those of local libraries, but spoke of those differences as being little more than technical variations. For all practical purposes they considered the work of both traditions as one.

Despite that closeness, however, the fact remains that through the first four decades of this century there were two separate traditions, not simply one. And the relationship between them may be described more accurately as a confederation of efforts rather than as a single network with strong communication links. Moreover, within the confederation the Library of Congress played a more or less passive role. It offered the products of its labor to the public as a kind of benevolence. Local librarians might use its gifts if they cared to do so, but they were under no obligation or pressure. The Library of Congress might also respond to the needs of the local tradition if that seemed appropriate, but its responses were primarily aids which enabled local libraries to use its subject cataloging products with better facility, not efforts to change its procedures because of suggestions from the local tradition. In short, the chief commitment of Library of Congress subject cataloging was to its own system. The local tradition benefited, but only in a derivative manner. This was understandable, the Library having all it could do to keep up with its own work.

At the same time, the vast growth in the amount of publication brought increasing pressure to bear on all aspects of cataloging, so much so, that by the 1930s the effectiveness and economy of subject cataloging came increasingly under scrutiny. It was this growth that helped bring about the efforts to explain the subject cataloging already described. It was this pressure that also raised what amounted to a reevaluation of the relationship between the two traditions. The essential result of the confederation had been to bring about a loose form of cooperative cataloging. And cooperative cataloging had, since the first meeting of the A.L.A. in 1876, always been promoted as one of the essential reasons for librarians and libraries to meet together and to pool their efforts.

In the face of rising economic pressures on subject cataloging, however, the casual relationship between the two traditions did not serve the needs of local libraries very well. One of the first manifestations of this realization was the call, increasingly heard throughout the 1930s, for the Library of Congress to communicate more effectively its subject cataloging changes. Still another manifestation was the growing realization by special libraries and by general libraries with special collection areas larger than those of the Library of Congress that their subject access needs were not being met by Library of Congress subject headings, and the feeling on the part of some of them that their needs might be met better by some other approach to the matter than dictionary subject catalogs.

These manifestations that the casual relationship between the two traditions was coming under increasing strain are important because they constituted the primary context of the work of David Judson Haykin, the chief of the Subject Cataloging Division of the Library of Congress from 1941 to 1952. Haykin's subject cataloging work was a direct response to the newly expressed needs. And the result of his labors was not only to reshape the relationship between the two traditions, but also to reinterpret the character of American dictionary subject cataloging itself.

David Judson Haykin

David Judson Haykin was born in 1896 in Novozybkov, Russia, the eldest son of Joseph L. and Grace R. Haykin.[1] He came to the United States in 1909 when the entire family emigrated and settled in Nebraska. Subsequently, he attended the University of Nebraska. Before earning his A.B. in chemistry in 1921, however, his college years had been divided by two years of active service in Europe with the Army Medical Corps. After a term as a senior library assistant at his alma mater, he attended the New York State Library School at Albany and received the B.L.S. in 1925. Afterwards, Haykin worked as the head cataloger of the New York State Library (1925–27) and of the Queens Borough Public Library (1927–29). While at Queens he also taught in the library school there. In 1930 Haykin set up the A.L.A. Office for Decimal Classification Numbers on Library of Congress Cards in Washington, D.C. And in 1932 he joined the Library of Congress staff, serving successively as the chief of the Division of Documents (1932–34) and of the Cooperative Cataloging and Classification Service (1934–40). During 1939 and 1940 he also served as the acting chief of the Catalog Division.

Perhaps in response to the same kind of pressures that were confronting the entire cataloging community, the Library of Congress reorganized its technical services operations during 1940. The most striking change was the operational separation of descriptive cataloging from subject access procedures. Previously, descriptive and subject cataloging had formed one operational unit, classification another. Under the new plan, descriptive cataloging was made a single unit and both subject cataloging and classification were brought together in a second unit called the Subject Cataloging Division.[2] When this change was made, Haykin was appointed the first chief of the newly organized subject unit. He officially began his duties on January 2, 1941, and continued at that post until September 1, 1952. Until his untimely death in May 1958, he continued at the Library as its specialist consultant in subject cataloging and classification. Between 1954 and 1956 he also served as the editor of the 16th edition of the Dewey Decimal Classification.

The importance of Haykin's influence on dictionary subject cataloging in the United States is comparable only to that of one other person

—J. C. M. Hanson. Like Hanson, Haykin combined solid cataloging experience with strong administrative decision making, and he appeared on the scene at a time in which his abilities were particularly needed and could be exercised. Thus, the results of his work also reverberated throughout the subject cataloging community so that in a comparable way the period since the 1940s might well be labeled the Haykin era much like the earlier period was called the Hanson era.

Haykin's work was also uniquely different from Hanson's. Where Hanson had found it necessary to create a dictionary subject catalog from little in the way of precedent, Haykin found it necessary to codify and normalize one that for all practical purposes had gotten out of control. In place of Hanson's freely exercised eclecticism, Haykin exercised forceful powers of rationalization which suggested a deep desire to impose control. Furthermore, the control he sought was not simply over the Library's own procedures, but over the activity of subject cataloging throughout the entire subject cataloging community. One result of his labor was, consequently, to bond the two subject cataloging traditions closely together. As it will be shown later, that accomplishment constituted both a strength and weakness of his work.

When Haykin began his subject catalog division duties in 1941, he brought to them a highly developed sense of two growing factors in subject cataloging. First, he, along with many others, recognized that cataloging in general and subject cataloging in particular were increasing in both the amount of labor needed and in their cost, neither of which showed any signs of abatement. Second, from the earliest years of his library career, Haykin also expressed a commitment to the necessity of cooperation as the most effective means of combating those increases. In his view, cooperation could be accomplished either as a common division of labor or as a network involving a centralized bureau. Earlier in his library career he spoke optimistically of major libraries sharing the burden of providing subject catalog copy, especially for technical subjects and foreign language materials needed by libraries which served researchers and scholars. A centralized bureau such as the Library of Congress could then edit the final copy and distribute it in the form of unit card sets. After he became an employee of the Library of Congress and, especially, after he became chief of the Subject Catalog Division, his faith in libraries sharing in the activity of providing subject catalog copy seems to have lessened considerably. Instead, he envisioned the role of the Library of Congress as the principal bureau from which such copy would emanate because that would ensure the lowest cost, the most speed, and the highest quality possible.[3]

With the expansion of centralized subject cataloging that emanated from the Library of Congress as the cornerstone of his vision of cooperation, Haykin immediately began to implement changes to ensure its success. He began by insisting on hiring subject catalogers who were also subject specialists. The annual report of the Librarian of Congress for the fiscal year ending June 30, 1941, noted that this division had already begun to "assemble a small group of subject specialists, each with a wide range of foreign languages, to perform the work of subject headings and classification."[4]

The second step in the change was to insist on the use of more and better subject terminology. The following year it was noted that "the gradual change in the current significance of different fields of subject matter and the appearance of publications dealing with new and developing subjects" made a corresponding increase in the number of new subject headings necessary.[5] The number of new headings adopted that year (1941/42) amounted to nearly 475, more than twice as many as the yearly average (about 190) of the previous decade. The year afterwards (1942/43) saw the figure double again, to about 950. And by the fiscal year 1943/44, new headings came to represent a floodtide, the number adopted that year numbering more than 1,500. Between 1943/44 and 1951/52, Haykin's last full year as chief, more than 15,500 new headings were added for an annual average of more than 1,700. Included in the totals was a spectacular rise to 2,508 new headings during the year 1950/51.[6]

Better service in representing the Library's subject headings to the wider cataloging community represented still another form of improvement for Haykin. The first step in that direction was the publication in 1943 of the fourth edition of the subject heading list. It represented the Library's headings through December 1940 and was the first revised edition to appear since 1928. This edition also included "refer from" cross-references ("xx" references) although they were placed in a separate volume. The references made the syndetic structure of the list fully available for the first time. Even before the edition had been published, supplements also began appearing on a quarterly basis, their regularity again a first. Five years later the fifth edition of the list was published. That edition integrated the "refer from" references into the main list and normalized typefaces and arrangement in a manner typical of more recent years. During the same period, Haykin also authorized and consulted closely on the Library's venture into a specialized field—a list of music subject headings for both general and special music collections and libraries.[7]

Improving the work of the Subject Catalog Division in this way was not only an important feature of Haykin's program for the success of national cooperative cataloging, but also an aspect of his work welcomed and appreciated by the cataloging community. But it was a relatively simple accomplishment compared to a far more important need—the control of quality by adhering to standardized dictionary subject catalog practice. One might suppose that this automatically implied the necessity of a subject cataloging code much like codes for descriptive cataloging. Indeed, as already noted, persistent calls for such a code or rumors that one was in progress had been made since the 1920s, and the attempts to explain subject heading work by Mann and others constituted an implicit statement of the need for one. In 1937 Haykin made passing reference to the fact that "the principles of subject cataloging have nowhere been fully stated as yet." But he also noted that the absence of an explicit statement of principles had not prohibited subject catalogers from adhering to a de facto code of subject rules "almost without exception." He concluded that principles of subject cataloging, although unstated, had been "fairly faithfully and consistently followed by all libraries."[8]

After Haykin became chief of the Subject Cataloging Division, how-ever, his earlier idealistic prognosis of the uniformity of subject cata-loging practice appears to have been moderated. He found that not even Library of Congress practice could be said to have the kind of uniformity he had earlier envisioned. His estimate of the situation ap-peared in the introductory pages of the fourth edition of the Library's list of subject headings:

> The Library of Congress list of subject headings had grown by a slow process of accretion. New headings were added to it as they were adopted in the course of cataloging the Library's books. There was not, to begin with, a scheme or skeleton list of headings to which addi-tions could be made systematically, completing and rounding out a system of subject headings for a dictionary catalog. Such a scheme could not have been devised at the time the Library's dictionary cata-logs were begun, because there was no solid body of doctrine upon which it could be based; the guiding principles which were then in print for all to read and apply were very meager and concerned them-selves with the form of headings and their choice. They did not provide the theoretical basis for a system of headings. Whatever measure of logic and consistency has been achieved in the headings is due to the continuity of oral tradition which stems from J. M. C. Hanson [sic], who was chief of the Catalog Division from 1897 to 1910, Charles Mar-tel, Chief from 1912 to 1930, and their associates in the Catalog division, and the occasional written instructions issued by them. The failures in logic and consistency are, of course, due to the fact that headings were adopted as needed, and that many minds participated in the choice and establishment of headings.[9]

Although Hanson's version of the dictionary subject catalog was a far more rational creation than Haykin suggested and control over the application of its procedures was far more effective than implied, its rationality was doubtless obscured by the fact that neither Hanson nor Martel recorded the subject cataloging procedures in a way that would have ensured their consistent application over a long period of time.[10] Nor, apparently, did they require a record of the conditions surrounding individual subject heading decisions. The latter was especially significant because the basis of so many headings was necessarily tied to how the meanings of particular terms and their classificatory positions were understood on the occasions when they were devised.

Those problems were exacerbated by still another factor that was unmentioned by Haykin but which undoubtedly had a significant effect on the subject heading procedures of the Library—that is, the changes in personnel the Library experienced during a time of significant changes in the general subject cataloging situation. To begin with, it seems reasonable to assume that, when created, the Library's subject catalog represented a reasonably adequate expression of subject access methodology for the subject access conditions of the time. One may also assume that the subject cataloging process functioned in a reasonably controlled manner (not without inconsistency, but rather with its own brand of allowable inconsistency) until at least the early or mid-1920s, chiefly because the two persons most responsible for its creation were continually present, Hanson until 1910 and Martel through the 1920s.

Martel's retirement from an administrative role in 1930 not only interrupted direct administrative continuity with the past, but also came at that critical point when the general parameters of subject cataloging work were beginning to change dramatically. As already noted in this study, notions regarding users had already shifted to a basis in types of libraries. And specific entry had already begun a drift to a positive rather than a negative emphasis. Significant increases in the numbers of publications to be handled by the Library, especially in terms of the specialized subjects they represented, as well as the growing importance of modern research ideals led to a corresponding shift in what was generally expected of subject access systems. Finally, questions regarding cost and efficiency in subject cataloging began to assert themselves seriously.

With these various changes taking place, it appears that for more than a decade, from the mid to late 1920s until Haykin became the chief of the newly created Subject Cataloging Division in 1940, the Library subject heading work functioned without strenuous leadership. There was no one so conversant with the beginnings of the subject heading system that subject heading practices could be rigidly disciplined in terms of their original emphases. And there was no one immediately available who could reinterpret the system in such a way as to be more amenable to the changing emphases then taking place. As more than a decade passed in which the Library's subject catalogers struggled to adapt an essentially older system to a changing situation, with only few explanations of its foundations and with more than enough work to do than would allow for the leisure to investigate its theoretical aspects, it is no wonder that the system experienced difficulties. The greater marvel of it was perhaps that the subject headings system functioned as well as it did, a tribute indeed to its founder, Hanson. Given that situation, it is also not difficult to see why Haykin might have been led to the conclusion that there had been little system to begin with.[11]

Haykin's concern was justified, therefore, although the reasons for the rise of difficulties were more complex than he suggested. He was also concerned because the problems inherent in the Library's subject cataloging work were not limited in their effect only to the Library of Congress. The growing dependence of other libraries on the bibliographical products of the Library of Congress, when combined with the forcefulness of the time-honored opinion that cooperation was the key to coping with cataloging difficulties, placed the Library of Congress in a critical position. If it suffered confusion and inconsistency, that confusion and inconsistency would be transmitted to the entire cataloging community.

There was little mystery as to what was needed. The annual report of the Librarian of Congress for the year 1942 stated:

> There is a definite need both in the Library of Congress and in other libraries for manuals on the use of our subject headings and our system of classification. Such manuals would state the theoretical basis for an approach to the subject analysis of books.[12]

In fact, Haykin himself noted that the very growth of awareness of the need for a manual tended by itself to improve the situation.[13] But producing a manual was not a simple prospect. In the same report that called for manuals of procedure, it was also stated that the staff was then too pressed to undertake such projects, even though the Library "recognizes a responsibility to make or help make them a reality."[14]

Part of the problem of subject heading practice was considered to be the large amount of subject expertise it demanded. The Librarian's report for the following year stated:

> The present practices by which "subject headings" are "assigned" by the staff of the Library's Subject Cataloging Division leave something to be desired both in the library and out of it. No matter how learned the Library's specialists may be—and some of them are men of an extraordinary breadth of learning—they cannot be familiar with the development of ideas and conceptions in all disciplines nor can they project the past history of ideas into the future as the masters of a subject field can do.[15]

The same difficulties applied to writing a manual. One possible solution to the problem was to convene "a congress of the various disciplines." Another was to conduct "a systematic review" of the subject headings in use through the coordinated efforts of "learned societies, special library groups, and individual scholars" who could then be enlisted for such a project. But alternatives such as these were impractical and, given the changes taking place, could only delay writing a manual still longer.[16]

In the end, Haykin himself took steps to write a manual of principles and practice. He was released from his regular duties for a short period in the latter part of 1946 to devote full time to it, hoping for completion early in 1947. The task took much longer than expected, however, so that it was not until 1951 that the manual, entitled *Subject Headings, a Practical Guide,* finally appeared.[17]

Haykin's Approach to Dictionary Subject Cataloging

Although aided in his efforts by regular discussions with the subject catalogers of the division, Haykin's *Subject Headings* were primarily the result of his own strenuous efforts at making a statement of the Library's subject cataloging practices. The importance of his work goes beyond its relationship to the Library, however, because Haykin effectively interpreted dictionary subject cataloging in a way not previously done. The effect was to lend his support to a general change that has taken place since the 1950s in how subject heading work is to be understood.[18]

Haykin divided the topic into principles (of which he named four: reader as the focus, unity, usage, and specificity) and practices. For this discussion it is more useful to examine his work in terms of the following two areas: (1) the traditional features of the dictionary subject catalog to which he adhered; and (2) the operating principles he followed.

TRADITIONAL FEATURES

Haykin adhered to several traditional features of the dictionary subject catalog. The most important of these was the use of conventional subject names as subject headings. Others included a controlled vocabulary that involved direct heading form, a syndetic system of cross-references, and the extensive use of subheadings.

The idea of conventional subject names, a tradition going back to the beginning of dictionary subject catalogs a century before, treated any subject heading as the commonly spoken name of a subject, much like the conventional but proper names by which one refers to particular persons or things. When viewed as a conventional subject name, a subject heading had a unitary quality that was inviolate. It came into being and was used as an essential whole rather than as an amalgamation of separate parts that retained their own meanings even though combined in a single unit.

This approach to subject naming, particularly where complex subject names were involved, placed Haykin squarely in the tradition first articulated by Cutter that subject names must have achieved societal status or recognition to be used as subject headings. One necessary role of the subject cataloger was, therefore, to be a searcher for conventional names and, with respect to complex names, a searcher for stabilized phrases that were commonly used. Only these could be considered "independent headings."19

This approach to subject naming also placed Haykin squarely in the tradition begun by Hanson that subject names when used as independent headings must be preserved in their normal grammatical connections. Like Hanson, however, Haykin also adhered to the idea that the integrity of a conventional subject name was not destroyed by manipulating it by inversion. For example, AMERICAN ART might be changed to ART, AMERICAN much like John Phelps Smith might be inverted to the form Smith, John Phelps without changing its meaning. Because of this practice, Haykin like Hanson, allowed the inversion of hundreds of phrase headings, the most common being those that began with national adjectives. What was to be avoided if at all possible was the conversion of a phrase heading into a string-of-terms by the use of subdivision. In other words, AMERICAN ART was not to be converted to the form ART–AMERICAN. The use of subdivision technique in this way deprived the original conventional name of its normal naming structure and had the ultimate effect of converting the name into separated terms with independent meanings.

One might approach subject naming in the latter way, of course, systematically analyzing the separated elements in terms of their semantic relationships to one another. But that was an approach common to classified catalogs and, particularly, to the newer developments in subject access that gained currency in the 1950s. It depended essentially on the atomizing of all complex subject names into their constituent elements and reconstituting them in an artificial syntax for use in a controlled search procedure. For Haykin, on the contrary, a dictionary subject catalog remained primarily a whole name catalog (not withstanding the manipulation of the whole names), a listing of commonly spoken subject names in alphabetical order.[20]

The remainder of the traditional features of the dictionary subject catalog to which Haykin adhered comprised normative dictionary subject catalog arrangements handed down from previous decades. But each was affected by the notion of conventional subject names, either directly or in a derivative fashion. First, the dictionary subject catalog did not list a document under just any conventional subject name—for example, under whatever name an author might have used in the work for its topic. Rather, where alternative name forms existed as synonyms or near synonyms, the dictionary subject catalog necessarily controlled the vocabulary possible by using a single name from among such alternatives.

Haykin explicitly described this feature as the principle of unity. It served as the basis for the catalog's potential to gather together in the same place in the catalog, documents that dealt with the same subject rather than allowing them to be scattered under various equivalent terms. This feature was deeply rooted in tradition, forming an essential feature of Cutter's and Hanson's systems. It also required that homonyms—subject names used in more than one way and for which no alternatives existed—be qualified (usually by a trailing parenthetical expression) so that the sense in which the term was being used was clear.[21]

The second traditional feature of arrangement was that names used as headings were to be placed directly rather than indirectly in the main alphabetical sequence of the catalog. In Haykin's thinking, an indirect heading meant placing a conventional subject name as the last element of a series of words that were related semantically in a hierarchically conclusive "echelon of terms." For example, given the subject name FROGS, indirectness would mean placing it at the end of an echelon of terms such as ZOOLOGY–VERTEBRATES–AMPHIBIANS–FROGS. When all such strings-of-terms were arranged alphabetically, the result was an alphabetico-classed catalog.[22]

This format had one strong advantage in Haykin's view, its capacity for collocating subject names on the basis of their class inclusion relationships. It was understood, however, that some subject names, unable to be identified in this way, would by default be entered directly. But Haykin also concluded that this format had serious disadvantages. It required a reader to know in advance the hierarchical level with which to begin any particular search; to know, for example, that to find books on FROGS one had to begin with the class ZOOLOGY. Lacking that information, the reader needed a system of "see" references interspersed in the main alphabetical sequence of headings to reveal where every indirectly entered conventional term was located. Because such a reference amounted to the same as direct entry, the searcher would have ended up searching in two places—the first direct, the second indirect—for the same information found in one place in the direct heading approach. In Haykin's opinion it was far more efficient to list documents once under their respective direct headings. Other disadvantages of the indirect method included necessarily elaborate and, by implication, confusing heading strings, as well as what Haykin considered often to be arbitrary choices of terms used in the intermediate positions in the various strings. These choices resulted in a catalog that was not strictly or scientifically classed, although it might appear and claim to be.23

A third traditional arrangement feature of Haykin's dictionary subject catalog was that it used a system of cross-references: "see" references from nonpreferred to preferred terms; and "see also" references from broader to narrower terms and between coordinate terms. "See" references were made necessary because of the need to control synonyms. "See also" references were necessary to help readers direct their searching to more appropriate narrower subject names or to suggest related avenues of searching. Haykin also supposed that "see also" cross-references might be used to conduct exhaustive searches. But he concluded that that was not their primary function and using them for that purpose was not very effective.24

A fourth and final traditional arrangement feature of Haykin's approach to dictionary subject catalogs consisted of the extensive use of subheadings to subarrange document classes for convenient searching. This feature included subarranging books listed under a directly entered subject name by terms that indicated the form in which the subject treatments of the books were made, the time period to which they were limited, or the place to which they were confined. Following Hanson, this feature also included the use of topical subheadings that qualified and thus limited the scope of entry terms. But topical subheadings were restricted in their use, at least ideally, to those that only supplemented the specification denoted by the entry term. If they by themselves scope-matched the topical contents of the books placed under them, they were not to be used. For example, a history of psychology could be appropriately placed under the entry term-subheading combination PSYCHOLOGY–HISTORY in which the entry term PSYCHOLOGY is supplemented in its scope-matching potential by the qualifier –HISTORY. The qualifier in this case is legitimate because even though it is a conventional subject name in its own right, it does not by itself scope-match the book. However, should a conventional subject name be available that matches the topical scope of a book by itself, such as HISTORIOGRAPHY, the history of doing history, the subsequent use of either a heading-subheading combination to indicate fully the topic of the book (HISTORY–HISTORY) or that particular conventional subject name itself in a heading-subheading combination (HISTORY–HISTORIOGRAPHY) would be inappropriate. Those uses of subheadings would constitute alphabetico-classed subentry.[25]

This particular approach to determining when indirect entry (i.e., subentry in Cutter's terminology) was not alphabetico-classed constituted a unique solution to the problem of how subarrangement practices in a dictionary subject catalog differed from those in an alphabetico-classed catalog. Its uniqueness resided in making the status of a subheading a function of the goal of scope-matching by means of conventional headings. When an entry term represented the limits of scope-matching in a conventional heading—that is, the absolutely best available approximation of the topical contents of a book in the form of a commonly used subject name—the subheadings placed under it would not constitute classed subdivisions. They could not be considered classed subdivisions because the most specific conventional subject name for the book had already been determined. And if one had already determined the most specific heading available, the subheading by itself could not then be considered a still more specific scope-match subject name. If it were, then having considered the entry term to be the most specific conventional heading available would have been an erroneous judgment, and the subheading would then function as a subdivision.

It should be noted that this approach to determining appropriate subheadings was not without its difficulties. It depended upon the subject cataloger's judgment of whether conventional subject names used as entry terms did in fact represent the limits of conventional subject name specificity. If entry term choices were poorly made because of haste, poor judgment, or lack of understanding, the subheading practice would be inconsistent, inadvertently allowing alphabetico-classed headings to be used. More important, if entry choices were affected by a conscious attempt to achieve collocation in a classified manner, some subheadings would represent conscious incursions of classification.

Hanson had not only knowingly allowed the use of classified headings, but said as much. Haykin also allowed the same kinds of headings, but he regularly avoided rationalizing them as conscious attempts to resort to classification. He claimed instead that such headings resembled alphabetico-classed headings "in their outward form only" and thereafter rationalized their use in other ways. In the midst of a series of examples involving the subdivision –RESEARCH, rationalized as alphabetico-classed in outward form only because no conventional subject names which included that word were available, he noted that HEART–DISEASES was also justifiable even though used in place of the conventional subject name HEART DISEASES. He implied, however, that it too was alphabetico-classed in outward form only. The reason for using the subdivided form was to group this subject with others on the heart in which nonclassed subheadings were allowable because only phrase forms were available. This was apparently justified by his words that such practices were allowable "for the purposes of the catalog, where it is desirable to conform to an existing pattern."[26]

Later he provided another example—CONSTRUCTION INDUSTRY–TAXATION instead of TAXATION OF THE CONSTRUCTION INDUSTRY—that he also suggested only appeared like an alphabetico-classed heading rather than actually being one. He noted that it had been "reduced to the physical form of an alphabetico-class heading for convenience of grouping the arrangement." He justified this particular example as "obviously not 'taxation as a division of the subject CONSTRUCTION INDUSTRY' " and noted more generally:

> Where usage does not offer a settled phrasing of a heading, or if the heading is involved and would present difficulties or uncertainties in filing, this division for reasons of structure rather than substance is permissible.[27]

The difficulty with his reasoning in each instance was that by his procedure of allowing topical subheadings only when no conventional subject names were available, these examples were in fact alphabetico-classed headings. Why he should have been so tenacious in appealing to other rationalizations is not clear.

OPERATING PRINCIPLES

Traditional features of the dictionary subject catalog provided one kind of constraint to Haykin's approach to subject cataloging. Another kind of constraint consisted of three operating principles invoked in the actual process of choosing subject headings for books: (1) the reader as the focus; (2) common usage; and (3) specificity. Of these, the first was the most important and the other two were deeply affected by it.

The Reader as the Focus. The concept of the reader as the focus was Haykin's way of indicating that the ultimate or principal source of information on which to base decisions in the dictionary subject cataloging process was the reader. By "the reader" Haykin meant the group for which any particular dictionary subject catalog was made. Since any single catalog might serve an array of variously defined groups, however, in practical terms "the reader" meant the numerically superior group, or at least the target group, being served. And by using the group being served as the ultimate or principal source of information for decision making, Haykin meant ascertaining the habits, needs, and conscious preferences of readers as they searched for subject information.[28]

Haykin considered the rationale behind this operating principle to be self-evident.

> The user of the catalog is the user of the library and, since the librarian's task is to make available the resources of this library to the user, the cataloger must, by the same token, make the catalog such that the reader can as quickly and as easily find out whether the library has the books he seeks. This much is axiomatic.[29]

In other words, the dictionary subject catalog must be constructed in such a way that it matches the readers' subject searching patterns because that would appear to be the most efficient way of helping them.

Haykin also considered this approach to subject cataloging to rest on "psychological rather than logical grounds."[30] He cited as support for the necessity of this approach the "biblio-psychology" writings of Nicholas A. Rubakin.[31] Rubakin (1862–1946), a participant in the socialist revolution in Czarist Russia earlier in the century, was a librarian and bibliographer who viewed "education as the fundamental vehicle for the liberation of the toiling masses."[32] Libraries played an important role because education in Rubakin's view came through reading, and reading could be promoted and enhanced by means of libraries. To support his contentions, Rubakin developed an elaborate theory of reading psychology which included among its elements the thesis that reading development was a function of the interaction between a person's psychological makeup and the mental images prompted by books. For the purposes of scientific analysis, however, readers were best classified in terms of sociologically defined groups.

One may assume that Haykin found the latter aspect of Rubakin's ideas particularly relevant because it suggested something of a scientific, or at least rigorously analytical, basis for viewing subject heading choices. Subject names, like reading, reflected the way people thought. But the patterns of thinking were best viewed as a function of groups of people rather than of individuals. Subject heading choices must consequently be based on the knowledge of the mental habits of the groups of people who would use them. Since Haykin did little more than mention the relevance of Rubakin's theories to his notion of the reader as the focus, it is not clear whether they functioned as a fundamental source of his ideas or only as a reinforcement of ideas he already possessed. It is obvious, however, that Rubakin's ideas fit in well with the view, increasingly widespread by the 1940s, that user considerations related to types of libraries or to their clienteles were fundamental to subject access work. Haykin's appeal to Rubakin may well have been his way of indicating that a commitment to user considerations had the potential of being more than a vague and sentimental notion. Haykin's statements about the reader as the focus appear, therefore, to constitute his attempt to state the general idea of user considerations in a more cogent way than it had been stated by writers in the past.

It should be carefully noted that Haykin's appeal to the idea of the reader as the focus was not a suggestion that the subject catalog was ultimately illogical. Such might be the case if Haykin had applied the idea to individuals rather than to groups of people. But Haykin stressed groups, not individuals, as the basis of his thought. What he was actually guarding against by his appeal to the idea was the view that readers' subject searching needs and habits should be made to conform to a singular logic that was concluded to be either in the nature of knowledge itself or an adequate characterization of all readers without any finer distinctions. His view suggested that there were in effect a variety of "logics" that were characteristic of groups of readers. The variety lay at the basis of, for example, the subject terms readers used in searching and the semantic relationships that were in operation as people engaged in the act of subject searching. To elicit subject cataloging principles and to construct subject catalogs which best served the readers were, in effect, to base them on those group-oriented mental conventions.[33]

Because the idea of the reader as the focus was so fundamental, Haykin applied it to all aspects of the dictionary subject catalog structure and to all aspects of subject cataloging activity. He referred to it as a way to justify the traditional features of the catalog which have already been discussed. The direct entry of independent headings was justified, for example, because readers tended to search directly for individually named subjects. They especially did not care to work through an index which required at the minimum a double search. Scientists and researchers were in Haykin's opinion not only especially likely to search that way, but also to search directly for the very narrowest topics. Likewise, the cross-reference structure described above in which mainly descending (broader to narrower) rather than ascending (narrower to broader) references were used was justified because, when readers did fail to look under the specific name of a topic, their tendency was to search primarily in a broader to narrower pattern. Thus, entering books under the specific topics they treated and referring only downward to those even more specific was the principal entry and reference structure needed.[34]

Other examples of Haykin's justification of traditional features of the dictionary subject catalog by appealing to the idea of the reader as the focus might also be made. But the most important application that Haykin made of the idea was to the actual procedures of subject cataloging. Haykin wrote that because the idea was "a cataloging axiom," fundamental subject cataloging rules followed directly from it.[35] Even more important, heading-by-heading choices were also affected. Haykin summarized the latter by stating that

> the degree of specificity of the heading, the choice and order of the language, and the arrangement of the headings in the catalog, must depend upon the intellectual equipment of the reader and his psychological approach to the catalog.[36]

The practical effect was to make each conscious decision of the subject cataloger dependent on something approximating a mind's-eye view of how the reader group being primarily served was most likely to search for any particular topic (that is, as to its degree of specificity) and for any particular heading (that is, as to its wording and its placement in the catalog). Earlier writers as far back as Esther Crawford had implied that the idea should be applied this thoroughly. And more recently, Pettee had stated the implications of the idea more directly. But it was left to Haykin to apply the idea in an explicit and thorough manner, referring to it constantly as he discussed each kind of subject cataloging choice.

Because of the thoroughness with which Haykin applied the idea of the reader as the focus, its importance in his subject access thinking cannot be overestimated. At the same time, his use of the principle was not without severe difficulties, a matter he was the first to admit. Interpreting the reader as a group and particularly as the numerically superior group a library served, while a useful notion especially for special libraries where the clientele was homogeneous, was not a useful notion for public libraries, where the clientele could only be described as a "miscellaneous public."[37] Haykin's solution to that problem was for catalogers to identify a target group as their chief focus. He wrote:

> Solution is sometimes reached by taking account of the lower intellectual levels of the population; in cities with dominant industries or occupations, the language of the industry of occupation is adopted for its subject field, other factors being applied to the choice of headings in other fields.[38]

The difficulty with his solution was that he suggested no criteria by which one might choose the most appropriate target group. Nor did he suggest what to do when more than one appropriate target group was identified.

Haykin also admitted that there was a notable absence of objective data concerning readers' preferences in many specific matters. Concerning the issue of how specific headings should be, Haykin stated as early as 1948:

> The literature of subject headings contains little evidence of studies made to determine what a reader looks under when he wants material on a given topic, whether, for example, he looks directly under the term which designates specifically the topic he is interested in or seeks to find it under a comprehensive heading.[39]

He repeated that opinion in 1951 and noted the following year that "there is no evidence to show that the approach is not based solely, or largely, on the personal factor, and that no common denominator can be found for the approach of readers who belong to a particular educational level, social strata, or age group."[40]

In 1951 Haykin also explained that the lack of objective data applied to other particular matters as well as to the problem of specificity.

> Very little by way of objective, experimental data is available on the general approach of the reader to the subject element of the dictionary catalog. There is little evidence to show what proportion of the users of the catalog employ it to find books by subject and how that proportion varies with different categories of readers and libraries. No valid data exist to show whether readers, and what categories of readers, seek books under a specific heading or a comprehensive subject. Further, we need to know how the reader is affected by the internal structure of subject headings—types of subdivision, methods of qualification. Possibly of secondary importance are the following problems: 1) the advantages and disadvantages of headings of the alphabetico-classed type;

2) the comparative merits of popular and scientific names, especially of popular English and foreign scientific names; and 3) the best position of references to related subjects with respect to the heading from which the references are made, . . .[41]

So severe was the lack of data that Haykin considered his list of problems to constitute something of a "no man's land."[42]

One might think that the lack of "objective, experimental data" would have caused Haykin to defer from resorting to the idea of the reader in the way that he did. The opposite was the case, however. The lack of data did not in and of itself invalidate the importance of the idea for him. This is evident in the way he regularly attributed the absence of data as a condition of past subject cataloging. In other words, previous subject catalogers had simply not done their homework thoroughly enough. That did not mean that the data could not be collected. One hears Haykin saying in those instances that the age of objective data collecting was just beginning and for those who might question the principle to be patient just a little longer.[43]

More important, Haykin also suggested that while objective data was not always available, that did not mean that useful data was lacking all altogether. Librarians had been collecting information about users for years in the form of their experience. Although that information had not been gathered in a scientific way, it did give some temporary indication, often remarkably accurate, of what the habits, needs, and preferences of readers were with respect to the various problems that subject catalogers faced. With that information had also come a considerable amount of experience in learning how the problems might be solved. Thus in almost every instance where Haykin referred to the lack of data, he also referred to the knowledge that had already arisen from the combined experience of librarians and how it provided a useful basis on which to proceed, at least until further studies could be made.[44] It was in this spirit that he added the hopeful note to his 1951 work that

> as further experience and objective study show principles and rules of practice to be faulty or inadequate, they will be displaced or modified. Meanwhile, the statements which are embodied in the following chapters represent the most valid current practice as evolved in the Library of Congress and the libraries which voluntarily follow it.[45]

Usage. The second operating principle in Haykin's approach to dictionary subject cataloging, one that was affected very clearly by the idea of the reader as the focus, was usage. By "usage," Haykin meant:

> The obligation of the cataloger is to choose the heading under which the readers are most likely to look for the subject represented by it.[46]

When, as already noted, readers are thought of in terms of the dominant group a library served, the idea of usage actually meant the usage common to that group. This was the sense of his term "common usage."

> The heading chosen must represent common usage, or, at any rate the usage of the class of reader for whom the material within the heading falls is intended.[47]

Because usage was to be considered in terms of groups, it required the cataloger to identify those characteristics that influenced the language of the particular group served.

> This choice would vary with the clientele of the library; its intellectual background based on social group, age, level of education, occupational interest, and the like. However, the principle, in each case, is the same; the terms used by the cataloger must correspond to usage, as far as possible and as far as that can be determined. This usage would vary with the public which the library must serve. A public library must somehow, in a sense, strike an average, that is use the language of the layman; a children's library must, as far as possible, limit itself to the language of the child and of the school; while the special library, such as the medical library, must base its choice on the usage of the specialists who it might serve. In any case, the choice should not be limited by the knowledge of the cataloger or his predilections, nor should it be based, generally speaking, on the desire of the cataloger to bring certain materials together on the grounds, say, that the subject matter is related. The latter is to be accomplished by classification, not subject headings.[48]

Haykin found that several practices flowed from the general character of common usage. To begin with, in American libraries the notion implied "current American usage." Foreign terms could be used, but only under certain conditions—for example, "when the concept is foreign to Anglo-American experience and no satisfactory term for it exists"; "when, especially, in the case of scientific names, the foreign term is precise, whereas the English one is not"; and also when a foreign term had been "incorporated into the English vocabulary."[49] Because common usage required currency, it also implied keeping up with changes which occurred in the meanings of terms. Haykin labeled this factor "semantic change." Semantic change led to the catalog being in a constant state of change as new terms led to the discontinuance of old ones. It also required the cataloger to have a ready source for determining the latest terms. He warned against the use of general dictionaries because they tended to become quickly outdated and did not always differentiate current from outdated terms. In their place Haykin called for the use of current periodicals.

> The surest sources of usage are periodicals on various subjects. If there is agreement on terms among those contemporaries who have competence in the subject and write on it for others, including readers of like competence, it is safe to use such terms.[50]

A final observation on Haykin's principle of common usage is that usage determination and thus the problem of semantics were in his thinking confined directly to choices of subject names considered as conventional headings. They did not include either the order of the words within such names or the order of terms used as subarrangement devices. Haykin had limited the notion of semantics to choices between terms as early as 1948. He noted at that time that semantics also technically included consideration of "the form of the heading" and that this was "fundamentally a matter of word order." But even though word order was an "important consideration," he concluded that its importance was "secondary" to semantics interpreted as the issue of the meanings of the names themselves.[51]

Haykin broached the topic of word and term order only obliquely in 1951 in his *Subject Headings*. He noted that the form which a subject heading was to take reflected "the idiosyncracies of the English language."[52] This implied that term format followed no identifiable general patterns in usage. And if there were no identifiable general patterns in usage, making general rules for such matters was impossible. The best that one could do was to make rules of limited application based on differing rationales. This general attitude concerning word and term order problems was reflected in the fact that Haykin did not address the issue at all in the section in his book on basic principles. He instead made only passing reference to some elements of it among those factors that were in the "no man's land" of matters needing further investigation. Elsewhere in his book, his attitude was reflected in those of his rules on the use of subheadings devised with only vague assumptions about known usage patterns. For example, Haykin's discussion of whether geographical subheadings should be direct or indirect constituted an extended appeal to differing rationalizations for why sometimes one and sometimes the other order was justified. He noted of indirect subdivision, for example, that it

> assumes that the interest and significance of certain subjects are inseparable from the larger area—the country or state—or that the study of subordinate geographic areas is best considered as contributing to the study of the larger area.

But, Haykin clearly did not favor indirect geographical subdivision and he maintained that ultimately "there can be no consistency in determining which headings are to be subdivided indirectly and which directly."[53]

Haykin's attitude toward word and term order may also have dictated his approach to the inversion of conventional headings. He preferred the uninverted forms of such headings because they represented "the normal order of words." But he also had little hesitancy in justifying inversion in particular situations by appealing to now one and now another user searching habit. Following Hanson, the only qualification that he made of the practice was that "the integrity of the commonly used phrase" be preserved. In other words, the grammatical order of the words in such phrases was not to be disturbed nor could the names be broken apart into separate terms.[54]

In 1952, perhaps in response to reviews of his *Subject Headings,* Haykin finally addressed the matter of word and term order very directly.

> It is a remarkable fact that a major part of the literature of subject headings in this country is devoted to the structure of subject headings rather than their meaning and use. The concept that headings must respond to the readers approach and must be based on usage has not received the attention it deserves. As a matter of fact, however, structure is a secondary consideration, since, if the readers approach were to be carefully investigated, it would be found that no case can be made for invariably adhering to particular patterns of word order.[55]

It is obvious from his remarks that he did not consider the matter to be very important, at least in comparison with the problem of word meanings. His conclusion differed little, therefore, from his first comment on it four years previously.

Specificity. The third and final operating principle in Haykin's approach to dictionary subject cataloging was specificity. To begin with, Haykin accepted the fundamental distinction that had been suggested by Knapp and Prevost and that had been more sharply described by Gull, that specific entry was in reality a dual concept. It dealt with both heading format—whether headings were direct and therefore not classed in structure—and specification—the extent to which a subject heading scope-matched the subject of a book. Haykin expressed his adherence to this interpretation of specific entry in his often quoted statement that "what distinguishes the subject heading in a present-day dictionary catalog from other forms is that it is both specific and direct."[56] Thereafter, when he spoke of specificity alone, he referred primarily to the scope-matching aspect of specific entry.

By separating extent of specification from heading directness in this way, Haykin provided the idea of specificity, and therefore specific entry as well, with an essentially positive rather than negative emphasis. He insisted on stating the idea of scope-matching in a positive way to guard against entering books as a matter of course under conventional subject headings broader than their subjects. To do such entry would result in undivided class entry. Undivided class entry was objectionable to Haykin on two counts. First, books so entered would be intermixed in the same subject heading file with others also given undivided class entry that had still other specific subjects, as well as with books whose subjects matched the entire scope of the entry term. To find a book on a particular specific subject in such a subject heading file, a user would have to search the entire file. This would be difficult if the file were long. Furthermore, success in finding books that were as specific as the user's request would depend on how expressive the titles of the books in the file were. Since in his opinion titles did not always express the contents of books accurately, success in such searches would be diminished. The second objection to undivided class entry was similar to Haykin's objection to indirect or divided class entry. Neither the user nor the cataloger would know for sure what the most appropriate class term under which to search or enter such books would be. In Haykin's view, "it is virtually impossible to set a standard for the breadth of a heading, if a specific one is not to be used."[57]

By combining a positive rendition of the scope-match equation with his insistence on the use of conventional headings placed directly in the main alphabetical sequence of the catalog (i.e., direct entry), Haykin gave substance to his explicit interpretation of specific entry as both direct and specific. The resulting procedure could therefore be described in the following way. Subject headings were first of all to consist of conventional subject names. These names were to match the respective scopes of the subjects being indicated rather than being broader than those subjects. And they were to be placed directly in the catalog's main alphabetical sequence of headings rather than indirectly as the last element of an echelon of terms.

The foregoing description of specificity and specific entry was fundamental to Haykin's work. But it remained only the starting point for entry decisions in his system because, despite the explicit and positive picture it portrayed, Haykin was also convinced that the idea of specificity had inherent limitations. Therefore, specific entry, interpreted as the entry of a book under a direct, scope-match heading, could not be applied to every situation. The fact that he began with a positive statement of the idea is important, however, because it made the exceptions to specific entry matters of conscious decision making rather than matters of total vagueness and confusion.

With respect to the specification element of specific entry, Haykin held the opinion that there were some situations in which the subject of a document was, for various reasons, too minute or narrow to be specified exactly. For example, he noted that books on the topic Raw silk would likely be looked for under the term SILK rather than under its specific conventional name in all but textile libraries. Likewise, subjects that represented varieties of a thing rather than a species, such as "the names of makes of automobiles"—for instance, Ford automobiles or Packard automobiles—would likely be looked for under their species name, AUTOMOBILES, rather than under their specific conventional names in all but automotive libraries.[58]

Limitations related to directness of entry occurred in the same way. Haykin concluded that there were some situations in which books on subjects with specific conventional names would not be searched for under those names in their regular order. Instead, they would be looked for under the noun in the subject name that represented the class of which the specific subject was only a part.

> It is unlikely that the reader will look under an adjective denoting language, ethnic group, or place for material on a subject limited by language, ethnic group, or place, although, in the case of ethnic groups particularly, the interest in the group may outweigh that in the subject. On this basis it has been assumed, although it has not been demonstrated, that a reader interested in French art or French anonyms and pseudonyms would be much more likely to look under ART, FRENCH (or ART–FRENCH) and ANONYMS AND PSEUDONYMS, FRENCH than under the respective uninverted forms, that is, the linguistic, ethnic, or local adjective, which may be considered the more specific approach to the subject.[59]

Limitations such as these are very important because they required Haykin, like his predecessors, to retreat from a positive interpretation of specific entry in at least some instances. Unlike his predecessors, however, for whom retreating from specific entry involved a good deal of confusion, retreating from specific entry for Haykin was in many respects an explicit and conscious matter because it was expressed clearly in terms of the twofold characterization of the notion.

The limitations Haykin set on specific entry also set his use of the principle apart from that of his predecessors in two other ways. First, his conclusion that the idea of specification was to be occasionally limited appears to account for his rephrasing of the basic scope-match equation where he significantly altered the referent in the equation— that is, the delineation of what is to be matched by a subject heading. Haykin's earliest statement of the scope-matching equation, made in April of 1948, appeared very much like statements found earlier in Mann and others in that it referred explicitly to the subject matter of a document as that which was being matched by a corresponding subject heading.

> The heading chosen to represent the subject matter of a book in an alphabetical subject catalog should be as specific as the concepts or objects treated, provided a term exists to express it.[60]

Later in 1948 and again in 1951, however, Haykin modified the way he stated the basic equation. Instead of calling for a match between a subject heading and the subject of a document, he called for a match between a subject heading and simply "the topic it [i.e., the subject heading] is intended to indicate."[61]

In some respects, the change in wording did not alter the basic equation. One may interpret the phrase "the topic it is intended to indicate" as the subject of the document in hand. Obviously, this is what Haykin had in mind when he stated that books "about" or "on" Canaries, Thomas Jefferson, Harvard University, the Taj Mahal, and the Battle of Bunker Hill, should be entered under the scope-matching subject headings CANARIES; JEFFERSON, THOMAS; HARVARD UNIVERSITY; TAJ MAHAL; and BUNKER HILL, BATTLE OF, 1775, the inversions in the two cases considered not to have changed their functions as conventional subject names.[62] It was this fundamental meaning that provided the equation with its positive tone. Haykin summarized the operation in the form of his rule, "The heading should be as specific as the topic it is intended to indicate. As a corollary, the heading should not be broader than the topic; . . ."[63]

It is noteworthy that by changing the basic equation from "scope-matching the subject of a document" to scope-matching the "topic it is intended to indicate," Haykin deleted any rigid requirement that what was being matched was in every instance the subject of a document. The practical effect of this was to allow the subject cataloger to avoid scope-matching when necessary. Rephrasing the formula in this way added a significant degree of vagueness, however, at least on an initial reading of his equation. If what was to be matched by a subject heading was not to be in every instance the subject of a document, one might legitimately ask what it should be. The injunction to scope-match viewed without further qualification could therefore be interpreted as much a requirement to choose a subject to indicate by means of a subject heading as it was a requirement to choose a heading that scope-matched the already "given" subject of a document. Haykin appears not to have viewed this issue as a problem, however. The question of what subject was to be scope-matched by a heading was itself determined by reference to the reader as the focus. One simply scope-matched the subject the reader was most likely to search for.

The second way that Haykin's limitations of specific entry set his use of the principle apart from that of his predecessors was that the principal basis on which to make decisions in the matter was, as just noted, the subject cataloger's consideration of the user. This source for making decisions is especially apparent when, in explaining the kinds of limitations described above, Haykin used such phrases as "to serve the best interests of the reader," "it is unlikely that the reader will look under [the more direct term]," and "it is questionable whether the reader would look under the specific term," as well as such phrases as "in all but a textile library" and "in an automotive library."[64] When to use a broader heading (i.e., when to specify a topic that was broader than the subject of a book) and when to use indirect heading forms were, in short, functions of one's understanding of the needs of particular groups of users.

In many respects, Haykin's justification of specific entry limitations by means of an appeal to the habits of readers did not lead to different results from those of his predecessors. For example, he wrote:

> to provide for material on raw silk, in any but a textile library under RAW SILK would separate it from very closely related material on other forms of silk; even SILK, RAW would be some distance away in the catalog from SILK, since it would follow all the subdivisions under the heading SILK.[65]

This provision was not unlike Hanson's desire to collocate related subjects on behalf of students and investigators. Elsewhere, Haykin flirted with the idea of specification based on document class size as found in the writings of Mann, Sears, and Pettee. Having already concluded that most readers would look for particular makes of automobiles under the term AUTOMOBILES, he added:

> It is, nevertheless, not unreasonable, at the same time, to single out FORD AUTOMOBILES, either *because of the number of books on the subject,* or because it may be considered a species, or special type of automobile.[66]

One result that was unique about Haykin's appeal to a consideration of the reader as a way to modify specific entry is that it gave him an overarching rationale that accommodated all previous rationalizations and methods. In fact, because the previous rationalizations, although not always explained as such, were ultimately based on user consideration, Haykin's appeal to the reader as the focus may be viewed as a summation of them and as a way to justify the variety of results they had produced over the years.

An even more important result is that it effectively extended the detailed application of user considerations in making subject heading decisions. The rationalizations of previous writers were limited in many respects. When Hanson modified specific entry by incorporating collocative devices, it was for a particular kind of user—the student and investigator. When Mann and others modified specific entry because of the desire to produce reasonably sized document classes, it was because users generally expected to find subject heading files of that kind. Haykin's appeal to the reader as the focus went beyond such limited objectives. More than simply providing an opportunity to make general subject heading decisions on the basis of an explicit rationalization concerning this or that particular group, it demanded that users be considered in specific entry decisions on a case-by-case, heading-by-heading basis. And with that demand, it in effect implied not simply that a single type of user be kept in mind or that a single kind of result be considered, but that all relevant user groups and all useful results be considered at each heading was formulated.

Ultimately, therefore, Haykin's interpretation of specific entry, while more clearly defined and more purposefully applied, had the potential of being more complicated than anything his predecessors had envisioned. When one considers how uncertain Haykin's idea of the reader as the focus was, the potential for this approach to specific entry to produce a variety of seemingly contradictory and ad hoc results was limitless. At the same time, however, it seems clear that Haykin was not disturbed by that possibility. He appears to have concluded that inconsistent variations would occur only as minor exceptions and that even if they constituted inconsistencies, they would be justified. Thus, he ended his explanation of the limits of specificity and specific entry by returning to the basic premise with which he had begun:

> As a general rule, however, when a term sanctioned by American usage is available for an object (or group of objects), a concept, or a relationship, it may be used as a subject heading.[67]

The limitation of specificity because the subjects of some books were too small or minute to be specified was only one problem that Haykin encountered in his application of the operating principle of specificity. Another source of difficulty arose from limitations inherent in using conventional subject names based on common usage. As already noted, the idea of conventional headings assumed that a subject heading consisted of a whole name in which grammatical integrity was preserved, rather than a string of coordinated but essentially separate elements. Conventional subject names might consist of single words or extended phrases of various types. In the form of phrases they served as a means of indicating document topics that could only be named by complex descriptions. As phrase names increased in complexity, however, the amount of variation in their formulations also increased. This made it more difficult to conclude whether one or another form had become established in common usage. In fact, the more complex conventional names became, the less likely any particular name might represent a clear choice for the scope-matching process. Even if validated, conventional subject names in phrase form made even greater problems when placed in the catalog. Given the often irregular nature of English usage, related topics with complex names were likely to be scattered all over the catalog according to how their established names happened to be constructed.

As already noted, Hanson had encountered the problem of complex names earlier in the century. In his opinion, names of this kind were the bane of the pure dictionary catalog idea because they so effectively promoted its scattering tendency. Hanson's solution was, whenever appropriate, either to manipulate complex conventional subject names (usually by inversion) in such a way as to collocate them with other related subjects or to not use them at all but to achieve specification and collocation by the alternative route of topical subdivision.

Resorting to topical subdivision as a way to achieve specification, and therefore collocation, appears to have become the more popular of the two alternatives in Library of Congress practice. A short note in the Cataloging Service's *Bulletin* in 1950 suggested that over the years Library of Congress subject catalogers had tended to balk at times in the task of assessing whether phrase names were established in favor of the use of subdivision.

> The Library of Congress determines the form of new subject headings solely on the basis of current usage as found in the periodical literature and books on the subject. In the past, many headings represented what might be termed "cataloger's choice," that is, they were chosen by the catalogers solely on the grounds that they exactly described the subject matter without regard to whether or not they were in common usage. The same sort of subject headings resulted when a

cataloger attempted to combine two related subjects under one heading.[68]

Examples of the headings that had resulted from the practice were CHILDREN–CHARITIES, PROTECTION, ETC.; REPORTS–PREPARATION; and WAGES–FAMILY ALLOWANCES, ETC. In keeping with the need to follow common usage, these were subsequently changed to CHILD WELFARE, REPORT WRITING, and FAMILY ALLOWANCES, respectively. Indeed, Haykin was firm in his conclusion that common usage phrase headings were to be given first consideration as the most appropriate way to indicate subjects the descriptions of which were complex. Thus, in his *Subject Headings* he wrote:

> Subdivision, as against the use of a word or phrase heading, is resorted to when no invariable, commonly used and accepted phrase is available with which to express the intended limitation of a subject.[69]

But the use of phrase headings in this way created severe problems. Haykin, like Hanson, found their tendency to scatter material to be severe enough to require their manipulation in the form of inversion. Unlike Hanson, however, Haykin did not rationalize inversion by a forthright appeal to the need to incorporate collocation into the dictionary subject catalog. In fact, he appears to have been adverse to using that argument at all. In 1948, when speaking of choosing conventional headings, he noted that choices should not be based

> on the desire of the cataloger to bring certain materials together on the grounds, say, that subject matter is related. The latter is to be accomplished by classification, not subject headings.[70]

Elsewhere, Haykin took considerable pains to point out how the dictionary subject catalog was essentially different from classification in its purpose and method and that, despite the similarity between some of its heading-subheading combinations and those found in alphabetico-classed catalogs, the combinations did not represent classification.[71]

Haykin's general statement about collocation suggests he was either not aware of or unwilling to admit the important role it had played in Hanson's creation of the Library's subject catalog. From the start, the very purpose of inversion had been to incorporate classificatory sequences in the catalog while staying within the bounds of conventional subject name usage. And regardless of whether Library of Congress subject catalogers had understood its genesis and explicit classificatory purpose over the years, it had become a long-standing practice in the Library's subject cataloging procedure. Haykin's aversion to the use of the rationalization may account for the fact that in several places in his *Subject Headings* he simply described the function of inversion as a collocating device without explaining its purposeful role as classification.[72] In the single instance in which he did attempt to explain the practice—the examples of French art and French anonyms and pseudonyms quoted earlier—he appealed not to the need to incorporate classificatory sequences in the catalog, but rather to writing headings in a manner that would match the way readers would search for a topic. In that particular case, it required headings that were indirect rather than direct. His appeal to user considerations in that case constituted a significant departure from Hanson in rationalizing inversion since it suggested that word order could be based directly on how users mentally conceived of subject names. That rationalization fit well into Haykin's general opinion about determining word order because it implied that appropriate word order was a function of the case in hand rather than of general patterns that were applicable to a broad range of subject terms.

An increased number of phrase headings of all kinds, regardless if used in a straightforward manner or inverted, also required a more demanding approach to the use of cross-references. For this reason, Haykin found it necessary in his discussion of the various forms of conventional phrase names to correlate the various cross-references that necessarily had to be made for each. It will be noted, however, that as the heading forms became more and more complex—for example, in the case of those that he listed as composite in form—Haykin found it less and less possible to reduce the cross-references required to some system.[73]

In the end, however, not even the ever-increasing use of complex phrase headings could accommodate the kinds of complex precoordination that was increasingly demanded of the subject naming process. Unlike Hanson, however, Haykin did not automatically resort to subdivision techniques to fill in where conventional phrase subject headings could not be found, even though he was aware of the potential for the use of subdivision techniques to precisely specify the subjects of documents in many cases.[74] Instead, he resorted to still another alternative technique—double or multiple entry. It was this alternative that lay behind the final clause in his description of specificity: "Rather than use a broader heading, the cataloger should use two specific headings which will approximately cover it."[75] In other words, if a phrase heading that matched the scope of the topical contents of a document was unavailable, the first alternative was not, as apparently it had been for Hanson, to list a subject name broader than the complex description and then subdivide it by some other term to make the result more specific, but rather to use two or more independent headings.

The types of duplicate or multiple entries Haykin had in mind here were not those that consisted of headings reversed in their term orders making direct access to the two main elements of the same heading possible—for example, UNITED STATES—FOREIGN RELATIONS—FRANCE and FRANCE—FOREIGN RELATIONS—UNITED STATES, or SWISS NEWSPAPERS (GERMAN) and GERMAN NEWSPAPERS—SWITZERLAND. Nor did it consist of those that gave access to two legitimately different foci in the same work—for example, HARVARD UNIVERSITY—SONGS AND MUSIC for a collection of the student songs of a particular school, but also STUDENTS' SONGS, AMERICAN because the same work illustrated American student songs in general.[76] Rather, it consisted of multiple entry for those subjects that contained multiple qualifications. Haykin described one of these kinds of subjects as that which consisted of a genus or species of a biological family that was restricted in scope to a place—for example, Gnatcatchers, a species of bird, limited in scope to California; or Poa, a genus of grasses, limited in scope to Scandinavia. For each of these, two entries were given: GNATCATCHERS and BIRDS—CALIFORNIA; POA and GRASSES—SCANDINAVIA.

The reasoning that Haykin gave for multiple entry of this kind was related to his estimate of readers' searching interests. In Haykin's mind the readers' interest in the particular genus or species was not primarily restricted by place even if such a limitation was evident in the books themselves. Rather, geographical limitation was associated mainly "with the order, family, or, in any case, the larger group into which the genus and species falls."[77] By analogy he extended this pattern to still other topics. For example, works restricted to a particular level of education and also to a place were given such dual headings as EDUCATION, HIGHER and EDUCATION—UNITED STATES; EDUCATION, SECONDARY and EDUCATION—UNITED STATES. Haykin was not entirely convinced of the appropriateness of this extension, however, and suggested that the direct subdivision by place of the primary headings was actually justified. But he appears to have balked at the prospect of intentionally using subdivision in that way.

A second and more important kind of multiple qualification was that which consisted of one subject with what amounted to two adjectival qualifications. Haykin listed one such type as "names of orders, classes, etc. of parasites which infest a particular host," and gave as examples: TAPEWORMS and PARASITES—MAN; NEMATODA and PARASITES—SHEEP.[78] Two headings were provided in each case because in Haykin's opinion the subjects gave distinct evidence of a "dual interest." He seems not to have considered combining all three terms together in single headings—for example, as in PARASITES—MAN—TAPEWORMS and PARASITES—SHEEP—NEMATODA—with appropriate cross-references or rotated forms. Haykin might also have listed as well headings about machinery which, like C. D. Gull's example of pumps qualified both by use and by structure, involved multiple aspects. For example, marine diesel engines were given the two headings in the Library's catalog DIESEL MOTOR and MARINE ENGINES, and diesel fuel pumps the two headings DIESEL MOTOR and FUEL PUMPS.[79]

Summary

There are other aspects of Haykin's approach to dictionary subject cataloging that might also be examined. The remainder of the chapters (those not explicitly discussed here) in his *Subject Headings,* for example, provided detailed discussions of such things as subject heading patterns for personal and geographic names, and filing. He also included a brief discussion of how Library of Congress subject headings might be adapted for use in special libraries and, with respect to personnel and procedures, how new headings might be established. With the latter he also listed the considerations he felt to be important in the use of specialists to generate new headings. To examine these various other aspects of his work, however, would only reinforce what has already been said of the fundamental characteristics of his system.

Those fundamental characteristics may be summarized in the following way. Haykin began with certain traditional structural features of the Library's dictionary subject catalog. These included such things as the use of conventional subject names, the use of controlled vocabulary choices where more than one conventional subject name was available, the predominant use of direct rather than indirect entry format, the use of a cross-reference structure, and the use of subdivision practices to subarrange subject heading files and also to further specify the subjects of books when no conventional subject names were available. His use of those traditional structural features were controlled by three basic operating principles: the reader as the focus, common usage, and a reasonably clear statement of specificity that was effectively distinguished from issues related to whether headings were direct or indirect.

Haykin's application of his operating principles made his interpretation of the Library's dictionary subject cataloging unique in many respects. It obviously gave to the Library's subject cataloging procedures a character essentially different from that which it had had earlier in the century. More importantly, it gave to the Library's procedures a basis for becoming more competitive in the changing subject access picture of the times. The result was to make his work, as well as critical responses to it, the central theme of dictionary subject cataloging discussion since that time.

CHAPTER 12

Dictionary Subject Cataloging since Haykin

Effects of Haykin's Work

Haykin's work had three important effects. First, it provided a definitive description of American and Library of Congress dictionary subject cataloging practice. Before his writings, the chief written sources available were Cutter's *Rules,* the relatively brief descriptions provided in the works of Mann and Sears, and the longer discussion Pettee had provided. With Haykin's *Subject Headings,* the entire process of dictionary subject cataloging work was for the first time described in an up-to-date manner and presented in a profusion of detail in comparison to previous efforts. Moreover, Haykin had prefaced his descriptions of practices with an explicit statement of principles and had thereafter referred regularly to those principles when discussing particular procedures. The effect was to provide both the practices and their rationales in one cohesive package.

Haykin's work did not embody an exhaustive treatment of the matter. This was recognized both by Haykin and his reviewers. Haykin later planned an even more extensive manual that not only would have reiterated his basic principles and practices, but would also have presented subject heading work in terms of separate fields of knowledge. His untimely death in 1958 found this project no further along than an outline and notes, however. Subsequent efforts by the personnel of the Subject Cataloging Division to continue it eventually languished.[1]

The second effect of Haykin's work was that as the most definitive statement of American dictionary subject cataloging ever made to that point, it became accepted as the normalized version of what dictionary subject cataloging comprised. As a result, all subsequent discussions of dictionary subject cataloging have been deeply colored by Haykin's views of the matter, either by referring to his work directly as the normative expression of theory and practice, a characteristic more common among writers in the 1950s, or by interpreting previous writers, most notably Cutter himself, in terms of Haykin's approach. The latter is nowhere more evident than where Cutter's statements about the "convenience of the public" came to be considered as synonymous with Haykin's notions of the reader as the focus. Viewing Cutter through Haykin's eyes also had the reverse effect of portraying Haykin's work as authoritatively descended from the past. The connection between Haykin and Cutter has also been fundamental to criticisms, beginning with Coates in 1960 and proceeding on the assumption that to effectively criticize present dictionary subject cataloging one must go directly to its supposed source—Cutter. It has been a Cutter interpreted through Haykin, however, rather than a Cutter understood in the context of his time.

It may reasonably be asked why Haykin's approach to the dictionary subject catalog assumed such an overwhelming position of authority—that it seemed not to occur to many that there could be a legitimate approach to dictionary subject cataloging different from that which Haykin and Library of Congress practice had come to represent. The answer to this question lies in the third effect of Haykin's work, that of coalescing the two traditions in subject cataloging practice—local subject cataloging and Library of Congress subject cataloging—in such a way as to make it appear that there had always been only one.

Earlier in this work it was noted that before 1940 the two traditions were related but in a relatively casual manner in which the Library of Congress played a more or less passive role. Haykin effectively changed that relationship in two respects. First, he made the Library's subject cataloging products more valuable, more readily available, and, in the end, virtually indispensable to libraries that represented the local tradition. This service was particularly vital for research and other academic libraries whose collections increasingly included the specialized kinds of documents to which Haykin insisted on giving better access. Second, Haykin's work as a spokesman also provided a statement of principles and practices which strongly suggested to the wider cataloging community that apart from occasional discrepancies the Library's subject cataloging products were relatively free from the same confusions that all subject catalogers faced, that they were instead securely based on an authoritative rationale. There was, therefore, good reason to have confidence in the products issued by the Library. And when this confidence was combined with the economic necessity of controlling the cost of subject cataloging, the result was a growth in the dependence of local catalogers on the Library of Congress which made it seem natural to speak of subject cataloging as a single tradition. It consisted of the Library of Congress in an authoritative position of leadership with local libraries confidently following, all doing their work more or less in the patterns set by the Library.

As dependency grew, local subject catalogers increasingly found it difficult to justify the option of doing their own subject cataloging differently, except perhaps in very specialized subject areas. But this resulted in accepting Library of Congress inconsistencies along with everything else. And by the late 1950s the problem of inconsistencies began to occupy more and more of the attention of subject-catalog commentators. In this respect, Francis J. Witty remarked in his review of the sixth edition of the Library's subject heading list:

> It seems a shame that the libraries of the United States are almost forced to go along with these inconsistencies since so many use LC cards and LC subject headings, and it would be almost financially impossible to catch these deviations before the headings are typed on cards.

Later in his review he even more aptly summarized the locked-in nature implied by a single subject cataloging tradition when he stated, "It is becoming more and more evident that as the Library of Congress goes, so go the libraries of the United States."[2]

The implications of Witty's latter statement and realization seem ominous, especially in hindsight. But during the 1950s they appear to have been overshadowed by a far more positive sense of gratitude. Pauline A. Seely, when reviewing Haykin's *Subject Headings,* reflected something of that spirit in her words:

> All in all, Mr. Haykin's book is such an excellent contribution to our professional literature and fills such a long-felt need that any quarrels with it are really only quibbles, born perhaps of the desire that it might have been just a little more detailed.[3]

And a notable review written by Carlyle J. Frarey of the sixth edition of the Library's subject heading list, the first for which comparisons could be made to Haykin's *Subject Headings,* exhibited the same tone by a strong tendency to exonerate the Library for whatever problems were noted.[4] In sum, the work of Haykin and the Library of Congress assumed a position of immense authority. It was gladly accepted, not simply in the absence of some better alternative in dictionary subject cataloging, but in the absence of any other viable alternative in dictionary subject cataloging at all. There was, in other words, little with which one could have compared it and therefore little means for its critical evaluation. It seems important here, at the same time, to offer some critical comments on Haykin's work, some of which were recognized by Haykin's contemporaries and some of which arise from the perspective offered by this work.

Critical Problems in Haykin's Approach

Given the century-long development of dictionary subject cataloging already presented, the most general and fundamental conclusion about Haykin's approach to subject cataloging is that it essentially differed from the approaches of his most significant predecessors, especially those of Hanson and Cutter. The differences were not simply related to catalog structure or even, for that matter, to obvious procedures. At those levels one will find many likenesses between Haykin and what went before him. Rather, the differences between Haykin and his predecessors resided at a deeper level altogther. They arose from a change in the context of subject access that led Haykin to use similar structures and procedures but in essentially different ways and with significantly different rationalizations.

THE CHANGE IN CONTEXT

This study has already demonstrated that Cutter devised his dictionary subject catalog in the context of a greatly circumscribed world of subjects. The dimensions of his world of subjects become more evident when one considers his view of subjects in and of themselves, in relation to documents, and in terms of how the public thought of them. He dealt with these factors by constructing a system similarly circumscribed. Conventional subject names were useful in his system because the universe of "subjects" that Cutter wished to give access to was limited and because he intended to enter documents only under the narrowest or most concrete conventionally named subject that each treated. The latter goal thus limited the number of complex subject names that Cutter had to devise. Finally, Cutter's structured understanding of "the public" led to his procedures being relatively unaffected by what today is called user considerations.

Hanson's approach to dictionary subject cataloging was also affected by its context. It involved significant departures from Cutter's work because of its loss of Cutter's structured view of subjects and of the public, because of its equating of the topical contents of books with the subjects that were to be indicated in a subject catalog, and perhaps most of all because of Hanson's general understanding of classification. The system that resulted from those changes in context was clearly a compromise. Hanson's understanding of specific entry meant that the entire subject content of each book should be indicated in the catalog by a subject heading. But this goal was circumscribed by his use of conventional subject names. His realization that usable conventional subject headings were not always available, especially for subjects whose descriptions were complex, and his dislike of scattering of related subjects throughout the catalog when conventional subject headings were available, led Hanson to use alternative procedures of subject indication. This approach not only gave the idea of specific entry a negative cast, but also gave Hanson significant opportunities to incorporate classificatory sequences in the catalog.

The ultimate rationale behind Hanson's incorporation of classification was the desire to make a catalog that was very helpful to the scholars and students that he concluded were the principal users of the Library of Congress's catalog. This modern-sounding recourse to user considerations was limited by the narrowness of its conception and application. Neither the books that were being cataloged nor the perceived needs of the special category of users called scholars demanded more than what were for Hanson a relatively simple and limited set of classification-based procedures. They did not, at least in his opinion, greatly compromise the integrity of the system as a whole.

Just as Hanson's work represented a departure from Cutter's, so also did Haykin's represent a departure from Hanson's. In this case, however, the change arose from what Haykin himself described as a virtual revolution that had taken place in the world of subject access. Haykin cogently described his perception of that change in a paper he gave at about the same time his *Subject Headings* was published which demonstrated the effect of the documentation movement on his thinking. In his opinion, the function of libraries had largely shifted from providing entertainment and general education to supplying specialized information needs, especially for researchers who were extending the boundaries of knowledge. The physical types of materials collected by libraries had also become greatly diversified. And the topical contents of library collections had largely shifted from works of literature and periodicals of broad subject matter to a wide variety of special materials that contained "highly specialized, sometimes abstruse units of subject matter." The changed context required that subject access "approach indexing in its method" and that it make use of mechanical devices to speed information delivery.[5] The change did not in Haykin's opinion presuppose that a change was also needed in the strategy necessary to indicate subjects of documents in catalogs, however. For him, the alphabetical subject headings of the dictionary subject catalog remained the best approach to the subject indication of knowledge in books and periodicals. All that was needed to make subject headings more responsive to their new situation was their more rigorous application.

Given this revised subject access context, Haykin invested the system he had inherited from Hanson with emphases designed to meet the changes. The severe difficulties that his revised emphases engendered provide both a basis for evaluating his work and a means of reviewing the critical reactions of subject access commentators since his day.

CONVENTIONAL SUBJECT NAMES

Haykin began as Hanson had with the general assumption that the entire topical content of each document was legitimately the subject that was to be indicated in the subject catalog. As already noted, however, by separating the problem of directness of entry from extent of specification within the general notion of specific entry, he was able to give specificity a positive rather than a negative tone. When coupled with an adherence to the use of conventional subject names as headings, however, his positive emphasis on specificity assumed an almost unsupportable burden.

Conventional subject names represented in many respects a reasonable assumption about subject access needs and habits. If the readers do indeed search for subjects by means of the "names" that have come to signify them in some stable manner, then it seems reasonable that indicating the subjects of documents by means of those names will provide an adequate means of access. It is this assumption that underlay Metcalfe's dictum that the chief method of dictionary subject cataloging is the arrangement of known names in a known (i.e., alphabetical) order.

The chief difficulty with this assumption is that not all the subjects of documents being added to a catalog have names that are conventional in the sense implied. Because of his emphasis on giving access to the subjects of books, Hanson had found this to be a notable problem earlier in the century. Haykin found the problem to be even worse, however, because of his insistence on giving access to the highly specialized subjects of highly specialized documents. The cataloger's burden of discovering usable conventional names for such topics, already a difficult task, became even more burdensome as the number of such topics increased. Also, when Haykin formally prescribed multiple entry as an equal or even better alternative than subarrangement techniques to achieve specification of topics, he did so without any criteria for when one or another of each of the two alternative methods should be used. Thus, he made the resulting specification procedure even more variable than it had been for previous writers, and to the outsider, even more unpredictable. When subsequently combined with variable procedures for retreating from specific entry altogether—for example, by means of inversion and other manipulations of conventional heading format and by means of the use and structure of subdivision—the resulting subject heading procedure became even more troubling and inscrutable in appearance than it had been previously. The process tended to be accepted regardless of its inscrutable nature by those who were fundamentally committed to the dictionary subject catalog in the first place. But it garnered sharp criticism from those who saw it as typical of dictionary subject catalog methods, that is, fundamentally illogical and inconsistent.

As early as 1953 in a review of Haykin's *Subject Headings*, E. J. Coates drew explicit attention to one of these difficulties when he noted that dependence on conventional subject names (i.e., names of "customary usage") did not yield very useful results for many of the subjects of highly specialized contemporary documents. He concluded:

> The day is surely past when clearly defined subject fields lacking a name capable of use as a catchword in an alphabetical sequence should be hidden away amongst material of general scope at the nearest generic head. A subject without a name can, and for maximum usefulness should, be indicated by a descriptive subheading.[6]

Coates's conclusion implied that Haykin's system had few alternatives to inclusive undivided class entry when usable conventional subject names were unavailable. But this was clearly erroneous because it did not take into account the other alternatives Haykin employed for indicating the subjects of books.

Coates's labeling of conventional subject names with the term "catchwords" did not do justice to Haykin's insistence on the use of compound subject names even in the form of extended phrases if they were adjudged usable. Equating conventional subject headings with catchwords suggested that dictionary subject catalogers were resigned to using only relatively simple one- or, at the most, two-word terms that were easily filed. One does find a tendency toward this practice in earlier writers such as Akers, Mann, and even Pettee. But even among those writers the tendency appears to have been largely an unconscious one, dictated perhaps by the desire to use simple examples. It was, however, clearly not what Haykin had in mind. The fact is that Library of Congress practice had been resorting to multiple-word extended phrase headings in increasing numbers since at least the 1940s.[7]

Seven years later Coates provided a more extensive analysis of Haykin's Library of Congress practices in his work *Subject Catalogues: Headings and Structure*. There, he recognized more fully the alternative procedures to specification available in Haykin's system. But he also submitted the entire specification procedure, together with the cross-reference structure of Library of Congress dictionary subject cataloging, to a scathing indictment for its failure to specify uniquely by means of single scope-matching headings the topical contents of individual documents and, from the standpoint of classification goals, for its failure to collocate related subjects in a coherent and systematic manner.

More importantly, Coates to his own satisfaction traced the ultimate source of the problems to Cutter. It was in that context that Coates concluded that Cutter and his nineteenth-century contemporaries, beset with "tidy minds," conceived of subjects as distinct and separate entities with stock names from among which the subject cataloger chose the one that came closest to describing the contents of any particular document.[8] Furthermore, concerning what appeared to Coates to be Cutter's method for determining term order in compound headings and in subdivided headings, he concluded:

> The difficulty and confusion in Cutter's thinking about subject headings arises from his intermittent failure to distinguish between the criteria applicable to a complete subject heading on the one hand and to an entry word on the other.[9]

In other words, Coates concluded that Cutter's apparent lack of interest and rigor in dealing with anything beyond the initial term in situations that from a modern point of view demanded strings of precoordinated terms was clearly a failure in logic and foresight on Cutter's part.

Within the context of mid-twentieth-century subject access ideas, Coates's conclusions about Cutter are understandable. If one begins with the premise that the entire topical content of each document is legitimately a subject to indicate and that the job of a subject cataloger is to indicate by means of coextensive headings each and every subject so invested with legitimacy, then Cutter's selective approach to subjects cannot but seem simplistic and bereft of logic and foresight. What Coates was not aware of was that Cutter's general conception of the universe of ideas, while no less populous or interrelated than his own, was circumscribed by the idea that only some among the total universe of such ideas were, technically speaking, subjects. Nor without a knowledge of Cutter's notion of subject structure could Coates have understood what Cutter meant by the specific subject of a document—the narrowest or most concrete "subject" treated in a book—and on that basis why he was not concerned with term order in precoordinated strings-of-terms except as term order considerations were relevant to whatever compound subject names were allowed.

The purpose of Coates's analysis of Cutter was to provide an etiology for current Library of Congress subject heading practice. Thus, he implied that Cutter's supposedly simplistic view of subjects and incomprehensible methodology had been more or less taken over without much thought by Haykin. But here too his analysis was faulty. Haykin, no less than Coates, had little idea of how essentially different Cutter's approach to subjects and their indication was from those who succeeded him. Nor did Coates realize that Haykin's approach to methodology owed more to Hanson than to Cutter. Finally, unaware of the evolution which had occurred over the years in subject heading practice, Coates also was not in a position to appreciate the importance of Haykin's positive emphasis on specificity. His lack of knowledge of that development appears to have caused him to undervalue the efforts Haykin had made to achieve scope-matching.

At the same time, by focusing on the limitations of conventional subject headings and the lack of order inherent in the alternatives to the use of conventional headings in Library of Congress practice, Coates identified one of the most persistent problems of Haykin's Library of Congress subject heading system—that is, that specificity, despite being interpreted primarily in a positive manner, was not achieved in any consistent or predictable manner. It was this limitation of specificity by the use of conventional headings that appears to have preoccupied most of the commentators on Library of Congress practice during the remainder of the 1950s, much more so, for example, than problems related to the collocation of related subjects. The writers did not always discuss the problem with Coates's clarity, however. Robert A. Colby, writing in 1954 about problems related to devising subject headings for the field of literary study, noted that some of the headings and subdivisions found in the Library of Congress list were simply not the most precise available according to scholars in the field. He also found fault with the use of multiple entry where it seemed to him that single headings would do. He was actually struggling with the limitations of conventional headings, although he appears not to have been aware of the problem in a categorical way.[10]

Writing in 1957, George Scheerer castigated dictionary subject cataloging methodology for its use of catchwords, a practice that in his opinion was patterned after language dictionaries. His subsequent list of the ills this practice had led to was notable not for its reasoned analysis but rather for its expression of an overall frustration that demanded some kind of scapegoat.

> The catchword, with the futile debate about direct and indirect entry, is still with us. To this day, as some LC cards demonstrate, cata-

logers use the leading words of the title as the key to the subject heading, sometimes overlooking the real subject of the book completely. They translate the title when necessary into the "natural phrase," and, to get the latter for the authority list, they search the cultural atmosphere for the current terminology or the jargon of the hour. It is no wonder that the subject catalog provides for librarians, catalogers, and the public a first-class guessing game.[11]

Here again, the essential issue was the technical problems that arose with the use of conventional subject names. But Scheerer, like Colby, did not speak of it in a clear categorical sense and his etiology of the practice was clouded because of his frustration.

NEWER DEVELOPMENTS IN SUBJECT ACCESS

Scheerer's description of dictionary subject cataloging focused on still another issue of particular importance. His dissatisfaction with subject heading practices was deeply predicated on his admiration for classified cataloging of the kind on which Coates and other British catalogers had been working and which was ultimately based on the ideas of S. R. Ranganathan. For Scheerer and others the attractiveness of Ranganathan's analytico-synthetic approach to subject indication resided in the seeming elegance with which it had combined a positive approach to specificity (i.e., specificity as coextensive item-specification) with a highly regularized syntax. To those like Scheerer who chafed at the way specificity was dealt with in dictionary subject cataloging and at the irregularity of the syntax that was involved, analytico-synthetic classification's control and regularization of subject access procedures approached the stature of a panacea.

Enthusiasm of that kind did not focus on the weakness of classified cataloging, however, because it was aimed not so much at analyzing that alternative as much as at describing what were perceived as unredeemable ills of dictionary subject cataloging. Dictionary subject cataloging was adjudged to be so deficient that any other method would have appeared better. In this context, the "any other method" that appeared better was classified cataloging (as perhaps natural language text processing might appear today), particularly as exemplified in the British National Bibliography.

To bolster his conclusion that classified cataloging was the best alternative, Scheerer also explained at length how, having preceded dictionary subject cataloging in time, classified cataloging was actually one of the parents of the dictionary subject catalog. This conclusion was also suggested to him by the fact that classification persisted in dictionary subject cataloging method, although in a veiled manner.

The implication was obvious, therefore, that dictionary subject cataloging represented an aberration from what was for Scheerer the best method.[12]

Scheerer's assessment of the development of subject cataloging was accurate in some respects, such as that dictionary and classified cataloging have been related in important ways. But as one may see in the development already presented here, he did not go nearly far enough. As a result, his tracing of parentage was more convenient for myth-making than for accurate historical analysis. It was just this kind of black-and-white analysis that motivated the work of John W. Metcalfe, who in three major works on subject cataloging between 1957 and 1965 attempted to set the record straight not only about the essential differences between the two subject cataloging methods, but also about what he concluded were the exaggerated claims made for the classified method.[13]

Unfortunately, all such argumentation was deeply hindered by its inability to examine dictionary subject cataloging in some categorical way. Thus, here too, Haykin's emphasis on a positive interpretation of specificity failed to gain the merit it deserved. Also missed were the effect of the source, changes in context, and the subsequent limitations inherent in Haykin's use of conventional subject names as subject headings.

When reviewing the limitations of Haykin's method, it is particularly important to recall that subject access took a decided turn in methodology during the 1950s. A major theme in that turn was the assumption that in order to achieve subject access control, complex subject names must be atomized into their component elements and then recoordinated, often according to a regularized syntax. The rules for syntax have varied, but ultimately they have tended to be rationalized on the basis of some kind of "natural" order, whether that is a natural order inherent in objects, a natural logical order inherent in types of concepts, or a natural linguistic order.

Haykin stood, in one sense, just on the other side of that divide, and he may well not have recognized it. At least this is suggested by his comment in 1952 that he found it "remarkable" that writers on subject access should be so concerned with "the structure of subject headings rather than their meaning and use."[14] In other words, given his commitment to the use of conventional subject names as *the* way to indicate subjects in catalogs, even for topics whose descriptions were complex, the issue of subject heading format receded into the background. Questions related to choosing the right conventional names were in his view the primary concern of subject catalogers. Questions regarding term order were "secondary" since in his opinion "no case can be made for invariably adhering to particular patterns of word order."[15]

By adhering to this conclusion, Haykin clearly placed Library of Congress methodology outside the tenor of the times. A methodology that begins with the assumption that term order among other things is not subject to stated and rigorously applied rules will have little in common with those that do. It may have been for this reason perhaps that Haykin more or less avoided the topic. It explains, for example, why he had next to nothing to say about what had occupied previous writers on subject heading work at length—that is, whether in place and topic combinations, one or the other should come first.[16] It also suggests why he never responded directly to Mortimer Taube's fundamental challenge to dictionary subject cataloging.

In a notable article in 1952, Taube, previously associated with the Library of Congress's Science and Technology Project but at the time of writing involved with the creation of his Uniterm indexing system, pointedly observed that Haykin's specific entry system could not by virtue of its limitation on subject subdivision specify topics that involved the coordination of more than two general terms. By way of a principle, he noted that

> the specificity achieved by the intersection, coordination, or logical product of terms of equal generality differs in principle from the specificity of a specific word or phrase and whatever degree of subdivision is allowed.[17]

Furthermore, he noted explicitly that multiple entry under the separate elements of such complex terms—for example, entry of a work on Radiation injuries to liver caused by gamma rays under LIVER–RADIATION INJURIES and GAMMA RAYS–PATHOLOGICAL EFFECTS—did not amount to specific entry because both of the resulting terms were broader than the topic of the work.

Taube's challenge, reiterated in many forms since his time, is not answerable in any logical way from the standpoint of Library of Congress practice. But if one assumes as Taube and others have that the main goal of a subject access system is to specify the subjects of documents precisely by means of single scope-matched or coextensive headings in either a pre- or post-coordinated manner, then any procedure such as Haykin's that enters works under headings broader than that has failed. Haykin may have felt no need to respond to the observation because providing single scope-matched headings for each document was not the single principal goal of the Library of Congress system. Instead, that goal was modified by adherence to conventional subject names as headings. And that adherence took precedence over the competing idea that complex subject descriptions were somehow to be fractured into their component elements so that in the end some pre- or post-coordinated string-of-terms adequate to the scope-matching task could be devised.

This did not mean that Haykin was untroubled by the problems associated with term order. But in keeping with the ultimate rationale that he continually resorted to for justifying all particular decisions, his solution to such problems lay in a far different direction than that involved in the kind of rigorous procedures used by classified cataloging and other post-1940s types of subject access systems. His solution resided instead in understanding the role of user considerations in subject access procedure.

USER CONSIDERATIONS

No single feature of Haykin's approach to dictionary subject cataloging bore as pervasive and heavy an imprint as his emphasis on user considerations. Saying this does not somehow place his approach to subject cataloging in a unique position. All modern subject access developments contain a notable emphasis on this idea. There is, however, an important difference in the way the idea was applied by Haykin and the way it has been applied by others.

Outside of Haykin, most applications of user considerations have involved an appeal to predetermined characterizations of users' habits in subject searching. These have consisted principally of characterizing the user as a specialist or scholar. Given users who regularly consider subjects to be elements of complex structures of subject relationships— that is, researchers and scholars more often than not working in the areas of science or technology—it stands to reason that a subject access instrument should present subjects in an orderly and consistent manner in terms of those same complex interrelationships. In other words, the system made for such users would be no less complex than the subject structures the users themselves conceptualize. This line of reasoning was particularly applicable to those whose subject access work was aimed at scientists and scholars and whose subject content areas were specialized in scope. But when one had to devise a general subject access system that served the widest possible range of users in terms of ability and interests and that included the widest possible range of topics, then the appeal to user considerations was necessarily much more nebulous.

Still, the idea that user considerations are critical has been too dear a concept to omit from discussions of subject heading practice. Thus,

Scheerer, realizing that a classified approach to subject access of the kind he was promoting had traditionally been predicated on service to a scholarly clientele rather than a range of users who were nonscholarly as well, solved the problem not by denying the value of user considerations but rather by concluding that the main body of users, especially in college and university libraries, were no longer the uneducated masses for which in Scheerer's analysis the dictionary catalog had originally been designed. By beginning with the assumption that users were more highly educated than previously and consequently interested in "subject exploration" rather than "quick reference," he set the stage for calling for a subject access instrument that was likewise as rigorous as the users it served—the classified catalog or at least a dictionary catalog constructed on rigorous principles.[18]

Haykin's approach to user considerations in the form of his general notion of the reader as the focus was at once far more realistic and far more inapplicable than those who began by predetermining who the user was. In fact, it may be said that Haykin extended the concept as close to its ultimate absurdity as possible without it breaking down altogether. In so doing, he differed in his use of the idea from any of his predecessors.

Haykin's emphasis on the reader as the focus was significantly different from Hanson's use of the idea and from Cutter's as well because it provided him with what was, in effect, a variable rationale for making particular decisions. Its variable nature was based on the fact that readers were for Haykin no longer divisible into the two or three simple and discrete categories that they had been for Hanson or Cutter or even into type-of-library categories favored by Mann and Pettee. Rather, they had become as numerous as the many sociologically distinct groups that could be identified among a library's variable clientele. That breadth combined with what more often than not amounted only to slim evidence of the presence or absence of reader's habits and needs made it possible for him to justify a wide variety of notable variations in such practices as extent of specification, subdivision patterns, and some of the forms of multiple entry, each already discussed above. The facility that this variable rationale provided Haykin also appears to have been the reason that he no longer had to appeal to the rationale Hanson had used, that is, that variations from the stated specific entry procedure were justified because of the need to incorporate classification sequences in an otherwise specific entry catalog. Haykin did not need to appeal to that rationale when the reader as the focus justified his alternatives so much more effectively.

Haykin's use of the reader as the focus in this variable way did not escape the notice of his contemporaries, particularly Paul S. Dunkin.

Following the lead of Marie L. Prevost, Dunkin attributed the source of the idea to Cutter's "convenience of the public." And, as noted earlier, while Dunkin did not contest the appropriateness of attempting to adjust subject access to readers' needs, he did point out the dire effects of the idea as an operating principle. In practice it functioned as the absence of principle rather than as the presence of one. Its vagueness arose from the inability to measure readers' habits and needs in such a way that the results could provide a reasonably sure basis for decisions. In the end, Dunkin's observations confirmed what Haykin had at one point only hinted at but then passed over, that readers' habits and needs in searching might ultimately be based "on the personal factor, and that no common denominator can be found for the approach of readers who belong to a particular educational level, social stratum, or age group."[19]

The same conclusion was at least implied in Oliver L. Lilley's notable 1955 article on the nature of specificity. Lilley concluded that if extent of specification was to be responsive to the approach of the reader, then it must ultimately anticipate the intellectual interests of readers on an individual basis. He concluded, however, that to do so was clearly impossible.[20] Other writers also noted the difficulties raised by the idea. But in no case did any writer go so far as to deny its necessity. As Dunkin was later to note, the idea that the reader was the focus belonged in the same category as "mother love" and "home," its rightness self-evident, but its applicability highly questionable.[21]

INCONSISTENCY

Haykin's appeal to the reader as the focus gave him a principle by which to rationalize particular decisions. But it also led to inconsistencies and, worse, to the condoning of previous inconsistencies in subject heading choices and format. It would be erroneous to conclude, however, that Haykin's procedures in this respect brought inconsistency to Library of Congress subject headings for the first time. As this study has already shown, the regular incorporation of inconsistencies went back to the discontinuity that existed between Hanson's two basic categories of users—scholars and nonscholars. Their needs were in fundamental conflict and to meet their needs Hanson devised alternative subject heading choice procedures that produced conflicting heading forms. During the decades that followed Hanson, when the number of distinct user categories increased to include the clientele of types of libraries, inconsistent variations in subject heading choices and format, rationalized on the basis of those categories, also increased. Despite such rationalizations, the idea of user considerations remained relatively vague, explained in only the most general terms. By the time Haykin arrived on the scene, the process of choosing subject headings had already taken on the appearance of an essentially haphazard activity that produced inconsistencies as a matter of course.

Haykin's attitude toward inconsistencies must be seen in light of this situation. His emphasis on the reader as the focus may be viewed as an attempt to correct the haphazard and vague rationalizations of procedure which had developed. In his view it was not enough to rationalize one's heading choices on only vague notions about the clientele of differing types of libraries. Without more strenuous efforts, headings would represent little more than the unconscious predilections of subject catalogers. Each individual heading choice instead had to conform consciously to what was known of the mental habits of the readers being served. At the same time, Haykin's emphasis on the reader as the focus also reinforced even more firmly the established assumption that heading choices and format would necessarily incorporate inconsistencies. Inconsistencies would occur because the patterns of use found among diverse groups of users were themselves inconsistent. Inconsistencies were not only justified, therefore, but mandated by the actual state of user needs. Haykin's contribution to the situation was not to deny inconsistencies but to require that they not be incorporated in a haphazard fashion. They were to be identified as rigorously as possible and thereby controlled.

Haykin's attitude toward inconsistencies was as a result somewhat middle-of-the-road. He constantly emphasized the positive side of his position by enjoining subject catalogers to carefully devise headings on the basis of the best available evidence of users' psychological subject searching habits. But he also took sharp issue with those who criticized subject heading procedure for allowing any inconsistencies at all, so much so that his attitude toward inconsistency appeared at times to be immoderate. Haykin was incensed, for example, when one critic of the Library of Congress subject heading list suggested that because Library of Congress subject headings contained inconsistencies at all, they were somehow woefully deficient. Haykin's answer was to defend inconsistency as the proper result of a reasonable method of considering the user.

Concerning the use of both topic subdivided by place and place divided by topic patterns of subdivision, he stated:

> The inconsistency of using headings of both types . . . in our catalogues does not disturb us in the least. We do not seek consistency of the kind which would either subdivide all headings by place or use all, or nearly all, subjects as subdivisions under names of places. Our aim is to bring together under names of places those topics which are

likely to be sought initially under names of places, and under subjects those which are likely to be sought primarily under subjects and secondarily under place. There are no objective data based on research which would show clearly in all cases which is the better choice.

Of inversion practices, Haykin admitted, "No consistency in the form of headings is sought by us. Each case is decided on its merits." And, finally, concerning phrases formulated differently when used in headings and when used in subheadings, he wrote:

> This again is a case of intentional inconsistency based on usage. We are not concerned about consistency between the wording of a main heading and the same concept used as a subdivision, as long as usage justifies the inconsistency and presumably helps the user of the catalogue find what he is after. In individual cases our inconsistency may be infelicitous, but the principle is sound.[22]

It is plain that Haykin was not overly troubled by the presence of inconsistencies in the Library of Congress system, at least not by those which were required by one's conscious effort to make headings conform to readers' subject searching habits. In fact, Haykin appears to have been so committed to finding headings that would within the constraints of conventional subject name usage most adequately indicate the many new topics of specialized documents appearing in his day, that the achievement of consistency in heading choices and format was the least of his considerations.

At the same time, it is noteworthy that Haykin's generally open attitude toward inconsistencies and variations in headings did not extend to the realm of cooperative cataloging. Inconsistencies that arose from different libraries making different heading choices, while occasionally justified on a local basis, if allowed equal status as cooperative subject cataloging copy, would ultimately destroy the uniformity necessary for the national cooperative cataloging effort.

The source for Haykin's opinion in this matter is not difficult to see. His sense of the single subject cataloging tradition that had become more of a reality through his efforts required a single agency to ensure quality and uniformity in the subject cataloging copy that would be used in the great majority of library dictionary subject catalogs. That agency was, of course, the Library of Congress, not because it was somehow inherently better than any other agency but because it was simply in the best position to assume the role. It had the staff, the money, the administrative structure, and the respect of the wider cataloging community to best accomplish the task. Given the central position of the Library in cooperative subject cataloging, it made little difference if justifiable inconsistencies were generated in the Library's own cataloging. As long as most libraries used the same results, common subject access in those libraries would be assured. Haykin captured the spirit of what he meant when, in commenting on British practices in librarianship and cataloging, he noted that "some of the generally accepted compromises (one might almost say axioms) of American cataloging are still moot questions among British librarians." Among the latter was the habit of using local systems of cataloging and classification.

> Thus, too, many a librarian—librarian rather than cataloger, by the way—still thinks in terms of his own kind of catalog, personally devised or improvised rules of entry and description, his own, or a personal choice, of a system of classification. The handicap of individual dogma and practice to union catalogs and to common access to books through catalogs constructed on the basis of common rules and through a universally accepted, though perhaps less than perfect, classification —this handicap is, of course, recognized, but it is not likely to lead to common action. British cataloging thought roams far and soars high, but is unlikely to lead to action on the basis of ready and universal access to library collections.[23]

Haykin's view of the needs of the national cooperative cataloging movement incorporated a serious paradox, however. By Haykin's own admission, the application of the idea of the reader as the focus as the most fundamental operating principle in subject heading work focused principally on individual libraries and the needs of their users. But this was contrary to his idea of a single cataloging tradition controlled and administered from a single point—the Library of Congress. Library of Congress subject catalogers could not logically make a single set of subject headings for all libraries or even for all types of libraries and also adhere to the principle that the reader as the focus represented. And even if, through some rationale, Haykin assumed that it was possible to ascertain the needs of all libraries and their users and come up with an "averaged" set of headings amenable to most of them, the fact that the first responsibility of the Library's subject catalogers was to make headings to meet the needs of the Library's own clientele made even that prospect impossible. In short, Haykin's idea of the reader as the focus and his belief in the necessity of a single cataloging tradition were diametrically opposed.

Haykin does not appear to have recognized this paradox. Considering its obviousness, at least in retrospect, one may wonder why he was so oblivious to it. Until further evidence is available, all reasons are speculative, of course, but one possibility is that Haykin simply thought of the Library of Congress as the prototype of all libraries. Headings made for it were thus equally usable in all libraries. Another possible reason is that in an era (post-World War II) when centralization, especially through agencies of the federal government, represented a new and useful solution to social problems, conflicts of this kind were simply not noticed, either by Haykin or by others. The immense task of making Library of Congress subject headings more modern and more readily available, combined with the economics local libraries faced in keeping up with the increasing load of subject cataloging, made conflicts related to uniformity and to the internal inconsistencies of the Library's subject heading system all but invisible. Furthermore, there was little with which one could compare either the Library's work or Haykin's synthesis of it, especially from a vantage point inside the tradition. And special libraries, potentially the best source of criticism, were increasingly divorcing themselves from dictionary subject cataloging in favor of solutions to subject access needs offered by the information science movement. In the end, there was comparatively little impetus for ongoing critical evaluation. With the appearance of Carlyle Frarey's state-of-the-art review of subject heading work in 1960, in fact, the quest for explanation of the nature of dictionary subject cataloging seems to have come to a close. Unfortunately, almost all substantive issues related to subject heading work were unresolved.[24] Dictionary subject cataloging, fraught with problems, remained a mystery. This depressing outlook did not deter local libraries from making use of Library of Congress subject heading copy, however, regardless of whether it was fully satisfying. With a ready source of such copy and no better prospects in sight, libraries simply proceeded with the business at hand.

Still, others clearly did not agree with Haykin when he stated that inconsistencies did "not disturb us in the least." Although libraries continued to use Library of Congress subject heading copy as a matter of course, by the mid-1960s new voices began to raise criticism of the Library's subject cataloging products. These generally focused not on theoretical issues but rather on identifying the nature and extent of inconsistencies. In fact, the period since the mid-1960s may be characterized as one continuous stream of criticisms of the Library's subject cataloging practices for inconsistencies identified at all levels of its subject catalog system.

Haykin's Continuing Influence

The influence of Haykin on the development of dictionary subject cataloging makes it appropriate to call the period since the 1940s "the Haykin era," just as the period after Hanson was called "the Hanson era." This conclusion is warranted because Library of Congress subject heading practice has generally continued to follow the complex of fundamental tenets which formed the basis of Haykin's work. The most important of those tenets include: (1) a commitment to conventional subject names as subject headings with all of the difficulties that such headings involve for compound subject descriptions; (2) specific entry as scope-matching, but only as a starting point, the principle being modified by the limits imposed by conventional subject names and by judgments about users' needs; and, most importantly, (3) the commitment to considering the user as a rationale for making subject cataloging decisions.

Evidence for the continuing presence of Haykin's tenets is at least suggested by the persistence of a considerable amount of variation and irregularity in subject heading structure, subdivision practice, and subject heading choice. Furthermore, variations and irregularities in these matters, well documented over the last two decades in a steady, dreary stream of articles and books that have been highly critical of Library of Congress practice, show little sign of abating to any significant degree. Evidence of this kind is indirect because it does not conclusively prove the influence of Haykin's tenets. One might as well attribute such results to the dead weight of practices Haykin may be seen as having codified. Still, the continuing and notable presence of such variations and irregularities and, more importantly, the use of Haykin's rationalizations for them strongly suggest that their persistence is due in no small measure to his work.

RICHARD S. ANGELL

A more persuasive form of evidence of the continuing influence of Haykin may be found in the official descriptions of Library of Congress subject cataloging practice made by Richard S. Angell, Haykin's successor as chief of the Subject Cataloging Division. In 1954 Angell made what amounted to a programmatic restatement of Haykin's goals as the basis of his own work. His emphasis on the compilation of the best possible lists of subject terms, especially through the cooperative efforts of specialists, reflected Haykin's view that the best route to better subject access would be through paying attention to the "semantics" of conventional subject names.[25] Angell's assignment of problems related to consistency in subject heading format (under the label of "predictability") to the status of problems that were then unsolvable and needful of future study reflected Haykin's identification of that issue as a matter of secondary importance.[26]

Angell also reiterated the tenet, obvious in Haykin, that specificity as an operating principle had distinct limitations. His statement of its limitations was expressed in somewhat different terms than Haykin's, but it amounted to the same thing. He contended that specificity could be viewed in two ways: the specificity that was "possible" and the specificity that was "desirable." By the first, he meant specifying documents in terms of estimates of their subject contents alone; by the second, specifying documents in terms of the subject demands that might possibly be made of the system as a whole. Angell's subsequent denial that subject access could be provided for either exhaustive searches or for future searches concerning aspects of subjects not "foreseen at the time of the original indexing" is an understandable limitation of the second kind of specificity. But his reference as well to examples of highly complex subject descriptions and his subsequent denial that they should necessarily be specified completely in terms of their descriptive complexity left little doubt that, just as Haykin had concluded, even the first kind of specificity was to be limited. And limitations of specificity in that sense was a fundamental tenet of Haykin's approach.[27]

Seventeen years later, in 1971, Angell, then speaking as the chief of the Library's Technical Processes Research Office, reiterated with only some changes of terminology the Library's commitment to essentially the same positions. For example, under the heading "Terminology" Angell reiterated the Library's commitment to conventional subject names "established" through common usage determinations, noting at the same time that obsolete terms should continually be updated. Later under the heading "Form and Structure of Headings" he also reiterated the continued preference for extended phrase headings over strings-of-terms that arose from subdivision practices, even though such phrase headings were often manipulated through inversion.[28]

Angell also reiterated the limitations of specificity in the system. He did so, however, in the light of the ongoing discussion which had taken place within the cataloging community during the intervening years. He noted something of what some writers had concluded was the inescapably "relative" nature of the idea. He also specifically pointed out what he considered to be the British approach to specificity in which the idea had been interpreted more rigidly in terms of single entry item specification. After these observations he concluded that

> we could more usefully deal with the problem of specificity if we substituted for "specific" the notion of "expressive." In this sense specificity is not an attribute of a subject access vocabulary as such (i.e., of its terms) but is rather a function of the total resources of the indexing system, and of the way in which it is used.

> In order to achieve expressiveness, American library practice, as exemplified in the list and practices of the Library of Congress, relies in considerable part on the resources of the English language. It uses natural language as naturally as possible. This accounts for the presence in the list of a variety of standard phrase forms, in which relationships between terms are made clear by the syntax of the language. In this respect the principle of common usage, which governs the choice of single terms is also invoked.[29]

Despite Angell's attempt to clarify the idea by using "expressiveness" in place of "specificity," the new term retained the same kind of vagueness Haykin's approach to the matter had included. To say, for example, that a subject heading should be expressive is meaningless until one states explicitly what is being expressed. And to the extent that he left the letter unstated, the indeterminate side of Haykin's specificity rule, that a subject heading was to be as specific "as the topic it is intended to indicate," remained unchanged.[30]

Angell's statement that specificity "is a function of the total resources of the indexing system and of the way it is used" might be interpreted as an indication of a new direction in the interpretation of the idea if one concluded that he was referring to a systems approach to specificity. In that approach specificity is viewed as a function of several interrelated factors rather than simply as a function of the single factor of the relationship of a subject heading to the topical scope of a document. But this does not seem to be what Angell had in mind. His statement appears instead to be no more than a veiled reference to the Library's use of multiple entry when no single conventional subject heading could be devised and when subdivision practices could not accommodate subject descriptions with multiple qualifications. He appears to have been suggesting, in other words, that even if no single subject heading were available to express "the subject" of a document, the document might still be considered to be specified within the system as a whole by the combination of headings under which it was placed.

When Haykin raised multiple entry to a status equal to or greater than subdivision as a way to accommodate complex subject descriptions, he did so without any explanation for the procedure. In the absence of any statement by Haykin, Angell's explanation of specificity in the preceding quotation offers something of a rationale for multiple entry. But on closer examination, Angell's explanation does no more than raise new problems. First, regardless of the fact that two or more terms or sets of subject terms are *thought of* as constituting an entire subject description, they do not actually accomplish the indication of that subject in terms of a particular document until the means have been made available to recoordinate them. But Library of Congress practice contains no systematic features to accomplish recoordination. Rather, it would have to depend on the ability of the catalog user to accomplish the task in a retrospective or "quasi" post-coordinate fashion. This may well have been what Angell meant when he attached to his statement the condition that specification was a function not only of the whole system, but also of "how it is used." One might, for example, look up one term under which a document was entered and then by scanning the titles at that location (or even the record of other subject headings on the cards) match the first term with a second to determine which documents within the document class more specifically match the search request. This practice is actually a time-honored procedure for using any catalog in which specification is not complete. Again, one might look up two terms separately and compare the documents in both document classes to see which ones appear in both places. This would be little more than an item-on-term matching procedure similar to Taube's original coordination process. Library of Congress practice does include some provisions for making cross-references that aid in the user's ability to coordinate terms, but these do not appear to have been made in any consistent manner. And even if they were consistently made, users would have to be trained in how to go about the coordination procedure. In summary, although Library of Congress subject catalogers might reasonably consider documents to have been fully specified within the system by the use of multiple subject headings, this belief is actually predicated on the assumption that the use of the system by searchers completes the coordination process. As noted, however, the means by which users might accomplish this are not readily available. As a result, retrieval of documents about subjects with complex descriptions given multiple entry under separate elements of the descriptions is at best only partially assured.

A second difficulty that arises with Angell's explanation of specification when used as a justification of multiple entry is that because it approaches complex subject descriptions as coordinations of other subject terms, at least in those instances in which multiple entry has been justified, it suggests an intrusion of yet another kind of subject indication in a subject catalog already overly complex by reason of its varied procedures. As noted earlier in the discussion of Hanson's methodology, Hanson's approach to subject relationships rested heavily on the meanings of particular terms within an enumerated classificatory structure. He in effect bypassed Cutter's approach to subject relationships that rested on a formal significance order between coordinated categories of subjects. The rationalization of multiple entry here represents in certain respects a return to Cutter's approach to subject relationships, at least in those instances where multiple entry is used, because it depends primarily on the simple coordination of terms (although without Cutter's significance order) taken from subject descriptions, rather than on the meanings of particular terms within an enumerative classificatory structure. To add this approach to subjects to the Library of Congress catalog is to intermix essentially different approaches to subject indication.

The third and last difficulty that arises from justifying multiple entry in this explanation of specification is that Angell, like Haykin, gave no firm indication of when either single or multiple entry should be used. Lois Chan explicitly noted this problem when she wrote:

> There are two approaches to representing a complex subject in the catalog: by using a complex heading which reflects all elements and facets of the subject or by using several headings, each of which brings out one or more of the elements or aspects. When a complex heading required by the document does not exist, the subject cataloger at the Library of Congress may propose a new heading as requird by the work. However, because there are no rules concerning specificity or co-extensivity, the cataloger may and often does choose the second approach. . . . In dealing with a complex subject for which no single heading exists, it is difficult to predict which approach will be taken by the Library of Congress.31

Chan's conclusion that the Library's choice in any one instance is not predictable is very accurate. One may legitimately argue with her statement, however, that there are "no rules concerning specificity or co-extensivity." She required that specificity be achieved only in the form of single precoordinated headings that by themselves fully scope-matched the topical contents of the documents being entered in the system. But Angell had directly denied that meaning of specificity, and Haykin had at least implied its denial. Furthermore, to conclude that the Library of Congress has no rules for specification is to misinterpret Haykin's own stress upon the principle. Of course, as already noted, Haykin's statement was hedged in by constraints related to conventional headings and the operating principle of the reader as the focus. The lack of predictability arises from those constraints rather than from the lack of rules per se. What is important here is that Angell's 1971 statement suggested that those constraints were still being observed. In the second paragraph of the above quotation taken from his article, Angell noted the continuing importance of conventional subject names (under the label of "natural language") and of the reader as the focus (under the label of "common usage") as the chief factors that affected subject heading choices and, therefore, specification. In other words, specificity, labeled "expressiveness" by Angell, remained modified by the same factors that had made it a variable and in some cases a vague operation for Haykin, and that together led to a lack of predictability as to which actual approach—single entry conventional heading, single string-of-terms, or multiple entry—should be followed in any one instance.

Thus far in tracing Angell's statements concerning the nature of Library of Congress practices, little has been said of the third of Haykin's tenets, the reader as the focus. As a matter of fact, one will find no explicit use of that phrase in either of Angell's presentations. The presence of that idea remained unchanged, nevertheless, except that Angell referred to it either as common usage, which he used more or less synonymously with Haykin's term, or by directly describing particular user considerations as the basis for particular practices.[32]

THE READER AS THE FOCUS

Haykin's controlling rationalization of the reader as the focus retained its important position for Angell, and it has persisted ubiquitously in the Library's subject cataloging over the last three decades. In many respects it has provided the reasoning behind some of the changes in particular practices. For example, Patrick Wilson suggested in 1979 that the appearance over the preceding decade of multiple entry under both specific headings and class inclusive headings spelled the end in selective situations of what he termed Haykin's idea of "exclusively specific entry."[33] In one sense, the practices that Wilson discussed did indeed represent a departure from Haykin. Although in selected cases Haykin did resort to multiple entry, one of which was class entry, he appears not to have sanctioned that practice where a single specific level entry was possible and appropriate.

At the same time, there are at least three good reasons why even this direct change from a particular pattern of Haykin's is still well within Haykin's tenets. First, for Haykin specific entry was not as "exclusive" as Wilson suggested. It was instead no more or less than a starting point to be modified where appropriate, rather than to be followed as a rigid procedure. Second, the modifications of specific entry that Haykin did sanction were almost all based on user considerations. Here, despite Wilson's claim that reasons for two-level entry are meager, it is plain that they have been justified on the same basis—usefulness to the supposed needs of particular kinds of users. Third, in contrast to Wilson's complaint that two-level entry is pursued selectively rather than consistently, one only need be reminded that inconsistency of this kind was apparently not overly troubling to Haykin. His approach to such matters required little more than judicious restraint based on matching subject heading practices to the large variety of user groups inherent in his idea of the reader as the focus, rather than consistency based on some overarching and singular logic of subject retrieval patterns.

Another example of the continuing presence of Haykin's principle of the reader as the focus is the movement over the last decade to replace terminology in the subject heading list which is deemed prejudicial to one or another group of users.[34] Having originated during a period of social protest during the 1960s and waged in a manner not unlike a moral crusade, this movement for change is plainly consistent with Haykin's principle. Its call for changing particular terms is no different, for example, than insisting on using subject headings that precisely serve specialist users.

At the same time, the movement to modify subject headings because of a perceived reader bias raises significant difficulties. First, the movement has focused on the paradox noted earlier, that Library of Congress subject catalogers make subject heading choices for all libraries when the idea of the reader as the focus actually requires a local emphasis in the choice of headings. The answer offered by the movement —the democratization of subject heading choices in which suggestions for headings devised within the wider cataloging community are to be used by the Library as cooperative subject cataloging copy—does not dissolve the paradox, however. It only substitutes another source for networkwide copy rather than insisting on focusing on the readers in local situations and devising headings accordingly. In other words, the new movement, no less than Haykin, accepts the tenet that a more or less singular set of subject headings may be used for all libraries.

Second, the democratization process itself engenders hidden difficulties suggested in the following questions. If the process of choosing subject headings must necessarily be democraticized so that user groups being served are represented in the choosing process, what is to prevent the choosing process from becoming only a quasi-democratic activity beset by uncontrolled lobbying, the winners being those who have the resources and the skill to exercise the most influence? Furthermore, can the process of choosing subject headings bear this kind of politicizing without more attention being paid to who is being represented and how that representation is being accomplished?[35]

A third difficulty with this new movement is that there has been almost no corresponding interest in or discussion of coordinating the changes that have been suggested for individual headings with other tenets implicit in the Library of Congress system, the most notable being its commitment to conventional subject names. In this respect one cannot help but note the wide variety of formats among suggested substitute headings, sometimes heading-subheading formats, sometimes wholesale inversions, and sometimes wholesale qualifications. The difficulty is not that such forms are not used in Library of Congress practice, but that their use among the suggested changes appears only to aggravate the kind of term order chaos already prevalent in the system. One might argue, of course, that since Haykin seems to have considered format of secondary importance, it should not be given greater weight in the present case. But with more persons than ever suggesting new terms with only scant attention paid to format and subdivision practice, the acceptance of new terms without rigorous attention to what patterns do exist raises the probability that even greater numbers of inconsistencies will arise.

Beyond Haykin

In contrast to those subject heading practices that confirm Haykin's continuing influence, other changes have occurred since the 1950s that might be construed as a move away from Haykin. But changes of the latter kind have been less noticeable in comparison and on the whole seem tenuous in their character.

One such change has been the application of computer technology to the Library of Congress subject heading system and the implication in doing so of moving toward a systems interpretation of the idea of specificity that is more aligned with contemporary systems approaches to subject indexing. In these approaches the effectiveness of a subject access system is viewed as a function of the interaction of various elements of the system. The elements are themselves related to input practices, file characteristics, search patterns, and, in keeping with information transfer models, those factors having to do with feedback that make the system cybernetic. Some of the elements are reasonably concrete (e.g., file characteristics), some are at best ambiguous (e.g., the nature of terminology and of searching patterns), and all may be conceived as variable in their respective roles within the system. Specificity, as only one of the elements of the system, is as contingent on other variables as any other element. Thus the question of what constitutes appropriate specificity (i.e., how specific should specific be?) may not be expressed simply as a straightforward match between the topical content of a document and a subject heading. Instead, it must be viewed as a function of all the elements of the indexing system. To borrow Angell's phrase, it must be seen as "a function of the total resources of the system and of how it is used."

This approach to specificity is most appropriate to a system based on a cybernetic model and has become possible at least in conception by the advent of computer technology. Library of Congress subject cataloging work has the potential for applying this approach to specificity, at least to the extent that it has developed its own computerized subject access systems using its subject headings as the basic vocabulary of those systems. At the same time, however, the vagueness that Haykin had earlier attributed to the idea of specificity remains, especially to the extent that the Library's dictionary subject cataloging remains a manual access system.

Another way in which one might suppose that change has been taking place in dictionary subject cataloging has arisen with what appears to be a growing propensity to speak of the dictionary subject catalog's headings as natural language.[36] This trend is important because of the high regard that natural language information systems have attained in recent years. Thus, it might seem that by pursuing natural language headings even more rigorously, contemporary dictionary subject cataloging practice could be considered to be in the vanguard of contemporary developments in subject access.

It should be said, however, that characterizing Library of Congress subject headings as natural language terms, even in part, is problematic at best. Part of the difficulty lies in the idea of natural language itself. If by the phrase one refers to a subject system "without vocabulary control" where whatever terms the authors of documents use to discuss their ideas are used as the vocabulary, then obviously dictionary subject catalog headings are not natural language headings.[37] They consist instead of a selected vocabulary chosen from among many alternative terms available. Of course, to the degree that subject headings are derived from the documents themselves, such as in the form of partial title added entries, this sense of natural language holds.[38] The uncontrolled approach to subject access is, however, generally limited in Library of Congress practice.

But even if by the phrase "natural language" one refers to a more general notion of using language the way people normally speak— that is, with normal grammatical constructions and phrasing—one still may not conclude that dictionary subject catalog headings consist of natural language, at least that part of them that are conventional subject names. Many headings may be accurately characterized in this broader sense of the term, but there are also many others in the system that are manipulated, especially by inversion. Regardless of how one might rationalize such manipulations, the resulting headings are not natural spoken or written language, at least not in English. To the extent that such manipulations are done in some partially systematic way, they differ only by degree from the artificial syntaxes common to such highly structured schemes as say, PRECIS or Farradane's relational indicators system.

Even should the manipulated headings be discounted, it is questionable whether those that remain could be considered natural language without some further qualification. The reason for this conclusion is that at least some of what Library of Congress practice uses as phrase headings—for example, phrases involving the propositions "in" or "as" or those that involve the effect of one thing on another in the form [object], EFFECT OF [substance, thing, etc.] ON—are really only formulaic contrivances that have only the appearance of natural language. But they are in reality no less structured than a vocabulary built with a rigorous citation formula where subheadings are separated by dashes or other special punctuation. Subject headings of this formulaic kind appear to arise not from the observation of actual use but rather from what Angell spoke of as using natural language "as naturally as possible," that is, using words and word order from everyday speech to express large classes of complex ideas in a way that approximates the appearance of regular language.[39] It appears that Library of Congress practice has placed an implicitly higher value on phrases contrived in this way than on others, such as those built through subdivision practice, for no other reason than their seemingly "natural" appearance. But regardless of the rationalization, headings of this kind also constitute a constructed and in many respects an artificial rather than a natural language vocabulary. Because of this fact it is only with difficulty that one may speak of contemporary dictionary subject cataloging as having a natural language vocabulary. At best it is a mixture of natural and artificial language with few guidelines for distinguishing the two.[40]

A final way in which one might suppose that change is taking place in contemporary dictionary subject cataloging practice and one that is surprising in being contrary to Haykin's general approach to the matter, is the extent to which a greater degree of regularization has been insisted on in subdivision practice. One mark of this change has been the publication in the eighth edition of the Library's list of headings of the most complete listing of commonly recurring subdivisions yet provided, complete with explanations of their use. The result is to enable the subject cataloger to build subject heading strings through a kind of building-block technique. An emphasis on regularization has also appeared in the recent shift to the principal use of "indirect" rather than "direct" local subdivision. The rationale given for this change—"the advantages of uniformity throughout the system" —is unusual because it raises consistency in heading format to a much higher level of importance than the "secondary" role that Haykin accorded it.[41] On the other hand, the new emphasis given to consistency may well be limited only to those measures that will make computerization of the subject heading files less troublesome.[42] If that is the case, the advent of computerization, while demanding more consistency than previously deemed necessary, will not ultimately demand the kind of consistency that would bring about a basic change from Haykin's tenets. In fact, the very capabilities of computers to succeed in searching by what may conveniently be called "brute force" may well militate against pursuing the kind of consistency normal for highly structured subject access systems.

However small, therefore, some changes outside the context of Haykin's tenets have indeed taken place. And these suggest that contemporary dictionary subject cataloging is not entirely static. But for the most part, contemporary practice remains deeply expressive of Haykin's work. Whether or not it should remain this way is a far different question. Any answer to that question must begin with an attempt to understand how contemporary practice has arisen. The present study represents an attempt to gain that understanding.

CHAPTER 13

Summary and Observations

This effort began by describing and questioning conventional wisdom concerning the origin and development of contemporary dictionary subject cataloging—that it was derived more or less directly from the work of Charles A. Cutter and that its chief weaknesses may be attributed to propagating the inconsistencies and inadequacies of Cutter's original system. This study has shown that dictionary subject cataloging has had a far more complex history than this view allows. The only sense in which present-day subject heading work may be said to derive from Cutter's work is in such formal matters as the use of conventional subject names as subject headings, a controlled vocabulary, and a cross-reference structure. At the far more important level of the fundamental ideas which give meaning to those formal aspects of the work, dictionary subject cataloging has undergone significant changes since Cutter's day.

One fundamental change has been in the idea of a subject. In a process covering several decades, Cutter's original discriminatory and classificatory view of subjects has been replaced by a view in which subjects are considered to be no less than properties of books themselves without other qualifications. Classification might be invoked in a posterior sense to bring order to subjects thus conceived, but it no longer holds the anterior and preemptive position it held in Cutter's thinking.

The loss of Cutter's discriminatory and classificatory referent had a corresponding effect on two other fundamental ideas in subject heading work. First, the nature of specific entry and the idea of specificity have changed in a manner in keeping with the change in subject referent. Specific entry in Cutter's system meant entering a book under the most specific subject that it treated, where a subject meant an established topic of thought and most specific meant the subject of the greatest concreteness when measured in terms of Cutter's categorical approach to subject structure and his significance order between those categories. This required a choice between subjects and only after

394

that a concern for how the name of the chosen subject should be written. With the change in subject referent, specific entry has come to mean entering books under a subject heading (or headings) that expresses their entire topical contents. Since there are no choices to be made between subjects (except where there is a desire to retreat from full specification because of other factors), subject heading work has become primarily the activity of naming the entire topical contents of books.

The second major effect of the shift in subject referent has been on the use of conventional subject names as subject headings. Unlike the change in specific entry, the most fundamental method of naming subjects has remained the use of conventional subject names. In Cutter's system the use of conventional subject names was a viable measure. By recognizing only established topics of thought as subjects and limiting specific entry to the most concrete subjects that books treated, Cutter made it highly probable that the conventional subject names needed for entry were both distinct and relatively uncomplicated in form. Cutter was not interested, in other words, in characterizing "the subjects" of books in the modern sense of the idea, although he did recognize the existence of complex descriptions of topics of books. In contrast, the subsequent need to express the subjects of books by means of subject headings that were, if possible, in the form of conventional subject names made unreasonable demands on the use of such names. Characterizing the subjects of books required conventional subject names of greater complexity. But the process of determining whether such names were commonly used became very difficult and indeterminate as their complexity increased. Even when identified, however, the tendency of such names to scatter related topics throughout the catalog far exceeded anything that Cutter had had to face. Cutter was not unaware of the scattering that took place even in his more limited use of such names. But he was able to ameliorate the effects of the scattering by the use of rigidly controlled subarrangement terms and cross-references that were also based on his categorical approach to subject structure and his significance order between categories of subjects. When subject catalogers who succeeded Cutter lost his classificatory referent, however, they also lost the rationale behind the use of such devices. Therefore, the devices could not be used with the same effect.

J. C. M. Hanson at the Library of Congress was more responsible than any other modern subject cataloger for adopting the changed subject referent and a scope-match interpretation of specific entry, although he did not appear to recognize the nature of the shift. He did recognize the problems engendered by the use of conventional subject names in the context of the new subject referent, however, and met those problems with a series of unique measures. One of his measures was to circumvent full-specification conventional subject names by the use of class entry combined with subarrangement terms. A second measure was to manipulate, especially by inversion, the complex conventional subject names he was obliged to use. A third measure was to purposefully choose class-subclass sequences in preference to such names.

The most striking result of his measures was to incorporate heading forms that not only brought a significant amount of classification into the dictionary subject catalog, but also did so in the heading structure of the system rather than only in the cross-references and subarrangement rationale. Hanson justified this procedure because of his desire to add a significant amount of collocation to a catalog that in his opinion would become no more than a chaotic index if restricted to the straightforward use of conventional subject names. But his classificatory solution to the scattering problem added a new complexity to the catalog because it included a significant amount of variation and inconsistency in the headings generated. The reason for the variation was that Hanson's view of classification required it. He approached subject order pragmatically in terms of separate fields of knowledge rather than on the basis of a systematically structured and unified system. Consequently, his classificatory decisions could not avoid appearing as ad hoc decisions that looked inconsistent when viewed from outside the system.

Another result of Hanson's measures was to add to the use of conventional subject names a second and competing method for achieving scope-matching—the use of strings-of-terms in the form of headings combined with subarrangement words. At least that is the way his subarrangement procedures appeared when displayed in the form of subject catalog copy. Over the long run it was this use of such heading formats rather than the classificatory motivation behind them that became the most important aspect of their use.

During the decades after Hanson's pioneering work, his hybrid version of the dictionary subject catalog came to be accepted as the normative expression of that catalog type. As catalogs grew in size, however, the extensive variations in subject heading form and the lack of clarity in the idea of specific entry inherent in his system caused an increasing amount of confusion. These factors, when combined with a growing information revolution that required more effective specification and greater control over heading format, prompted investigations that served in various ways to further change the nature of dictionary subject cataloging. Beginning with Margaret Mann in 1930, for instance, the aspect of specific entry that has to do with specification came to be stated positively as the scope-match idea which is standard today. And with Haykin's work at the Library of Congress during the 1940s, greater emphasis than ever has been placed on scope-matching as an answer to the question of what a subject heading is supposed to indicate. At the same time, the specification element of specific entry has never entirely freed itself from limitations imposed on its scope-matching goal. Sometimes the limitations have arisen from a desire to produce document classes of reasonable size. At other times they have been rationalized by claiming that users do not always require full specification in the sense that scope-matching requires. And at still other times, scope-matching has been limited because of resistance to the use of complex strings-of-terms, substituting for them the use of multiple entry terms. Multiple entry terms used in this way have been rationalized by the belief that they specify a work in their aggregate, even though the terms constitute class entry when considered separately.

In contrast to the clarification characterizing the matter of specification, the question of how subject headings should be written has undergone far fewer changes. The most significant change was Haykin's renewed emphasis during the 1940s on the use of conventional subject names. As a result of that emphasis, Library of Congress cataloging work placed greater emphasis on determining conventional subject names to begin with rather than on automatically resorting to Hanson's alternative of class entry combined with subarrangement terms. At the same time, the manipulation of conventional subject names, particularly by the use of inversion, and the use of strings of-terms as a method of specification have also continued. But they have tended to be justified by appeals to user considerations rather than by appeals to the classificatory rationalization Hanson had used. One may surmise that the continued use of such variable forms has occurred because the weight of tradition has required it. However, the effect of their continued use has been to continue the variation and unpredictability in heading form that is one of the most distinctive characteristics of dictionary subject cataloging today.

A second major area of change in a century of dictionary subject catalog development—one that rivals the shift in subject referent in its importance—has been the role of user considerations in subject heading work. Cutter's understanding of the public was an overarching concept that arose from a comprehensive theory of how human mental processes function. Its basic characteristic was its unity. The subjects which all users sought were elements of a single unified universe of subjects differentiated only by their relative concreteness or generality. The readers who constituted the public were divisible into levels of mental activity but formed a unity in that they all thought about subjects in the same way—in terms of the increasing levels of generality that subjects represented. The chief result of this unity was that it enabled Cutter to justify making a single subject access system for all users.

Cutter did not subsequently choose the dictionary subject catalog made according to his specifications because it was the only practicable form, however. He might have used a systematically classed or an alphabetico-classed catalog to achieve the desired results. But the state-of-the art of those catalog forms was not such that it would have served his goal of specifying each book by its most specific or concrete subject, even by means of subentry. Furthermore, he faced the practical matter that the largest number of readers were those who would most easily use a catalog which placed a premium on entry (not subentry) under the most specific (i.e., concrete) subjects which books treated. That did not mean that advanced readers had no use for such an entry system. They too looked for subjects of greater concreteness as well as for subjects of greater generality. But the subject relationships and collocation patterns, which placed concrete subjects in their proper relationships with all other subjects in the universe of knowledge and which advanced readers depended on in their searching, would be displayed only in the abbreviated form of subarrangement if Cutter's specific entry system were followed. Therefore, Cutter added to his specific entry system an infrastructure of cross-references to collocate the specific subjects otherwise entered directly in the catalog. The collocation patterns in cross-references were also rigidly controlled because they too reflected his understanding of categorical subject structure and significance order.

By beginning his entry system with the subjects at one end of a spectrum which included all subjects—that is, with the most specific or concrete subjects that books represented—and relating all other subjects of greater generality to that specific or relatively concrete starting point, Cutter in effect coordinated the subject access needs of all users in a single cohesive system. He was able to do this because he ultimately saw the world of subjects which various levels of readers sought and the patterns in how they sought those subjects as complementary, not contradictory. He was able to proceed in this way because, in terms of a modern analogy, he concluded that all readers played in the same ball game by the same set of rules.

With Hanson and his contemporaries at the turn of the century, the unity on which Cutter based user considerations became fractured. Users came to be divided into two distinctly different groups: scholars and students, and average or general readers. The two groups of readers no longer had a common bond such as that found in Cutter's unified view of human mental activity. Thus, their subject searching patterns were no longer compatible in any practical sense. In fact, the subjects for which they searched, judged on the basis of their content rather than by their respective levels of concreteness or generality, were plainly different. Scholars and students were identified by content-related fields of knowledge. General or average readers were identified by the way they searched, that is, looking for simple subjects of relatively small extent as discrete entities unrelated to other topics.

One result of this difference in user considerations was to view subject access provisions designed for the respective groups as difficult to combine in a single system. Smaller and medium-sized public libraries, the branches of large urban libraries, and children's libraries, by consensus the chief locations of average readers, were generally thought to need simple subject catalogs which provided direct access to the simply named and not-too-minute subjects for which average readers searched. In contrast, dictionary subject catalogs made for large libraries, by consensus the chief locations of students and scholars, were to provide access to the more minute subjects with complex names that students and scholars sought. In addition, a dictionary subject catalog made for the latter group required strenuous efforts to collocate subjects in a way helpful to those who used it. Special efforts at collocation were needed because of the severe scattering that resulted from attempting to indicate the entire topical contents of books in subject headings.

J. C. M. Hanson at the Library of Congress attempted to combine both needs in one catalog, but he admittedly aimed at the advanced group. The result was a catalog that stressed scope-matching of the subjects of books regardless of the complexity in the subject naming required. It also incorporated a considerable amount of collocation, not simply by means of the cross-references Cutter had used, but by introducing collocation devices in subject heading formats themselves. Other writers such as Theresa Hitchler and those responsible for compiling the third edition of the A.L.A. *List* aimed their work at the average reader. Because subject catalogers by the first decade of the century were already becoming dependent on subject heading copy and lists to do their work, however, and because subject heading format found in those sources was already becoming significantly influenced by Library of Congress heading patterns, the headings subject catalogers used often had the flavor of a catalog made for the advanced group of readers. Their only recourse was to modify in limited ways either the headings they found in such lists or the way that such headings were assigned.

Another result of the difference between the two groups of readers was a growing conviction that subject heading format and specificity had to be tailored to the thinking patterns of those who searched for subjects. Hanson expressed this idea in part by his insistence that collocation could best be achieved on the basis of fields of knowledge. Public librarians such as Hitchler and especially Esther Crawford expressed the same conviction about choices and forms of headings in relation to average readers. The division of all readers into only two groups did not prove to be a very helpful basis on which to make such choices, however. Thus, by the 1920s the idea of making subject heading choices and formats responsive to readers came to be based on the type of library readers frequented. On that basis, it was concluded that public libraries needed one set of headings, college libraries another, children's libraries still another, and special libraries yet others.

By mid-century, the assumption that user considerations were necessarily an intimate part of subject cataloging thought and method had become firmly entrenched in dictionary subject catalog work. But by then the character of user considerations had changed in even more significant ways. First, efforts to differentiate users by types of libraries were eventually abandoned in favor of two basic categories of users —specialists, including scholars of all sorts whether they frequented special libraries or other more general libraries which supported research, and nonspecialists or general readers. The two categories are plainly reminiscent of the twofold categorization of readers at the turn of the century. But they differed in that the discontinuity that characterized earlier thinking had become a chasm during the later period. The two types of users were now considered essentially different in what they sought as well as how they searched. The source of this definitive separation was doubtless the rise of academic, industrial, and governmental research in which users had information needs deemed so technical and specialized as to put them in a world of their own in terms of subject access requirements. Regardless of the source, however, the result was to make it appear impossible to devise a subject access system to serve both kinds of readers at the same time. To extend an analogy used earlier, the two kinds of readers no longer even played in the same ball game let alone used the same rules.

This interpretation of user considerations also led to the growing identification of the dictionary subject catalog with nonspecialists. The needs of specialists were viewed as so rarefied as to preclude the possibility that the dictionary subject catalog could be useful. One reason for this conclusion was the confused state that dictionary subject cataloging entry procedures and format had arrived at by mid-century. Specialists, it was judged, simply needed more order and specificity than dictionary subject catalog practice provided. Another reason for the conclusion was that even if dictionary subject catalogs could provide a consistent level of specificity, the idea of scope-matching no longer met the needs of specialists now viewed as operating on the level of "micro-thought" rather than the "macro-thought" associated with the subjects of entire documents. Still another reason for the conclusion was that the dictionary subject catalog had been used by "general" libraries for so many decades that it had simply become identified with the needs of nonspecialists rather than specialists. The irony of this conclusion was that the true nature of Hanson's innovations at the beginning of the century had been to design a hybrid catalog particularly useful to scholars and students. That by the 1950s it should be considered by some as little more than a modified catchword index can be accounted for only as a quirk of history involving the loss of corporate memory.

One result of the identification of the dictionary subject catalog with general readers was to provide some of the motivation for the spate of alternative subject access systems developed since the 1950s. Another was to place the dictionary subject catalog in a seemingly permanent position of inferiority, a limbo that no number of reforms instituted since the 1940s by the Library of Congress, the acknowledged leader in promoting that catalog type, has been able to overcome. The chief reason for this failure may well be the third characteristic that the idea of user considerations had gained by the 1950s, that is, its pervasive quality. It is true that previous writers had described the ideal of making subject heading choices and formats responsive to user considerations. But their comments tended to be only of the most general kind. In the hands of David J. Haykin, however, user considerations (the reader as the focus) were made fundamental to all other subject cataloging decisions, thereby gaining the status of being the preeminent operating principle in subject heading work. Haykin saw the subject cataloger's task as one of identifying the dominant or target group a library served, assessing the psychological patterns that that group followed in searching for subjects, and thereafter making not simply general decisions on the basis of the knowledge gained but heading-by-heading choices. That this was an acceptable interpretation of the role of user considerations was borne out by its acceptance in the subject cataloging community at large. In fact, no less an authority than Cutter himself, especially in his words about the convenience of the reader, was invoked in support of the interpretation.

The difficulties of this use of the idea of user considerations have not gone unnoticed, however. For example, Haykin gave no indication of how a dominant user group was to be identified and admitted that hard data on which to base subject heading decisions was not readily available. What he really appealed to as the basis for decision making were traditional ideas that subject catalogers had had about users over many years. Even were such data available, however, the usefulness of the idea for particular libraries was extremely limited given their commitment to follow Library of Congress choices. Applying user considerations to the local library subject cataloging situation plainly contradicts the need for centralized subject cataloging. Finally, while the idea of user considerations might seem theoretically justifiable, its use has often been only a rationalization of past, often inconsistent decisions or present ad hoc policies. These difficulties suggest that ultimately the ideal of making heading choices responsive to the needs of users is really only a principle that may be invoked by the Library of Congress itself, given its central position as a source of subject cataloging copy, and that at best it plays the role of a principle that really is not a principle, but rather the absence of principles.

With the latter issue, it is plain that dictionary subject cataloging has arrived at a point exactly opposite from where it began with Cutter a century earlier. Cutter had stated in a prefatory note to his subject rules on entry:

> If there is no obvious principle to guide the cataloger, it is plain there will be no reason why the public should expect to find the entry under one heading rather than another, and therefore in regard to the public it matters not which is chosen. But it is better that such decisions should be made to conform when possible to some general system, as there is then more likelihood that they will be decided alike by different catalogers, and that a usage will grow up which the public will finally learn and profit by, as a usage has grown up in regard to the author entry of French names containing De, Du, La, etc.[1]

Cutter's initial words about the lack of an obvious principle to guide the cataloger is one of the most apt descriptions of present-day dictionary subject cataloging ever made, even though they are one hundred years old. The entry process in contemporary subject heading work, in which one confronts the question of what a subject heading should indicate, is notably erratic. Although that process begins with the general assumption that scope-matching the topical contents of works is its goal, the principle is never explained in an obvious way, and it is regularly subverted by the use of entry under non-scope-match headings rationalized in a variety of ways.

Entry form in contemporary subject heading work, in which one confronts the question of how a subject heading should be written, suffers even more severely. One finds a large substratum of conventional subject names. But many of these have been manipulated, especially by inversion, for the sake of achieving collocation. And to these have been added an equally large number of heading-subheading combinations in the form of strings-of-terms, the clear purpose of which is to provide an alternative method of scope-matching when conventional subject names are not available or desirable. The most notable aspect of the resulting mixture of heading forms is that their use is ultimately highly unpredictable and, within certain limits, even contradictory.

Finally, the cross-reference structure of contemporary dictionary subject catalogs, in which one confronts the question of how subjects should be related, also suffers the same sort of erratic appearance. It reflects and perpetuates the highly variable approach to classificatory order begun by Hanson eighty years ago. Thus, the cross-references and the use of collocation by heading structure, with which cross-references in a sense compete, are of dubious systematic value.

Cutter was convinced that the lack of an obvious principle on which to base entry and format choices (and the collocation system as well because it reflected his entry system) would make the resulting subject system superfluous for users as far as its predictive value was concerned. The user would not be able to develop search strategies on the basis of regular patterns of entry and heading format. In the present situation that result is even more forbidding. Its lack of predictability is a problem not only for users, but also for librarians who either use it on behalf of readers or who must attempt to teach its use. In fact, the lack of predictability makes the dictionary subject catalog as presently practiced essentially unteachable and nearly unlearnable. It can be learned, of course, but the effort required is like that of the wise old fisherman who has learned after years of effort when to fish, where to fish, and how to fish in order to get reasonable results some of the time. The problem is, what librarian, reader, or even subject cataloger, having the necessary measure of tenacity, will invest that kind of effort, especially when the explanations of the tool are generally so inadequate and the time necessary to do so is so constrained by other needs?

In contrast to the above situation, Cutter suggested that the decisions required to build a dictionary subject catalog "conform when possible to some general system." Given Cutter's generally ironic writing style, the phrase "when possible" should not be taken to mean that he thought the task not really possible or even hardly possible. Quite to the contrary, the foregoing commentary on his work suggests that he considered the task much more possible than not. He was able to do so because behind his dictionary subject catalog was an essentially rational view of subjects and users that, when made the basis of the catalog, would yield a highly rational system. More importantly, he believed that the rational nature of the resulting system would ultimately appeal to and shape the nature of its use.

This belief represents an essential difference between his day and the present. The chief justification for the basically erratic and nonsystematic nature of the dictionary subject catalog in the present day is that it follows a basically unsystematic public. Extended logically, this means that the public's catalog is nonsystematic because the public is nonsystematic, or worse, that the public catalog is irrational because it reflects an irrational public. On that basis, no cataloger who wished to serve the public by making a catalog reflecting the public's thinking could make a rational system. And any who claimed to have done so would be considered deluded. No one really believes such a train of thought, however. In fact, should this sort of thinking be true, then millenia of educational endeavors have been only delusions. Furthermore, not even the present-day dictionary subject catalog really follows that logic. Its erratic character has arisen not from following a singularly nonsystematic public, but rather from following a variety of systematizations and rationalizations that are often in conflict with one another and that have arisen from decades of decisions made without a fully explained master plan. It likely serves as well as it does because its kaleidoscopic nature ensures at least as much success as failure over the long run. That being its strength, there may be good reason not to tamper with it too much. Another generation or two certainly cannot alter its effectiveness either negatively or positively to any great degree by still more layers of rationalizations. And when the immense economic aspects of change and the vague hope that the sheer brute force of computer technology will overcome any structural problems are also considered, there appears to be good reason to leave the matter as it is. The dictionary subject catalog as presently made will simply continue to help some while hindering others, showing its rational face at one time and its irrational at another. Given that approach, questions concerning if, when, or how it might ultimately break down under its own weight are really beside the point.

If, on the other hand, a change is desirable, an understanding of its past development suggests that at a minimum the following issues must be faced in one form or another. To begin with, it is the opinion here that the role of user considerations, at least in the way they are presently conceived and applied, must be allowed to die an honorable death. The most critical aspect of this matter needing reform is the notion that user considerations provide a reasonable basis for making heading-by-heading decisions (or even groups-of-headings-by-groups-of-headings decisions) related to extent of specification or heading formats. Outside of a continual and massive data gathering effort that in some magical way could assess how people actually frame their subject searching thoughts, there is simply no basis for that kind of rationalization. Even should such an effort be conducted, the results, as Esther Crawford found as early as 1907, would be filled with pitfalls in instrumentation and would be of highly dubious value. Furthermore, the appeal to user considerations in that ideal sense has never really been accomplished. Instead, such decisions have really been made on the basis of the prejudices and ideas of librarians, these masquerading under the name of their experience. At best the only aspect of subject heading work that might benefit from carefully drawn user surveys is that involving choices between natural language synonyms where some terms imply a prejudicial point of view or where terms are obviously limited in their technical connotations to a relatively small proportion of the entire public.

Another current aspect of user considerations needing serious review involves the division of the public into two fundamentally different groups, general users and specialists. The use of this kind of thinking as a basis for entry and format choices is questionable for no other reason than the dubious character of the idea of the general reader. All things being equal, there is no such being as a general user insofar as that category constitutes little more than the absence of those qualities attributed to specialists. Seen in that way, the idea of a general user has no predictive value of any merit. Even if there are such beings as general users, however, the connotations implicit in their definition as a category—that is, either the lack of any reasonable amount of intellect or skill in the use of language or the lack of any familiarity with a particular subject area—suggests that they would constitute a nonproductive basis on which to make cataloging decisions.

A more seemingly accurate and useful way to describe catalog users is to view all users as exhibiting specialist tendencies of one sort or another, some highly developed, others hardly developed at all. All specialists are related to the general communities of persons who find an interest in a particular subject area and thus use the literature related to that area. This is the case regardless of whether such general communities of interest are highly formalized in their structure, entrance requirements, and participation (as in academic or technical fields of research) or are highly informal in the same matters (as in such fields as model railroading, needlepoint, home auto repairs, and the like). The only real differences between one catalog user and another lies in the natural technical terms (i.e., the jargon) that they use because of their participation in one or another specialist community and in the precision with which they frame their inquiries. Viewed in this way, the public is a cohesive entity in the same way (but not on the same basis) that Cutter viewed it. And it is that public and the specialist communities the public represents for whom catalogs and particularly their entry and format choices are or should be made.

If both of the foregoing aspects of user considerations are discountenanced or revised in the manner indicated, the way would be free to meet other important structural and procedural requirements of the dictionary subject catalog on different, hopefully more systematic bases. The first of these other requirements is the nature of the entry process itself. It is imperative that a useful and reasonably unequivocal meaning be given to what a subject should indicate— that is, to its specification goal. Cutter originally used the term "specific entry" to mean just such a specification goal although he did so on the basis of a measure that is no longer meaningful. But since his time, a change in subject referent has made both stating and following a specification goal a matter of great confusion. The chief difficulty has not been the total lack of a goal. There has been at least a tacit emphasis on scope-matching over that period. Rather, it has been that neither an explicit statement of that meaning nor an explanation of the particular conditions under which it should not be met has ever been made. This has left the process of specification open to wide variation, sometimes because of the limitations of the vocabulary available to meet the goal and at other times because of less than explicit appeals to supposed user needs. None of this suggests that determining an appropriate specification goal will be an easy matter. Specifying "the subject" of a document is open to question, for instance, because the idea of "the subject" of a book is itself a fuzzy notion. Even should one conclude that documents do have properties called subjects, the very individuality of the subjects, like the individuality of humans, leads to the absurd situation of the subjects of no two books being exactly alike. Therefore, all documents would theoretically end up in single document classes. Still, the idea that a document has a cohesive subject is of considerable operational merit at least in a great many situations.

If scope-matching is used as the specification goal, one need is that the literary unit underlying it be noted (and perhaps encoded in automated systems) in such a way as to give an indication of what is being specified. A second need is to make it possible to use redundant multiple entry when and where merited. Marcia Bates suggested that present Library of Congress subject headings are non-redundant, representative of essentially one-place subject indication.[2] While her statement is not entirely accurate in particular cases, it is true as a general description of the system, and as such meets the traditional economies of manual subject card catalogs. The day of such stringent economies is long over, however, not only in machine systems, but also to a limited extent in manual systems as well. A third need in a system specifying the entire topical contents of documents (or of other allowable literary units) is for explicit instructions about nonredundant multiple entry. This would recognize the existence of documents which have more than one subject although only a single literary unit, as in a book on dogs and cats or one on painting and sculpturing. Fourth, there is a need for a capacity to truncate specification under stated conditions. Catalog use is, after all, also affected by file length as well as by how completely subject headings describe or otherwise indicate subject content. Thus, it is imperative that such truncation be provided for, although on a systematic basis. A regularized procedure for truncating, perhaps not unlike the use of apostrophes in decimal classification copy, might be formulated. However, the systematization of such a procedure would depend on the next consideration, the requirements for a regularized approach to vocabulary.

A second general requirement to be met in a dictionary subject catalog freed from untenable user considerations is for a regularized approach to vocabulary. At the head of the list of issues in this area is the need to address the priority that has historically been given to the use of conventional subject names, especially in the form of complex subject descriptions. There can be little question that conventional subject names have validity in a great many cases. The chief difficulty in their use is to determine where that validity ends and speculation based on the simple desire to produce headings which look like conventional subject names begins. What is certain is that no demonstrable basis for supposing that names constructed on the principle of using natural language "as naturally as possible" produced headings any more justified or even useful to the public than headings formally structured on some other principle.[3] Another difficulty with the use of conventional subject names is the denial of their use even when available either because of the desire to follow past patterns involving strings-of-terms or because of the failure to look seriously for such names. One solution to their use would be to set up rigid requirements for their establishment, related, for example, to the number of documents in which they appear. Another solution would be to forego their initial use altogether in favor of a systematically structured vocabulary of the sort found in string indexing systems.

Another aspect of making a regularized vocabulary is to provide some means for a systematic citation order of the components of headings, not simply for individual types of headings as is now done, but in an overall sense on the basis of categories into which words might be systematically placed. This one innovation alone would appear to be the single most useful way to improve the predictive value of subject heading form. It is one that Cutter followed, and it is the basis of all modern structured vocabulary systems. A final aspect of making a regularized vocabulary is the basis of choice between equivalent terms. Of special merit in this respect is the need to follow what has already been alluded to, that language preferences be based on the fields to which topics belong rather than on the basis of supposed levels of intelligence of readers, especially of the fictitious general reader. An interface with other terms, such as those that arise in popular treatments and those that amount to little more than slang, might then be restricted to an equivalent term reference structure. In this way, the catalog might more usefully follow the needs of specialists—that is, of the specialist aspects of all readers' searching—as its basic point of vocabulary preference.

The third and last major requirement to be faced in a dictionary subject catalog freed from untenable user considerations is for a regularized approach to subject collocation. At present, subject collocation is accomplished in two competing ways: by the use of heading format such as inversion or the construction of strings-of-terms sequences, and by the use of "see also" cross-references. One difficulty with this approach, besides that of determining which method should be followed in individual cases, is the mixture of purposes that attends heading format decisions. One must decide without any sure guidelines not only what kind of heading to use—that is, conventional subject names or strings-of-terms—but also whether a conventional subject name or an element of a string-of-terms is a likely candidate for collocation needs and thus manipulation through inversion. Another difficulty is that the long-held conviction that a conventional subject name remains a conventional subject name even though inverted is actually a supercilious distinction. An inverted heading is no more a conventional subject name than is a string-of-terms heading. This conclusion is supported by the growing consensus of practice to interfile all such terms regardless of their structure. Consequently, inverted headings function as strings-of-terms regardless of their format. Still another difficulty in the present approach to collocation is the absence of precision in denoting relationships that are involved. It is obvious, for example, that the term "see also" is capable of many meanings and that the lack of a more specific way of differentiating those meanings detracts from its usefulness.

One way to accommodate the need for collocation without violating the process of making heading format decisions is to restrict it to cross-references, preferably removed entirely from the catalog and made available in the form of a thesaurus which would become part of a necessary presearch strategy for all serious catalog consultation. That a separate search through a vocabulary list is viable and necessary seems to be recognized in part by the practice now common in many libraries of placing the subject heading list on which the catalog is based in some prominent place near the catalog, even though it is questionable whether such lists are all that useful in the way they are presently constructed. The need for a thesaurus showing term relationships, even if only in the form of a terminal display, is also a standard part of the procedure of consulting an automated data base. It seems in this respect that no less should be provided for the dictionary subject catalog as well.

The use of the kinds of alternatives suggested here constitute only one approach to changing what now exists. Others would require steps no less complex. A change made on any such bases, especially those outlined here, will obviously produce a catalog different than the dictionary subject catalog as it is now found. Certainly, it will result in a catalog unlike the unsystematic dictionary subject catalog now produced. It will be tempting to think of any proposed change as a move altogether away from Cutter's idea of a specific entry catalog. But that is a fallacious conclusion. Cutter's idea of a specific entry dictionary subject catalog has not been followed for decades. In fact, it would be advisable to discontinue the use of the phrase "specific entry" altogether because its meaning, having changed so decisively over the years, causes more confusion than it is worth. Furthermore, one might reasonably suppose that were Cutter present today, he would indeed applaud such a change, given his belief in the necessity of making a catalog on a systematic basis.

More importantly, others might argue that the proposed changes would spell the end of the dictionary subject catalog made with the reader in mind, especially the general user, when making particular decisions. But this is certainly an unfounded argument since it is difficult at best to demonstrate that such choices have ever been made with any hard data about users. Furthermore, there are good reasons why appreciable benefits may be expected from such a change. First, there seems to be at least some evidence that catalog use is shaped by and follows catalog practice; thus, users will adapt to what is provided just as they have adapted to the present hybrid catalog. Cutter observed this factor in his words quoted earlier in this chapter. And the more recent study of catalog use conducted by Marcia Bates also suggested that success in catalog subject searching is especially affected by familiarity with the catalog, not because it was prestructured on some basis or another.[4] If this factor is true, and there seems little reason to doubt it, then users will at least not be hindered by a more systematically structured catalog and, given a familiarity with it that would be based on its greater predictability, their use of it stands a good chance of being enhanced. Second, even if the success rate in readers' searching is not improved in particular cases, the fact that the nature and patterns of a more systematically structured dictionary subject catalog could be taught with some facility would certainly help those who are in a position to learn, especially librarians. Third, a systematically structured dictionary subject catalog cannot help but be an aid in automated systems if for no other reason than the savings it would provide in more regularized programming and in computation time. Fourth, it seems appropriate, at least to this writer, that the time has come to take seriously the professional nature of subject information systems engineering. In few, if any, other professions does one find the participants in the profession shaping their services and tools in such a way as to make them amenable to use by nonprofessionals. In the same way, a subject information system, including a dictionary subject catalog, should be as complex and structured as is needed to accomplish the objectives deemed necessary to it. If it is necessary for nonprofessionals to use such systems, that may be accomplished by creative approaches to instruction, especially the use of automatic tutorials built into occasions of use. None of this denies the fact, of course, that any change would be costly, both in terms of the dollar amounts needed and in terms of the flurry caused by still another round of discussions related to catalog closings and the like. But a decisive and well-reasoned change has a very good chance of making such costs and struggles well worth the effort.

Notes

PREFACE

1. Thomas Reid, *Essays on the Intellectual Powers of Man* (Cambridge, Mass.: M.I.T. Press, 1969), pp. 463–531.

2. Patrick Wilson, *Two Kinds Of Power: An Essay on Bibliographical Control*, University of California Publications; Librarianship: 5 (Berkeley: University of California Press, 1968), especially chapter 5, "Subjects and the Sense of Position."

3. Charles A. Cutter, *Rules for a Dictionary Catalog*, 4th ed., U.S. Bureau of Education, *Special Report on Public Libraries*, Part II (Washington: U.S. Government Printing Office, 1904). Hereafter cited as *RDC*. The first edition (1876) had the title *Rules for a Printed Dictionary Catalogue*. The second (1889) and third (1891) editions had the title *Rules for a Dictionary Catalogue*. Citations to particular rules and to their discussions, besides using page numbers, will include rule numbers and reference to the discussion itself if that is the source. For example, *RDC*, R161, p. 66, means *Rules*, 4th ed., rule 161 itself; *RDC*, R161, disc., p. 66, refers to Cutter's discussion appended to the rule.

CHAPTER 1. STATEMENT OF THE PROBLEM

1. *RDC*, "Preface to the Fourth Edition," p. 5.

2. David J. Haykin, "Cooperative Cataloging in North America—Problems and Possibilities," *Cataloging and Classification Yearbook* 6 (1937): 30.

3. George Scheerer, "The Subject Catalog Examined," *Library Quarterly* 27 (July 1957): 192.

4. Paul Dunkin, *Cataloging U.S.A.* (Chicago: American Library Association, 1969), p. 9.

5. Carlyle J. Frarey, "Subject Headings," in *The State of the Library Art*, ed. Ralph R. Shaw, vol. 1, part 2 (New Brunswick, N.J.: Graduate School of Library Service, Rutgers, The State University, 1960), especially pp. 63–67.

6. Mary Dykstra, "The Lion That Squeaked," *Library Journal* 103 (September 1, 1978): 1572.

7. John W. Metcalfe has drawn the lines between the two groups in the form of his historical survey, *Information Retrieval, British and American,*

1876–1976 (Metuchen, N.J.: Scarecrow Press, 1976). For the purposes of this work, the most notable persons in the first group include E. J. Coates and S. R. Ranganathan. Those of the second group include Richard Angell, James C. M. Hanson, David J. Haykin, Paul S. Dunkin, Margaret Mann, John W. Metcalfe, and Julia Pettee.

8. Margaret Mann, *Introduction to Cataloging and the Classification of Books* (Chicago: American Library Association, 1930), p. 177. Mann repeated the statement in the second edition of her work (Chicago: A.L.A. 1943), p. 143, the only substantive change being that the entry should be under "the most specific subject heading *available* (emphasis added). This definition did not appear at all in her 1928 preliminary edition, *The Classification and Cataloging [sic] of Books,* mimeographed preliminary ed. (Chicago: American Library Association, 1928), p. 180.

9. Various words, such as subject, topic, and theme, are commonly used in an interchangeable way to refer to what Wilson, *Two Kinds of Power,* especially pp. 69–77 and notes 17–18, conveniently calls the "aboutness" of a work. Cutter, in *RDC,* Definitions, "Subject," p. 23, defines the term subject "as the theme or themes of the book, whether stated in the title or not." Such words will be used interchangeably here as well, although "topical content" and "entire topical content" turn up more than any other terms. Nevertheless, as Wilson notes, the idea of "the subject" of a book is a very difficult one. To this might be added that the difficulty of the idea is further complicated by our own understanding of how a subject heading or subject name is said to relate to a subject. On the one hand, one might suppose that subject and subject heading are synonymous, or at least, nearly so; that when one speaks of the subject of a book, what is meant is no more nor less than the words used to name the subject. In this view, subjects are only words. This conclusion might well be arrived at for no other reason than the fact that it is impossible to speak of any particular subject without naming it. Even a notation has no meaning unless it is converted to words. Julia Pettee, in "A New Principle in Dealing with Subject Matter Needed?" *Journal of Cataloging and Classification* 10 (January 1954): 17–18, seems to come close to this equation in her insistence that subject headings are in the end only words called names and a subject cataloger is primarily an analyst of how people use those naming words. On the other hand, most writers, and perhaps common sense as well, seem to assume that subject headings refer to some thing besides themselves. Therefore, they are to be considered independent of what they indicate. The "what" in the phrase "what they indicate" refers to a subject. The very idea that a subject heading could be called a "summarization" as in E. J. Coates, *Subject Catalogues, Headings and Structure* (London: The Library Association, 1960, 1969 printing), p. 17, "a succinct abstract" as in *Sears' List of Subject Headings,* 11th ed., ed. Barbara M. Westby (New York: H. W. Wilson Co., 1977), p. xii, or a "distillation," as suggested by students in the advanced cataloging class at the Louisiana State University, School of Library and Information Science, of "the subject" of a work, suggests not only that the two things are different but that the relationship between them is one of lesser to greater. A subject heading repre-

sents the subject of a work in some lesser, more cryptic way. Or, alternatively, the relationship may be explained by calling it symbolic. Jay E. Daily, in "Subject Headings and the Theory of Classification," *American Documentation* 8 (October 1957): 272, suggests that a subject heading or a subject classification notation is no more than a symbol that simply represents a class of things. As such, a symbol should not only not be confused with what it represents, but should be seen for what it is, a completely arbitrary thing, the meaning of which is set by tacit or sometimes formal agreements among people. Phyllis A. Richmond, in "Cats: An Example of Concealed Classification in Subject Headings," *Library Resources and Technical Services* 3 (Spring 1959): 109, perhaps reflecting on the implications of Pettee's statement noted above, differentiates between subject and subject heading by calling the first an "idea" and the second only "words." Furthermore, she suggests that to not make such a distinction "leads to ludicrous as well as dangerous errors." In sum, most writers differentiate between subjects and subject headings (or subject terms). That differentiation will be assumed here as well, mainly because the writings of subject catalogers could not easily be discussed from any other viewpoint.

10. E. J. Coates, in "Alphabetical Subject Catalogues," review of *Subject Headings, a Practical Guide,* by David J. Haykin, *Journal of Documentation* 9 (March 1953): 62, following the ideas of S. R. Ranganathan, was perhaps one of the first to suggest that "coextensive" be used to describe the scope-match relationship that is described here as fundamental to contemporary dictionary subject cataloging. While the term has found increasing acceptance over the years and, more recently, in Lois M. Chan, *Library of Congress Subject Headings: Principles and Application,* Research Studies in Library Science, no. 15 (Littleton, Colo.: Libraries Unlimited, 1978), p. 36, and elsewhere, where she has used it to describe the specificity goals of Library of Congress subject cataloging, its use has not been universal, especially among writers on dictionary subject cataloging. For example, Richard S. Angell, "Library of Congress Subject Headings—Review and Forecast," in *Subject Retrieval in the Seventies: New Directions,* ed. H. Wellisch and T. D. Wilson (Westport, Conn.: Greenwood Publishing Company, 1972), p. 150, suggested only that the word "expressive" be used for the term "specificity." This may owe to the fact that having arisen from rigorous classification procedure, and used most often in classification oriented indexing, the term "coextensive" has acquired other connotations that do not apply to specific subject heading practice. The most notable of these connotations has been the assumption that a document is not specified adequately unless a single string-of-terms has been provided that scope-match it. This has been called item-specification. For a highly useful summary of this, as well as of all the various meanings of specificity that have grown up over the years, see John Balnaves, "Specificity," in *The Variety of Librarianship: Essays in Honour of John Wallace Metcalfe,* ed. W. Boyd Rayward (Sydney: Library Association of Australia, 1976), pp. 47–56. For the reasons given here, "coextensivity" will not be used in the present work.

11. This second step is actually included in the diagram in Figure 1. The

idea of scope-matching infers it. The emphasis here is on fitting the subject term formally into the vocabulary of the subject heading system.

12. The example is taken from David J. Haykin, *Subject Headings, A Practical Guide* (Washington, D.C.: U.S. Government Printing Office, 1951), p. 3.

13. The examples here are taken from *RDC*, headnote to "B. Entries Considered as Parts of a Whole," p. 79.

14. The first example is from Anthony C. Foskett, *The Subject Approach to Information*, 3rd ed. (Hamden, Conn.: Linnet Books, 1977), pp. 73, 84–86. The second is from Boston Athenaeum, *Catalogue of the Library of the Boston Athenaeum*, [ed. C. A. Cutter], 5 vols. (Boston: The Athenaeum, 1874–82), 1:444, a work by W. Falconer entered under CALCULUS *(in Medicine)*.

15. Foskett, who follows Coates in the matter, punctuated the string-of-terms only with commas.

16. *RDC*, R161, and disc., pp. 66–67.

17. *RDC*, R161, disc., p. 67.

18. *RDC*, R164–65, and disc., pp. 68–69.

19. More complete specification of this work in Cutter's system might be achieved through the subarrangement of entries under NEW ENGLAND, specifically by labeling all works on ornithology by the subheading –ORNITHOLOGY. But doing so was in Cutter's opinion a function only of file length. Therefore, directions for doing so are not included here but rather are given in R340, p. 123, where arrangement of subject entries is discussed. Even there, however, the subarrangement is only suggested and, at that, only when the entire file of NEW ENGLAND entries totalled enough to enable the cataloger to break it up into smaller sections of between twelve and twenty entries each. Furthermore, even should the NEW ENGLAND file contain enough entries to merit its subarrangement, this does not ensure that –ORNITHOLOGY will be the first or most appropriate subheading to employ.

20. *RDC*, R165, disc., p. 68.

21. *RDC*, R175, disc., p. 75.

22. Coates, *Subject Catalogues*, p. 32.

23. Ibid., p. 33.

24. Coates, "Alphabetical Subject Catalogues," p. 62.

25. John W. Metcalfe, *Information Indexing and Subject Cataloguing: Alphabetical-Classified, Coordinate-Mechanical* (New York: Scarecrow Press, 1957), p. 28 and passim.

26. *RDC*, R161, disc., p. 67.

27. Dunkin, *Cataloging U.S.A.*, pp. 71–73.

28. *RDC*, R175, disc., p. 74, and R176, disc., p. 76, respectively.

29. See, for example, the long lists of entries under United States and Great Britain in the Boston Athenaeum, *Catalogue*.

30. *RDC*, R340–43 and their respective discussions.

31. Cutter did not discuss the technical difference between classed subdivision and subarrangement by "aspect" as Metcalfe does in *Information Indexing and Subject Cataloguing*, and in *Subject Classifying and Indexing of Libraries and Literature* (New York: Scarecrow Press, 1959), especially

pp. 273–78 under the title "Subject Specification and Qualification." His ideas are reiterated by R. K. Olding, "Form of Alphabetico-specific Subject Headings and a Brief Code," *Australian Library Journal* 10 (July 1961): 127–37, and discussed critically in Elaine Svenonius, "Metcalfe and the Principles of Specific Entry," in *The Variety of Librarianship: Essays in Honour of John Wallace Metcalfe*, ed. W. Boyd Rayward (Sydney: Library Association of Australia, 1976), pp. 171–77. Cutter did imply the difference, but one must piece together several of his comments to see it. That piecing together forms the main content of chapters 2–6 ahead.

32. *RDC*, introductory paragraph to "2. Choice Between Different Names," p. 69.

33. *RDC*, "Preface to the Fourth Edition," p. 6.

34. *RDC*, R169a, p. 70.

35. *RDC*, R175, disc., p. 74.

36. *RDC*, R175, p. 72.

37. *RDC*, R175, disc., p. 74.

38. *RDC*, R169a–e, p. 70.

39. *RDC*, R169, disc., p. 70.

40. *RDC*, R175, p. 72.

41. *RDC*, R175, disc., p. 75.

42. Coates, *Subject Catalogues*, p. 35.

43. *RDC*, headnote to "B. Entries Considered as Parts of a Whole," and R187–88, pp. 79–80.

44. The original study was my "Charles Ammi Cutter: Nineteenth Century Systematizer of Libraries," (Ph.D. dissertation, University of Chicago, 1974). It was supplemented by later findings related to the place of Scottish common sense philosophy in Cutter's thinking, the latter included in the introductory chapter of Cutter, *Charles Ammi Cutter: Library Systematizer*, ed. F. Miksa, The Heritage of Librarianship Series, no. 3 (Littleton, Colo.: Libraries Unlimited, 1977).

45. *RDC*, headnote to "A. Entries Considered Separately," p. 66, at the beginning of his subject cataloging rules.

46. Cutter conceived of most of the basic features of his subject access work in both subject cataloging and classification during the 1870s, a period during which he advanced from his thirty-third to his forty-third years, and in which he enjoyed his greatest personal success both at the Boston Athenaeum and among his colleagues in the newly formed American Library Association.

47. Julia Pettee included a single historical chapter in *Subject Headings: The History and Theory of the Alphabetical Subject Approach to Books* (New York: H. W. Wilson, 1946), pp. 22–52. But it essentially stopped at the beginning of the twentieth century. Metcalfe, *Information Retrieval*, pp. 89–107, went one step further by including a brief survey of Library of Congress practices after Cutter, summarizing their relationship in the phrase, "the subject cataloging that was Cutter and became Library of Congress" (p. 105). However, most of his comments about Library of Congress subject cataloging are restricted to the period since the 1940s and to the work of D. J. Haykin. Metcalfe has come as close as anyone in observing that there are

distinct differences between Cutter's work and the work of those who followed him. His analysis of Cutter is relatively extensive when all of his various works are compiled. But it is nonetheless limited because the sources of Cutter's thinking remained hidden to him. Furthermore, the overall influence of Metcalfe's various works on subject cataloging development has been somewhat limited because of a difficulty in his style that makes reading many of them a trying experience. British writers such as Coates, *Subject Catalogues,* and Foskett, *Subject Approach to Information,* have treatments notable for the way they assume Cutter and Library of Congress practice to be for all practical purposes the same. Dunkin, *Cataloging U.S.A.,* and Leonard Jolley, *The Principles of Cataloguing* (New York: Philosophical Library, 1961) ch. 5, pp. 98–125, make even fewer distinctions between the two. Finally, Carlyle Frarey was at one time working on a historical analysis of subject heading work for a D.L.S. at Columbia University that might have offered light on the matter (Frarey, "Subject Headings," p. 8 and endnote 9). Unfortunately, this was never completed.

48. S. R. Ranganathan, *Theory of Library Catalogue,* Madras Library Association Publication Series, no. 7 (London: Edward Goldston, 1938), passim, especially pp. 78–99. Ranganathan coupled Cutter with Margaret Mann's then recently published textbook, *Introduction to Cataloging and the Classification of Books* and treated them together.

49. British writers committed to analytico-synthetic classification as the proper approach to subject access have, following the lead of Ranganathan, been most representative of the scapegoat approach to dictionary subject cataloging. Their treatments have ranged in tone from the scholarly treatment offered by Coates in his *Subject Catalogues* to the cute myth offered by D. Batty in "Christopher Robin: Animadversions on American Cataloguing and Indexing." *Catalogue & Index,* no. 14 (April 1969): 4–6.

CHAPTER 2. SUBJECTS AS SUBJECTS ALONE

1. Patrick Wilson offers some reflections on the notion of subjects in *Two Kinds of Power,* chapter 5, especially pp. 69–77. He limits himself essentially to the idea of "the subject" of a document—that is, its "aboutness." But his footnotes provide very helpful sources in the literature of philosophy for pursuing the matter further. C. L. Drake broached the topic more directly in "What Is a Subject?" *Australian Library Journal* 9 (January 1960): 34–41, where he took issue with Metcalfe's distinction between classifying subjects and classifying information about subjects. Drake's distinction between subjects as found in enumerative classification schemes and subjects as found in books is close to what is said here, although his expression of the difference was not offered primarily as a way to analyze the idea of a subject itself but rather as a way to contest Metcalfe's views presented in *Information Indexing and Subject Cataloguing,* paragraphs 539–40. Metcalfe also addressed the issue later in "When Is a Subject Not a Subject?" in *Toward a Theory of Librarianship: Papers in Honor of Jesse Hauk Shera,* ed. C. H. Rawski (Metuchen, N.J.: Scarecrow Press, 1973), pp. 303–38. But there he tended

only to show the variety of meanings attached to the term by other writers rather than to analyze it in some definitive way. A more recent treatment will be found in Ingetraut Dahlberg, "On the Theory of the Concept," in *Ordering Systems for Global Information Networks,* ed. A. Neelameghan (Bangalore: FID/CR and Sarada Ranganathan Endowment for Library Science, 1979), pp. 54–63. Although not directly on the subject of "subjects," Victor H. Yngve, "Stoic Influences in Librarianship: A Critique," *Journal of Library History* 16 (Winter 1981): 92–105, will also be found to bear on the issue.

2. *RDC,* Definitions, "Subject," p. 23.

3. *RDC,* Definitions, "Class," disc., p. 16.

4. *RDC,* R161, disc., p. 67.

5. *RDC,* Definitions, "Class," disc., p. 16.

6. *RDC,* Definitions, "Subject," disc., p. 23.

7. *RDC,* Definitions, "Class," p. 15.

8. *RDC,* Definitions, "Class," disc., pp. 16–17.

9. Ibid., p. 16.

10. *RDC,* Definitions, "Syndetic," p. 23.

11. Charles A. Cutter, "Library Catalogues," in *Public Libraries in the United States of America, their History, Condition, and Management, Special Report,* Part I (Washington: U.S. Government Printing Office, 1876), p. 564. Cutter's *Rules* were part II of the same report. The fourth edition of the *Rules* is cited here simply because that is the edition that is most readily available. The almost thirty years between the first and the fourth editions make little difference in the subject cataloging portion of the *Rules,* however since few changes of any significance were made in them. The fact is that Cutter's *Rules* and his article on "Library Catalogues" in part I of the *Special Report* must be read together to gain a proper understanding of what Cutter was getting at in subject access.

12. *RDC,* R187, disc., p. 79.

13. *RDC,* R188, p. 80.

14. Cutter, "Library Catalogues," p. 532.

15. Ibid., p. 540.

16. Cutter does not appear to consider the possibility, for example, of a null class or even of a class with only one member in it, at least not when speaking of subjects alone. On the other hand, he may well have considered these possibilities in compiling "book classes." The reason for Cutter's apparent lack of interest in a more rigorous approach to logical categories, at least from a modern point of view, may well have been the state of instruction in logic during his Harvard College years (1851–55). Logic was not taught as a philosophical discipline at that time. Rather, it was taught only as an element of rhetoric, usually by recourse to texts such as George Campbell, *The Philosophy of Rhetoric* (first published 1776) and Richard Whately, *Elements of Logic* (first published 1826). Even with the use of Whately, however, the use of logic was limited to the way it embellished public argument rather than as a discipline in and of itself. Logic was not transferred to the Harvard philosophy faculty until the 1860s, after the works of Sir William Hamilton, John Stewart Mill, George Boole, and Augustus DeMorgan had

finally taken their effect between the late 1840s and the 1850s. Afterwards, a more typical treatment of logic, including discussions of class differentia, connotation and denotation, etc., would be that found in the popular text by W. Stanley Jevons, *Lessons in Logic*. But that shift appears to have passed Cutter by. A useful survey of the type of instruction that was given at Harvard, especially during Cutter's years there, will be found in Benjamin Rand, "Philosophical Instruction in Harvard University from 1636–1906—II," *Harvard Graduates Magazine* 37 (January 1929): 188–200. Further light is shed by G. Stanley Hall, "On the History of American College Textbooks and Teaching in Logic, Ethics, Psychology and Allied Subjects," American Antiquarian Society, *Proceedings*, New Series 9 (April 1894), especially pp. 146–52; and by Elizabeth Flower and Murray G. Murphey, *A History of Philosophy in America*, 2 vols. (New York: Capricorn Books and G. P. Putnam's Sons, 1977), 1: 365–93.

17. *RDC*, Definitions, "Class," p. 17.

18. *RDC*, Definitions, "Subject," p. 23.

19. Cutter, "Library Catalogues," p. 540.

20. *RDC*, Definitions, "Class," footnote, p. 17.

21. Cutter, "Library Catalogues," p. 547.

22. *RDC*, R175, disc., p. 74.

23. Ibid.

24. Ibid., pp. 74–75.

25. The caption title for *RDC*, R164–65, p. 68, is "Choice between subject (or form) and country." Within the two rules themselves Cutter referred to the same thing as choice between "the local and the scientific subject," between "country and scientific subject" and between "general subject" and "place." They all functioned as synonyms, however, for general subjects on the one hand and individual subjects in the form of places on the other.

26. *RDC*, R165, disc., p. 68.

27. *RDC*, R175, disc., p. 75.

28. Ibid.

29. Ibid., p. 74.

30. *RDC*, Definitions, "Class," footnote, p. 17.

31. A more complete discussion of the influence of this philosophical movement in America and, especially, of its role in Cutter's total work as well as a useful list of sources may be found in Cutter, *Charles Ammi Cutter: Library Systematizer*, pp. 29–43, 66–69. Two other works especially useful for understanding the philosophical ideas of the movement are Flower and Murphey, *A History of Philosophy in America*, vol. 1, pp. 203–393, and Bruce Kuklick, *The Rise of American Philosophy; Cambridge, Massachusetts, 1860–1930* (New Haven: Yale University Press, 1977), pp. 5–45. Works of particular Scottish philosophers referred to here are Thomas Reid, *Essays on the Intellectual Powers of Man*, and Dugald Stewart, *The Collected Works of Dugald Stewart*, ed. Sir William Hamilton, vols. 2–4, 6: *Elements of the Philosophy of the Human Mind*, and *Outlines of Moral Philosophy* (Edinburgh: Thomas Constable, 1854–55). The *Outlines* were first published in 1793. The *Elements* were published in 1792 (v. 1), 1814 (v. 2), and 1827 (v. 3).

32. It may also be of some interest to librarians that Scottish influence could be said to extend to the present-day library movement insofar as modern mathematical logic as first devised by George Boole was based on his adaptation of Sir William Hamilton's analysis of the syllogism.

33. Cutter's academic records in the Harvard University Archives provide information on the courses and the Scottish philosophical texts that his courses required. Besides his coursework in mental and moral philosophy, he was also exposed to Scottish thinking in his courses on rhetoric and the use of textbooks such as George Campbell's *The Philosophy of Rhetoric,* New edition (New York: Harper and Brothers, 1854). Cutter's interest in the Scottish philosophers for the period 1855 to 1868 is also reflected in the circulation records of the Harvard College Library, also in the archives. Besides the works of the Scots themselves, Cutter also borrowed various works of Theodore S. Jouffroy and Victor Cousin, French representatives of the Scottish school. His book borrowing, while not conclusive evidence of his own thinking, is significant nonetheless because some of it coincides with his work on Abbot's alphabetico-classed catalog of the college's library. When one reads the various authors cited here, especially the work of Reid, the parallels to Cutter's subject rules and, especially, to his terminology are striking.

34. A pertinent modern discourse on the perception of individuals may be found in P. F. Strawson, *Individuals, an Essay in Descriptive Metaphysics* (London: Methuen, 1959).

35. Stewart, *Outlines,* in his *Collected Works,* v. 2, p. 24.

CHAPTER 3. SUBJECTS IN RELATION TO WORKS

1. *RDC,* Definitions, "Class," disc., p. 15.

2. Ibid., pp. 15–16. Of course, more than this is normally associated with the classification of books, especially the collocation of subject document classes to form a logical system of classes. Cutter discussed these other aspects of classification under the rubrics "classifying the subject-lists to make classes," and "classifying the classes to make a systematic catalog." But "classification of books to make subject lists" (that is, making subject document classes) remained for him the most fundamental operation. E. Wyndham Hulme presented similar views at the turn of the century in a series of papers on subject cataloging and classifying, usefully summarized in Joel M. Lee, "E. Wyndham Hulme: A Reconsideration," in *The Variety of Librarianship: Essays in Honour of John Wallace Metcalfe,* ed. W. Boyd Rayward (Sydney: Library Association of Australia, 1976), pp. 101–13.

3. *RDC,* Definitions, "Class," disc., p. 16.

4. *RDC,* Definitions, "Specific Entry," p. 22.

5. *RDC,* R161, p. 66.

6. In "The New Catalogue of Harvard College Library," *North American Review* 108 (January 1869): 106, Cutter had described the entry practice of the dictionary catalog as, "Each book is put under as specific a subject as possible." He meant the same thing when he spoke of the dictionary cata-

log's "fundamental principle of putting everything under the most specific subject." (p. 110). He was attempting to describe the dictionary catalog in the only words he then had at his disposal, the terminology of classification. By 1876 he had come up with a shorthand way of indicating the same thing —that is, specific entry. Thus, in "Library Catalogues," p. 532, where he quoted the section of p. 106 from his "New Catalogue" article at length, he omitted the longer sentence description altogether. In both "Library Catalogues" and in his *Rules* where he did refer directly to the dictionary catalog's basic principle, he simply called it specific entry.

7. Cutter's use of the phrase "specific subject" covered the longest span, occurring first in his "New Catalogue" article in 1869 and as late as "Some Hints on Subject Cataloging in Dictionary Style," in A.L.A., *List of Subject Headings for Use in a Dictionary Catalog*, 2nd ed. (Boston: Published for the A.L.A. Publishing Section by the Library Bureau, 1898), pp. 197–98. (The entire list hereafter cited as A.L.A., *List* (1898)). Cutter used the term "special subject" much less frequently and, with respect to entry practice, only in the formal definition of specific entry just cited.

8. Cf. Elaine Svenonius, "Metcalfe and the Principles of Specific Entry," p. 172. Following Metcalfe, Svenonius points out both the centrality and the perplexing nature of the idea of specific entry in Cutter's work.

9. Cutter, "Library Catalogues," p. 530.

10. *RDC*, Definitions, "Classed Catalogs," p. 17.

11. *RDC*, R161, disc., p. 66.

12. *RDC*, R165, disc., p. 68, and R176, disc., p. 76.

13. Listed by author in the Boston Athenaeum catalog as, Cust, *Lady* Mary Ann. *The cat, its history and diseases*. 2d ed. London, 1870. 8° Its subject entry was CAT, *The*, where it was listed with only one other work, J. F. Fleury's, *Les chats; histoire, moeurs, etc.*

14. *RDC*, R161, disc., p. 67 (first two examples); R175, disc., p. 74 (next two examples); Boston Athenaeum catalog (last example) under the phrase as it reads.

15. The method employed to accomplish this characterization, whether, for example, single or multiple-term specification, is not in question at this point. Nor is the question of its possibility a matter of concern here, even though, as Patrick Wilson has noted in his *Two Kinds of Power*, pp. 69–77, the idea of "the subject" of a book is fuzzy. The fact is that librarians and patrons alike have supposed it to be possible.

16. *RDC*, Definitions, "Class," disc., p. 16. Emphasis added.

17. Cutter, "Library Catalogues," p. 528. Emphasis added.

18. *RDC*, Definitions, "Subject entry," p. 23. Emphasis added.

19. *RDC*, R172, p. 71. Emphasis added.

20. Cutter, "Library Catalogues," p. 536. Emphasis added.

21. Cutter, "New Catalogue," p. 106; cf. Cutter, "Library Catalogues," p. 532.

22. Cutter, "Library Catalogues," p. 546, footnote.

23. *RDC*, R177, p. 76, and R165, p. 68. Emphasis added.

24. *RDC*, Definitions, "Class," disc., p. 16.

25. *RDC,* R161, disc., p. 67.

26. Coates, *Subject Catalogues,* p. 33.

27. Ibid. Coates, along with nearly all modern writers, concludes that the chief difference between Cutter's day and the present with respect to subject access is that Cutter and his contemporaries dealt only with relatively simple subjects whereas moderns deal with complex subjects. The idea that in barely one hundred years subjects have become complex is rather elusive, however, especially when one attempts to define the idea of a complex subject more exactly. It might be assumed, for example, that cats is a simple subject whereas the manufacture of multiwall kraft paper sacks for the packaging of cement is complex, or even very complex. (Foskett, *Subject Approach to Information,* p. 84, concludes that it is much more complex than at least the heat treatment of aluminum.) But, how might one tell? Complexity is certainly not a function of the objects of thought themselves. Were that so, there would be distinct limitations on what could be compared. One might compare subjects based on concrete objects such as cats and parameceum and conclude that cats are the more complex organisms of the two. But how different is the complexity of cats and dogs, or perhaps more usefully, cats and DC-10s? And this sort of measure does not apply at all when comparing concrete subjects with abstract subjects or abstract subjects with other abstract subjects. It would be absurd to ask, for example, which subject was more complex, Cats or Love, Love or History? Complexity in subjects is likewise not a function of either an informal or a formal measure of thought necessary to make a subject clear in one's thinking, such as, for example, the sheer amount of thought expended or the extent of a disciplined reasoning process. A measure of that sort would not only be relative to the person doing the thinking but would be viewed as inconclusive and superfluous. In the end, it would appear that what is meant by subject complexity actually has little to do with subjects themselves. Instead, it is only a reflection of the ease or difficulty with which subjects are named, described, or otherwise referred to. Subjects referred to by means of simple, familiar words or names are considered simple subjects. Those referred to by means of involved, unfamiliar words or names are considered complex. Cats is considered a simple subject because its "name" is short and familiar. The manufacture of multiwall kraft paper sacks for the packaging of cement is considered complex because its name is long and involved and perhaps not familiar. Should the latter acquire a catch-name such as the manufacture of C-sacks (L-sacks being reserved for multiwall kraft paper sacks for the packaging of lime, etc.), and become familiar among a wide group of people, it would become in time a simple rather than a complex subject. For these various reasons, it seems superfluous to speak of complex subjects as if the term means any useful measure of subjects themselves. To be more precise, one might usefully speak only of subjects with complex descriptions as opposed to subjects with simple descriptions. Of course, on this basis, one might still conclude that there has been a shift since the nineteenth century, the difference now being stated as people in the twentieth century speak more often of subjects with complex descriptions. As the discussion progresses, however, it will be seen that this

difference is not one of any change in mental capacities, but rather only one having to do with how the idea of a subject is defined in the first place.

28. Reid, *Essays on the Intellectual Powers of Man,* Essay 5, "Of Abstraction," especially pp. 463–510.

29. Ibid., p. 463.

30. It should be noted that although "DC-10" is a proper name, its conventional use in that manner does not make it the name of an individual in the same way that, say, Floyd Brown, or the Fellowship Church of Baton Rouge refer to particular individuals. Strawson has referred to this as "non-particulars" that become entrenched as individuals, in *Individuals,* pp. 230–34.

31. A particularly useful study of the classification of subjects in the entire Medieval period will be found in James A. Weisheipel, "Classification of the Sciences in Medieval Thought," *Mediaeval Studies* 27 (1965): 54–90; and Richard McKeon, "The Organization of Sciences and the Relations of Cultures in the Twelfth and Thirteenth Centuries," in *The Cultural Context of Medieval Learning,* ed. J. E. Murdoch and E. D. Sylla, Boston Studies in the Philosophy of Science, v. 27 (Dordrecht; Boston: D. Reidel Publishing Company, 1975), pp. 151–92. See also James A. Weisheipel, "Developments in the Arts Curriculum at Oxford in the Early Fourteenth Century," *Mediaeval Studies* 28 (1966): 151–75, for a useful description of logic textbooks during the later medieval period.

32. Lisa Jardine, *Francis Bacon, Discovery and the Art of Discourse* (London: Cambridge University Press, 1974), pp. 17–58, describes the movement to simplify logical method by modifying dialectic textbooks between 1450 and 1550. Afterwards, she discusses Bacon's contributions in the light of those modifications. See also Paolo Rossi, *Francis Bacon: From Magic to Science* (Chicago: University of Chicago Press, 1968), especially chapters 4–6.

33. Jose Ortega y Gasset, "The Mission of the Librarian," in *Of, By and For Librarians,* Second Series, ed. John David Marshall (Hamden, Conn.: Shoe String Press, 1974), pp. 197–203.

34. S. R. Ranganathan, in his *Theory of Library Catalogue,* was perhaps the first to suggest the relationship. Phyllis Richmond, in "Cats: an Example of Concealed Classification in Subject Headings," extended the conclusion far beyond Cutter to alphabetical subject heading work in general. Her list of sources is very useful.

CHAPTER 4. SUBJECTS AND THE PUBLIC

1. *RDC,* R161, disc., p. 67.

2. *RDC,* R164, p. 68; cf. R169, p. 70, where he refers to choosing a subject name that "is most familiar to the class of people who consult the library."

3. Cutter's most notable statement occurs in *RDC,* R175, disc., p. 74, where he states, "When there is any decided usage (*i.e.,* custom of the public to designate the subjects by one of the names rather than by the others) let it be followed."

4. *RDC,* headnote to "2. Choice Between Different Names," p. 69.

5. *RDC,* "Preface to the Fourth Edition," p. 6.

6. Cutter's statement elicits a scenario in which simple cataloging rules without exception come into conflict with the public's general and deeply rooted habits (i.e., "habitual way of looking at things"). But he noted in the following paragraph that the focus of his concern was whether or not the preliminary rules written by the A.L.A. advisory committee on cataloging paid enough attention to the "habits of users." It is interesting to note that those rules, ultimately issued as the 1908 *Catalog Rules,* were limited to descriptive cataloging. Moreover, most of the context of *RDC,* "Preface to the Fourth Edition" was concerned with the descriptive cataloging related to the new Library of Congress card service. Finally, Cutter was completely wrapped up in rectifying his fourth edition to the new descriptive cataloging changes then taking place. In contrast, there were no substantive changes in his subject cataloging rules throughout the four editions of his work. All of this strongly suggests that his mind was on descriptive cataloging when he wrote the statement.

7. See chapter 1, pp. 21–22.

8. "Cultivated" does not turn on the issue of "manners," although as Scottish philosophy became influential in America, and as the nineteenth century wore on, an emphasis on manners eventually became very important. It is that emphasis on manners that underlies the view in which New England patricians are portrayed as elitist and priggish. In an earlier work, *Charles Ammi Cutter: Library Systematizer,* pp. 35–43, I used the term "enculturated" for what was meant here. I am now more inclined to use "cultivated" as the most useful term available, despite the confusion that may result from confusing it with an emphasis on manners. For a decidedly negative interpretation of this characteristic among librarians, see Dee Garrison, *Apostles of Culture: The Public Librarian and American Society, 1876–1920* (New York: The Free Press, 1979), chapters 1–3. Garrison views the idea of cultivation totally in a later Victorian sense of manners.

9. Stewart, *Elements of the Philosophy of the Human Mind,* in his *Collected Works,* v. 2, p. 59.

10. Ibid., p. 203.

11. Cutter, "Library Catalogues," p. 541.

12. Ibid.

13. Ibid.

14. Ibid., p. 530.

15. Ibid., pp. 529–30, 541, 547–48, 550. Cf. also Cutter's description of college library users in "New Catalogue," especially pp. 116–20.

16. Cutter, "Library Catalogues," p. 550.

17. Ibid., p. 543.

18. Ibid., p. 547.

19. Ibid., p. 545; cf. pp. 531–32.

20. Ibid., p. 531.

21. Of course, it should also be noted that Cutter lived in a time when the general literacy rate in the United States was apparently much lower than what it is now. In fact, general elementary education was just becoming organized in Cutter's day. High schools were relatively few in number, and

a college education was restricted to a relatively small proportion of the population. Moreover, an enormous number of immigrants and people otherwise on the move were placing severe strains on a society that was shifting noticeably from an agrarian to an urban-industrial base. Perhaps in that context, Cutter's categories of the public were more realistic than one realizes.

22. Cutter, *Charles Ammi Cutter: Library Systematizer*, pp. 29–43, and passim among Cutter's writings, especially pp. 228–37. Cf. Cutter, "Library Catalogues," p. 550.

23. Cutter, "Library Catalogues," p. 550.

24. Cf. *Dewey Decimal Classification and Relative Index*, edited under the direction of Benjamin A. Custer, 3 vols. (Albany, N.Y.: Forest Press, 1979), vol. 3 (Index), passim.

CHAPTER 5. SUBJECT CATALOGS AND CATALOGING

1. *RDC,* Definitions, "Catalog," p. 15.

2. *RDC,* Definitions, "Subject catalog," p. 23.

3. *RDC,* Definitions, "Classed catalogs," disc., p. 18.

4. *RDC,* Definitions, "Dictionary catalog," p. 19.

5. *RDC,* Definitions, "Entry," p. 19.

6. *RDC,* Definitions, "Reference," p. 21.

7. Cf. *RDC,* Definitions, "Entry," pp. 19–20, for the various subelements of his definition of entry.

8. *RDC,* Definitions, "Under," p. 24.

9. *RDC,* Definitions, "Heading," p. 20.

10. Ibid. Emphasis added.

11. Cf. *RDC,* Definitions, "Dictionary and other alphabetical catalogs," p. 19, where Cutter says of entering books under subject names that are in fact classes (i.e., general rather than individual subjects), "Whenever a book treats of the whole subject of a class, it is *specifically* entered under that class." Emphasis added.

12. *RDC,* R340, disc., p. 123.

13. Coates, "Alphabetical Subject Catalogues," p. 63, suggested that calling them subdivisions instead of simply subheadings was unwise because technically the dictionary catalog does not employ subdivisions.

14. It will be noted that Cutter did not indicate on his chart that alphabetico-classed catalogs also had "specific headings," although he did note along the side that they as well as dictionary and systematically classed catalogs had "specific subjects." The reason for not indicating the presence of specific headings on the chart was probably owing to a lack of space to show how diversely alphabetico-classed catalogs treated specific headings. In the dictionary catalog, specific headings were always alphabetically arranged. In the systematically classed catalog, they were always logically arranged. In the alphabetico-classed catalog, they were sometimes logically and sometimes alphabetically arranged, they sometimes provided entry, sometimes

subentry. There was plainly little enough space on the chart to indicate all of that.

15. *RDC*, Definitions, "Dictionary and other alphabetical catalogs," p. 19.

16. In addition to these efforts, Cutter also reclassified and recataloged the Harvard Divinity School Library collections while a student librarian there (1857–59). And concurrently with his work at the Harvard College Library, he indexed several books for the additional earnings it brought. See Miksa, "Charles Ammi Cutter, Nineteenth Century Systematizer of Libraries," pp. 27–32, 43–95, and especially 84–95.

17. Charles C. Jewett, *Notices of Public Libraries in the United States of America* . . . Printed by Order of Congress, as an appendix to the Fourth Annual Report of the Board of Regents of the Smithsonian Institution (Washington: Printed for the House of Representatives, 1851); Hermann Ludewig, "Bibliographie und Bibliotheken in den Vereinigten Staaten von Nord-Amerika. Zweiter Artikel. Bibliotheken in den Vereinigten Staaten," *Serapeum* 7 (no. 8, April 30, 1846): 113–23; (no. 11, June 15, 1846): 161–72. Cutter's "Library Catalogues" article actually consists of three sections. The text of his discussion of cataloging theory came first on pages 526–52. This was followed by an eight-page discussion of cataloging costs and other practical considerations. A third section consisted of a series of eleven tabulated summaries of types of catalogs and their characteristics and data related to costs of catalogs (pp. 560–76). A twelfth table on pages 577–622 in that section consisted of the list of catalogs themselves.

18. A comparison of Cutter's list of catalogs with the one in Jim Ranz, *The Printed Book Catalogue in American Libraries, 1723–1900*, ACRL Monograph Series, no. 26 (Chicago: A.L.A. 1964), pp. 117–28, reveals that Cutter omitted nineteen catalogs or supplements between 1723 and 1875. But this amounted to a statistically insignificant loss compared to the 1,010 items that he did include, especially since fourteen of the nineteen were from the earlier period (i.e., 1723–1850) and at least some of those were represented in Cutter's list by other catalogs from the same libraries.

19. Ranz, *The Printed Book Catalogue,* especially pp. 23–30, 55–75. The purpose of Ranz's study was to assess the rise and decline of printed catalogs. Nevertheless, his work documents at least in part the rising dominance of the dictionary catalog as well.

20. See ahead, Figure 7, line 7.

21. Cutter, "Library Catalogues," p. 529.

22. Cambridge (Mass.) High School, Library, *A Classed Catalogue of the Library of the Cambridge High School,* [compiled by Ezra Abbot] (Cambridge: John Bartlett, 1853), p. v.

23. Cutter, "New Catalogue," p. 118.

24. Cutter, "Library Catalogues," pp. 529–30; cf. also Tables V–VII, pp. 564–67.

25. Ibid., p. 530.

26. Ibid., pp. 531–32.

27. Ibid., p. 529.

28. Ranz, *The Printed Book Catalogue,* pp. 37-39, 42-43.

29. Ibid., p. 64.

30. Cutter, "Library Catalogues," pp. 532-33; cf. Tables V-VII, pp. 564-67.

31. Ibid., p. 533.

32. *RDC,* R172, disc., p. 71. Cutter did not supply the source of his quotation but it likely came from the introduction to a catalog he had examined.

33. Cutter, "Library Catalogues," p. 538; cf. also *RDC,* "Objects," p. 12. Object 1.C states: "To enable a person to find a book of which . . . the subject is known,"—that is, a known-item search for a particular book by means of its title word. Object 2.E states: "To show what the library has . . . on a given subject,"—that is, a search for a subject document class. Dunkin, *Cataloging U.S.A.,* pp. 66-67, explicitly pointed out that this conflict of objects has not always been noted. And even Cutter did not seriously deal with the first of the two, making it subservient to the second. Although Dunkin pointed out the conflict, he obviated the first object to a certain degree by interpreting the means to its accomplishment as a matter of indicating "the specific subject of the book" rather than what it really requires, access to a book by a subject word (usually in the title) that is an identification tag derived from the book rather than assigned to it.

34. Cutter, "Library Catalogues," pp. 536-37.

35. Ibid., p. 533. Cutter estimated that nine-tenths of all dictionary catalogs lacked this control. He did not give a basis for his estimate, however, whether, for example, it was an extrapolation based on those he had personally examined.

36. Ibid., p. 536.

37. Ibid., p. 532.

38. Ibid., p. 550.

39. *RDC,* headnote to "B. Entries Considered as Parts of a Whole," p. 79.

40. Ibid.

41. Cutter, "Library Catalogues," p. 532.

42. Ibid., pp. 532-33.

43. Cutter, "New Catalogue," especially pp. 116-17; Cutter, "Library Catalogues," pp. 543-47.

44. Cutter, "Library Catalogues," p. 540.

45. Cutter, "New Catalogue," p. 116.

46. *RDC,* R161, disc., p. 67.

47. *RDC,* R175, disc., p. 74. Emphasis his.

48. *RDC,* Definitions, "Dictionary and other alphabetical catalogs," disc., p. 19.

49. A more detailed account of Cutter's Harvard years will be found in Miksa, "Charles Ammi Cutter, Nineteenth Century Systematizer of Libraries," chapters 1-2.

50. Cutter's claim to have to come to "swear by" Abbot's system was made in a lecture given by him at the Columbia School of Library Economy, February 16, 1888. The lecture was recorded in shorthand notes by Melvil Dewey, MS, Columbia University Library, M. Dewey Papers, and by George Watson Cole, MS, American Antiquarian Society, G. W. Cole Papers. Cutter's argu-

ments about incorporating some of Abbot's system into the Boston Athenaeum catalog are found in "Librarian's Report on the Best Method of Copying Mr. Lowell's Catalogue," in Cutter, *Charles Ammi Cutter: Library Systematizer*, p. 168. A more complete account of the changes that he did incorporate into the catalog and, especially, of the reaction of the trustees of the Athenaeum to them will be found in Miksa, "Charles Ammi Cutter, Nineteenth Century Systematizer of Libraries," chapter 5.

51. Ezra Abbot, "Mr. Abbot's Statement Respecting the New Catalogues of the College Library," in *Report of the Committee of Overseers of Harvard College Appointed to Visit the Library for the year 1863* (Boston: Press of George C. Rand and Avery, 1864), p. 55.

52. Ibid., pp. 55–59.

53. *RDC*, Definitions, "Dictionary and other alphabetical catalogs," disc., p. 19.

54. *RDC*, Definitions, "Syndetic," p. 23.

55. *RDC*, Definitions, "Dictionary and other alphabetical catalogs," disc., p. 19.

CHAPTER 6. CUTTER'S SUBJECT RULES

1. See examples under countries in the Boston Athenaeum catalog and cf. *RDC*, R175, disc., p. 75.

2. See chapter 1, pp. 21–22.

3. Cutter, "New Catalogue," pp. 119–20.

4. Cutter referred to these words as "This rule of 'specific entry' " in the discussion that followed them. Cf. also *RDC*, Definitions, "Specific entry," p. 22: "*Specific entry*, registering a book under a heading which expresses its special subject as distinguished from entering it in a class which includes that subject."

5. Cutter did not intend that titles should never be referred to in determining what books treated of, but only that titles should not be referred to exclusively. Cf. *RDC*, R172, p. 71; Definitions, "Title," pp. 23–24; Cutter, "New Catalogue," p. 120; and Cutter, "Library Catalogues," p. 540.

6. This conclusion is only speculation. The real issue is not the sheer number of books or articles written on a topic, but whether the topic had been discussed and named, perhaps in the context of other subjects.

7. Cutter variously called the second part of the combination dealt with here by the names "subject" (as opposed to a country), "scientific subject" (as opposed to a "local" subject), and "general subject" (as opposed to a place). He also included the word "form" in the caption to the rule and one may suppose that, given his separation of form entry from subject entry, he meant in this instance form considered as a subject (i.e., "about" the form) rather than form as a literary or practical arrangement (i.e., "in" a form). The variation in labels seems of little account. The important thing is that all the labels were combined with an individual subject and therefore were less concrete. Another aspect of his discussion is interesting, although one may only speculate about its implications. Cutter noted in a second paragraph

that the idea of giving countries precedence over general subjects was a principle that was not uniformly adhered to in catalogs "as the more obvious 'specific' rule is obeyed." This suggests that Cutter's insistence that places as well as persons were to be treated as individual subjects was not as widely recognized as he cared to admit. Later, in his rules for arrangement (*RDC*, R345, disc., p. 127), Cutter referred to the precedence given to countries over general subjects as "the tendency of the dictionary catalog . . . towards national classification; that is, in separating what relates to the parts of a subject, as is required by its *specific* principle, it necessarily brings together all that relates to a country in every aspect, as it would what relates to any other individual." (Emphasis his.) One might wonder if his emphasis on places in this way was a result of his observation of cataloging practice or only a philosophical distinction. That his contemporaries did not agree with him in his conclusions in the matter will become obvious in the succeeding chapters here.

8. Cutter, "Library Catalogues," pp. 537–38.

9. *RDC*, R172, disc., p. 71.

10. *RDC*, R175, disc., p. 74.

11. Cutter supplied this particular example in *RDC*, R339, p. 122, in his section on arrangement. The rule itself reads, "Care must be taken not to mix two subjects together because their names are spelled in the same way."

12. The notion that Cutter's commitment to specific entry was compromised by this criterion has arisen from interpreting Cutter's *Rules* through the filter provided by Library of Congress practice. Within the Library of Congress tradition, a classificatory approach to this rule appears to have had its beginning particularly in the work of J. C. M. Hanson, the original designer of the Library of Congress subject catalog. Hanson's significantly different attitude toward specific entry will be discussed in chapter 8.

13. Modern readers will find Cutter's differentiation between Ancient Egypt and Modern Egypt superfluous without some understanding of Cutter's view of subjects. Coates, *Subject Catalogues,* p. 35, apparently thought this when, upon quoting the statement here, especially Cutter's qualification of it as a "plausible" statement, he responded, "He might indeed!" Coates's response and obvious amusement may well have gotten the best of him, however. He misquoted Cutter here, inserting Ancient history for Ancient Egypt. Perhaps because Cutter used Ancient history later in the same rule, Coates simply confused them. But one cannot help but wonder if Coates, not being aware of Cutter's classificatory framework of reference, simply was not being very careful with Cutter's text, having found there notions that he already had concluded were absurd. (Cf. misquotations of R175, p. 74, on the same page and of R343, p. 123, on the following page in Coates's work.) Cutter's example of Ancient and Modern Egypt made sense to him, given his presuppositions concerning subjects. On the other hand, his own footnote on the matter, where he concludes "Individuals should not be divided," was not as clear a conclusion as it might appear, even for Cutter's system. The

notion that a place as an individual could have constituent parts—for example, Massachusetts in relation to its individual towns—has already been noted. Of course, Ancient and Modern Egypt differ only in terms of time periods, not constituent localities. Ancient history in relation to Modern history is also not a good comparison because Cutter viewed those as two different places (Antiquities: History and, one supposes, the Modern world—History), both analogous to Europe: History (cf. *RDC*, R175, disc., p. 75).

14. Chan, *Library of Congress Subject Headings*, p. 55.

15. The way one sees the sequence of Cutter's arguments in the entire rule 174–175 section will significantly affect the interpretation one gives to Cutter's attitude toward compound subject names. The failure to comprehend Cutter's notion of subject structure and significance order will also seriously affect the interpretation. But the latter is in the present case even more seriously exacerbated by the former.

First, it appears that most commentators have taken the entire discussion following the statement of rule 175 to be chiefly related to inversion. But this is clearly not the case. Cutter discussed the two provisions of the third option, inversion and reduction of a compound subject name to a single word synonym (in that order) beginning immediately after the statement of his rule to the middle of page 74, ending with the words " . . . Lyceum system, etc." Thereafter, he turned to the problem of choosing between synonymous compound subject names, finishing the discussion on that note. The evidence for this is (1) inversion is no longer mentioned at all in the last part of the rule discussion; and (2) the examples he referred to in the last part of the rule are keyed to the second, rather than the third option (i.e., to b, c, and d, rather than to b alone). As such, they have to do with Cutter's rule because Cutter's rule combined the first two options. The reason why the entire discussion after rule 175 has been ordinarily taken to refer to inversion is most likely because Cutter's measure for determining when not to invert (pp. 72–74) and for determining what synonymous compound subject name to choose among alternatives (pp. 74–75) are, as the treatment here shows, the same. They are both based on an analysis of the choices to be made in the light of his subject structure and significance order.

Second, most commentators have supposed that because all subsequent discussion after rule 175 deals chiefly with inversion, the main emphasis of his entire rule was deciding whether or not to invert. As the commentary here will demonstrate, however, inversion was in fact a minor theme. It amounted to a rarely used provision that was far overshadowed by Cutter's main interest—entering most compound subject names directly as they read.

Third, commentators have failed to discern the difference between the provisions of the second and third options, especially the differences in their respective provisions for inversion. It is no wonder that it looks like Cutter contradicts himself by saying on the one hand invert the headings and, on the other hand, inversion is wrong. As the discussion here will show, what he really said was invert some headings if their inversion is not of the wrong type, that is, inversion as practiced in the third option. The same difference applies to the provision for reduction of phrase names to an equivalent single word.

16. Cutter's criticism is given on page 74 of his discussion. It comes after his discussion of inversion in the third option because he reversed the order of his treatment of that option's two principal provisions. The reason why he reversed them is not stated explicitly, but it is likely that he discussed this form of reduction last because he concluded that by itself it had some value. It dealt with choosing between subject names as they read and, in that form, one could always argue that one or another single-word synonym was at least as well known or even better known than the compound subject name involved. Cutter seems not to have been averse to using this approach in the Boston Athenaeum catalog (which, by his own admission, did not always follow his *Rules*). Of the single-word synonyms that Cutter listed on pages 72 and 74 as examples of this form of reduction, he used Physics for Natural philosophy, with a reference from the latter to the former. He also used Intellect, Hygiene, and Sociology, but he did not refer to those terms from Intellectual philosophy, Sanitary science, and Social sciences, respectively. He may not have referred from the first because it was practically contiguous in the catalog with its replacement term. The other two omitted references seem strange, however, although they may have been the result of confusion as the work progressed. A reference at the end of the "Science" entries (See also . . . Social science) was not changed. It remains a moot point as to whether Cutter used these terms because he "reduced" them to equivalent single-word synonyms or because he thought them to be the most commonly used terms in the first place. But, his lack of cross-references seem to be an outright mistake.

17. Dunkin, *Cataloging U.S.A.*, pp. 87–88, listed Cutter's objections to Schwartz's noun rule in an orderly sequence. He labeled the fourth objection—Cutter's analysis of how persons looked for subjects and particularly their concentration on single subject names—with the phrase, "Logic will not bother the user," and suggested afterward that it was "sheer supposition." Cutter was not trying to cover up a consciously illogical provision by referring to the illogic of patrons' thinking, however. His user psychology suggested that most users (all of the first category—desultory readers—and perhaps some of the second category as well) simply approached subjects as single subject names without thinking about their classificatory relationships. Thus, it was logical for Cutter to suppose that Morbid anatomy would not be a problem whether written directly or as Anatomy, *Morbid*. His argument was sheer supposition only insofar as his entire user psychology was sheer supposition.

18. Cutter may well have had in mind Marshall Hall's *Mutual Relations Between Anatomy, Physiology, Pathology, and Therapeutics, and the Practice of Medicine* (London, 1842) for this example. In the Boston Athenaeum catalog, this book was given subject entry under the four component subjects. The bibliographical descriptions were abbreviated but were not analyticals because the imprint was included in each case. Cutter's suggestion of placing

it only under Medicine would appear therefore to be a hypothetical case. If anything, he preferred multiple entry under the specific subjects.

19. Cutter, "Library Catalogues," p. 541.

20. Ibid., p. 548.

21. *RDC*, headnote to "B. Entries Considered as Parts of a Whole," p. 79; Cutter, "Library Catalogues," p. 548.

22. *RDC*, "General Remarks," p. 11. The differences between them were not based on the number of books in the collections to which they gave access, but rather to how much printed copy was allowed each item. "Short" was usually one line for a title if in one column, or two lines if in two columns. "Medium" usually did not exceed four lines. And "Full" often went to six or seven lines for each item.

23. This is emphasized here because it is a common practice in today's catalogs to truncate the descending cross-reference structure at what Cutter would have considered to be the narrowest general subject, but not to continue to the individual subjects in the catalog in each case. If continued at all, the usual practice is to include only "Example" or "General" crossreferences.

24. *RDC*, R165, disc., p. 69.

25. Quoted in Cutter, *Charles Ammi Cutter: Library Systematizer*, p. 150.

26. One will find some reflection of this in the "Relative Index" of the Dewey Decimal Classification in those instances where places are identified primarily in terms of their area number rather than all the various places in the schedule where they may be enumerated and also in those instances where many concrete general subjects (e.g., copper) have truncated index entries consisting of common superordinate chains. For example, references from Aluminum, Beryllium, and Copper technologies to their "Social and economic aspects" are not given in each location but rather are referred to the common superordinate chain "Secondary industries" which is itself connected to the relevant entry locations in the social sciences. See *Dewey Decimal Classification*, 19th ed., v. 3, passim.

27. Cutter, "Library Catalogues," p. 548. When comparing Abbot's catalog with his own dictionary system, Cutter remarked, "Under each system, he who wishes to find *all* that the library contains on a given topic must usually consult several parts of the catalogue and spend time and thought in the search." (Ibid., p. 540. Emphasis his.)

28. Cutter, "New Catalogue," p. 116.

29. Cutter, "Library Catalogues," p. 531, footnote.

30. *RDC*, R343, disc., p. 127 (emphasis his); cf. R165, disc., pp. 68–69; and "New Catalogue," pp. 110–11.

31. *RDC*, R175, disc., p. 75; cf. headnote to "B. Entries Considered as Parts of a Whole," p. 79.

32. Cutter included the idea of making a synoptic table as a final separate table in *RDC*, 1st ed., R87; and *RDC*, 2nd and 3rd ed., R121. In the fourth edition, however, he simply appended a long final discussion to R188 (on ascending references) arguing against it.

CHAPTER 7. THE TRANSITION FROM CUTTER TO THE TWENTIETH CENTURY

1. American Library Association, *List of Subject Headings for use in Dictionary Catalogs* (Boston: Published for the ALA Publishing Section by the Library Bureau, 1895). (Hereafter cited as A.L.A., *List* (1895).)

2. Cutter presented a cogent explanation of this reasoning in an address to the fourth A.L.A. Conference at Washington, D.C., in 1881, "Classification on the Shelves," *Library Journal* 6 (April 1881): 66. The fact is shelf classification preceded subject catalogs as the most widely followed method of subject access not only in the form of older fixed arrangements, but even with the modern classification inaugurated by the Decimal Classification. In a sense, the latter forced the issue of catalog subject access because as shelf classifications became increasingly "minute" in their structures to accommodate ever-increasing numbers of new books, their complexity made them increasingly less useful for the straightforward searching out of particular subjects. Cf. William C. Lane, "Present Tendencies of Catalog Practice," *Library Journal* 29 (December 1904): 136, who used the term "aristocratic" to differentiate between classed and dictionary subject catalog access.

3. Pettee, *Subject Headings*, "Preface," p. 3. It appears that one or more words have been omitted between "syndetic" and "had not."

4. A.L.A., *List* (1895), "Preface," p. iv. Julius Kaiser, *Systematic Indexing* (London: Pitman, 1911), also made use of the idea of concretes in his concrete-process structure of headings. Kaiser's work was not widely known, however, perhaps because by his admission it had to do with information indexing of special records rather than subject cataloging and that admission placed it beyond the interest of librarians in general libraries.

5. American Library Association, Committee on an Index to Subject Headings, Report, *Library Journal* 6 (April 1881): 114–15. For a fuller accounting of the work of the committee and of the difficulties of the A.L.A. in 1880, see Miksa, "Charles Ammi Cutter, Nineteenth Century Systematizer of Libraries," pp. 443–45, 653–56. Bowker authored the article "On a Co-operative Scheme of Subject-entry, with a Key to Catalog Headings," *Library Journal* 3 (November 1878): 326–29; Perkins, the article "Classification in Dictionary Catalogues," *Library Journal* 4 (July/August 1879): 226–34; and Noyes, the Brooklyn Library's alphabetico-classed catalog entitled *Analytical and Classed Catalogue of the Brooklyn Library* (Brooklyn: 1878–80), all of which more or less turned on the kinds of classificatory distinctions that Cutter had made.

6. The decision to form a committee to reconsider subject headings is recorded in the Proceedings of the 1892 A.L.A. Conference, *Library Journal* 17 (August 1892): C30–C31. The first report of the new A.L.A. Committee on an Index to Subject Headings, with discussion, will be found in *Library Journal* 18 (September 1893): C79–C82. The committee was particularly concerned with modifying the effect of Cutter's rules 164–165.

7. A.L.A. Committee on an Index to Subject Headings, Report and Discussion, *Library Journal* 19 (December 1894): C138–C139; A.L.A. *List* (1895), "Preface," p. iv.

8. Beginning in the spring of 1892, Cutter experienced difficulties in his professional life that did not begin to be resolved substantially until August 1894 when he assumed his duties as the first librarian of the Forbes Library in Northampton, Massachusetts. He traveled in Europe during May and June 1893, and again from October to August 1894. A full accounting of this troubling period in his life will be found in Miksa, "Charles Ammi Cutter, Nineteenth Century Systematizer of Libraries," pp. 257–71, 705–65. Suffice it to say that by the end of this period in his life, Cutter's national role in the A.L.A. was so reduced and his work at the Forbes so overwhelming that he had neither the time nor the inclination to involve himself in the work of the committee with anything approaching his former enthusiasm for such work. Cutter's "Some Hints on Subject Cataloging in Dictionary Style," included in the A.L.A., *List* (1898), pp. 197–98, provided only a brief statement of the main subject cataloging emphases of his *Rules*.

9. Cutter's early voice occurred in the form of a published controversy in which he defended Abbot's Harvard College alphabetico-classed catalog as well as subject catalog access in general. See Miksa, "Charles Ammi Cutter, Nineteenth Century Systematizer of Libraries," pp. 76–78, 424–32. Between 1878 and 1886, Cutter devised a classification scheme for the Boston Athenaeum. Besides the scheme itself, he also developed his "Author Tables," better known since then as his "Cutter numbers." After 1886, he changed his Athenaeum scheme (especially its notation) into his better known Expansive Classification, the seventh "expansion" of which he was working on at his death in 1903. The work was never completed, but it ultimately influenced the Library of Congress Classification scheme. Some sense of Cutter's productivity in classification may be gained from the selections on that topic included in Cutter, *Charles Ammi Cutter: Library Systematizer*, pp. 238–88, and in the bibliography on pp. 314–37. A narrative account of his classification work will be found in Miksa, "Charles Ammi Cutter, Nineteenth Century Systematizer of Libraries," chapter 7.

10. See especially Kuklick, *The Rise of American Philosophy*, Part 1, in which "the fall of one orthodoxy in Cambridge and the rise of another" (p. 27) is traced. See also Flower and Murphey, *A History of Philosophy in America*, vol. 1, pp. 365–87.

11. C. A. Cutter, "Classification on the Shelves: with Some Account of the New Scheme Prepared for the Boston Athenaeum," and "The Expansive Classification," in Cutter, *Charles Ammi Cutter: Library Systematizer*, pp. 252 and 287, respectively.

12. Cutter, "Some Hints on Subject Cataloging in Dictionary Style," p. 197.

13. The shift in societal values that characterized the Progressive Era has been the subject of a large number of both general works and works dealing with particular areas of society. See especially Garrison, *Apostles of Culture*, pp. 3–15; cf. *Charles Ammi Cutter: Library Systematizer*, p. 66, note 10, for a useful list of sources.

14. Cf. Garrison's treatment of Dewey in *Apostles of Culture*, chapters 6–10. Some indication of the shift in library leadership will be found in

Miksa, "Charles Ammi Cutter, Nineteenth Century Systematizer of Libraries," pp. 615–753.

15. Miksa, "Charles Ammi Cutter, Nineteenth Century Systematizer of Libraries," pp. 594–614, 815–22; *RDC*, "Preface to the 4th Edition," p. 6.

16. *RDC*, Definitions, "Dictionary and other alphabetical catalogs," p. 19.

17. *RDC*, R161, disc., p. 67.

18. Ibid.

19. Intrinsically related subject terms are those related in terms of their meanings. For example, Mammals and Cats are related intrinsically because of connotations and denotations implicit in the terms themselves. Extrinsically related subject terms are those related on the basis of assigned or extrinsic connections. For example, the heat treatment of aluminum contains two terms related only by the action of putting them together to describe an industrial process. They are not intrinsically related by definition. A. C. Foskett, the source of the latter example, describes the two kinds of relationships as "semantic" or "syntactic" in his *Subject Approach to Information,* pp. 62–63. The most notable problem that early classed catalogs faced was how to represent places when they were only extrinsically related to the general subject at hand. A perusal of the third volume of *A Catalogue of the Library of Harvard University in Cambridge, Massachusetts,* 3 vols. (Cambridge: E. W. Metcalf, 1830–31), and *A Catalogue of the Maps and Charts in the Library of Harvard University in Cambridge, Massachusetts* (Cambridge: E. W. Metcalf, 1831), two of the better prepared classed catalogs of the earlier period, shows that places were denoted as subclasses only under general subjects that implied geographical subdivisions (e.g., HISTORY; GEOGRAPHY, TOPOGRAPHY, STATISTICS; the various parts of JURISPRUDENCE, GOVERNMENT AND POLITICS; MAPS AND CHARTS) whereas places were not used at all as subdivisions under other topics such as the parts of NATURAL HISTORY even though they were often indicated in the titles of books as parts of the subject matter. Other classed catalogs often did not go even that far in including places as elements of subject hierarchies.

20. Drake, "What Is a Subject?" p. 36. The context of Drake's statement was his analysis of John W. Metcalfe's understanding of a subject in the then recently published *Subject Classifying and Indexing of Libraries and Literature.* Metcalfe had attempted to demonstrate that subject classifying was not a process of subdividing subjects by logical differentia related to the objects involved, but was rather only sorting information (i.e., books) by subject or subject aspect. In the course of critically examining Metcalfe's ideas, Drake briefly noted the ideas about two kinds of subjects quoted here. Metcalfe's attempt to distinguish subject subdivisions from subject aspects by appealing to the idea that all classification really did was to sort out information about subjects was in many respects an attempt to deal with Cutter's use of subarrangement terms without a knowledge of Cutter's ideas about subject categories and significance order.

21. Ibid.

22. *Dewey Decimal Classification and Relative Index,* 19th ed., vol. 1, pp. xxvii–xxxvi and xxxix ff., respectively.

23. For example, Ezra Abbot's Harvard College Library alphabetico-classed card catalog and the *Analytical and Classed Catalogue of the Brooklyn Library*, compiled by Stephen B. Noyes, both appear to have appealed to something of the idea of significance order based on concreteness that Cutter followed. Of course, both men had been educated in the same tradition which Cutter had been exposed to. In fact, Noyes had been only two years ahead of Cutter at Harvard College, and had also worked at the Boston Athenaeum. Abbot had been Cutter's mentor.

CHAPTER 8. HANSON AND THE LIBRARY OF CONGRESS

1. A.L.A., *List* (1895), "Preface," p. iii. The second edition issued in 1898 contained 192 changes in headings. Some of these were in the area of medicine. But most amounted only to "alterations in spelling or compounding of words to conform to the Century dictionary, the standard adopted by the Publishing Section." A.L.A., *List* (1898), "Preface to the second edition," p. vi. This second edition was subsequently reissued several times. Plans for a third edition began in 1906 with the appointment of an advisory committee of seven members. Two more were added later. Esther Crawford did the actual compiling and editing from late 1906 to mid-1909. She was succeeded by Mary Josephine Briggs who completed the work two years later. A.L.A., *List of Subject Headings for Use in Dictionary Catalogs,* 3rd ed. (Chicago: A.L.A., 1911), "Preface," p. iii. (Hereafter cited as A.L.A., *List* (1911)).

2. Mary W. MacNair, "The Library of Congress List of Subject Headings," *Bulletin of the A.L.A.* 6 (July 1912): 231.

3. J. C. M. Hanson, "The Subject Catalogs of the Library of Congress," *Bulletin of the A.L.A.* 3 (July 1909): 389; A.L.A., *List* (1911), "Introduction," pp. vi–vii.

4. Library of Congress, *Subject Headings Used in the Dictionary Catalogs of the Library of Congress* (Washington: U.S. Government Printing Office, Library Branch, 1910–1914); Library of Congress, *List of Subject Headings, Additions and Revisions,* no. 1–14, December 1908–November 1917 (Washington: U.S. Government Printing Office, Library Branch, 1908–1917); Library of Congress, *Subject Headings Used in the Dictionary Catalogs of the Library of Congress,* 2nd ed. (Washington: U.S. Government Printing Office, Library Branch, 1919).

5. An exemplary and exhaustive biography of Hanson may be found in Edith Scott, "J. C. M. Hanson and His Contribution to Twentieth-Century Cataloging," (Ph.D. dissertation, University of Chicago, 1970). A briefer treatment will be found in *Dictionary of American Library Biography,* s.v. "Hanson, James Christian Meinich (1864–1943)," by John Phillip Immroth.

6. There is no one place that one may point to in Hanson's relatively few published writings and declare that it preeminently illustrates the shift in meanings that took place between Cutter and Hanson. By any measure, the shift in meanings was subtle and not a matter of overt reflection on the part of catalogers. Evidence of the shift in Hanson is of two kinds. First, there is absolutely no mention of Cutter's distinctions in Hanson's writings.

Considering their importance to the way Cutter's system functioned, their absence is indicative of significant change. Second, given the conclusion that a different framework of ideas was in effect, one must deal with how Hanson meant certain statements if he did not see them as Cutter had. For example, when comparing the 1869 Library of Congress printed alphabetico-classed subject index with his own endeavor, in "Subject Catalogs of the Library of Congress," p. 385, Hanson quoted from the previous publication to the effect that it was "the readiest available key to the books upon every subject which the Library of Congress embraces." Considering the period from which that catalog dated and the persons who made it—Frederic Vinton and A. R. Spofford, both of whom came from the same kind of earlier nineteenth century milieu which Cutter had experienced—it is difficult to interpret Hanson's statement in any other way than as a confirmation of the idea that of all the subjects that had been established up to that time, the 100,000 plus books of the Library of Congress represented many of them. Hanson immediately shifted his attention to the situation at hand, however. The thousands of books added since the 1860s, which brought the Library's collections to nearly one million volumes, represented "an enormous increase in the literature of many subjects." One does not find in this statement a more or less accidental relationship between subjects and the books that contain them. Rather, one finds a strong emphasis on books per se representing new subjects; that is, increases in the numbers of books were the same as increases in the numbers of new subjects. The same may be said of statements of Hanson's found elsewhere on other topics. The problem with the second kind of evidence is that it is eisegetical—read into the text. It does not constitute objective evidence. Still, faced with the need to explain the lack of Cutter's fundamental ideas, the imposition of this interpretation seems warranted, at least until some other more inclusive explanation is proposed.

7. *RDC,* Definitions, "Subject heading," p. 23.

8. After giving the reasons for choosing the dictionary rather than the classified subject catalog, Hanson immediately launched into a description of the chief problem facing the subject catalogers, that of having an adequate font of subject names at their disposal. The A.L.A. *List* was used as a starting point, but with the recognition that "considerable modification and specialization would have to be resorted to." Thus, other sources of subject names were kept handy, including the indexes of the Decimal and Expansive classification schemes, a list of the headings used at Harvard College Library, the subject index to the dictionary catalog of the Sydney (Australia) Public Library, and Fortescue's subject index of the British Museum Library catalog. In addition to these, numerous other reference books were also consulted. The purpose of all such sources seems obvious enough. If the topical content of any particular book could be confirmed by a common name in some other source, the name could be used in the catalog. Even with a wealth of sources, however, Hanson had to admit that "hundreds of subjects come up from day to day on which no information can be found outside of the work in which the new topic is first suggested" ("Subject Catalogs of the

Library of Congress," p. 387). The underlying equation is obvious as well. New books were equal to new topics which were equal to new subjects. The chief problem was how to name them.

9. Hanson, "Subject Catalogs of the Library of Congress," p. 390; cf. p. 387 as well as the previous note above.

10. Ibid., p. 390; also Hanson's remarks in A.L.A. Catalog Section discussion, *Bulletin of the A.L.A.* 2 (September 1908): 868–70.

11. Hanson, "Subject Catalogs of the Library of Congress," p. 390.

12. Ibid.

13. Ibid.

14. Ibid.

15. It should be especially noted that Hanson's evaluation of specific entry, while accurate for his own subject catalog, was not accurate for Cutter's. In Cutter's dictionary subject catalog an altogether different situation prevailed. Specific entry did not mean representing "the subjects" of books, but only the most concrete subjects treated in them. Scattering was present, but was, in effect, controlled by a cross-reference structure that, based on a significance order between categories of subjects, could relate subjects in a systematic and orderly manner.

16. Documents and descriptions related to Cutter's classification work and thinking may be found in brief form in Cutter, *Charles Ammi Cutter: Library Systematizer*, pp. 57–61, 238–88, and in a lengthier treatment in Miksa, "Charles Ammi Cutter, Nineteenth Century Systematizer of Libraries," pp. 486–614.

17. Two examples of user-oriented class order occurred in music and area studies. In his approach to the classification of music, Cutter opted for arrangement first by musical form and only secondarily by composer, rather than like the Harvard College Library, first gathering all the works of a composer together. His rationale for doing so was that his Forbes Library readers asked for music by form. See: Charles A. Cutter, "Shelf Classification of Music," *Library Journal* 27 (February 1902): 68–69. He also made it possible in his *Expansive Classification* to shift books from their normal discipline order to an area studies sequence by the simple expedient of beginning the class number with the area notation. Thus, German philosophy, history, statistics, natural sciences, fine arts, etc., could be gathered in one place on the shelves. He thought this to be especially useful to college libraries that supported curricula that emphasized studies of a place. See Charles A. Cutter, "Suitability of the Expansive Classification to College and Reference Libraries," *Library Journal* 24 (July 1899): C48–C49.

18. Hanson's experience with, estimates of, and use of the *Expansive Classification* are detailed in Scott, "J. C. M. Hanson," chapters 4, 6–7, passim.

19. For a discussion of Hanson's earlier educational experiences, see Scott, "J. C. M. Hanson," ch. 2. He published two reports on the departmental library problem at the University of Chicago: "Some Observations on the Departmental Library Problem in Universities, with Special Reference to the University of Chicago," *Bulletin of the A.L.A.* 6 (July 1912): 280–92; and "Study

of the Departmental Libraries at the University of Chicago, 1912–1917—Observations and Experiences," *Bulletin of the A.L.A.* 11 (July 1917): 211–21.

20. The categories are not mutually exclusive, of course. Geographical subclasses are often alphabetically arranged or in combinations of systematic and alphabetico-classed sequences. Form arrangement sometimes has alphabetically arranged elements. Chronological arrangements of either type stand alone as a uniquely different approach but when complex often involve subsequences of the other arrangements. Alphabetical arrangement is by far the most common device, however, popping up as the chief method to sequence arrays of a variety of topics.

21. "Martel's seven points," while nowhere adequately explained in the literature (cf. Lois M. Chan, *Immroth's Guide to the Library of Congress Classification*, 3rd ed., Library Science Text Series (Littleton, Colo.: Libraries Unlimited, 1980)), is the closest that Hanson and Martel came to providing a basic ordering principle. It indeed reoccurs throughout the scheme from the broadest to the narrowest topics. But its use as a pattern was highly variable. It began with the idea that general works should precede those narrower in scope. When fully represented this meant that the first six categories (i.e., points) almost always preceded the seventh. For the most part this pattern also placed general form division materials (dictionaries, periodicals, collections, etc.) first within the general materials and more often than not began those materials with periodicals. But beyond that, the other categories of materials followed no stated order. Furthermore, the first six categories of materials are more appropriately called clusters, their composition and completeness varying from subject area to subject area. They are also joined by a variety of free-floating categories (e.g., exhibitions, museums, etc.) that belong to no particular category. Finally, there are kinds of materials included among them, notably in the "general-special" sections of the "general works" cluster that often function as a miscellaneous category including topics that by any measure of consistency belong in the special topics section (Martel's seventh point), or so it seems to this writer. In the end, therefore, "Martel's seven points" bear only the vaguest resemblance to a consistent and repetitive pattern of collocation.

22. One still finds vestiges of this older view of scholarship in the realm of earned degrees. The highest earned degree in American universities remains the Doctor of Philosophy, although specialist advanced degrees denoting special fields have become more numerous. A doctor of philosophy degree has retained its association with an overall view of knowledge, rather than simply with one specialty. In this respect, it denotes the state of being a philosopher and, therefore, one notable for wisdom in general—regardless, of course, of whether that is in fact the case.

23. Hanson, "Subject Catalogs of the Library of Congress," p. 390.

24. Ibid.

25. *RDC,* R161, disc., p. 67; R164–65, disc., p. 68.

26. INTERLIBRARY LOANS is, in one sense, not a scope-match conventional heading at all. Rather, it is narrower than the concept of Lending of books.

Of course, perhaps the very notion of book lending meant library book lending.

27. The first edition of the Library's list of subject headings used the second of the two sequences. The order of the last two terms makes little difference here, however, because together they were subordinated to Postal service.

28. Hanson discussed both of these examples in 1909 in his "Subject Catalogs of the Library of Congress," p. 390. He also discussed the example on the Eastern question the previous year in his recorded remarks in the A.L.A. Catalog Section discussion, *Bulletin of the A.L.A.* 2 (September 1908): 868–70.

29. A brief note of the difficulties that early classed catalogs had with the class order of places in relation to topics was provided in chapter 7, note 19.

30. The seventh expansion of Cutter's *Expansive Classification* came the closest to the Library's needs, but even it was not detailed enough. Furthermore, it was unfinished at the time of the Library's search for a usable scheme. See Scott, "J. C. M. Hanson," chapters 6–7.

31. Hanson, "Subject Catalogs of the Library of Congress," p. 388. That changes in subject headings resulted from changes in the classification scheme seems strongly indicated in a footnote to the second subject headings additions and revisions list issued in April 1909: "For convenience of reference all headings used under *Photographic* and *Photography* are given, i.e. headings formerly adopted as well as additions and changes resulting from the recent recataloging of TR" (Library of Congress, *List of Subject Headings, Additions and Revisions* no. 2 [April 1909]: 6). The recataloging of photography books in the Library's collections had apparently finally been completed. This caused some revisions of the TR schedule and, consequently, enough changes in photography subject headings that it was decided to publish the revisions of that entire section of subject headings.

32. Cf. Library of Congress Classification Z4–Z8, Z696–Z697. The actual sequence in the latter appears to be Library science-Collections (i.e., functional treatment of the library's collections, including all standard library operations)-Classification (i.e., of books).

33. As the succeeding discussion will show, variations based on rationalizations other than dependence on the classification scheme make it impossible to claim consistency within any of the topical areas in Figure 10. Furthermore, since a close examination of the Library's classification scheme is well beyond the scope of this work, the number of correlations noted here are relatively limited. The examples chosen have been hampered by the unavailability of the very earliest schedules of the classification scheme in every instance. Nevertheless, by the use of the oldest schedules available and by limiting the examples to those topical areas that seem to have been reasonably stable over a number of years, the conclusions drawn here seem warranted. Doubtless, however, more detailed comparative work in correlating the two systems would establish the conclusions with greater firmness.

34. Hanson, "Subject Catalogs of the Library of Congress," p. 387.

35. Ibid. He referred to the report of the A.L.A. Committee on an Index to Subject Headings, *Library Journal* 18 (September 1893): C79–C80. Distinguishing here between "place" and "general subject" follows Cutter's terminology. To distinguish only between "place" and "subject" as Hanson and the committee report did suggests strongly that a place is something other than a subject.

36. Hanson, "Subject Catalogs of the Library of Congress," p. 387. Anderson's views are contained in Sydney, Public Library of New South Wales, *Guide to the System of Cataloguing of the Reference Library. . . ,* 3rd ed. (Sydney: W. A. Gullick, 1898); Sydney, Public Library of New South Wales, *Subject Index of the Books in the Author Catalogues for the Years 1869–1895* (Sydney: Turner & Henderson, 1903). Hanson reviewed the latter work very positively in *Library Journal* 29 (April 1904): 197.

37. Hanson, "Subject Catalogs of the Library of Congress," p. 387.

38. The topics Coast defenses and Fortifications were both in the Military Science (UG) schedule of the classification scheme. Both were subdivided geographically and both should have been used as class entry terms. Likewise, Finance and Appropriations and expenditures, both topics in the Public Finance (HJ) schedule of the classification scheme, were also subdivided geographically. They too should both have been used as class entry terms. Variations such as these could also not be explained as exceptions based on differentiating between those topics to be entered under general subject (sciences, technology, and most of economics) and those to be entered under place. That pattern required at least the first pair to be consistent and at least strongly suggested that the second pair be consistent as well.

39. Hanson, "Subject Catalogs of the Library of Congress," p. 387.

40. I would venture the axiom that a reference structure used primarily as a means to "correct" or otherwise provide alternatives to an otherwise unsystematic approach to subject collocation will eventually be viewed as only a random infrastructure and not be highly regarded. The remainder of this study will reinforce the assertion that the cross-reference structure of Library of Congress subject headings has generally not been taken seriously. As a matter of fact, it cannot be viewed in any way other than that stated above.

41. The problem of differentiating between subject subdivisions on the one hand and topical subheadings on the other hand necessarily arises from one's definition of specific entry because the notion of a specific subject assumes that class inclusion can be recognized. John W. Metcalfe has made perhaps the most concerted effort to interpret Cutter's basic notion of specific entry and thus to distinguish between the two kinds of subheadings. See his *Information Indexing and Subject Cataloging,* pp. 124-27; *Subject Classifying and Indexing of Libraries and Literature,* pp. 272–77; and "When Is a Subject Not a Subject?" pp. 310–12. His approach to the matter was echoed in Olding, "Form of Alphabetico-Specific Subject Headings and a Brief Code," pp. 127–37, and seriously challenged by Drake, "What Is a Subject," pp. 34–36. Svenonius, "Metcalfe and the Principles of Specific Entry," pp. 171–73, summarized Metcalfe's view, but concluded that "it tightens Cutter's rule in a way which probably follows Cutter's intent, though it is perhaps a sophisti-

cation he could not have imagined" (p. 173). It is interesting to note that subheadings have come to be understood in common parlance as either aspects or subdivisions to topics. Chan, *Library of Congress Subject Headings,* pp. 63–65, says that only genus-species and whole-part relationships are characteristic of classed catalog subdivision practice. All other topical subdivisions, such as AGRICULTURE–TAXATION and HEART–DISEASE, are simply aspects or facets of a subject. But this is surely a troublesome distinction since the idea of facets is ordinarily used in the sense of a logically distinguished subclass. For example, B. C. Vickery, in *Faceted Classification, a Guide to Construction and Use of Special Schemes* (London: Aslib, 1960), p. 12, describes facets as "mutually exclusive" groups of terms, "each derived from the parent universe by a single characteristic of division. We may look upon these facets as groups of terms derived by taking each term and defining it, *per genus et differentiam,* with respect to its parent class." His reasoning may in fact be applied to the present examples to show why they are subdivisions and not simply aspects. The reasons why –TAXATION and –DISEASES may not appear to be subdivisions may actually be because of the vagueness in the way the terms are listed. AGRICULTURE, when defined as an economic activity, certainly has a subclass of operations impinging on it that include –TAXATION. And HEART, when placed in the general class MEDICINE (rather than simply HUMAN ANATOMY) certainly has a subclass of diseases. If, however, HEART and AGRICULTURE were simply viewed as elements of the general classes HUMAN ANATOMY and TECHNOLOGY respectively, then the subclasses could be considered not intrinsic and therefore only aspects. The vagueness of the difference between aspects and subdivisions was further illustrated to this writer in a provocative though wholly unscientific way when he asked colleagues to identify which of the subheadings in Figure 10 were only aspects and which (if any) were subdivisions, with no other explanation to go on than their casual understanding of the difference. The result was not a little confusing and strongly suggested that there is little real understanding of classificatory distinctions that would make differentiating between subdivisions and aspects of a topic a useful device.

42. Hanson, "Subject Catalogs of the Library of Congress," p. 390.

43. Forty years later, David J. Haykin, one of Hanson's successors, used the above argument as a way to justify topical subheadings in his work *Subject Headings,* p. 36. Chan, *Library of Congress Subject Headings,* p. 64, reiterated Haykin's reasoning and claimed that subheadings used to carry out specification "resemble alphabetico-classed entries in their outward form only." Besides the comments here, this use of subarrangement is also discussed in chapter 11.

44. Hanson's enthusiasm for and use of classed subarrangement should not be considered strange. Among the basic resources that he used for subject names was the Harvard College Library's list of subject headings compiled under the direction of William C. Lane. The better part of that list was alphabetico-classed, having been originally based on the work of Ezra Abbot and Charles Cutter some thirty years earlier. When one considers Hanson's concern about the general increase of subjects ("Subject Catalogs of the

Library of Congress," pp. 385–86) and his concern that these be collocated, not scattered, the alternative offered by alphabetico-classed headings such as those found in the Harvard list must have seemed like reasonable choices.

45. Hanson, "Subject Catalogs of the Library of Congress," p. 390. The more fundamental question of why some topics were scattered and others gathered is even less answerable, buried as it is in Hanson's generally pragmatic approach to classification described earlier.

46. The three examples of the formulaic phrase heading in Figure 10D, column b—JEWS IN AFRICA, JEWS IN CHICAGO, and JEWS IN THE UNITED STATES —are like the tip of an iceberg. In the first edition of the Library's subject heading list, that formula includes sixty-six phrases on two complete pages (pp. 513–14). Their formulaic phraseology followed the classification scheme (DS135) in that it represented the last two elements of the sequence HISTORY– ASIA–PALESTINE/THE JEWS–JEWS OUTSIDE OF PALESTINE–[Place].

47. Hanson's protest to MacNair is recorded in Scott, "J. C. M. Hanson," p. 290.

48. See RDC, R174–175, but see also the discussion of that rule in chapter 6.

49. Hanson, "Subject Catalogs of the Library of Congress," p. 389.

50. Ibid., p. 390.

51. Ibid.

52. Ibid., pp. 390–91.

CHAPTER 9. DICTIONARY SUBJECT CATALOGING BEFORE 1940

1. One need only read cursorily through a selection of A.L.A. conference proceedings during the first decade of the twentieth century, especially comments made in the Catalog and College Sections discussions, to catch the decided nature of the following view of readers. Of particular merit are the following items from the 1902 College Library Section meeting: N. D. C. Hodges, "Bibliographies vs. Dictionary Catalogs," Library Journal 27 (July 1902): 178–80; Alice B. Kroeger, "Dictionary Catalogs vs. Bibliographies," Library Journal 27 (July 1902): 180–82; and comments by various persons including Hodges and especially F. J. Teggart, in Library Journal 27 (July 1902): 183–86.

2. Mildred A. Collar briefly summarized this issue in "The Classification and Cataloging of Children's Books," Library Journal 28 (July 1903): 65.

3. J. C. M. Hanson expressed acute awareness of the conflicts in his "Printed Cards of the Library of Congress, their Various Uses, and Practical Difficulties Experienced in their Use," Library Journal 28 (July 1903): 192. He raised the possibility then, as he was to do again in 1909 in his "Subject Catalogs of the Library of Congress," pp. 390–91, that some accommodation might be made for other libraries by printing special cards of a different nature. But this was never able to be done. Gardner M. Jones again raised the issue of incompatibility during the Catalog Section discussion in Library Journal 31 (August 1906): 237. But it was Artena M. Chapin, "Cataloging in a Small City Library," Bulletin of the A.L.A. 5 (July 1911): 219, who raised

the question of whether Library of Congress cards in general, including subject headings, were worth the trouble at all. Developments subsequent to the first decade decided the issue decisively in favor of using Library of Congress copy.

4. Theresa Hitchler, *Cataloging for Small Libraries,* A.L.A. Publishing Board, Library Handbook, no. 2 (Boston: The Board, 1905). A greatly expanded second edition was published in 1915: *Cataloging for Small Libraries,* rev. ed. (Chicago: A.L.A. Publishing Board, 1915). And a third, relatively unchanged edition was published in 1926. The citations here are principally from the first edition. William Warner Bishop, "Subject Headings in Dictionary Catalogs," *Library Journal* 31 (August 1906): 113–23. Except for the addition of section captions in the text, Bishop's advice on subject headings was unchanged in the form of chapter 7 of his *Practical Handbook of Modern Library Cataloging* (Baltimore: Williams & Wilkins, 1914). Here, citations are from the original article. His text was reissued in 1927 in a second edition of his book, but the chapter on subject headings remained unchanged.

5. Hitchler, *Cataloging for Small Libraries,* p. 19.

6. Ibid.; in her 1915 edition, p. 42, Hitchler expanded these comments to include the suggestion that different subject terms, presumably more simplified, should not be made for children's libraries, these being for her a variant kind of smaller library.

7. Bishop decisively separated the needs of the larger library from the smaller. Of the latter he stated in "Subject Headings," p. 113, that it in fact "need not bother itself greatly about principles of subject entry," chiefly because its staff and patrons alike would depend on shelf classification and current bibliography.

8. Ibid.

9. Ibid., p. 114.

10. Hitchler, *Cataloging for Small Libraries,* p. 19.

11. Ibid., p. 18.

12. Bishop, "Subject Headings," pp. 114–15.

13. Ibid., p. 115. It should be noted that Hitchler, in *Cataloging for Small Libraries,* was certainly cognizant of Cutter's *Rules,* to the extent, at least, that she included many of his definitions in her glossary, "Bibliographical and Typographical Terms," pp. 39–62. This provides at least one explicit connection between her work and a classificatory approach to subjects. On the other hand, she did not explain her notions about subjects in any theoretical way in the text of her work. There, she was plainly intent on writing simple instructions.

14. Bishop, "Subject Headings," pp. 116–17. Bishop's specific resolution of the place-topic problem was the same as Hanson's at the Library of Congress with the exception that Hanson allowed some ad hoc variations from the basic pattern.

15. Ibid., p. 115.

16. Ibid.

17. Ibid.

18. Esther Crawford, in "The New Edition of A.L.A. Subject Headings," *Library Journal* 32 (January 1907): 25, noted that the decision was publicly announced by the A.L.A. Publishing Board in December 1906.

19. Hitchler, *Cataloging for Small Libraries,* p. 8.

20. Ibid., emphasis added.

21. Crawford, "The New Edition of A.L.A. Subject Headings," pp. 25–26.

22. Esther Crawford, "A.L.A. Subject Headings," *Library Journal* 32 (October 1907): 435.

23. Ibid.

24. Ibid.

25. Ibid.

26. Ibid.

27. Ibid.

28. Ibid., p. 436.

29. Esther Crawford, "A.L.A. Subject Headings—II," *Library Journal* 32 (November 1907): 500–1; "A.L.A. Subject Headings. III," *Library Journal* 32 (December 1907): 560–61.

30. The issue of consistency bore the onus of a theoretical versus practical conflict. That which was theoretically consistent was likely to be impractical and that which was practical was likely to be theoretically inconsistent. Andrew Keogh wrote in 1908 that a catalog "is designed to answer certain questions with the least trouble to the user. It should be a labor-saving and not a trouble-making device . . . Theoretical considerations should therefore always give way to the facility of use." (Quoted in Elva S. Smith, *Subject Headings for Children's Books in Public Libraries and in Libraries in Elementary and Junior High Schools* (Chicago: A.L.A., 1933), p. ix.) Mary J. Briggs, in "The A.L.A. List of Subject Headings," *Bulletin of the A.L.A.* 6 (July 1912): 228, compared subject heading work with that of making the 1908 code of descriptive cataloging rules and found that whereas the latter was amenable to consistency, the former was not. "But who can frame a code of rules or formulate principles through which consistency in subject headings may be attained? And is consistency so absolutely necessary or desirable? Is not the ideal catalog the one which is best adapted to the needs of the majority of its users; which is so arranged that the reader can find what he wants in the shortest possible time, even at the sacrifice of absolute consistency."

31. Briggs, "The A.L.A. List," p. 229.

32. Ibid., p. 230.

33. Interestingly, Briggs's speech was followed by one by Mary M. MacNair, the editor of the Library of Congress's list, "The Library of Congress List of Subject Headings," pp. 231–34.

34. Briggs, "The A.L.A. List," p. 231.

35. The single exception to this period of quiescence in public discussion was the publication of Margaret Mann's *Subject Headings for Use in Dictionary Catalogs of Juvenile Books* (Chicago: A.L.A. Publishing Board, 1916).

36. "Training for Cataloging Work," *Bulletin of the A.L.A.* 9 (September 1915): 262–72.

37. A brief account of children's subject heading work during the first three decades of the twentieth century is given in Smith, *Subject Headings for Children's Books,* pp. viii–ix. The relationship between Mann and Smith in the development of such lists was important. Both began library work at the Carnegie Library of Pittsburgh in 1903 and collaborated for some sixteen years before Mann left the institution in 1919. Smith helped to produce some of the earlier lists issued by the library, but Mann published the first strictly children's subject cataloging guide in 1916. Afterward, Smith augmented the text of Mann's work to produce her 1933 volume. Smith summarized how she changed Mann's emphases on page xxix.

38. Minnie E. Sears, ed., *List of Subject Headings for Small Libraries, Compiled from lists used in nine representative small libraries* (New York: H. W. Wilson Company, 1923).

39. Minnie E. Sears, ed., *List of Subject Headings for Small Libraries, Compiled from lists used in nine representative small libraries,* 2nd ed., rev. & enlarged (New York: H. W. Wilson Company, 1926). This edition was reprinted in 1928.

40. Hanson, "Subject Catalogs of the Library of Congress," pp. 393–96; T. Franklin Currier had broached the issue of insufficient specification in large catalogs in "Too Many Cards under a Subject Heading," *Library Journal* 35 (September 1910): 412–13, and his concern was repeated by William Warner Bishop in "Two Unsolved Problems in Library Work," *Library Journal* 37 (January 1912): 10–11. Bishop's concern about insufficiently specified books actually lay at the base of his treatment of subject cataloging in his 1906 remarks in "Subject Headings."

41. Henry B. Van Hoesen, ed., *Selective Cataloging: Cataloger's Round Table, American Library Association, July 3, 1924* . . . (New York: H. W. Wilson, 1928). All of the various problems here are discussed or alluded to in one way or another.

42. The role of the administrator and the problem of costs came to be more and more prominent throughout the 1930s. See for example the entire change in point of view in William M. Randall, "The Technical Processes and Library Service," in *The Acquisition and Cataloging of Books: Papers Presented before the Library Institute at the University of Chicago, July 29 to August 9, 1940,* ed. William M. Randall (Chicago: University of Chicago Press, 1940), pp. 1–29.

43. The categories are much more complex, of course, especially when subtypes and hybrid types are admitted. But the basic four have persisted. It remains to be seen if the information revolution of the last two decades will effectively change the nomenclature of library types into something altogether different, based, for example, on kinds of information service rather than kinds of institutional affiliation.

44. As noted in the text, the discussion about the public library "type" and how its distinctive characteristics came to be understood is speculative. What is needed is a sociological analysis of the library as an institution to clarify this matter. The history of libraries in the twentieth century has by and large been written as a series of studies of types of libraries with little

attention paid to how the types of libraries have come to be differentiated. An account of the origin of types of libraries and, therefore, types of clienteles, would greatly benefit librarians' understanding of the effective domain of libraries and would lead to a fruitful examination of what has been up to now an all too simplistic approach to the characterization of users.

45. Mann, *Subject Headings,* p. 3.

46. Ibid., pp. 3–4.

47. Ibid., p. 3.

48. The quoted definitions of simple terms occur throughout the entire section on simple terms in Smith, *Subject Headings for Children's Books,* pp. xix–xx.

49. Ibid.

50. Ibid., p. xix.

51. Ibid.

52. Ibid., p. xx.

53. Mann, *Subject Headings,* pp. 3–4.

54. Smith, *Subject Headings for Children's Books,* p. xx.

55. Mann, *Subject Headings,* p. 4.

56. Smith, *Subject Headings for Children's Books,* p. xx.

57. Ibid., p. xxiv; Mann, *Subject Headings,* p. 28.

58. Cf. Mann, *Subject Headings,* pp. 21–23.

59. Smith, *Subject Headings for Children's Books,* p. xxiv.

60. Ibid., p. xx.

61. The following summary of characteristics related to special libraries and the documentation movement is purposefully left at a highly generalized level. To examine the movement in greater detail is beyond the scope of this work because special libraries and the documentation movement have not been a direct factor in dictionary subject catalog development. For a useful general view of the development of the special library and documentation field, especially from the standpoint of education for librarianship, see Jesse H. Shera, *The Foundations of Education for Librarianship,* Information Science Series (New York: Wiley–Becker and Hayes, 1972), pp. 163–94, 274–95. Samuel Brandford's *Documentation* (London: Crosby Lockwood & Son, 1948), on the other hand provides a useful view from inside the documentation movement. In addition, the historical essay on the development of the documentation movement by Jesse H. Shera and Margaret E. Egan in the second edition of Bradford's work (Crosby, Lockwood & Son, 1953, pp. 12-27) contains the thought-provoking thesis that traditional librarianship abrogated its information science responsibilities when it allowed periodical indexing to be severed from book subject cataloging at the turn of the century. None of this is to say that there has been no connection at all between special libraries, documentation, and information science on the one hand and dictionary subject cataloging on the other. One of the purposes of the present work is to attempt to show such connections regardless of the fact that they appear always to have been tenuous and shadowy, more an influence related to the general social background of dictionary subject cataloging than any direct borrowing.

62. Cutter, "Library Catalogues," pp. 540 and 548.

63. Bradford, *Documentation* (1948), p. 11.

64. Cf. Harriet D. MacPherson, "Building a List of Subject Headings," *Special Libraries* 24 (March 1933): 44–46.

65. An interesting and notable early direct criticism of dictionary subject catalogs for special libraries may be found in A. F. C. Pollard and S. C. Bradford, "The Inadequacy of the Alphabetical Subject Index," in *Proceedings of the Seventh [ASLIB] Conference* (London: Aslib, 1930), pp. 39–54. Direct criticisms of this sort and the resolution of subject access needs by appeals to classified cataloging were in the 1930s more likely to be found among British rather than American authors. In America, the wholesale separation of special libraries from dictionary subject cataloging appears not to have taken place until after World War II. That they were closer together during the 1930s is suggested by two papers by Julia Pettee in which the special library use of dictionary subject cataloging is more or less taken for granted: "Subject Headings: an Introductory Paper," *Special Libraries* 23 (April 1932): 151–56, and "The Philosophy of Subject Headings," *Special Libraries* 23 (April 1932): 181–82. Of course, one might argue that Pettee could hold such opinions because she was a special librarian in a theological library rather than in a science or technological special library.

66. Grace O. Kelley, "The Subject Approach to Books: An Adventure in Curriculum," *Catalogers' and Classifiers' Yearbook* 2 (1930): 9–23; cf. Susan G. Akers, "A Decade of Teaching Subject Headings," *Catalogers' and Classifiers' Yearbook* 4 (1934): 85–92, where essentially the same attitude prevails.

67. For the identification of academic libraries with cultural uplift goals, see Orvin Lee Shiflett, *Origin of American Academic Librarianship* (Norwood, N.J.: Ablex Publishing Corporation, 1981), p. 273.

68. The Association of Research Libraries was founded in 1932 and thereafter promoted the special research academic library as a group apart from simply academic libraries in general.

69. Dorcas Fellows, *Cataloging Rules, with Explanations and Illustrations,* 2nd ed., rev. and enl. (New York: H. W. Wilson, 1922). The Fellows text was a revision of the Library School Rules first issued by Melvil Dewey in the late 1880s but revised here from Library School Bulletin 36 (1915). It depended chiefly on reiterating older rules (e.g., Cutter's *Rules*) for the statement of practice and then discussing at length such clerical matters as spacing in typing cards, kinds of cards to make within any one unit entry set, etc.

70. Susan G. Akers, *Simple Library Cataloging* (Chicago: A.L.A., 1927); Margaret Mann, *Introduction to Cataloging and the Classification of Books* (Chicago: A.L.A., 1930). A preliminary mimeographed edition of Mann's work was issued in 1928 under the title *The Classification and Catologing [sic] of Books,* primarily for eliciting critical comments from the cataloging community. A second edition was issued in 1943 and for many years functioned as *the* standard teaching text in library schools. Unless otherwise noted, citations are from the 1930 edition, cited hereafter simply as Mann, *Introduction*. Minnie E. Sears, *List of Subject Headings for Small Libraries, Compiled from lists used in nine representative small libraries,* 3rd ed., rev.

& enlarged, including a new section, "Practical Suggestions for the Beginner in Subject Heading Work" (New York: H. W. Wilson Company, 1933). Cited hereafter as Sears, *List of Subject Headings* (1933). Since Smith has already been discussed in the context of children's libraries and Akers is for the most part very brief on subject heading work, most of the discussion will center on Mann and Sears.

71. Mann, *Introduction,* p. 177; cf. Akers, *Simple Library Cataloging,* p. 32, where she states that the most appropriate heading for a book is that "which most truly represents the content of the book or a certain part of the book, that is, the most specific heading possible." Sears, *List of Subject Headings* (1933), p. xii, wrote, "The first step in the work is to determine the real subject of the book, that is, what the author had in mind when he wrote the book"; and on p. xiii, coupled this with the entry process by declaring, "The matter of translating the subject of the book into the proper specific subject heading is the great difficulty of subject heading work. The first exact rule is what is known as the rule of *specific entry.* Enter a book under the most specific term (i.e., subject heading) which accurately and truly fits the subject presented in the contents of the book." Emphasis hers.

72. Sears, *List of Subject Headings* (1933), p. xiii.

73. Ibid.; Mann, *Introduction,* pp. 176–77, 178–79, for examples using the subject PSYCHOLOGY, and cf. p. 183 for the example DRAMA.

74. Cf. Mann, *Introduction,* p. 183; Sears, *List of Subject Headings* (1933), p. xvi. Of course, given the general confusion by the 1930s about the difference between subarrangement and subdivision, this may not have been seen as a problem of subject specification. Still, Sears stated explicitly that topical subdivisions were used "in order to make the headings more specific" (p. xvi) and that being the case, the failure to use a topical subdivision amounted to purposefully providing class entry.

75. On recall as the number of items retrieved, especially for small libraries, see Mann, *Introduction,* p. 179; on experience, see Sears, *List of Subject Headings* (1933), p. xiii.

76. *RDC,* "Objects," p. 12.

77. *RDC,* R161, disc., p. 67. Emphasis his.

78. Mann, *Introduction,* p. 177. Emphasis hers.

79. Smith, *Subject Headings for Children's Books,* p. xx, after warning against making headings that are "unnecessarily minute," described such subjects as those "which include divisions so small that it is quite improbable they will be discussed separately." She meant that it was fruitless in such catalogs to subdivide too minutely. It should also be noted that Smith's explicit reason for avoiding "unnecessarily minute" headings was not their lack of gathering capacity but rather that children simply did not think of such subjects.

80. Sears, *List of Subject Headings* (1933), p. xiii.

81. Mann, *Introduction* (1943), p. 143.

82. That the latter was the case at the Library of Congress is discussed in chapter 11.

83. Mann, *Introduction,* p. 191.

84. Akers, *Simple Library Cataloging,* p. 32.

85. Sears, *List of Subject Headings* (1933), pp. xiv-xv.

86. *RDC,* R169, p. 70.

87. Mann, *Introduction,* p. 3.

88. Ibid., pp. 3–4.

89. In the second edition of her work, Mann more specifically referred to the first group as "special libraries." See Mann, *Introduction* (1943), p. 3.

90. Akers, *Simple Library Cataloging,* p. 5; Sears, *List of Subject Headings* (1933), p. xii.

91. College libraries, as distinguished from university libraries, tended to be characterized as part of the scholarly group despite their generally small size. And one may question whether there was such a thing as a special collection used chiefly by general readers. Not much can be found in the literature delineating that category.

92. Mann, *Introduction,* p. 173.

93. *RDC,* headnote to "B. Entries Considered as Parts of a Whole," p. 79; cf. also R175, disc., p. 75, where Cutter noted that the "main object" of a dictionary catalog was "ready reference." One has cause to wonder how Mann arrived at her interpretation because Cutter nowhere said anything about general readers wanting a "definite bit of information" or that the subject searches of general readers could be characterized as not being general or exhaustive, at least not in the sections of his *Rules* noted here. Here, all Cutter did was to characterize scholarly readers as those whose subject searches were extensive and thorough and that a cross-reference system would aid them in that effort. He also noted that the dictionary catalog had another object to pursue, "facility of reference." Two things must be noted here of Cutter's words: first, he characterized only scholarly searching, not nonscholarly; and second, he characterized the object of the dictionary catalog not as opposite that of a classed catalog, but merely as different from it. Now, if one begins with the assumption that Mann apparently held (probably following Hanson), that scholarly and general readers were opposites not simply different in degree (as Cutter had suggested), then it would seem reasonable that any characterization of scholarly readers (such as the one Cutter made here) need only be reversed to characterize its opposite kind. That is in fact where Mann appears to have gotten her characterization of general readers—that they searched neither thoroughly nor extensively and looked for subjects as separate rather than as connected ideas. Furthermore, if the classed catalog and the dictionary catalog are also seen as opposites in the same manner of reasoning, then one need only reverse the chief characteristics of the classed (subjects collocated) to arrive at the chief characteristic of the dictionary (subjects not collocated, or not classed or standing alone). This was all a far cry from Cutter's chief characterization of the dictionary catalog, that it gave facility of reference to the most concrete subjects, not simply that it gave facility of reference to separately taken subjects.

94. Sears, *List of Subject Headings* (1933), pp. xvi–xvii.

CHAPTER 10. REVOLUTION IN SUBJECT ACCESS

1. Since the 1940s, in fact, standard American textbooks on cataloging such as those issued by Eaton, Wynar, and Piercy, as well as reissues of Akers, have assumed a tradition well nigh independent of the critical writers in the field of subject cataloging. They have tended to present subject cataloging work as little more than variations of Mann or Haykin with little theoretical substance of note. Perhaps more could not be expected. As the course of this inquiry will show, critical writing on subject heading work, though rigorous through the 1950s, ultimately drew few firm conclusions. Since 1960 it has in fact devolved to a documentation of Library of Congress inconsistencies. The cutting edge of subject access thinking has been for all practical purposes coopted by persons working in indexing and automated information retrieval.

2. The findings of twenty-seven use studies made between 1931 and 1951 (many of them done as theses) are summarized and evaluated in Carlyle J. Frarey, "Studies of Use of the Subject Catalog: Summary and Evaluation," in *The Subject Analysis of Library Materials,* ed. Maurice F. Tauber (New York: School of Library Service, Columbia University, 1953), pp. 147–66. Only five studies are listed for the 1930s, however. The remaining twenty-two were made between 1940 and 1951. Of the twenty-seven studies, sixteen were focused on university, college, or research needs. Frarey later added another thirteen studies to his total and expanded the idea of user studies considerably in his "Subject Headings" (1960), pp. 8–13, 22–24, and note 104, pp. 76–78.

3. Hitchler, *Cataloging for Small Libraries* (1905), lists Cutter's *Rules* in her bibliography (p. 35), follows them in the matter of filing (pp. 27–32), and draws on them for definitions (pp. 39–62). But she recommended only "Some Hints on Subject Cataloging in Dictionary Style" (p. 18) for subject cataloging instructions. Bishop, *Practical Handbook of Modern Library Cataloging,* p. 111, note 2, simply states, "Cutter's *Rules* contain some admirable chapters on the theory of subject entry." Cutter is not cited as an aid by either Akers, *Simple Library Cataloging,* or by Smith, *Subject Headings for Children's Books.* Sears, *List of Subject Headings* (1933), pp. xi–xii, cites Cutter as a general aid and also more specifically in reference to choice between subject names. Fellows, *Cataloging Rules,* p. 40, notes that the principles she uses are "taken largely from *Cutter,* where a very full discussion of the topic may be found." But then, after citing three other persons, only one of two principles that she lists—choice between synonyms—reflects Cutter directly. Only Mann, *Introduction* (1930), of the various textbook writers refers several times to Cutter. But even she limits reference to him to specific problems. In fact, she cautioned students about his subject rules in general, stating, *"Rules for a dictionary catalog* by C. A. Cutter, is the only printed code covering the rulings for subject headings and while this should be referred to by students, their attention should be called to the fact that much of the reasoning used by Cutter was based on that formerly applied to a classified catalog, and that many of the illustrations are out of date" (p. 176). Her view of the difference between Cutter and contemporary work was

perceptive, although as shown here in the previous chapter, that did not help her to avoid including some of his reasoning in her own system.

4. On the use of lists see Mann, *Introduction,* pp. 195–97; cf. Akers, "A Decade of Teaching Subject Headings," pp. 85–92; and also Henry Black, "The Problem of Subject Headings," *Catalogers' and Classifiers' Yearbook* 6 (1937): 86–90.

5. Fellows, *Cataloging Rules,* p. 40, noted in 1922 that "an extended treatment of principles is now (July 1921) being prepared for publication by Mary E. Hyde, instructor in the New York State Library School." Akers, "A Decade of Teaching Subject Headings," p. 85, repeated the statement and noted (p. 88) that a text promised so many years before would soon be coming out under the auspices of the A.L.A. Committee on Cataloging and Classification. During the 1940s, the need for a code was often mentioned. David J. Haykin's *Subject Headings,* issued in 1951, appeared to have filled the need, at least in part. But it too was to be superseded by an even more thorough work. Hopes for that final volume were expressed during the mid-1950s, but were dashed by Haykin's untimely death in 1958.

6. S. R. Ranganathan, *Theory of Library Catalogue,* p. 92. The results of his critique were not unimportant. British writers schooled in Ranganathan's thought not only assumed the same essential connection in the 1950s, but also the ridiculing tone as well, although without recourse to Ranganathan's laws and canons as a critical measure.

7. Maurice F. Tauber, "Subject Cataloging and Classification Approaching the Crossroads," *College and Research Libraries* 3 (March 1942): 150. Cutter did not, of course, set down the procedures in 1904, the date of the fourth and posthumous edition of his *Rules.*

8. Patricia B. Knapp, "The Subject Catalog in the College Library, the Background of Subject Cataloging," *Library Quarterly* 14 (April 1944): 110. This article was the first of two that provided "the essential portion" of Knapp's master's thesis: "The Subject Catalog in the College Library; an Investigation of Terminology" (Master's thesis, University of Chicago, 1943). The second of the two articles was entitled with the thesis title proper: "The Subject Catalog in the College Library; an Investigation of Terminology," *Library Quarterly* 14 (July 1944): 214–28.

9. Ibid., pp. 110, 115. The rules of Cutter's upon which Knapp focused particular attention were R175 (on compound headings) and R164–165 (on choices between subject and country). Knapp actually mentioned only ten of Cutter's twenty-eight subject rules.

10. Pettee, *Subject Headings,* p. 47. Pettee was comparing subject rules with rules for descriptive cataloging, the former lacking, the latter plentiful. She had previously written on Cutter's connection with the development of a theory of author main entry and perhaps keenly felt the absence of generally accepted subject rules. Curiously, however, Pettee rarely if ever mentioned Cutter in her earlier writings on subject headings.

11. Randall, "The Technical Processes and Library Service," nowhere called for studies of the users in types of libraries per se. But his over-

whelming insistence on finding out "what sorts of patrons there are and what they need to know about books" (p. 22) as one of the fundamental bases of library research, when combined with his various examples, leaves little doubt as to the direction such research must take, that is, according to individual libraries as examples of types of libraries. Frarey, "Studies of Use of the Subject Catalog: Summary and Evaluation," p. 148, noted that a previous call for such research by Randall at the 1930 Los Angeles A.L.A. conference may well have been the kickoff point for such studies. But since only five of the studies that Frarey listed in his summary were conducted before 1940 and twenty-two were after 1940, he concluded (pp. 151–52) that Randall's first call was abortive and that the second call in the article cited above was what really took effect. In his 1960 *Subject Headings,* p. 10, Frarey reiterated his opinion, suggesting that Randall had given the outline in 1940 as to what such user studies should focus on. Especially important forum proceedings were recorded in the *Journal of Cataloging and Classification* 8 (December 1952): 131–58 ("Symposium on Subject Headings"), and in *The Subject Analysis of Library Materials,* which consisted of the proceedings of an institute held in 1952, jointly sponsored by the Columbia University School of Library Service and the A.L.A. Division of Cataloging and Classification.

12. Pettee, *Subject Headings,* p. 66.

13. Ibid., pp. 66–67.

14. Ibid., p. 67.

15. Ibid., p. 84.

16. Ibid., see variously pp. 83, 153–54, and 161. Cf. also p. 168. The word "casual" in "casual informative literature" is not defined.

17. Ibid., pp. 83–84.

18. Ibid., p. 68. The main outlines of a dictionary subject catalog made for nonscholars and thus only for informational purposes are found in chapter 5, pp. 68–92.

19. Ibid., p. 81.

20. Ibid., p. 83. The main outlines of a dictionary subject catalog made for scholars are found in chapter 6, pp. 83–99. But since this was Pettee's primary interest, she extended her comments by dealing with special problems in chapters 7–8.

21. Ibid., p. 80.

22. Jean K. Taylor, "Reflections and Observations on Subject Analysis: the Public Reference Librarian," in *The Subject Analysis of Library Materials,* ed. Maurice F. Tauber (New York: School of Library Service, Columbia University, 1954), p. 169. Cf. Pettee, "A New Principle in Dealing with Subject Material Needed?" pp. 17–19, who suggested that subject catalog use was primarily a function of kinds of thinking rather than, one supposes, a type of library.

23. This terminology became more frequent by the end of the 1940s and was referred to in the Columbia University conference of 1952, *The Subject Analysis of Library Materials,* particularly in Frarey, "Studies of Use of the Subject Catalog: Summary and Evaluation." It seems to have become established by the 1954 A.L.A. forum on "Standards for Subject Headings," the

papers of which were printed in the *Journal of Cataloging and Classification* 10 (October 1954): 175–202. And Paul S. Dunkin, in "Criticisms of Current Cataloging Practice," *Library Quarterly* 26 (October 1956): 295, excerpted precisely that emphasis from Frarey when reviewing subject heading development in 1956.

24. Dunkin, "Criticisms of Current Cataloging Practice," p. 293.

25. Ibid., p. 301. The idea that the user and common usage were primary considerations in Cutter's subject heading system was not often discussed before the mid-1940s. Before that time considerations of usage seem to have been more or less taken for granted. Even Knapp's 1944 studies on college library catalog use and Pettee's 1946 *Subject Headings* assumed the reality of user considerations and did not, therefore, closely examine Cutter's words on the matter. The first American writer who did closely connect Cutter with the idea of usage was Marie L. Prevost in "An Approach to Theory and Method in General Subject Indexing," *Library Quarterly* 16 (April 1946): 140–51, where she was very critical of the idea. After her article, other writers seem to have taken for granted the connection of user considerations with Cutter, as if those who came after Cutter were indoctrinated by him. Dunkin, after referring to Prevost in the article cited here, summarized and expressed with eloquence what had become accepted opinion.

26. Cf. Carlyle J. Frarey, "The Role of Research in Establishing Standards for Subject Headings," *Journal of Cataloging and Classification* 10 (October 1954): 186, 188; David J. Haykin, "What It Takes to Be a Subject Cataloger," *Journal of Cataloging and Classification* 10 (January 1954): 34; Katherine Ball, "Economics in Subject Cataloging: Bibliographies as a Substitute for Subject Cataloging," *Journal of Cataloging and Classification* 8 (December 1952): 145–47.

27. Cf. May G. Hardy, "The Library of Congress Subject Catalog: An Evaluation," *Library Quarterly* 22 (January 1952): 40–50; George Scheerer, "The Subject Catalog Examined," pp. 187–98.

28. Melvin J. Voigt, "The Researcher and his Sources of Information," *Libri* 9 (1959): 177–93.

29. Paul S. Dunkin, "Cataloging and the CCS: 1957–1966," *Library Resources and Technical Services* 11 (Summer 1967): 286.

30. Dunkin, *Cataloging U.S.A.*, p. 141.

31. Ibid., p. 142. Emphasis added.

32. *RDC*, R161, disc., p. 67.

33. Ibid.; R175, disc., p. 75. Emphasis Cutter's.

34. Sears, *List of Subject Headings for Small Libraries, including Practical Suggestions for the Beginner in Subject Heading Work,* 5th ed. (New York: H. W. Wilson Company, 1944), p. xxviii.

35. Library of Congress, *Subject Headings used in the Dictionary Catalogs of the Library of Congress,* 4th ed., ed. Mary Wilson MacNair, 2 vols. (Washington: The Library, 1943), 1: passim.

36. Knapp's 1943 University of Chicago thesis, as cited above in note 7, was issued in two parts in the 1944 *Library Quarterly*. In the discussion here, her findings related to the nature of the catalog are in the first article, which

is cited as "Subject Catalog"–I. Findings related to the subject searching patterns of students are found in the second article, which is cited as "Subject Catalog"–II.

37. Knapp, "Subject Catalog"–I, p. 112. Emphasis added.

38. Whether Knapp ever intended an extreme approach to specific entry might be debated because it is not obvious whether her use of "primary" in her conclusion that scope-matching met "the primary rule of specific entry" meant "most fundamental" or "most important." If she meant "most fundamental," then she was in effect discounting any other interpretation of the idea such as that headings should also be not classed. If she meant only "most important," then she could have meant that while a heading must first scope-match the content of the books, it might also then have to meet other criteria as well.

39. Knapp, "Subject Catalog"–I, p. 112.

40. Marie L. Prevost, "An Approach to Theory and Method," p. 140. She quoted *RDC*, "Preface to the Fourth Edition," p. 6. On whether Cutter specifically meant his words to be applied to the subject system, see above, chapter 4, pp. 73–74.

41. Prevost, "An Approach to Theory and Method," pp. 142–44. Prevost's noun rule was much more sophisticated than the one proposed by Jacob Schwartz in the previous century and contested by Cutter (*RDC*, R175, disc., pp. 72–74). Schwartz dealt primarily with adjective-noun phrases. Prevost was not dealing with known and accepted two-word phrases that simply involved one noun and one adjective. Instead, she attempted the much more ambitious project of reducing any complex subject heading to a noun (whatever that might be) with its qualifiers. As ambitious as her project was, however, it retained the very definite limitation of being useful only as a way to discipline an already formulated list of subject headings. She did not, in other words, provide a method for determining what the fundamental idea in any subject description should be, but rather only a method for reformulating headings once their fundamental foci had already been determined. The fundamental idea in Agricultural libraries, for example, could have been either Agriculture or Libraries (the way she had it). That its fundamental idea was Libraries was already established by the emphasis in the list in which it was found, the subject heading list of the Library of Congress. For a useful discussion of Prevost's "noun approach," see Dunkin, *Cataloging U.S.A.*, pp. 88–90.

42. Prevost, "An Approach to Theory and Method," pp. 141–42.

43. Ibid., p. 145.

44. Ibid., p. 144.

45. Ibid., p. 145.

46. On Farradane, cf. Foskett, *Subject Approach to Information*, pp. 74–76; Coates, *Subject Catalogues*, pp. 45–50.

47. Prevost, "An Approach to Theory and Method," pp. 145, 150.

48. C. D. Gull, "Some Remarks on Subject Headings," *Special Libraries* 40 (March 1949): 83–88. The relationship between Gull working on the Library's Science and Technology Project and David J. Haykin, chief of the

Library's Subject Cataloging Division at that time, has not been investigated. It is likely an important one insofar as their respective interpretations of specific entry are very similar. Haykin's ideas are discussed in the next chapter in the context of Library of Congress general subject heading development. Gull is treated separately here because his clear expression of the idea of specific entry was published first in 1949. Furthermore, Gull's expression of the idea of specific entry had a closer tie to the developments of the 1950s in indexing, considering Mortimer Taube's criticism of them.

49. Gull, "Some Remarks on Subject Headings," p. 84.

50. Ibid. The symposium was held in December 1947. The arguments that Gull offered comparing direct and indirect headings began on p. 84 and continued to p. 86.

51. Ibid., p. 83.

52. Gull made use of the same limitation when, in criticizing direct headings, he noted that when quarterly indexes were prepared, there were "many headings for which there is only one entry per heading" (p. 85). The implication was that full specification was not desirable if it produced single-item files. That was a condition more likely to occur in the quarterly indexes that had fewer numbers of entries than in the entire catalog.

53. Ibid., pp. 87–88.

54. Eleanor J. Aronson, "Cataloging in a Large Reports Organization," *American Documentation* 3 (April 1952): 114–17; Mortimer Taube, "Specificity in Subject Headings and Coordinate Indexing," *Library Trends* 1 (October 1952): 219–23. Taube's harsh but matter-of-fact treatment of the multiple entry procedure was referred to enough times by other writers during the 1950s to give it an important place in the history of subject access, at least among American writers. It was particularly important because of the way it contrasted a new way of thinking with what had been traditional. Thus, it plays the role of an important landmark showing the point at which the older and newer approaches to subject access parted. It was not by any means the only such marker. For example, an article by B. C. Vickery, "The Structure of a Connective Index," *Journal of Documentation* 6 (September 1950): 140–51, appears to have played a similar role, although it compared the older with the newer traditions in a more general and abstract way and led in its reasoning to the need for a classified approach to subject access. And, of course, there were still other writings of importance that presented the new ideas far more thoroughly than these two articles. These are especially important, however, for the conscious transition in thought that they represented.

55. Since the purpose of describing new developments in subject access since the 1950s is to provide only enough background to draw general conclusions about the importance of the developments for dictionary subject cataloging, the survey itself is brief and without specific documentation. Highly useful summaries of the various systems as well as citations of the appropriate literature will be found in F. Wilfred Lancaster, *Information Retrieval Systems: Characteristics, Testing, and Evaluation* (New York: Wiley, 1968), chapters 2–3, and *Vocabulary Control for Information Retrieval*

(Washington, D.C.: Information Resources Press, 1972), chapters 2–5; and Foskett, *The Subject Approach to Information,* passim. A useful survey of more recent developments in natural language indexing will be found in F. Wilfred Lancaster, "Vocabulary Control in Information Retrieval Systems," in *Advances in Librarianship,* vol. 7, ed. M. J. Voigt and M. W. Harris (New York: Academic Press, 1977), pp. 1–40.

56. It is ironic that Cutter's subject heading system, criticized so harshly in 1938 by Ranganathan in his *Theory of Library Catalogue,* actually had more in common with Ranganathan's work than Ranganathan realized—given, that is, the interpretation of Cutter in the present work. Ranganathan, like Cutter, began with the assumption that the universe of subjects was a unitary whole, capable of expansion, but not otherwise composed of disparate and unrelated parts. He also assumed, like Cutter, that the universe of subjects was orderly and that the order inherent in it was what one expressed in a classification of subjects. Most important, Ranganathan, like Cutter, saw the order of the subjects within the universe of knowledge as a function of categories of subjects and their relationships, an idea-level approach to subject collocation. The details of their respective schemes were, of course, very different. Cutter's canonical classes were traditional to say the least. His facets, built around a theory of knowledge acquisition and structured as a scale of concreteness, were likewise from a former period of thinking and limited in the elegance with which they accommodated what is implied by the notion of a subject. And the limitations of his categories of subjects made it impossible for him to characterize subject relationships with the power that Ranganathan's more complex structure achieved. Still, Cutter proceeded with what amounted to a citation order for the subjects in his subject heading system that was not unlike the citation order found in analytico-synthetic methods. It is unfortunate in the end that Ranganathan was able to see Cutter's work only through the haze that came from interpreting Cutter through American contemporary practice, especially with its emphasis on what Ranganathan would have called a verbal rather than idea-level analysis of subject relationships and on an all encompassing importance given to user considerations apart from any developed theory of users themselves.

57. Lancaster, "Vocabulary Control in Information Retrieval Systems," pp. 25–26.

58. S. R. Ranganathan, "Library Classification Through a Century," in *Classification Research; Proceedings of the Second International Study Conference,* ed. Pauline Atherton (Copenhagen: Munksgaard, 1965), pp. 20ff.

59. Pollard and Bradford, "The Inadequacy of the Alphabetical Subject Index," especially pp. 42–43.

60. Ranganathan, *Theory of Library Catalogue,* especially pp. 84–85. Others since Ranganathan have noted the relationship of classification and subject headings. See especially Richmond, "Cats: An Example of Concealed Classification in Subject Headings," pp. 102–12. More recently, G. Bhattacharyya, "Cutter's Procedure for Specific Subject Indexing," *Library Science with a Slant to Documentation* 11 (June 1974): 77–91, after faithfully collating and analyzing various definitions in Cutter's *Rules,* concluded that Cutter's

method for devising subject headings at least implied and was dependent on classificatory principles. He did not go as far as the conclusions in the present work, however.

61. Cf. Raynard Swank, "Subject Catalogs, Classifications, or Bibliographies? A Review of Critical Discussions, 1876–1942," *Library Quarterly* 14 (October 1944): 316–32.

CHAPTER 11. HAYKIN AND THE LIBRARY OF CONGRESS

1. The biographical information on Haykin included here is taken from *Dictionary of American Library Biography*, s.v. "Haykin, David Judson (1896–1958)," by Leonard Ellinwood. Beyond that brief sketch, there is little on Haykin besides obituaries. More importantly, no critical study of his work has been made despite the significant role he has played in the development of American subject heading work. Haykin's life and work also stand as a significant parallel to the career of Seymour Lubetzky, Haykin's junior by two years. Both were Russian emigrees, though Lubetzky came to the United States much later in life than Haykin. Both earned degrees at American colleges and library schools. Both ended up at the Library of Congress, Haykin in 1932, Lubetzky in 1943. And both applied their considerable intellectual skills to the task of providing theoretical rationalizations of, and where possible, procedural discipline to, Library of Congress cataloging processes that had grown in a seemingly helter-skelter fashion since the beginning of the twentieth century.

2. Library of Congress, *Annual Report of the Librarian of Congress for the Fiscal Year Ending June 30, 1941* (Washington, D.C.: The Library, 1942), p. 206, strongly suggests that the organizational change was made principally to deal more efficiently with the growing volume and variety of items being processed.

3. The development of Haykin's views on how cooperation could best be accomplished may be effectively seen by sequentially reading the following articles by him: "Some Problems and Possibilities of Cooperative Cataloging," *Bulletin of the A.L.A.* 21 (October 1927): 355–58; "Cooperative Cataloging in North America—Problems and Possibilities," *Catalogers' and Classifiers' Yearbook* 6 (1937): 26–35; and "Way to the Future: Cooperative and Centralized Cataloging," *College and Research Libraries* 3 (March 1942): 156–62.

4. Library of Congress, *Annual Report of the Librarian of Congress for the Fiscal Year Ending June 30, 1941,* p. 206.

5. Library of Congress, *Annual Report of the Librarian of Congress for the Fiscal Year Ending June 30, 1942* (Washington, D.C.: The Library, 1943), p. 142.

6. Specific totals for new headings added each year began appearing only with the 1944/45 annual report. But percentage comparisons given in the reports for 1942/43, 1943/44, and 1944/45 allow the previous years' totals to be approximated: 1944/45 (1,862) represented a 22.6 percent increase over 1943/44 (i.e., 1,519); 1943/44 (1,519) represented a 60 percent increase over 1942/43 (i.e., about 950); 1942/43 (about 950) represented twice the number

of 1941/42 (about 475) and also five times the annual average of 1932/33 to 1941/42 (i.e., about 190 per year). The total for the decade between 1942 and 1952, nearly 17,000 new headings (about 1,700+ per year average), is impressive when compared with the previous decade when the yearly average was under 200 new headings and the grand total for the entire decade was barely 2,000.

7. Normalized typefaces and arrangement included the use of the markers sa, x, and xx for reference listings, and in the main alphabetical sequence, the use of boldface type for preferred headings and lightface type for non-preferred headings. The Library of Congress, *Music Subject Headings Used on Printed Cards of the Library of Congress* (Washington: The Library, Subject Cataloging Division, 1952), differed from a list of literature headings published in 1926 in that it was not simply extracted from the already extant main list of headings but rather represented a concerted effort to discipline music subject and form headings.

8. Haykin, "Cooperative Cataloging in North America—Problems and Possibilities," p. 30.

9. Library of Congress, *Subject Headings Used in the Dictionary Catalogs of the Library of Congress,* 4th ed., vol. 1, p. iii.

10. Haykin appears to have been above all else an administrator who was not nearly as concerned about where the subject system had come from as about where it was going. As a result he seems not to have understood the nature of Hanson's original work on the system very well. His apparent lack of a substantive understanding of Hanson's work shows up not only in the present instance, but also (as will be shown later in the present chapter) in his misunderstanding of the relationship of the subject heading system to the classification of subjects. Haykin both specifically denied or avoided discussing the intentional classificatory aspects of the Library's subject catalog, despite the fact that Hanson had intended that effect at least in a controlled way. Haykin's consistent lack of reference to Cutter's *Rules* in his various writings on subject headings (cf. Chan, *Library of Congress Subject Headings,* p. 14) may also have arisen not because he thought them to be too fundamental to cite or because he did not think Cutter's work relevant to the Library's situation as he found it, but rather because he simply was not all that conversant with them.

11. The foregoing portrayal of developments in Library of Congress subject heading work will necessarily remain tentative until someone carefully examines evidence internal to the Library, especially regarding the main idea here, that the Library's subject heading system began to encounter serious difficulties by the end of its third decade rather than from its beginnings, and furthermore, that it did not just sort of accumulate in the more or less haphazard manner that Haykin implied.

12. Library of Congress, *Annual Report of the Librarian of Congress for the Fiscal Year Ending June 30, 1942,* p. 143. It is taken for granted that if Haykin was not the author of this statement as well as others regarding subject cataloging developments at the Library, he at least agreed with them essentially.

13. Library of Congress, *Subject Headings Used in the Dictionary Catalogs of the Library of Congress,* 4th ed., vol. 1, p. iii.

14. Library of Congress, *Annual Report of the Librarian of Congress for the Fiscal Year Ending June 30, 1942,* p. 143.

15. Library of Congress, *Annual Report of the Librarian of Congress for the Fiscal Year Ending June 30, 1943* (Washington, D.C.: The Library, 1944), p. 46.

16. Ibid.; Library of Congress, *Annual Report of the Librarian of Congress for the Fiscal Year Ending June 30, 1944* (Washington, D.C.: The Library, 1945), p. 79.

17. That Haykin was released "as of August 12, 1946" to work on it full-time is recorded in the Library of Congress, *Annual Report of the Librarian of Congress for the Fiscal Year Ending June 30, 1946* (Washington, D.C.: The Library, 1947), p. 278. The same report (p. 284) noted that the Subject Cataloging Division had been reorganized to include among three new sections the Science and Technology Section, the eventual location of C. D. Gull's work.

18. Haykin stated in *Subject Headings,* "Preface," p. v., that "Principles and rules here stated represent, in considerable part, the views of the catalogers of this country. In particular they represent the thinking of the staff of subject catalogers at the Library of Congress brought out during weekly and occasional conferences where new headings and old practices are freely discussed." The first statement reflected Haykin's view that there was actually only a single subject cataloging tradition in the country rather than two. That he helped to merge the two actual traditions more completely will be dealt with in the next chapter. As to the second statement, taken at face value it suggests that Haykin was little more than an amanuensis in a cooperative endeavor among the Library's subject catalogers. But this was a role that simply was not typical of the man. To what extent the views in the work did represent the views of others as well as of Haykin or whether he simply viewed others as agreeing with him whether they did or not will have to await further investigation. Until evidence arises to the contrary, it must be assumed that the views in the work represent Haykin's approach to subject heading work first, regardless of who else contributed to them.

19. Haykin, *Subject Headings,* p. 22, and elsewhere. Haykin also used the term "commonly used phrase" (p. 24 and elsewhere) to mean the same thing.

20. Ibid. Cf. p. 21, and Haykin's statement on p. 27 that "subdivision, as against the use of a word or phrase heading, is resorted to when no invariable, commonly used and accepted phrase is available with which to express the intended limitation of a subject." Haykin's use of inversion is everywhere apparent, but see especially pp. 22–25. The use of conventional subject names as subject headings is different from common usage. The latter requires the use of conventional subject names but may be more narrowly defined as an operational principle concerned with choosing between such names.

21. Ibid., pp. 7–8. Cf. also the various places where he discusses the uses of parenthetical qualifiers.

22. Ibid., p. 3.

23. Ibid., pp. 2–4. He also discussed advantages and disadvantages of format in "Let's Get Down to Fundamentals," *Bulletin of the Medical Library Association* 36 (April 1948): 84–85; and in "Subject Headings: Principles and Development," in *The Subject Analysis of Library Materials,* ed. Maurice F. Tauber (New York: School of Library Service, Columbia University, 1953), pp. 45–48.

24. Haykin, *Subject Headings,* pp. 13–20; Haykin, "Subject Headings: Principles and Development," pp. 51–52.

25. Haykin, *Subject Headings,* pp. 27–36, especially 27 and 35–36 on topical subdivision. Cf. also Haykin, "Subject Headings: Principles and Development," pp. 50–51.

26. Haykin, *Subject Headings,* p. 36.

27. Haykin, "Subject Headings: Principles and Development," p. 51.

28. Haykin's most cohesive statement on the reader will be found in his *Subject Headings,* p. 7. Other earlier statements may be found in "Let's Get Down to Fundamentals," pp. 82–83, and, with Helen E. Bush, in "Music Subject Headings," Music Library Association, *Notes* 2nd Series 6 (December 1948): 41. These three sources do not exhaust his words on the topic, however. Haykin referred to the idea of the reader as the focus constantly in all aspects of subject heading work, so that to get the broadest exposure to how he viewed it, the entire corpus of his writings must be surveyed. This is especially true of *Subject Headings* where references to the reader will be found on almost every page.

29. Haykin, "Let's Get Down to Fundamentals," p. 82.

30. Haykin, *Subject Headings,* p. 7.

31. Haykin formally cited Rubakin's work only twice, both times in 1948: "Let's Get Down to Fundamentals," p. 83, and "Music Subject Headings," p. 41. At that point in time, however, only one item among Rubakin's formidable literary output (almost 775 items) had been translated into English, a popularizing article entitled "Reader, Know Thyself," *Library Journal* 59 (April 15, 1934): 344–46. Most of Rubakin's formal discussions of bibliopsychology were available in either French or Russian. Haykin, fluent at least in Russian, probably used texts in that language. English-language materials now available consist of *Nicholas Rubakin and Bibliopsychology,* ed. S. Simsova, World Classics of Librarianship (Hamden,. Conn.: Archon Books, 1968); Alfred E. Senn, *Nicholas Rubakin, a Life for Books,* Russian Biography Series, no. 1 (Newtonville, Mass.: Oriental Research Partners, 1977); and S. Simsova, "Nicholas Rubakin," in *Four Studies in Soviet Librarianship,* ed. G. Harris, Occasional Papers, no. 3 (London: Library Association, International & Comparative Librarianship Group, 1977), pp. 7–18. The extent to which Haykin was actually influenced specifically by Rubakin's theories must await further investigation.

32. Senn, *Nicholas Rubakin,* p. 10.

33. The most direct statement of the idea's group orientation is found in Haykin, *Subject Headings,* p. 7, where he not only places the reader and "the desire to arrange entries in some logical order" in opposition, but also notes

as well that "as far as possible, these rules should provide a direct approach to the topic for *most* of the clientele of the library, references serving the needs of minorities among readers. . . ." Emphasis added.

34. Haykin's references to readers' preferences for direct entry are found whenever he compared direct and indirect entry. In "Subject Headings: Principles and Development," pp. 46–48, 51–52, he noted that readers could actually be divided into two groups, those such as scientists who tended to go directly to the specific topic of their interest no matter how narrow, and those who started at a subject broader than their topic. The broader-to-narrower reference structure as well as direct and very specific headings were, therefore, both justified.

35. Haykin, *Subject Headings*, p. 7.

36. Haykin, "Let's Get Down to Fundamentals," p. 82.

37. Haykin, "Subject Headings: Principles and Development," p. 48.

38. Haykin, *Subject Headings*, p. 4.

39. Haykin, "Let's Get Down to Fundamentals," p. 83.

40. Haykin, "Subject Headings: Principles and Development," p. 47.

41. Haykin, *Subject Headings*, p. 4.

42. Ibid.

43. Ibid., and cf. his concluding remarks on subject heading development in "Subject Headings: Principles and Development," pp. 53–54.

44. Cf., for example, Haykin, *Subject Headings*, pp. 9–11, where the interplay between the lack of data and the need to follow experience is more than evident in Haykin's discussion of specificity.

45. Ibid., pp. 5–6.

46. Haykin, "Let's Get Down to Fundamentals," pp. 83–84.

47. Haykin, *Subject Headings*, p. 8.

48. Haykin, "Let's Get Down to Fundamentals," p. 84.

49. Haykin, *Subject Headings*, pp. 8–9.

50. Ibid.

51. Haykin, "Music Subject Headings," p. 51.

52. Haykin, *Subject Headings*, p. 21.

53. Ibid., p. 30.

54. Ibid., pp. 23–24.

55. Haykin, "Subject Headings: Principles and Development," p. 50.

56. Haykin, *Subject Headings*, p. 4.

57. Ibid., pp. 9–10. Upon first examination it might appear that Haykin's argument in favor of direct and specific entry and against any alternative to it, such as undivided class entry, is skewed. There were in actuality two alternatives to his preferred direct and specific heading INCOME TAX for a work on income tax. The one he listed, TAXATION, represented undivided class entry. Another, TAXATION–INCOME TAX, which he did not list, represented divided class entry (or as Cutter would have said, specific subentry). By not listing both alternatives, one might conclude that his argument was shortsighted and biased. The difficulty is lessened, however, when it is recognized that Haykin's argument at that point was really not about directness or in-

directness per se, but only about the use of conventional subject names that by themselves were broader or narrower than the topic at hand. He had already dispensed with indirect classed entry in his introductory remarks five pages previously. Here, he was only concerned with specificity per se. His examples both consisted of direct headings, however. Cf. "Let's Get Down to Fundamentals," p. 83.

58. Haykin, *Subject Headings,* p. 10.

59. Ibid., p. 11. Haykin's closing clause, "which may be considered the more specific approach to the subject" makes little sense. He really seems to have meant "the more direct" not "the more specific" approach to the topic, unless, that is, he confused the two aspects in his thinking.

60. Haykin, "Let's Get Down to Fundamentals," p. 83.

61. Haykin, "Music Subject Headings," p. 41; Haykin, *Subject Headings,* p. 9.

62. Haykin, *Subject Headings,* pp. 10–11.

63. Ibid., p. 9.

64. Ibid., pp. 10–11.

65. Ibid., p. 10.

66. Ibid., p. 11, emphasis added.

67. Ibid. It seems certain that despite the uncertainty in the way Haykin expressed the goal of specificity, later interpretation of it has stressed the basic scope-match ideal. Cf. Charles C. Bead, "Subject Headings: How and When They Are Established and When They Are Changed," *Music Library Association Technical Reports* 3 (October 1975): 45: "Current LC subject-heading practice calls for specific entry, i.e., entry under a heading which expresses the topic of a work precisely rather than under a broader, generic heading."

68. "Cataloger's Choice," Library of Congress, *Cataloging Service,* Bulletin 22 (June 1950): 3.

69. Haykin, *Subject Headings,* p. 27.

70. Haykin, "Let's Get Down to Fundamentals," p. 84.

71. Cf. Haykin, *Subject Headings,* pp. 1–4, 35–36, 89; Haykin, "Subject Headings: Principles and Development," pp. 45–46.

72. Cf. Haykin, *Subject Headings,* pp. 22–24, 73–74.

73. Ibid., pp. 21–24.

74. Haykin, "Music Subject Headings," p. 42.

75. Haykin, *Subject Headings,* p. 9.

76. Ibid., pp. 57–59.

77. Ibid., p. 59.

78. Ibid., p. 60.

79. Library of Congress, *Library of Congress Catalog; Cumulated List of Works Represented by Library of Congress Printed Cards—Books: Subjects, 1950–1954* (Ann Arbor, Mich.: J. W. Edwards, 1955), s.v. DIESEL MOTOR, FUEL PUMPS, and MARINE ENGINES. The first set of headings was for *Marine Diesel Engine Standards* (New York: Diesel Engine Manufacturers Association, 1940); the second for *Fuel Injection Systems* (New York: Diesel Publications, 1950).

CHAPTER 12. DICTIONARY SUBJECT CATALOGING SINCE HAYKIN

1. Haykin's design for a more complete code will be found in his "Project for a Subject Heading Code . . . Revised September 1957" (Typescript, Library of Congress, 10 pp.). The intention of the Subject Cataloging Division to carry on his work was summarized briefly by Maurice F. Tauber in "Subject Headings and Codes," *Library Resources and Technical Services* 3 (Spring 1959): 97–98.

2. Francis J. Witty, Review of *Subject Headings Used in the Dictionary Catalogs of the Library of Congress,* 6th ed., *Catholic Library World* 30 (April 1959): 435.

3. Pauline A. Seely, "Subject Headings Today," Review of *Subject Headings, A Practical Guide,* by D. J. Haykin, *Library Journal* 78 (January 1, 1953): 22; cf. review by B. Bassam, *Journal of Cataloging and Classification* 8 (September 1952): 120–21. An exception to the wholehearted approbation of Haykin's work was provided in a review by Wyllis E. Wright, *College and Research Libraries* 13 (July 1952): 282, who noted critically that Haykin's disclaimer that his work followed actual Library of Congress practice in every instance "seems too general . . . to cover the failure to discuss the variations and inconsistencies of LC headings which unduly complicate the explanation of subject headings to the library user." The only thoroughly critical review of the work was by E. J. Coates in his "Alphabetical Subject Catalogues," pp. 58–63. Coates wrote from a British point of view that was deeply indebted to the new trends then occurring in subject access.

4. Carlyle J. Frarey, Review of *Subject Headings in the Dictionary Catalogs of the Library of Congress,* 6th ed., *Library Resources and Technical Services* 3 (Spring 1959): 156–61.

5. Haykin, "What It Takes to Be a Subject Cataloger," p. 34. The paper was "Presented at a meeting of the Northern Ohio Catalogers at the East Cleveland Public Library, November 8, 1952."

6. Coates, "Alphabetical Subject Catalogues," p. 62.

7. Pettee, *Subject Headings,* p. 57, gave the impression that subject headings were not much more than catchwords when she paraphrased Cutter's specific entry rule as "Enter under specific topic" and then defined a topic as "a concept or particular nucleus of thought, usually expressed by a word, about which all aspects are gathered." Later, when describing the names that were to be used as subject headings, she wrote, "A topic must have a good filing name to have an independent entry in the dictionary catalog" (p. 61). A "good filing name" can mean little other than a simple or at least common catchword. That there had been a shift towards the greater use of phrase subject names was noted by Jay E. Daily in "Subject Headings and the Theory of Classification," pp. 271–72.

8. Coates, *Subject Catalogues,* p. 32.

9. Ibid., p. 37.

10. Robert A. Colby, "Current Problems in the Subject Analysis of Literature," *Journal of Cataloging and Classification* 10 (January 1954): 19–28.

11. George Scheerer, "The Subject Catalog Examined," p. 192.

12. Ibid., pp. 190–94.

13. Metcalfe's three principal works are *Information Indexing and Subject Cataloging, Alphabetical-Classified, Coordinate-Mechanical* (1957); *Subject Classifying and Indexing of Libraries and Literature* (1959); and *Alphabetical Subject Indication of Knowledge* (1965). A more recent work, *Information Retrieval, British and American, 1876–1976,* provides something of a chatty historical narrative that places the chief antagonists, alphabetical catalogers versus classified catalogers, in useful, sometimes amusing, perspective.

14. Haykin, "Subject Headings: Principles and Development," p. 50.

15. Ibid.

16. Bartol Brinkler, "The Geographical Approach to Materials in the Library of Congress Subject Headings," *Library Resources and Technical Services* 6 (Winter 1962): 50, noted that in contrast to other earlier writers on the topic, Haykin devoted only one paragraph to the matter in his *Subject Headings.*

17. Taube, "Specificity in Subject Headings and Coordinate Indexing," p. 222.

18. Scheerer, "The Subject Catalog Examined," p. 188. Finding users to be just as one's subject system requires them to be is something of an occupational hazard of subject access workers, affecting even the more notable. Ranganathan, for example, in his *Library Catalogue, Fundamentals and Procedure,* Madras Library Association Publication Series, no. 15 (London: G. Blunt, 1950), pp. 439–48, drew up a twofold idealization of subject searchers that, not unexpectedly, supported the need for a classified display of subjects. His "findings" were also, of course, quite different than those of Cutter.

19. Haykin, "Subject Headings: Principles and Development," p. 47; Dunkin later summarized his own thought on the matter of user considerations in his *Cataloging U.S.A.,* pp. 140–43. In the end, he allowed the problem of needing to determine readers' habits to stand as a perplexing conundrum.

20. Oliver L. Lilley, "How Specific Is Specific," *Journal of Cataloging and Classification* 11 (January 1955): 3–8. Cf. also his "Evaluation of the Subject Catalog," *American Documentation* 5 (April 1954): 41–60; and "The Problems of Measuring Catalog Use," *Journal of Cataloging and Classification* 10 (July 1954): 122–31.

21. Dunkin, *Cataloging U.S.A.,* p. 141. Cf. the work of Carlyle J. Frarey in "Practical Problems in Subject Heading Work: A Summary," *Journal of Cataloging and Classification* 8 (December 1952): 154–58; "The Role of Research in Establishing Standards for Subject Headings," pp. 179–90; his already cited "Subject Headings" (1960); and his later "Dilemma of Subject Analysis for Modern Library Service," in *Reference Research and Regionalism, selected papers from the 53rd Conference, Texas Library Association* (Austin, Tex.: The Association, 1966), pp. 54–60. Cf. as well Wyllis E. Wright, "Standards for Subject Headings: Problems and Opportunities," *Journal of Cataloging and Classification* 10 (October 1954): 175–78; and Hilda Steinweg, "Medical Subject Heading Terminology," *Journal of Cataloging and Classification* 12 (July 1956): 171–80, especially p. 179.

22. "The Library of Congress List of Subject Headings: Rejoinder to Mr. Chakrabarti," *Indian Librarian* 9 (June 1954): 15–16.

23. David J. Haykin, Review of *Cataloging Principles and Practice*, ed. M. Piggott, *Library Journal* 80 (July 1955): 1564. By 1955 Haykin had also assumed the editorship of the Dewey Decimal Classification. In "Book Classification and the Problem of Change," *College and Research Libraries* 16 (October 1955): 370–74, he expressed the same sense of being troubled by those who deviated locally from the work being done editorially on the decimal system at the Library of Congress. He noted that local variations could be justified occasionally, but deplored them anyway because in his opinion most librarians "reject outright changes in the system, yet . . . indulge in less valid and generally less justifiable change" (p. 373). The DDC (meaning his own work) represented the best changes and he wished that local librarians would use them. His entire attitude towards cooperation seems in many respects reminiscent of that of Melvil Dewey during the late nineteenth century. For Dewey, the means to an end (some particular system) was not nearly as important as the end itself (cooperation) because the means had been decided on as the best by the best minds available.

24. Frarey, "Subject Headings," especially "Summary and Areas of Investigation," pp. 63–67.

25. Richard S. Angell, "Standards for Subject Headings," *Journal of Cataloging and Classification* 10 (October 1954): 195–96.

26. Ibid., pp. 191–93.

27. Ibid., pp. 193–94.

28. Richard S. Angell, "Library of Congress Subject Headings—Review and Forecast," pp. 148–49, 153–54.

29. Ibid., p. 150.

30. See chapter 11, pp. 356–57.

31. Chan, *Library of Congress Subject Headings*, p. 40.

32. Angell, "Library of Congress Subject Headings—Review and Forecast," sections on "Specificity" (p. 150) and "Terminology" (pp. 148–49) for use of the phrase "common usage." In the section "Form and Structure of Headings" Angell, like Haykin, justified the inversion of phrase headings in some instances because it was assumed "that the searcher would prefer this collocation of entries to the dispersion of the direct forms" (p. 154).

33. Patrick Wilson, "The End of Specificity," *Library Resources and Technical Services* 23 (Spring 1979): 116–22.

34. Cf. the work of Sanford Berman, especially his *Prejudices and Antipathies; A Tract on the LC Subject Headings Concerning People* (Metuchen, N.J.; Scarecrow Press, 1971); and, more recently, Joan K. Marshall, *On Equal Terms: A Thesaurus for Non-sexist Indexing and Cataloging* (Santa Barbara, Calif.: ABC Clio, 1977).

35. The problem of representation is even further exacerbated by the fact that those most vocal in calling for changes remain librarians rather than users. It is reasonable to ask whether the subject heading choice process is really that much further advanced by substituting librarians outside the Li-

brary of Congress for those inside. None of this is intended to suggest that changing terminology considered to be prejudicial is wrong, rather only that it is far more problematic than it might have at first seemed.

36. Cf. Angell, "Library of Congress Subject Headings—Review and Forecast," p. 150; Chan, *Library of Congress Subject Headings,* pp. 45, 152.

37. Lancaster, "Vocabulary Control in Information Retrieval Systems," p. 17.

38. Cf. Library of Congress, *Cataloging Service,* Bulletin 121 (Spring 1977): 16.

39. Angell, "Library of Congress Subject Headings—Review and Forecast," p. 150.

40. Chan, *Library of Congress Subject Headings,* p. 45, appropriately describes the headings of the Library of Congress system as "a mixture of natural and an artificial language." She includes in the artificial language categories inverted, qualified, and strings-of-terms headings. She does not, however, distinguish between phrases that occur as names and those that are contrived in the formulaic sense noted here.

41. Library of Congress, *Cataloging Service,* Bulletin 121 (Spring 1977): 14.

42. Angell, "Library of Congress Subject Headings—Review and Forecast," p. 151, noted that "the geographic code developed as a part of MARC format has a built-in hierarchy, with the result that all subject headings in our machine-readable records to which this code has been assigned are in effect divided "Indirect." One can only wonder whether the eventual shift to indirect subdivision was as much affected by this machine facility as it was by any other factor.

CHAPTER 13. SUMMARY AND OBSERVATIONS

1. *RDC,* headnote to "A. Entries Considered Separately," p. 66.

2. Marcia Bates, "Factors Affecting Subject Catalog Search Success," *Journal of the American Society of Information Science* 28 (May 1977): 168.

3. Angell, "Library of Congress Subject Headings—Review and Forecast," p. 50.

4. Bates, "Factors Affecting Subject Catalog Search Success," p. 167.

Selected Bibliography

Abbot, Ezra. "Mr. Abbot's Statement Respecting the New Catalogues of the College Library." In *Report of the Committee of Overseers of Harvard College Appointed to Visit the Library for the Year 1863*, pp. 35–76. Boston: Press of Geo. C. Rand & Avery, 1864.

Akers, Susan G. "A Decade of Teaching Subject Headings." *Catalogers' and Classifiers' Yearbook* 4 (1934): 85–92.

_____. *Simple Library Cataloging*. Chicago: American Library Association, 1927.

American Library Association. *List of Subject Headings for Use in Dictionary Catalogs*. Boston: Published for the A.L.A. Publishing Section by the Library Bureau, 1895.

_____. _____. 2nd ed., rev. 1898.

_____. _____. 3rd ed. Chicago: American Library Association, 1911.

American Library Association. Committee on an Index to Subject Headings. [Reports] *Library Journal* 6 (April 1881): 114–15; 18 (September 1893): C79–C82; 19 (December 1894): C138–C139.

Angell, Richard S. "Library of Congress Subject Headings—Review and Forecast." In *Subject Retrieval in the Seventies: New Directions*, edited by H. Wellisch and T. D. Wilson, pp. 143–62. Westport, Conn.: Greenwood Publishing Co., 1972.

_____. "Standards for Subject Headings—A National Program." *Journal of Cataloging and Classification* 10 (October 1954): 191–97.

Aronson, Eleanor J. "Cataloging in a Large Reports Organization." *American Documentation* 3 (April 1952): 114–17.

Ball, Katherine. "Economies in Subject Cataloging: Bibliographies as a Substitute for Subject Cataloging." *Journal of Cataloging and Classification* 8 (December 1952): 145–47.

Balnaves, John. "Specificity." In *The Variety of Librarianship: Essays in Honour of John Wallace Metcalfe*, edited by W. Boyd Rayward, pp. 47–56. Sidney: Library Association of Australia, 1976.

Bates, Marcia. "Factors Affecting Subject Catalog Search Success." *Journal of the American Society for Information Science* 28 (May 1977): 161–69.

Bead, Charles C. "Subject Headings: How and When They Are Established and When They Are Changed." *Music Library Association Technical Reports* 3 (October 1975): 43–56.

Bhattacharyya, G. "Cutter's Procedure for Specific Subject Indexing." *Library Science with a Slant to Documentation* 11 (June 1974): 77–91.

Bishop, William Warner. *Practical Handbook of Modern Library Cataloging.* Baltimore: Williams & Wilkins, 1914.

_____. "Subject Headings in Dictionary Catalogs." *Library Journal* 31 (August 1906): 113–23.

_____. "Two Unsolved Problems in Library Work." *Library Journal* 37 (January 1912): 7–11.

Black, Henry. "The Problem of Subject Headings." *Catalogers' and Classifiers' Yearbook* 6 (1937): 86–90.

Boston Athenaeum. *Catalogue of the Library of the Boston Athenaeum, 1807–1871.* [Edited by C. A. Cutter.] 5 vols. Boston: The Athenaeum, 1874–1882.

Bowker, Richard R. "On a Co-operative Scheme of Subject-entry, with a Key to Catalog Headings." *Library Journal* 3 (November 1878): 326–29.

Bradford, Samuel. *Documentation, with an Introduction by Jesse H. Shera and Margaret E. Egan.* London: Crosby Lockwood & Son, 1953.

Briggs, Mary J. "The A.L.A. List of Subject Headings." *Bulletin of the A.L.A.* 6 (July 1912): 227–31.

Brinkler, Bartol. "The Geographical Approach to Materials in the Library of Congress Subject Headings." *Library Resources and Technical Services* 6 (Winter 1962): 49–64.

Brooklyn Library. *Analytical and Classed Catalogue of the Brooklyn Library: Authors, Titles, Subjects, and Classes.* [Compiled by S. B. Noyes.] Brooklyn: 1878–1880.

Cambridge (Mass.) High School. Library. *A Classed Catalogue of the Library of the Cambridge High School.* [Compiled by Ezra Abbot.] Cambridge, Mass.: John Bartlett, 1853.

Chan, Lois M. *Library of Congress Subject Headings: Principles and Application.* Research Studies in Library Science, no. 15. Littleton, Colo.: Libraries Unlimited, 1978.

Chapin, Artena M. "Cataloging in a Small City Library." *Bulletin of the A.L.A.* 5 (July 1911): 218–20.

Coates, E. J. "Alphabetical Subject Catalogues." Review of *Subject Headings; A Practical Guide,* by D. J. Haykin. *Journal of Documentation* 9 (March 1953): 58–63.

_____. *Subject Catalogues: Headings and Structure.* London: The Library Association, 1960.

Colby, Robert A. "Current Problems in the Subject Analysis of Literature." *Journal of Cataloging and Classification* 10 (January 1954): 19–28.

Collar, Mildred A. "The Classification and Cataloging of Children's Books." *Library Journal* 28 (July 1903): 57–68.

Crawford, Esther. "A.L.A. Subject Headings." *Library Journal* 32 (October 1907): 435–36; (November 1907): 500–1; (December 1907): 560–61.

_____. "The New Edition of A.L.A. Subject Headings." *Library Journal* 32 (January 1907): 25–26.

Currier, T. Franklin. "Too Many Cards Under a Subject Heading." *Library Journal* 35 (September 1910): 412–13.

Cutter, Charles Ammi. *Charles Ammi Cutter, Library Systematizer.* Edited by F. Miksa. The Heritage of Librarianship Series, no. 3. Littleton, Colo.: Libraries Unlimited, 1977.

_____. "Library Catalogues." In *Public Libraries in the United States of America, their History, Condition and Management; Special Report, Part I,* pp. 526–622. Washington: U.S. Government Printing Office, 1876.

_____. "The New Catalogue of the Harvard College Library." *North American Review* 108 (January 1869): 96–129. (Portions of this article are reprinted in Cutter, C. A. *Charles Ammi Cutter, Library Systematizer,* pp. 153–61.

_____. *Rules for a Dictionary Catalog.* 4th ed. U. S. Bureau of Education. *Special Report on Public Libraries—Part II.* Washington: U.S. Government Printing Office, 1904.

_____. "Some Hints on Subject Cataloging in Dictionary Style." In American Library Association, *List of Subject Headings for Use in Dictionary Catalogs,* pp. 197–98. 2nd ed., rev. Boston: Published for the A.L.A. Publishing Section by the Library Bureau, 1898.

Daily, Jay E., "Subject Headings and the Theory of Classification." *American Documentation* 8 (October 1957): 269–74.

Drake, C. L. "What Is a Subject?" *Australian Library Journal* 9 (January 1960): 34–41.

Dunkin, Paul S. "Cataloging and the CCS: 1957–1966." *Library Resources and Technical Services* 11 (Summer 1967): 267–88.

_____. *Cataloging U.S.A.* Chicago: American Library Association, 1969.

_____. "Criticisms of Current Cataloging Practice." *Library Quarterly* 26 (October 1956): 286–302.

Dykstra, Mary. "The Lion That Squeaked." *Library Journal* 103 (September 1, 1978): 1570–72.

Fellows, Dorcas. *Cataloging Rules, with Explanations and Illustrations.* 2nd ed., rev. and enlarged. New York: H. W. Wilson Company, 1922.

Flower, Elizabeth, and Murphey, G. Murray. *A History of Philosophy in America.* 2 vols. New York: Capricorn Books, G. P. Putnam's Sons, 1977.

Foskett, Anthony C. *The Subject Approach to Information.* 3rd ed. Hamden, Conn.: Linnet Books, 1977.

Frarey, Carlyle J. "The Dilemma of Subject Analysis for Modern Library Service." In *Reference Research and Regionalism; Selected Papers from the 53rd Conference, Texas Library Association,* pp. 54–60. Austin: The Association, 1966.

_____. "Practical Problems in Subject Heading Work: a Summary." *Journal of Cataloging and Classification* 8 (December 1952): 154–58.

_____. Review of *Subject Headings Used in the Dictionary Catalogs of the Library of Congress,* 6th ed. *Library Resources and Technical Services* 3 (Spring 1959): 156–61.

_____. "The Role of Research in Establishing Standards for Subject Headings." *Journal of Cataloging and Classification* 10 (Otcober 1954): 179–90.

_____. "Studies of Use of the Subject Catalog: Summary and Evaluation." In *The Subject Analysis of Library Materials,* edited by Maurice F. Tauber, pp. 147–66. New York: School of Library Service, Columbia University, 1953.

_____. "Subject Headings." In *The State of the Library Art,* vol. 1, part 2, edited by Ralph R. Shaw. New Brunswick, N.J.: Graduate School of Library Service, Rutgers, The State University, 1960.

Gull, C. Dake. "Some Remarks on Subject Headings." *Special Libraries* 40 (March 1949): 83–88.

Hanson, J. C. M. "The Printed Cards of the Library of Congress, their Various Uses, and Practical Difficulties in their Use." *Library Journal* 28 (July 1903): 189–92.

_____. Review of *Index of the Books in the Author Catalogues for the Years 1869–1895,* Sydney, Public Library of New South Wales. *Library Journal* 29 (April 1904): 197.

_____. "The Subject Catalogs of the Library of Congress." *Bulletin of the A.L.A.* 3 (July 1909): 385–97.

Hardy, May G. "The Library of Congress Subject Catalog: An Evaluation." *Library Quarterly* 22 (January 1952): 40–50.

Haykin, David J. "Book Classification and the Problem of Change." *College and Research Libraries* 16 (October 1955): 370–74.

_____. "Cooperative Cataloging in North America—Problems and Possibilities." *Catalogers' and Classifiers' Yearbook* 6 (1937): 26–35.

_____. "Let's Get Down to Fundamentals." *Bulletin of the Medical Library Association* 36 (April 1948): 82–85.

_____. "Project for a Subject Heading Code . . . Revised September 1957." Typescript. Library of Congress. 10pp.

_____. "The Library of Congress List of Subject Headings; Rejoinder to Mr. Chakrabarti." *Indian Librarian* 9 (June 1954): 14–17.

_____. Review of *Cataloguing Principles and Practice,* edited by M. Piggot. *Library Journal* 80 (July 1955): 1564.

_____. "Some Problems and Possibilities of Cooperative Cataloging." *Bulletin of the A.L.A.* 21 (October 1927): 355–58.

_____. *Subject Headings, a Practical Guide.* Washington: U.S. Government Printing Office, 1951.

_____. "Subject Headings: Principles and Development." In *The Subject Analysis of Library Materials,* edited by Maurice F. Tauber, pp. 43–54. New York: School of Library Service, Columbia University, 1953.

_____. "Way to the Future: Cooperative and Centralized Cataloging." *College and Research Libraries* 3 (March 1942): 156–62.

_____. "What It Takes to Be a Subject Cataloger." *Journal of Cataloging and Classification* 10 (January 1954): 34–39.

Haykin, David J., and Bush, Helen E. "Music Subject Headings." Music Library Association. *Notes,* 2nd Series 6 (December 1948): 39–45.

Hitchler, Theresa. *Cataloging for Small Libraries.* A.L.A. Publishing Board, Library Handbook, no. 2. Boston: A.L.A. Publishing Board, 1905.

_____. _____. Rev. ed. Chicago: A.L.A. Publishing Board, 1915.

Hodges, N. D. C. "Bibliographies *vs.* Dictionary Catalogs." *Library Journal* 27 (July 1902): 178–80.

Jardine, Lisa. *Francis Bacon, Discovery and the Art of Discourse.* London: Cambridge University Press, 1974.

Kelley, Grace O. "The Subject Approach to Books: An Adventure in Curriculum." *Catalogers' and Classifiers' Yearbook* 2 (1930): 9–23.

Knapp, Patricia B. "The Subject Catalog in the College Library, an Investigation of Terminology." *Library Quarterly* 14 (July 1944): 214–28.

————. "The Subject Catalog in the College Library, the Background of Subject Cataloging." *Library Quarterly* 14 (April 1944): 108–18.

Kroeger, Alice B. "Dictionary Catalogs *vs.* Bibliographies." *Library Journal* 27 (July 1902): 180–82.

Kuklick, Bruce. *The Rise of American Philosophy: Cambridge, Massachusetts, 1860–1930.* New Haven: Yale University Press, 1977.

Lane, William C. "Present Tendencies of Catalog Practice." *Library Journal* 29 (December 1904): 134–43.

Library of Congress. *Subject Headings Used in the Dictionary Catalogues of the Library of Congress.* Washington: U.S. Government Printing Office, Library Branch, 1910–14.

————. [Supplement]. *List of Subject Headings. Additions and Revisions, no. 1–14, December 1908–November 1917.* Washington: U.S. Government Printing Office, Library Branch, 1908–17.

————. *Subject Headings Used in the Dictionary Catalogs of the Library of Congress.* Edited by Mary Wilson MacNair. 4th ed. 2 vols. Washington: The Library, 1943.

Lilley, Oliver L. "Evaluation of the Subject Catalog." *American Documentation* 5 (April 1954): 41–60.

————. "How Specific Is Specific?" *Journal of Cataloging and Classification* 11 (January 1955): 3–8.

————. "The Problems of Measuring Catalog Use." *Journal of Cataloging and Classification* 10 (July 1954): 122–31.

MacNair, Mary W. "The Library of Congress List of Subject Headings." *Bulletin of the A.L.A.* 6 (July 1912): 231–34.

MacPherson, Harriet D. "Building a List of Subject Headings." *Special Libraries* 24 (March 1933): 44–46.

Mann, Margaret. *The Classification and Catologing [sic] of Books.* [Mimeographed preliminary edition]. Chicago: American Library Association, 1928.

————. *Introduction to Cataloging and the Classification of Books.* Chicago: American Library Association, 1930.

————. ————. 2nd ed. Chicago: American Library Association, 1943.

————. *Subject Headings for Use in Dictionary Catalogs of Juvenile Books.* Chicago: A.L.A. Publishing Board, 1916.

Metcalfe, John W. *Information Indexing and Subject Cataloging: Alphabetical-Classified, Coordinate-Mechanical.* New York: Scarecrow Press, 1957.

_____. *Information Retrieval, British and American, 1876–1976.* Metuchen, N.J.: Scarecrow Press, 1976.

_____. *Subject Classifying and Indexing of Libraries and Literature.* New York: Scarecrow Press, 1959.

_____. "When Is a Subject Not a Subject?" In *Toward a Theory of Librarianship; Papers in Honor of Jesse Hauk Shera,* edited by Conrad H. Rawski, pp. 303–38. Metuchen, N.J.: Scarecrow Press, 1973.

Miksa, Francis L. "Charles Ammi Cutter: Nineteenth Century Systematizer of Libraries." Ph.D. dissertation, University of Chicago, 1974.

Olding, R. K. "Form of Alphabetico-Specific Subject Headings and a Brief Code." *Australian Library Journal* 10 (July 1961): 127–37.

Perkins, Frederic B. "Classification in Dictionary Catalogues." *Library Journal* 4 (July/August 1879): 226–34.

Pettee, Julia. "A New Principle in Dealing with Subject Matter Needed?" *Journal of Cataloging and Classification* 10 (January 1954): 17–19.

_____. "The Philosophy of Subject Headings." *Special Libraries* 23 (April 1932): 181–82.

_____. "Subject Headings: an Introductory Paper." *Special Libraries* 23 (April 1932): 151–56.

_____. *Subject Headings: The History and Theory of the Alphabetical Subject Approach to Books.* New York: H. W. Wilson Co., 1946.

Pollard, A. F. C., and Bradford, S. C. "The Inadequacy of the Alphabetical Subject Index." In ASLIB, *Proceedings of the Seventh Conference,* pp. 39–54. London: ASLIB, 1930.

Prevost, Marie Louise. "An Approach to Theory and Method in General Subject Indexing." *Library Quarterly* 16 (April 1946): 140–51.

Randall, William M. "The Technical Processes and Library Service." In *The Acquisition and Cataloging of Books: Papers Presented Before the Library Institute at the University of Chicago, July 29 to August 9, 1940,* edited by William M. Randall, pp. 1–29. Chicago: University of Chicago Press, 1940.

Ranganathan, S. R. *Library Catalogue, Fundamentals and Procedure.* Madras Library Association Publication Series, no. 15. London: G. Blunt, 1950.

_____. "Library Classification Through a Century." In *Classification Research; Proceedings of the Second International Study Conference . . . ,* edited by Pauline Atherton, pp. 15–35. Copenhagen: Munksgaard, 1965.

_____. *Theory of Library Catalogue.* Madras Library Association Publication Series, no. 7. London: Edward Goldston, 1938.

Ranz, Jim. *The Printed Book Catalogue in American Libraries, 1723–1900.* ACRL Monograph Series, no. 26. Chicago: American Library Association, 1964.

Reid, Thomas. *Essays on the Intellectual Powers of Man.* Cambridge, Mass.: The M.I.T. Press, 1969.

Richmond, Phyllis Allen. "Cats: An Example of Concealed Classification in Subject Headings." *Library Resources and Technical Services* 3 (Spring 1959): 102–12.

Rubakin, Nicholas. *Nicholas Rubakin and Bibliopsychology.* Edited by S. Simsova. World Classics of Librarianship. Hamden, Conn.: Archon Books, 1968.

Scheerer, George. "The Subject Catalog Examined." *Library Quarterly* 27 (July 1957): 187–98.

Scott, Edith. "J. C. M. Hanson and his Contribution to Twentieth-Century Cataloging." Ph.D. dissertation, University of Chicago, 1970.

Sears, Minnie Earl, ed. *List of Subject Headings for Small Libraries, Compiled from Lists Used in Nine Representative Small Libraries.* New York: H. W. Wilson Co., 1923.

————. ————. 2nd ed., rev. and enlarged. New York: H. W. Wilson Co., 1926.

————. ————. 3rd ed., rev. and enlarged, including a new section, "Practical Suggestions for the Beginner in Subject Heading Work." New York: H. W. Wilson Co., 1933.

————. *List of Subject Headings for Small Libraries, Including Practical Suggestions for the Beginner in Subject Heading Work.* 5th ed., with the addition of Decimal Classification Numbers by Isabel Stevenson Munro. New York: H. W. Wilson Co., 1944.

————. *Sears' List of Subject Headings.* 11th ed. Edited by Barbara M. Westby. New York: H. W. Wilson Co., 1977.

Seely, Pauline A. "Subject Headings Today." Review of *Subject Headings, a Practical Guide,* by D. J. Haykin. *Library Journal* 78 (January 1, 1953): 17–22.

Senn, Alfred E. *Nicholas Rubakin: A Life for Books.* Russian Biography Series, no. 1. Newtonville, Mass.: Oriental Research Partners, 1977.

Smith, Elva S. *Subject Headings for Children's Books in Public Libraries and in Libraries in Elementary and Junior High Schools* . . . . Chicago: American Library Association, 1933.

Steinweg, Hilda. "Medical Subject Heading Terminology." *Journal of Cataloging and Classification* 12 (July 1956): 171–80.

Stewart, Dugald. *The Collected Works of Dugald Stewart.* Edited by Sir William Hamilton. Vols. 2–4, 6: *Elements of the Philosophy of the Human Mind,* and *Outlines of Moral Philosophy.* Edinburgh: Thomas Constable, 1854–55.

Svenonius, Elaine. "Metcalfe and the Principles of Specific Entry." In *The Variety of Librarianship: Essays in Honour of John Wallace Metcalfe,* edited by W. Boyd Rayward, pp. 171–89. Sydney: Library Association of Australia, 1976.

Swank, Raynard. "Subject Catalogs, Classifications, or Bibliographies? A Review of Critical Discussions, 1876–1942." *Library Quarterly* 14 (October 1944): 316–32.

Sydney. Public Library of New South Wales. *Guide to the System of Cataloguing of the Reference Library;* . . . . 3rd ed. Sydney: W. A. Gullick, 1898.

————. *Index of the Books in the Author Catalogues for the Years 1869–1895.* Sydney: Turner & Henderson, 1903.

Taube, Mortimer. "Specificity in Subject Headings and Coordinate Indexing." *Library Trends* 1 (October 1952): 219–23.

Tauber, Maurice F. "Subject Cataloging and Classification Approaching the Crossroads." *College and Research Libraries* 3 (March 1942): 149–56.

————. "Subject Headings and Codes." *Library Resources and Technical Services* 3 (Spring 1959): 97–112.

Taylor, Jean K. "Reflections and Observations on Subject Analysis: The Public Reference Librarian." In *The Subject Analysis of Library Materials,* edited by Maurice F. Tauber, pp. 167–90. New York: School of Library Service, Columbia University, 1954.

Van Hoesen, Henry B., ed. *Selective Cataloging: Cataloger's Round Table, American Library Association, July 3, 1924.* New York: H. W. Wilson Co., 1928.

Vickery, B. C. "The Structure of a Connective Index." *Journal of Documentation* 6 (September 1950): 140–51.

Voigt, Melvin J. "The Researcher and His Sources of Scientific Information." *Libri* 9 (1959): 177–93.

Weisheipel, James A. "Classification of the Sciences in Medieval Thought." *Mediaeval Studies* 27 (1965): 54–90.

Wilson, Patrick. "The End of Specificity." *Library Resources and Technical Services* 23 (Spring 1979): 116–22.

————.*Two Kinds of Power: An Essay on Bibliographical Control.* University of California Publications; Librarianship: 5. Berkeley: University of California Press, 1968.

Witty, Francis J. Review of *Subject Headings Used in the Dictionary Catalogs of the Library of Congress,* 6th ed. *Catholic Library World* 30 (April 1959): 434–35.

Wright, Wyllis E. Review of *Subject Headings, a Practical Guide,* by D. J. Haykin. *College and Research Libraries* 13 (July 1952): 281–82.

————. "Standards for Subject Headings: Problems and Opportunities." *Journal of Cataloging and Classification* 10 (October 1954): 175–78.

Index